Jamaica

a Lonely Planet travel survival kit

Christopher Baker

Jamaica

1st edition

Published by
   Lonely Planet Publications
   Head Office: PO Box 617, Hawthorn, Vic 3122, Australia
   Branches: 155 Filbert St, Suite 251, Oakland, CA 94607, USA
                   10a Spring Place, London NW5 3BH, UK
                   71 bis rue du Cardinal Lemoine, 75005 Paris, France

Printed by
   Colorcraft Ltd, Hong Kong

Photographs by
   All photographs by Christopher Baker except:
   Lee Abel
   Jan Butchofsky Houser
   Dave Houser

   Front cover: wood carving, Dave Houser

Published
   August 1996

Although the author and publisher have tried to make the information as accurate as possible, they accept no responsibility for any loss, injury or inconvenience sustained by any person using this book.

National Library of Australia Cataloguing in Publication Data

Baker, Christopher P., 1955-.
   Jamaica.

   Includes index.
   ISBN 0 86442 372 1.

   1. Jamaica – Guidebooks.
   I. Title. (Series: Lonely Planet travel survival kit).

917.292046

Christopher P Baker

Christopher grew up in Yorkshire, England. He earned his BA (Honors) in geography at the University of London and gained his first serious suntan in Morocco on a research expedition. He returned to the Sahara in 1976 and also participated in an exchange program at Krakow University in Poland. He later earned master's degrees in Latin American Studies (Liverpool University) and education (Institute of Education, University of London).

Chris first bummed his way around Jamaica in 1978 during a six-month sojourn in the Caribbean, Mexico, and North America. In 1980, he settled in California, where he received a Scripps-Howard Foundation Scholarship in Journalism to attend the University of California, Berkeley.

Since 1983 Chris has made his living as a professional travel and natural sciences writer for publications such as *Newsweek*, *Islands*, *Elle*, the BBC's *World Magazine*, *National Wildlife*, *Geographical Magazine*, and *Caribbean Travel & Life*. He has authored many travel guidebooks and has contributed chapters to *The Nature Company Guide: Ecotourism*, *The Beginner's Guide to Getting Published*, and *I Should Have Stayed Home*, an anthology of works by travel writers.

Chris is a member of the Society of American Travel Writers and has been honored with several awards for outstanding writing, including the prestigious Lowell Thomas Travel Journalism Award for 'Best Travel News Investigative Reporting 1993' and the Benjamin Franklin Award 1995 for 'Best Travel Guidebook.' He regularly lectures aboard cruise ships.

Chris recently discovered the joys of motorcycle touring and in 1996 traversed Cuba on two wheels to write *Mi Moto Fidel: My Faithful Motorcycle*, a literary travelogue about journeying through his favorite country.

From the Author

Fervent thanks are due to many friends and others who helped in researching and writing this book. Above all, thanks to Fay Pickersgill and the staff of the Jamaica Tourist Board; Suzanne McManus and John Issa of SuperClubs; Dulcie Moody and Michael Campbell of Island Car Rentals; Anne Townsend, Paulette Haughton, and Sebastian Tickle of Caribic Vacations; Gail Jackson of Negril Tree House; and Jillian Shaffer of Peter Martin Associates.

I'd also like to thank Johny Abbott and Lorraine Fong of the Jonraine; Jack Abela of Dragon Bay; Cheryl Andrews; David Barlyn of Island Outpost; Vernon Chin of Toby Inn; Maureen Collins of Treasure Beach Hotel; Audrey Cooke-Brown of Christar Villas; Cathleen Decker of Jensen/Boga Inc and Air Jamaica; Evelyn Deluce of Bozell Public Relations; Hilari Dobbs and Richard Kahn of Kahn Associates; Robbie Epstein of Strawberry Hill; Ernst Forstmayr of Blue Lagoon; Rosalie Goodman of Goblin Hill; Tammy Hall of Good Hope; Lorna Hamilton of Ciboney; Andrea Hutchinson of Network Public Relations; Virginia LaCroix of Trans-

Jamaica Airlines; Deanne Lucy and Richard Lumsden of Intercaribe; Barbara Lulich of Jamaica Grande; Andre McGann of Doctor's Cave Beach Hotel; 'Jean' McGill of Rio Grande Attractions; Diana McIntyre-Pike of the Astra Country Inn; Marcella Martinez of Martinez Associates; Michael Poynter and Carol Hay of Wyndham Kingston; Paula Reid of Club Jamaica; Joanne and Kevin Robertson of Coyaba; Judy Schoenbein of Appleton Estates; Fred Schwartz of Vacation Network; Gary Sewell of the Transport Authority; Brian Shiels of Morgan's Harbour; Gordon "Butch" Stewart, Sarah-Greaves Gabbadon, and all the staff of Sandals; Jennifer Tomlinson of Terra Nova Hotel; Sarah and Jason of Jake's; and others to whom I apologize for my oversight.

Thanks also to my great friend Sheri Powers and to the many other friends and travelers who shared insights and experiences along the way.

From the Publisher
This first edition was edited and produced in Lonely Planet's office in Oakland, California. Kate Hoffman wrangled with the text and maps, with ample assistance from the worldly Don Gates. Carolyn Hubbard zeroed in on bloopers, proofing with gusto. Michelle Gagne and Laini Taylor pitched in with editing and proofing.

Chris Salcedo handily drew the maps, researched illustrations, and laid out the pages. Much thanks to Richard Wilson for sharing his layout savvy with Chris. Hugh D'Andrade, Hayden Foell, and Mark Butler used their pens and scratch boards to illustrate. Alex Guilbert trained his eagle eye on the maps, and Scott Summers polished the pages. Hugh designed the *boonoonoonoos* cover.

Contents

Map Legend

BOUNDARIES

— — — — International Boundary

— ‥ — ‥ — Parish Boundary

AREA FEATURES

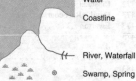

Park

NATIONAL PARK   National Park

HYDROGRAPHIC FEATURES

Water

Coastline

River, Waterfall

Swamp, Spring

ROUTES

Freeway

Major Road

Minor Road

Unpaved Road

Trail

Ferry Route

Railway, Railway Station

Metro, Metro Station

ROUTE SHIELD

A1 Highway

SYMBOLS

✪ NATIONAL CAPITAL	✈ Airfield	Gas Station	✿ Park
◉ Parish Capital	✈ Airport	⸖ Golf Course	)(Pass
	∴ Archaeological Site, Ruins	⊕ Hospital, Clinic	⊶ Picnic Area
● City	⑨ Bank, ATM	❶ Information	★ Police Station
● Town	✕ Battefield	⚒ Lighthouse	⬛ Pool
	�🏖 Beach	✳ Lookout	✉ Post Office
■ Hotel, B&B	● Bus Depot, Bus Stop	⛏ Mine	☒ Shipwreck
▲ Campground	⊟ Cathedral	⚑ Monument	❖ Shopping Mall
⌂ Chalet, Hut	⌒ Cave	▲ Mountain	🏛 Stately Home
❤ Hostel	✝ Church	🏛 Museum	☎ Telephone
⌂ Shelter	◎ Embassy	♪ Music, Live	▣ Tomb, Mausoleum
▼ Restaurant	⸙ Fishing, Fish Hatchery	← One-Way Street	🎋 Trailhead
⚐ Bar (Place to Drink)	⤬ Foot Bridge	⊖ Observatory	⚘ Winery
▬ Café	✣ Garden	P Parking	🦌 Zoo

Note: not all symbols displayed above appear in this book.

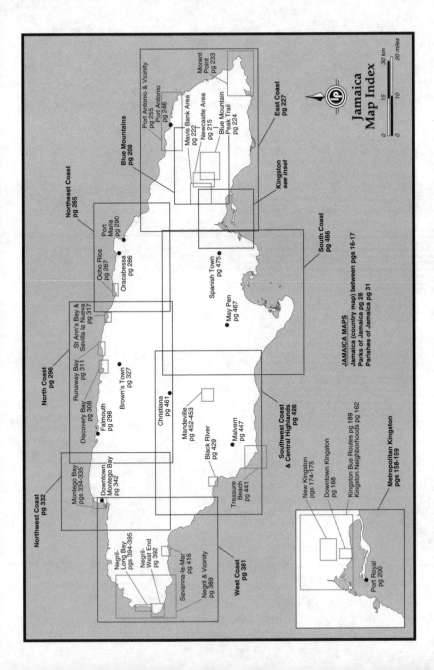

Jamaica
Map Index

Northwest Coast pg 332

Montego Bay pgs 334-335

Downtown Montego Bay pg 342

Negril-Long Bay pgs 394-395

Negril-West End pg 392

Negril & Vicinity pg 389

Savanna-la-Mar pg 416

West Coast pg 381

North Coast pg 296

Runaway Bay pg 311

Discovery Bay pg 308

Falmouth pg 298

St Ann's Bay & Sevilla la Nueva pg 317

Brown's Town pg 327

Christiana pg 461

Northeast Coast pg 265

Port Maria pg 290

Ocho Rios pg 267

Oracabessa pg 286

Blue Mountains pg 208

Port Antonio & Vicinity pg 255

Port Antonio pg 246

Mavis Bank Area pg 222

Newcastle Area pg 215

Blue Mountain Peak Trail pg 224

Morant Point pg 233

East Coast pg 227

Kingston *see inset*

South Coast pg 466

Spanish Town pg 475

May Pen pg 467

Mandeville pgs 452-453

Malvern pg 447

Black River pg 429

Treasure Beach pg 441

Southwest Coast & Central Highlands pg 426

JAMAICA MAPS
Jamaica (country map) between pgs 16-17
Parks of Jamaica pg 28
Parishes of Jamaica pg 31

New Kingston pgs 174-175

Downtown Kingston pg 168

Kingston Bus Routes pg 189
Kingston Neighborhoods pg 162

Metropolitan Kingston pgs 158-159

Port Royal pg 200

0   15   30 km
0   10   20 miles

Introduction

Jamaica enjoyed a reputation for exoticism long before Harry Belafonte lauded it as the 'Island in the Sun.' Swashbuckling movie hero Errol Flynn and his Hollywood pals cavorted here in the 1930s and 1940s, and England's equivalents – Noel Coward, Lawrence Olivier, and Sean Connery – had a penchant for this vibrant and colorful Caribbean island. Their interest attracted others, but even before the turn of the 19th century, visitors flocked to its shimmering beaches, ethereal mountains, and tropical climate.

Why choose Jamaica when there are more than 30 other Caribbean islands? Jamaica still has an allure matched only by Cuba and a diversity that few others islands can lay claim to.

Each of the island's four major resort areas and several minor ones has its own mood and character. Compare sleepy Port Antonio with its air of tropical lassitude, to Negril, every beach bum's idea of paradise, with its seven-mile, crescent-shaped, white-sand beach, carnal red sunsets, and reputation for bacchanalian living.

Many islands have lovelier beaches (and more of them), but Jamaica has its fair share of stunners fringed by coral reefs. It also has the widest range of accommodations in the Caribbean with something for every taste and budget. You can camp atop a coral cliff, choose a private villa with your own private beach, laugh your vacation away at a party-hearty, all-inclusive resort, or pursue a genteel lifestyle at a secluded retreat where butlers still call you 'm'lord' and 'm'lady.'

Water sports are well developed. So, too, are horseback riding, sport fishing, golf, and lazy river runs by bamboo raft. There are ample opportunities for birding, hiking, and many other off-beat adventures. You'll find colonial-era plantation homes and work-a-day plantations to explore, along with centuries-old botanical gardens, forts, and other historical sites. And the bustling markets are a whirligig of color and motion.

Stray from the north-coast resorts, and you'll discover radically different environments and terrains – perfect for exploring when you burn out on the beach.

Most of Jamaica is rugged and mountainous, reaching 7200 feet in the Blue Mountains, where the world's most sought-after coffee is grown. Pockets of wild, mysterious, thickly jungled terrain are so forbidding that during the 17th and 18th centuries bands of fiercely independent runaway slaves – the Maroons – survived here. Swampy wetlands harbor endangered crocodiles and manatees. Parched cactus-covered savannas line the south coast, where traditional fisher folk draw their *pirogues* and nets up on otherwise lonesome dark-brown beaches. And visitors familiar with sleepy Caribbean capital cities are surprised to find bustling Kingston a cornucopia of cosmopolitan culture that belies Jamaica's justly earned reputation for laid-back, parochial ease.

The Jamaican experience arises from its complex culture, which aspires to be African in defiance of both the island's location and colonial heritage. The island's evocative and somber history is rooted in the sugar-plantation economy: the slave era weighs heavy still in the national psyche.

To many people, Jamaica means reggae and Rastafarianism, both full of expressions of hope, love, anger, and social discontent. Behind the Jamaica Tourist Board's clichés lies a country beset with widespread poverty. Jamaica is a densely populated island struggling to escape dependency and debt. Colorful music and religion are opiates during hot nights, when Jamaicans move with a sensual ease, and everyone – dreadlocked local and clean-cut visitor alike – finds their nirvana in various combinations of reggae, reefers, and rum.

Much has been written about crime and safety. Too much. True, Jamaica is a volatile society, but violence rarely intrudes on the foreign visitor. It is mostly restricted to drug wars and impassioned political feuds in the ghettoes of Kingston. And harassment by over-zealous hustlers is at worst merely a nuisance.

Most visitors return home with memories of a warm, gracious people with a quick wit and a ready smile. The island enjoys harmonious race relations: its motto is 'Out of many, one people.' The rich African heritage runs deep. So, too, the British legacy – from the ubiquitous games of cricket to the names of the island's now defunct counties: Middlesex, Surrey, and Cornwall. Indian, Chinese, Middle Eastern, and other cultures have added to the island's cultural mix, nowhere more so than in its zesty cuisine – another fabulous Jamaican highlight.

Jamaica's appeal lies in its distinctive, simple, evocative style and easy Caribbean pace. Travel with an open mind, and you'll have 'no problem, mon!'

Facts about Jamaica

HISTORY

Jamaica has a colorful and painful history, marred since European settlement in the early 1500s by an undercurrent of violence and tyranny. The Spanish who arrived in 1509 quickly decimated the peaceful indigenous population and established a plantation-based economy that the English would later perfect. Three hundred years of slavery – of blood, sweat, and tears – under feudal colonial tutelage left a legacy of antagonism, cultural malaise, and destitution, spurring a push for national dignity. These conditions have shaped many of the events since emancipation.

The Arawaks

Around 700 AD, an Amerindian group called the Arawaks arrived and settled the island now known as Jamaica. The Arawaks had originated in the Guianas of South America perhaps 2000 years earlier. After developing seafaring skills, they had gradually moved north through the Caribbean island chain over several centuries.

The Arawaks were a short, slightly built race averaging a height of about five feet. They had bronze skin, broad faces, and shiny black hair. They prized pointed skulls (to attain this exalted shape, babies heads were pressed between slats of wood) and wore their hair in a topknot.

The Arawaks lived in egalitarian communities in conical thatched shelters located near river mouths. Their villages were comprised of several family clans and headed by a *cacique*, whose hereditary yet largely nominal title was passed down by primogeniture. Arawak society was communal, and materialism an alien concept.

(They gladly gave what gold they had to the greedy Spaniards who arrived in Columbus' wake; the Arawaks had only a limited amount of gold for ornamentation, obtained mostly in trade with other islands.)

Columbus described the gentle Arawaks as 'honest and content with what they have . . . a peaceful and generous people.' They thrived on an abundance of fish and shellfish, fruit, and cassava. The women engaged in food gathering, while the men hunted, fished, and tilled the fields. The Arawaks were skilled agriculturalists who rotated their crops to prevent soil erosion. Jamaica's fertile soils yielded yams, corn (maize), beans, spices, and cassava, which they leached of poison and baked into cakes and even fermented into beer.

The Arawaks had neither the wheel nor a written language, and they used neither beasts of burden nor metals (except for crude gold ornamentation). However, the abundance of food provided plenty of time for the pursuit of leisure. The Arawaks evolved skills as potters, carvers, weavers, and boat builders (Columbus remarked at the scale of their massive canoes – up to 100 feet long and capable of holding up to 50 people – hewn from the silk cotton tree). The Arawaks were particularly adept at spinning and weaving cotton into clothing (which they traded with neighboring islands) and hammocks – an Amerindian invention. The early Spanish even had the Arawaks weave sailcloth for their ships. The Indians also wove ropes, carpets, and watertight roofs from the stringy bark of the calabash tree.

A ball game called *batos* formed an important focus of social life. The game, roughly resembling volleyball, was played in stone plazas called *bateyes* using a ball made of rubber – a novelty to the Spaniards – and the Arawaks bet on the games. The Spaniards also noted other habits: the Indians would get fired up by maize alcohol, smoke dried leaves, and snort a powdered drug blown up the nostrils through a meter-long tube called a *tabaco*.

Religion played a central role in Arawak life. They worshipped various gods who were thought to control known forces such as rain, sun, wind, and hurricanes, and were represented by *zemes*, idols of humans or animals. One god was supreme: Yocahú, the sun god (also the 'Giver of Cassava'). They believed in a glorious afterlife and would sometimes strangle their dying chieftains to speed them to heaven, an idyllic place called *coyaba*, where pestilence, drought, hurricanes and other troubles were unknown. The deceased were buried in caves, where their bones were often placed in large jars.

More than 230 Arawak sites have been unearthed in Jamaica, most notably at White Marl, three miles east of Spanish Town (now the site of the Arawak Museum). The little that remains of their culture is limited to pottery shards; petroglyphs of frogs, lizards, turtles, humans, and abstract designs (most notably on the ceiling of Mountain River Cave near Guanaboa Vale in St Catherine); and words such as canoe, cannibal, hammock, hurricane, and tobacco.

The Coming of Columbus

Christopher Columbus (Cristoforo Colombo) sighted the islands of the Caribbean on October 12, 1492, during the first of his four New World voyages to find a westward route to the East Indies. Until then, the Old World was unaware of the existence of the Americas.

Until his death, Columbus remained convinced that these islands were the easternmost outposts of Asia. He had traveled west to reach them, so he named them the West Indies. Everywhere he landed, Columbus found indigenous peoples – the peaceful Arawaks and warring Caribs – and he called them 'Indians.'

The explorer set sail on his second voyage for the New World with an armada of 17 ships on September 5, 1493. Before reaching Jamaica, he 'discovered' Puerto Rico, where he made his first contact with Caribs, a war-mongering people he described as 'ferocious.'

By the time Columbus 'discovered' Jamaica on May 5, 1494, the Arawaks inhabited the entire island they called Xaymaca ('land of wood and water'). There were perhaps 100,000 Arawaks in Jamaica when Columbus landed in today's St Ann's Bay, which he named Santa Gloria 'on account of the extreme beauty of its country.'

At the time of Columbus' landing, the easternmost islands of the Caribbean had been swept by warlike Caribs, from which the region gets its name. Like the Arawaks before them, the Caribs had originated in northern South America and swept north through the Caribbean, slaughtering and enslaving the Arawaks wherever they found them. The Caribs never reached Jamaica where, it is claimed, the Arawaks had never experienced war and had no weapons.

The newcomers from the Old World, however, encountered a hostile reception. After anchoring the night offshore in Bahía Santa Gloria, Columbus sailed down the coast to a horseshoe shaped cove (today's Discovery Bay), where he had his crossbow men fire on another hostile group of Arawaks, killing several. He also set a fierce dog – the first the Arawaks had ever seen – on the Indians, thus establishing the vicious tone of future colonial occupation. Columbus took possession of the island for Spain and christened it Santo Jago. The Arawaks soon reappeared with peace offerings and feasted the strange newcomers throughout their brief stay.

On May 9, Columbus sailed on to El Golfo de Buen Tiempo (the Gulf of Good Weather), today's Montego Bay and then sailed away to Cuba. He returned later that year and explored the west and south coast before again departing.

Columbus returned nine years later on his fourth and final voyage to seek a passage to Asia. Columbus – titled the 'Viceroy of the Indies' – was by now out of favor at court. No gold, ivory, or other wealth had been found in any quantities during his explorations, and the Crown and other underwriters of his expensive expeditions wished to see a return on their investment. Unfortunately, Columbus' worm-eaten ships were falling apart. One, the *Gallega*, he abandoned off Panama. Another sank off Hispaniola. As he headed for Hispaniola, storms forced him to seek shelter in Jamaica, and he barely made it to Santa Gloria Bay. The two remaining vessels were so worm-riddled that Columbus and his 120 crewmen (including his son Ferdinand and brother Bartholomew) were forced to abandon ship and watched both vessels capsize and sink.

The luckless Spaniards spent almost a year marooned. The Arawaks wisely gave them a wide berth. Melancholy set in, and they suffered desperately from disease and malnutrition. Finally, two officers succeeded in paddling a canoe to Hispaniola, where they were imprisoned by the jealous governor, who sent a vessel to Jamaica to see if Columbus was dead. The skipper passed by Santa Gloria Bay, where he left a message for Columbus that no vessel could be spared to rescue him. Eventually the officers were released from jail, and they chartered a ship to rescue the now broken explorer and his men. On June 29, 1504, Columbus sailed away, never again to return to Jamaica or the New World.

Spanish Settlement

For a while Jamaica was Columbus' personal property. When he died in 1506, the title passed to his son Diego, whose descendants to this day carry the honorary title of Marquis of Jamaica. Diego appointed one of his father's lieutenants, Don Juan de Esquivel, as governor. In 1510, Esquivel began to colonize the island. He established a capital called Nueva Sevilla (New Seville) near present-day St Ann's Bay, where Columbus' vessels are believed to have sunk in 1503. Unfortunately, Nueva Sevilla was built near a swamp and proved an unhealthy and unproductive site. In 1534, the Spanish uprooted and created a new settlement on the south coast to serve

as their capital, which they named St Jago de la Vega (today's Spanish Town). The new capital grew quickly and became a center of social life. Little remains today of the original settlement, which was reclaimed by nature.

The settlers raised cattle and pigs on large ranches on the savanna of the south coast. They shipped lard derived from the fat of wild pigs, which roamed in large numbers in the interior hills. They also introduced two things that would profoundly shape the island's future: sugar and slaves imported from Africa.

The First Slaves

The Spaniards had exacted tribute from the Arawak, whom they enslaved, decimating the indigenous population through hard labor and ill-treatment. Many Indians chose to kill their children and commit suicide by drinking poisonous cassava juice rather than succumb to the ordeal of Spanish rule. European diseases decimated the Indians, too, for they had no resistance to the common cold, influenza, and more deadly ailments. Within a few decades the Indian population had been entirely wiped out. (Years later, in 1598, the governor, Fernando Melgarejo, proposed setting aside a special area where the last few Arawaks could live unmolested, but he was overruled.) Thus, the Spaniards took to importing slaves: the first shipment of African slaves arrived in 1517. The Spaniards turned to the Catholic religion to justify their actions. They converted their slaves and convinced themselves that the bleak life of a Christian slave was superior to that of a free heathen.

The island was ostensibly ruled by a governor and a council, or *cabildo*, of elected members. The two were constantly at odds. A third authority was the Church. Rivalry between the troika weakened the colony, which received little support from the Spanish Crown. Although small settlements at Oristan (Bluefields, near Savanna-la-Mar) and Esquivel (today's Old Harbour) were established, the Spaniards never developed Jamaica. It languished as a post for provisioning ships moving between Spain and Central America. The weak colony was constantly harassed by French, English, and Dutch pirates, who had begun to operate in Caribbean waters even before the first Spanish settlement in Jamaica was laid. Jamaica remained an undeveloped backwater, a third-rate colony ripe for invasion.

The English Invasion

In 1654, Oliver Cromwell, Lord Protector of England, devised his ill-fated 'Grand Western Design' to destroy the Spanish trade monopoly and accrue English holdings in the Caribbean. He amassed a fleet, jointly led by Admiral William Penn (father of the founder of the US state of Pennsylvania) and General Robert Venables, to conquer the Spanish-held Caribbean islands. The expedition was ill-equipped and badly organized. Its 'wicked army [of] . . . common cheats, thieves [and] . . . lewd persons' was severely repulsed in April 1655 by Spanish forces on Hispaniola at the loss of more than 1000 men. The two leaders were as ill-chosen as the men they commanded. The historian Germán Arciniegas recorded that 'Penn smiled every time Venables made a blunder, and Venables made a blunder every time he gave an order or mapped a campaign.'

After their disastrous debacle, they sailed to thinly populated, weakly defended Jamaica, intent on a prize to appease Cromwell. On May 10, 1655, Venable and Penn's expeditionary force of 38 ships landed 8000 troops at Caguaya, near the Spanish capital of St Jago de la Vega. The Spaniards held off the English for a while under a ruse that they were considering their terms of surrender. Instead, they stripped them of all their possessions and simply retreated north over the mountains, from where they set sail to Cuba, abandoning the island to the English. The English troops promptly set about destroying the city.

Before leaving, the Spanish also freed their slaves and encouraged them to harass the English. These *cimarrones* ('wild

ones') took to the hills, where they mastered hit-and-run guerrilla warfare and defended their freedom fiercely until finally granted autonomy a century later. A small band of Spanish loyalists under General Cristobal Ysassi also fought a guerrilla war against the English. In 1658 Spanish forces arrived from Cuba to assist Ysassi. The decisive battle at Rio Bueno was won by the English under Colonel Edward D'Oyley, who had sailed around the island with 750 men. Ysassi escaped, and after two futile years of guerrilla warfare he, too, fled to Cuba. With the destruction of St Jago, the English wiped out virtually all traces of the Spanish occupation. Many Spanish place names remain, however.

English Settlement

Cromwell sought to consolidate his new holding by enticing settlers with promises of land grants and supplies. In December 1656, for example, 1600 English arrived from Antigua to settle the area around Port Morant at the eastern tip of Jamaica. The region proved too swampy. Within one year, three-quarters of the settlers had succumbed to malaria and other swamp fevers.

Others settlers fared better and a viable economy began to evolve as trade was established with other islands and the home country. The island was under military rule, and many soldiers wished to settle down as colonists. This desire and the tensions and rivalry between supporters of Cromwell and those who favored restoration of the monarchy helped spawn a mutiny of troops in August 1660. D'Oyley lost no time in suppressing the insurrection and executed the two colonels in charge of the rebellious regiments.

In 1661, following the restoration in England, D'Oyley was appointed governor directly responsible to King Charles II. Ironically, he was directed to release the military forces from duty and to promote economic prosperity. By 1662, 4000 colonists had arrived, forming an electorate that created a governing council. It soon found itself at odds with the governor. The English government encouraged

Northeast of Savanna-la-Mar, the mineral waters of Roaring River
spring from the ground and flow through fields of water hyacinths.

Montego Bay Marine Park
Highly rated dive sites ranging from shallow patch reefs to stunning walls

Cockpit Country
Five hundred square miles of deeply pitted, otherworldly terrain, a must for hearty hikers accompanied by guides

Negril Beaches
The best for laid-back sunning by day and live reggae by night

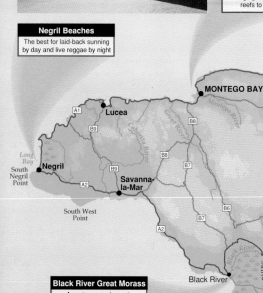

Falmouth

Runaway Bay

MONTEGO BAY

B11

B10

B5

Discovery Bay

A1

Lucea

B9

Cabarita River

Montego River

Great River

B8

Martha Brae River

B11

Brown's Town

B10

B5

B3

Long Bay

South Negril Point

Negril

B8

B9

B7

Savanna-la-Mar

A2

B8

B7

B6

B10

Christiana

B3

South West Point

A2

B7

B6

B5

B4

Black River

Don Figuerero Mountains

A2

Mandeville

A2

Black River Great Morass
A vast swamp, home to crocodiles, manatees, and countless birds

Black River

Santa Cruz Mountains

Malvern

Treasure Beach

Milk River

Treasure Beach
Known islandwide for the graciousness of its laid-back residents

Alligator Pond
A mountain-fringed bay and thriving fishing village full of Jamaican charm

Long Bay
A pristine 15-mile coastline of cacti, mangroves, and reeds, a naturalist's delight

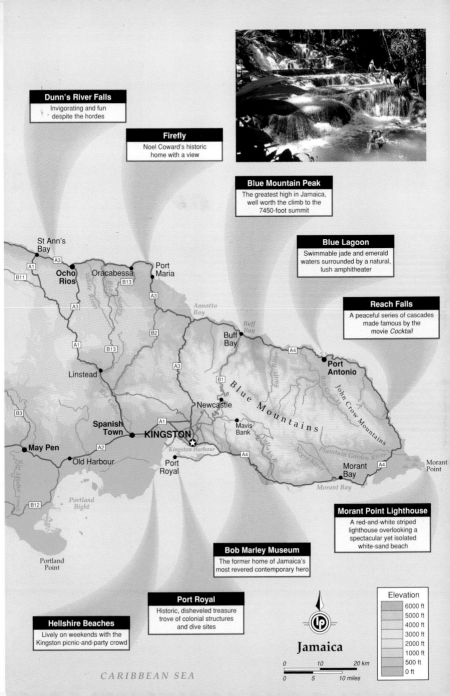

Dunn's River Falls
Invigorating and fun despite the hordes

Firefly
Noel Coward's historic home with a view

Blue Mountain Peak
The greatest high in Jamaica, well worth the climb to the 7450-foot summit

Blue Lagoon
Swimmable jade and emerald waters surrounded by a natural, lush amphitheater

Reach Falls
A peaceful series of cascades made famous by the movie *Cocktail*

Morant Point Lighthouse
A red-and-white striped lighthouse overlooking a spectacular yet isolated white-sand beach

Bob Marley Museum
The former home of Jamaica's most revered contemporary hero

Port Royal
Historic, disheveled treasure trove of colonial structures and dive sites

Hellshire Beaches
Lively on weekends with the Kingston picnic-and-party crowd

St Ann's Bay
A1
A3
B11
Ocho Rios
Oracabessa
B13
Port Maria
A3
White River
Rio Nuevo
Annotto Bay
A3
B2
Buff Bay
Buff Bay
A1
B13
A3
Suff River
A4
Port Antonio
Linstead
B1
Blue Mountains
John Crow Mountains
Rio Grande
B3
Newcastle
Rio Cobre
Spanish Town
A1
KINGSTON
Kingston Harbour
Mavis Bank
Mabis R
Negro River
Plaintain Garden River
Morant Point
May Pen
A2
Old Harbour
Port Royal
A4
Morant Bay
A4
Rio Minho
Morant Bay
B12
Portland Bight

Portland Point

CARIBBEAN SEA

Jamaica

0   10   20 km
0   5   10 miles

Elevation
6000 ft
5000 ft
4000 ft
3000 ft
2000 ft
1000 ft
500 ft
0 ft

Seeking the spirit in the wood

A vender of 'sex potents' (for men only)

MoBay entertainment – or was it the jerk?

Enterprising higgler at Sandals Resort

Giggling schoolgirls studying tourists

investment and further settlement, which hastened as profits began to accrue from cocoa, coffee, and sugarcane production.

In 1687, Sir Hans Sloane, a prominent London physician, published a scholarly description of Jamaica that did much to popularize the island. A new wave of settlement began, including felons exiled to Jamaica as punishment and impoverished Scots and Welsh who arrived as indentured laborers. Tradesmen also arrived, along with merchants, skilled craftsmen, and would-be planters eager to cash in on the growing fortunes of this fecund island, which was being turned into a vast sugar plantation.

Rise of the Buccaneers

During the 17th century Britain was constantly at war with France or Spain. Since the Royal Navy couldn't effectively patrol the Caribbean, the Crown sponsored individual captains – privateers – to do the job. It issued Letters of Marque authorizing privateers to capture enemy vessels and plunder enemy cities. Jamaica, lying so close to Cuba and Hispaniola, was an ideal base.

Many of the privateers – buccaneers (from *boucan*, the Spanish word for smoked meat) – had evolved as a motley band of seafaring miscreants, political refugees, and escaped criminals who had gravitated to the tiny isle of Tortuga, northwest of Hispaniola. Here they coalesced and established a thriving trade with passing ships. They lived a relatively sedentary life raising hogs and cattle. They also hunted wild boar in the hills of Hispaniola and sold the smoked meat, along with tallow and hides.

The Spanish authorities resented their presence. When the Spanish made a savage attempt to suppress them, the buccaneers were forced from Tortuga to Tortola. They formed the Confederacy of the Brethren of the Coast, committed to a life of piracy against the Spaniards. Gradually they replaced their motley vessels with captured Spanish ships and grew into a powerful and ruthless force. Before long they were

raiding far and wide and were a feared force throughout the Antilles.

Initially, the English joined with the Spanish in attempts to suppress the buccaneers. But the outbreak of the Second Dutch War against Holland and Spain in March 1664 caused England to rethink its policy. Jamaica was vulnerable to attacks. Hence, the newly appointed governor, Sir Thomas Modyford, contrived for the Brethren to defend the island (historian Edward Long later wrote: 'It is to the Bucaniers that we owe the possession of Jamaica at this hour'). Port Royal and Kingston Harbour became their base, and their numbers swelled astronomically.

Port Royal prospered and within a decade was Jamaica's largest city. It became an immensely wealthy yet rough and sordid den of iniquity, reportedly with more brothels and alehouses than any other city on earth. One buccaneer, John Esquemeling, recorded how he 'saw one of [these pirates] give unto a common strumpet five hundred pieces-of-eight only that he might see her naked.'

At sea the buccaneers adopted strict rules of honor, as well as insurance policies for those wounded in battle – the loss of an eye or a finger earned 100 pieces of eight or one slave, the loss of a right arm earned 600 pieces of eight or eight slaves, and so on.

They were also ruthless against the Spanish. The privateers' extremes of violence and debauchery are hinted at by Esquemeling, in his eye-witness description of the sacking of Porto Bello:

Having shut up all the Soldiers and Officers, as prisoners, into one room, they instantly set fire unto the powder . . . and blew up the whole Castle . . . with all the Spaniards that were within. This being done, they . . . fell to eating and drinking after their usual manner, that is to say, committing in both these things all manner of debauchery and excess. These two vices were immediately followed by many insolent actions of Rape and Adultery committed upon many very honest women, as well married as virgins; who being threatened with Sword, were constrained to submit their bodies to the violence of these lewd and wicked men.

A ruthless young Welshman named Henry Morgan quickly established his supremacy over the mercenary mob and guided the buccaneers and Port Royal to their pinnacle (Morgan, it appears, had been shipped from Wales to Barbados as an indentured servant and made his way to Tortuga to join the Brethren).

Morgan and his cutthroats pillaged many Spanish towns through the Americas before crowning an illustrious career by sacking Spain's premier New World City: Panamá. Spain and England had just signed a peace treaty, however, and Morgan's actions earned the ignominy of King Charles. After being recalled to England to stand trial, the daring buccaneer and his mentor were cleared of disgrace (Modyford was imprisoned for a brief term as a salve to Spain) and reunited in Jamaica, Morgan as governor and Modyford as chief justice. Morgan, now knighted, became a rich landowner with property throughout Jamaica. He was charged the responsibility for suppressing privateering as an officially sanctioned activity. Even so, he caroused in Port Royal, where he succumbed to dropsy (edema) and was entombed at Port Royal in 1688.

With England at peace with its rivals, buccaneers were now regarded as pirates. Mother Nature lent a hand in their suppression when a massive earthquake struck Port Royal on June 7, 1692, toppling much of the city (and Morgan's grave) into the sea. More than 2000 people – one-third of Port Royal's population – perished. Many of the survivors pitched camp across the bay at the site of today's Kingston. Although Port Royal was rebuilt, the pirates were forced back to sea again.

French Invasions

The English constructed forts all around Jamaica's coast to defend against pirates and European invaders. The island was seen as a worthy prize by France, with whom England remained in near-constant war. In 1694 a French invasion fleet under Admiral Jean du Casse, the buccaneer governor of Saint-Domingue (Haiti), took advantage of Jamaica's weakness following the earthquake and raided several points along the Jamaican coast, laying waste to many plantations. And in August 1702, a French fleet under du Casse and English fleets under Admiral John Benbow, sailing from Port Royal, fought a six-day battle to a stalemate off the coast of Colombia. Benbow obstinately refused to retire, despite the desertion of four of his captains, two of whom were later court-martialed and shot.

The First Maroon War

By the end of the 17th century, Jamaica, which the English had consolidated as a slave colony, was also under siege from within. The first major slave rebellion occurred in 1690 in Clarendon Parish, where many slaves (mainly of fiercely independent, warlike Cormorante tribes of the African Gold Coast) escaped and fled into the mountains. They joined the descendants of slaves who had been freed by the Spanish in 1655 and had eventually coalesced into two powerful bands in the Blue Mountains and in the Cockpit Country of southern Trelawny (then part of St James Parish).

In 1663, the English had offered full freedom and land grants to all the African slaves brought over by the Spanish who would surrender, but the Maroons (from the Spanish word *cimarrón*, or 'wild ones') refused. For the next 76 years the communities of Maroons plagued the English. They raided the plantations from their remote redoubts and served as magnets for runaway slaves. Their daring grew with their numbers, and some 44 Acts of the Assembly were passed to deal with their intransigence.

For decades the English militia skirmished with bands of Maroons in what came to be known as the First Maroon War. Finally, in 1729, the English launched an offensive to eradicate the Maroons, but the thickly jungled mountains were ill-suited to English-style open warfare. The Maroons had perfected ambush-style guerrilla warfare; they were an invisible enemy operating in bands that communicated with secret calls and by *abeng* horn.

After a decade of fruitless and costly campaigning, the English (aided by dogs and *mestizo* trackers brought in from Central America) gained the upper hand. As the English soldiers squeezed the hardy Maroons into smaller and smaller territories, they decided to come to terms. On March 1, 1739, Colonel Guthrie and Cudjoe, the Cormorante leader of the Maroons of Trelawny, signed a peace treaty granting the Maroons autonomy and 1500 acres of land. In return, the Maroons agreed to cease harassing the English. They also agreed to chase down runaway slaves as bounty hunters, and to assist the English in quelling rebellions. The Maroons of the Blue Mountains under a leader named Quao signed a similar treaty one year later. Though the Maroons were temporarily spent as a force, they had sealed their status as the symbol of Jamaica's fierce independence (see the sidebar Windward Maroons in the Blue Mountains chapter).

Pesky Pirates

Pirates added to the colony's problems. Several pirates rose to infamy for their cruelty, daring, and, occasionally, their flamboyant ways.

Every English schoolchild has heard of 'Blackbeard,' whose real name was Edward Teach. This brutal giant of a man

The ferocious Blackbeard sported proto-dreads.

terrorized his victims by wearing flaming fuses in his matted beard and hair. And 'Calico Jack' Rackham, although equally ruthless, became known for his fondness for calico underwear (see the Calico Jack sidebar in the Southwest Coast chapter). Like many pirates, Rackham was captured and executed; his body was hung in an iron frame on a small cay off Port Royal (the cay is still called Rackham's Cay).

For the next hundred years pirates plagued the Caribbean, plundering ships of all nations and coming ashore to raid the sugar plantations that were sprouting all over Jamaica.

King Sugar

Many officers in Cromwell's army had received land grants. They and subsequent English settlers employed slaves to clear the land for raising indigo, tobacco, and cocoa. But one crop above all was best suited to the soil and climate: sugar. During the course of the 18th century, Jamaica became the largest sugar producer in the world.

Throughout the period, Jamaica was ruled by a governor appointed by the monarch, and by an elected assembly of planters, who were usually at loggerheads with the governor. The island was divided into 13 parishes (their boundaries remain today), the local affairs of which were administered by a council of leading planters. The Crown's interests at the parish level were looked after by an appointed custos (see the Local Government section under Government & Politics below). The colonialists' main interest lay in fostering the sugar and slave economy. Small-scale farmers diminished in numbers as they were squeezed from productive land by more powerful sugar planters.

Many Jamaican planters were absentee landlords who lived most of the year in England, where they displayed an ostentatious lifestyle and formed a powerful political lobby. Aided by protective tariffs in England that taxed sugar products from other islands and kept Jamaica sugar prices artificially high, they fostered and maintained for the West Indian 'sugar colonies' an importance all out of proportion to their size. The planters built sturdy and handsome mansions – 'great houses' – often in the latest Georgian fashion high above their canefields, where they could catch the cooling breezes and watch over their estates. These plantations usually consisted of boiling houses, distilleries, and other factory buildings made of stone, with stone aqueducts to supply water. Rows of squalid barracks and huts for the slaves were also constant features. Towns grew up around the major ports, which were centers for trade with North America and Europe. Jamaican sugar, rum, and molasses were exchanged for lumber, pickled fish, salted meats, flour, and other supplies.

Slavery
Slavery came to dominate Jamaican life. By 1700 there were perhaps 7000 English

in Jamaica and 40,000 slaves. One century later, the number of whites had tripled, but they ruled over 300,000 slaves.

The transition to plantation labor wasn't easy for slaves newly arrived from Africa. The average slave had to be 'broken in' for two or three years. More than 500,000 slaves were imported during the 18th century, yet six slaves died for every one born. Tens of thousands were worked to death. Others died of exposure, disease, or malnutrition. Slaves were put to work in the fields without respect for gender. Although the majority of slaves were field laborers, others were put to work building factories, houses, and roads. The more fortunate were chosen as domestic servants, cooks, footmen, butlers, and grooms.

During their few free hours, slaves cultivated their own tiny plots. Sunday was a rest day, and slaves gathered to sell yams and other produce at the bustling markets. If fortunate, a slave might save enough money to buy his freedom, which a master could also grant as he wished (free blacks were issued a pass and had to wear a blue cross on their shoulders). The offspring of white men and slave women were know as 'free-coloreds' and were accorded special rights.

The planters ran their estates as vicious fiefdoms under the authority of an overseer, who enjoyed relatively free reign. White planters lived in constant fear of slave revolt. To forestall ferment, slaves were denied permission to congregate, and families were separated to break down clan systems. Planters burned slaves to death, strangled them, and employed other tortures to terrorize the slave population into obedience. The extreme treatment was eventually regulated by slave codes, but plantation society remained tied to the rule of the whip.

Rebellions & Revolutions
The slaves despised their 'massas' (masters) and struggled against the tyranny imposed on them at every opportunity. Insurrections were put down with the utmost severity.

The Slave Trade

English merchants dominated the trade that supplied the West Indies with slaves from West Africa. They operated an immensely profitable triangular route. The ships normally set sail from Bristol or Liverpool for Africa carrying trinkets to barter for blacks who were captured or sold into slavery in their homelands. Most were from the Ashanti, Cormorante, Mandingo, and Yoruba tribes.

At first, traders bought captured warriors and other prisoners of local chieftains. As demand soared, huge raids swept through West Africa, and captives were chained together and driven like cattle to the coast. There they were held in stockades before being loaded onto ships for the sordid 'middle passage' across the Atlantic.

The voyage was a dreadful ordeal that lasted anywhere from six to 12 weeks. The captives were kept chained below, where they lay amid their excrement and vomit, shoulder to shoulder. Not an inch of space was wasted. Inevitably, they weakened and sickened, and many died of disease in the festering holds. Others committed suicide. The captives who were still alive were fattened up as the boat reached port.

The slaves were oiled to make them look healthy before being auctioned. Their prices varied between £25 and £75 for unskilled slaves; slaves who had been trained as carpenters and blacksmiths fetched a premium – often £300 or more. The most wretched had a worth of no more than a shilling.

Kingston served as the main distribution point for delivery to other islands. Of the tens of thousands of slaves shipped to Jamaica every year, the vast majority were re-exported.

The slave ships then returned to England carrying sugar, molasses, and rum. ■

---

43   Kingston, Nov 23, 1803
FOR SALE, *for Cash, Bills of Exchange, or Produce.*
343 Prime Young and Healthy
N E G R O E S.
Imported in the ship Roz, from Angola
BOGLE, JOPP, & CO

---

50   Kingston, Dec 10, 1803
TO BE SOLD, *for Cash or Bills of Exchange*
225 Choice Young Congo
S L A V E S.
Imported in the ship Bedford, Capt. Lane
SHAW, INGLIS, & MILLS

---

46   Kingston, Nov 11, 1803
TO SALE, *for Cash, Produce, or approved Bills of Exchange,*
315 Young Healthy
S L A V E S.
Imported in the ship Folly, James Blake, Master, from Congo
FAIRCLOUGH, BARNES, & WILSON

---

37   September 8, 1803
F O R   S A L E
Six Young Healthy and well-disposed
N E G R O E S,
Coopers by trade.
For particulars apply to
JOHN STONE

---

44   October 8, 1803
FOR SALE, *by Personel agreement, in the parish of St. James,*
1 0 0   Prime NEGROES,
Acustomed to Plantation Work; among whom are several valuable Tradesmen. For terms apply to
Meese Atkinson, Knobers & Co.

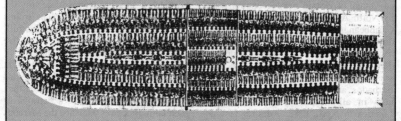

Tacky's Revolt, the first major uprising, erupted on Easter Monday in 1760 in Port Maria in St Mary Parish. Tacky was a tribal leader of the fiercely independent Cormorante tribe from the African Gold Coast. Before dawn, Tacky and a small band of followers murdered the fort storekeeper and stole a supply of muskets and arms. They then moved inland, murdering white settlers and urging slaves to revolt. The rebellion rippled through the western parishes as slaves joined the uprising. When word reached Spanish Town, the governor dispatched troops and called upon the Maroons to aid in suppressing the revolt. Tacky was killed, and many of his followers committed suicide rather than face capture. But the flames of rebellion flickered for months before finally being extinguished. White society enacted a swift and violent retribution (see the Easter Rebellion sidebar in the Northeast Coast chapter for further details).

The spirit of independence fomenting abroad also affected Jamaica, such as during the American War of Independence, which began in 1775. Sympathies in Jamaica lay with the 13 American colonies. When the colonies declared independence, the Jamaican House of Assembly petitioned King George on their behalf. Britain blockaded North America's eastern seaboard, cutting it off from trade with Jamaica, which relied on food imports from North America. As many as 15,000 slaves may have died of starvation as a result of the food shortages, which prompted the introduction of breadfruit from the South Seas as a staple for slaves.

Meanwhile, France and Spain took advantage of Britain's preoccupation with its North American colonies to recapture Caribbean islands that Britain had acquired during the preceding half-century of rivalry. By the end of the War of Independence in 1781, Britain had lost all its possessions in the West Indies except Antigua, Barbados, and Jamaica. France and Spain, now in alliance, attempted to invade Jamaica in April 1782. Admiral George Rodney set sail from Port Royal with a naval fleet and in a three-day running engagement off Dominica soundly defeated the enemy fleet in the Battle of the Saints. Rodney returned to Port Royal with the French flagship *Ville de Paris* in tow and the Count de Grasse, Admiral of France, as his prisoner. Rodney was rewarded with a barony and a £2000 annual pension. His feat is commemorated by a grand marble monument and statue in Spanish Town square.

The Tide Turns

In Europe, the French Revolution of 1789 spread a spirit of subversion worldwide, not least in the French colony of St Domingue, where slaves successfully ejected the French colonialists and established their independence, becoming the first free black state under the black general Toussaint L'Ouverture. In 1793, England attempted to turn back the tide by invading Haiti and managed to hold on to it for four years before being repulsed.

The example of Haiti fostered a sense of black pride and spurred new uprisings throughout the Caribbean. In Jamaica, Maroon sentiments were running high. A Second Maroon War broke out in 1795 after two Trelawny Maroons were sentenced to flogging for stealing pigs. The slaves who inflicted the punishment had been runaways that the Maroons had captured and returned to the British authorities. The proud Maroons were incensed at the insult; they felt deceived by colonial authorities, and simmering tensions boiled over. When threats against the residents of Montego Bay were issued in Trelawny Town, the new governor, the Earl of Balcarres, declared martial law and sent troops to destroy the Maroons' provision grounds. The troops were caught in a fatal ambush, and a full-scale war broke out that was to last five months, disrupting the entire island.

Eventually colonial authorities brought in bloodhounds from Cuba. The Maroons quickly surrendered on a pledge that they could retain their land. In a betrayal of good faith, Balcarres banished the Maroons to Nova Scotia, from which they were eventually sent to Sierra Leone, becoming the first New World Africans ever repatriated to Africa (about 60 later returned to Jamaica as free men). An English barracks was erected in Trelawny Town, forever ending the Maroon threat.

The Demise of Slavery

The turn of the century saw growing anti-slavery sentiment, influenced in part by the liberal shock waves of the French Revolution. A humanitarian spirit and a sense that slavery conflicted with Christian ideals was evolving in England, supported by abolitionist parliamentarians such as William Wilberforce.

Throughout the 1700s, the Church of England, the sole denomination in Jamaica, supported slavery. By the early 19th century, the arrival of Nonconformist missionaries and the emergence of the evangelical clergy within the established Church fostered a rising movement for abolition. They faced mounting hostility and even violent reaction from the 'plantocracy.' The Colonial Church Union (an unholy alliance between the planters and church establishment) hoped to delay emancipation by silencing the nonconformist missionaries and destroying their places of worship. Several missionaries were killed by hired thugs.

British Parliament banned the slave trade in 1807. Although the planter-dominated Jamaican House of Assembly vigorously opposed efforts to end slavery, sentiment in England was shifting against the intransigent planters. It would take little to sway Parliament to vote for abolition.

The Christmas Rebellion

That moment occurred in the wake of the Christmas Rebellion, which erupted in 1831 as the last and largest of the slave revolts in Jamaica. The rebellion was inspired by 'Daddy' Sam Sharpe, an educated slave and lay preacher who used his prayer meetings to incite passive resistance.

Though Sharpe had hoped for a peaceful uprising, the rebellion turned violent. As many as 20,000 slaves joined the revolt, which spread throughout the island, leaving in its wake enormous destruction. Plantations were razed to the ground and planters murdered. Once again, martial law was declared and troops were employed with vicious force to suppress the uprising. The governor persuaded the slaves to surrender on a promise of full pardon using the ruse that Parliament had voted to abolish slavery. Once the slaves had laid down their arms, more than 400 slaves were hanged; hundreds more were whipped.

The accounts of retribution fostered a wave of revulsion in England and helped the abolitionist cause. Parliament finally abolished slavery on August 1, 1834. (See the Christmas Rebellion sidebar in the Northwest Coast chapter.)

The Era of Emancipation

To ease the transition from a slave economy to one based on wage labor, Parliament conditioned the slaves' freedom: slaves had to serve a six-year unpaid 'apprenticeship' for their previous masters. In response slaves simply left the estates. The apprenticeship system was soon abandoned and the slaves set free unconditionally in 1838.

Economic chaos followed. Although Parliament voted £20 million to compensate the slave owners, the planters now had to pay their laborers. They offered starvation wages. Most slaves chose to leave the estates and fend for themselves. Aided by missionaries, many slave communities formed 'free villages' on uncultivated land.

The plantocracy attempted to sustain the crippled estates by importing indentured laborers from China and India (indentured laborers also built the island's first railroad, which opened in 1845). Other laborers came from Germany, Ireland, and Scotland. Many thousands of free Africans were also attracted to Jamaica as laborers. Few of these immigrants, however, chose to work the plantations. Instead, they lived a harsh life as subsistence farmers – the forebears of today's still impoverished agrarian class.

Jamaican sugar faced growing competition from Brazil, Cuba, and other islands. Likewise, beet sugar was now being grown cheaply in Europe (sugar production peaked in 1814 at 34 million pounds). Then Britain adopted a Free Trade policy, and Jamaican sugar lost the protection it had previously enjoyed; the Sugar Equalization Act of 1846 removed all protective measures on sugar imports to Britain. Many estates ceased cultivation and either were overrun by natural vegetation or were broken up into smaller holdings.

The old order had been toppled, undermining the planters' economic power. Nonetheless, the white plantocracy maintained its political power. Blacks, though free, had no political voice. By law, only titled property owners could vote. Blacks were routinely denied land claims by courts still lorded over by white magistrates schooled in the plantation mentality. The magistrates continued to mete out harsh 'justice' to a free but marginalized peasantry relegated to the least fertile lands. The majority of the population endured miserable economic conditions and squalor. Rural settlements were entirely lacking in sanitation, and epidemics of cholera and smallpox washed across the island in 1850 and 1852, reaping 32,000 people among the destitute black underclass.

A mulatto (mixed race) class had by now emerged. Mulattos had been enfranchised in 1830 and granted full rights equal to English citizens in 1832. Many mulattos received a good education and rose into the middle classes. Most looked up to the white society of their fathers. They were a privileged class and enjoyed the benefits of political power. Others sided with the oppressed, whose cause was taken up vociferously in the 1860s by a mulatto lawyer and liberal assemblyman, George William Gordon.

Morant Bay Rebellion
Jamaica's economy, already weakened by emancipation, degenerated further during the American Civil War (1861 – 1865), when naval blockades cut off vital supplies that sustained the island. Desperation over economic conditions, high food prices, and injustice finally boiled over in 1865. A demonstration in Morant Bay led by a black Baptist deacon named Paul Bogle descended on the town courthouse. The militia fired into the crowd, killing dozens of people, and a violent rebellion ensued. Several planters were murdered.

Governor Edward Eyre and his followers used the Morant Bay Rebellion as a pretext to get rid of Assemblyman Gordon. He was arrested, shipped to Morant Bay, swiftly tried by a kangaroo court, and promptly hung alongside Paul Bogle. More than 430 other rebels were executed, countless scores were flogged, and thousands of homes razed in retribution.

The brutal repression provoked an outcry in Britain. Eyre was recalled to England and dismissed from the colonial service, but not before being forced to persuade the Jamaican Assembly to vote its own dissolution. The island reverted to Parliament's control as a Crown Colony, with ultimate power in the hands of a series of liberal governors, marking the beginning of a more enlightened era.

Judicial reform was followed by the foundation of an educational system and civil service. Irrigation projects drained lowland marshes, which were converted to productive land, and a Lands Department was established to assist local farmers in buying government land. Telegraph communications were established in 1869. Money was allocated for an extensive new road system. The nation's capital was even moved from Spanish Town to Kingston. And Jamaica's economy began to recover, thanks to the lowly banana.

Banana Boom & Bust
In 1866 a Yankee skipper, George Busch, arrived in Jamaica and loaded several hundred stems of bananas, which he transported to Boston and sold at a handsome profit. He quickly returned to Port Antonio, where he encouraged production and soon had himself a thriving export business. Captain Lorenzo Dow Baker followed suit in the west, with his base at Montego Bay. Within a decade the banana trade was a booming business, so much so that Port

'Mr Tally Mon, tally me bananas...'

Antonio was a busier port than Liverpool. Everyone rushed to grow 'green gold.' The coming of banana boats was announced by a conch shell, the sound of which reverberated through the hills – a signal for country farmers to cut the fruit and rush down to the harbor by river or donkey.

Baker's small enterprise evolved into the Boston Fruit Company, and eventually, through merger, into the United Fruit Company, the giant that would control the economies of Central America's 'Banana Republics.' In 1927 production peaked and 21 million stems were exported. By then the big Yankee corporations had succeeded in squeezing out small-scale Jamaican farmers.

To pay the passage south to Jamaica, banana traders promoted the island and took on passengers. Thus, the birth of the banana-export trade also gave rise to the tourism industry.

Labor Unrest

Despite general progress, conditions for the working poor in Jamaica had remained appalling throughout this period. A series of natural disasters added salt to the wound. A great earthquake that toppled much of Kingston on January 14, 1907, also killed more than 800 people. Hurricanes devastated the island in 1915, 1916, and 1917.

In the 1930s events came to a head as the ripples from the Great Depression were felt around the world. Sugar sales plummeted, and banana exports followed suit. The vast majority of Jamaicans were unemployed and destitute; fewer than 20% earned any income at all. Strikes and riots erupted throughout the Caribbean, spilling over in Jamaica in 1938 when a demonstration at the West Indies Sugar Company factory at Frome, in Westmoreland, got out of hand. A battle between police and thousands of unemployed seeking work left several people dead. Strikes and looting erupted throughout Jamaica.

Birth of Modern Politics

This was a period, too, when Jamaican nationalism was growing. Native-son Marcus Garvey's call for black self-reliance were stirring resistance to paternalistic colonial government. In 1938 amid the clamor, a charismatic labor leader, Alexander Bustamante, formed the Bustamante Industrial Trade Union (BITU), the first trade union in the Caribbean (see the sidebar on Alex Bustamante in the Southwest Coast chapter). That same year, Bustamante's dissimilar cousin, Norman Manley, formed the People's National Party (PNP), the first political party on the island (Bustamante would form his own party – the Jamaica Labor Party (JLP) – in 1943). Separately they campaigned for economic and political reforms.

Prompted by the exigencies of WWII, when the Caribbean islands supplied food and raw materials to Britain, the British government enacted a policy to stimulate economic and social development in the Caribbean. Adult suffrage for all Jamaicans and a new constitution that provided for an elected government were introduced in 1944 (Bustamante's JLP won Jamaica's first election). In 1947 virtual autonomy was granted, though Jamaica remained a British colony under the jurisdiction of Parliament and the Crown – a prelude to full independence.

When the PNP took power in 1955, Manley began to steer Jamaica towards independence within a Caribbean federation. 'It is impossible to assume that each island, even the largest, could by itself be in a position to provide the basic necessities of a modern state,' said Manley in March 1945. With Manley's blessing, the British government established the West Indies Federation in January 1958 to unite the former Caribbean colonies as a single political entity and build a measure of stability to guide their independence.

Independence

Bustamante, however, declared the JLP opposed to membership and pressured for secession from the federation. In 1961, Prime Minister Manley allowed voters to decide by referendum. Bustamante was vindicated, Jamaica seceded, and a new constitution was drawn up. When Jamaica withdrew from the federation, the self-interest of its remaining members led to its collapse.

On August 6, 1962, Jamaica gained its independence in a ceremony witnessed by Vice President Lyndon Johnson and Princess Margaret. At midnight, the Union Jack came down in the National Stadium in Kingston, replaced by Jamaica's new flag: black (for the people), green (for the land), and gold (for the sun).

Turbulent Years

Immediate post-independence politics were dominated by Bustamante and Manley, whose parties grew ideologically apart. The JLP tilted towards the USA and free-market policies. Buoyed by the rapid growth of the bauxite industry, Jamaica experienced a decade of relative prosperity and growth, which continued under the administration of Donald Sangster (who died shortly thereafter) and Hugh Shearer – Bustamante's successors (Shearer was related to both Bustamante and Manley).

Following Manley's death in 1969, the PNP espoused increasingly radical social policies under the leadership of his son, Michael. In 1972, the PNP came to power under the election theme 'Time for a Change.' (Manley, an eloquent, handsome figure and charismatic, gifted speaker, had traveled to Ethiopia, where Emperor Haile Selassie had given him a staff – a 'rod of correction,' Manley called it.)

Manley attempted to make Jamaica a 'democratic socialist' nation. He initiated greater state control over the economy, including the bauxite industry, resulting in a deservedly greater share of revenues for the island. Manley introduced a statutory minimum wage and legislation favoring workers' rights. A literacy campaign, socialist health care, and other liberal economic and social reforms proved popular with the masses.

Unfortunately, the move toward socialism caused a capital flight at a time when Jamaica was reeling from the shock of the world's oil crisis and worldwide depression. Inflation roared above 50%, foreign investors pulled out, unemployment skyrocketed, and Jamaican society became increasingly polarized.

Outbreaks of violence erupted and finally boiled over into full-fledged warfare during the campaigns preceding the 1976 election. Heavily armed gangs of JLP and PNP supporters began killing each other in the partisan slums of Kingston, where party loyalties are more keenly territorial than in Europe and North America. Manley was forced to declare a state of emergency, but his PNP won the election by a wide margin that Manley took as a mandate supporting his socialist agenda.

The US government was hostile to the socialist path Manley was taking. He particularly antagonized the US by developing close ties with Cuba, and a six-day state visit by Fidel Castro in 1977 and the arrival of Cuban doctors, educators, and technical experts were seized upon by conservatives determined to thwart the communist association. The CIA developed plans to topple the Jamaican government. Western companies began to pull out, and the economy went into a steep decline. Tens of thousands of skilled workers and professionals fled the island, taking their money with them. Businesses closed down. Severe scarcities of even the most basic consumer items became common.

The IMF and World Bank refused to provide further loans to support the government deficit or to finance Manley's social programs. In 1977 they demanded a draconian austerity program. Manley, caught between a rock and a hard place, began to reverse his policies, alienating the PNP rank and file. A small right-wing clique of the Jamaica Defense Force even attempted an unsuccessful coup d'etat! Gun battles raged in Kingston. Armed police and soldiers patrolled the streets, and army helicopters whirred overhead. Street searches became routine.

Middle-class Jamaicans still speak with animosity of the Manley years, when a brain drain and capital flight almost bankrupted the country and the country lived under siege.

About Face

In 1980, the voters decided it was time for a change, but not before witnessing the most violent year since the 1865 Morant Bay Rebellion. Almost 700 people were killed in the election campaign, mostly in Kingston 'garrisons' ruled by party vigilantes (see the Corruption & 'Garrison' Politics section below). Tourism withered.

Under Boston-born, Harvard-educated Edward Seaga, the PLP inherited a country on the verge of bankruptcy and mired in domestic unrest. Seaga had promised 'deliverance.' He set himself the task of reversing Manley's policies. His efforts to restructure the economy included an austerity program and a painful devaluation of the dollar that created further hardships. Seaga also severed diplomatic relations with Cuba and nurtured strong ties with the Reagan administration, which offered Jamaica financial support. Soon, Jamaica's economic downward spiral slowed and a recovery began.

Nonetheless, Seaga's popularity waned due to the social costs of his retrenchment policies, which included severe cuts in education and health spending. Thus, when the US launched its military invasion of Grenada in autumn 1983, Seaga called a snap election to take advantage of a sudden boost in popularity and the absence of Michael Manley, who was touring abroad. The PNP boycotted the sudden election.

For the next six years (1983 – 1989), Jamaica had a one-party parliament. It was also a one-man show: Seaga held the positions of Prime Minister, and Minister of Finance and Planning, Minister of Information, Minister of Culture, and Minister of Defence. The cult of personality, government corruption, and growing poverty and unemployment in the midst of an economic revival turned the electorate against him.

In September 1988, Hurricane Gilbert tore across the island – the first such storm to do so since 1951. The most violent hurricane this century devastated crops islandwide, damage to property exceeded US$300 million, and one-quarter of Jamaica's population was left homeless.

Manley Mark II

Meanwhile, Manley's political thinking had changed from anti-American firebrand to middle-of-the-road populist promoter of free enterprise and tourism. Manley dubbed himself a 'mainstream realist.' Jamaica was still a polarized society, but one in which the middle and upper classes alone had benefited from the economic recovery; the vast majority of Jamaicans were poorer. In 1989 voters gave Manley a second term (the election period was relatively violence free), during which he took a leaf from Seaga's book, further deregulating the economy, reducing the scope of state involvement, and pursuing liberal-conservative economic policies.

Manley retired from politics in 1992 due to ill health, handing the reins to his deputy, Percival James Patterson – Jamaica's first black prime minister.

In the last election, held on March 30, 1993, the PNP won by a landslide (it took 52 out of 60 seats) against an ailing JLP, which suffered from internal feuding. The next elections are scheduled for 1998.

GEOGRAPHY

At a size of 4411 sq miles, about equal to the US state of Connecticut, or one-twentieth the size of Great Britain, Jamaica is the third largest island in the Caribbean and the largest of the English-speaking islands. It is one of the Greater Antilles that make up the westernmost and largest of the Caribbean islands (the Lesser Antilles, made up of dozens of smaller islands, lies further east and curl south like a shepherd's crook).

Jamaica lies 90 miles south of Cuba, 600 miles south of Miami, and 100 miles west of Haiti. It is within the tropics, 18° north of the equator between latitudes 17° 43' and 18° 32' north and longitudes 76° 11' and 78° 21' west.

The island is roughly ovoid in shape and measures 146 miles east to west; widths vary between 22 and 51 miles, with a sagging underbelly. Despite its relative small size, Jamaica boasts an impressive diversity of terrain and vegetation, although few visitors venture afield to experience this array. Columbus described it as 'the fairest isle that eyes beheld; mountainous . . . all full of valleys and fields and plains.' It *is* beautiful, with views worthy of a Winslow Homer painting.

The Coast
Jamaica is rimmed by a narrow coastal plain pitted with bays everywhere except in the south, where broad flatlands cover extensive areas and there are long ruler-straight stretches. Most of the developed resorts huddle along the north coast and to a lesser degree the west and northeast, where white-sand beaches are edged up against the shore by mountains. North coast vegetation is lush, more so to the east along the island's windward coast.

The south coast offers sharply contrasting terrain, including several areas of parched savanna plus two large swampy areas: the Great Morass, a vast wetland fed by the Black River and inhabited by timid crocodiles; and Long Bay, a remote strip of marshland that harbors Jamaica's last manatee population. In places, mountains muscle right up to the coast, dividing broad plains dominated by market gardens and sugarcane fields. Since coral reefs here are far offshore, there are few white-sand beaches. Mostly they are of gray-brown sand. East of Kingston, the coastal plain

again narrows and is backed by the Blue Mountains and John Crow Mountains.

Isolated, uninhabited coral cays speckle the sea off the southern coast, including the Pedro Cays – important nesting sites for colonies of boobies, terns, and other seabirds.

The Uplands
Inland is mostly mountainous. Almost half the island is at elevations of over 1000 feet. The mountains run through the island's center, rising gradually from the west and culminating in the tortuous Blue Mountains in the east, capped by Blue Mountain Peak at 7402 feet. Mountainous spurs and plateaus extend from the central chain and Blue Mountains to the south coast (cliffs reach 1500 feet in places).

The limestone interior is dramatically sculpted of deep vales and steep ridges. Much of the central uplands is dominated by basket-of-egg topography, highlighted by the Cockpit Country, a virtually impenetrable tract pitted with bush-covered hummocks, vast sinkholes, underground caves, and flat valley bottoms. The drama of this classic karst topography is not obvious from ground level, but from a plane its eerie grandeur is startling. The Cockpits are well known, but the same topography blankets much of the interior spine.

The limestone plateau rises to the island's backbone, which has a distinctly alpine feel at higher elevations. Here the terrain, deep-valed and wooded in deciduous and coniferous trees, is reminiscent of parts of central Europe.

GEOLOGY
Jamaica was born of volcanic activity.

Until about 190 million years ago, the earth's surface consisted of a single ocean and one great land mass: Pangaea (Greek for 'all earth'). Then the giant continent began to break up under the strain of hot, viscous magma (molten rock) welling up from deep within the earth. The earth's crust separated into thick 'plates' that have been inching apart and colliding at a snail's pace ever since – a process known as plate tectonics.

Jamaica and the other islands of the Greater Antilles were first pushed up from the seabed by a great volcanic welling about 140 million years ago, as the Caribbean plate jostled with the North American plate, creating huge friction and volcanic activity. During periods of inactivity, weathering wore the new land down. The island subsided beneath the sea about 100 million years ago before reemerging some 80 million years later during renewed volcanic activity, when the Caribbean plate changed direction, creating new forces (as well as the Blue Mountains, and the 24,720-foot-deep Cayman Trench west of Jamaica). The island continues to rise, in places as much as one foot every 1000 years.

Jamaica is situated in an earthquake zone. Frequent quakes shake the island, often with devastating effect: Port Royal was completely destroyed in 1692, and Kingston was devastated in 1907. Eastern Jamaica suffers frequent tremors. Unfortunately the country has been late in the day in bringing building codes up to par. Many thermal springs usher from fissures along the south coast.

The island is cut by about 120 rivers, many of which are bone-dry riverbeds for much of the year but become raging torrents after heavy rains, washing silt onto the lowland plains and causing great flooding. Only 12 are major – if still modest – rivers.

Two-thirds of the island's surface is composed of limestone (the compressed skeletons of coral, clams, and other sealife) that is in places several miles thick and covered by thick red-clay soils rich in bauxite. Most was laid down during the geological period when Jamaica was covered in sea and conical clams up to six feet across built great colonies on the seabed. The limestone takes on diverse and extraordinary forms, as in the vast shield-shaped Hellshire Hills and, most dramatically, in Cockpit Country, a 500-sq-mile region of northwest Jamaica.

Since limestone is unusually soft and porous, rainfall tends to soak into the rock rather than form rivers. As it soaks in, it dissolves the calcium carbonate, creating a tortuously pitted surface and great networks of dramatically sculpted underground caverns. (Water is aided in this action by reacting with limestone and carbon dioxide in the air to form a weak solution of carbonic acid, which speeds the erosion process; vegetation grows in the cracks and further breaks down the rock.) Where the caverns have become too large to support the rock above, the roofs collapse to form vast sinkholes, or depressions.

The limestone filters rainfall, purifying Jamaica's water supply.

CLIMATE

One of Jamaica's greatest allures is its idyllic tropical maritime climate. Seasons are virtually nonexistent, but weather patterns can change quickly, especially during hurricane season (see below). Visitors can call ☎ 924-0760 for north coast weather information; call ☎ 924-8055 for south coast information.

Temperatures

The temperature along the coast averages a near-constant 80° to 86°F year-round. Temperatures fall steadily with increasing altitude but even in the Blue Mountains average 65° or more. Monthly temperatures range less than 6°F, with February and March usually the coolest months. Down by the shore you're cooled by a warm trade wind – known as the 'doctor breeze' – that blows by day. A less noticeable nocturnal offshore breeze is known locally as 'the undertaker.' Cool 'northers' can also blow during December to March, when cold fronts that bring freezing conditions to Florida can affect Jamaica (on extreme occasions, temperatures may drop into the 60s).

Rainfall

Rainfall averages 78 inches. However, there are considerable variations nationwide, with the eastern (or windward) coast receiving considerably more rain than elsewhere. Parts of the John Crow and Blue Mountains receive an average of 300 inches a year (Bowden Pen, in the Upper Rio Grande Valley, holds the record with 496 inches in 1959 to 1960).

A 'rainy season' begins in May or June and extends through November or December, with the heaviest rains in September and October. However, rain can fall at any time of year – normally in short, heavy showers, often followed by sun.

By contrast, the southern coast lies in a rain shadow and in places is semibarren. The Treasure Beach area is particularly dry and can even experience drought in some years, as in 1994, when a drought afflicted the entire island.

Humidity is relatively high year-round, ranging from 63 to 73% in Kingston, and 71 to 77% in Montego Bay.

Hurricane Season

Although Jamaica lies in the Caribbean 'hurricane belt,' relatively few of the hurricanes that sweep the region touch Jamaica. The last great storm to hit the island was Hurricane Gilbert, which roared ashore in 1988, causing immense damage and killing 45 people.

Officially the hurricane season lasts from June 1 to November 30. August and September are peak months. A traditional rhyme is 'June too soon, July stand by, August prepare you must, September remember, October all over.'

ECOLOGY & ENVIRONMENT

Ecotourism has come late to the Caribbean: the islands depend heavily on resort-based, sun-seeking tourists. Only a decade ago, visitors had to look hard for protected areas. Today, national parks and wildlife reserves are rising from Miami to Maracaibo on the neap of an eco-sensitive wave. Jamaica has been especially late in the day in discovering that its wilderness is something to safeguard.

True, the Wildlife Protection Act (1974) gave protection to crocodiles, manatees, the yellow snake, and several other endangered species. And the Beach Protection Act was enacted in 1978 to forestall removal of sand by hotel developers creating artificial beaches. But only in 1991 was a regulatory body – the Protected Areas Resource Conservation Project (PARC) – created and entrusted with developing national parks. PARC is a joint venture between the Jamaican government and the US Agency for International Development (USAID). The island has one marine and one terrestrial national park, but as yet the latter is

The Big Blows

Caribbean hurricanes begin off the coast of Africa, forming as winds rush toward a low-pressure area and begin to swirl around it due to the rotational force of the earth's spin. They move counterclockwise across the Atlantic, fed by warm winds and moisture, building up force in their 2000-mile-run toward the Caribbean.

On the islands, the first stage of a hurricane's approach is called a 'tropical disturbance.' The next stage is a 'tropical depression.' When winds exceed 40 mph, the system is upgraded to a 'tropical storm' and is usually accompanied by heavy rains. The storm becomes a hurricane if winds exceed 74 mph and intensifies around an eye (a center of calm).

Hurricanes can range from 50 miles in diameter to devastating giants more than 1000 miles across. Their energy is prodigious – far more than the mightiest thermonuclear explosions.

Hurricanes are tracked by the National Hurricane Center in Miami, Florida. Satellite weather forecasts provide advance warning, but it is difficult to predict a storm's path.

If a hurricane warning is announced, stay sober. A hurricane is no time to be partying. You'll need your wits about you both during and after the storm.

For current weather information, you can call WeatherTrak at ☎ (900) 370-8725. ■

little more than a park in name (see National Parks below).

Coastal mangrove and wetland preserves, montane cloud forests, and other wild places are strewn across Jamaica, yet few travelers visit the island to get close to nature. Those that do are poorly served by wildlife reserves. Ecological treasures such as Long Bay's stunning swamplands – the last refuge of endangered manatees – go untapped. Eco-consciousness among the Jamaican population (and government) is at best embryonic, and existing legislation is largely ineffectual.

Many of Jamaica's endemic wildlife species are gone forever and many other species, including those that inhabit coral reefs, are endangered by such threats as pesticides, siltation, and other agricultural runoff; by the toxic byproducts of the alumina-processing industry; and by urban development that causes habitat loss. For example, the government Urban Development Council is blithely pushing a massive planned city into the Hellshire Hills – a forbidding, parched habitat of jagged limestone covered with the last rare remnant of 'dry limestone forest' that only a tough iguana could love. In fact, the Hellshires are the only place where the endangered Jamaican iguana hangs on to life by a thread.

The past few years have seen a stirring of eco-awareness. Jamaicans are beginning to adopt a more cautious attitude toward unrestrained hotel construction. For example, fears that Negril was becoming overdeveloped led to a two-year moratorium on construction in 1992; the measures were relaxed in 1994 after measures to protect the environment were implemented, including a new sewage system. More attention is also being given to community involvement. Entrepreneurs are beginning to open up nature spots to a more sophisticated audience that wants to escape the resort routine. And organizations such as the Jamaica Association of Dive Operators (JADO), the Jamaica Conservation and Development Trust, and the Negril Coral Reef Preservation Society are becoming increasingly active in conservation.

Jamaica's rich natural diversity is a boon, and it's a pity to miss out on it. If you're keen to get close to nature, you can find plenty to keep you enthralled. You'll also be doing Jamaica a good turn. Nature tourism is one of the most practical ways to save wild places and their wildlife from more erosive exploitation: it provides a way of reconciling economic development with species protection while giving the local communities a stake in conservation.

Ecological Treasures

The Caribbean has beaches, but it also has bush. No other island's interior gives its beaches as much competition as Jamaica's.

You can forsake sandals for hiking boots to follow mountain trails, shower in remote waterfalls, and shoot birds through the lens of a camera. Birdwatchers and botanists should flock to the Blue Mountains, where forests of towering antediluvian tree ferns, rhododendron dells, and cloud-swathed thickets dripping with mosses and orchids can easily be experienced along a warren of trails in Hollywell 'National Park' and along the well-maintained seven-mile trail to the summit of Blue Mountain Peak (7402 feet), which offers rare elfin forest stunted by extremes of cold.

Other prize areas include the totally uncharted Cockpit Country and the recently created but as yet undeveloped Font Hill Reserve, which like many swampy habitats in Jamaica teems with crocodiles and waterfowl. Negril's Great Morass (amazingly untapped yet literally a stone's throw from Negril's beaches) and the as-yet-undiscovered Long Bay swamps both harbor crocodiles, exotic birdlife, and other unique and much-imperiled wildlife that could be seen with comparative ease – if only some bright entrepreneur would cotton on! For now, your only sure bet is to penetrate the Black River Morass by boat from the town of Black River or check out Canoe Valley (Alligator Pond), another wetland that harbors endangered manatees.

Much of the north coast, of course, is fringed by coral reefs more beautiful than a forest of gems.

Ten Tips for Environmentally Conscious Travelers

Don't litter. Remember: take only photographs, leave only footprints. If you see litter, pick it up. Support recycling programs.

Respect the property of others. Never take 'souvenirs' such as shells, plants, or artifacts from historical sites or natural areas. Treat shells, sea urchins, coral, and other marine life as sacred.

Don't buy products made from endangered species. Many species of plants and animals are killed to make trinkets for tourists. By buying products made of tortoise shell, coral, or bird feathers, you are contributing to the decimation of wildlife. Shop with a conscience (see the sidebar on Shopping in the Facts for the Visitor chapter).

Keep to the footpaths. When hiking, always follow designated trails. Natural habitats are often quickly eroded, and animals and plants disturbed by walkers who stray from the beaten path.

Don't touch or stand on coral. Coral is extremely sensitive and is easily killed by snorkelers and divers who fail to honor this law of nature: human contact is deadly. Likewise, boaters should never anchor on coral – use mooring buoys. That's the law!

Sponsor environmental consciousness in others. Try to patronize hotels, tour companies, and merchants that act in an environmentally sound manner. Consider their impact on waste generation, noise levels and other pollution, energy consumption, and the local culture.

Help local communities gain a share of tourism revenues. Many local communities are hard-pressed in their survival and derive little benefit from Jamaica's huge tourism revenues. Educate yourself on community tourism and ways you can participate (see the Community Tourism sidebar in the Southwest Coast chapter). Use local guides wherever possible.

Respect the privacy of others. Don't intrude on others' lifestyles or privacy. Ask permission when taking photographs of individuals or before entering private property.

Respect the community. Learn about the customs of the region and support local efforts to preserve their environment and traditional culture.

Tell others. Politely intervene when other travelers are acting in an environmentally or socially detrimental manner. Educate them about the potential negative effects of their behavior. ∎

Felling the Forests

Virtually the entire island was smothered with forest and marshland when Columbus landed. Enough remains to remind you what Xaymaca looked like in 1494. But the island has been ravaged during the intervening 500 years. Forests were felled and wetlands drained for King Sugar and, later, for bananas. Jamaica's hardwoods were logged, too, to supply English (and Jamaican) furniture designers and craftsmen (much-sought-after Jamaican mahogany is the hardest variety in the world, and today it is almost all gone). Tourist resorts

and teeming populations engaged in survival edge up against much that remains.

Saving Jamaica's forests is not simply an aesthetic consideration: the nation's water supply depends on halting deforestation.

The sad news is that the island is losing its forest cover at a rate of 5.3% per year, according to a 1994 study of worldwide deforestation by the Food and Agricultural Organization (FAO) and World Resources Institute (WRI). Jamaica's rate of deforestation is by far the highest of any country in the world – more than twice that of Costa Rica and more than four times that of Mozambique, the highest in Africa.

In June 1992, the Natural Resources Conservation Authority Act established the NRCA, a regulatory body responsible for 'effectively managing the physical environment of Jamaica so as to ensure conservation.' The body also has the duty of promoting ecological consciousness among Jamaican people and of managing the national parks and protected areas.

Explaining to a destitute farmer that he can't cut trees to grow crops is difficult at best. Enforcement of regulations is virtually nonexistent, and the government has no official tree-planting program to replace what is lost (the Forest Department's tree nursery at Twickenham Park produces only a fraction of its seedling-producing capability). Such efforts have relied on nonprofit organizations such as the Jamaica Agricultural Society, which initiated a massive tree-planting campaign in 1995 (the Canadian government agreed to provide J\$170 million to finance the Trees for Tomorrow project, a scheme to maintain and restore Jamaican forests). And private enterprises such as Silver Hills Nursery, near Nonsuch in Portland, are popping up to provide a stock of fruit and lumber tree seedlings (see the East Coast chapter). Owner, Englishman Frank Swindells, also educates Jamaica's youth to have an appreciation of the value and necessity of environmental protection and the role that forests play in the enhancement of their environment.

Community Involvement

'Meet the People.' That's the new cry of Caribbean governments wishing to stimulate tourism that complements and supports local communities and thereby helps preserve the cultural heritage. For example, Jamaica's Community Tourism efforts (pioneered by Diana McIntyre-Pike, director of Countrystyle Ltd, a company that specializes in cultivating a marriage between tradition and tourism) urges visitors to take meals, outings, work-visits, and

Meet the People

Two decades ago, the Jamaica Tourist Board developed the Meet the People program, so that visitors to the island could interact with Jamaicans in their home environment and gain an appreciation for island life. Normally this involves being invited to an afternoon tea, dinner, or cocktail party; joining a family at a church service; sightseeing; or even a few hours of sharing the host's work environment.

About 600 volunteer families participate. The families are interviewed by JTB officials, and their premises inspected to ensure that they meet the program's standards. The JTB tries to match ages, professions, and hobbies of host and visitor. Since the JTB wishes to put Jamaica in the most positive light, you can expect to see middle-class or even upper-class life (the governor's wife regularly participates in the program). The hard life and poverty that is the lot for half of the population is *not* open to view through the JTB program.

There's no charge, but a small gift (or picking up at least a portion of any tab) is considered a common courtesy. ∎

accommodations with local villagers. Doing so channels income into needy hands and helps build community pride and cohesion.

Rural communities are also being encouraged to partake in preserving their natural heritage and, by doing so, to benefit from the ecotourism boom. Nature-guide training, and environmental and cultural awareness programs are growing, as in the Blue Mountains, where PARC is attempting to encourage community involvement in the evolution of the Blue Mountains – John Crow National Park as a potential eco-escape.

FLORA & FAUNA
Plants, Fruits & Flowers

Jamaica boasts more than 3000 species of flowering plants (including 200 species of orchids), of which at least 827 are endemics found nowhere else. The British

Isles, many times larger, can only manage a relatively puny one-twentieth that number. Jamaica is also renowned for having some 60 bromeliad species; dozens of epiphyte species (air plants) such as Old Man's Beard, which grows along power lines; and 550 species of ferns.

Impatiens color roadsides at cooler heights. Periwinkle grows everywhere and is commonly used in bush medicines. Many native plants are used in herbal medicines, teas, and spices, among them cerasee, a climbing vine of the cucumber family; world-renowned Jamaican ginger; and pimento, Jamaica's only indigenous spice and a member of the myrtle family (periwinkle is also in this family).

A great many species are exotics introduced from abroad. Two of the most obvious are the ubiquitous bougainvillea, whose tissue-paperlike blossoms blaze purple, pink, and orange; and the equally widespread poinciana, introduced from Kew Gardens in 1858. Ackee, the staple of Jamaican breakfasts, was brought by African slaves. But cocoa and cashew are natives of Central America and the West Indies, as is cassava, a root crop that was once a staple for indigenous peoples. Bombay mango, despite its name, flourishes only on tiny Jamaica. And a native pineapple from Jamaica was the progenitor of Hawaii's pineapples (the fruit even appears on the Jamaican coat of arms).

Another true-blooded native is bladderwort, a carnivorous plant that lures insects into its bladder where they trigger a trap door and are gradually digested. Another endemic 'carnivore' is the duppy flytrap, a climbing vine that bears an eight-inch-wide, heart-shaped purple flower (the largest in Jamaica). The hollow flower exudes a noxious smell that attracts flies. The flies enter through a tiny hole and are trapped inside by hairs pointing inward. The duppy plant doesn't consume the fly, however. In its struggle to escape, the fly becomes smothered with pollen; eventually the hairs collapse, allowing the fly to escape.

Many visitors are surprised to find cacti flourishing in the parched south, especially in the Hellshire Hills and around Treasure Beach. The opuntia cactus, or prickly pear, is popular with many poor Jamaicans, who roast and eat it (it supposedly tastes like roast pork).

Jamaica has several unique species, including the queen of the night cactus, which blooms spectacularly, and God okra, an endemic climbing cactus that bears a scarlet edible fruit called 'vinepear.' Other endemics are the melon cactus, which has a melonlike base topped by a magenta flower; phallic dildos, commonly used as hedges in the Treasure Beach region; and the *Rhipsalis baccifera* cactus, locally called spaghetti cactus.

Tree Species

The national flower is the dark blue bloom of the lignum vitae tree, found mostly in the dry southern plains and coastal foothills. Its timber is the heaviest of all known woods and much in demand by carvers, but the bark, gum, fruit, leaves, and blossoms also serve useful purposes, including medicines for gout and syphilis. Its beautiful blossom attracts large numbers of butterflies.

The national tree is blue mahoe, an endemic form of hibiscus with a ruler-straight trunk reaching 70 feet. It derives its name from the blue-green streaks in its beautiful wood, which is favored by carvers and craftsmen. Mahoe also blossoms splendidly, with blooms blazing from yellow to red. Another dramatically flowering tree is the vermilion 'flame of the forest' or *spathodea* (also called the 'African tulip tree').

Jamaica has long been known for the quality of its hardwoods. The native mahogany, which grows predominantly in limestone areas, is considered the highest grade mahogany in the world. It and ebony (known for its dark heavy wood perfect for carving) have been logged and decimated during the past two centuries. Both are now extremely rare. Ebony can be recognized by its burst of vermilion-bright flowers after rains.

Other native trees include the massive silk cotton, the huge buttress flanks of which are unmistakable. It's said to be a favored habitat of *duppies* (ghosts). Another dramatic tree is the strangler fig, or ficus, which begins life as an ephiphyte on the branches of other trees. It sends down woody roots that attach themselves to the ground and expand – as if from some Hollywood horror movie – to totally engulf the host tree. Eventually they smother the host, which may die and rot away, leaving a thriving free-standing ficus the hollow trunk of which may become a habitat for bats, rodents, and other species.

You can recognize the native calabash tree by its large gourd, which is dried and carved into craft items such as storage dishes or 'shake-shakes' (maraccas) filled with stones. Logwood, introduced to the island in 1715, also grows wild in dry areas. Its wood produces a dark blue dye. Logwood was grown commercially in great quantities during the 19th century, when the value of logwood exports exceeded that of sugar. Another intriguing tree is boarwood, named for a folk belief that wild boars, when injured, will gash the bark with their tusks and rub their wounds on the sap. It is restricted to the Blue Mountains.

Palms are ubiquitous, except at the highest reaches of the Blue Mountains. There are many species, including the stately royal palm (a Cuban import), which grows to over 100 feet and even has a reserve named for it in the Great Morass near Negril. Other species are endemic, such as the thatch palms, the leaves of which produce fiber rope used in wicker.

Much of Jamaica's leeward coast is fringed by mangroves – the only tree able to survive with its roots in saltwater. All four New World species are found here. The hardy plant puts down a circumference of slender stilt roots, forming a great tangle that helps build up the shoreline and prevent erosion by trapping sediment. It also provides a rich compost for algae and other microorganisms that draw crustaceans and spawning fish in vast numbers. Many creatures are specially adapted to survive in the mangroves.

The endangered hutia favors nocturnal pursuits.

Mammals

Jamaica has very few mammal species. Small numbers of wild hogs still roam remote pockets of the John Crow Mountains. And there are 23 species of bats (called 'rat-bats') but not the vampire. These furry mammals usually hide by day inside caves or beneath tree limbs, then emerge at night to feed on fruit or to scoop insects on the wing.

Otherwise the only native land mammal is the endangered Jamaican hutia, or coney, a large brown-colored rodent akin to a guinea pig. Once a favorite food source of Arawak Indians, it has since been hunted to near extinction by man and mongoose. Habitat loss now restricts the highly social, nocturnal beast to the Blue Mountains, Hellshire Hills, and a few other remote areas of eastern Jamaica. It lives underground and is rarely seen.

The most obvious mammals are all imports, such as cattle and the ubiquitous goat. Jamaica has its own hardy cattle hybrids, such as red poll. The mongoose is the animal you are most likely to see, usually scurrying across the road. This weasellike mammal was introduced from India in the late 19th century to control rats, but it reproduced quickly and turned its attention on domestic fowl and native animal species. It's now considered a destructive pest. By destroying the harmless yellow snake, birds, lizards, and other species, the mongoose has disturbed the ecological balance. Even the rat, the scourge of sugar plantations, was introduced, albeit accidentally as a stowaway aboard the first ships.

Amphibians & Reptiles

Jamaica has plenty of slithery and slimy things. The largest and most enthralling to see are crocodiles (incorrectly called 'alligators' in Jamaica). They're found in the wild in wetlands and mangrove swamps along the south coast, most notably Font Hill Reserve, the Black River Morass, and Long Bay. Ruthless hunting in recent centuries has reduced their numbers considerably. Although protected, they are still taken illegally for food (see the Crocodiles sidebar in the Southwest Coast chapter).

Lizards are everywhere in their bright green, dusky brown, and speckled, rainbow-colored suits. Jamaica has 24 species of lizards, mostly small but some attaining 20 inches or more, and even five feet for the iguana. The Jamaican iguana hangs on to survival in the remote backwaters of the Hellshire Hills (see the Iguana sidebar in the Kingston chapter). Some lizards – the anolids – can change color as camouflage. One species, the smooth-scaled galliwasp, is superstitiously considered to have a fatal bite. Some Jamaicans still believe that if bitten, you must reach water before the lizard to avoid death (a West African belief). My favorites are the geckos, charming but noisy little creatures that can often be seen hanging on your ceiling by their suction-cup feet.

Jamaica has five species of snakes, none poisonous. All are endangered thanks mostly to the ravages of the mongoose, which has entirely disposed of a sixth species – the black snake. Count yourself lucky to see the nocturnal yellow snake (a constrictor called 'nanka' locally), which can grow to eight feet. Most other species rarely exceed one foot long.

The island also harbors 17 species of frogs (including four tree-frog species and two species of whistling frogs) and one toad. The giant toad, called the 'bull frog' was introduced from Barbados in 1844 by a planter who hoped that the species would

eat rats that were destroying his cane. The plump toad, which weighs up to 1.2 kg, is an equal-opportunity consumer: anything bite-size and animate is food. Uniquely, all Jamaica's 14 species of endemic frogs do *not* undergo a tadpole stage; instead, tiny frogs emerge in adult form directly from eggs.

Insects

There are mosquitoes and bees, but most bugs are harmless. A brown scarab beetle called the 'newsbug' flies seemingly without control (when it flies into people, locals consider it a harbinger of important news).

Many insect species are quite beautiful, not the least of which are Jamaica's 120 butterfly species and countless moth species (called 'bats' locally), of which 21 are endemic. The most spectacular is the giant swallowtail *(papillio homerus)*. This native, with a wingspan of six inches that qualifies it as one of the world's largest butterflies, flies only at higher altitudes. Its sole habitat is the John Crow Mountains and the eastern extent of the Blue Moutains (and in the Cockpit Country in smaller numbers). The species is endangered.

You're sure to come across fireflies (called *blinkies* and *peeny-wallies)* flashing luminously in the dark. The phosphorescent green flashing is used like semaphore to guide potential mates. About 50 species are found in Jamaica, each of which has its own individual gender-specific signal so that males and females can tell each other apart and prevent mating with other species. Upper-class women (humans, not fireflies) used to wear live fireflies as necklaces. Peeny-wallies were also placed en masse in jars to act as lanterns – eerie!

Birds

Jamaica is popular with birders. The island has 240 bird species, of which 27 species and 21 subspecies are endemic. Several endemic species have become extinct in recent years, including the Jamaican black-capped petrel and parakeet. Others, such as the Jamaican blackbird and ring-tailed pigeon, are endangered. Almost every species of Jamaican bird is now protected by law.

Stilt-legged, snowy-white cattle egrets are a common sight. They usually accompany cattle and are often seen riding piggyback, long bills jabbing at flies. John crows are also found all over Jamaica. The ungainly bird is not actually a crow but a vulture known to residents of the US as the turkey buzzard. It is feared in Jamaica, perhaps because of its undertaker's plumage, bald red head, and hunched shoulders. It's a subject of several folk songs and proverbs, including one applied to a poor man who pretends to be well-to-do: 'John crow say 'im a dandy man but 'im only have so-so feather.' Local lore states that you can predict the approach of rain when John crows take to the air.

In the mountains you may hear the mournful note of the solitaire or spy the Jamaican eleania or Blue Mountain vireo; lower down are the Jamaican euphonia; rare yellow-billed and black-billed parrots; grassquits; the beautiful little black-cloaked, yellow-breasted bananaquit (also called the 'beany bird' or 'sugarbird'); and the mockingbird, which imitates the calls of other birds and sings by night (earning the moniker 'nightingale'). It is particularly vocal before sunrise, when its poetic songs may be rebutted by some of the most unpoetic terms in the Jamaican dialect.

That sneaky thief on your breakfast table is the kling-kling, or shiny black Greater Antillean grackle, with eyes like Spanish beads and a kleptomaniac's habits in hotel dining rooms. Another bird with questionable ethics is a shiny black member of the oriole family known as the cowbird. The female practices 'brood parasitism' – she seeks out a suitable nest of another species and adds her own egg to those of the builder, who incubates the entire clutch. Unfortunately, the cowbird's egg usually incubates first and dominates the nest. Introduced only in recent years, the cowbird is already having a deleterious affect on other bird species.

Patoo (a West African word) is the Jamaican name for the owl. Many islanders superstitiously regard owls as a harbinger of death. Jamaica has two species: the screech owl and the endemic brown owl. It also has four endemic species of flycatchers, a woodpecker, and many rare species of doves, including the crested quail dove, or 'mountain witch,' that wears a multi-hued cloak of black, purple, cinnamon, and bronze. Many resident species have developed behavior patterns unique to the island. The Jamaican tody (locally called 'robin redbreast'), a wren-size, lime-green bird with white chest and scarlet throat, nests underground at the end of a two-foot-long tunnel.

Jamaica, which lies on a migration route, is visited in both spring and autumn by birds such as vireos, flycatchers, thrushes, and the black-bellied plover en route between summer and winter habitats. Birders can also spot whistling ducks, herons, gallinules, and countless other waterfowl in the swamps.

Large, graceful pelicans can be seen diving for fish, while frigate birds – sometimes called the man o' war bird – soar high above. They have a wingspan of over six feet; long, hooked beaks add to their sinister appearance. Offshore cays vibrate with the honking and caterwauling of seabirds such as boobies and noddy terns.

Enchanting hummingbirds are immediately identifiable by their vivid plumage and the buzz of their rapidly vibrating wings. These splendid treasures can fly sideways, backwards, and even upside-down, their wings a filmy fast-beat blur.

Jamaica has four of the 16 Caribbean species of hummingbirds (all hummingbirds are found only in the New World). The crown jewel of West Indian hummingbirds is undoubtedly the streamertail, the national bird, which is indigenous to Jamaica. This beauty boasts shimmering emerald feathers, velvey black crown with purple crest, and long, slender, curved tail feathers. It is known locally as the 'doctor-bird,' apparently for its long bill that resembles a 19th-century surgical lancet. The red-billed streamertail inhabits the west, while the black-billed lives in the east. It adorns Jamaican two-dollar bills and the logo of Air Jamaica.

The Jamaican mango hummingbird, particularly abundant around Kingston and Montego Bay, can often be seen sipping nectar from the wild banana and poor man's orchid. Another dazzler is the vervain hummingbird, dark-green and so small and quick in flight that it is almost invisible (it is the world's second smallest bird).

Folklore says that hummingbirds have magical curative powers, and Jamaican sorcerers still turn the birds' tiny bodies into charms to protect their possessions from thieves.

Birdwatching Sites Good sites include Marshall's Pen (outside Mandeville), Font Hill Reserve and Great Morass (near Black River), Rockland Bird Feeding Station (near Montego Bay), and Salt Pond and Great Salt Pond (near Treasure Beach). There's an aviary in Hope Botanical Gardens in Kingston, and Enchanted Gardens (a resort in Ocho Rios) has a large walk-in aviary.

The Gosse Bird Club is a valuable information source. Contact Audrey Downer (☎ 922-2253) or Robert Sutton (☎/fax 963-8569). Sutton and his son lead birding tours into Cockpit Country and other select sites. In the USA, contact Field Guides, PO Box 160723, Austin, TX 78716, ☎ (512) 327-4953, fax (512) 327-9231, which offers organized birding tours.

There are many good books and field guides to Jamaican birds, including *Birds of the West Indies* by James Bond and the more up-to-date *Birds of Jamaica* by Downer & Sutton (see the Books section in the Facts for the Visitor chapter).

Marine Life

Jamaica's marine life is as varied as its habitats. The immense undersea world is enthralling. Frondlike orange gorgonians (named for the trio of snaked-haired Greek goddesses) spread their fingers upwards toward the light. There are contorted sheets of purple staghorn and lacy outcrops of tubipora such as delicately woven Spanish

mantillas, sinuous boulderlike brain corals, and soft-flowering corals that sway to the rhythms of the ocean currents.

Over 700 species of fish zip in and out of the exquisite reefs and swarm through the coral canyons: wrasses, parrotfish, snappers, bonito, kingfish, jewelfish, and scores of others whose names you may never learn but whose beauty you will forever remember. The smaller fry are ever-preyed upon by barracudas, giant groupers, sharks, and tarpon. Farther out the cobalt deeps are run by sailfish, marlin, and manta rays.

Jamaica's variety of aquatic life is astonishing. However, some of those creatures survive as well as they do in part because they pose hazards to humans. See Dangers & Annoyances in the Facts for the Visitor chapter.

Coral Ecology Corals are tiny animals with a great gaping mouth at one end surrounded by tentacles to gather food. The polyps live protected by an external skeleton the production of which is dependent upon algae that live inside the polyp's tissue. The creatures live in vast colonies that reproduce both asexually by budding (many species are dimorphic – both male and female), and sexually through a synchronous release of spermatozoa (when this happens the surrounding waters become milky). Together they build up huge frameworks – the reefs.

A reef is usually composed of scores of different species and shapes, each occupying its own niche. However, all corals can only flourish close to the ocean surface, where they are nourished by sunlight in clear, unpolluted waters above 70°F.

When it dies, the coral's skeleton turns to limestone that another coral polyp may use as a foundation to cement its own skeleton. The entire reef system is gnawed away by parrotfish and other predators that browse on the coral. A reef will repair itself, but much of Jamaica's reef system has been severely damaged (and continues to be) by the discharge of wastes and agricultural runoff, such as phosphates and nitrate nutrients that encourage algae blooms and seagrasses that choke coral growth.

Coral reefs are the most complex and sensitive of all ecosystems and take thousands of years to form. The rainbow-hued reefs are divided into life zones gauged by depth, temperature, and light; each zone harbors distinct fish, coral, and other species. Jamaica's reefs are prodigal places, especially along the north coast, where the waters are scintillatingly clear and the reef is almost continuous (few rivers empty silt into the sea). Here, much of the reef lies within a few hundred yards of shore.

Reef systems are broken and far from shore off the south coast, where the shelf extends up to 20 miles from land.

Marine Turtles Three species of marine turtles – the green, hawksbill, and loggerhead – find Jamaica's beaches appealing as nest sites, although only the beautiful and relatively small hawksbill does so with regularity. Turtles migrate hundreds of miles to nest and lay the eggs for tomorrow's turtles, as they have for at least 150 million years.

Arawak Indians considered them a delicacy, and traps called 'turtle crawles' can be seen around the coast. The Arawaks' subsistence needs had as little impression on the vast aquatic herds as the North American Plains' Indians had on the buffalo. Columbus' 'discovery' of the West Indies, however, opened up the waters to rapacious hunting of turtles, which are now endangered.

Unfortunately, Jamaican fishermen still catch turtles for meat, and the hawksbill's lustrous shell is much sought after for jewelry. You may see turtle shells hanging in bars or even for sale. Remember: it is strictly illegal to sell or purchase turtle products of any kind. To do so only encourages their decimation.

Marine Mammals The Caribbean monk seal, once common in Jamaican waters, was last seen in 1952 on the Pedro Cays. Unfortunately, the endangered West Indian manatee is heading for a similar fate. The shy and gentle creatures were once common around the island and formed a staple of the Arawak Indian diet. Only about 100 still survive in Jamaican waters, mostly in the swamps of Long Bay (you can see them with relative ease at Alligator Pond, also known as Canoe Valley).

Manatees are warm-blooded marine mammals with a huge bloated body (like plump wine sacks), a blunt snout, and a paddlelike tail. They have a voracious appetite and can consume 100 pounds of water hyacinths and other floating vegetation daily. They can reach 12 feet in length and weigh over 1000 pounds (see the Manatee sidebar in the South Coast chapter).

National Parks

Jamaica's embryonic park system comprises two national parks plus a fistful of other wilderness areas granted varying and relatively minimal degrees of protection. Several additional national parks have been touted for years. See the National Parks map for proposed sites. Vital pristine regions are threatened with commercial development due to lack of enforcement of regulations.

For information about hiking in Jamaica's national parks, see Hiking in the Activities section of the Facts for the Visitor chapter.

Montego Bay Marine Park This 15.3-sq-mile park was established in May 1990 to preserve and manage Montego Bay's coral reefs, mangroves, and offshore marine resources. It stretches from Donald Sangster airport to the Great River. Fishing is banned with its perimeter, and water sports are restricted to designated areas.

Blue Mountains – John Crow National Park This 300-sq-mile park, established in 1993, contains half of the total acreage in Jamaica's proposed national parks. Its formation heralds a brave attempt to halt devastating deforestation. The park includes the forest reserves of the Blue and John Crow Mountain Ranges and spans the parishes of St Andrew, St Thomas,

Parks of Jamaica

0   15   30 km
0   10   20 miles

National Park
Proposed National Park
Marine Park
Proposed Marine Park

Portland, and St Mary. Forty percent of the higher plant species are endemic to the area, and the forests harbor many endangered species, including the Jamaican hutia, giant swallow-tail butterflies, and yellow-billed parrots.

Critical to its success is the participation of the community. Only 15 poorly equipped park rangers police the park. There are few facilities, and as yet the park has gone unnoticed by nature lovers, despite its many attractions, most notably its montane forests rich in birdlife. In an effort to stimulate ecotourism and to maximize its benefits for the community, locals from the buffer zones have been trained as guides.

Botanical Gardens

Jamaica has more botanical gardens than any other Caribbean island, and with good reason. They were established during the colonial era to propagate exotic fruit crops introduced from England's far-flung empire, including breadfruits first brought from Tahiti by Captain William Bligh in 1793 to be grown as a staple for slaves (see Food in the Facts for the Visitor chapter).

Leading gardens include Castleton and Cinchona, both in the mountains above Kingston; Hope Botanical Gardens, in Kingston; and Coyaba and Shaw Park, both in Ocho Rios. The Natural History Division of the Institute of Jamaica (12 East St, Kingston, ☎ 922-6020) has a herbarium of over 125,000 plant specimens.

GOVERNMENT & POLITICS

Jamaica inherits its political institutions from Britain. It is a stable parliamentary democracy within the Commonwealth – in many regards a little England in miniature, attested to by the black parliamentary speaker wearing his white wig, with a gold scepter at his side. There's nothing English, however, about the passion that dominates Jamaican politics.

Although Jamaica is independent, its titular head of state is Queen Elizabeth II of England. She is represented by a Jamaican-born governor general (often referred to as 'GG' by islanders) appointed on the advice of the prime minister and a six-member Privy Council. The governor's duties are largely ceremonial and include appointing the prime minister, who is always the leader of the party winning a majority in national elections.

Executive power resides with a cabinet

appointed and led by the prime minister and responsible to Parliament. Parliament consists of a bicameral legislature – a 60-member elected House of Representatives, and a nominated 21-seat Senate, of which 13 members are appointed by the prime minister and eight by the leader of the opposition. The House may override a Senate veto, but a two-third majority vote in both houses is required to change Jamaica's constitution.

A full parliamentary term is five years. The governor general, however, may call a national election at his discretion at any time at the request of the prime minister (that usually means when timing seems propitious for the ruling party). Jamaica has a 'first past the post' electoral system; there is no proportional representation. All adults ages 18 and over may vote.

Political Parties

Post-independence Jamaican politics has been largely a struggle between two parties: the People's National Party (PNP) and the Jamaica Labour Party (JLP).

People's National Party The PNP is a social-democratic party closely affiliated to the National Worker's Union. It was formed in 1938 under the leadership of barrister Norman Washington Manley, who headed the party for 31 years before being succeeded by his son Michael, a prominent journalist and trade unionist. Its leader is the current prime minister, PJ Patterson.

Jamaica Labour Party Despite its name, the JLP is a conservative party with ties to the Bustamante Industrial Trade Union. Founded in 1943 by labor leader Sir Alexander Bustamante, it is currently led by ex-Prime Minister Edward Seaga, a dynamic promoter of free enterprise who preaches limited government involvement in the economy. Seaga has connections with one of Jamaica's oldest and best-known 'garrison' constituencies. Violent flare-ups in and around Seaga's West Kingston constituency in 1995 served to remind voters that the party leader was instrumental in the creation of one-party enclaves ('garrisons') in which favors are dispensed by politicians and the electoral is kept in the party's sway by violence and intimidation.

Despite his economic successes, Seaga's arrogant and confrontational style has alienated many of his party followers and turned away voters in recent years (a poll in mid-1995 showed that the JLP had only 16% of the voters behind it). Seaga has faced significant opposition in recent years from fellow MPs and party members. The infighting that beriddles the party came to a head in mid-1995 when 11 dissident MPs called on Seaga to resign as party leader.

National Democratic Movement In October 1995, Bruce Golding, former JLP chair and Seaga's heir-apparent, resigned and formed a new party: the National Democratic Movement. Golding launched his new party with a promise to enact radical constitutional changes to ensure greater accountability and continuity in government policies.

Other Parties There are a handful of minor parties, including the communist Worker's Party of Jamaica.

The Prevailing Mood

Third parties have never won significant support. An independent poll published in mid-September 1995, however, suggests that this may be changing: voters have grown weary of the old paternalist style of politics. Decades of violent politics, confrontation, corruption and mismanagement have led voters to embrace change, and the two parties must now work harder to win over supporters.

The poll found significant dissatisfaction with the two-party system and MPs. Under prevailing conditions, the National Democratic Movement would poll 20%, the JLP 18%, and the PNP 21% in an election. The poll also showed a rise from 6 to 18% in the numbers of people who stated they would not vote and of uncommitted voters from 29 to 37%.

Corruption & 'Garrison' Politics

The one thing the PNP and JLP have shared in common is a flair for corruption and pandering – what Jamaicans call 'politricks.'

Largesse & Intimidation Election time in Jamaica can be a volatile affair. Kingston can become the victim of what my friend and fellow travel writer Lynn Ferrin calls Jamaica's 'drop-dead politics.' Fortunately, things have calmed down since the late 1970s and early 1980s, when scores of Jamaicans lost their lives in partisan killings in 'garrison constituencies.'

During the heady 1970s, individual politicians literally developed strangleholds over some low-income areas in Kingston by pandering to 'dons' (gang leaders) who would deliver blocks of votes in exchange for government contracts and other largesse such as jobs and housing. Political discipline was enforced by bullying and the barrels of Armalite and M-16 rifles. Even reggae superstar Bob Marley was a target of a machine-gun attack on his home on the eve of the December 1976 election!

Politicians could once claim that they controlled the gangs by rewarding them with construction and other contracts on a partisan basis. Budgetary constraints in recent years, however, have reduced the largesse they can dole out. The gangs they gave birth to still engage in periodic political killings that mar Kingston. In October 1994, for example, a brief turf war broke out when 'dons' in Seaga's West Kingston constituency became concerned that residents were shifting political loyalties from the JLP to the PNP. Intimidation to enforce party loyalty ended in six people being shot dead.

According to a police commissioner's report released in October 1995, gangs in East Kingston (the former constituency of Michael Manley) with political connections have been terrorizing local businesses, which they take over.

Corruption Graft is a way of life in Jamaican politics. Many of the funds of the government's 'social and economic support program,' for example, become a gravy train for contractors with political connections. The pork-barrel problem is compounded by the fact that leading officials of government agencies are usually political appointees eager to cash in for themselves before the next change of government. Examples abound of large-scale get-rich-quick schemes and shameless conniving worthy of Anancy, the Jamaican folktale spider-hero.

In May 1995, for example, the floodgates broke on the National Water Commission scandal, when it was revealed that an estimated 40% of revenues collected for water use from private citizens disappears into the hands of NWC officials.

That same month, a cash-for-visa scheme that involved prominent members of the PNP's Youth Organization was exposed. The leadership had been selling written 'recommendations' virtually guaranteeing US visas to would-be emigrants for US$950 apiece, often at the behest of MPs representing their constituents. An investigation implicated a number of senior party officials.

The biggest area of pork-barrel politics is in road construction. Each administration announces massive road reclamation programs, but corrupt contractors usurp the money. According to the *Jamaica Herald* (May 20, 1995) 'more than half of the J$3 billion allocated to road construction will go directly into the pockets of a cabal of road contractors.'

In 1988, scheming politicians even usurped international relief funds after Hurricane Gilbert 'mashed up' Jamaica. Mayors and MPs courted voters in the forthcoming elections by commandeering relief supplies, which they handed out as 'personal donations.'

Local Government

Jamaica is divided into 12 parishes: St Thomas, Portland, St Mary, St Ann, Trelawny, St James, Hanover, Westmoreland, St Elizabeth, Manchester, Clarendon, and St Catherine. There are two corporate

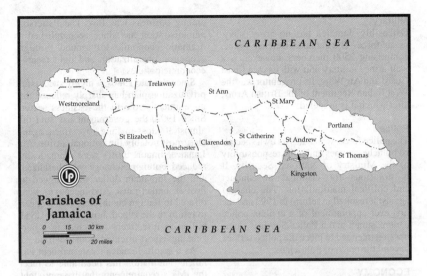

Parishes of Jamaica

areas as well: Kingston and St Andrews. Each parish has an elected council responsible for local administration. The parishes were initially created by British colonialists and headed by a *Custos Rotulorum*, the monarch's representative. The honorary title, which means 'Keeper of the Rolls,' is now largely ceremonial and granted to the senior justice of the peace.

The Judiciary

Jamaica's judicial system is based on English common law and practice.

Local justices of the peace and resident magistrates' courts administer justice at the parish level. Each parish has one magistrate's court (St Andrew has three and Kingston four). In addition, there is a special family court, revenue court, traffic court, and a gun court that handles violent crimes involving firearms. A court of appeals reviews appeals, which can then be appealed to the Supreme Court headed by the chief justice (appointed by the governor general on recommendation from the prime minister). Resident magistrates and judges making up the Court of Appeals and Supreme Court are also appointed by the governor general upon the advice of a bipartisan Judicial Service Committee. The final appeal body is the Judicial Committee of the Privy Council in the United Kingdom.

There are five prisons, administered by the Prisons Department of the Ministry of Youth and Community Development. Conditions within the prisons are notoriously bad, particularly in St Catherine Prison in Spanish Town. In 1994 the United Nations' Committee on Human Rights condemned Jamaica for prison conditions and the ill-treatment of prisoners.

Reinstating Capital Punishment

In January 1995 the government announced that it was reintroducing hanging after a six-year hiatus following a UK Privy Council ruling that capital punishment was legal. At the time, 272 people were on death row. That same month, the Jamaican Court of Appeals upheld that flogging is permissible. The last official flogging was ordered in 1970 – the two guards who carried out the sentence were both murdered within a year! ■

Military

Ostensibly, Jamaica has no army, navy, or air force. The Jamaica Defence Force, comprising 2500 members, however, is a well-armed military unit with its own Coast Guard and Air Wing. Its progenitor was the West Indian Regiment of the British Army, after which it is modeled.

Police

The police force, which has its own specialist branches, comes under the responsibility of the Ministry of National Security. It is notorious for criminal misconduct and political manipulation. The charges against it resulted in reform in 1993 and the first-ever appointment of a civilian police commissioner and a Police Services Commission intended to place the police service beyond the reach of politicians.

ECONOMY

Jamaica's economy is highly developed compared to those of most Caribbean members. It has an active stock market, many international banks, a large skilled work force, and a relatively broad-based economy. The economy, however, is dependent on imported consumer goods and raw materials that have exceeded earnings from tourism, bauxite, sugar, and bananas, all of which are susceptible to erratic worldwide demand (tourism and bauxite accounted for 78% of foreign exchange earnings from 1970 to 1990). The island has had to face an acute balance-of-payments crisis and is beleaguered by a massive foreign debt. Jamaica has also suffered from high inflation and persistent unemployment.

The USA is Jamaica's major trading partner, accounting for 36% of the island's exports and 52% of its total imports.

Government Policy

There was a marked decline in prosperity during the 1970s and 1980s, when gross domestic product (GDP) fell considerably. In the early 1990s inflation briefly hit 106%, interest rates on commercial loans averaged 60%, there were no foreign reserves in the central bank, and confidence among business was low. The Patterson administration has since accomplished a dramatic economic turnaround through economic liberalization and tight macroeconomic policies.

Since the late 1980s, a highly successful privatization plan has sharply reduced the government's role in the business sector. Since 1992, the government has sold off almost 300 loss-making government agencies, most notably the national airline, Air Jamaica. Import tariffs were dramatically reduced. Foreign exchange was liberalized, and the Jamaican dollar was allowed to float at market rates. And incentives were offered to foreign businesses, which began to return to the island, bringing over US$1 billion in investment and creating a burgeoning export-oriented industrial base.

As a result, Jamaica's external debt has fallen. The nation has been able to meet the IMF's requirements that have brought Jamaica renewed funding. And Jamaica's equity market performed so well in 1992 and 1993 that the Jamaica Stock Exchange became the fastest growing stock market in the world.

It hasn't been painless: in 1992, the government's efforts to reduce the budget deficit and inflation in compliance with IMF conditions caused social and industrial unrest. The government has attempted to use tough monetary policies such as high interest rates to control liquidity and reduce pressure on the Jamaican dollar. Economic indicators vindicated the government's policy: the dollar exchange rate, which had fallen from J$8 per US$1 in 1990, stabilized at J$22 per US$1 in 1992, and inflation was cut to 15% by the end of 1993.

Although the devaluation has stimulated export-oriented businesses, the heavy debt burden, reduction in real incomes, and stringent monetary policy have hampered economic growth, which stalled in 1993 (growth slowed from 5.5% in 1990 to 0.8% in 1994; manufacturing declined by 0.5%). Another rapid slide in the value of the Jamaican dollar also began in mid-1993. By the end of 1995, the Jamaican dollar had lost almost 50% of its value, and stood at J$38 to the US dollar, adding to the nation's balance of payments woes. Nonetheless, the Patterson administration had accumulated US$435 million in international reserves at the close of 1995 – the first foreign reserves since 1977!

The Foreign Debt Burden

On the eve of independence Jamaica had no external debt. Massive government programs were covered by massive foreign borrowing of more than US$5 billion in the 1970s and 1980s. Today Jamaica's foreign debt stands at about US$4 billion (down from US$4.5 billion debt in 1993). The debt is one of the highest per capita debt burdens in the world at US$1800 per person (versus a GDP of only US$1475 per person). It eats away at foreign currency earnings, 40% of which are paid to meet interest and capital repayments.

Hamstrung by Poverty

Despite its relatively developed economy, Jamaica is one of the poorest islands in the Caribbean. Although its GDP was US$3.73 billion in 1993, its meager per capita GDP of US$1475 reflects the nation's continuing battle with poverty (Barbados has a per capita GDP of US$5100; Trinidad and Tobago's is US$3300). One-third of Jamaican families officially live below the poverty line. A significant number work a small patch of land, coaxing scallions, yams, some carrots, thyme, a little coffee, and perhaps some *ganja* from subsistence-size plots of poor quality. And unskilled workers are abysmally poorly paid (the average minimum wage is US$18 for a 40-hour week). The official unemployment figures (18% in 1994) are overly optimistic. As much as one-third of the working population is unemployed, with another one-third freelancing in what is called the 'informal sector' (prostitution, higglings, and hustling). An estimated 300,000 of the country's 2.5 million people work as higglers – pavement vendors who sell everything from buttons and cosmetics to clothes and electronic items.

The vast majority of workers lack any vocational training. Even for trained tradespeople, there is limited work in the boondocks: when a large-scale project arrives, outside contractors usually bring in their own crews, and locals are left on the margins. Many adults remain in the boonies, earning pennies but not starving, unable to significantly better their lives. The ambitious are lured by the city, where the lucky few will find work. A life of disappointment, however, lies ahead for a huge percentage of young men and women with no jobs but plenty of dreams.

The continual slide in the value of the Jamaican dollar has had a devastating impact on the purchasing power of poor families in an economy reliant on goods imported from the USA. And the number of people has grown faster than the economy that sustains them. Real incomes have gradually declined since 1980 for the low-paid and irregularly or casually employed. Many families can no longer afford even the basic necessities. Jamaica has *no* general unemployment benefits (about 125,000 of the abject poor do receive food coupons, however).

In 1993 the United Nations' Human Development Index listed Jamaica's quality of life and social development as 69th in the world (the USA placed sixth and the UK 10th). Three-quarters of all houses have no indoor plumbing; only half have electricity. Laundry is typically done in the nearest river.

Major Industries

Tourism Tourism is the country's most important source of foreign currency (earnings rose to US$965 million in 1995, up from US$917 million in 1994). It also directly employs over 72,000 Jamaicans (plus 217,000 indirectly). The impact of tourism extends into many fields: for example, agriculture supplies food, and linen and household commodities are needed for hotels.

Mass tourism was given a boost when President Kennedy imposed a US trade embargo on Cuba in 1961. Today, Jamaica receives more visitors than all but two other Caribbean nations: the Bahamas and Puerto Rico. Despite the continued embargo, Cuba was set to oust Jamaica into fourth place in 1996 (see the Cuba Sí sidebar in the Northwest Coast chapter).

Tourism is a fragile and volatile industry, susceptible to upset by natural disasters such as Hurricane Gilbert in 1988 and bad publicity over crime and violence. During the early 1980s tourism withered due to political violence on the island. The decline spurred an aggressive 'Come Back to Jamaica' advertising campaign. Arrivals topped one million for the first time in 1987. Visitor numbers increased by 58.4% between 1988 and 1993 (cruise-passenger visitors, who traditionally account for slightly more than one-third of arrivals, increased by 70%). Arrivals fell 1.6% in 1994 following a number of highly publicized killings of visitors, while unseasonably warm weather in much of the US during the winter of 1993 – 1994 also kept snowbirds at home. Arrivals reversed in the first quarter of 1995, and a record 1.14 million visitors arrived in 1995, 65% of whom came from the USA (the UK accounted for 12% of the market). Over 30% of visitors come on charter packages.

The government has taken concrete steps toward planning for future growth in tourism. The physical environment of many resort areas has come under pressure in recent years, so the Ministry of Tourism established a Tourism Action Plan (TAP) in 1988 to manage tourism growth. All proposed resort developments, for example, must now meet TAP requirements to ensure community input. A human resources division was set up to train government staff, such as immigration officers, airport porters, and others who liaise with tourists. TAP has installed street signs, opened up vendors markets, and in mid-1995 even established two dozen litter wardens in Ocho Rios. And TAP's Project Department was given a mandate to facilitate restoration of attractions.

A new entertainment complex is planned in Montego Freeport. Airport improvement and expansion includes a new terminal at Donald Sangster airport in Montego Bay. In 1994 a new 30,000-sq-foot cruise terminal opened in Montego Bay with two new cruise berths (for a total of five). The deepwater facilities were also being improved at Ocho Rios, which in mid-1995 received a J$57 million facelift.

Although JTB officials claim that Jamaica's problems get more than their fair share of negative publicity, the truth is that the problems faced by visitors are real. Late in the day, industry figures have pulled their heads from the sand and are taking bold steps to alleviate such problems as harassment by hustlers.

Other efforts by the JTB include plans to polish Jamaica's attractions (76 attractions – rafting, stables, farms, caves, and great houses among them – are on file at the JTB). According to a recent study, attractions bring in 47% of total tourism revenue.

The JTB is beginning to promote 'cultural tourism' and more specialized vacations, led by the ecotour market – Jamaica has incredible ecotourism potential, though its crop of existing eco-attractions is comparatively unsophisticated. It has also touted the restoration of historic towns such as Falmouth, Port Royal, and Spanish Town as Jamaican Williamsburgs. And the JTB and Kingston's hoteliers, who have traditionally relied on business traffic, are beginning to aggressively market Kingston as an exciting cultural center. Attempts to promote Kingston, however, may be premature. Relocating the Reggae Sunsplash festival from Montego Bay to Kingston in 1993, for example, attracted visitors to the city, but many went home with a less than savory impression.

Bauxite Bauxite – red gold – was for three decades the bedrock of the Jamaican economy. The ore, which is used to produce aluminum, is abundant on the island. Jamaica has estimated reserves of 2.5 billion tons – 7% of world reserves and enough to last another century at current production rates.

The industry was birthed during WWII, when mining grew rapidly to supply the aircraft industry. The rapid post-war expansion of the world's civil aviation industry maintained the momentum. By 1957 Jamaica was the world's No 1 source of bauxite. During the 1970s it accounted in certain years for over 45% of Jamaica's net earnings and almost 30% of GDP, and supplied nearly two-thirds of US requirements for aluminum.

The industry was controlled by a handful of US and Canadian companies. Since the bauxite companies were selling to their parent companies, which processed the ore abroad, they vastly undervalued the bauxite and thereby reduced their royalty and tax payments to the Jamaican government. The crafty device, called transfer pricing, robbed Jamaica of a reasonable share of its natural wealth. In 1974, the Manley administration resolved this by indexing the price of bauxite to the price of aluminum ingots (the government also gained a 51% controlling influence).

A collapse of the worldwide market in the late 1970s to mid-1980s had a devastating impact on the Jamaican economy, but the industry began to recover in the mid-1980s. Jamaica's production rose to 11.94 million tons in 1994, the highest level attained since 1960. However, earnings have not kept pace due to the reduction in the world price of bauxite.

Today, Jamaica is the world's third largest producer of bauxite and processed alumina. Only Australia and Brazil produce more. The industry employs barely 1% of the work force, yet accounts for one-quarter of the government's income.

Agriculture

Agriculture is by far the most important source of employment (40% of the labor force), despite its relatively low contribution to GDP (less than 10%). Agriculture's share of export earnings has fallen from about 50% in 1970 to 20% in recent years.

At first sight, a visitor would guess that this fecund land should be able to feed its population (of the island's 2.7 million acres, 1.68 million is suitable for agriculture). However, most of the best land is used to grow sugar or bananas for export, a legacy of the colonial plantation era. Necessary foodstuffs for domestic consumption are imported or produced in small quantities by subsistence farmers on marginal, usually mountainous land.

The sugar and banana industries have seen significant increases in production in recent years, sponsored in part by the US government's Caribbean Basin Initiative, which since 1983 has fostered economic growth in the region by excluding Caribbean products from import duties.

In the late 1800s, Jamaica was the world's largest banana producer, but the industry has gradually declined during this century. Exports averaged 78,000 tons annually in the 1970s but fell to 28,000 tons the following decade. Jamaica's banana crop was devastated by hurricanes in both 1980 and 1988. The industry has since seen a recovery and has taken advantage of an expanding banana market. Jamaica exported 78,577 ton of bananas in 1994, earning US$40 million.

Sugarcane is another major crop – almost one-third of Jamaica's agricultural land (203 sq miles) is planted in sugar. During the 1970s, one-quarter of the population was dependent on the sugar economy! The sugar economy remains the largest employer in Jamaica, but it pays subsistence wages. Formerly the engine of the Jamaican economy, the industry has declined steadily since 1965, when production peaked at 501,000 tons. Production began to increase again in the early 1990s and reached 240,000 tons in 1994 (export earnings were US$98 million). In 1993 and 1994 the Jamaican government sold off four of its five state-owned sugar factories, and it is anticipated that modernization should lead to an increase in production.

The sugar economy remains susceptible to devastation by both rain and wind, and the vicissitudes of market prices: the world price for sugar was 29 cents a pound in 1980; within four years it had plummeted to four cents a pound.

Hallowed Grounds

Since coffee grows well on well-watered, well-drained slopes in cooler yet tropical climates, it is no surprise that it thrives in the Blue Mountains. Here the combination of slope, aspect, soil type, and clmatic conditions conspire to produce a distinctly flavored coffee acclaimed by many connoisseurs as the best in the world.

Blue Mountain coffee is lighter and sweeter than other coffees and yet more robust, with a unique woody flavor. It also has less caffeine. There is enormous variation in quality, however, even within the Blue Mountains. Not all Blue Mountain coffee lives up to its reputation or its astronomical price.

Coffee plants, which are native to Ethiopia, were first cultivated in the French West Indies in 1717; virtually the entire Caribbean coffee stock is derived from a single plant introduced to Hispaniola that year. In 1728 Governor Sir Nicholas Lawes introduced coffee to Jamaica at Temple Hall Estate, and other planters followed suit, prompted by the growing demand in Europe, where coffee shops were the rage. (So popular did West Indian coffee become that the satirist Alexander Pope could quip, 'Coffee which makes the politician wise,

LEE ABEL

Jamaica is growing more and more food for export and less and less for domestic consumption. Hence, food imports continue to rise and today account for two-thirds of domestic consumption. Unfortunately, preferential trade benefits for sugar and bananas are being lost as the European Union (EU) phases out preferred trade agreements. Jamaica now needs to find and develop new niche markets. Increasing attention is being given to allspice (pimento), citrus, coffee, ginger, cocoa, rum, ornamental flowers, and cattle, which together amounted for about US$30 million in exports in 1995. Citrus projects have expanded rapidly in the past 20 years. And an export-oriented papaya and mango fruit farm was established in 1993.

Most of the nontraditional export crops are supplied by small-scale farmers. Small holdings are the backbone of the local economy: the vast majority of Jamaica's 160,000 farmers cultivate less than five acres (the average holding is 1.55 acres). Their productivity is relatively insignificant. Small-scale farmers are hampered by poverty. They cannot afford the debilitating loans or the high cost of fertilizers, fuel, mechanized equipment, and other agricultural inputs. Agricultural projects rarely reach down to the grassroots; the Jamaican government lacks the administrative ability or chutzpah to implement community organization.

Fishing Although Jamaica has a fishing industry, it is mostly comprised of small-scale, village-level entrepreneurs who in and see through all things with his half-shut eyes.') Production was boosted by the arrival of French planters fleeing the revolution in St Domingue (Haiti) in 1801, and it peaked in the boom years – 1800 to 1840 – when production rose to 17,000 tons a year. For a time Jamaica was the world's largest exporter.

Emancipation in 1838 doomed the plantations. Many slaves left the estates and planted their own coffee. As steeper slopes were planted, coffee quality began to decline. The upsurge of free trade and the end of England's preferential tariffs for Jamaican coffee further damaged the industry at a time when high-quality coffee from Brazil, a relative new-comer, was beginning to sap Jamaica's market share. A series of hurricanes this century did further inestimable damage. By the close of WWII, Jamaica's coffee industry was on its last legs.

There has been a resurgence in the popularity of Blue Mountain coffee in recent years under Japanese stimulus and aided by the Jamaican Coffee Industry Board, set up to ensure quality. Blue Mountain coffee is a treasured commodity in Japan, where the beans sell for US$50 or more per pound. To stimulate production, Japanese companies offered growers development loans at 4 and 5% interest. They also bought plantations, such as Craighton Estate. In doing so they have cornered the market (more than 90% of Blue Mountain coffee is sold to Japan at a preferential rate of US$7.50 a pound; the Japanese sell it to the domestic market at almost a 1000% premium).

Although the Coffee Industry Board purports to maintain strict standards and regulates the use of the name Blue Mountain coffee, the policy is a farce. The board operates four processing plants in the Blue Mountains. The factories are supplied by scores of small-scale farmers who are required by law to sell to the coffee board at whatever price the board chooses to pay (about half what the Japanese buy it for), regardless of the world market value. Blue Mountain coffee growers cannot legally sell their coffee anywhere else. And only beans processed at the four plants may be sold as 'Blue Mountain coffee.'

Unfortunately, the four factories blend the high-quality beans with lesser quality Lowland and Mountain beans (the terms correspond to the elevation at which the coffee is grown). Many independent producers complain that their superior beans are thus degraded and even poor beans end up being sold as 'Blue Mountain coffee.' Hence, many small holders refuse to sell to the central processors and cure and roast their own beans (often over a smoky wood fire), which they sell privately (and illegally) at bargain prices. ■

their small, flimsy craft find it difficult to compete with the large mechanized fleets of competing nations that fish the nearby waters. Hence, Jamaica imports about 50% of fish sold on the island at a cost of about US$23 million a year. The waters of the Caribbean have been overfished, adding to local woes.

Jamaica is developing a commercial aquaculture, with fish farms raising tilapa and tarpon. The island has about 1977 acres of ponds.

Manufacturing Manufacturing, which has grown at an average of 2.5% per year since 1990, contributes 18% of GDP and employs about 11% of the active work force.

The low per capita GDP and the island's relatively small population (2.6 million)

provide a limited consumer base for domestic industry; Jamaica faces an uphill battle to develop and sustain homegrown industries. Nonetheless, investment incentives have resulted in the growth of sizable processed-goods and textile industries (the latter employs more than 20,000 people). Jamaica's garment exports increased 159% from 1992 to 1994, when they earned US$474 million (Jamaica is one of the biggest suppliers of underwear to the US market).

There are four free-trade zones – one in Montego Bay, one in Spanish Town, and two in Kingston – where foreign companies are entitled to special incentives. A state-of-the-art telecommunications facility, Digiport International, opened in 1989 at Montego Freeport, attracting several

North American data processing and software companies.

POPULATION & PEOPLE

Jamaica's population is currently estimated at 2.6 million (2.37 million in the census of 1991), of which about 680,000 live in Kingston. At least another two million Jamaicans live abroad. Emigration has served as an escape valve that balances the high birth rate of 24 per 1000. This rate has also been reduced by vigorous programs implemented by the National Family Planning Board. Jamaica's population grew 1.7% annually in the 1980s (it had declined to 0.9% in 1990), but without emigration it would have been 2.3%. One-third of the population is under 14 years of age. About 50% of the population live in urban environments.

A Diverse People

The nation's motto – 'Out of Many, One People' – reflects the nation's diverse heritage. Tens of thousands of West Africans, plus large numbers of Irish, Germans, and Welsh arrived throughout the colonial period, along with Hispanic and Portuguese Jews. Following emancipation in 1838, Chinese and Indians arrived as indentured laborers from Hong Kong and Panamá. The majority remained when their contracted service was over. All intermarried with Africans.

Still, Jamaica is overwhelmingly black. More than three-quarters of the population is of supposedly pure African descent. Another 15% are of Afro-European descent, with the remainder made up of Afro-Chinese and Chinese (1.5%), East Indian and Middle Eastern (3.5%), and European (4%) minorities.

White visitors will find themselves a tiny minority. This can be unnerving if theirs is the only white face for miles around, and children and even adult men start shouting 'whitey!' (don't worry, it's usually a matter-of-fact statement of surprise, not a term of abuse).

Jamaica proclaims itself a melting pot of racial harmony. Indeed, the island is relatively and refreshingly free of racial tensions. Still, insecurities of identity have been carried down from the plantation era. Class divisions in Jamaica are still related to color.

The Black Color Scale

Middle-class Jamaicans will tell you that Jamaicans measure people not by the color of their skin but by the depth of their integrity. Color in Jamaica is the ultimate status symbol in a society that exhibits great admiration for status symbols. This is a legacy of the plantation era, when whites sired mulatto ('brown') children with slave mistresses (white women may have had slave lovers, but they made certain they did *not* have their children). These offspring were usually favored by their fathers. By law they were 'free-colored' and eventually held the same legal rights as their fathers.

The plantocracy developed a scale of 'whiteness' that described the mulattos' relative status. Though originally used by the planters, the lexicon passed into general parlance that expressed the percent of black blood: sambo (three-quarters), mulatto (half), quadroon (one-quarter), octaroon (one-eighth), and musteefino (one-sixteenth). Jamaicans still have a name for every nuance of shade. A partial list includes white, off-white, high yellow, coolie-royal, chinee-royal, red, brown, high brown, and black. 'She black, black, black, so 'til' means she's *very* dark indeed!

Tourists should be cautious about using Jamaican terminology, as the interpretation can vary according to context and may carry a pejorative connotation, much as the word 'nigger' in the USA has different connotations when used by whites (always derogatory) and blacks (sometimes considered self-deprecating humor.) Interestingly, black visitors to Jamaica are easily and rapidly identified as tourists and are treated just like white tourists.

Today there is a general sliding scale by which the lighter one's shade of skin, the more skilled and prosperous one is assumed to be. Jamaican politics and businesses have always been dominated by whites and light-skinned 'browns.' The first *black* prime minister was elected only in 1992. The very poorest Jamaicans are usually very dark. Many darker Jamaicans still attempt to 'lift' their color by marrying a lighter skinned person, and it's not uncommon for newspapers and magazines to attempt to slander or flatter public figures by darkening or lightening their photographs.

Minorities

Whites Whites are divided into 'white Jamaicans' and 'Jamaican whites.' Many of the former (immigrants from Europe, mostly England) seem to cling to a grandiose illusion of the good old days when Britannia ruled the waves and Jamaica. Most Jamaican whites (island-born) are really 'off-whites.' They contain a trace of black blood but prefer to be considered white and many are very sensitive about this. The greatest misfortune that can occur is to sire a 'throwback' child of dark complexion or to break out in brown pigmented patches (known as 'mulatto blasts') as these Jamaican whites approach middle age.

The island also has a significant number of poor Jamaican whites: the descendants of Welsh, Scottish, Irish, and German indentured laborers who arrived following emancipation and never made good. The majority are the offspring of about 1100 Germans who arrived between 1834 and 1838. A large colony settled in Seaford, in Westmoreland, where for many generations they refused to intermarry with blacks. This unique extant enclave of Germans is now much-diminished and affected by inbreeding.

You'll also come across many brown-skinned, green-eyed, blond-haired mulattos (so-called 'red' people, a pejorative term) around Treasure Beach in St Elizabeth – the descendants of Scottish seamen, it is said, who were stranded here.

Indians Indians constitute one of the largest ethnic minorities in Jamaica. About 36,400 Indians (mostly Hindus from Northern India) migrated to Jamaica as indentured laborers contracted to work for a specific period in return for cash or land – between 1838 and 1917. They were concentrated in the old sugar parishes of Westmoreland, Clarendon, and St Thomas. They lived a life of semislavery and conditions were so appalling, with much malnutrition and tuberculosis, that the Indian government forbade further migration in 1917. After serving their tenure of indentureship, many Indians moved to Kingston where they rented land, eventually hired laborers, and generally prospered as merchants. The arrival of new migrants ensured that cultural practices such as the *pujas* (prayers) and religious celebrations were kept alive, although many families changed their names to escape the stigma of the caste system. Later this century, another group of independent immigrants arrived and formed a mercantile community known as the 'Bombay Merchants.'

Though small in numbers, the Indians' legacy is profound. Their contributions include the curries that are now an island staple and *ganja*, which they introduced to the island along with the word itself.

Chinese Many Chinese also arrived in Jamaica as indentured laborers during the post-emancipation era. Today their descendants (less than 1% of the population) are predominant in the restaurant trade, real estate, and the business community. Several family dynasties are among the wealthiest of Jamaicans. Sadly, Jamaica's Chinese population is now only about 5000; the vast majority – as many as 35,000 by some estimates – left during the turmoil of the 1970s, most headed for the USA.

Middle Easterners Likewise 'Syrians,' a generic Jamaican term for those of Levantine extraction, have made good economically and politically (the PNP party leader and ex-premier, Edward Seaga, is Lebanese). Most are descendants of Lebanese who arrived around the turn of the century and established themselves in the garment industry and as general merchants.

Jews Jews have a long heritage in Jamaica. They first arrived in significant numbers during the Spanish colonial period, when they were forced to flee the Inquisition. They were also persecuted in Jamaica, where they assumed new identities and had to practice their religion in secret. Hence, many Jews assisted the English during the 1655 invasion. They were permitted to remain and practice Judaism freely, and quickly established an early influence in political affairs.

There are probably fewer than 1500 Jews in Jamaica today, though their influence has remained inordinately greater than their numbers (in 1849, when eight of the 47 members of the House of Assembly were Jewish, the Assembly became the first legislative body in the world to adjourn for Yom Kippur).

EDUCATION

During the late 19th century, the British established in Jamaica the foundations of what developed into an admirable education system, based on the British model of schooling. The Manley administration gave priority to enhancing educational standards in the 1970s. Critics say the Jamaican education system has since been dismantled. There is no doubt that Jamaica's educational system is in crisis.

Spending per student fell from an average of US$120 in 1980 to US$97 by 1987 (compared to US$600 in Barbados and US$550 in Trinidad) during which time the portion of the government budget spent on education dwindled from 18 to 11%. Low salaries fail to attract quality teachers. Few schools have computers or advanced teaching aids now commonplace in schools in more developed societies. Many rural schools lack even basic sanitation. In many schools, the student/teacher ratio is very high. The problem is compounded by lack of transportation. Many children in rural areas must travel many miles to reach school, and it is common to see groups of schoolchildren walking barefoot in the rain.

To solve this, the government has attempted to get private industry involved through its Adopt-a-School Program, launched in 1989. In May 1993, the World Bank and IMF together approved loans of US$60 million to support reform of Jamaica's education system.

Although primary education is free and compulsory to the age of 14, the financial crisis in education has adversely affected students' academic success. About 60% of Jamaican schoolchildren (mostly in rural areas) do not complete primary education. Of those that do, more than half are functionally illiterate (officially, adult literacy is estimated at 85 to 90%, though this includes a great percentage who can do little more than sign their name). There's a shortage of secondary-school places, so primary school-leavers must take competitive exams for placement, as must secondary school-leavers hoping to attend university or vocational college.

Jamaican schoolchildren perform at miserably low levels in maths and English in the Caribbean Examinations: in the 1994 examinations, only 23% of Jamaican students attained the Grade II level of proficiency required by private-sector companies and tertiary institutions. Many well-to-do families send their children to private schools.

ARTS

Jamaica is a center of Caribbean art. Kingston, in particular, has a vitalic cultural energy. There's a strong intellectual-tradition and a large middle class to support the arts. Music, dance, drama, and fine arts have flourished tremendously since independence in 1962, and quintessentially Jamaican styles have evolved. The island's rich artistic heritage reaches back to pre-Columbian days, when the Arawak Indians etched petroglyphs on the ceilings and walls of caverns.

Anyone limiting themselves to resort entertainment could leave the island assuming that fire-eaters, limbo dancers, calypso bands, and painted fish and carved gourds are Jamaica's artistic staples, but a much richer artistic tapestry awaits discovery. Few visitors venture to Kingston, where the sophistication of visual and performance arts may come as a surprise.

Visual Arts

Jamaica's 'plastic arts' (ceramics, sculpture, paintings, woodcarving, and textiles) lagged behind performing arts for many years, but they have caught up in recent decades. The National Gallery is the starting point for any understanding of Jamaican art. It houses the nation's largest collection of historical and contemporary art, arranged in separate rooms chronologically and by artist. The larger towns and cities also support commercial art galleries. The exceptional ones are noted under the towns where they are located.

The history of Jamaican art has its origins in the 18th and 19th centuries, when itinerant artists such as Philip Wickstead and George Robertson roamed the plantations, recording that life in a idyllic, romanticized light and always from a Eurocentric point of view that totally ignored the African heritage. Satirist William Hogarth was one of few artists to portray the hypocrisy and savagery of plantation life.

Until the 1920s, leading artists were establishment figures. The artistic forum continued to look to Europe for inspiration and reflected little of the yearnings and turmoil of Jamaican history. The turbulent decade, however, was a heady time of growing nationalism and black pride. Fueled by homegrown yearnings for a distinctive Jamaican identity, a new national consciousness and artistic movement arose. Artists began to edge away from the Eurocentric model and developed their own indigenous expressions, most strongly shaped by themes of poverty, bondage, striving, and other realities of Jamaican life. The so-called 'Jamaica School' sought to capture the island's essence on canvas.

A pivotal event occurred in 1939 when about 40 well-known artists stormed the annual meeting of the Institute of Jamaica, an organization established to encourage the arts, science, and culture.

They demanded an artistic unshackling from European aesthetic prescriptions. One of the artists, a lawyer named Robert Braithwaite, pointed to the portraits of the English governors on the wall and exclaimed, 'Gentlemen! We have come to tell you to tear down these pictures and let the Jamaican paintings take their place.'

Edna Manley, a leader of the group, was instrumental in the radical change. Manley – Jamaica's leading sculptor – was born in England to a Jamaican mother. As the wife of Norman Manley, Jamaica's future and first prime minister, she was very much an establishment figure but no less Jamaican for it. During the formative years between 1922 and 1940, Manley and another artist, Koren der Harootian, nurtured the fine-art movement by freeing themselves from English aesthetics.

Manley organized art classes at the Institute of Jamaica, which evolved into the Jamaican School of Art and later into the Edna Manley School of the Visual Arts. This resulted in the opening of commercial galleries, which, in turn, encouraged self-taught artists. Manley's successor, Karl Craig, expanded the school in the 1970s. It became the embryo for the National Gallery of Jamaica, which today houses a splendid collection of Manley's works in the Roy West Building on Kingston's waterfront. Manley herself remained at the forefront of sculpture and art until her death at 86 in 1987.

The Jamaican School evolved two main groups: the island-themed primitives (labeled 'intuitives') and a more internationalist group of painters schooled abroad. The former is exemplified by the works of self-taught artists such as John Dunkley, whose explorations of Biblical and folkloric icons have been inordinately influential, and 'Kapo' Mallica Reynolds. Many self-taught intuitive artists have risen from the ghettoes. Dunkley (born in 1881) was a Kingston barber who painted his entire shop – furniture, walls, and all – in Jungian-style vines, flowers, and abstract symbols. Dunkley later turned to canvas. His untempered interpretations of Jamaica life inspired many subsequent intuitive artists whose efforts were purely home-grown. Like many artistic geniuses, Dunkley did not grow rich on his art. Today, years after his death, collectors pay big money for his works.

Bishop Mallica 'Kapo' Reynolds is the most renowned of the intuitive artists. Kapo was a leading Revivalist cult leader (see the Religion section below) who painted 'ecstatic landscapes and mystical visions.' He was imprisoned in the 1930s for practicing *obeah* (black magic) and later suffered a seizure that left him paralyzed below the waist. Nonetheless, his career spanned 50 years. One of his works was presented to Emperor Haile Selassie in 1966; another – *A New Spring* – was a wedding gift to Prince Charles and Princess Diana. He died at 78 in 1989. Kapo and other intuitive masters are well represented in the National Gallery.

Contemporary Jamaican artists such as Michael Escoffery, Carl Abrahams, Barrington Watson, and Christopher Gonzalez have earned world-renown for their museum pieces. Gonzalez's life-size memorial bust of Jamaican National Hero George William Gordon and full figure eight-foot-tall bronze statue of Bob Marley can be viewed at the National Gallery in Kingston.

Gonzalez and many other avant-garde artists studied abroad in the 1960s and 1970s and returned inspired by new ideas that they wedded to their nationalist spirits. No collective visual style defines Jamaican painters, but many emphasize historical roots in their works. The international success of reggae music has had a profound effect on Jamaican visual arts. Rastafarians are common subjects, as are market higglers, animals, and religious symbols merged with the myths of Africa.

One of the more unusual artists is Everald Brown, who has an unmistakable niche. Brown creates sculptures in stone kindled by 'divine inspiration,' especially from the stones that 'speak' to him near his home in Murray Mountain, St Anns. He also creates unique musical instruments, such as his Talking Drum and Star Guitar.

Many anonymous artists lavish their métier on murals, which are everywhere. Bars, shops, restaurants, and rum shops islandwide copy the Jungian-style of John Dunkley (usually with vines crawling along a black wall) or display whimsical alfresco trompe l'oeil cartoons dramatizing Jamaican life.

Colloquially, the pop-style wall murals are known as 'yard art,' after the 'yards' of Kingston ghettoes, where powerful politically inspired murals are painted in big, bold colors that can be absorbed at a glance. Many are threatening, no-nonsense parochial messages. Others are more cheery, adding color and humor to otherwise depressing environments.

Muralist skills are exemplified by the giant mural on the Assembly Hall at the University of the West Indies campus in Kingston. Another work, this one by famous artist Karl Parboosingh, appears on the outer wall of the Frame Centre in Kingston.

In addition to the fine arts, Jamaica's crafts industry supports tens of thousands of artisans. Island artisans offer a cornucopia of leatherwork, ceramics, shell art, beadwork, and basket-weaving and other straw-work made of native thatch palm. Although much of it is tawdry kitsch, mass-produced with little skill or pride, some is surprisingly sophisticated – even museum quality. One company, Things Jamaica Ltd, has worked for more than 30 years to expand Jamaica's craft industry by accepting only the highest quality works; its efforts have strongly influenced industry standards.

Thousands of self-taught woodcarvers hew intuitive carvings in lignum vitae, blue mahoe, and other hardwoods. The crafts stalls that line north-coast roads are menageries of palette-bright fishes, toads, sphinxlike cats, and magnificent roosters, often painted with bright pointillist dots. The most popular subjects are giant Rasta heads, oversized fish and giraffes, and almost life-size wooden men with larger than life-size phalluses.

Literature

While the island has produced no writer of world-renown, Jamaican does have its literati. Most are well known in the Caribbean but not much further afield: John Hearne *(The Sure Salvation)*, Roger Mais *(Brother Man)*, and Orlando Patterson *(The Children of Sysyphus)*, whose novels provide fascinating insights into Rastafarian culture.

Most writers and playwrights are haunted by the ghosts of Jamaica's past, mostly its slave history and the ambiguities of Jamaicans' relationship to Mother England. Novels have tended to focus on physical survival in a grim colonial landscape and escape to the mother country, which often proves even more grim.

In recent years, a number of Jamaican women have gained notice: Christine Craig *(Mint Tea)*, Patricia Powell *(Me Dying Trial)*, and Vanessa Spence *(The Roads Are Down)*, for example. Coping is still the main theme, as it was in the 'migrant literature' of the 1950s, but the setting is mostly contemporary, and the oppressors are the men within their characters' lives.

Music

From hotel beach parties to the raw 'sound system' disco of the working-class suburbs, Jamaica reverberates to the soul-riveting sounds of calypso, soca, and reggae. Music is everywhere. The buses are practically mobile discos. Streetside stores blast rap-reggae to wake the dead. Story-tall speakers in rural village squares make the telegraph poles shake.

Reggae may have put Jamaica on the musical map, but the nation's musical heritage runs much deeper. It is also constantly evolving, setting the tone and pace for the world to follow and underpinning Jamaica's sizable recording industry. Kingston has become the 'Nashville of the Third World,' and recording studios pump out dozens of new titles each month.

African Roots Jamaican music draws on its rich heritage of folk music introduced by African slaves. Although slaveholders attempted to suffocate African culture, traditional music survived. Particularly important were the 'talking drums' *(burru)*, which were used to pass information, and folk songs derived from the canefields, where songs developed to ease the back-breaking labor. The songs have been kept alive this century by day workers (see the Day Work section under Society & Culture below), and by professional groups such as the Jamaica Folk Singers and National Dance Theatre Company singers.

Over generations, European elements such as the French quadrille introduced by planters were absorbed and fused into the African music and dance, creating a uniquely Caribbean style. Its earliest expressions were in *jonkanoo* celebrations held at Christmastime, when drums, rattles, the *abeng* horn and conch shell came together in a riotous carnival, later accompanied by fife and flute, then fiddles and horns (see the Jonkanoo sidebar in the Facts for the Visitor chapter). Jamaicans still play tambours (drums), bamboo flutes, and other African instruments, as they have since the days of slavery. The use of *akete* drums and rattles in the kumina religion would later find their way into reggae music.

Calypso Calypso is often associated with Jamaica, partly because of Harry Belafonte's fame (initiated with the 1957 release of his 'Banana Boat Song' and 'Islands in the Sun'). The steel drum lies at the heart of calypso, and many hotels feature a steel-drum band in their weekly repertoire of entertainment. The music, however, really belongs to Trinidad.

Mento The earliest original Jamaican musical form was *mento*, a folk calypso that emerged at the turn of the 19th century as an accompaniment to a dance derived from the French quadrille and English-inspired Maypole dances. The music fused calypso with Cuban influences – the guitar, banjo, shakers, and rumba box (adapted from the African thumb piano, with metal straps for strings) – introduced by Jamaican migrant workers. Mento was slow and rhythmic, with raunchy lyrics that perfectly suited the undulating groin-to-groin movements (called 'dubbing') from which today's intimate, grinding 'wine' style of Jamaican dance derives.

Mento developed a faster pace during the 1940s and 1950s and became as popular throughout Jamaica as reggae is today. It was even popular at high-society gatherings. (Mento is kept alive during Heritage Week's 'Mento Yard,' hosted in a different parish each October and featuring traditional folk groups and mento bands.)

By the late '50s, the music was fading under a wave of popular North American music, particularly early boogie-woogie and rhythm and blues, which bore similarities to Jamaican rhythms. Jamaican musicians (many of whom had been weaned in military bands and were playing to tourists in north-coast hotels) began playing experimental sounds, mixing the American R&B sound with calypso-mento. The new music was given an onomatopoeic name for the *ska-ska-ska* noise of the piano.

Ska Though short-lived, ska was uniquely inventive and unmistakenly Jamaican. It was mostly instrumental: horn-driven, with a danceable double-time beat. The music's own unique bobbing dance style (also called ska, or skanking) became an overnight sensation, with shuffling feet seemingly moving like crankshafts and arms pumping like pistons.

Ska was adopted by the poor and dispossessed, as it still is in down-at-heels backwaters such as Port Royal. Soon, lyricists edged the instrumentalists aside, marrying the music to social protest for the first time in lyrics. The trend was exemplified by a group led by Bob Marley, a young singer who was recording ska hits such as 'Rude Boy' (named for the thugs then taking over Kingston's ghettoes). Ska was dominated by Don Drummond, lead trombonist of the Skatalites, whose compositions defined ska

in the same manner that Bob Marley's music would later dominate reggae. Drummond converted to Rastafarianism, influencing dozens of other musicians, before murdering his lover and being committed to a mental asylum in 1969.

Radio stations spread ska to North America and Europe, and performers such as Toots & the Maytals, and Byron Lee and the Dragonaires became household names. In England, ska found a strong following among Jamaican immigrants and gained prominence when Millie Small had a multi-million-sale smash hit in 1964 with 'My Boy Lollypop.'

Rock-Steady Gradually ska was slowed down to half speed and became a more syncopated, melodic music that harked back to mento. The dance style was more languid, with minimal movements that gave the new 'ska' its own name: rock-steady.

Rock-steady was short-lived, basically spanning 1966 to 1970. Leading exponents were Desmond Dekker ('Israelites'), Jimmy Cliff ('You Can Get It If You Really Want'), and Leroy Sibbles and his band, the Heptones, who gave the sound a heavy bass. Others charged rock-steady with angrier lyrics.

Reggae Reggae is the heartbeat of Jamaica – a brand of music as strongly identified with the island as R&B is with Detroit or jazz with New Orleans. It's a major factor in the Jamaican economy, at no time better demonstrated than during Reggae Sunsplash and Reggae Sumfest, when almost one-quarter million visitors arrive from overseas to dance and sway in delirious union to the soulful, syncopated beat.

Reggae evolved in the ghettoes of Kingston, born of the tensions and social protest simmering violently in the late 1960s. Jamaicans will tell you that reggae means 'comin' from de people,' a phrase coined (as was the name *reggae* itself) by Frederick 'Toots' Herbert, of Toots and the Maytals, in his first single, 'Do the Reggay,' in 1968. They'll also tell you that

Reggae Royalty

During Bob Marley's lifetime, the reggae superstar was one of the world's greatest musical influences, and after his death, his name has become synonymous with Jamaica.

Robert Nesta Marley was born on February 6, 1945, in the tiny village of Nine Miles in St Ann Parish. His mother, Cedella, was a Jamaican, his father white and English-born. He deserted the family while Robert was still a youngster.

In his teens, Bob Marley moved to Trench Town, a poverty-ridden ghetto in Kingston, where he joined with Junior Braithwaite, Peter (Tosh) Macintosh, and his childhood friend Neville ('Bunny') Livingstone in a group, the Wailing Rude Boys, named for the militant young thugs – the rude boys – then rampaging in Kingston. The group later shortened its name to the Wailers. They recorded ska and rock-steady tunes that had met with limited success. Marley married, and his wife, Rita, became the leader of a backup group called the I-Threes with Judy Mowatt and Marcia Griffiths.

In 1967 the Wailers briefly broke up. After living with his mother in Wilmington, Delaware, Marley returned to his home parish where he tried farming. North American singer Johnny Nash, who had seen Marley perform on TV, set out to find the reclusive singer. Nash signed Marley (now a Rastafarian) and began producing Marley's ground-breaking melodies that the world now knows as reggae.

In 1970 the Wailers formed their own company, Tuff Gong. They also signed up with wizard music promoter Chris Blackwell's Island Records and in 1973 released two smash hit albums: *Catch a Fire* and *Burnin'*. The albums catapulted Marley's music from the stark slums of Trench Town into the consciousness of the world, aided the following year by British rock-star Eric Clapton's version of the Marley hit 'I Shot the Sheriff.' Reggae soared to the top of the world charts. Marley followed this success with other blockbuster albums: *Rastaman Vibration, Exodus,* and *Survival.*

Marley's stature was such that he was courted by politicians during a period when Jamaica was seething with violence and animosities. In 1976 he was nearly killed during an assassination attempt at his home in Kingston. Two days later, Marley held a concert in which he induced political archrivals Edward Seaga and Michael Manley to link arms with him in a plea to stop the sectarian violence (an act he repeated in 1978 at his One Love concert).

By 1980, multimillionaire Marley had attained superstardom. Despite this, Marley never forgot nor forsook his roots. A consistent voice against racism, oppression, and injustice, Marley became the musical conscience of the world. Throughout the Third World, he was received as a messiah. On April 17, 1980, for example, Marley led a triumphant concert to celebrate Independence Day at the transformation of Rhodesia into Zimbabwe. On the eve of his death, he was awarded the Order of Merit, Jamaica's highest honor.

The Honorable Robert Nesta Marley, OM, died of brain cancer on May 11, 1981, at Miami's Cedars of Lebanon Hospital at the age of 36. Dressed in a blue denim suit and a tam of red, green, and gold, his body lay in state at Kingston's National Arena, a Bible in one hand, a guitar in the other. He was laid to rest in a crypt within a whitewashed chapel next to the one-room cottage where he lived as a boy. The cortege stretched for 50 miles!

Marley died without making a will. Sadly, his fortune has been the source of ongoing legal battles between family members. Nonetheless, in his homeland, Marley's name is hallowed and he is revered almost as a god. ■

reggae is about 'truth and rights.' The music expresses a yearning for respect, self-identity, and affirmation amid poverty. Its lyrics are distinct in their political, social, and religious messages full of metaphor, expressions of anger, and praise of Jah.

Reggae is associated above all with one man: Robert Nesta Marley. Marley had established himself as an early leading

After the Wailers split up, Bunny Wailer, Bob Marley, and Peter Tosh had successful solo careers.

influence, with his creative style and unique stage presence. He adopted Rastafarianism, injecting his music with greater soul and more poignant lyrics that helped spark a worldwide 'Third World consciousness.' In 1972 he came under the wing of genius record producer Chris Blackwell. Blackwell produced Marley's *Catch a Fire* and *Burnin'*, which both rocketed up the charts and put reggae – and Marley – on the map (see the Bob Marley sidebar).

Though Marley died in 1981, reggae has gone from strength to strength. International stars such as Eric Clapton and Paul Simon even began to incorporate reggae tunes into their smash hit albums. Though no other artist has attained Marley's stature, reggae's success has spawned dozens of international stars: Toots and the Maytals, Peter Tosh, Jimmy Cliff (whose movie *The Harder They Come* helped thrust reggae onto the world stage), Third World, Burning Spear, and Black Uhuru. Marley's wife,

Rita, and four of their children (performing as the Melody Makers) have continued to hold aloft the family flame, as has Ziggy Marley, Bob's eldest son and one of at least 10 children sired by the singer.

Not all reggae stars are Jamaican. Reggae has a huge following in Scandinavia and Japan, where homegrown performers are bursting onto the scenes. Foreign performers such as Maxi Priest, Steel Pulse, UB40, and Linton Kwesi Johnson, all from England, are at the vanguard. Nor do all reggae artists embrace social commentary in their music. Latterday artistes such as Maxi Priest, Gregory Isaacs, and Freddie McGregor have popularized a beautifully melodic, romanticized reggae called Lover Rock.

Purely instrumental reggae is known as dub music. Jamaican DJs invented their own lyrics to 'dub' over the music, initially in a verse form that has since evolved into dancehall.

Dancehall The current in-vogue working-class music is dancehall – a kind of Caribbean rap music. It is named for the loosely defined venues at which 'toasters' (rapper DJs) set up mobile discotheques, usually comprising two decks, an amplifier and mixer, and enormous speakers. The music they play is a hybrid of reggae and rap music of the 1990s' urban ghettoes is the USA, usually with a monotonous yet always fast-paced, compulsive beat.

Many of the artists add vocals (and often musical overtones) to already existent rhythms. The form harks back to the 1950s when DJs traveled about the island with their mobile discotheques and chatted over the music they played. Back then the relatively few DJs were mostly colorful show-stealers sporting often outrageous costumes and performing acrobatics. They paid compliments or 'toasts' to the crowd and became known as 'toasters,' with a style all their own. Such DJs as Lord Stitch, Big Youth, and Count Machukie rose to such fame that their toasts were recorded on vinyl, often by 'dubbing' onto the B sides of established singles.

The lyrics are generally sexually explicit (known as *slack)* and often glorify violence. An albino named Yellowman (Winston Foster) is the undisputed king of slack. Violence charged dancehall-rap is epitomized by Buju Banton, whose single 'Boom Bye Bye' was denounced for advocating murdering gays. Banton's misogynist and homophobic lyrics caused the police commissioner to issue a decree banning radio and TV stations from playing songs that advocate gun violence. Many contemporary artists have countered the worrisome trend with socially conscious lyrics known as dub poetry.

Today's dancehall adherents have their own uniform. For the men, massive gold chains and jewelry called 'cargo' are de rigueur, as are gold-rimmed sunglasses and ornate hairdos. For women (or 'queens'), less is more: often bright-dyed, fancy hairstyles or wigs, and show-stopping outfits, often skin-tight and always skimpy. The undisputed reigning queen of 'queens' is Carlene, a dyed-blond, light-skinned mulatto with an outrageous (and successful) sense of self-promotion.

Soca Hailing from Trinidad, this fast-paced dance music fuses soul and calypso. Though soca has a pedigree going back two decades, it gained prominence in Jamaica only recently at Carnival. It is now the music of choice at resort discos and upscale discos in 'uptown' Kingston (dancehall is the music of 'downtown').

Theater & Dance

Jamaica has a rich heritage of theater and dance. An alchemy of outside influences, it is second only to Cuba in the Caribbean. Amateur theaters and dance companies are scattered throughout Jamaica, and Kingston-based companies often tour the parishes. Kingston's scene is vibrant enough to sustain half a dozen or more concurrent productions. Many of the larger, upscale hotels also feature their own productions.

Theater productions, often performed in patois, are difficult for visitors to understand. They're often bawdy and farcical, with a tendency to portray the trials of the poor.

Dance embraces forms from indigenous African dances to contemporary and classical. Among Jamaica's many internationally acclaimed groups are the Little Theater Movement, the National Dance Theater Company, the Jamaica Folk Singers, the National Chorale, the University Players, and Sistren, an all-women group that performs politically charged productions focusing on the plight of women.

Theater and dance receive substantial government support, including funds from the Institute of Jamaica's Cultural Development Commission. Formal training is sponsored under the aegis of the Jamaica School of Dance, Jamaica Musical Theater Company, and Jamaica School of Drama.

National Dance Theater Company The NDTC, Jamaica's most acclaimed dance troupe, is based in the Little Theater. Its dancers, musicians, and singers have earned praise around the world under the direction of Professor Rex Nettleford, who founded the company in 1962 as an offshoot of Jamaica's independence celebrations. It explores African themes and forms, often in vividly imaginative costumes, through performances based on Jamaican history and daily life. The NDTC's season usually runs mid-July to mid-August, with a weeklong miniseries in November/December and a medley of religious works at dawn on Easter Sunday.

National Pantomime Begun in 1941 the National Pantomime, the oldest annual production in Jamaica, is traditionally held in the Ward Theater. The production – a monument of folk theater and irreverent family entertainment – is staged by the Little Theater Movement, the oldest theatrical company in the Caribbean. The performers are all volunteers.

The pantomime has its roots in the British tradition, in which performances were based on childhood fairytales and stories such as 'Cinderella' and 'Jack and the Beanstalk.' Over the years it acquired Jamaican subjects. Folkloric characters such as Bredda Anancy and Bredda Tacooma, who originated in West Africa, soon began to appear on the Jamaican pantomime stage, as did adapted versions of Jamaican folktales.

Contrary to its name, the performance has nothing to do with mime. Pantomime is a musical comedy – a blend of lively song, dance, and words that lampoon Jamaican foibles, historic events, and well-known figures in Jamaican life. The island's leading playwrights, composers, and actors donate their time and skills to produce this world-class sendup. The audience gets drawn in, volubly so! The lyrics are in patois, so most visitors have difficulty understanding.

SOCIETY & CULTURE
Traditional Culture

Few traces of Arawak culture remain of the original Jamaican people. Many Arawak words have been passed down into common parlance, including the island's Arawak name: Xaymaca.

The strongest legacy has descended from the African slaves who brought their superstitions, folk stories, music, and religious beliefs. Most slaves came from Ghana and neighboring regions of West Africa, and Yoruba and Ashanti. Many African traditions from these regions survive in various guises. 'Jamaicatalk' is laced with African words. Storytellers have maintained an oral literature of folk tales, such as Anancy stories. And superstitions (often derived from a belief in *obeah)* have remained particularly undiluted. For example, when asked about his or her health, a Jamaican usually replies 'not too bad'; many Jamaicans are unwilling to tempt fate and the intervention of duppies (ghosts) with overly positive statements.

The African Caribbean Institute of Jamaica (ACIJ) was established in 1972 to study the island's African heritage.

Anancy Anancy is Jamaica's unlikely leading folk hero. This devious spider is the subject of many tales, still frequently told to children at bedtime. The folktales originated with the Ashanti tribe of Ghana but have become localized through the centuries. A song usually accompanies the tale. In fact, many of Jamaica's traditional folksongs derive from Anancy stories. Every tale usually ends with the cryptic 'Jack Mandora me no choose none,' a saying of obscure origin the meaning of which is open to interpretation.

Like Brer Rabbit, Bredda (brother) Anancy survives against the odds in a harsh world by his quick wit, sharp intelligence, cunning, and ingenuity. He personifies the qualities of survival so admired by Jamaicans. Anancy, his wife Crooky, and his son Tacooma frequently appear in the annual Christmas pantomime.

Several books trace the evolution and meaning of Anancy stories, including *The Art of Jamaican Oral Narrative Performances* by Laura Tanna.

Dealing with Duppies

Many Jamaicans believe in *duppies*, the ghosts or spirits of the dead that appear only at night. The term is derived from the Africa Twi tribal word *dupon* for the roots of a tree. The superstition is based on an African belief that humans have two souls. One goes to heaven for judgment; the other lingers on earth, where it lives in trees and sends shivers down the spines of superstitious Jamaicans.

Duppies are a force of either good or evil, and can be captured and used to either help, as in *myal,* or harm, as in *obeah.* Talismans are used to manipulate them. For example, many Jamaicans still place a crossed knife and fork and a Bible near young babies at night to keep away an evil, blood-sucking, witchlike duppy called Ol' Hige. Like vampires, evil duppies are also terrified when folks 'cut ten' (make the sign of the cross).

You may even come across rural Jamaicans carrying a handful of matches or stones that they can drop on the road if they think they're being followed by a duppy. Duppies are incurably curious and will stop to see what has been dropped; since they can't count beyond three, local folklore says that they'll count the first three objects and then have to start at the beginning again.

Many rural Jamaicans remain terrified of another duppy – the Whistling Cowboy, who can kill you if he breathes on you. He rides a three-legged horse, so be careful if you hear *itty-itty-hop-itty-itty-hop.* ∎

Folk Healing Traditional folk healing is still very much alive. Healers, called 'balmists,' can be either male or female and are often associated with *obeah* cults. They rely on native herbs mixed into concoctions the recipes for which have often been handed down through many generations. Red flags fly outside their 'balmyards' to chase away evil spirits.

Day Work Jamaicans also still participate in day work, in which villagers perform a common task such as building a house or planting a field. The custom, which originated from the Dahomey region of West Africa, was an early source of many Jamaican folk songs created to lighten the work. These songs utilize the African-derived call-and-response pattern, with verses sung by a leader, or *bomma*, and a chorus, or *bobbin*.

Names & Name-Calling Few Jamaicans still give a child a 'Born Day Name,' a West African tradition of naming by the day of the week. For example, the name Cudjoe (the name of the 18th-century Maroon leader) meant 'Monday.' However, such names are still in use as uncomplimentary descriptive terms. For example, someone born on Friday is often called a

cuffee (stupid); a *quashie* (bumpkin) is someone born on Sunday.

Nine Nights Many Jamaican elders still observe nine nights, a 'wake' held on the ninth night after someone's death to ensure that the spirit of the deceased departs to heaven. If such a ceremony is not performed, his or her spirit (or duppy) will hang around to haunt the living. The wake is usually accompanied by hymn singing and superstitious rituals such as turning over the mattress of the deceased or sweeping out the house.

Modern Culture

Most visitors have very limited contact with Jamaicans and then usually only on the beaches and in restaurants, hotels, and discos. The social reality of everyday Jamaica is hidden. Your interaction with Jamaicans will be richer if you open your ears and mind in trying to understand the social conditions and dilemmas that have shaped the unique Jamaican character. An appreciation for the ironic helps, as do empathy and compassion.

Jamaica has a profound class system despite a unifying sense of national pride. At its heart is an unwritten color code that may not be very noticeable to foreign visitors (see the Black Color Scale section under Population & People above).

The Jamaican Character Jamaicans are an intriguing contrast. The majority are the most gracious people you'll ever meet: happy-go-lucky, helpful, courteous, genteel, and full of humility. Jamaican children are almost without exception well-behaved and extremely polite. You'll rarely see bad behavior among children of school age: they have an English-style civility that they share with a majority of senior citizens.

However, a significant minority is composed of the most sullen, cantankerous, obstreperous, and confrontational people you could ever wish not to meet. Foreign visitors are often shocked at the surliness and seeming indifference they so often encounter. The Jamaicans' renowned belligerent independence can trace its roots all the way back to the Maroons. Charged memories of slavery and racism have continued to bring out the spirit of anarchy latent in an ex-slave society divided into rich and poor.

You'll not meet many Jamaicans without strong opinions, and they're not sheeplike with them. The clash of opinions boils over in debates over politics. Private differences don't stay that way for long – part of the national psyche is an instinct to get involved in others' 'bisniss.' When Jamaicans are not pleased, they tell you in no uncertain terms.

The Jamaican character can seem schizophrenic and perplexingly volatile. Many Jamaicans are particularly quick to take imagined offense. Their in-your-face response is often quite aggressive and psychologically disturbing for visitors. Hustlers often use this to devastating effect on tourists: 'What matter? You got sometin' against me?' The best defense is to defuse the situation by joking back. Jamaicans appreciate a quick wit. They're also quick to acknowledge their own faults and other absurdities.

Wit & Humor Among the most marvelous treasures in the Jamaican cultural trove are a love of color and drama, a sharp intellect, and above all a keen sense of humor. The Jamaican's sarcastic and sardonic wit is legendary. Often it is laced with sexual undertones. Jamaicans like to make fun of others, often in the most subtle yet no-punches-pulled way, but they accept being the source of similar humor in good grace. Individual foibles and physical abnormalities inspire many a knee-slapping jibe.

The lusty humor will sometimes be directed at you. Take it in good humor. Their deprecating and self-deprecating humor is never meant to sting. You'll be an instant hit if you give as good as you get, but the key is subtlety, not malice.

Sex & Family Life Jamaicans are sexually active and at an early age (5% of mothers have their first child before they are 15 years old). Noncommittal sexual relationships are the norm, especially among the poorer classes. Like many aspects of Jamaican life, this is a carryover from slave days, when slaves were encouraged to have children but were denied permanent relationships (it was common for planters to separate 'husband' and 'wife').

It is still common for a poor couple to marry only late in life, if at all. Most couples live together, often on an ephemeral basis. Thus it is not unusual for women to have children by several men and for men to sire families with several women. Almost two-thirds of children are born out of wedlock. A lower-class woman is considered a 'mule' – sterile – if she hasn't had a child by her twenties.

Pumping It Up

Many Jamaican men are preoccupied with their libido, or 'nature,' and have concocted all kinds of juices ('sex potents') for maintaining their health. With names like Front-End Lifter, Tear-Up Mattress, and Brek-Down Bed, they leave little to the imagination. Most look like bottled diarrhea and are usually made of Irish moss (a type of sea algae) and other herbal ingredients. ∎

Jamaicans are direct about sex. If a Jamaican wants to sleep with you, he or she will let you know. On the Lonely Planet travel video *The Jamaican Experience*, host Ian Wright is asked by the woman giving him an aloe massage: 'So shorty, you wanna go in de bushes?' You'll need to be just as direct with your response to get a 'No!' across. Don't beat about the bush in the hope of not hurting someone's feelings. It doesn't work. If love beneath the palms sounds enticing, expect to be asked for a 'likkle sometin" to help feed the kids (this is true of men and women). My experience is that Jamaican women like to cut to the chase. Romance takes a backseat to raw physical passion.

Women in Jamaica Jamaica is a matriarchal society in the African (and slave plantation) tradition. The sexes lead independent lives, at least among the lower classes. In the slave system, men were ·commonly sold and separated from their lovers and children. Even women slaves were commonly sold, never to see their children again. When that happened, the grandmother, aunt, or another family member would care for the child. The tradition continues: it is common for a woman to leave her children in the care of a relative for months or even years at a time while she takes up with another man or for reasons of employment or hardship.

Jamaican women are strong and fiercely independent. Many couples in relationships maintain their own separate property. Numerous Jamaican women complain that this brings men's insecurities to the surface. A large percent of Jamaican men expect women to play a subservient role; they feel threatened by Jamaican women, especially educated women whom they consider too independent.

In 1993, 12.7% of the women in the labor force had reached senior management and professional level, compared to only 8% of male workers.

Work & Living Conditions The two generations since independence have seen a remarkable change, not least a growing disparity in incomes. There has been a steady move away from an agrarian society to an increasingly industrialized and urbanized one marked by massive migration into Kingston, where a burgeoning underclass has been forced to live in slums.

The majority of Jamaicans live a marginal existence in ramshackle villages and rural shacks, sometimes in pockets of extreme and sobering poverty. There are pockets of malnutrition but no starvation – the island is too fecund for that. Jamaicans have only to reach out and pluck bananas and coconuts, and fish is available on the end of a line. On market days, country higglers will get up before dawn, load up their yams, carrots, and chocho (a native squash), trek from the hills to the main roads, and catch rides to the main market towns – all to earn a few pennies.

It is hard for the majority of Jamaicans to gather even the most meager resources. They languish under economic hardships. The aspirations of most poorer Jamaicans remain compromised, and despite notable exceptions, individuals are generally reluctant to take risks. Some sociologists have suggested that one of the reasons behind this can be traced back to slavery, when blacks were robbed of their sense of initiative and browbeaten into resignation to circumstance. Many low-income Jamaicans have been unable to find a way out of poverty, so they hustle. They hang out on the streets waiting for an opportunity to present itself.

In contrast, Jamaica has a significant middle and upper class, who conspicuously live in the hills above Kingston and Montego Bay. These two classes often live with a surprising lack of contact with the harsh reality in which the majority of Jamaicans live and can muster little empathy. North American values and consumer tastes have strongly influenced Jamaica's middle classes. The cultural and political elite is drawn from a relatively small number of families. White families are still predominantly in charge of business and political affairs. Menial and manual labor is still abhorred by many non-blacks as a symbol of inferior status.

This is a legacy of colonial days, when whites ran the administration and businesses. Historians argue that in the post-emancipation period, the British exploited color gradations in hiring and the associated social privilege, because a 'divide and rule' policy had become an imperative for running the British Empire. Jamaica became a color-coded society. Available school places, for example, were reserved for whites and 'high browns,' or 'outside *piknis*' (mulatto children, usually the illegitimate offspring of a white man and a black woman). As late as the 1950s, black girls were rarely employed in offices, which led to demonstrations for change. The police force was white, as were the Anglican and Catholic Church clergy.

On the eve of independence, whites were still at the top. The middle-class business-people, traders, and professionals were mostly minorities or of mixed ethnic background. The vast pool of labor, subsistence farmers, and the unemployed were black. Thus status, self-esteem, and stigmas became associated with work.

Crime & Violence Jamaica has witnessed a dramatic increase in violent crimes in the past two decades. The Pan American Health Organization reported that in 1990 there were 55 murders per million people worldwide; Jamaica's murder rate is four times higher, second only to the USA. The moral decay that has swept younger culture worldwide has done so to devastating effect in Jamaica. Fortunately, violence rarely infringes on visitors.

Much of the violence is related to the drug trade, particularly in Kingston, where Western-style street shootouts between gangs and police are common. There are even parts of Kingston where the police dare not venture! Police officers are frequently brutally murdered. (In turn, many police members are guilty of summary justice and violent excesses; 145 of the 700 reported murders in Jamaica in 1990 were victims who died in police custody!)

Dos & Don'ts
Do be direct. Jamaicans prefer it. They're among the most direct people you'll ever meet. If you beat around the bush, they may not get your point.

Do relax. Tropical time happens at a slower pace. 'Soon come' is a favorite expression meaning 'it'll happen when it happens.' Don't expect that you can improve the situation by being rude or throwing tantrums. Most Jamaicans will simply shrug their shoulders.

Do be empathetic. Try to understand the hardships that the majority of Jamaicans face. Don't try to take advantage of an individual's plight.

Don't call Jamaicans 'natives'. Jamaicans may be natives of the island, but the term is laden with racial connotations that can be taken as slurs. 'Islanders' or simply 'Jamaicans' is more appropriate.

Do ask before snapping a photo. Many Jamaicans enjoy being photographed, sometimes for a small fee, but others prefer not to pose for tourists. For more on this topic, see the Photographing People section under Photography & Video in the Facts for the Visitor chapter.

RELIGION

You don't have to peer inside the *Guinness Book of Records* to discover that Jamaica has the greatest number of churches per sq mile in the world (more than 80% of Jamaicans profess to be Christians). There seems to be a church every few hund red yards, with virtually every imaginable denomination in the world represented. The Church serves as an important social center in Jamaican communities. The gospel is a source of hope, with its talk of equality and redemption in the afterlife. The African legacy also runs deep on the island, and religious beliefs brought by slaves linger, often interwoven like a weft in the warp of Christian ideology.

Religious tolerance has evolved only as a modern Jamaican tradition. The colonial plantocracy (and Anglican church establishment) was totally indifferent to the spiritual welfare of the slaves. They did not consider blacks to be human beings in possession of souls. Ever-fearful of slave uprisings, they attempted to vanquish the slaves' African heritage by banning religious gatherings and aggressively thwarting missionary efforts at religious conversion. Nonetheless, missionary zeal gathered pace in the half-century preceding emancipation in 1834 as Baptist and Methodist preachers arrived to spread abolitionism alongside their own version of the word of God. A period of Christianization known as the 'Great Revival' followed emancipation.

Christianity

On weekends, it's common to see adults and children walking along country roads holding bibles and dressed in their finest togs – the girls in white, the men in somber suits, the women in heels, hats, and bright-colored satins. On Sundays every church in the country seems to overflow with the righteous, and the old fire-and-brimstone school of sermonizing is still the preferred mode. Bible-waving congregations sway to and fro, roll their heads, and wail and shriek 'Hallelujah!' and 'Amen, sweet Jesus!,' while guitars, drums, and tambourines help work the crowds into a frenzy.

The majority of the population (38%) belong to the Anglican Church of Jamaica, formerly the Church of England, which has dominated religious life since 1655; the English ruling class ensured that each parish had an Anglican church. Baptists (18%), Methodists (6%), and Presbyterians (5%) claim significant adherents, as they have since slavery, when missionaries were at the forefront of the fight for abolition. Every town of any significance also has a Roman Catholic Church. The Spanish introduced Catholicism, which was banned by the English between 1655 and 1792. Eight percent of the population today is Catholic, mostly Chinese, East Indians, and Middle Easterners. There are also Pentecostals, Quakers, Christian Scientists, Seventh Day Adventists, and other fundamentalists, who have made serious inroads in recent years at the behest of aggressive proselytizing.

Revivalist Cults

Jamaica has several quasi-Christian, quasi-animist sects. Their spiritual beliefs and practices resemble the voodoo religions of Haiti – the blood of the Holy Sacrament, as it were, mixing with the blood of the sacrificial goat. They are generically named Revivalist cults after the Great Revival that swept Jamaica in the 1860s, during which many blacks converted to Christianity. Revivalism is popular among the poorest classes, but is looked down on by educated Jamaicans.

The cults are derived from animist beliefs of West Africa. (Animism has nothing to do with animal spirits; the name is derived from the Latin word *anima*, for soul.) These beliefs are based on the tenet that the spiritual and temporal worlds are a unified whole. A core belief is that spirits live independently of the human or animal body and can inhabit inanimate objects. These earthly spirits, which can communicate themselves to humans, are usually morally neutral; it is the service to which humans call them that determines whether they will be a force of good or evil.

Many Jamaicans, regardless of religious faith, commonly consult practitioners who claim to be able to invoke the assistance of spirits and ghosts (duppies). Some practitioners operate as 'balmists,' using 'black magic' (called *obeah*, an Ashanti word from West Africa) for medicinal purposes, to enact revenge, to influence impending court cases, or to ensure a successful romance on behalf of a supplicant. Firm believers will sometimes heal or fall sick and even die due to their faith in the power of *obeah*. Since it is occasionally used for murder and other evil, *obeah* has been banned since slave days. Although usually associated with evil practice, obeah can also be used for good, when it is called *myal*.

Pocomania The most important Revivalist cult is Pocomania, a uniquely Jamaican spirit cult mixing European and African religious heritage. The cult is organized into hierarchical bands that hold their meetings at consecrated 'mission grounds' (or 'seals') and are overseen by a 'leader' or 'shepherd' (or 'mother' if female), who often doubles as a herbalist healer.

The ritual meetings are lively, colorful affairs involving prayers, dances, and rhythmic drumming that becomes frenzied, whipping up such a fervor that adherents may go into a trance, often aided by rum and ganja. Then, a worshipper may become 'possessed' by a spirit who becomes his or her guardian. Dancers who have fallen into a trance utter bleats and screams and all kinds of incomprehensible jibberish. They have even been known to publicly throw sexual inhibitions aside and even cause themselves serious injury.

Kumina This is the most African of the Jamaican religious cults. It was introduced by free Africans who arrived as laborers following emancipation and settled predominantly in St Thomas, where the spirit cult remains strongest.

Based on the worship of hundreds of ancestor spirit-deities, Kumina focuses on appeasing wandering spirits (duppies) of dead people who did not receive proper rites and are a menace to society. Kumina ceremonies are performed for all sorts of social occasions. Goats are frequently sacrificed. Drums are particularly powerful during Kumina ceremonies, which use a ritual Bantu language from the Congo (now Zaire), where the cult originated. As with Pocomania, dancers become possessed by spirits.

Rastafarianism

Jamaica is often summed up as 'reggae, rum, and rastas.' The Rastafarians, with their uncut, uncombed hair grown into long sun-bleached tangles known as 'dreadlocks' or 'dreads,' are synonymous with the island in the sun. There are perhaps as many as 100,000 Rastafarians in Jamaica. They adhere to an unorganized religion – a faith, not a Church. The Rastafarians' profound influence has far outweighed their small numbers.

Garveyism Rastafarianism evolved as an expression of poor black Jamaicans seeking fulfillment during the 1930s, a period of growing nationalism and economic and political upheaval. It was boosted by the 'back to Africa' zeal of Marcus Garvey's Universal Negro Improvement Association, founded in 1914 (see the Marcus Garvey sidebar in the North Coast chapter). Rastafarians regard Garvey as a prophet. The black nationalist had predicted that a black man – a Redeemer – would be crowned king in Africa. Haile Selassie's crowning as emperor of Abyssinia (now Ethiopia) in 1930 fulfilled Garvey's prophecy and established a fascination with Ethiopia that lies at the core of Rastafarianism.

Many Garvey supporters saw their Redeemer in Selassie, and they quoted Biblical references in support of Selassie's claim to be the king of all Africans. He traced his family tree back to King Solomon and the Queen of Sheba, and took the title 'King of Kings, Lord of Lords, Conquering Lion of the Tribe of Judah.' These Garveyites believed Selassi was God incarnate. They adopted Selassie's precoronation name, Ras Tafari: Ras (prince) and Tafari (to be feared).

One charismatic leader, Leonard Percival Howell, consolidated his Rastafarian faith and began a proselytizing tour. Howell was sentenced to jail under sedition charges for preaching that Jamaicans should pledge allegiance to the King of Africa, not the King of England. Freed from jail in 1940, Howell established the first Rastafarian community – the Pinnacle – in West Kingston. His followers adopted the 'dreadlocked' hair style of several East African tribes – an allegory of the mane of the Lion of Judah.

Rastafarian Tenets A document began to circulate in the 1950s outlining the 'Twenty-One Points' that defined the Rastafarian philosophy and creed. The first tenet was that the African race was one of God's chosen races, one of the twelve tribes of Israel descended from the Hebrews

Holy Smoke!

Ganja (marijuana) is an omnipresent fact of a Jamaican vacation. The weed that grows throughout the island has been cultivated for its narcotic effect since 1845, when indentured Indian laborers brought the first seeds from Asia (the English called it 'Indian hemp'). Its use spread rapidly among the plantation workers. Since it induced indolence and reduced productivity, it was outlawed at an early stage. Nonetheless, islanders have used it ever since. Today, an estimated 60% of Jamaicans smoke it on a regular basis.

Many Jamaicans don't see ganja as a drug but as a medicinal and religious herb. To Rastafarians it is a source of wisdom, a holy herb. Ganja use crosses all social strata; it is no less common for friends of the highest income levels to offer guests an after-dinner 'tote' than it is for the urban poor, who often smoke spliffs the size of bazookas.

For Jamaica's impoverished farmers, growing ganja ('poor man's friend') is one of the few sure ways of earning money. The remote interior provides ideal conditions; the five-lobed plant thrives in Jamaica's rich red soil. And the main export market – the USA – is nearby.

First the seedlings are meticulously raised under protective cover and then transplanted into fields (guano (bat dung) used as a fertilizer supposedly produces the most prolific plants). There they mature in five or six months, reaching heights as great as 10 feet! Ganja is planted between other crops by small-scale farmers, and in larger plots by more serious entrepreneurs who can earn US$10,000 per kilo. Each acre can yield up to four kilos. Once harvested, the plants are pressed to extract hash oil, and the leaves are then dried. Distributors collect the dried and baled ganja, which they transport to lonesome boat docks and remote airstrips for rapid shipment to the USA. Legitimate businesses sometimes act as covers (many respected businesspeople in Jamaica reportedly got their start in drug trafficking). Even cruise ships and scheduled airlines are often used, sometimes with the help of corrupt officials.

The US embassy estimates that during the early 1980s, the annual wholesale value of Jamaica's ganja crop exceeded US$1.5 billion. At the time, it may well have been Jamaica's major source of foreign exchange! Since 1986 the Jamaican government has attempted to crack down on drug trading at the behest of the US Government, supported by the US Drug Enforcement Agency (DEA). Efforts to eradicate the crop include spraying nurseries with weed killers.

Many people argue that ganja's contribution to the economy is too vast and vital to eradicate, and there are reasons to believe that the ganja trade has had tacit approval at the government level. Nonetheless, the DEA claims that Jamaica's ganja exports have fallen by two-thirds since 1986, but Jamaica is no beneficiary. The small farmers have borne the worst of the crunch. The demise of ganja has fostered the use and trading of other drugs, especially crack and cocaine.

Illicit drug sales on the streets are commonplace, and most street hustlers and roadside stalls will have a small spliff or bag of ganja on hand. If they like you, some Jamaicans may even give you a 'small sometin' of ganja – often enough to get the entire hotel high! The strongest varieties are Burr, Cotton, and Lamb's Breath, which are marketed in the USA as *sinsi* (short for *sinsemilla*, Spanish for seedless), the highest grade (pardon the pun).

If you're tempted to sample the local crop while on the island, remember that the possession, use, or sale of any drug is strictly illegal, and foreigners are not exempt from the heavy punishments. ∎

and displaced. Jamaica is Babylon, and their lot is exile in a land that cannot be reformed. A second tenet states that God, who they call *Jah*, will one day lead them from Babylon to Zion (the Promised Land, or Ethiopia). A third addresses the divinity of Haile Selassie and his status as the Redeemer chosen to lead Africans back to Africa.

Rastafarians have adapted traditional Christian tenets to fit their philosophical mold. They believe that in its original form the Bible told the history of the African peoples, but that it was stolen and rewritten by whites to suppress and dominate blacks. This interpretation underpins the Rastafarians' mistrust of white society and elements of Christian philosophy, especially of redemption after death. Rastafarians believe that heaven is on Earth in the present. (They also casually dismiss Selassie's appalling human rights record and harsh, despotic rule. Though Selassie died in 1975, a commonly held belief is that he still lives among them unidentified in a new guise.)

Meanwhile they wait for redemption. Reggae – a music born of their nonviolent protest against oppression – and *ganja* (the Holy herb) kill the time. *Soon come!*

Ganja & Good Living Rastafarians believe that ganja provides a line of communication with God. Again, they look to the Bible, specifically Psalm 104.14, which says 'He causeth the grass to grow for the cattle, and herb for the service of man.' Most but not all adherents smoke *ganja* copiously from cigar-size reefers *(spliffs)* and the holy *chalice*, a bamboo pipe made of a goat's horn. Through it they claim to gain wisdom and inner divinity.

In recent years, Rastafarianism has concerned itself less with redemption than with resolution of the problems of the poor and dispossessed on the island. It advocates a peaceful fight against oppression, against Babylon, defined as the 'establishment' and powerfully exemplified by Bob Marley, the Rastafarian reggae superstar, in his song 'Babylon System':

Babylon system is the vampire
Sucking the blood of the sufferers
Building church and university
Deceiving the people continually
Me say them graduating thieves
And murderers, look out now
Sucking the blood of the sufferers.

Despite its militant consciousness, Rastafarianism is not a political movement. True Rastas preach love and nonviolence and live by strict Biblical codes that advocate a way of life in harmony with Old Testament traditions. They are vegetarians who follow strict dietary laws. Strict adherents are teetotalers, too. They also shun tobacco and the staples of western consumption. Those who copy Rastafarian style but bring ill-repute are referred to as 'wolves.'

Rastafarian Sects Adherents are grouped into regional sects that cleave to the strict codes to greater or lesser degrees. The Bobo Ashantis that live above Bull Bay follow a strict ascetic life. A sect known as the Twelve Tribes of Israel (Bob Marley was a member) is composed primarily of more accomplished, well-to-do Jamaicans who have managed a greater accommodation with Babylon. It has branches around the world. The Ethiopian Zion Coptic Church, a fringe sect that has become heavily involved in the drug trade, is shunned by traditional Rastas, who deem the Coptics 'wolves.'

A Unique Lexicon A fourth tenet of Rastafarianism is the belief that God exists in each person, and that the two are the same. Thus the creed unifies divinity and individuality through the use of personal pronouns that reflect the 'I and I.' ('One blood. Everybody same, mon!') 'I' becomes the *id* or true measure of inner divinity that places everyone on the same plane. Thus 'I 'n' I' can mean 'we,' 'him and her,' 'you and they.'

Rastafarians have evolved a whole lexicon of their own, which has profoundly influenced 'Jamaica Talk' (see below).

LANGUAGE

Officially English is the spoken language. In reality, Jamaica is a bilingual country and English is far more widely understood than spoken. The unofficial lingo, the main spoken language of the poor Jamaican, is *patois* (PA-twah) – a musical dialect with a uniquely Jamaican rhythm and cadence. Patois evolved from the Creole English and a twisted alchemy of the mother tongue peppered with African, Portuguese, and Spanish terms and, in this century, Rastafarian slang. Linguists agree that it is more than pidgin English, and it has its own identifiable syntax.

Patois is deepest in rural areas, where many people do not know much standard English. Although it is mostly the lingua franca of the poor, all sectors of Jamaica understand patois, and even polite, educated Jamaicans (who tend to speak with a lilting Queen's or Oxford English) lapse into patois at unguarded moments. Most Jamaicans will vary the degree and intensity of their patois according to with whom they're speaking.

Understanding Patois

When Jamaicans speak patois, the discussion may be incomprehensible to travelers.

Like Yorkshire folk, Jamaicans often drop their 'h's' (thus, 'ouse' instead of house) and add them in unexpected places (for example, 'hemphasize'). Jamaicans have great difficulty pronouncing 'th' and usually drop the 'h' here, too: hence, 't'ree' for 'three,' 't'anks' for 'thanks,' and 'rat' for 'wrath.' 'The' is usually pronounced as 'de' and 'them' as 'dem.' They also sometimes drop the 'w,' as in 'ooman' (woman).

In patois, the word 'up' intensifies meaning: thus, cars 'mash up.' Jamaicans also often use transliteration, as in 'flim' for 'film,' and 'cerfiticket' for 'certificate.' They rearrange syllables and give them their own inflections. Patois is usually written phonetically.

Since you'll not be able to walk far without being asked for money, it helps to know enough patois to comprehend what you're hearing. Expect to hear 'gi mi a smallers no bass' ('give me some money now boss'); 'bass' means boss and is often used to address persons in authority or those able to dispense favors.

Jamaican patois is imbued with sexual slang, often of an extremely sexist nature. Cuss words also abound, especially the word *rass*, an impolite term that originally meant 'backside' or 'arse' but the meaning of which now varies according to circumstance. It's a word visitors to Jamaica should know, as it's one of the most commonly used (and misunderstood) words. Generally it is a term of abuse, as in 'im a no good rass!' (mild), or when used with Jamaicans' most offensive yet common derogatory term, 'im a rass blood clot' (a menstrual pad, or 'pussy clawt'). It can also be used as an endearment ('hey, rass, gi mi smallers') or in a similar vein to describe a superlative ('dat gal pretty to rass, mon!').

Patois is not gender specific. Everyone, everything is simply 'im' or 'dem.' Possessive pronouns such as my and mine are often replaced with 'a fi,' which can also be an intensifier, as in 'a fi mi bike' (it's *my* bike).

The most interesting way to collect a dictionary full of patois is in 'rum bars' or aboard the local buses.

Colonial Carryovers

Many words in the Jamaican lexicon are carryovers from the early English colonial days – true Shakespearean English. The language is imbued with terms otherwise considered archaic. One of the most obvious is 'chain,' the old English measurement (22 yards), which is still used liberally though not necessarily accurately. You may also be served a drink in a 'goblet.'

A few pronouns derive from slave days. Thus visitors can expect to be called 'massa' (master) or 'mistress.' The term 'pickaninny' is still used for children, despite its racist connotations in western culture; for example, the bus conductor might say 'pickney stan' up an gi big people seat.'

African Heritage

Scores of words have been passed down from Africa, mostly from the Ashanti, Cormorante, and Congolese languages. Thus, a

Jamaican may refer to a fool as a 'bo-bo.' A commonly used word is 'nyam,' which means 'to eat.'

Sayings & Proverbs

Jamaicans use plenty of metaphor and proverbs. They will tell you 'cockroach no business in a fowlyard' (mind your own business'). If a Jamaican tells you, 'de higher monkey climb, de more 'im expose,' he or she is telling you that you're acting pretentiously, exposing more than you should.

Some phrases you'll hear may not mean what they suggest. 'Soon come,' for example, is a common refrain, but don't hold your breath! The phrase *really* means the subject will arrive eventually – almost the opposite of what you would expect. Likewise, 'jus' up de road' or 'jus' a likkle distance' can mean miles or the other side of town.

The most common greeting is 'everyt'ing cool, mon?' or 'everyt'ing *irie*?'

Jamaica Talk

Here's a sampling of words you'll be sure to hear while strolling through the streets.

Babylon – the establishment, white society
bandulu – hustler, criminal
batty – bottom or rear end, as in 'yu batty too big, mon!' (as heard from a woman who doesn't give a damn for your looks)
boonoonoonoos – fabulous, greatest
boops – a man who keeps a woman in idle splendor (guys, watch out if a girl tells you 'mi wan' you fi mi boops')
boopsie – a woman with a sugar daddy

chalice – a Rastafarian's holy ganja pipe (also known as a **clutchie**)
clawt, claat – used in one of the strongest and most frequently heard Jamaican expletives (see Understanding Patois above)
cool runnings – no problem
cool yu foot – slow down, relax
cris – from crisp, meaning top-rate; 'im a cris, cris t'ing!' ('he's handsome!'), heard from a woman who fancies a man

de – the
do – please, as in 'do, me a beg yu'

downpresser – a Rastafarian term for an oppressor
dunzer – money; also known as **smallers**
duppy – ghost

facety – cheeky, impertinent, as in 'yu facety, yu know gal!' ('you're rude, girl!')
fiyah – a Rastafarian greeting

ganja – marijuana; also known as 'de 'oly 'erb,' 'wisdom weed,' 'colly weed,' 'kaya,' 'sensie,' and 'tampie'
gravilishas – greedy

'im – he, she, her, his, it
irie – alright; a term used to indicate that all is well; also the equivalent of 'groovy'; also a greeting ('everyt'ing irie?')
I-tal – natural foods, health food, purity

Jah – God; an Old Testament name, popular with Rastafarians
Jamdung – Jamaica (also known as *Jah-Mek-Ya*, as in God's work)

kingman – husband
kiss mi . . . – not an invitation, but a common profane exclamation, as in 'kiss mi rass!'

level vibes – no problem
lion – upright, usually for a righteous Rastafarian

massah – mister; derived from 'master' of slave-era days and now used for any male but particularly one in authority
marga – thin (from meager), as in 'da boy deh mawga' ('that man there is skinny')
mash up – to have an accident

naa – won't, as in 'mi naa go dung deh' ('I won't go down there')
natty – dreadlocks, also called *natty dread*

one love – parting expression meaning unity

pickney – child or children, shortened version of pickaninny
pollution – people living in spiritual darkness

posse – a group of young adults who form a clique

rass – a backside, and one of the most violent cuss words; generally used to abuse someone or something, preceded or followed by expletives; also used to denote large size (see Understanding Patois above)
rhaatid – like rass, but a gentler and more commonly used expletive; meaning depends on intonation and facial expression
riddim – Jamaica's reggae has it, as do Jamaican men and women
roots – coming from the people or communal experience

satta – invitation to sit, usually to meditate
smaddy – somebody
soke – fool around, as in 'no soke wi' mi' ('don't mess with me')
swimp – shrimp
spliff – a joint (as in ganja, not elbow)

tea – any hot drink
t'ink – think

wine – sensuous dance movement; body contact considered integral to a good time
wolf – a Rastafarian imposter

Zion – Ethiopia, the promised land

Facts for the Visitor

PLANNING
When to Go
Jamaica is a year-round destination, though there are seasonal differences to consider. Weatherwise, temperature isn't a factor in determining when to go. Rainfall, however, *is* – especially if you plan on spending time in the east coast and Blue Mountains. The so-called rainy season extends from May to November, with two peaks: in May/June and October/November. Although this time of year is a little more humid than others, rain usually falls for short periods (normally in the late afternoon), and it's quite possible to enjoy sunshine for most of your visit.

Tourism's 'peak season' runs from mid-December to mid-April, when hotel prices are highest. This is the busiest (as well as the driest) season, when 'snowbirds' from Canada and the northeastern USA flock south.

Be aware that some hotels are booked solid during Christmas and Easter. You can save wads of money (40% or more at some hotels) and will find fewer foreign visitors if you visit 'off-season,' the remainder of the year. This is when the Jamaicans take their vacations, more Europeans arrive, and there are relatively few North Americans.

What Kind of Trip
Options range from bumming around on the cheap to pre-paid packages at a ritzy beach resort where butlers and valets wear white gloves. The vast majority of visitors opt for something in-between: a pre-arranged, modestly-priced hotel in a well-developed resort town, where they can linger on the beach with occasional forays to attractions further afield.

There's nothing wrong with visiting Jamaica simply to laze on a beach, sip rum cocktails, and get a tan. Most visitors opt for this type of vacation. The island's homegrown 'all-inclusive' resorts provide particularly good options for escapism. The downside is that your contact with the *real* Jamaica is at a minimum. The experience is 'canned.'

A more enriching experience comes from immersing yourself in Jamaica. Meeting Rastafarians, playing dominoes in a rum shop, exploring off the beaten track, visiting a Kingston dancehall . . . such experiences will allow you to know and appreciate the warm and colorful Jamaican character.

Jamaica is not well set up for special-interest vacationers. Birders, hikers, cavers (spelunkers), artists, and others with special interests will find relatively few tour companies catering to their needs. Still, the market is evolving, and you can always do your own thing with relative ease.

Maps
The Jamaica Tourist Board (JTB) publishes a 1:350,000-scale 'Discover Jamaica' road map in association with Esso. No topographical details are shown, and some of the sites of tourist interest are marked in the wrong place. The same is true of a similar road map published in association with Texaco, which has the advantage of showing topographical detail and greater road details. Both include separate street maps of Kingston and major towns. Shell also publishes a road map to Jamaica. You can pick these maps up at the respective gas stations or at any JTB office.

The most accurate maps of all are the Jamaica Ordnance Survey maps published by the Survey Dept (☎ 922-6630) 23½ Charles St (PO Box 493), Kingston 10. The most useful are the 1:50,000 scale topographical maps, which cost US$5 each. Unfortunately, only a few of the 20 sheets are currently in print. You'll need to pay at the cashier's office on the 3rd floor; it's open Monday to Thursday, 9 am to 1 pm and 2 to 3 pm.

Spring Break Fever

Beach parties, free concerts, and fun in the sun lure thousands of North American college students every spring. The JTB launched its 'Spring Break' program in 1989, with a host of activities specifically designed for the spring-break crowd and sponsored by Appleton Rum and Red Stripe beer. The idea is to have fun, often interpreted as get boozed up and get laid!

For information, contact Campus Vacations (☎ (718) 834-9670 or (800) 659-7377), Reggaejam Campus Travel (☎ (813) 985-7944 or (800) 873-4423), or Student Travel Services (☎ (607) 272-6964 or (800) 648-4849). Companies such as Sunsplash Tours and Sunburst Holidays (see Charter Flights in Getting There & Away) also cater to the party-hearty crowd by offering weeklong packages to Negril and Montego Bay, starting at about US$450 per person, including round-trip airfare, airport transfers, accommodations, parties and concerts, etc. Trips are generally offered throughout March and April. ■

You can also order individual Ordnance Survey sheets from:

France
Espace IGN, 107 rue la Boétie, 75008 Paris (☎ (1) 43-98-85-00)
USA
Maplink, 25 E Mason St, Santa Barbara, CA 93101 (☎ (805) 965-4402, fax (805) 962-0884 or toll free fax (800) 627-7768)

Rand McNally, 8255 N Central Park, Skokie, IL 60076 (☎ (708) 329-6594, fax (708) 673-0530)
UK
Ordnance Survey International, Romsey Rd, Maybush, Southampton SO9 4DH (☎ (0703) 792000, fax (0703) 792404)

Sanfords, 12-14 Long Acre, London WC2E 9LP (☎ (0171) 836-1321, fax (0171) 836-0189)

The Survey Dept also sells larger-scale topographical and planimetric city and regional maps, and provides photographic map services. A single-sheet 1:250,000-scale topographical map costs a whopping US$150, but you can also order this reduced to 1:500,000 scale for US$50 plus US$2 per 100 sq inches.

For information about maritime maps and charts, see the Yacht section under Sea in the Getting There & Away chapter.

What to Bring
Travel light! Jamaica is a hot, tropical country and you shouldn't need much clothing. My motto is: if you can't take your main bag as a carry-on onto an aircraft, you've packed too much for a one-week visit. This depends on where you stay, however. The fancier the resort, the more you will want to pack a selection of fancy clothes.

Airlines are strict about baggage allowance and carry-ons. The dimensions of checked luggage should not measure more than 62 linear inches (length plus width plus height), with a 70 pound weight limit. The maximum size for a carry-on bag is usually 45 linear inches. A duffel-style bag with zippered pockets is handiest, though small suitcases are also good. Garment bags are ideal if you plan on staying at one resort. It's best to avoid backpacks with external metal straps. Make sure your luggage is padlocked before parting with it, and don't leave anything of value in external pockets. Theft from baggage at Montego Bay airport is very high; the baggage handlers cannot be trusted! A small daypack is also handy.

Clothing Loose-fitting, lightweight cotton clothing is best because it allows air flow in the hot humid climate. Tight clothing tends to make you sweat more and can get uncomfortable, as will synthetics like nylon. T-shirts and tank-tops are the perfect wear for outdoors and are best worn without being tucked in.

White is the best color for reflecting the sun's rays, but has the disadvantage of getting dirty quickly. A long-sleeved shirt and long pants are useful in case you get a sunburn. You'll also need long pants for the more upscale discos and restaurants.

Don't forget one or two pairs of shorts, which can be your normal daywear, and swimwear, which should be restricted to the beach. Dress more modestly in towns. This is particularly true of conservative Kingston, where women may attract unwanted attention commensurate with the amount of flesh they expose. Topless bathing (even a birthday suit) is allowed at some resort hotels and on the beach in Negril.

A light sweater might prove handy at night – you'll certainly need one in the upland areas – and if you're hiking in the Blue Mountains, bring a heavy sweater and wind-breaker.

Some hotels require casual evening wear at dinner. Several of the ritzier hotels even require jackets (and ties in winter) for men, and elegant dresses for women while dining. Such hotels *do not* allow shorts or jeans in the dining room. Elsewhere, however, fancy togs are taken more as a statement of the wearer's insecurities or snootiness. They also mark you as wealthy, leaving you more open to potential robbery or higher prices when bargaining for souvenirs (if you can afford expensive clothing, surely you can afford a couple of extra dollars for a wooden carving).

Speaking of money, it's a good idea to carry your cash in a money-belt beneath your clothing.

You'll get by with a pair of sneakers, sandals, or flip-flops (thongs), and a pair of lightweight casual shoes for evening wear. In the interest of conservation *and* for personal safety, you should refrain from walking on coral, but elasticated canvas and rubber 'reef-walking' shoes are ideal for wading.

If you plan on hiking, prepare for variable weather conditions. Rain can fall at any time of year, especially in mountainous areas. Higher peaks are often pelted by wind-driven rain, and you should dress accordingly. Pack a windproof jacket, a sweater, and, ideally, a lightweight rainjacket. At lower altitudes, lightweight cotton clothing will suffice. Trousers rather than shorts are best for hiking through bush, as they protect against thorns. Generally, sneakers or tennis shoes are fine for hiking. Even better are the new breed of lightweight canvas hiking boots. You'll want something sturdier than sneakers to handle the sharp limestone of the Cockpit Country and Hellshire Hills.

Not all hotels provide laundry services. You may need to wash your underwear and socks in your sink and hang them to dry.

Toiletries & Supplies You should bring all toiletries with you. But you don't need to overdue it. Women, for example, may find an excess of make-up is uncomfortable in the humid tropical heat. As a minimum, your basic kit should include toothpaste, toothbrush, dental floss, deodorant, shampoo and conditioner, skin creams, make-up, tampons, contraceptives, and a basic health kit (see Health below).

Few hotels in Jamaica provide complimentary toiletries. Don't forget a washcloth: many hotels don't have them. Unless you're staying at an upscale hotel, consider bringing a beach towel. Better yet, buy one in Jamaica. You can also buy any toiletry you may need in Jamaica, although at a higher price than North America or Europe.

Don't forget a spare pair of glasses or contact lenses (bring your prescription, too, though getting spectacles or contacts replaced can take over a week), and any medicines you may require. Pharmacies should be able to fill any prescriptions you require. Many drugs that are available by prescription-only in the USA can be bought over the counter in Jamaica.

A flashlight is useful in the event of an electrical black-out (very common), or to find your way along unlit streets or paths at night. I also consider a Swiss Army knife essential.

Other essentials include resealable plastic bags (handy for toiletries), a small laundry bag (for dirty underwear and wet clothes), a fold-up umbrella (which will also prove a handy parasol), plus a brimmed hat or baseball cap for shade (alternatively you can buy a straw hat in Jamaica).

It's better to bring items such as laundry detergent, notepads, pencils, batteries, etc with you; they're available in major towns, but don't rely on finding them when you want to buy them.

Camping Supplies & Sporting Gear

Jamaica does not cater to campers. Although a few places rent tents, you should bring everything you need. Make sure your tent is bug-proof and that it can withstand a good downpour. There's not much worse than having mosquitoes buzzing around or a flood to contend with. Most campsites have cooking facilities or are near to inexpensive restaurants, so there should be no need to bring cooking gear unless you plan on camping in the boondocks.

Essential supplies are a flashlight, mosquito repellent, Swiss Army knife (with corkscrew), water bottle, thin rope to use as a washing line, and a lightweight sleeping bag. Also consider a lantern or candles and waterproof matches. See Camping below.

Most resorts with golf or tennis facilities rent equipment, as do dive shops for scuba and snorkeling. However, you may wish to bring your own gear.

RESORT AREAS & BEACHES

The JTB has divided the island into seven 'resort' areas, though only four are true, beach-based resorts. Between them, these areas boast virtually the entire crop of hotels. All can be reached via primary roads. Visitors to Jamaica always ask, 'Which is the best beach?' The answer is elusive, partly because many of the finest beaches are privately owned and access is limited. Others are fronted by hotels that jealously guard them. Here's a list of the 'resort' areas and some public beaches where you can bronze your buns:

Kingston The nation's bustling capital is more of a business locale than a tourism center. However, it *is* the center of island culture and is surprisingly sophisticated.

Most of Jamaica's museums and art galleries are here, as well as some important historical buildings. Kingston receives few tourists and gives visitors a strong sense of Jamaican reality.

Mandeville This historic agricultural and residential town lies in the cool elevations of the mountainous interior. Its appeal is with visitors who shun the beach resorts in favor of birding, scenic mountain drives, hiking, and interactions with local families. Mandeville is the center for community-based tourism. Near at hand lie the Great Morass (a vitally important swamp area) and Treasure Beach (an offbeat south coast resort for travelers seeking a budget or 'alternative lifestyle' experience).

Montego Bay The second largest city in Jamaica, MoBay, as the city is popularly called, has more hotel rooms than anywhere else on the island. It's the main tourist center, with several modest public beaches and a good choice of hotels. MoBay is on the northwest coast. I consider it overrated.

There are three main beaches in town and a fourth minor one. All are popular with locals and provide a good opportunity to mingle. **Cornwall Beach** is a small white-sand beach in the center of town. It offers plenty of water sports and a popular bar. **Doctor's Cave Beach** is a larger sibling to Cornwall. It also has water sports, snack bars, and other facilities. **Walter Fletcher Beach** is less popular with tourists, but a favorite of locals. It's narrower than Cornwall and Doctor's Cave. There are concessions. **Dead End Beach** is a slender sliver used almost exclusively by locals.

Several small beaches extend east of town, but they are virtually the private domains of resorts such as Sandals Montego Bay, which has indisputably the best private beach on the island.

Negril Jamaica's liveliest resort, Negril also boasts the most stunning beach on the island. It's far enough from everywhere else to have its own unique, fun-in-the-sun appeal. Live reggae shows, spectacular sunsets, and a *laissez*, let-your-hair-down attitude make this a favorite of budget and college-age travelers. Some of the finest all-inclusive resorts are also here, including Hedonism II (the wildest resort in Jamaica) and Swept Away (the island's pre-eminent fitness-focused resort). Negril is also renowned for scuba diving and water sports. Accommodations run the gamut from camping and budget cottages to ritzy.

My vote for most appealing beach in Jamaica goes to **Long Bay**. The curved white-sand beach is about five miles long. A coral reef lies within wading distance offshore, and the water is as calm as a millpond. Virtually the entire beachfront is developed with low-rise hotels, cottages, thatched bars, restaurants, and water-sport concessions: none are taller than the palm trees that loom over the beach its entire length. **Bloody Bay** is Long Bay's smaller, slightly less appealing, less developed, but nonetheless attractive neighbor.

Ocho Rios Situated along the north coast, 'Ochi' is the main destination for cruise ships. The town itself is unappealing despite its two beaches, but there are plenty of historical sites, botanical gardens, and other attractions within a few minutes' drive. Accommodations range from budget guesthouses to some of Jamaica's finest all-inclusive resorts. Ocho Rios was due to receive a major facelift in 1996.

In the center of town, **Turtle Beach** fronts the harbor. The sand is attractive, but this is one place where you can expect to be hassled by hustlers and annoyed by the whir of jet skis. It has water-sport concessions. **Mallard Beach**, a smaller neighbor, is mostly the domain of hotels, each of which covets their own sliver. You'll find several pretty beaches east and west of town, including **Mammee Bay**.

Port Antonio Secluded at the lush north-eastern tip of Jamaica, this formerly bustling banana port has long been popular with Hollywood stars and other luminaries,

but has remained small and relatively un-developed. Offbeat Port Antonio is a center for bamboo raft trips and is developing as a center for hiking in the Rio Grande valley and Blue Mountains. It has several deluxe resorts, but its highlights are its fully staffed, upscale villas.

Three small beaches (one where you can get an all-over tan) line the perimeter of **Navy Island**. East of town **Frenchman's Cove** and **San San Beach** are both attractive yet tiny white-sand beaches in the cusp of headlands. They're secluded and tend to draw an exclusive clientele from nearby upscale resorts and villas.

Eight miles east of Port Antonio, **Winnifred Beach** is popular with locals. There are rustic eateries and bars. Continuing east you'll come to **Boston Beach**, famous for jerk stalls. This small beach is washed by waves good enough to surf. It is mostly the domain of locals, as is **Long Bay**, a white-sand beach in a beautiful setting. The beach is undeveloped and, being on the windward side of the island, has large waves and a dangerous undertow.

Runaway Bay This small, secluded resort town, midway between MoBay and Ocho Rios, is famous for its coral reefs and polo facilities. Here you'll find many hotels and all-inclusives, including family resorts.

OTHER ESCAPES

South Coast Most of the beaches along the south coast are long gray-sand beaches, less pretty than their northern neighbors, but appealing for their colorful fishing boats and isolation. Few have any tourist facilities, so you should come prepared with drinks and foods. The best selection is around **Treasure Beach**. Others can be found at **Morant Bay**, **Alligator Pond**, **Whitehouse**, and **Bluefields**, which has one of the few – albeit very narrow – white-sand beaches along the south coast.

You'll find several attractive white-sand beaches on the east side of the **Hellshire** peninsula. They're extremely popular with Kingstonians on weekends and get very lively. Likewise, **Lime Cay**, a small coral island only a short boat ride from Port Royal, is rimmed by white sand and has scintillating waters that attract picnickers.

To the Interior Other areas also stand out for their unique appeal: the Blue Mountains and the Cockpit Country, in south Trelawny Parish. These offer unique physical settings and are idyllic escapes from the package-tour syndrome; here you can experience firsthand the *real* Jamaica. Only the first two have any facilities.

Jamaica Heritage Trail The recently formed Jamaica Heritage Trail Ltd (a joint venture between TAP and seven financial institutions) is developing an islandwide heritage trail linking sites of historical and architectural significance. JHTL chose Falmouth as its first site. The town has the largest collection and some of the finest examples of Georgian architecture in Jamaica. Port Royal and Spanish Town also have a fabulous wealth of historical buildings. Unfortunately, the majority of buildings are terribly run down and tourism facilities are meager. Hopefully by the time you read this, Jamaican decision-makers will have come to appreciate that these three towns are untapped treasures.

THE BEST

Alligator Pond – Literally hidden away from the world in its own mountain-fringed bay, this small, atmospheric fishing village is the most uniquely Jamaican spot on the entire coastline. Sure, the beach is an unappealing brown, but its marvelously lonesome, and a fabulous wildlife-rich marshland lies to the east.

Black River Boat Trip – A leisurely cruise into the Great Morass with a naturalist guide brings you face to face with crocodiles, waterfowl, and other beautiful critters. Trips depart from the town of Black River.

Cuba Excursion – If you like Jamaica, you'll *love* Cuba, which lies a 90-minute flight to the north. Several tour companies offer one-, two-, and multi-day excursions to this fascinating and friendly island of sensual charms. Your visit will occur during a transitional period when change is sweeping the nation, but it is still the Cuba of recent history that most people have heard about but never seen. Be prepared to be pleasantly surprised by reality as opposed to Yankee-inspired defamation. By the way: Yankees are welcome! (See the sidebar Cuba Sí! in the Northwest Coast chapter for more information.)

Dunn's River Falls – Cruise ship passengers swarm like lemmings to this tumbling cascade outside Ocho Rios, but climbing the slippery limestone tiers is exhilarating fun, hordes or not.

Firefly – Jamaica has many fine historical attractions, but the former home of Noel Coward, near Port Maria, is my favorite. The vistas from his hilltop home didn't inspire his song, 'A Room with a View,' but they could have.

Helitour Over Cockpit Country – The Cockpit Country is Jamaica's most dramatic landscape. Since it is incredibly difficult to access, seeing it from on high is the way to go. Do it slowly, by helicopter from Montego Bay or Ocho Rios. Wow!

Hiking to Blue Mountain Peak – When a break from the beach is required, a walk on the wild side will introduce you to another Jamaica. Highlights include cloud-shrouded forests and a view from the 7450-foot summit that makes all others seem fainthearted efforts. For those flush with money, a night or two at Strawberry Hill seems like Heaven; for the impecunious, there's Maya Lodge, touted as one of Jamaica's foremost budget retreats.

Negril – Jamaica's best beach, best sunsets, best nightlife. What more could you want?

Reggae Sunsplash or Reggae Sumfest – Five days of world-class entertainment and color-blind revelry elevate these two musical shindigs to an almost religious experience.

Treasure Beach – Oozing with laid-back, off-the-beaten-track ambiance, this loosely knit south coast community is a haven of Jamaican graciousness and calm. The beaches win no prizes, but who cares! Jake's is the place to stay.

THE WORST

This is where I lose friends and make enemies. Many hotels and attractions are dismal letdowns, despite being lauded. Here are a few:

Accompong – It's hyped, but there's *nothing* unique or different about this tiny hamlet that touts itself as the capital of Maroon culture.

It's a harpy to get to and after your troubles, disappointment might be the only reward. I'll eat my words on January 6, when the village comes alive with festivities.

Downtown Kingston – Despite its numerous historical edifices, Kingston's teeming downtown can seem unwelcoming and possibly even scary for first-time visitors. Others may thrill to its seething energy. Several sites are letdowns.

Folly – One of Port Antonio's much-touted attractions is nothing more than a derelict, mildewed wreck. It's a favorite of photographers for fashion shoots and music videos. If you have a model and camera in hand, fine. Otherwise, skip it!

Montego Bay – Gulp! Do I mean it? Well, it all depends on where you stay. Many resort towns are much worse, but as Jamaica's *premier* resort, I can't understand the appeal. The resort is only marginally attractive. The public beaches are mediocre. Many hotels are dowdy and devoid of life. And unless street parties are your gig, entertainment is lackluster. (I could say the same for Ocho Rios and Port Antonio.) Fortunately, the shopping is good and there are some splendid attractions close at hand. Couples staying at Sandals Montego Bay or Jack Tar Village needn't worry.

Tivoli Gardens & the Ghettoes – A sociologist could have a field day, but Kingston's ghettoes are off-limits to outsiders.

TOURIST OFFICES

The Jamaica Tourist Board (JTB) has six offices in Jamaica plus offices in key cities around the world. These serve as information centers, and their staff members are usually very helpful in answering questions. You can request maps and literature, including hotel brochures, however they do not serve as reservation agencies.

Roadside information booths have also recently been established in major resorts along the north coast and Negril.

Tourist Offices Abroad

The JTB has offices in these locations:

Canada
 1 Eglinton Ave E No 616, Toronto, ON MAP 3A1 (☎ (416) 482-7850, fax (416) 482-1730

France
 c/o Target International, 52 Ave des Champs Élysées, 75008, Paris (☎ (1) 45-61-90-58, fax (1) 42-25-66-40)

Germany
 c/o Pan Consult at Falkstrasse 72-74, 6000 Frankfurt/Main 1, (☎ (069) 70-74-065, fax (069) 70-1007)

Italy
 c/o Sergat Italia SRL, Via Monte Dei Cenci 20 7/A 01186, Rome (☎ (6) 654-01-336, fax (6) 687-3644)

Japan
 The Carrington Group, Ginza Yamato Building, 9th floor, 7-9-17 Ginza, Chuo-ku, Tokyo 104 (☎ (03) 289-5767)

Spain
 c/o Sergat España SL, Apdo-Correos 30266, 08034 Barcelona (☎ (3) 280-5838, fax (3) 280-4520)

UK
 1-2 Prince Consort Rd, London SW7 2BZ (☎ (0171) 224-0505, fax (0171) 224-0551)

USA
 Atlanta 300 W Wieuca Rd NE No 100A, Atlanta, GA 30342 (☎ (404) 452-7799, fax (404) 452-0220)
 Boston 21 Merchants Row, Boston, MA 02109 (☎ (508) 845-6021, fax (508) 845-6017)
 Chicago 500 N Michigan Ave No 1030, Chicago, IL 60611 (☎ (312) 527-1296, fax (312) 627-1472)
 Dallas 8214 Westchester No 500, Dallas, TX 75225 (☎ (214) 553-5188, fax (214) 553-5183)
 Detroit 26400 Lahser Rd No 114A, Southfield, MI 48034 (☎ (810) 948-9667, fax (810) 948-1860)
 Los Angeles 3440 Wilshire Blvd No 1207, Los Angeles, CA 90010 (☎ (213) 384-1123, fax (213) 384-1780)
 Miami 1320 S Dixie Hwy No 1100, Coral Gables, FL 33146 (☎ (305) 666-0557, fax (305) 666-7239)
 New York Headquarters 301 Second Ave, New York, NY 10017 (☎ (212) 866-9727 or (800) 233-4582, fax (212) 866-9730)
 Philadelphia 1315 Walnut St No 1505, Philadelphia, PA 19107 (☎ (215) 922-0642, fax (215) 922-0643)
 For a free Jamaica Vacation Kit PO Box 9032, E Setauket, NY 11733-9032 (☎ 800-526-2422)

Local Tourist Offices

The JTB headquarters is in Kingston at 2 St Lucia Ave (☎ 929-9200, fax 929-9375). It's surprisingly poorly stocked with literature, perhaps because Kingston isn't a major tourist destination. In addition, you'll find JTB offices at:

Black River
    Hendrik Bldg, 2 High St, Black River PO (☎ 965-2074, fax 965-2076)
Montego Bay
    Cornwall Beach, PO Box 67, Montego Bay (☎ 952-4425, fax 952-3587)
Negril
    Shop No 20, Adrija Plaza, Negril PO (☎ 957-4243, fax 957-4489)
Ocho Rios
    Ocean Village Shopping Centre; PO Box 240, Ocho Rios (☎ 974-2582, fax 974-2559)
Port Antonio
    City Centre Plaza, PO Box 151, Port Antonio (☎ 993-3051, fax 993-2117)

VISAS & DOCUMENTS
Passport

US and Canadian citizens do not need passports for visits up to six months. However, they *do* need two pieces of identification, including proof of citizenship (or permanent residency), such as a birth certificate, voter's registration card, or driver's license with photo ID.

All other visitors *must* arrive with a passport. British citizens need passports that will still be valid six months from their date of arrival.

It's a good idea to carry your passport with you, out of the reach of thieves. Otherwise, leave it in a safety deposit box in your hotel, along with your other valuables.

Visas

No visas are required for entry to Jamaica for citizens of European countries (including Turkey), the USA, Canada, and Mexico.

Photocopies

You should make two photocopies of your most valuable documents before leaving home. Make sure you include your passport, driver's license, airline ticket, hotel vouchers, health insurance, etc. Keep one copy at home. Carry the second copy with you, but separate from the originals.

Getting Married in Jamaica

Jamaica is a popular destination for honeymooners, many of whom tie the knot on the island. It's often promoted as an ideal place to get married, and its requirements to do so are easily met. There is no blood test requirement, for example, and unlike many other Caribbean destinations which require residency up to one week, Jamaican law allows couples to marry after only 24 hours on the island.

In addition to proof of citizenship (such as a certified copy of a birth certificate that includes the father's name), you'll need certified copies of the appropriate divorce or death certificates, if one or both of you is divorced or widowed, and written parental consent if either partner is under 21 years of age. These documents must be notarized.

Most major hotels and tour operators will make all arrangements, although they usually ask couples to send notarized copies of required documents at least one month in advance. Major resorts usually have special package prices that include the wedding ceremony, government tax, and wedding expenses (SuperClubs' Grand Lido and Sans Souci Grand Lido will even pick up the entire tab if you choose to get married while staying at either resort). They can also arrange a wedding at short notice with a justice of the peace. If you prefer a religious ceremony, advance planning with a member of the clergy is required.

Alternately, you can apply in person at the Registrar Office at 37 Market St, Montego Bay, or the Ministry of National Security & Justice (☎ 922-0080) at 12 Ocean Blvd, Kingston. It's open Monday to Thursday, 8:30 am to 5 pm, until 4 pm on Friday. The paperwork costs US$150. ∎

Travel Permits

No travel permits are required. However, you'll need to fill out an immigration card upon arrival (usually this is handed out on board the aircraft, but if not, you'll find them in the arrivals lounge). You will need to show it when you depart, and also for bank transactions and currency exchange.

Cruise-ship passengers are cleared en masse by the cruise company.

Onward Tickets

Immigration formalities require that you show a return or ongoing airline ticket when arriving in Jamaica.

Travel Insurance

However you're traveling, it's worth taking out travel insurance. You may not want to insure that grotty old army surplus backpack, but everyone should be covered for the worst possible case: an accident, for example, that requires hospital treatment and a flight home. If you are planning to travel for a long time, travel insurance may seem rather expensive, but think of it this way: if you can't afford insurance, you certainly won't be able to afford to deal with a medical emergency overseas.

A travel insurance policy that covers theft, loss of baggage, and medical treatment is a good idea. You might also consider trip cancellation insurance if you have booked a pre-paid package with cancellation penalty clauses. Any travel agent can recommend an appropriate package.

When purchasing medical insurance, consider a policy that pays for medical services immediately and directly. Otherwise you may have to pay on the spot, then claim for reimbursement once you return home. Check if the policy covers ambulances or an emergency flight. If you have to stretch out you will need two seats and somebody has to pay for them! Also check to see if there are exclusions for any 'hazardous activities' you may be contemplating, such as renting motorcycles, scuba diving, or even trekking.

Driver's License & Permits

To drive in Jamaica, you must have a valid International Driver's License or a current license for your home country or state valid for up to six months. You can obtain an International Driver's License by applying with your current license to any Automobile Association office. The IDL is valid in Jamaica. In the USA it costs US$10 and can be issued on-the-spot at AAA offices (two passport photographs are required).

A North American driver's license is valid for up to three months per visit from the date of entry. A UK license, however, is valid for up to one year, while a Japanese driver's license is valid only one month.

Hostel Card

Jamaica has no youth hostel system. Unless you plan on combining your visit to Jamaica with other destinations that have youth hostels, you can leave your IYHF card at home.

The same is true for student, youth, and seniors' cards. Nobody in Jamaica honors them.

EMBASSIES
Jamaican Embassies Abroad

In the USA, the Jamaican embassy is at K St NW No 355, Washington, DC 20006 (☎ (202) 452-0660, fax (202) 452-0081).

In the UK, the Jamaican High Commission is at 1-2 Prince Consort Rd, London SW7 2BZ (☎ (0171) 823-9911, fax (0171) 408-2545).

Foreign Embassies in Jamaica

At press time, more than 40 countries had official representation in Jamaica. All are located in Kingston. If your country isn't represented in this list, check in the Kingston telephone directory.

Australian High Commission
    64 Knutsford Blvd, Kingston 5 (☎ 926-3550, 926-3551)
Austrian Consulate
    2 Ardenne Rd (☎ 954-3290 or 929-5259)
Barbados Consulate
    56½ Duke St (☎ 923-9221)
British High Commission
    26 Trafalgar Rd, Kingston 10 (☎ 926-9050)
Canadian High Commission
    Royal Bank Limited Bldg, 30 Knutsford Blvd, Kingston 5 (☎ 926-1500)
Cuban Embassy
    9 Trafalgar Rd, Kingston 10 (☎ 978-0931)
Danish Consulate General
    449 Spanish Town Rd (☎ 923-9028 or 923-5051)

French Embassy
   13 Hillcrest Ave, Kingston 6 (☎ 927-9811)
German Embassy
   10 Waterloo Rd, Kingston 10 (☎ 926-6728)
Haitian Consulate General
   2 Munroe Rd (☎ 927-7595)
Honduran Embassy
   7 Lady Kay Drive (☎ 925-6544)
Israeli Consulate
   60 Knutsford Blvd, Kingston 5 (☎ 926-8768)
Italian Embassy
   10 Rovan Drive, Kingston 6 (☎ 925-4371 or
   978-2173)
Japanese Embassy
   32 Trafalgar Rd, Kingston 10 (☎ 929-7534)
Netherlands Embassy
   53 Knutsford Blvd, Kingston 5 (☎ 926-2026)
Norwegian Consulate
   6 Newport Blvd (☎ 923-4811)
Spanish Embassy
   25 Dominica Drive, Kingston 5 (☎ 929-6710)
Swedish Consulate
   20 Bell Rd (☎ 923-7114)
Swiss Consulate
   105 Harbour St, Kingston 5 (☎ 922-3347)
Trinidad & Tobago High Commission
   60 Knutsford Blvd (☎ 926-5730)
US Embassy
   Jamaica Mutual Life Centre, 2 Oxford St,
   Kingston 2 (☎ 929-4850 or 926-5679, fax
   926-6743)

In addition, the US government maintains a consular office in Montego Bay (St James Plaza, 2nd floor, Gloucester Ave, ☎ 952-0160 or 952-5050), as do Canada (29 Gloucester Ave, ☎ 952-6198) and Britain (☎ 953-2231).

If need assistance with immigration formalities, contact the Jamaican Immigration Office, Overton Plaza, 3rd floor. It's hours are Monday to Thursday, 8:30 am to 1 pm, and 2 to 5 pm.

Entering Jamaica

You are allowed to import the following items duty free: 25 cigars, 200 cigarettes, one quart liquor (except rum), one pound of tobacco, and one quart of wine. The following items are restricted: firearms, drugs (except prescription medicines), flowers and plants, honey, fruits, coffee, and meats and vegetables (unless canned).

You are allowed to bring in a reason-able amount of personal belongings free of charge. However, you may need to show proof that laptop computers and other expensive items are for personal use. You should declare these upon arrival.

Only animals born and bred in the UK may be brought in; all others must be quarantined for six months upon arrival.

Leaving Jamaica

US citizens can purchase up to US$600 duty-free per person, provided they have not used the allowance within the last 30 days. In addition, you may import 200 cigarettes, 100 cigars (except from Cuba), plus one liter of liquor or wine. Art, handicrafts, antiques, and certain other items are exempt from duties under the Generalized System of Preferences. For more specific information, contact the US Customs Service at PO Box 7407, Washington, DC 20044.

Canadian citizens are once a year allowed a C$300 allowance, plus 200 cigarettes, 50 cigars, two pounds of loose tobacco, and 40 ounces of liquor. In addition, you can mail unsolicited gifts valued up to C$40 per day. The booklet *I Declare* provides more information: contact the Revenue Canada Customs Dept, Communications Branch, Mackenzie Ave, Ottawa ON, K1A 0L5.

British citizens may import goods worth up to £200 in addition to 100 cigarettes, 50 cigars or 250 grams of loose tobacco, and two liters of wine plus one liter of spirits (depending on alcohol proof). For further information, contact Her Majesty's Customs & Excise Office, New King's Reach House, 22 Upper Ground, London SE1 9PJ.

MONEY

The Jamaican dollar – called *jay* – is the basic currency and the only legal tender in the country (except for duty-free goods, which must be purchased with foreign currency). However, prices are often quoted in US dollars, which are widely accepted. European currencies are usually frowned upon. You can bring in as much money as you wish (however, you're not allowed to take out any Jamaican money upon departure).

It's always wise to check whether a quoted price is in Jamaican or US dollars, particularly when using taxis.

Costs

Jamaica is relatively inexpensive as Caribbean destinations go. How much you spend, however, depends on your sense of style. Even hard-core budget travelers will need at least US$20 a day. Roadside stalls and budget restaurants sell jerk pork and other local meals for as little as US$2. A hand of bananas or half a dozen mangoes will cost about US$0.50. More touristy restaurants, however, can be expensive as many of the ingredients they use are imported: expect to pay at least US$8. Grocery shopping can be expensive for the same reason; stick to local produce if possible.

Transport costs vary. Car rentals are expensive by North American standards, beginning at about US$45 a day for the smallest vehicle, excluding insurance. A gallon of gas costs about US$1.70, about the same price as a 50-mile bus journey. Bus travel is inordinately cheap. Taxi service is expensive, but unlicensed taxis will carry you for whatever fare you can bargain them down to.

Accommodations will be your biggest expense. It is possible to find budget accommodations for as little as US$10 a night, though most charge US$20 or more, even for spartan conditions. Medium-standard hotels range from about US$30 to US$60, and top-class accommodations can run as high as US$200 or more nightly. Check to see if government tax is extra.

Discounts If you want to save money, consider visiting in 'summer,' or low-season (mid-April to mid-December), when hotel prices plummet and airfares are often reduced. Another good way to stretch your dollars is to rent a villa or cottage with several other people.

Your Pocketful of Gold by Jacqueline Marie is a discount voucher book covering tours, sights, and attractions throughout the island (PO Box 793, Mundelein, IL 60060, (☎ (800) 972-4620).

The Traveler Club is a Jamaican frequent travelers' club that offers discounts on items from fast food to insurance. New members receive a free US$10 phone card. For information contact ITS Tours, 18 Ripon Rd, Kingston 5 (☎ 926-6540), or any branch of CIBC Ltd bank.

Carrying Money

Cash Carry as little cash as needed when away from your hotel. Keep the rest in a hotel safe. You can rely on credit cards and traveler's checks for most of your purchases. However, you'll need cash for most transactions in rural areas and at gas stations.

Don't carry your cash where it can be seen. Avoid carrying wallets in your back pockets. Put them in your *front* pocket. Even better, you should carry cash in a money belt or pouch, worn *inside* your clothing. Set a small sum (say US$100 or so) aside for emergencies in case you get ripped off.

Traveler's Checks Traveler's checks are widely accepted in Jamaica. You can purchase them at virtually any bank, lending institution, or currency-exchange service worldwide prior to departing for Jamaica. Three of the most popular and widely accepted traveler's checks are American Express, Barclays Bank, and Thomas Cook.

Some hotels, restaurants, and exchange bureaus charge a hefty fee for cashing traveler's checks.

To report lost American Express traveler's checks, call ☎ (800) 221-7282. For lost Thomas Cook checks, call ☎ (800) 223-7373.

ATM Cards Automated teller machine (ATM) cards are a good way to obtain incidental cash. You punch in your personal identification number (PIN) and the amount of the withdrawal, which issues local currency (your home account is automatically debited).

Don't rely on your ATM card, however. Unfortunately, few local banks are linked to international networks such as Cirrus or Plus. Some Scotiabank branches have this facility, but I've found my ATM cards don't work at all locations.

Check with your local bank before departing for Jamaica to find out how you may be able to utilize your ATM card.

Credit Cards Major credit cards are widely accepted throughout the island. Visa and MasterCard are the most commonly accepted, followed by American Express, Diners Club, and Discover.

You can use your credit card to get cash advances at most commercial banks, but anticipate a lengthy wait and, usually, a small interest or transaction fee.

American Express is represented by Stuart's Travel Service, which has four offices in Jamaica: in Kingston (☎ 926-4291), Montego Bay (☎ 952-4350), Negril (☎ 957-4887), and Ocho Rios (☎ 974-2288).

To report lost or stolen credit cards, call:

American Express	☎ (800) 528-4800
AmEx Gold	☎ (800) 528-2121
Diners Club	☎ (800) 525-9135
MasterCard	☎ (800) 826-2181
Visa	☎ (800) 336-8472
Visa Gold	☎ (800) 847-2911

International Transfers If you need emergency cash, you can arrange a telegraphic or mail transfer from your account in your home country, or from a friend or family member. You can also arrange a transfer in advance through your local bank.

Western Union has offices in major towns islandwide (for the nearest location, call ☎ toll free 991-2056/7/8/9, or 926-2454 in Kingston).

Currency
The unit of currency is the Jamaican dollar, the *jay*, which uses the same symbol as the US dollar ($). Jamaican currency is issued in bank notes of J$1, J$2, J$10, J$20, J$50, and J$100. Coins are issued for 10 cents, 20 cents, 25 cents, 50 cents, J$1, and J$5.

The symbol for cents (¢) is also the same as in the US.

One-cent and five-cent coins are still in circulation, but are being phased out. The smaller denomination coins are virtually valueless and many cashiers simply round up to the nearest dollar when giving change.

You'll occasionally hear old names used, such as *quattie*, the name for the 1½ penny coin introduced in 1834, *fippance* (three pence coin), and *mac* (shilling). They most often appear in folksongs and tales.

A significant number of counterfeit bills are in circulation, and banks and shopkeepers are fairly savvy at identifying them.

Currency Exchange
The official rate of exchange fluctuates daily and as of January 1996 was about J$38 to US$1, and J$50 to £1.

The Jamaican dollar has been in gradual decline against the US dollar since September 1991, when the government discontinued its hard-currency auction system previously used to maintain a fixed exchange rate. The Jamaica dollar, which had briefly stabilized at about J$33 to US$1, fell about 20% in value during the last three months of 1995.

Changing Money
Nine commercial banks maintain branches throughout the island, so you will rarely be far from a bank. Those in major towns maintain a foreign exchange booth, and foreign currency may be exchanged for Jamaican dollars during regular business hours. Bank hours are generally 9 am to 2 pm, Monday to Thursday, and Friday 9 am to 3 pm. Some banks close at 2 pm and reopen from 3 to 5 pm on Fridays. A few local banks also open 9 am to noon on Saturday.

You can also change money at most hotels, or at licensed exchange bureaus in the airports and at a few other select locations in major resort towns (a chain called Cambio has several outlets in supermarkets). The rate in hotels is usually between 2 to 5% lower than at the banks, and varies widely between hotels.

Often you'll be given big denomination

bills (J$500 and up). Smaller bills, however, are preferable, especially if you intend on exploring the boondocks, where change for such large bills may be in short supply.

Save all your foreign exchange receipts, as you'll need to show a record of your transactions when changing Jamaican dollars back to your national currency.

Black Market
Plenty of young Jamaican men are eager to change Jamaican dollars in street transactions. It's strictly illegal, however, and hardly worth it: the black market rate in 1995 was only 5 to 10% better than the official exchange rate, and street trading has its risks. If you choose to deal, try to bargain for the best rate you can. Don't accept the first rate offered.

Be very cautious: *never* hand over your money until you have counted *every* Jamaican bill handed to you. The following trick is often used on foreigners: as you each hand over your money, the Jamaican shouts 'Police!' and runs; the foreigner's reaction is usually to beat a hasty retreat, but upon counting his or her money finds a few Jamaican dollar bills enfold bill-size pieces of newspaper!

You're not helping the struggling Jamaica economy, however, by trading on the black market. By doing so you'll undermine the government's attempts to stabilize the Jamaican dollar's official value.

Tipping & Bargaining
Tipping hasn't reached the crazed levels of the USA. However, a 10% tip is normal in hotels and restaurants, and bellhops at most hotels expect a tip for bringing baggage to your room (US$0.50 per bag is plenty). The Sandals and SuperClubs resorts and a few other all-inclusive resorts have a strictly enforced no-tipping policy; their staff can lose their jobs for accepting tips.

Some restaurants automatically add a 10 to 15% service charge to your bill, in which case there's no need to leave an additional tip. Check your bill carefully, as often the charge is unscrupulously hidden.

Most prices in shops are fixed. However, bargaining – *higgling* – is a staple of street and market life in Jamaica. Bargaining with higglers is one of the livelier aspects of getting to know the island culture. Sometimes the bargaining gets a bit brisk, even bad-tempered.

Taxes
The government charges a General Consumption Tax of 15% on hotels, restaurant bills, and most purchases in stores.

A J$500 departure tax is charged at airports (you can pay in Jamaican dollars or other national currency).

POST & COMMUNICATIONS
Mail
Every town and most villages have a post office; there are over 300 nationwide. The smaller ones (called postal agencies) issue stamps and receive and send letters and parcels, but otherwise have few facilities. Larger post offices are full-service, with telegram facilities, a philatelic bureau, and savings' bank bureau. Some have fax facilities.

Post offices are open Monday to Friday, 8 am to 5 pm. Postal agencies are usually open Monday, Wednesday, and Friday, mornings only, although times vary according to agency.

Postal Rates Jamaica is one of the cheapest countries in the world from which to mail letters and postcards. Postcards cost J$0.90 to anywhere in the world; aerograms cost J$0.80. Airmail letters to the USA and Canada cost J$1.10 per half ounce for letters; to UK and Europe it costs J$1.40 per half ounce; and to Africa, Asia, or Australia, J$1.80. Local letters within the country cost J$0.50.

Sending Mail Public postboxes are few and far between. You will need to go to a post office to mail your postcards and letters. Alternately, you can leave them with the front desk clerk at most hotels.

Jamaica proves the adage that you get what you pay for. The stamps may be pretty and cheap, but the service is *sloooow*! Always use airmail unless you have a valid reason not to. Airmail to North America usually takes about 10 days to two weeks, and a few days longer to Europe. Surface mail can take forever (at least two months). Even a letter from Montego Bay to Kingston can take a week.

Ensure that any parcels are adequately secured. Postal theft is common, so don't tempt fate by mailing loosely taped packages. *Never* mail cash or valuables in the post. If you want to mail valuable documents, use UPS or Federal Express.

When sending mail to Jamaica always include the addressee's name, address or post office box, town, and parish, plus 'Jamaica, West Indies.'

Receiving Mail You can have mailed addressed to you 'Poste Restante' care of a major central post office, such as Montego Bay.

Express Mail Services There are several express mail services (including Federal Express) listed in the yellow pages.

UPS has offices in the following locations:

Kingston
    5 Altamont Terrace (☎ 968-8288)
Mandeville
    Shop No 33, Manchester Shopping
    (☎ 962-5135)
Montego Bay
    No 3 Miranda Ridge, 36 Gloucester Ave
    (☎ 979-0292)
Negril
    Shop No 10, Adrija Plaza (☎ 957-9198)
Ocho Rios
    LOJ Complex, 1 Newlin St (☎ 974-0204)
Savanna-la-Mar
    82A Great Georges St (☎ 955-9637)

UPS offers a money-back guarantee of 24-hour delivery to North America and parts of Europe, plus free customs clearance. The offices are open daily, 7 am to 7 pm.

Telephone
Jamaica has a fully automated telephone system; all services are completely digital.

The service is not up to North American standards, however, and crackles are other strange noises are frequent. Disruptions are not unknown. Telephone communications are handled by Telecommunications of Jamaica (TOJ), a privately owned holding company for the Jamaica Telephone Company (TelCo) and Jamaica International Telecommunications Ltd. (Additional service for foreign companies in the Montego Freeport is provided by Jamaica Digiport International, owned jointly by AT&T, Cable & Wireless, and Telecommunications of Jamaica.)

Jamaican numbers all have seven digits, which you dial for calls within the same area code. For calls to other area codes, dial 0 then the seven digit number. Remember, only 1.6% of the population has a telephone.

If you wish to call Jamaica from abroad, dial the country code (809 for most of the Caribbean) and then the area code and local number.

Public Telephones Even remote villages are served by public telephones, which often serve the entire community. You'll also find public telephones at TOJ offices in most major towns. Offices are usually open Monday to Friday, 8 am to 4 pm, and until noon on Saturdays (see page 5 of the telephone directory for a full list of TOJ offices). Its head office is at 51 Half Way Tree Rd, Kingston 5 (☎ 926-9700).

To use a public phone, pick up the receiver and wait for the clicking tone before dialing. You deposit your coins *after* a connection; only then can you begin talking.

Phone Cards Most public phones now use Jamaica TelCo phone cards, which have virtually replaced coin-operated public call boxes. The cards can be handy if you're making several calls, but it can be a hassle if you want to make one quick call and you have to go scout out where to buy a phone card because that's all the public phone will accept.

The plastic cards are available from retail stores, hotels, banks, and other outlets displaying the 'phone cards on sale' sign. There's always an outlet close by the phone, even in the boondocks. The card is paid for in advance in denominations of J$20 to J$500.

To make a call, simply lift the receiver and insert the card picture-side face up into the special slot in the telephone unit. Then dial 113; when you hear the tone, press the # button, then dial your number. Then, wait for the other party to start talking before pressing the 'Press to Talk' button.

When calls are made, the telephone shows the balance remaining on a digital screen, and deducts the charges from the value of your card. Some phones are cantankerous and don't always accept the cards, at least not at first try.

International Calls The easiest way to call home is usually from your hotel. Almost all the larger or more upscale hotels have direct dial calling; elsewhere you may need to go through the hotel operator, or even call from the front desk.

Hotels add a 15% government tax for overseas calls. They also impose their own service charge at sticker-shock rates! Some hotels even block access to home-direct service so that they can jack up your bill.

You can save money by using a 'home-direct' service such as AT&T USADirect, MCI CallUSA, or Sprint Express. You dial an access number from any telephone to reach a US operator who links your call. You can bill to your home phone, phone card, or collect to whoever you're calling. AT&T USADirect phone booths are located at several key locales in Jamaica, and most upscale hotels have signed up with AT&T to offer direct service from room phones. Many Jamaican operators still tell you that you can't use your calling card to call internationally. If this happens, try another operator!

For countries that cannot be dialed direct, call the international operator at ☎ 980-0000.

Never give your calling card number to anyone other than the operator, as scams are frequent.

You can no longer receive collect calls from overseas.

To place collect or calling card calls, simply dial the appropriate code below:

Country	Service	Code
USA	AT&T USADirect	☎ 872
	MCI CallUSA	☎ 873
	Sprint Express	☎ 875
Canada	Canada Direct	☎ 876
UK	BT Direct	☎ 874

Cellular Phones You can bring your own cellular phone into Jamaica, but you'll be charged a customs fee upon entry (this is refunded when you leave). You can also rent cellular phones from TOJ, which has four Cellular Customer Care centers:

Kingston
    115 Constant Spring Rd (☎ 969-9855)
Mandeville
    24 Hargreaves Ave (☎ 962-9855)
Montego Bay
    36 Fort St (☎ 979-9855)
Ocho Rios
    Mutual Life Bldg (☎ 974-9855)

Cellular coverage is available only in specific areas. The airtime charge is US$3 per minute.

Boatphone, a subsidiary of London-based Cable & Wireless, also provides a cellular network throughout the Caribbean for yachts and cruise ships. By dialing '*0 SND' in Jamaica, you can register your cellular phone for instant service. You can arrange billing direct to your credit card. For information, call ☎ (800) 262-8366 from the USA; ☎ (800) 567-8366 from Canada; or ☎ (809) 480-2628 or 462-5051 from elsewhere. In Jamaica, call ☎ 968-4000.

Boatphone offers discount rates for use over a six-week period or longer, and rents top-quality cellular phones and fax machines.

Fax & Telex
Many towns have private fax services; these are listed in the regional chapters. You can also send faxes from hotels and major post

offices, and from the TOJ centers, from where you can also send telegrams.

Most hotels and large businesses have telex service, but this is rarely used in the current era of faxes. In addition, many larger, more modern hotels provide modem access for guests who travel with their laptop computers.

BOOKS

Information on bookshops throughout Jamaica can be found in the regional chapters.

West Indies Book Unlimited, PO Box 2315, Sarasota, FL 34230 (☎ 813) 954-8601) sells Caribbean-related books, including fiction and out-of-print, hard-to-find books.

Macmillan Caribbean, a division of Macmillan Press, publishes a wide range of general guides and special-interest books about the Caribbean. You can order a catalog by contacting Macmillan Caribbean, Houndmills, Basingstoke, Hampshire RG21 2XS, England (☎ (0256) 29242, fax (0256) 20109).

The following books provide worthwhile background reading.

Lonely Planet

Eastern Caribbean – travel survival kit by Glenda Bendure and Ned Friary will prove invaluable if you're planning to do some island hopping.

Other Guidebooks

There are about one dozen English-language travel guidebooks to Jamaica, plus many other Caribbean guidebooks with chapters on Jamaica.

Insight Guides' Jamaica (APA Publications) is the most richly illustrated guide. It also has the most detailed introduction to the country, with splendid treatment on island culture written by a team of native writers. It's a handy sightseeing guide, too, though weak on nitty-gritty details.

Tour Jamaica by Margaret Morris (The Gleaner Company) is an excellent guide for anyone exploring on foot or by car. The large-format book is full of intriguing history on sites often off the beaten path. She details 19 recommended tours. It's been out of print for several years, but rumor has it that a new edition will soon be printed.

Adventure Guide to Jamaica by Steve Cohen (Hunter Publishing) is an indispensable guide for anyone interested in off-the-beaten-track exploration and activities. Cohen clearly loves the island and its people.

Best Dives of the Caribbean by Joyce & Jon Huber (Hunter Publishing, Edison, New Jersey) provides a valuable introduction for scuba divers, including general practicalities on travel. Its Jamaica chapter is very shallow. Likewise, *Adventuring in the Caribbean* by Carrol Fleming (Sierra Club Books, San Francisco) provides only fleeting coverage on Jamaica.

Kay Showker's *Outdoor Traveler's Guide to the Caribbean* (Stewart, Tabori & Chang, New York) is an excellent guide for ecotourists, with detailed information on specific locales in Jamaica for birders, hikers, and nature lovers.

The US Dept of State publishes *Tips for Travelers to the Caribbean* (Publication No 9906, BCA), available from the Superintendent of Documents, US Government Printing Office, Washington, DC 20402 (☎ (202) 783-3238).

Travel

Very few travel books have been written about Jamaica, at least during this century.

An early travelogue that provides a colorful insight into the life and times of colonial Jamaica is Lady Maria Nugent's *Journal of Residence in Jamaica, 1801–5*. In a similar vein is *Journal of a West Indian Planter* by Matthew 'Monk' Lewis, written in 1834.

Ian Fleming Introduces Jamaica, published in 1965 and now out of print, is a collection of essays edited by Morriss Cargill. Various authors describe aspects of Jamaican life.

Jamaica the Blessed Island by Lord Olivier (Faber & Faber) recalls the noted actor's viewpoints and experiences as a favored vacation spot. Likewise, swash-buckling Hollywood hero Errol Flynn, who lived in Jamaica for many years, recalls his colorful experiences in his biography *My Wicked, Wicked Ways*.

History & Politics

A revival of appreciation in Jamaica's past in recent years has fostered publication of several worthy history books. One of the leading publishers is the Institute of Jamaica.

Jamaica Surveyed by Barry W Higman (Institute of Jamaica, Kingston), a history professor at the University of the West Indies, analyzes contemporary prints, diagrams, and topograph plans alongside historical estate maps to investigate changes in land use patterns during the past three centuries.

Views of Jamaica (Institute of Jamaica, Kingston) features rare illustrations of plantations and townscapes by the renowned 19th century artist, Joseph Bartholemew Kidd (a prominent founder of the Scottish Academy of Art).

In a similar vein is *A Picturesque Tour of the Island of Jamaica*, originally published in 1825 (recently reprinted by Mill Press), and featuring beautiful illustrations of an idealized Jamaica by James Hakewill.

Edward Long's three-volume *The History of Jamaica* written in 1774 remains a definitive study of the early colonial era. *The Annals of Jamaica* is a similar, two-volume work by George Bridges, published in 1828.

Two good books that tell the fascinating tale of the Maroons are *The History of the Maroons* by RC Dallas, a two-volume set published in 1803, and Carey Robinson's *The Fighting Maroons of Jamaica* (Collins). Robert Leeson's *The Cimaroons* (Collins) is another serious yet engaging study of the Maroons. *The Sun & the Drum* by Leonard Barrett (Sangster) traces the African influence on Jamaican culture.

Jamaica and Voluntary Laborers from Africa 1840-66 by Mary Elizabeth Thomas (University of Florida Press) tells the tale of indentured labor immigration, while *Alas Alas Kongo* by Monica Schuller (Johns Hopkins University Press) records how free Africans were lured to Jamaica in the post-emancipation era.

Buccaneers of America, first published in 1684, is an entertaining eyewitness account of the sordid acts of the infamous buccaneers told by John Esquemeling, who partook in the misdeeds. Surprisingly little has been written on the pirate era. However, the era is covered well in *Port Royal* by Clinton V Black (Institute of Jamaica Publications). The book provides a detailed and entertaining account of the riseand fall of Port Royal. Black also authored*Tales of Old Jamaica* (Longman Caribbean), which tells the tale of 10 of Jamaica's most notorious scoundrels, including Annie Palmer, the 'White Witch of Rose Hall.'

Tony Sewall's *Garvey's Children: The Legacy of Marcus Garvey* (Macmillan Caribbean) provides a look at the rise of black nationalism inspired by National Hero Marcus Garvey. The theme is also discussed in *Colour, Class and Politics in Jamaica* by Aggrey Brown (Transaction Books).

Dread: The Rastafarians of Jamaica by Joseph Owens (Sangster, Kingston) and *Rastafari: For the Healing of the Nation* by Dennis Forsythe (Ziaka Publications) are both noteworthy books on Jamaica's most talked-about creed.

Alexander Bustamente and Modern Jamaica by George Eaton (Kingston Publishers) follows the rise of nationalism to its logical conclusion: independence and the birth of a nation under the fostership of National Hero Alexander Bustamante.

Flora & Fauna

There's no shortage of books on the natural history of Jamaica and the Caribbean islands. *Flowering Plants of Jamaica* by C Dennis Adams (University of the West Indies) has detailed descriptions of individual species, accompanied by illustrations. *Caribbean Flora* by the same author (Nelson), is in a similar vein, as are *Wild Flowers of Jamaica* by AD Hawkers & B Sutton, and *Flowers of the Caribbean* and *Trees of the Caribbean*, both by GW

Lennox & SA Seddon. All three are published by Macmillan Caribbean.

Serious botanists with a practical bent should check out *Caribbean Wild Plants & Their Uses* by Penelope Honeychurch (Macmillan) and *200 Conspicuous, Unusual or Economically Important Tropical Plants of the Caribbean* by John Kingsbury (Bullbrier Press).

Birders are well represented by *Birds of Jamaica: A Photographic Field Guide* by Audrey Downer & Robert Sutton (Cambridge University Press). This richly illustrated guide is well written, with general introductory sections and species by species accounts.

James Bond's classic *Birds of the West Indies* is another reference for serious birdwatchers. It was recently republished as *Peterson's Field Guide to Birds of the West Indies* (Houghton Mifflin) in a lavishly illustrated version.

Other books on birds include *The Birds of Jamaica* by DB Stewart (Institute of Jamaica Publications), *Familiar Jamaica Birds* by Anna Black (Jamaica Information Services), and *Gosse's Jamaica 1844–45: Excerpts from a Naturalist's Sojourn in Jamaica*, printed in 1851.

If you're into snorkeling or diving, a standard reference should be Eugene Kaplan's *Peterson Field Guide to Coral Reefs* (Houghton Mifflin). In the same series is *Fishes of the Caribbean* by Ian Took. Both are comprehensive books with detailed information on ecosystems, habitats, and individual species.

Cuisine

There are many books on Jamaican cooking that will help you recreate your favorite island dishes in your own kitchen.

Two of the best are *Real Taste of Jamaica* by Enid Donaldson (Ian Randle), and *Traveling Jamaica with Knife, Fork & Spoon: A Righteous Guide to Jamaican Cooking* by Robb Walsh & Jay McCarthy (Crossing Press). The latter is a collection of anecdotes and recipes from the backcountry and the kitchens of snooty resorts.

Jerk Barbecue from Jamaica by Helen Willinsky (Crossing Press) is a must for preparing a sizzlingly successful barbecue, while *Cooking with Caribbean Rum* by Laurel-Ann Morley (Macmillian) and *Cooking with Red Stripe* by the brewing company, Desnoes & Geddes, provide intriguing recipes using beer and rum.

Architecture

Several books have been written on Caribbean and Jamaican architecture. *Jamaican Houses: A Vanishing Legacy* by Geoffrey de Sota Pinto (de Sota Pinto Publishers) has brief descriptions and black and white prints of Jamaica's most important historical houses.

Caribbean Style by Suzanne Slesin and Stafford Cliff (Clarkson N Potter) and its pocket-sized companion, *Essence of Caribbean Style*, explain the evolution and elements of the Caribbean vernacular in architecture. The lively text is supported by stunning photography.

Folklore & Folktales

If you want to understand something of traditional folktales, read *Jamaican Folk Tales & Oral Histories* by Laura Tanna (Institute of Jamaica Publications). This collection includes tales of Anancy, the popular spider-hero of Jamaican folklore, as does Louise Bennett's *Anancy and Miss Lou* (Sangster) and *Anancy Stories and Dialect Verse* (Pioneer Press).

Jamaica Talk, 300 Years of the English Language in Jamaica by Frederic Cassidy (Macmillan Caribbean) will provide you with an understanding of English as spoken in Jamaica. *Jamaican Proverbs* by Martha Beckwith (Negro University Press) will help you translate the esoteric sayings that Jamaicans are sure to throw your way.

General

The *A–Z of Jamaican Heritage* by Olive Senior (The Gleaner Company) is an encyclopedia on Jamaica. It's been out of print for some years, but provides a handy compendium for background reading, with valuable descriptions of esoterica.

In Focus Jamaica: A Guide to the People, Politics & Culture by Marcel Bayer (Latin America Bureau) provides an accurate and concise, yet detailed account of Jamaican reality.

If you're interested in learning about the life of reggae superstar Bob Marley and his influence on Jamaican music, read *Catch a Fire: The Life of Bob Marley* by Timothy White (Omnibus Press, London). It chronicles the musician's rise from rural poverty to international stardom, and analyzes the forces that shaped Marley's political and spiritual evolution.

A more sensational text is *Marley & Me: The Real Story as Told by Mike Henry* by Don Taylor (Kingston Publishers), who tells a controversial, behind-the-scenes tale of Marley's youth, family, politics, and the women in his life.

A handy booklet for planning your trip is *Consumer Reports Travel Buying Guide*, published by the Consumers' Union (New York). This annual pocket-sized book provides aid in finding discounts and avoiding pitfalls.

American Traveling Abroad: What You Should Know Before You Go by Gladson Nwann (World Travel Institute) is another handy international travel resource guide for US citizens planning a vacation. Virtually no stone is left unturned, with chapters on customs, health, security, seniors, etc.

Lastly, a series of short pocket-guides designed to help visitors understand Jamaican life is published by Jamrite Publications, Kingston, including the *How to be Jamaican Handbook* by Kim Robinson, Harclyde Walcott, & Trevor Fearon. *Ganja in Jamaica* by Vera Rubin & Lambros Comitas (Moulton & Co) will edify you on the mysteries of *de holy 'erb*.

CD/ROM

Virtually There: Caribbean is a CD/ROM designed to take you on a 'virtual vacation.' Jamaica and 18 other Caribbean islands are featured. The CD/ROM is issued by Sabre Interactive and is intended primarily for travel agents to show to their clients, but you can buy it through retail computer stores.

Wondering where to stay? Check out *Resorts of the Caribbean* and *Villas of the Caribbean*, two interactive CD/ROM travel guides produced by Straight Line Medium Inc (☎ (804) 784-2690), in association with Island Hideaways. Both feature an encyclopedic library of accommodations covering 20 islands. They sell for US$29.95; if you order both together, the second is half price.

ONLINE SERVICES

The explosion in recent years of communications in cyberspace (via computer interface) has fostered dozens of travel sites on Internet providers such as CompuServe and America Online. The World Wide Web (WWW) has scores of travel-related homepages (resource files). They are no substitute for a good guidebook, but many provide excellent information for planning your trip. They also give you a chance to exchange information and otherwise gossip with other travelers in-the-know via email (electronic mail).

Here's a list of good starting points to find information on the the web:

Lonely Planet
   This website is especially good for practical tips on preparing for your trip.
   (http://www.lonelyplanet.com)
CPSCaribNet
   Has facts and things to see and do for more

than two dozen Caribbean islands, including Jamaica. It has information on accommodations and special interest activities, real estate, yachting, and investing.
(http://www.cpscaribnet.com)

Yahoo
Allows you to use a search-word such as 'Caribbean' or 'Jamaica' to draw up as many sites as exist containing those keywords.
(http://www.yahoo.com)

Jamaica Tourist Board
The homepage has six categories of information, and additional construction is planned.
(http://www.jamaica–tours.com/jamaica/)

GNN Travel Center
Global Network Navigator is one of the largest and most far-reaching resources.
(http://nearnet.gnn.com/gnn/meta/travel/index.html)

American Society of Travel Agents
Find out which companies specialize in particular types of trips.
(http://www.ASTAnet.com)

Adventure Travel Society
Lists reputable adventure-travel companies by activity and destination.
(http://www.adventuretravel.com/ats/)

Specialty Travel Index
Also lists adventure-travel companies.
(http://www.spectrav.com)

Great Outdoor Recreation Page
If you plan on hiking, mountain biking, or the like, try this site with extensive listings on maps, gear, and outfitters.
(http://www.grop.com)

TravelMag
Has information for independent, down-to-earth travelers.
(http://www.travelmag.co.uk/travelmag/)

TapOnline
More information on independent travel.
(http://www.taponline.com)

Shoestring Travel
A forum for budget travelers.
(http://turnpike.net/metro/eadler/index.html)

Council Travel
Lists international airfares from US cities.
(http://www.ciee.org/cts/ctshome.htm)

College Travel
Check out student airfares.
(email: wolvie@prairienet.org)

Air Charter Guide
Find out student airfares in the directory on charter aviation worldwide.
(http://www.guides.com/acg)

FILMS

Jamaica has had star billing in dozens of films and its status as a favored location for Hollywood and music video shoots has fostered a minor industry, pumping in as much as US$10 million a year into the economy. Some of the movies below will give a taste of the landscapes and lifestyle.

The island has had strong links to James Bond movies ever since novelist Ian Fleming concocted the suave, macho spy 007 at his home near Oracabessa. The Bond movies *Dr No* and *Live and Let Die* were both shot on location on Jamaica's north coast.

Portions of *20,000 Leagues Under the Sea* were filmed in Jamaica. So too, were scenes from *Papillon* with Steve McQueen and Dustin Hoffman, employing many of Seaford's residents of German heritage as extras. *Lord of the Flies*, *Flipper*, *Prelude to a Kiss*, and *Search for Tomorrow* were also filmed in Jamaica.

Native-born singer Jimmy Cliff rocketed to fame in the movie *The Harder They Come*, in which he starred as a 'rude boy'

Jimmy Cliff starred in and sang the theme song of the movie *The Harder They Come*.

(armed thug) in Kingston's ghettoes. Cliff also starred alongside comedian Robin Williams in the movie *Club Paradise*, filmed around Port Antonio. In recent years Port Antonio has become something of an international star in its own right. *Clara's Heart* (starring Whoopie Goldberg), *Hammerhead* (starring Denzel Washington), the John Candy-Disney Productions movie *Cool Runnings*, *Cocktail* (starring Tom Cruise), *The Mighty Quinn*, *Blue Lagoon* (starring Brooke Shields), *Treasure Island* (starring Burt Lancaster), and *Wide Sargasso Sea*, a sultry tale of post-emancipation Jamaica, were all filmed wholly or in part around Port Antonio.

Port Antonio is also a favorite location spot for music videos starring Grammy-winning Jamaican dancehall artist Shabba Ranks.

Several US soap operas have also used Jamaican locales. *Going to Extremes* was filmed in St Ann's Bay and reportedly employed almost 5000 Jamaicans as extras.

NEWSPAPERS & MAGAZINES
Foreign Publications
Leading international newspapers such as the *International Herald Tribune*, *The Times* (of London), *Figaro*, and *USA Today*, plus leading magazines such as *Newsweek*, *Time*, and *The Economist* are stocked by many hotel gift stores, pharmacies, and stationery stores throughout Jamaica. You'll also be able to find many international consumer magazines. However, they're pricey – usually about three times the cost at home.

Before you go, take a look at some magazines about Jamaica and the Caribbean. *Caribbean Travel & Life* is a beautiful, full-color, bi-monthly magazine covering travel throughout the Caribbean. It has feature articles and resort reviews, plus is packed with money-saving tips and advertisements. I'm one of the contributing editors.

Caribbean World is a similar magazine, pubished quarterly and with an up-market focus.

Caribbean Week is a high-quality, bi-weekly news magazine that covers travel, politics, fashion, economics, and other trends throughout the region. It's in-depth reporting (by regional journalists) is aimed at the serious student of Caribbean affairs.

Jamaican Publications
The Gleaner is a high-standard, conservative daily that has been around since 1834. Coverage is mostly national, with a passing nod to international events. Its circulation is about 45,000 daily (the *Sunday Gleaner* has a circulation of about 95,000). The Gleaner Company also publishes a trashy afternoon tabloid – *The Star* – in a similar vein as the major English tabloids, and the slightly more erudite *New York Daily News*.

In January 1993, well-known Jamaican entrepreneur Gordon 'Butch' Steward (founder of the Sandals resorts) launched the *Jamaica Observer*, a moderate-quality tabloid published on Wednesday and Friday.

There are several regional newspapers, including the *North Coast Times*, which serves St Ann and St Mary Parishes. The *Western Mirror* serves Montego Bay and is published on Wednesday and Saturday.

The *Jamaica Tourist Guide* is a 16-page newspaper geared to international visitors. It's published monthly by The Gleaner Company. It features news reports, articles, and personality profiles, plus regional listings of things to do and places to see. You can obtain free copies in many hotel lobbies.

Published bi-weekly, *The Vacationer* is a newsletter-style publication for travelers, similar to the *Jamaica Tourist Guide*. Complimentary copies are available at hotel desks and JTB offices.

RADIO & TV
The Jamaica Broadcasting Corporation operates the national television service (there are two channels: JBC One and JBC Two) as well as an FM channel. The JBC's AM channel was privatized in 1994. A Public Broadcasting Corporation has been established to produce quality TV materials, but to date productions are of relatively low standard. In late 1995, the

government began a debate on whether to allow private cable companies to set up in Jamaica.

Most hotels offer satellite or cable TV, and CNN and ESPN are staples. Some hotels subscribe to HBO and other North American cable stations.

In 1995 there were three regional and three national radio stations. Call-in talk shows are very popular, and there is considerable political debate on the air.

Radio Jamaica Rediffusion (RJR) is a public service station that broadcasts 24 hours a day. It mixes talk shows, political analysis, and cricket coverage with reggae and popular music. RJR also broadcasts Fame FM, a popular music station.

Reggae lovers should tune-in to Irie FM, which plays non-stop reggae music. It has a fairly strong political content. (Amazingly, many reggae songs – including Bob Marley's – were banned for many years.) Love FM plays a lot of North American and romantic reggae. KLAS FM (89.5) and Power 106 FM are the two other stations.

Reception is variable throughout the island and is affected by terrain.

PHOTOGRAPHY & VIDEO

Jamaica is about as photogenic as a destination gets, and there are no restrictions on taking photographs, even at airports. You'll want plenty of film. The landscapes and seascapes are fabulous, as are the sunsets. Many locals enjoy posing for photos.

Film & Equipment

Bring the equipment you'll need from home. If you do have to buy something you'll find camera stores in most major towns, especially in Montego Bay and Ocho Rios, where duty-free stores sell cameras and lenses at prices that offer only marginal savings. Most shops sell a range of basic filters, including UV and polarizing filters – essentials for getting the most out of Jamaica's tropical conditions.

Film is extremely expensive – about double what you'd pay in North America – so ensure you bring enough to last. Even amateur photographers can easily shoot two

or more rolls a day. Most photo supply stores and drugstores sell a limited range of film. Print film is widely available, but slide (transparency) film is rarer, and usually limited to Kodak's Ektachrome or Agfachrome. Fuji film is virtually impossible to find in Jamaica. Many places, however, leave film sitting in the sun; avoid this like the plague, as heat and humidity rapidly deteriorate film. Don't forget to check the expiration date, too. Once you've finished a roll of film, try to keep it cool and have it developed as soon as possible. One or two weeks is OK, but if you'll be traveling around for several weeks, consider having your film developed on the island, or mailing it home for development (you can purchase pre-paid mailers for this purpose).

Every photographer has the same enemy in Jamaica – humidity. Carry silica gel packages in your camera bag to soak up humidity.

Photography

Your greatest potential disappointment when you receive your processed photographs is the possibility of a washed-out look due to overexposure. The bright tropical light can fool even the most sophisticated light metering systems. Your meter may not be set up to register the dazzling ambient light surrounding the subject it's reading from. Sand and water are particularly reflective.

A separate hand-held meter can provide more accurate readings. It's also often a good idea to 'stop down' one F-stop to reduce the light and thereby get richer color saturation. Most effective of all is to take photographs in early morning and late afternoon, to avoid the harsh shadows and the glare of the sun.

The type of film you use will also make a huge difference to the color rendition. Use Fujichrome Velvia, which gives the best color saturation of any film. It's not cheap, but it pays big dividends. Kodachrome 25 and 64 also give excellent color rendition; the former is great for bright conditions, but is too 'fast' to handle dark conditions or great contrasts of light and shade.

When photographing people, you'll need to compensate for the contrast between dark faces and bright backgrounds; otherwise they may turn out as featureless black shadows. The darker a person's skin is, the more light you will need to reflect onto their faces. Many modern cameras have a fill-in flash for this purpose. Alternately, invest in a small hand-held reflector. If you're taking really close up shots, you can even ask your subject to hold the reflector (out of the camera frame, of course).

Video
Video cameras and tapes are widely available in photo supply stores in main resort towns and in Kingston. Prices are significantly higher than you may be used to in North America or Europe.

Photographing People
The majority of Jamaicans delight in having their photographs taken, and will be happy to pose for your camera. Many make fantastic subjects in their bright Caribbean colors and sometimes flamboyant dress. Higglers – 'market mammies' – are especially intriguing subjects, as are Rastafarians.

However, many Jamaicans of all ages do not like having their picture taken, especially if they're not dressed in their Sunday best. Others have religious proscriptions. If they don't want to be photographed, they may let you no this in no uncertain terms, and can get quite volatile if you persist. Honor their wishes with good grace.

It is a common courtesy to ask permission. Expect to be asked to pay a small 'donation' to take photographs. Whether you agree to this or not is a matter of your own conscience, but honor someone's wishes: if you don't want to pay, don't take the shot!

In markets it is considered good manners to purchase a small item from whomever you wish to photograph. Don't forget to send a photograph to anyone to whom you've promised to do so.

Airport Security
Your baggage will be inspected when you depart Montego Bay and Kingston airports.

It's a good idea to have your film hand-inspected, since X-ray machines can fog films. Most modern X-ray machines will not produce any noticeable fogging if your film passes through only once or twice, but why take the risk? If your baggage will be passed through several X-ray machines during the course of your travels, you should definitely have it hand-checked. Otherwise, invest in a lead-lined film pouch, which you can buy at most camera stores.

Don't forget to have your camera hand-inspected if it has film inside.

TIME
In spring and summer, Jamaica is six hours behind Greenwich Mean Time and one hour ahead of New York. However, the island does not adjust for daylight-saving time. Hence, when the United States is on daylight-saving time, the time in Jamaica is five hours behind London, the same as Eastern Standard Time.

ELECTRICITY
Most hotels operate on 110 volts (50 cycles), the same as in the USA and Canada. However, some establishments operate on 220 volts (50 cycles), as in the UK. The more upscale hotels can usually provide a transformer and adapter, although don't expect this to be the case for budget properties.

Sockets throughout Jamaica are usually two-or three-pin to US standard. Occasionally, particularly in some older establishments, you may find three-square-pin sockets.

WEIGHTS & MEASURES
Jamaica has been making tentative moves to shift from the Imperial system to the metric. Distances are still shown on some maps in miles and inches, although official documents now speak of kilometers and centimeters. Road speed limits are still given in miles per hour, however, but a few signs have also begun to appear in metric. Because of this period of transition, information in this book is sometimes in metric, sometimes in Imperial. This may

be confusing, but hopefully the conversion chart at the back of the book will help out.

The antiquated English 'chain' is still the most commonly used measure of distance in Jamaican parlance. It equals 22 yards, and is used with relative accuracy in giving directions. If someone tells you that something is 'five or six chains' then you can expect this to be fairly accurate. However, 'a few chains' can means anywhere up to a mile or more.

Liquids are generally measured in pints, quarts, and gallons; and weights in grams, ounces, and pounds. However, metric measures are now increasingly being used. Most imported food items are in metric.

LAUNDRY

Self-service, coin-operated laundries are as rare as the Mauritian dodo. Drop-off laundries are more widely available in major resort towns. Elsewhere local women may offer their services, although you may need to seek them out.

Most hotels can arrange next-day or two-day laundry. Usually they will send your clothes out to be washed. For the better hotels, this will be to a professional laundrette. For more modest establishments, expect your laundry to be washed in a river and beaten over rocks. In the latter case, don't expect your clothes to be ironed.

HEALTH

Jamaica poses few health risks. The water is chlorinated and potable (though it's wise to drink purified water in the boondocks), and food hygiene standards are generally high. Your greatest threats are dehydration and an excess of sun and booze.

Travel health depends on your predeparture preparations, your day-to-day health care while traveling, and how you handle any medical problem or emergency that does develop. With a little luck, some basic precautions, and adequate information, few travelers experience more than upset stomachs.

While the discussions of diseases may provoke anxiety, they are provided for your enlightenment and are not necessarily a reflection of the prevalence of particular diseases or threats.

Travel Health Guides

There are a number of worthwhile books on travel health:

- *Staying Healthy in Asia, Africa & Latin America*, Moon Publications – Probably the best all-around guide to carry, as it's compact but very detailed and well organized.
- *Travelers' Health*, Doctor Richard Dawood, Oxford University Press – Comprehensive, easy to read, authoritative and also highly recommended, although it's rather large to lug around.
- *Where There is No Doctor*, David Werner, Hesperian Foundation – A very detailed guide intended for someone, like a Peace Corps worker, going to work in an undeveloped country, rather than for the average traveler.
- *Travel with Children*, Maureen Wheeler, Lonely Planet Publications – Includes basic advice on travel health for younger children.

Predeparture Preparations

Health Insurance An insurance policy to cover theft, loss and medical problems is a wise idea. There are a wide variety of policies and your travel agent will have recommendations. The international student travel policies handled by STA Travel or other student travel organizations are usually a good value. For more details about health insurance, see the Travel Insurance in the Visas & Documents section above.

Medical Kit A small, straightforward medical kit is a wise thing to carry. A possible list of kit supplies includes:

- Aspirin or Panadol – for pain or fever.
- Antihistamine (such as Benadryl) – useful as a decongestant for colds, allergies, to ease the itch from insect bites or stings or to help prevent motion sickness.
- Antibiotics – carry the prescription with you.
- Kaolin preparation (Pepto-Bismol), Imodium, or Lomotil – for stomach upsets.
- Rehydration mixture – for treatment of severe diarrhea. This is particularly important if traveling with children, but is recommended for everyone.
- Antiseptic such as Betadine – for cuts and grazes.

- Calamine lotion – to ease irritation from bites or stings.
- Bandages and Band-Aids – for minor injuries.
- Scissors, tweezers, and a thermometer (note that mercury thermometers are prohibited by airlines).
- Insect repellent, sunscreen, lip balm, and water purification tablets.

If you require a particular medication take an adequate supply, as it may not be available locally. Take the prescription or, better still, part of the packaging showing the generic rather than the brand name (which may not be locally available), as it will make getting replacements easier. It's a wise idea to have a legible prescription with you to show you legally use the medication.

In Jamaica, if a medicine is available it will generally be available over the counter and the price will be much cheaper than in Europe or North America. However, be careful to ensure that the expiration date has not passed and that correct storage conditions have been followed. It may be a good idea to leave unwanted medicines, syringes, etc with a local clinic, rather than carry them home.

The best medical kits on the market are made by Adventure Medical Kits (PO Box 43309, Oakland, CA 94624, ☎ (510) 632-1442 or (800) 324-3517, fax (510) 632-1284). Their comprehensive kits range from an 'Expedition' pack, with everything but the operating table, to specialized kits for families, white-water enthusiasts, mariners, cyclists, and day-trippers. They come with medical information booklets containing state-of-the-art medical advice and instructions on wilderness, pediatric, travel, and emergency medicine.

Immunizations No vaccinations are required to enter Jamaica unless you have visited the following locations within the previous six weeks: Asia, Africa, Central and South America, Dominican Republic, Haiti, and Trinidad & Tobago. Check with the JTB or through your travel agent before departure to see what current regulations may be. Yellow fever is not a threat in Jamaica, but immunization may be required of travelers arriving from infected areas, chiefly in Africa and South America. Protection lasts 10 years.

Certain vaccinations can be a good idea and can provide protection against diseases you might meet along the way. All vaccinations should be recorded on an International Health Certificate, which is available from your physician or government health department. Tetanus & Diptheria, Typhoid, and Infectious Hepatitis are vaccinations you may want to look into. Your doctor may still recommend booster shots against measles or polio, diseases still prevalent in many developing countries. The period of protection offered by vaccinations differs widely and some are contraindicated if you are pregnant.

Plan ahead for getting your vaccinations: some require an initial shot followed by a booster, while others cannot be given together. It is recommended you seek medical advice at least six weeks prior to travel.

Basic Rules
Care in what you eat and drink is the most important health rule; stomach upsets are the most likely travel health problem (between 30 and 50% of travelers in a two-week stay experience this) but the majority of these upsets will be relatively minor. Don't become paranoid; trying the local food is part of the experience of travel, after all.

Water Jamaica has its own natural purification system in its limestone base through which rainwater percolates. Water is generally safe to drink from faucets throughout the island. However, sanitation conditions in some outlying and backcountry areas are poor, and in the more extreme areas of the eastern parishes you should avoid drinking the water. The same is true for ice, particular that sold at street stands as *bellywash* or *snocones*, shaved ice cones sweetened with fruit juice. If you don't know for certain that the water is safe always assume the worst.

Reputable brands of bottled water or soft drinks are generally fine. Only use water from containers with an unbroken seal – not caps or corks. Take care with fruit juice, particularly if water may have been added. Milk should be treated with suspicion, as it is often unpasteurized. Boiled milk is fine if it is kept hygienically and yogurt is always good. Tea or coffee should also be OK, since the water should have been boiled.

Water Purification This is rarely needed in Jamaica. However, if you're camping or using hovel-like budget accommodations and are unsure of your water supply, then you should purify it. The simplest way is to boil it vigorously for five minutes.

If you cannot boil water it should be treated chemically. Chlorine tablets (Puritabs, Steritabs, or other brand names) will kill many but not all pathogens, including giardia and amoebic cysts. Iodine is very effective in purifying water and is available in tablet form (such as Potable Aqua), but follow the directions carefully and remember that too much iodine can be harmful. Tincture of iodine (2%) can also be used. Four drops of tincture of iodine per liter or quart of clear water is the recommended dosage; the treated water should be left to stand for 20 to 30 minutes before drinking.

Food Jamaican restaurants pose relatively few hygiene problems. The same holds true for most food bought off the street. Salads and fruit should be washed with purified water or peeled where possible. Ice cream is usually OK, but beware of street vendors and of ice cream that has melted and been refrozen. Thoroughly cooked food is safest, but not if it has been left to cool or if it has been reheated. Shellfish such as oysters and clams should be avoided as well as under-cooked meat, particularly in the form of mince. Steaming does not make shellfish safe for eating.

If a place looks clean and well run and if the vendor also looks clean and healthy, then the food is probably safe.

Nutrition Make sure your diet is well balanced. Eggs, tofu, beans, lentils, and nuts are all safe ways to get protein. Fruit you can peel (bananas or ortaniques for example) is always safe and a good source of vitamins. Try to eat plenty of grains (rice) and bread. Remember overcooked food loses much of its nutritional value. If your diet isn't well balanced or if your food intake is insufficient, it's a good idea to take vitamin and iron supplements.

Jamaica's is a hot climate, so make sure you drink enough – don't rely on feeling thirsty to indicate when you should drink. Not needing to urinate or very dark yellow urine is a danger sign. Always carry a water bottle with you on hiking trips.

Everyday Health In Jamaica's back-waters, clean your teeth with purified water rather than straight from the tap. Wash your hands before eating. Avoid overexposure to extremes: keep out of the sun at its peak, dress warmly if hiking to Blue Mountain peak. Avoid potential diseases by dressing sensibly. You can get worm infections from walking barefoot or dangerous coral cuts by walking over coral without shoes. You can avoid insect bites by covering bare skin when insects are around, by screening windows or beds or by using insect repellents. Seek local advice: if you're told the water is unsafe due to jellyfish, crocodiles or sharks, don't go in. In situations where there is no information, discretion is the better part of valor.

Medical Treatment
An embassy or consulate can usually recommend a good place to go for such advice. So can five-star hotels, although they often recommend doctors with five-star prices. (This is when that medical insurance really comes in useful!) In some places standards of medical attention are so low that for some ailments the best advice is to get on a plane and go somewhere else.

Climatic & Geographical Considerations
Sunburn In the tropics you can get sunburned surprisingly quickly, even in cloudy weather. Many people ruin their holiday by getting badly burned soon after they arrive

in Jamaica. You can easily spot them: they're the ones looking like boiled lobsters. *Don't underestimate the power of the tropical sun*, no matter how dark your skin color. Use a sunscreen with a protective factor of 15 or more. Take extra care to cover areas which don't normally see sun – eg, your feet. Be *very* careful if going topless and/or bottomless. Build up your exposure to the sun gradually. A hat provides added protection, and you should also use zinc cream or some other barrier cream for your nose and lips.

Calamine lotion is good for mild sunburn. Aloe vera also helps. You'll find plenty of Jamaican women selling aloe on beaches at major resorts. They'll give you a massage using a peeled aloe leaf for US$5 or so – it feels great!

Prickly Heat Prickly heat is an itchy rash caused by excessive perspiration trapped under the skin. It usually strikes people who have just arrived in a hot climate and whose pores have not yet opened sufficiently to cope with increased sweating. Keeping cool but bathing often, using a mild talcum powder, or even resorting to air-conditioning may help alleviate symptoms until you acclimatize.

Dehydration & Heat Exhaustion You'll sweat profusely in Jamaica. Take time to acclimatize to high temperatures and make sure you get sufficient liquids. You'll lose quite a bit of salt through sweating. Salt deficiency is characterized by fatigue, lethargy, headaches, giddiness, and muscle cramps and in this case salt tablets may help. Vomiting or diarrhea can also deplete your liquid and salt levels. Anhydrotic heat exhaustion, caused by an inability to sweat, is quite rare. Unlike the other forms of heat exhaustion it is likely to strike people who have been in Jamaica's hot climate for some time, rather than newcomers.

The key is to maintain an adequate level of liquids. Avoid booze by day, as your body uses water to process alcohol. Drink water, soft drinks, or – best of all – coconut water straight from the husk.

Heat Stroke This serious, sometimes fatal, condition can occur if the body's heat-regulating mechanism breaks down and the body temperature rises to dangerous levels. Long, continuous periods of exposure to high temperatures can leave you vulnerable to heat stroke. You should avoid excessive alcohol or strenuous activity when you first arrive in Jamaica.

The symptoms are feeling unwell, not sweating very much or at all and a high body temperature. Where sweating has ceased the skin becomes flushed and red. Severe, throbbing headaches and lack of co-ordination will also occur, and the sufferer may be confused or aggressive. Eventually the victim will become delirious or covulse. Hospitalization is essential, but meanwhile get victims out of the sun, remove their clothing, cover them with a wet sheet or towel, and fan them continually.

Fungal Infections Hot weather fungal infections are most likely to occur on the scalp, between the toes or fingers (athlete's foot), in the groin (jock itch or crotch rot) and on the body (ringworm). You get ringworm (which is a fungal infection, not a worm) from infected animals or by walking on damp areas, like shower floors.

To prevent fungal infections, wear loose, comfortable clothes, avoid artificial fibers, wash frequently, and dry carefully. If you do get an infection, wash the infected area daily with a disinfectant or medicated soap and water, and rinse and dry well. Apply an antifungal powder like the widely available Tinaderm. Try to expose the infected area to air or sunlight as much as possible and wash all towels and underwear in hot water as well as changing them often.

Cold Too much cold is just as dangerous as too much heat, particularly if it leads to hypothermia. This will only affect you if you're hiking to Blue Mountain Peak or elsewhere at higher elevations in Jamaica's mountains. If so, be prepared for cold, wet or windy conditions.

Hypothermia occurs when the body loses heat faster than it can produce it and the core temperature of the body falls. It is surprisingly easy to progress from very cold to dangerously cold due to a combination of wind, wet clothing, fatigue, and hunger. It is best to dress in layers; silk, wool, and some of the new artificial fibers are all good insulating materials. A hat is important, as a lot of heat is lost through the head. A strong, waterproof outer layer is essential, as keeping dry is vital.

To treat hypothermia, first get the person out of the wind and/or rain, remove their clothing if it's wet and replace it with dry, warm clothing. Give them hot liquids – not alcohol – and some high-calorie, easily digestible food. Do not rub victims but place them near a fire or in a warm (not hot) bath. This should be enough for the early stages of hypothermia, but if it has gone further it may be necessary to place victims in warm sleeping bags and get in with them.

Motion Sickness Eating lightly before and during a trip will reduce the chances of motion sickness. Find a place that minimizes disturbance – near the wing on aircraft, close to midship on boats, near the on buses. Fresh air usually helps, reading or cigarette smoke doesn't. Commercial anti-motion-sickness preparations, which can cause drowsiness, have to be taken before the trip commences; when you're feeling sick it's too late. Ginger is a natural preventative and is available in capsule form.

Jet Lag Travelers arriving in Jamaica from North America will feel relatively minor effects, if any. Those coming from Europe and further afield will be more susceptible.

The effects will usually be gone within three days of arrival, but there are ways of minimizing the impact of jet lag:

- Rest for a couple of days prior to departure; try to avoid late nights and last-minute dashes.
- Try to select flight schedules that minimize sleep deprivation; arriving late in the day means you can go to sleep soon after you arrive. For very long flights, try to organize a stopover.
- Eye drops and nasal sprays can help alleviate the ill effects of 'dry,' recirculated cabin air.
- Avoid excessive eating and alcohol during the flight. Instead, drink plenty of non-carbonated, non-alcoholic drinks such as fruit juice or water.
- Make yourself comfortable by wearing loose-fitting clothes and perhaps bringing an eye mask and ear plugs to help you sleep.

Diseases of Poor Sanitation

Diarrhea A change of water, food, or climate can all cause the runs. Despite all your precautions you may still have a bout of mild travelers' diarrhea but a few rushed toilet trips with no other symptoms is not indicative of a serious problem. Moderate diarrhea, involving half-a-dozen loose movements in a day, is more of a nuisance. Dehydration is the main danger with any diarrhea, particularly for children. Fluid replacement remains the mainstay of management. Weak black tea with a little sugar, soda water, or soft drinks allowed to go flat and diluted 50% with water are all good. With severe diarrhea a rehydrating solution is necessary to replace minerals and salts. Commercially available oral rehydration salts are very useful. Stick to a bland diet as you recover.

Lomotil or Imodium can be used to bring relief from the symptoms, although they do not actually cure the problem. Only use these drugs if absolutely necessary – eg, if you *must* travel. For children Imodium is preferable, but under all circumstances fluid replacement is the main message. Do not use these drugs if the person has a high fever or is severely dehydrated.

Giardiasis The parasite causing this intestinal disorder is present in contaminated water. The symptoms are stomach cramps, nausea, a bloated stomach, watery, foul-smelling diarrhea and frequent gas. Giardiasis can appear several weeks after you have been exposed to the parasite. The symptoms may disappear for a few days and then return; this can go on for several weeks.

Dysentery This is caused by contaminated food or water and is characterized by severe diarrhea, often with blood or mucus in the stool. There are two kinds of dysentery: bacillary, characterized by a high fever and rapid onset, headache, vomiting and stomach pains; and amoebic, which is often more gradual in the onset of symptoms, with cramping abdominal pain and vomiting less likely; fever may not be present. A stool test is necessary to diagnose which kind of dysentery you have, so you should seek medical help urgently.

Cholera Jamaica has not had a cholera outbreak in many years, although it is present on Haiti and in nearby Central American countries, where large-scale outbreaks occurred in 1994 and 1995. Cholera vaccination is not very effective. The bacteria responsible for this disease are waterborne. Outbreaks of cholera are generally widely reported, so you can avoid such problem areas. Attention to the rules of eating and drinking should protect the traveler.

Viral Gastroenteritis This is caused not by bacteria but, as the name suggests, by a virus. It is characterized by stomach cramps, diarrhea, and sometimes by vomiting and/or a slight fever. All you can do is rest and drink lots of fluids.

Hepatitis Hepatitis A is a very common problem amongst travelers to areas with poor sanitation. With good water and adequate sewage disposal in most industrialized countries since the 1940s, very few young adults now have any natural immunity and must be protected with the new vaccine Havrix or the short-lasting antibody gamma globulin.

The disease is spread by contaminated food or water. The symptoms are fever, chills, headache, fatigue, feelings of weakness and aches and pains, followed by loss of appetite, nausea, vomiting, abdominal pain, dark urine, light-colored feces, jaundiced skin and the whites of the eyes may turn yellow. In some cases you may feel unwell, tired, have no appetite, experience aches and pains and be jaundiced. You should seek medical advice, but in general there is not much you can do apart from rest, drink lots of fluids, eat lightly and avoid fatty foods. People who have had

hepatitis must forego alcohol for six months after the illness, as hepatitis attacks the liver and it needs that amount of time to recover.

Hepatitis B, which used to be called serum hepatitis, is spread through contact with infected blood, blood products, or bodily fluids, for example through sexual contact, unsterilized needles, and blood transfusions. Other risk situations include having a shave or tattoo in a local shop, or having your ears pierced. The symptoms of type B are much the same as type A except that they are more severe and may lead to irreparable liver damage or even liver cancer.

Although there is no treatment for hepatitis B, an effective prophylactic vaccine is readily available in most countries. The immunization schedule requires two injections at least a month apart followed by a third dose five months after the second. Persons who should receive a hepatitis B vaccination include anyone who anticipates contact with blood or other bodily secretions, either as a health care worker or through sexual contact with the local population, particularly those who intend to stay in Jamaica for a long period of time.

Hepatitis Non-A Non-B is a blanket term formerly used for several different strains of hepatitis, which have now been separately identified. Hepatitis C is similar to B, but is less common. Hepatitis D (the 'delta particle') is also similar to B and always occurs in concert with it; its occurrence is currently limited to IV drug users. Hepatitis E, however, is similar to A, and it is spread in the same manner, by water or food contamination.

Tests are available for these strands, but are very expensive. Travelers shouldn't be too paranoid about this apparent proliferation of hepatitis strains; they are fairly rare (so far) and following the same precautions as for A and B should be all that's necessary to avoid them.

Typhoid Contaminated water and food are responsible. Vaccination against typhoid is not totally effective and it is one of the most dangerous infections, so medical help must be sought. An outbreak of typhoid struck the southwest corner of Jamaica in 1992 and was attributed to contaminated dairy products.

In its early stages typhoid resembles many other illnesses: sufferers may feel like they have a bad cold or flu on the way, as early symptoms are a headache, a sore throat, and a fever which rises a little each day until it is around 40°C or more. The victim's pulse is often slow relative to the degree of fever present and gets slower as the fever rises – unlike a normal fever where the pulse increases. There may also be vomiting, diarrhea or constipation.

In the second week the high fever and slow pulse continue and a few pink spots may appear on the body; trembling, delirium, weakness, weight loss and dehydration are other symptoms. If there are no further complications, the fever and other symptoms will slowly go during the third week. However you must get medical help before this because pneumonia (acute infection of the lungs) or peritonitis (perforated bowel) are common complications, and because typhoid is very infectious.

The fever should be treated by keeping the victim cool and dehydration should also be watched for.

Worms These parasites are common in rural, tropical areas and a stool test when you return home is not a bad idea. They can be present on unwashed vegetables or in undercooked meat and you can pick them up through your skin by walking in bare feet. Infestations may not show up for some time, and although they are generally not serious, if left untreated they can cause severe health problems.

Diseases Spread by People & Animals
Tetanus This potentially fatal disease is present in Jamaica as in other undeveloped tropical areas. It is difficult to treat but is preventable with immunization. Tetanus occurs when a wound becomes infected by a germ which lives in the feces of animals or people, so clean all cuts, punctures or animal bites. Tetanus is also known as

lockjaw, and the first symptom may be discomfort in swallowing, or stiffening of the jaw and neck; this is followed by painful convulsions of the jaw and whole body.

Sexually Transmitted Diseases There's a high prevalence of venereal diseases in Jamaica. Sexual contact with an infected sexual partner spreads these diseases. While abstinence is the only 100% preventative, using condoms is also effective. Gonorrhea and syphilis are the most common of these diseases; sores, blisters, or rashes around the genitals, discharges or pain when urinating are common symptoms. Symptoms may be less marked or not observed at all in women. Syphilis symptoms eventually disappear completely but the disease continues and can cause severe problems, and even death, in later years. The treatment of gonorrhea and syphilis is by antibiotics.

There is no cure for herpes and there is also currently no cure for AIDS.

Condoms are widely available in pharmacies and general stores throughout Jamaica. Nonetheless, they may not be available when you need them. It's a good idea for both men and women to take condoms with them. After all, this is Jamaica, you are on vacation, and who knows what passionate moment might brighten your travel experience.

HIV/AIDS HIV, the Human Immunodeficiency Virus, may develop into AIDS, Acquired Immune Deficiency Syndrome. HIV is a relatively small yet not insignificant problem in Jamaica. Any exposure to blood, blood products, or bodily fluids may put the individual at risk. In Jamaica, transmission is predominantly through heterosexual sexual activity. Apart from abstinence, the most effective preventative is always to practice safe sex using condoms. It is impossible to detect the HIV-positive status of an otherwise healthy-looking person without a blood test.

HIV/AIDS can also be spread through infected blood transfusions; most developing countries cannot afford to screen blood for transfusions. It can also be spread by dirty needles – vaccinations, acupuncture, tattooing, and ear or nose piercing can potentially be as dangerous as intravenous drug use if the equipment is not clean. If you do need an injection, ask to see the syringe unwrapped in front of you, or better still, take a needle and syringe pack with you overseas – it is a cheap insurance package against infection.

Fear of HIV infection should never preclude treatment for serious medical conditions. Although there may be a risk of infection, it is very small indeed.

Insect-Borne Diseases

Malaria Fortunately malaria isn't present in Jamaica. It's spread by mosquito bites, but among Caribbean islands is relegated to Hispaniola (Haiti and Dominican Republic) and, to a lesser degree, Cuba.

Dengue Fever Although extremely rare, dengue fever is present on all Caribbean islands. There is no prophylactic available for this mosquito-spread disease. A sudden onset of fever, headaches, and severe joint and muscle pains (hence it's colloquial name, 'broken bone disease') are the first signs before a rash starts on the trunk of the body and spreads to the limbs and face. After a further few days, the fever will subside and recovery will begin. Serious complications are not common.

Try to avoid being bitten by mosquitoes. The mosquitoes that transmit dengue fever most commonly bite from dusk to dawn and during this period travelers are advised to wear light colored clothing, wear long pants and long sleeved shirts, use mosquito repellents containing the compound DEET on exposed areas, avoid highly scented perfumes or after-shave, and use a mosquito net – it may be worth taking your own.

Chagas' Disease In rural areas this parasitic disease is transmitted by a bug that hides in crevices and palm fronds and often takes up residence in the thatched roofs of huts. It comes out to feed at night. A hard, violet-colored swelling appears at the site of the bite in about a week. Usually the body overcomes the disease unaided, but sometimes it continues and can eventually lead to death years later. Chagas' disease can be treated in its early stages, but it is best to avoid thatched-roof huts, sleep under a mosquito net, use insecticides and insect repellents, and check for hidden insects.

Typhus Typhus is spread by ticks, mites, or lice. It begins as a bad cold, followed by a fever, chills, headache, muscle pains, and a body rash. There is often a large painful sore at the site of the bite and nearby lymph nodes are swollen and painful.

Check your skin carefully for ticks after walking in a danger area, such as a tropical forest. A strong insect repellent can help, and serious walkers in tick areas should consider having their boots and trousers impregnated with benzyl benzoate and dibutylphthalate.

Cuts & Scratches

Skin punctures can easily become infected in hot climates and may be difficult to heal. Treat any cut with an antiseptic such as Betadine. Where possible avoid bandages and Band-aids, which can keep wounds wet. Coral cuts are notoriously slow to heal, as the coral injects a weak venom into the wound. Avoid coral cuts by wearing shoes when walking on reefs, and clean any cut thoroughly with sodium peroxide if available.

Bites & Stings

Bee and wasp stings are usually painful rather than dangerous. Calamine lotion will give relief or ice packs will reduce the pain and swelling. There are some spiders with dangerous bites but antivenins are usually available.

There are various fish and other sea creatures that can sting or bite dangerously or that are dangerous to eat. Again, local advice is the best suggestion. Fortunately, Jamaica has no venomous snakes. What it does have in abundance in specific beach locales is no-see-'ums.

No-See-'Ums These well-named irritants are almost microscopically small fleas that hang out on beaches and appear around dusk (especially after rain) with a voracious appetite. Their bite is out of all proportion to their size. You'll rarely, if ever, see the darn things, despite the fact that they seem to attack en masse, seemingly when you're not looking. They prefer the taste of ankles, and have a predilection for diners at open restaurants by the shore. Cover your ankles if possible. Most insect repellents don't faze them. A better bet is a liberal application of Avon's Skin So Soft, a cosmetic that even the US Army swears by.

Jellyfish Local advice is the best way of avoiding contact with these sea creatures with their stinging tentacles. Dousing in vinegar will de-activate any stingers that have not 'fired.' Calamine lotion, antihistamines, and analgesics may reduce the reaction and relieve the pain.

Bedbugs & Lice Bedbugs live in various places, but particularly in dirty mattresses and bedding. Spots of blood on bedclothes or on the wall around the bed can be read as a suggestion to find another hotel. Bedbugs leave itchy bites in neat rows. Calamine lotion may help.

All lice cause itching and discomfort. They make themselves at home in your hair (head lice), your clothing (body lice), or in your pubic hair (crabs). You catch lice through direct contact with infected people or by sharing combs, clothing, and the like. Powder or shampoo treatment will kill the lice and infected clothing should then be washed in very hot water.

Scabies Scabies is an infestation of microscopic mites and is acquired through sexual contact, but may also be transmitted through linen, towels, or clothing. Scabies is very common in Jamaica among people living in rustic conditions.

The first signs – severe itching caused by infestation of eggs and feces under the skin – usually appear three to four weeks after infestation (as soon as 24 hours for second infestations) and is worse at night. Infestation appears as tiny welts and pimples, often in a dotted line, most commonly around the groin and lower abdomen, between the fingers, on the elbows and under the armpits. Other bacterial skin infections may occur.

Treatment is by pesticidal lotions (prescription-only in the USA) sold over-the-counter at local pharmacies in Jamaica. The entire body must be covered. Often two treatments within 48 hours are required. Personal hygiene is critical to exterminating the mites. At the same time as using the treatment, you must wash *all* your clothing and bedding in hot water.

Leeches Leeches may be present in damp rain forest conditions; they attach themselves to your skin to suck your blood. Hikers often get them on their legs or in their boots. Salt or a lighted cigarette end will make them fall off. Do not pull them off, as the bite is then more likely to become infected. An insect repellent may keep them away.

Women's Health

Poor diet, lowered resistance due to the use of antibiotics and even contraceptive pills can lead to vaginal infections. Wearing skirts or loose-fitting trousers and cotton underwear will help to prevent infections while traveling in hot climates.

Yeast infections, characterized by a rash, itch, and discharge, can be treated with a vinegar or even lemon-juice douche or with yogurt. Nystatin suppositories are the usual medical prescription.

Trichomoniasis is a more serious infection; symptoms are a discharge and a burning sensation when urinating. Male sexual partners must also be treated, and if a vinegar-water douche is not effective, medical attention should be sought. Metronidazole (Flagyl) is the prescribed drug.

If you are pregnant, take note that most miscarriages occur during the first three months of pregnancy, so this is the most risky time to travel as far as your own health is concerned. The last three months should also be spent within reasonable distance of good medical care.

You may find that your periods become irregular or even cease while on the road. Remember that a missed period in these circumstances doesn't necessarily indicate pregnancy. There are health posts or family planning clinics in urban centers throughout Jamaica, where you can seek advice and have a urine test to determine whether you are pregnant or not.

Health Facilities

Jamaica's health service is administered jointly by Parish Councils and the Ministry of Health and Environmental Control. Together they operate 23 general hospitals and seven specialist hospitals. Hospitals are located in most major towns and cities, including Kingston, Montego Bay, Falmouth, Mandeville, and Port Antonio. The nearest hospital to Ocho Rios is in St Ann's, about 10 miles west; the nearest hospitals to Negril are 20 miles away, in Lucea and Savanna-la-Mar. Most maintain 24-hour emergency wards.

You'll find health clinics in towns throughout the island. In addition, most large hotels have resident nurses, plus doctors on call.

The following are the leading hospitals (* denotes private hospitals):

Kingston
Andrews Memorial Hospital*	☎ 926-7401
Bustamante Hospital for Children	☎ 926-5721
Kingston Public Hospital	☎ 922-0210
Medical Associates Hospital*	☎ 926-1400
Nuttall Memorial Hospital	☎ 926-2139
St Joseph's Hospital*	☎ 928-4955
University of West Indies Hospital	☎ 927-1620

Mandeville
Hargreaves Memorial Hospital*	☎ 962-2040
Mandeville Hospital	☎ 962-2067

Montego Bay
Cornwall Regional Hospital	☎ 952-5100
Doctor's Hospital*	☎ 952-1616

Port Antonio
Port Antonio Hospital	☎ 993-2646

St Ann's Bay/Ocho Rios
St Ann's Bay Hospital	☎ 972-0150

Ambulances

The emergency number for public ambulances is ☎ 110.

The St John's ambulance brigade also provides a free ambulance service in Kingston (☎ 926-7656) and Ocho Rios (☎ 974-5126). Deluxe Ambulance Service has a 24-hour emergency service in Kingston (☎ 923-7415).

Wings Jamaica also provides a local and overseas 24-hour air ambulance service (☎ 923-6573 or 923-5416), as does Karvinair Air Ambulance (☎ 978-4913).

Medical Assistance Organizations

Many companies offer medical assistance for travelers. Most maintain 24-hour emergency hot-line centers that connect travelers to professional medical staff worldwide. Many also provide emergency evacuation, medical attention, and payment of on-site medical treatment. Some provide services for a set annual membership fee; others offer varying coverage levels.

The Council on International Education Exchange (CIEE) offers low-cost short-term insurance policies called 'Trip Safe' to holders of the International Student Identification Card (ISIC), International Youth Card (IYC), and International Teachers Identification Card (ITIC).

North American medical assistance organizations include:

Access America
    This company offers travel insurance and 24-hour emergency, travel, medical, and legal assistance. PO Box 6600 W Broad St No 11188, Richmond, VA 23230 (☎ (800) 284-8300)
Air Ambulance Professionals
    You can receive 24-hour worldwide medical transportation, with all flights staffed by 'aeromedically certified medical attendants.' Ft Lauderdale Executive Airport, 1575 W Commercial Blvd, Annex 2, Ft Lauderdale, FL 33309
ICT Travelers Assistance
    ICT offers free medical aid, including ambulance, hospitalization, medication, and emergency evacuation. PO Box G-759, Station G, Calgary AB, T3A 2G6, Canada (☎ (403) 228-4685, fax (403) 228-6271)

International Association for Medical Assistance
  for Travelers
    IAMAT is an information service to assist
    travelers needing medical attention. In the
    USA, 417 Center St, Lewiston, NY 14092
    (☎ (716) 754-4883). In Canada, 40 Regal Rd,
    Guelph ON, N1K 1B5
MEDEX/TravMed
    This company advises on where to obtain
    medical assistance. It monitors and pays for
    health care, and can arrange for emergency
    medical evacuation and repatriation. ITAA,
    PO Box 10623, Baltimore, MD 21285
    (☎ (800) 732-5309)
Travel Assistance International
    TAI emergency service includes on-the-spot
    payment for medical expenses, medical evac-
    uation, medication, repatriation of children,
    and other travel expenses. 1133 15th St NW
    No 400, Washington, DC 20005 (☎ (202)
    331-1609, fax (202) 331-1588)
Travel Care International
    This company specializes in medical evacua-
    tions around the world. PO Box 846, Eagle
    River, WI 54521 (☎ (715) 479-8881)
Worldcare Travel Assistance Association
    Worldcare provides medical assistance, hos-
    pital coverage, and evacuation. It provides
    immediate payment of medical costs
    abroad, plus round-trip airfare for a family
    member during hospitalizations of over 10
    days. 605 Market St No 1300, San Fran-
    cisco, CA 94105 (☎ (415) 541-4991 or
    (800) 666-4993)

TOILETS

The few public toilet facilities that do exist
are places to avoid.

Many Jamaican men think nothing of
pissing in public.

WOMEN TRAVELERS
Attitudes toward Women

'Political correctness' hasn't yet filtered
down through Jamaican society. Many
Jamaican men display behavior and attitudes that might shock Western women and
feminists. They'll often make a vocal
public display of a women's bodily assets:
*'Hey, Miss World . . . Yo' big roun batty get
mi so, so 'ard!'* Whether or not you accept
it as such, it's meant as a compliment.
Jamaican women can be equally forthright.
Casual sexual liaisons are a norm in

Jamaican society, especially in poorer
classes where there's little equivocation;
little of the romancing typical of most
Western couplings. If a Jamaican finds you
attractive, he or she is likely to point out
your physical attributes and offer a straightforward invitation to sexual bliss.

Many foreign women welcome these
advances, as evidenced by the proliferation
of 'rent a dreads' – basically, Jamaican
good time guys, or gigolos – on the arms of
North American and European women.

If this behavior is offensive, don't beat
about the bush for fear of hurting the man's
feeling. Give him an inch, so to speak, and
he'll take a yard. Jamaicans respect direct-
ness. Say 'No!' in certain terms. He'll most
likely take your rejection in good humor,
with a bawdy jibe at your lack of good
taste.

More educated Jamaican men tend to be
more respectful.

Safety Precautions

Women traveling alone can reduce unwanted attention by dressing modestly
when away from the beach. You should
avoid walking alone at night, hitchhiking,
and otherwise traveling alone in remote
areas. If you're driving alone, be discreet
about those you choose to give rides to.

Organizations & Resources

Women's organizations in Jamaica include:

Woman's Crisis Center
    18 Ripon Rd, Kingston 5 (☎ 929-2997)
Women's Center of Jamaica Foundation
    42 Trafalgar Rd, Kingston 10
    (☎ 929-7608)
The Woman's Club
    101 Hope Rd, Kingston 6 (☎ 927-0678)
Women's Resource & Outreach Center
    47 Beechwood Ave, Kingston 5
    (☎ 929-6945)

Good resources abroad include the Inter-
national Federation of Women's Travel
Organizations, 4545 N 36th St No 126,
Phoenix, AZ 85018 (☎ (602) 956-7175).
The *Handbook for Women Travelers* by
Maggie & Gemma Ross (Piatkus Books)

and *The Traveling Woman* by Dean Kaye (Doubleday & Co) are also replete with handy tips and practicalities.

GAY & LESBIAN TRAVELERS

Jamaica is an adamantly homophobic nation. In fact homosexual intercourse between men is illegal. Intolerance has found its way into the lyrics of several leading reggae and dancehall artists, such as Buju Banton and Shabba Ranks, whose advocacy of 'gay bashing' reflects – and no doubt sponsors – the bigoted mind-set.

I cannot recall ever having seen any overtly gay Jamaicans – intolerance is too great. Most Jamaican gays are still in the closet.

Likewise, the attitude of the majority of Jamaicans towards HIV and AIDS is insufferably narrow, and sympathy for those struck by the disease is pitifully lacking.

Organizations & Resources

I'm not aware of any gay and lesbian support groups in Jamaica, but the following organizations can provide information and assistance in planning a trip:

Gay & Lesbian Travel Services Network
    2300 Market St No 142, San Francisco, CA 94114 (☎ (415) 552-5140, fax (415) 552-5104, email: gaytvlinfo@aol.com)
International Gay Travel Association
    PO Box 18247, Denver, CO 80218 (☎ (303) 860-9105)
International Gay & Lesbian Association
    208 W 13th St, New York, NY 10001 (☎ (212) 620-7310)
    81 rue Marche au Charbon, 1000 Brussels, Belgium (☎ 32-2-502-2471)

Ferrari Publications produces several travel guides for gays and lesbians, including the *Spartacus International Gay Guide* (PO Box 37887, Phoenix, AZ 85069, ☎ (602) 863-2408, fax (602) 439-3952). Another valuable resource is *Odysseus: The International Gay Travel Planner* (PO Box 1548, Port Washington, New York, NY 11050, ☎ (516) 944-5330, fax (516) 944-7540).

DISABLED TRAVELERS

Disabled travelers will need to plan their vacation carefully, as few allowances have been made in Jamaica. However, things have begun to change in recent years, partly as a result of lobbying by Derrick Palmer, director of Disabled Persons International at 11 Carlton Crescent (PO Box 220, Kingston 6, ☎ 929-2073 or 929-0575).

Only a small percentage of hotels in Jamaica have facilities for disabled travelers. The JTB or Derrick Palmer can provide a list of hotels with wheelchair ramps, etc. Check with the individual hotel before making your reservation. Fortunately, many hotels are one-story affairs. Most hotels and restaurants in Negril are at ground level.

New construction codes mandate ramps and parking spots for disabled people at shopping plazas and other select sites.

Organizations & Resources

Contact the following for more information:

Society for the Advancement of Travel for the Handicapped
    Annual membership costs US$45. They publish a quarterly magazine *Access to Travel* (subscriptions cost $13). 347 Fifth Ave No 610, New York, NY 10016 (☎ (212) 447-7284, fax (212) 725-8253)
American Foundation for the Blind
    15 W 16th St, New York, NY 10011 (☎ (212) 620-2000)
Travel Information Service
    Provides an information pack (US$5) listing accessible hotels, restaurants, and attractions. Moss Rehabilitation Hospital, 1200 W Tabor Rd, Philadelphia, PA 19141 (☎ (215) 456-9600)
Air Transportation of Handicapped Persons
    A free pamphlet distributed by the US Dept of Transportation. Write: Free Advisory Pamphlet No AC12032, Distribution Unit, US Dept of Transportation, Publications Division, M-4332, Washington, DC 20590
The Wheelchair Traveler
    A handy newsletter. 23 Ball Hill Rd, Milford, NH 03055, (☎ (603) 673-4539)

SENIOR TRAVELERS

One-third of travelers worldwide are over 50, and travel companies court seniors with discounts, usually passed on to members of seniors' organizations. Most US airlines offer senior discount programs for travelers 62 or over. Some car rental companies also extend discounts – ask and you may receive!

Unfortunately, Jamaica seems virtually devoid of seniors' discounts. Only a handful of hotels offer them. There's no harm in asking, but don't be surprised to get 'no' for an answer.

SAGA International Holidays (120 Boylston St, Boston, MA 02116, ☎ (800) 343-0273) and Golden Companions (Box 754, Pullman, WA 99163, ☎ (509) 334-9351) specialize in all-inclusive tours for seniors, although neither had trips to Jamaica in 1995.

Organizations & Resources

The American Association of Retired Persons (AARP) offers discounts on hotels, car rentals, etc, through its Purchase Privilege Program (1909 K St NW, Washington, DC 20049, ☎ (800) 441-7575). It also arranges travel for members through AARP Travel Experience. Annual membership costs US$8. The Golden Age Travelers Club offers similar services (Pier 27, The Embarcadero, San Francisco, CA 94111, ☎ (800) 258-8880).

Another handy source of tips on seniors discounts is the monthly newsletter of the National Council of Senior Citizens (925 15th St NW, Washington, DC 20005, ☎ (202) 347-8800).

TRAVEL WITH CHILDREN

Jamaica courts the family traveler aggressively, and the larger hotels compete by providing facilities for children. Most hotels provide a babysitter or nanny by advance request. Several all-inclusive resorts, such as Poinciana (Negril), FDR Resort (Runaway Bay), and Breezes Boscobel Beach (Boscobel, near Ocho Rios) cater specifically to families and have a full range of activities and amenities for children. Most hotels also offer free accommodations or greatly reduced rates for children staying in their parents' room (a child is usually defined as being 12 years or younger, but some count those 16 or younger).

It's a good idea to pre-arrange necessities such as cribs, baby-sitters, cots, and baby food.

Villas and apartments are good options for families. Most come fully staffed, allowing you to leave the children with the housekeeper if you feel comfortable doing so (you'll need to check that this is in accordance with rental terms).

Travel with Children by Lonely Planet cofounder Maureen Wheeler (Lonely Planet Publications) gives you the low-down on preparing for family travel. Another handy resource is *The Family Travel Guide Catalog* published by Carousel Press. You can also subscribe to *Family Travel Times Newsletter* (80 Eighth Ave, New York, NY 10011, ☎ (212) 206-0688).

USEFUL ORGANIZATIONS

Jamaica Information Service This service dispenses all kinds of information, mostly geared to domestic issues such as housing law, government regulations, health issues, etc. The head office is at 58a Half Way Tree Rd, Kingston 10 (☎ 926-3740, fax 926-6715), and there are offices in most major cities. I've found most to be well-stocked with pamphlets.

Jamaica National Heritage Trust A branch of the Institute of Jamaica, the trust is dedicated to preserving, restoring, and maintaining more than 300 declared monuments nationwide. Its offices are at 79 Duke St, Headquarters House, in Kingston (PO Box 8934; ☎ 922-1287, fax 967-1703). It maintains the Jamaica Archives (☎ 984-2581) and Archives Record Dept (☎ 984-3041) in Spanish Town. Both are treasure troves for tracking down family histories and other historical data.

Institute of Jamaica This institute (☎ 922-6020) has reading rooms at 12 East St, Kingston. It publishes the *Jamaica Journal* and is responsible for maintaining six small museums in the Kingston area: the Arawak Museum and Old Kings House (in Spanish Town), Fort Charles, the National Museum of

Historical Archaeology, and the Forces Museum in Upton Park Camp.

British Council Brits who sorely miss their favorite newspaper will find the latest dailies available in the information library at this office in the First Mutual Life Bldg at 64 Knutsford Blvd (☎ 929-6915, fax 929-7090).

DANGERS & ANNOYANCES

For all its tropical beauty and charm, Jamaica has plenty of petty annoyances and can even be psychologically intimidating and scary. It helps to have a sense of humor.

The JTB publishes a pocket-sized pamphlet, 'Helpful Hints for your Vacation,' containing concise tips for safer travel.

In addition, the US State Dept publishes travel advisories that advise US citizens of trouble spots (Citizens Emergency Center, Room 4811, Dept of State, Washington, DC 20520-4818). Advisories are available by recorded telephone message ☎ (202) 647-5225) or by fax (202) 647-3000), and at US embassies and consulates abroad. You can also get advisories on the Internet (http://www.stolaf.edu/network/traveladvisories.html). However, the warnings are often out of date.

Undertows Those gorgeous coral reefs beg to be explored, and the turquoise waters are seductive sirens. How can you resist the temptation? You don't have to . . . but be aware that many places have dangerous undertows. This is particularly true along the east and south coasts, where you should never swim alone off isolated beaches. Long Bay is especially dangerous for its whipping undertows. Seek local advice about conditions before swimming.

Hurricanes Public warnings will be issued if a hurricane is due to come ashore. In the event of a hurricane, seek shelter in the sturdiest structure you can find. (For more on hurricane seasons, see the Climate section in Facts about Jamaica.)

Fearsome Flora The manchineel tree, which grows along the Jamaican shoreline,

produces small applelike green fruits. Don't eat them – they're highly poisonous! Take care not to sit beneath the tree either, as the raindrops running off the leaves onto your skin can cause blisters.

Critters to Beware Sea urchins cluster in great numbers on the seabed. Their porcupinelike spines are designed for defense. If you step on one, the 'quills' will pierce your skin and break off. They're agonizingly painful. You must remove the spine and treat the wound with antiseptic (it's a good idea to see a doctor, too).

Jamaica's benign-looking reef system harbors other nasty critters, not least the bristleworm, whose brittle bristles act like those of a prickly-pear cactus: one touch and you're impaled by tiny needles that detach as keepsakes. A white-tipped, yellowish brown, coral-look-alike (which isn't actually a coral), fire coral is so named for the severe burning sensation it causes when brushed up against.

Moray eels – plump gray-green critters – like nothing so much as an undisturbed life in their nooks and crannies amid the reef. They're curious creatures, though, and pop their heads out to keep an eye on things. Mindless divers often reach out to pet them. *Don't!* Their bite can do devastating damage.

The deadly scorpionfish is also present. It sits on the seabed and resembles the rocks and corals around it and is thus difficult to spot. Its raised spines inflict venom that can be fatal to humans. Likewise, stingrays often lie buried in sand; if you tread on one, its tail may slash you with a venomous spike. When wading in sandy shallows, it's a good idea to *slide* your feet along the sea bed to avoid stepping on the otherwise harmless rays.

Poisonous jellyfish also pulse in Jamaica's waters in late summer.

Swimming is usually no problem in the presence of sharks. Mostly, they're harmless nurse sharks. Fortunately, these dangerous-looking beasts (which can grow up to 12 feet long) are well fed and wary. Still, they'll attack in self-defense if provoked or cornered. Give them plenty of room.

Two-thirds of coral species are poisonous – another reason to remember, *hands off!*

See the Health section on some hints on how to relieve the stings and scratches.

Cockroaches This being the tropics, cockroaches are everywhere in Jamaica. Many are veritable giants! Even the fanciest hotels have them. You may not be used to them, and many visitors find the ugly bugs repugnant. However, they're not really a health problem, except in restaurants, where they can contaminate food.

'Hey, Whitey!' If you're white, Jamaicans will call you 'whitey!' or their own witty names: 'Hey! Kenny Rogers,' or 'Yo! Miss World.' Jamaican children in remote areas will call out 'whitey' as your drive by. They mean no offense.

Soon Come! The service in many five-star hotels, especially the all-inclusive resorts, is superb. But much of the rest of Jamaica has yet to discover that good service equates to good business. Two hoteliers in particular – Gordon 'Butch' Stewart and John Issa – have been at the forefront of elevating standards of quality and service. If you can't handle occasional surly service and the fact that things happen when they happen, you're in the wrong place. A phrase you'll hear often is 'Soon come!,' which really means: 'Hey, relax . . . what's the rush?'

My friend, Jamaican-born photographer Cookie Kincaid, told me a story that exemplifies Jamaicans' lackadaisical approach to life: a tourist had arrived at Kingston airport and went to a car rental company to pick up a car he'd reserved through his travel agency. There was no record of his reservation, and no cars were available. The receptionist was no help: 'Me know not'n' about it, mon!,' she said, brushing him off disdainfully. Eventually he persuades her to call her head office. She sits with the phone to her ear for an eternity. He watches, exasperated, as she files her nails with the phone all the while tucked in the crease of her neck. Eventually he asks her if anyone has answered yet. 'No, mon,' she replies, 'de phone line is busy!'

Driving Hazards Many Jamaican drivers rank high among the world's rudest and least cautious drivers. Jamaica has the third highest fatality rate for drivers in the world – behind Ethiopia and India – with a staggering 343 fatalities per 100,000 cars (compared to 26 per 100,000 in the US, and 22 per 100,000 in the UK). For tips on road safety, see the Driving Conditions section under Car & Motorcycle in the Getting Around chapter.

The main coastal highway is generally in good repair. However, be prepared for potholes, the consistent bane of secondary roads. Signs are few and far between, so you may need to ask directions frequently. Slow down for those hairpin bends!

People standing beside the road and animals that are inclined to dash in front of you are other obstacles to avoid.

Harassment Most Jamaicans are cheery, helpful, law-abiding folks with a concern to make a foreign visitor's experience as positive as possible. Jamaica's biggest on-going problem, however, is the large number of hustlers who harass visitors. A hustler is someone who makes a living by seizing opportunities, and the biggest opportunity in Jamaica is *you*!

Hustlers walk the streets looking for potential customers to whom to sell crafts, jewelry, or drugs, to wash cars, give aloe vera massages, or offer any of a thousand varieties of services. They don't wait for you to come to them: they come to you. A sibilant *sssssst!* to catch your attention is the first indication that hustlers have their eyes on you. If you as much as glance in their direction, they'll attempt to reel you in like a flounder.

Aggressive persistence is key to their success and shaking them off can be a wearying process.

Don't underestimate the hustlers' understanding of human psychology. Jamaican hustlers are experts in consumer psychology. They have an instant answer for any excuse you might throw. Putting a guilt trip on you is a favorite trick. 'Sssst . . . . Hey mon! Remember me?' is another clever line to introduce and link themselves to you. Many hustlers show a total disrespect for visitors who reject their services by saying: 'Hey mon, why you disrespect me?'

The problem is so severe that a white Jamaican hotelier told me that many older people who've been coming to Jamaica for years no longer visit because they are still being hassled by the same hustlers who hassled them the last time. 'Jamaicans have ruined their own show,' he told me.

Play to the Jamaicans innate sense of humor. A wise crack can often break the icy confrontation and earn you respect. Alternately, a good defensive gambit is to play like a savvy local: 'Cho mon, doant harass de touris'!' Most hustlers are aware of the JTB's efforts to eradicate the problem.

If you want a hassle-free time, check into an all-inclusive resort. However, even though they prohibit vendors from trespassing, hustlers simply paddle in by canoe or on surf boards to sell their goods and services in the shallows.

In off-the-tourist-beat Kingston, you'll rarely be hassled. Here, hustlers tend to gravitate to captive audiences, such as at traffic lights, where two or three young men will feverishly begin to wash your car at a red light, even if you adamantly say 'No!'

If you hire a guide, don't expect him to do more than keep you from getting lost or keep other hustlers at bay. Establish parameters such as what he'll provide and for how much up front.

Protecting Tourism
The JTB emphasizes public education to stress the backward linkages of tourism to agriculture and other supply industries. A National Tourism and Education Training Council has been set up to educate youngsters to degree level. In 1993, the Ministry of Tourism initiated a Montego Bay Resort Patrol. And in 1995, J$67 million was allocated to projects aimed at curbing visitor harassment and increasing security and ease-of-passage in Ocho Rios. ∎

Drug Trade Marijuana *(ganja)* is everywhere in Jamaica, and you're almost certain to be approached by hustlers selling drugs on the streets. Cocaine has recently become widely available, too. In Ocho Rios, pushers are a constant plague. Clearly, enough visitors buy drugs to make the trade worthwhile.

Be warned that possession and use of drugs in Jamaica is strictly illegal and penalties are severe. Almost every day of the year, foreigners carrying drugs are arrested for street trading by undercover agents, and as they attempt to board aircraft at Kingston and Montego Bay airports. The arrests are announced on radio news shows. If you *do* buy drugs in Jamaica, don't be stupid enough to try to take any out of the country.

Also be aware that smoking a Jamaican spliff or chillum will pack an almighty punch compared to those skinny little joints you're used to back home. It's not unknown, too, to find that the cocaine you sniff is actually Ajax, or that your ganja has been sprayed with paraquat, is laced with crack cocaine, or is really dried croton.

Jamaican smugglers have earned notoriety for hiding contraband in cruise passengers' luggage! Until recently this was easy due to lack of security. In 1995, new cruise piers were completed in Montego Bay and all luggage going on the cruise ship and airport was sent by bonded truck. However, to solve the issue once and for all, Regency Cruises (the only company to homeberth in Jamaica) ceased business later that year.

If you plan on hiking or exploring the off-the-beaten-path, it's wise to do so with a local guide. Many areas in the hinterland are centers for ganja production. The US Drug Enforcement Agency (DEA) works closely with both the Jamaica Defence Force and Ministry of National Security to suppress the trade, and strangers (especially white travelers) are often suspected of being DEA undercover agents. If you accidentally stumble across a ganja plantation, you could put your life in jeopardy!

Crime Most Jamaicans are extremely law-abiding citizens. Their sense of honor and pride runs deep, and their tolerance of thieves and criminals is extremely low. The Gun Court, for example, is very popular (its trials are not public, and the punishments for anyone convicted of a crime with a gun are harsh). Jamaicans have even been known to stone or beat to death thieves caught in the act.

Nonetheless, the island's pervasive poverty fosters crime. Jamaica, and in particular Kingston, has the worst reputation in the Caribbean for violent crime. This is mostly related to drug wars fought in the ghettoes far from tourist centers, and violent crime intrudes very little on the visitor. The island as a whole is generally safe and the vast majority of travelers return home without having suffered any mishaps whatsoever.

Most crime against travelers is petty, opportunistic crime. Take sensible precautions with your valuables. Carry your wallet in your front pocket, or better, in a money belt or similar pouch beneath your clothing. Steer clear of ghettoes, where you can easily get into serious trouble. And don't wander on unlit streets at night, when you should stick close to main thoroughfares.

Muggings do occur, and several visitors have been robbed in their cars or hotel rooms. You should take adequate precautions. Keep hotel doors and windows securely locked at night. Don't open your door at night to anyone who cannot prove his or her identity. If you are going to be camping, take care in choosing your site. It is unsafe to camp in the wild, especially alone or in small groups. Be cautious if invited to see the 'real Jamaica' by a stranger. Use your discretion.

Crime against visitors has dropped 53% since the initiation of 'Operation Shining Armour' in June 1994 – a collaborative effort by the Ministry of Tourism and Ministry of National Security to combat the crime problem. Police operations were beefed up in tourist resorts. Villas and apartments were required to be fitted with security systems wired to a central police command. Major hotels also have security guards to protect the grounds (if you're renting an out-of-the-way private villa or cottage, check in advance with the rental agency to establish whether security is provided).

LEGAL MATTERS

Jamaica's drug and drunk-driving laws are strictly enforced. Don't expect leniency because you're a foreigner. Jamaican jails are Dickensian, and a stay here can ruin your vacation . . . and your life! Still, if you run afoul of the law and are arrested, insist on your rights to call your embassy in Kingston to request their assistance. They should be able to help with finding a lawyer, advising relatives, and providing counsel.

BUSINESS HOURS & HOLIDAYS

Most business offices are open Monday through Friday, 8:30 am to 4:30 pm. Very few offices are open on Saturdays.

Most stores open at either 8 or 9 am and close at 5 pm, except Saturday, when they are open until noon. Generally shops are closed on Sundays, except pharmacies.

Public holidays are the following:

New Year's Day	January 1
Ash Wednesday	varies
Good Friday	varies
Easter Monday	varies
Labor Day	varies
Independence Day	August 5
National Heroes' Day	October 19
Christmas	December 25
Boxing Day	December 26

SPECIAL EVENTS

Jamaica hosts a full calendar of musical, artistic, cultural, and sporting events. The JTB publishes an annual 'Calendar of Events,' available from their offices worldwide.

The two biggest events are Reggae Sunsplash and Reggae Sumfest, held about one week apart in July/August. Several international tour operators have special packages built around the two musical events. Leading companies in the USA include Sunburst (☎ (800) 223-1277) and Island Flight Vacations (☎ (800) 426-4570).

Reggae Sunsplash Jamaica's most famous festival has fallen on hard times in recent years. Until recently, Montego Bay was the venue for this annual five-day reggae extravaganza, featuring nightly performances by such famous performers as Ziggy Marley, Burning Spear, Buju Banton, and Shabba Ranks. The event was initially hosted at Jarrett Park, an open-air entertainment center in Montego Bay. Sunsplash grew so popular – drawing in 100,000 or so visitors – that a special forum, the Bob Marley Performing Center, was built on Howard Cooke Drive.

In 1993 the event moved to a specially built venue, Jamworld, at Portmore outside Kingston. It was a disaster. Kingston proved less appealing to worldly reggae fans than Montego Bay. Synergy Productions, which had been staging Reggae Sunsplash since it began in 1978, was reportedly $1 million in debt after the Kingston debacle. In 1995 a group of private investors rescued the troubled event, which moved to Dover Raceway at St Ann, near Ocho Rios, ending with a beach party at Puerto Seco Beach in Discovery Bay.

The music usually doesn't begin until late at night and can continue until dawn. Tickets for the events range from US$7 to US$15. A three-day ticket cost US$60 in 1994, and a week-long ticket cost US$100. For information, call Synergy at ☎ (800) 937-7527.

Reggae Sumfest When Reggae Sunsplash moved to Kingston in 1993, a great sucking sound was heard as a new festival, Reggae Sumfest, rushed in to fill the vacuum. Sumfest has pushed Sunsplash offstage. For five nights each July or August, Montego Bay is transformed into a hive of activity. Hotels are booked solid, beaches overflow, and the night reverberates with music. Sumfest traditionally begins with a beach party on Walter Fletcher Beach and has four different theme nights, including 'Dance Hall Night,' the night the locals look forward to, when the dancing is almost X-rated.

Tickets, which go on sale about two weeks before the concert, are US$7 (for the beach party) to US$25 per night. Full-week bracelets that allow the wearer to attend all events cost between US$100 to US$150 per person. For information, call Summerfest Productions at ☎ (800) 979-1720.

Carnival In recent years Jamaica has enthusiastically adopted the Carnival of the eastern Caribbean. Although it only began in 1991, it is now a tourist attraction in its own right. Mostly, however, it is a big blow-out for the Jamaican masses. There's reggae and calypso, but dancehall soca is more important.

Be prepared to throw inhibitions to the wind. Jamaican revelers are not shy about wearing as little as possible, nor about *winin'* (making sexual contact while dancing) with absolute strangers.

The five-day event has a different theme each day, ending with the Last Hurrah.

Designers seek to make their bands the most outstanding, the most glittering, the most daring. Some designers choose controversial topics, while others go for fun and fantasy. It wouldn't be carnival without the outrageous. Hence some designers (and many of the crowd) strip down their creations to near nudity.

Other Events Most of the events below follow a predictable schedule. Many annual events occur at the cusp of months and the specific month may vary year to year from those given below. The JTB can provide phone numbers and dates for specific events (see Local Tourist Offices above).

The following are some of the leading events:

January

National Pantomime – an ingenious and witty satirical pantomime hosted annually in the Ward Theater in Kingston, from December 26 through the end of January (as it has for over 50 years). It continues through the end of April at the Little Theater, in Kingston.

Accompong Maroon Festival is a festival, dating from the 19th century, of music and dancing. It's held in Accompong, St Elizabeth and honors the Maroon tradition each January 6 –

the anniversary of the treaty signed between Maroon leader Cudjoe and the British. (☎ 952-7950)

Best of Harmony Hall is a showcase of paintings and carvings from Jamaica's leading artists hosted by Harmony Hall, Ocho Rios (☎ 975-4222).

White River Reggae Bash, at White River Reggae Park, Ocho Rios, is an annual one-day concert featuring Jamaica's leading reggae stars. (☎ 929-4089)

High Mountain 10K Road Race attracts local and overseas amateurs and professionals who compete in the island's largest bicycle road race. It's held at Williamsfield, Manchester. (☎ 963-4211)

Negril Sprint Triathlon, hosted by the Jamaica Triathlon Federations takes place at the Swept Away resort, Negril. This annual competition comprises a half-mile swim, 15-mile cycle race, and a three-mile run. The entry fee of US$75 includes pre- and post-triathlon events such as a Welcome Pasta Party. (☎ 957-4040)

Red Stripe Cup Cricket Competition features national teams from English-speaking Caribbean islands at Sabina Park, Kingston

The *Jamaica School of Dance Concert Season*, at the Little Theater, Kingston, features creative dancing based on Caribbean movements and themes. (☎ 922-5988)

February

Carib Cement International Marathon attracts top national and international athletes who run through the streets of Kingston. Entry fee is US$3.

Pineapple Cup Yacht Race, hosted by the Montego Bay Yacht Club, is when international competitors race to be first across the line from Miami to Montego Bay, a distance of 800-plus miles. (☎ 952-6101)

Bob Marley Birthday Bash, held every February 6, features top-rankin' reggae artists such as Ziggy Marley. It is usually hosted at the Bob Marley Museum in Kingston, but occasionally at Nine Miles, in St Ann. (☎ 923-9380)

Shell/Sandals Limited Overs Cricket Competition brings together the national teams of Jamaica, Barbados, and Trinidad & Tobago to bat it out at Sabina Park, Kingston.

UWI Carnival takes place at the University of West Indies campus, Kingston, and features a week-long carnival of reggae, calypso, and steel bands from throughout the Caribbean. There's also a crowning of the Carnival King and Queen.

March

JAMI Awards is the annual Jamaica Music Industry function featuring guest performers and lead artists in reggae, folk, gospel, jazz, and classical.

Jamaica Orchid Society Spring Show, held in the Assembly Hall on the UWI campus, Kingston, is a three-day flower show and orchid-lover's delight.

Miss Universe Jamaica Beauty Pageant takes place in Kingston to determine who will represent Jamaica in the Miss Universe Contest.

Negril West End Reggae Festival is when leading Jamaican and international reggae stars descend on Negril to perform at Hog Heaven. (☎ 957-4991)

April

Montego Bay Yacht Club Easter Regatta is a colorful annual competition and celebration featuring boats from throughout the Caribbean. (☎ 952-6101)

Harmony Hall Easter Crafts Fair brings out the best of Jamaican foods, drinks, arts, and crafts to be displayed and sold at Harmony Hall, Ocho Rios. (☎ 975-4222)

Devon House Craft Fair, at Devon House, Kingston, features colorful displays of arts, crafts, textiles, and foodstuffs.

Jamaica Carnival (see details above).

Motor Sports Championship Series at Dover Raceway, St Ann, is the first in a series of championship auto and motorcycle races.

Cable & Wireless Test Cricket is an international test cricket match featuring the West Indies team. It's held at Sabina Park, Kingston.

May

Manchester Horticultural Society Show is held at the Manchester Horticultural Showground, Mandeville. Displays of flowers and foliage plants and competitions are hosted by this horticulturalist society, founded in 1868. (☎ 962-2328)

Portland Annual Flower Show at Crystal Springs, Portland, adds further color to this already beautiful venue.

June

All-Jamaica Tennis Championships is a series of championships hosted late May through mid-July at the Eric Bell Tennis Complex, Kingston. (☎ 929-5878)

International Jazz Festival is held at various venues in Ocho Rios. Jazz musicians from throughout the Caribbean, Europe, and North

America play at hotels, beaches, and open-air grounds. (☎ 927-3544)

Motor Sports Championship Series at Dover Raceway, St Ann, is the second in a series of championship race meets.

July

National Dance Theater Company's Season of Dance is when Jamaica's internationally acclaimed National Dance Theater Company explores traditional and modern dance forms at the Little Theater, Kingston. (☎ 926-6603)

Reggae Sunsplash (see details above).

August

Denbigh Agricultural Show is held at the Denbigh Showground, May Pen, Clarendon. Here, Jamaica's leading farm and cattle exposition displays the best of the island's agricultural products.

Independence Day Parade Jamaicans take to the streets of Kingston to celebrate with dancing, a colorful Jonkanoo, and street parades.

Motor Sports Championship Series at Dover Raceway, St Ann, is the third in a series of championship race meets.

Hi-Pro Family Polo Tournament & International Horse Show at Chukka Cove, St Ann, is a combination event featuring top Jamaican and international riders.

Portland Jamboree brings life to sleepy Port Anonio for the nine-day festival including a float parade, street dancing, and arts and food fair.

Reggae Sumfest (see details above).

September

Miss Jamaica World Beauty Pageant, held at the National Arena, Kingston, is a gala crowning pageant to decide who will represent Jamaica in the Miss World contest. (☎ 927-7575)

Fossil Open Polo Tournament is a two-day event featuring some of the international polo circuit's top riders, held at Chukka Cove, St Ann.

October

Jamaica Open Pro Am Golf Tournament draws top local and overseas players. It's hosted by Wyndham Rose Hall Golf Club, Montego Bay.

Jamaica German Society Oktoberfest Even this ex-British Caribbean outpost has oom-pah-pah music and beer-swilling by the stein, held at the German Society Headquarters, Kingston. (☎ 927-6408)

International Marlin Tournament is Jamaica's premier sport fishing event. It takes place each early-October from the Port Antonio Marina and attracts anglers from throughout North America and the Caribbean. (☎ 923-8724)

Motor Sports Championship Series at Dover Raceway, St Ann, is the fourth in a series of championship meets.

December

Motor Sports Championship Series at Dover Raceway, St Ann, is the final meet, featuring motorcycles and more than a dozen classes of cars, with world-class riders and drivers.

Devon House Christmas Fair is highlighted by colorful displays of Jamaican arts, crafts, and culinary delights at Devon House, Kingston.

Johnnie Walker World Golf Championship, at the Tryall Golf, Tennis & Beach Club, draws the best international golfers in the world. They compete for the coveted title of World Champion, with the world's largest prize.

ACTIVITIES

Jamaica has a panoply of sports and special interest activities for those to whom bumming on the beach spells boredom. Some of the facilities are world-class, such as with golf. Others, such as hiking and bicycling, are relatively undeveloped as organized activities.

Hiking

One can spend weeks exploring the countryside. Jamaica's embryonic organized trail system, relegated mainly to the Blue Mountains – John Crow National Park, is popular for hiking, with miles of trails. Elsewhere, there are rough bridle tracks used by locals spanning remote areas nationwide. Thousands of miles of these narrow trails bustle with foot traffic. Following them into the interior is a tremendous way to meet Jamaicans who have been little touched by outside influences. They're almost invariably extremely welcoming and open, though you may meet a few more wary individuals.

The rugged and dramatic Cockpit Country and Hellshire Hills are little explored, yet tailor made for experienced backcountry hikers! You'll also find plenty of

Jonkanoo

Jonkanoo is a traditional Christmas celebration in which revelers parade through the streets dressed in masquerade. It was once the major celebration on the slave calendar.

The festivity, which had its origins among West African secret societies, evolved on the plantations among slaves who were forbidden to observe their sacred traditions. The all-male cast of masqueraders hid their identity: some dressed as demons, others wore papier-mâché horse heads, and many were on stilts. The elaborate carnival was accompanied by musicians with drums, fifes, flutes, and rattles.

At first, jonkanoos were suppressed by the colonial government, fearing they might get out of hand and lead to slave uprisings. Later, planters encouraged jonkanoos, which gradually adopted European traits. Creole elements found their way into the ceremony, and Morris dancing, polka, and reels were introduced. During its early 19th-century heyday, the jonkanoo featured processions of 'set girls,' groups of young women dressed identically and elaborately in a specific color (also according to color of skin). It declined again following emancipation when church and state suppressed the jonkanoo as a vulgar pagan rite. It was discouraged throughout this century, too, until recent years. It is now being revived as an important part of Jamaican culture and is reappearing in towns and villages at Christmas.

Christiana, in Manchester Parish, hosts perhaps the liveliest jonkanoo on the island.

Costumed spectators are expected to offer donations and food and drink to the performers. ∎

bridle trails close to the major north coast resorts.

Most trails are hilly, rugged, and often overgrown by bush. You'll find hiking even a short walk demanding: the oppressive heat and humidity can turn what seems like an easy stroll into a grueling trudge. Allow considerably more time than you would in temperate climates to cover a similar distance. This is especially true since distances that appear short on a map can be deceptive. And take locals' assurances that your destination is 'jus' around de corner' or 'a likkle distance' with a grain of salt.

Travel light. And always carry plenty of water, as you're sure to sweat profusely, and dehydration can set in quickly. Don't attempt to hike further than your state of physical health will allow. Bear in mind that many isolated roads and paths become quickly overgrown (consider buying a machete for off-the-beaten-path hiking). And remember that weather conditions can change quickly, especially in mountainous areas, where sudden torrential downpours can turn hiking trails into mud. Carry a windbreaker and a sweater or jacket in hilly areas. And be sure to take plenty of insect repellent, plus a small first aid kit for hiking in out-of-the-way places.

Rarely will you be far from habitation. However, it's easy to succumb to a false sense of security. It's easy to injure yourself in Jamaica's backcountry, and phones and first aid will seldom be close at hand.

Always follow established trails: Jamaica's mountain terrain is too treacherous to go wandering off the track, as thick vegetation hides sinkholes and great crevasses. Seek advice from locals about trail conditions before setting out.

Consider hiring an experienced local guide when hiking in remote areas, not least because the danger of stumbling upon a commercial patch of ganja is ever-present, and carries with it serious consequences! You can hire guides at many local rum shops.

Jamaica Alternative Tourism, Camping & Hiking Association is the only organization catering to hikers; besides selling trail maps, it provides guides and camping equipment for rent (PO Box 216, King ston 7, ☎ 927-0357). JATCHA is headed by Peter Bentley, who also owns Sense Adventures, which offers guided hikes. Peter is as knowledgeable about hiking in Jamaica as anyone. He can arrange guides to accompany you anywhere in the country. He's a naturist: if Peter comes with you, don't be surprised if he swaggers along by your side dressed only in his birthday suit and sneakers! Peter also sells *A Hiker's Guide to the Blue Mountains* by Bill Wilcox. Steve Cohen's *The Adventure Guide to Jamaica* provides details on hiking routes in the Blue Mountains and elsewhere.

The Touring Society of Jamaica (☎ 944-8325), based at Strawberry Hill, also offers guided hikes into the Blue Mountains. These are shorter and less arduous than Bentley's programs, and usually feature visits to coffee farms and other points of interest.

More rugged hikes into the Blue Mountains are offered by Valley Hikes, PO Box 89, Port Antonio (☎/fax 993-2543) which has trips up to nine days long through the Rio Grande Valley.

Hiking in the National Parks Only a handful of hardy hikers have trod the Blue Mountain pathways, but the potentials are immense.

Most hikers choose to follow the well-trodden path to the summit of Blue Mountain Peak (see the Blue Mountain chapter). The park, however, embraces hundreds of miles of bridle trails used by locals. Routes vary from an easy morning stroll to minor expeditions. The Protected Areas Resource Conservation Project (is also developing a trail system (including a Blue Mountain Ridge Trail, akin to the Appalachian Trail of the eastern USA), with hiking trails categorized as 'guided,' 'non-guided,' and 'wilderness trails.'

A fascinating complex of bridle trails leads into the mountains. From Gordon Town you can climb to the heights of Flamstead, once the lookout point from which Horatio Nelson surveyed ships approaching Port Royal. Another popular trail from Gordon Trail leads through the gorge of the Hope River to Newcastle army camp, from where you can continue to the top of Catherine's Peak (5056 feet). Half a dozen trails also converge on the Cinchona Botanical Gardens.

Other relatively well-trodden trails include Rose Hill Rd to Hollywell, Hardwar Gap to Silver Hill, Ecclesdown to Windsor Forest, Seamans Valley to Moore Town, and Bellevue to Millbank.

There are a few trails suited only to experienced trekkers; a couple require advance planning, such as the path to Nanny Town, the remote Maroon redoubt on the wild, totally uninhabited mid-level northern slope of Blue Mountain Peak. The path is cleared occasionally but quickly retaken by undergrowth. This and other trails in the Rio Grande Valley (which separates the two mountain ranges) are being opened up by Rio Grande Attractions Ltd, based in Port Antonio (see the East Coast chapter).

Horseback Riding

Horseback riding is a great way to explore Jamaica. Stables are located in most resort areas, and most hotels can arrange rides. Many lead through working plantations. Others venture further afield along bridle trails that lead into the rugged mountains. Prices range from US$20 to US$40 for two-hour rides.

The 50-acre Chukka Cove Equestrian, near Runaway Bay and Ocho Rios, is the island's premier riding facility, with eight pastures and a stable of 40-plus horses (☎ 972-2506). It offers tuition from basic riding to dressage, as well as polo, and also has the most developed horse-trekking trips into the interior.

Good Hope Plantation (near Falmouth) also has a large stable, plus miles of trails through the plantation and into the wooded highlands at the edge of Cockpit Country. Likewise, organized trail rides are offered at Rocky Point Stables (☎ 953-2286) at Half Moon Resort & Golf Club, and White Witch Stables (☎ 953-2746), both near Montego Bay, and Prospect Plantation (☎ 974-2373) near Ocho Rios, where 1½-hour and two-hour guided rides are available.

Several stables in Negril offer a more offbeat riding experience, as does Mayfield Ranch, near Treasure Beach.

See regional chapters for further details.

Scuba Diving

Jamaica's shores are as beautiful below the water surface as they are above, especially along the north coast, where the treasures range from shallow reefs, caverns, and trenches, to walls and drop-offs just a few hundred yards off-shore. Jacques Cousteau described the Montego Bay area as having 'some of the most dramatic sponge life in the Caribbean.' Negril, on the west coast, is another favorite spot with a diverse reef system. There are ship wrecks (plus aircraft and even cars), especially around the rarely dived Hellshire cays and Port Royal, which even boasts a sunken pirate city to explore!

All the favorite stars are on show: moray eels, grunts, barracudas, stingrays, turtles, and an impressive array of hard and soft coral formations. Most dive locations are within a 20-minute boat ride from shore. The reefs off the southern coast, where the island shelf extends up to 20 miles and river sedimentation pollutes the inshore waters, are much further out to sea.

Jamaica's waters offer exceptional visibility and water temperatures above 80°F year-round. Wet suits are not required for warmth, though they come in handy to prevent scrapes on coral.

There are dozens of licensed dive operators offering rental equipment and group dives from customized dive boats. Most belong to the Jamaica Association of Dive Operators (JADO). 'Resort courses' for beginners are offered at most major resorts, but you can also take a certification course. Guided dives led by qualified dive masters can be arranged through dive centers at virtually any of the all-inclusive resorts, or independent dive companies.

Never go diving with one of the freelance guides that solicit business on beaches. Since 1986, when Jamaica enacted water-sport licensing laws, dive operators have been required to adhere to strict safety standards.

The cost averages about US$35 per dive, or US$50 a day for a two-tank dive, for certified divers. Be sure to bring your dive card. Introductory half-day resort courses normally cost about US$50, and a full PADI (Professional Association of Diving Instructors) certification course will cost upwards of US$300.

The only decompression chamber on the island is at the University of West Indies Marine Laboratory in Discovery Bay (☎ 973-2241).

Montego Bay Montego Bay was the site of Jamaica's first marine sanctuary. Most dive sites are close to shore and vary from teeming patch reefs to awe-inspiring walls beginning in as little as 35 feet of water.

Negril Negril is a popular dive site, with miles of coral reefs now protected within the Negril Watershed Conservation Area. The best diving is a 10-minute boat ride from shore. Visibility reaches up to 100 feet. Aside from tunnels and overhangs, there are plane wrecks and drift diving. Most of the upscale resorts have their own scuba operations, and there are plenty of scuba concessions along the beach and West End.

North Coast The wall at Falmouth runs within half a mile of shore and is riddled with tunnels and caverns. A favorite is Chub Castle, which starts fairly shallow with a top decorated by soft corals and basket sponges; its wall is strung with rope sponges and black coral. Runaway Bay shares the same wall and offers similar conditions plus sunken planes and even two Mercedes cars!

Further east, at Ocho Rios, there's Devil's Reef, a pinnacle that drops more than 200 feet; and Caverns, a shallow reef about a quarter-mile long with nurse sharks in residence and the wreck of the 140-foot minesweeper, *Kathryn*. Resort Divers (☎ 974-5338, fax 974-0577), Shop No 6, Island Plaza, Ocho Rios, is a five-star, full-service pro-shop, servicing six hotels between Negril and Ocho Rios, where they offer free pick-up from cruise ships.

Port Antonio The east coast isn't as well developed for scuba diving, but there are some excellent sites. You'll find scuba facilities at Dragon Bay and San San Beach.

Port Royal If the thought of searching for pirate treasure appeals, check into the Buccaneer Club, at Morgan's Harbor. They offer dives to the Sunken City – the pirate capital that sank during an earthquake in 1692. There's also excellent coral diving nearby.

Snorkeling

Snorkeling equipment can be rented at most beach hotels and resorts for under US$10 a day.

Sailing

Most beachside resorts provide small sailboats called Sunfish, either as part of the hotel package rate or for a small hourly rental fee.

Sailboats, yachts, and cruisers can be rented by the day or week from marinas and small beachside companies almost anywhere along the north coast, as well as at Port Royal, near Kingston.

Sport Fishing

Jamaica's ocean waters are a pelagic playpen for schools of blue and white marlin, dolphin fish, wahoo, and tuna. Deep-water game fish run year-round through **marlin alley**, the deep Cayman Trench that begins as close to shore as two miles and plummets to fathomless depths. Sport fishing is popular and rewarding.

June and August are the prize months for sailfish and marlin. Seven blue marlin tournaments are held annually, highlighted by the prestigious Port Antonio International Marlin Tournament held each October.

Several operators set out from Montego Bay, and Ocho Rios. Most provide hotel transfers.

Few foreigners fish the south coast, where Jamaica's major fishing banks are located. Port Royal, near Kingston, has a marina with sport fishing boats for hire. Otherwise, consider hiring one of the more rustic fiberglass motorboats used by local fishermen based at Alligator Pond, Treasure Beach, or Whitehouse.

In general, sport fishing in Jamaica is slightly cheaper than elsewhere in the Caribbean. Rates range from US$300 to US$350 for half a day to US$600 or more for a full day, with bait and tackle provided. You normally provide your own food and drinks. Most charter boats require a 50% deposit (if you cancel, do so at least 24 hours before departure to avoid losing your deposit). Some boats keep half the catch. Discuss terms with the skipper prior to setting out. Never book your trip or negotiate arrangements with bystanders on the dock or beach.

Freshwater fishing is popular among locals. Jamaica remains untapped as a freshwater and fishing destination for foreigners. A growing number of inland resorts, however, raise tilapia, tarpon, and snook.

Surfing

Jamaica is *not* a surfer's paradise. If you're seeking the ultimate wave, look elsewhere. There are a few spots on the east coast, however, where surfers can find decent waves coming in from the Atlantic. Boston Beach, 10 miles east of Port Antonio, is acknowledged as the best spot. Other worthwhile places nearby include Long Bay and tiny Christmas Beach.

Golf

Jamaica's big strength is golf. It has more courses than any other Caribbean island, and has been attracting golfers since the mid-1800s when the first course was laid in the cool highlands at Mandeville.

At press time, Jamaica had 10 championship courses, some of which are regular stops for the PGA and LPGA tours. Green fees range from US$5 to US$50 in summer, and US$8 to US$80 in winter. Most courses have clubs (which cost US$5 to US$20 depending on the course), plus carts and caddies for hire. Tee times are normally easy to acquire. All the courses are open to the public.

The West

Negril Hills Golf Club overlooks the Great Morass. Jamaica's newest course opened in 1994 and features undulating fairways, water hazards, and lush swampy surrounds. If you plop your ball in the water, forget it. The crocodiles probably got to it first. Vital statistics: 18 holes, 6333 yards, par 72 (☎ 957-4638).

Tryall Golf Club is Jamaica's pre-eminent course. It is 12 miles west of Montego Bay, where it was designed on the site of a 19th century sugar estate. The course runs parallel to the sea and winds into the surrounding hills, with some fabulous views. It is noted for its rolling fairways and unforgiving greens. Facilities include a club house, bar, restaurant, pro-shop and beach club. Vital statistics: 18 holes, 6760 yards, par 71. Contact the Tryall Golf, Tennis & Beach Resort at ☎ (800) 742-0498, or the club house at ☎ 952-5111.

Montego Bay

Half Moon Golf Club, on the eastern outskirts of Montego Bay, was designed by the acclaimed designer Robert Trent Jones. It's a long, relatively flat course, with narrow fairways and small, undulating greens close to the sea. Facilities include a club house, restaurant and bar, plus a pro shop. Vital statistics: 18 holes, 7115 yards, par 72. Contact ☎ (800) 626-0592, or the club house at ☎ 953-2560.

Ironshore Golf & Country Club, just east of Montego Bay, is a 6633-yard, par 72 course designed by the famous links designer, Robert Moote. Ironshore is noted for its blind-shot holes. Contact ☎ 953-2800.

Wyndham Rose Hall Country Club is located on the Rose Hall Estate, east of Montego Bay, and grants tremendous ocean vistas. The sharp doglegs and windy conditions put a premium on club selection. The course is home of the Jamaican Open and the International Junior Golf Championship. There's a club house, plus a restaurant, bar, and pro-shop. Vital statistics: 18 holes, 6598 yards, par 72. Contact Wyndham Rose Hall (☎ (800) 822-4200) or the clubhouse (☎ 953-2650).

North Coast

Runaway Bay Golf Course is run by SuperClubs, the all-inclusive resort chain. The 6884-yard, par 72 course features elevated tees and well-placed bunkers. It has a club house, restaurant, and pro shop, and is the setting for the island's only golf school, the Jamaica Jamaica Golf School (☎ 973-2436). Instruction is available

for all levels (and is included for guests) at the Breezes Runaway Bay all-inclusive resort (formerly Jamaica Jamaica). For information, call ☎ 973-2561.

Upton Golf & Country Club is run by the Sandals resort chain. It is 700 feet up in the cool hills, two miles east of Ocho Rios. The splendidly scenic course boasts elevated tees plus a club house, bar, pro shop, and restaurant. Vital statistics: 18 holes, 6600 yards, par 71. Call Sandals at ☎ (800) 726-3257, or the clubhouse at ☎ 974-2528.

East

San San Golf & Country Club is a nine-hole course near Port Antonio. It was being restored at press time and may re-open by the time you read this. For the latest details, call ☎ 993-9345.

Kingston

Caymanas Golf Club, six miles west of Kingston, was the island's first 18-hole championship course. The 6844-yard, par 72 course features elevated tees and uphill shots to small, bunkered greens. Contact the clubhouse at ☎ 926-8144.

Constant Spring Golf Club, in a residential suburb of Kingston, was laid out in 1920 on a defunct sugar plantation, the ruins of which can still be seen. The 6196-yard, par 70 course is short and is noted for tight fairways and contoured greens. There's a club house, restaurant, bar, and pro shop. Contact the club at ☎ 926-8144.

Southwest Coast & Central Highlands

Manchester Country Club is a venerable nine-hole course laid out over a century ago on the outskirts of Mandeville, more than 2000 feet above sea level. It has 18 tee boxes. The clubhouse can be reached at ☎ 962-2403.

Jamaica hosts several leading international golf tournaments, including the Johnnie Walker World Championship held each mid-December at Tryall Golf Club. (The championship is the richest in golf, with a first prize of $550,000; in 1994 the total purse was $3 million.) Spectator admission is free, and a free shuttle runs from the Montego Bay Parish Library and selected hotels to Tryall.

Golfing Around in Jamaica Ltd (☎ 926-7206, fax 929-5078), 54 Brentford Rd, Kingston 5, offers four-, five-, and eight-day golf packages.

Caving

Jamaica has spelunkers salivating. The island is honeycombed with limestone caves and caverns, particularly in the western parishes. Some 400 of an estimated 900 caves on the island have been at least partly explored and mapped by the Geological Survey Dept and Jamaica Caving Club.

A few caves are steadfast tourist attractions, with guided tours and occasional refreshment stands. These include Runaway Caves (Green Grotto) near Runaway Bay, Roaring River near Savanna-la-Mar, and Somerset Caves and Nonsuch Caves near Port Antonio. Lesser-known caves include Ghourie Caves, Coffee River Cave, Ipswich Caves, Windsor Caves, and Oxford Caves – all are located on the fringe of Cockpit Country; guides are available, but there are no other facilities.

Many of the caves were once used by Arawak Indians for burial and ceremonial purposes, and petroglyphs add to the artistic appeal of the caverns. The most important of these is Mountain Valley Cave, in the Guanabacoa Valley north of Spanish Town. Many of the caves are also roosts for bats. They're harmless, but you have to contend with the stench of their manure, which locals collect for fertilizer.

Use extreme caution if exploring non-commercial caves. Many rivers and streams disappear underground and flow through the cave systems. During heavy rains the water level can rise rapidly and greatly, trapping and drowning unwary spelunkers and Indiana Jones-type adventurers.

Take powerful flashlights and spare bulbs and batteries.

An indispensable guidebook is *Underground Jamaica* by Professor Alan Fincham. For further information, contact the Jamaica Caving Club, which was once very active but apparently is somewhat quiescent these days (c/o Dept of Geology, University of the West Indies, Mona, Kingston, ☎ 927-6661).

Cycling

Relatively few people explore Jamaica by bicycle, and few Jamaicans use bicycles. The island is perfect for mountain biking, however. Mountain bikes can be rented at every major resort, although you'll have to search hard to find a top-class bike or equipment for touring. Far better for serious touring is to bring your own bike. Most airlines will let you ship it at no extra charge (and will provide shipping cartons). See Getting Around for more details.

Once you arrive you'll find very few bicycle repair shops. Hence, you'll need to carry an adequate repair kit plus plenty of spare parts such as inner tubes if you intend to roam off the beaten track. Travel as light as possible. And wear a helmet! Although there is little traffic away from resort areas and main roads, conditions are hazardous. Roads are covered with loose gravel, and are narrow and twisting, with many potholes and blind spots where you can anticipate being surprised by a Jamaican appearing like a bat out of hell!

Half-day bicycle tours in the mountains are offered by Blue Mountain Tours (152 Main St, Ocho Rios, ☎ 974-7075, fax 974-0635; or PO Box 84, Port Antonio, ☎ 993-2242) and High Hope Adventures (16 Top Rd, St Ann's Bay, ☎ 972-2997, fax 972-1607). Longer mountain bike tours through the central highlands are offered by JJ's Tours, with nights at the Hotel Villa Bella; one-, two-, and three-day trips cost US$60, US$70, and US$80 (c/o Hotel Villa Bella, PO Box 473, Christiana, ☎ 964-2243, fax 964-2765).

Sense Adventures (PO Box 216, Kingston 7, ☎ 927-0357) can custom-plan a bicycle tour, including guides if desired, as can Blue Mountain Tours.

The following towns have bicycle supply and repair shops:

Falmouth
    The Bicycle Shop, 12 Duke St (☎ 954-4114)
Kingston
    God Bless Cycle, Port More Mall, Shop 58, Portmore (☎ 988-7430)
Linstead
    Nook n Kranny, 1 Gillette St (☎ 985-9718)

Mandeville
OMG Auto & Cycle, 2 Perth Rd (☎ 962-5832)
May Pen
Aldokin's Hardware, 71 Manchester Ave (☎ 986-4392)
Montego Bay
Rapid & Sheffield, 30 Pimento Way (☎ 979-8158)
Ocho Rios
Cycletronics, 75 Main St (☎ 974-1281)
Savanna-la-Mar
Smiley's Cycle, 15 Ricketts Ave (☎ 955-3275)
Foote's Bike Rental, Rose St (☎ 955-4029)
Spanish Town
Auto & Bicycle Maintenance, 84 Young St (☎ 984-6683)
Winners Cycle Auto Stores, 12 Greendale Blvd, Shop 12 (☎ 984-8702)

Windsurfing

Most large beach hotels provide windsurfing equipment for rent or use free of charge. You can also rent sailboards from beach concessions at major resort towns from Negril to Ocho Rios. Wind conditions, however, are tame: ideal for beginners, but a bit too dull for serious adherents.

Kayaking

Despite its immense potential, Jamaica has barely been tapped as a venue for canoeing and kayaking. There are more than 120 rivers, many with white-water sections that provide challenging runs for kayakers. Few have been scouted. The Great River, west of Montego Bay, is one of the few that has.

Peter Bentley, founder of Sense Adventures (PO Box 216, Kingson 7, ☎ 927-0357), is the most knowledgeable person on the island. He's an enthusiastic kayaker and can provide information and recommendations for canoeists. His company also rents inflatable kayaks called Sea Eagle Explorers, and arranges guides plus guided canoe trips.

WORK

Visitors are admitted to Jamaica on the condition that they 'not engage in any form of employment on the island or solicit or accept any order for goods or services, for or on behalf of any persons, firm or company not carrying on business with the island.' So says the immigration stamp placed in your passport. Professionals can obtain work permits if sponsored by a Jamaican company, but casual work is virtually impossible to obtain.

Amigos de las Américas is a nonprofit voluntary service organization that works on public health projects in the Caribbean (5618 Star Lane, Houston, TX 77057, ☎ (713) 782-5290 or (800) 231-7796, fax (713) 782-9267). Young volunteers spend from four to eight weeks in a village. The program is open to anyone over 16 years.

ACCOMMODATIONS

For accommodations to meet every budget and style, few Caribbean islands can match Jamaica for diversity.

Where you stay can make or break your vacation, so it pays to research thoroughly. Price is only one guide – many hotels of similar price vary dramatically in ambiance and value. Far too many hotels in Jamaica are overpriced and/or soulless. But there are also some splendid bargains at all price levels, from cozy budget guest houses for US$10 nightly to ritzy all-inclusive resorts such as Grand Lido in Negril, where your maid will float hibiscus petals in the toilet bowl before turning down your linen sheets.

Twice a year the JTB publishes a guide and rate sheet to leading hotels and guest houses nationwide. You can obtain it from JTB offices worldwide, or from the JTB information booth upon arrival at the airports in Montego Bay or Kingston. The 140 or so establishments listed have been inspected and are 'JTB approved,' as are at least 300 guest houses nationwide. Many accommodations that are not JTB licensed are perfectly OK.

Rates & Seasons

Prices throughout this book are given in US dollars, and are normally for double rooms in low season unless otherwise stated.

Low season (summer) is usually mid-April to mid-December; high or peak season (winter) is the remainder of the year, when hotel prices increase by 40% or more.

Unless otherwise stated, all prices used refer to room only, or European Plan (EP). Many hotels have a tiered price system according to peak, shoulder, and low seasons, while others (usually the most select hotels) have year-round rates. Some properties also discount room rates based on the number of nights you stay. *Ask what discounts may be available and feel free to suggest your own.*

There are several advantages to traveling in low season, not least the price discounts. The more popular hotels are often booked solid in high season; at other times of the year not only can you find rooms, but you are often given the run of the house on rooms.

Some hotels will quote rates as Continental Plan (CP; room and breakfast), Modified American Plan (MAP; room plus breakfast and dinner), or American Plan (AP; room plus three meals daily). Don't forget to check if the quoted rate includes tax and service charge; if not, a compulsory 12.5% government General Consumption Tax (and possibly a 10 to 15% service charge) may be added to your bill.

In making a selection, consider which facilities your ideal hotel should have. If you're a serious golfer, consider paying a little more to stay at a dedicated golf resort. There are several dedicated scuba resorts, too.

Many hotels fill up during the winter, when it is advisable to book several months in advance. This is especially true if you're reserving by mail, which can take several weeks. It's best to phone, fax, or use a travel agent or hotel representative (see below) when making reservations from your home country.

Reservations

You can make reservations directly with hotels, but you'll find it just as easy to use a travel agency or hotel representative, such as TravelJam Reservation & Information Service, which represents almost two dozen upscale properties islandwide (1449 Lexington Ave No 3A, New York, NY 10128, ☎ (800) 554-7352).

In North America, the JTB operates a Jamaican Reservation Service at 1320 S Dixie Hwy No 1180, Coral Gables, FL 33146 (in the USA, ☎ (800) 526-2422; in Canada, ☎ (800) 432-7559).

Several Jamaican hotels that do not anticipate filling their rooms sell blocks of rooms in advance to wholesalers at bulk discounts, which the latter pass along as huge savings. Try The Room Exchange, which has dozens of properties to choose from (in the USA, ☎ (800) 846-7000, fax (212) 760-1013).

The Jamaica Hotel & Tourism Association represents hoteliers and other lodgings owners and tourism service providers (2 Ardenne Rd, Kingston 10, ☎ 926-3635, fax 929-1054).

Most hotels accept payment by credit card or traveler's check.

Camping

With few exceptions, Jamaica is not developed for campers. Negril is the only resort area with a choice of camping facilities, although a few isolated campsites are also scattered elsewhere. Many budget properties will let you pitch a tent on their lawns for a small fee. Some even rent tents. Most have shower, toilet, and laundry facilities. Costs begin at about US$5 per night, but US$10 is the average.

It is unsafe to camp wild in Jamaica: the threat of robbery or rape is too great. This includes beaches. If you insist on camping away from organized sites, ensure that you're within sight and sound of other visitors or hotels. The JTB or JATCHA (see Hiking above) can provide information on safe sites. However, the JTB has not licensed any properties as 'JTB approved' to date.

Hostels

Jamaica has no youth hostel association and there are no hostels on the island. The closest you'll find to the concept is Maya Lodge, in Jack's Hill on the outskirts of Kingston, and Hummingbird Heaven, outside Ocho Rios.

Guest Houses

Guest houses are the lodgings of choice for Jamaicans when traveling. Usually they're small, fairly simple, no-frills, family-run properties with a live-in owner who provides breakfast and sometimes dinner. What they lack in facilities they make up for in character – or at least, they should.

Unfortunately, the term is much abused in Jamaica. Some so-called guest houses are no more than a couple of dingy rooms with shared bathrooms (most guest houses have shared bath). Others are self-contained apartments. Still others are indistinguishable from hotels or faceless motels. Standards and prices vary enormously.

If what you need is a roof over your head, guest houses are an inexpensive option for value-wise lodgings, and they're good places to mix with locals. Don't expect to be right on the beach, though.

The *Jamaican Herald* and *The Gleaner* newspapers list guest houses under 'Boarding Accommodation' and 'Guest House' headings in their classified sections.

Family Stays

You can also make your own arrangements to stay with individuals or families that do not rent rooms as a normal practice. You should use your discretion. There are many scalawags and scoundrels eager to part visitors from their money, or worse; if you don't feel secure, don't accept an offer. The JTB's 'Meet the People' program, while not specifically designed to provide accommodations with Jamaican families, is a good starting point. Participants have been screened by the JTB, which can assist in arranging overnight stays. Diane McIntyre-Pike can also arrange family stays through her Community Tourism program based at the Astra Country Inn in Mandeville (62 Ward Ave, Mandeville, ☎ 962-3265).

Hotels

Jamaican hotels run the gamut, but terms such as 'deluxe' or 'first-class' have been so abused that it is unwise to rely on a hotel's brochure or promotional literature. Reporting on whether a hotel has air-con, TVs, and a swimming pool tells you nothing about its ambiance. Hence, I've tried to provide in-depth descriptions of hotels to help you make a more informed decision based on ambiance as much as amenities.

Some of the first, and certainly the most elegant, hotels in the Caribbean were established in Jamaica. It still has a large selection of stylish hotels based on European design, although many of the long-touted favorites now look jaded.

A consortium of more than three dozen smaller intimate hotels recently formed the Inns of Jamaica group for marketing purposes. Most are upscale. The biggest of these has 50 rooms. Contact JTB offices for a brochure.

The Elegant Resorts of Jamaica represents a handful of exclusive properties, including Half Moon Golf, Tennis & Beach Club, Round Hill Hotel & Villas, and Trident Villas & Hotel. Membership has been in flux in 1995.

All-Inclusive Resorts

All-inclusive resorts are cash-free, self-contained hotels or village resorts: you pay a set price and (theoretically) pay nothing more once you set foot inside the resort. Even unlimited booze is usually included.

All-inclusives offer a pampered vacation, but tend to shelter guests from mingling with locals and discovering the colorful, gritty, real Jamaica. If you want to get out and explore on your own, you're free to do so, of course. Most resorts also offer their own shopping and scenic bus tours.

All-inclusive resorts were invented in Jamaica and perfected to suit the needs of couples, families, and singles. Two companies dominate the scene: Sandals and SuperClubs. The renowned rivalry between them has fostered the highest standards based on supreme service. Together they set the benchmark that others attempt to reach, with varying degrees of success.

However, caution is needed when choosing an appropriate 'all-inclusive resort,' as all may not be as it seems. Many properties have jumped onto the 'all-inclusive' bandwagon for marketing purposes. Check carefully for hidden charges for water sports, laundry, and other activities or services *not* included in the price. Rates begin at about US$100 per day for the less expensive resorts.

Sandals Sandals has traditionally been a couples-only chain: no singles or families are allowed (nor gay or lesbian couples, for that matter). The company's various resorts boast the highest occupancy rates of any hotels in the Caribbean!

In 1995 the company broke ground on its first family resort – Beaches, in Negril – and is scheduled to build a second family resort near Bluefields, on the southwest coast. Sandals markets its resorts as 'ultra-inclusives.'

For more information on Sandals, contact:

Canada
    4211 Yonge St No 320, Willowdale ON, M2P
    2A9 (☎ (416) 223-0028, fax (416) 223-3306)
France
    Tropic Travel, 71 rue d'Aboukir, 75002 Paris
    (☎ 33-1-42-36-42-52, fax 33-1-42-36-48-35)
Germany
    Arnulfstrasse 44, 80335 Munich (fax 49-89-
    550-1916)
UK
    32 Ives St, London SW3 2ND (☎ (0171)
    581-9895, fax (0171) 823-8758)
USA
    Unique Vacations, 6150 SW 76th St, Miami,
    FL 33143 (☎ (305) 284-1300 or (800) 726-
    3257, fax (305) 667-8996)

SuperClubs Each of SuperClubs' six 'Super-inclusive' resorts caters to a specific market segment. In December 1995, the company announced that it would market three of its more budget-oriented properties under the 'Breezes' title, while its Sans Souci Lido and Grand Lido Negril resorts would remain deluxe flagships.

For more information on SuperClubs, contact:

Canada	☎ (800) 553-4320
UK	☎ (0992) 447420
	fax (0279) 506616
USA	☎ (800) 859-8009
	fax (305) 925-0334

Rentals
Jamaica boasts hundreds of private houses for rent, from modest cottages to lavish beachfront estates. In fact, more than 40% of the island's accommodations are 'self-catering,' a higher ratio than any other Caribbean island. Most are located in the north coast tourist resorts and, to a lesser degree, the coastal strip between Savanna-la-Mar and Treasure Beach. Many villas near Montego Bay, Ocho Rios, and Runaway Bay are in self-contained villa communities. They're a great way for self-sufficient travelers to establish their independence and are very cost-effective if you're traveling with family or a group of friends. Many 'self-catering' rentals actually come with a cook and/or maid included, or as an option. Others come with a kitchenette and you do your own cooking, laundry, etc.

You can rent cottages and villas directly from owners or villa-rental companies. Good sources are the classified ad sections of *Caribbean Travel & Life* and *Islands* magazines. A good starting point is the Jamaican Association of Villas & Apartments (JAVA), which represents about 80% of the 400 or so properties available island-wide, and is responsible for marketing rental units. Contact them in Jamaica at PO Box 298, Ocho Rios (☎ 974-2508, fax 974-2967). Other offices include:

UK
    TC Resorts, 21 Blandford St, London W1H
    3AD (☎ (0171) 486-3560, fax (0171) 486-
    4108). You can make bookings through JAVA.
USA
    1370 Washington Ave No 301, Miami Beach,
    FL 33139, ☎ (305) 673-6688 or (800) 845-
    5276, fax (305) 673-5666)

Other villa-rental companies include:

At Home Abroad
    405 E 56th St No 6H, New York, NY 10022
    (☎ (212) 421-9165)
Exclusive Villa Resort
    PO Box 1372, Montego Freeport
    (☎ 951-6232)
Selective Vacations Service
    PO Box 335 (154 Main St), Ocho Rios
    (☎ 974-5187, fax 974-2359; in the USA
    ☎ (800) 262-2727)

Villa Leisure
  PO Box 1096, Fairfield, CT 06430 (☎ (203) 222-9611)
Villas by Linda Smith
  8029 Riverside Drive, Cabin John, MD 20818 (☎ (301) 229-4300)
Villawise
  PO Box 17 (103 Main St), Ocho Rios (☎ 974-5877, fax 974-5362)

Several of Jamaica's most elegant resorts offer villa rentals in private homes on the resort grounds. The advantage is that guests have access to all resort facilities. These include Half Moon Club, Round Hill, and Tryall Golf, Beach & Tennis Club, all near Montego Bay, and Trident Villas and Goblin Villas near Port Antonio.

Usually, upscale villas have private pools, TV/VCRs, stereos, and often a tennis court. They're almost always fully staffed with a maid, cook, and gardener. Some even include a butler and laundress. A night watchman is recommended. Most staff are trained, and are almost always courteous, deferential, and willing to please.

Your villa rental agency should supply you with complete details on staff arrangements, including guidelines for tipping. It's customary to give the staff one night off per week. You should also tip each staff member separately according to the service they've provided. However, an unwritten ranking states that the cook gets the largest tip and the laundress the least. Most villa rental agencies recommend that the combined gratuity should total about 7 to 15% of the villa rental cost.

When choosing location, consider the distance from the airport, how close you want to be to a major town (convenient for food shopping, restaurants, etc), and whether you want easy access to golfing and other activities. Some villas near major resorts come with access to the latter's facilities. Many villas are located in the hills, where they offer the advantage of cool breezes and spectacular views. They're also cheaper.

Rental rates vary from as low as US$100 per week for budget units with minimal facilities. More upscale villas usually begin at about US$750 weekly for a two-bedroom cottage and can run US$5000 or more for a four-bedroom estate sleeping eight or more people. Rates fall as much as 30% in summer. A large deposit (usually 25% or more) is required to confirm your reservation; full payment is normally required one month before your rental begins.

You'll pay a premium for being down by the beach. Expect to pay more, too, if your villa is pre-provisioned with food. It's usual to buy your own food (costs generally run about US$100 per person per week). Your cook may stock the food for your first dinner and breakfast, and should be reimbursed. He or she normally accompanies you on your shopping spree – a great way to learn about local food items and Jamaican dishes. If you let the cook do your shopping, be sure to give *explicit* written instructions, and ask for a strict accounting.

FOOD

Jamaica's homegrown cuisine is a fusion of many ethnic traditions and influences. The Arawak Indians were the first island residents to grill meats and fish. They also brought callaloo, cassava, corn, sweet potatoes, and several tropical fruits to the island. The Spanish adopted native spices, later enhanced by spices brought by slaves from their African homelands. East Indian immigrants brought hot and flavorful curries, often served with locally made mango chutney. *Roti*, a bread of Indian origin, is also popular served with a dollop of curried goat or chicken in the middle and eaten folded. Middle Eastern dishes and Chinese influences have also become part of the national menu. And basic roasts and stews followed the flag during three centuries of British rule, as did Yorkshire pudding, meat pies, and hot cross buns.

The Jamaicans have melded all these influences into dishes with playful names.

A fair amount of Jamaican cuisine is an adventure in tongue-lashing. A key ingredient is pimento (or 'allspice'), which is indigenous to Jamaica, where it grows most profusely in hilly limestone areas. It

berries on a glossy-leaved tree related to the bay and clove.

A key island condiment is savory, piquant Pickapeppa sauce, the recipe for which is a closely guarded secret. The basic ingredients, however, include tomatoes, onions, raisins, tamarind, mangoes, red-hot peppers, cane vinegar, thyme, and other spices.

Out to Eat

Restaurants range from wildly expensive to humble roadside stands and bamboo shacks where you can eat simple Jamaican fare for as little as US$1. Hole-in-the-wall restaurants often serve fabulous local fare; don't be put off by their often basic appearance (unless they're overtly unhygienic). Most serve at least one vegetarian meal (often called I-tal, a Rastafarian inspiration for 'pure' or health food).

Restaurants that are geared to the tourist trade are generally overpriced, partly because much of the food they serve is imported. Most hotels incorporate Jamaican dishes in their menus, although these are often tame versions of the spicy island cuisine. Even more upscale restaurants serving continental fare meld Jamaican staples into their menus. Virtually anywhere, you'll be able to find ackee and saltfish, for example.

Dress is casual at even the most exclusive restaurants, where you will be expected to dress 'elegantly casual,' meaning no jeans. A few of the more traditional upscale resorts may require jackets and ties for men at dinner.

Food bought at grocery stores is usually expensive. Many of the canned and packaged goods are imported and cost up to three times what you might pay at home. Bottled water is also expensive. You'll find plenty of dirt-cheap fresh fruits, vegetables, and spices on sale at markets and roadside stalls islandwide. Likewise, you can usually buy fish (and lobster *in season*) from local fishermen. If you have some favorite food items – perhaps you can't live without bottled prunes? – consider taking them with you . . . just make sure they're preserves, or otherwise non- 'live' agricultural products.

Many of the more popular upscale resorts sell evening passes that allow you to eat and drink in their restaurants, bars, and nightclubs for a single fee.

Plenty of restaurants serve continental cuisine, and virtually every town of any size has fast-food joints such as McDonald's, Burger King, and Kentucky Fried Chicken. Their local equivalents are Mother's and King Burger.

By far the best selection of restaurants is in Kingston, although Ocho Rios and Montego Bay also have an excellent selection.

Ackee & Saltfish

A typical Jamaican 'plantation breakfast' is ackee and saltfish, the national dish. Ackee is a tree-grown fruit (native to Africa) the golden flesh of which bears an uncanny resemblance to scrambled eggs when cooked. Served with johnny cakes (delicious fried dumplings) and callaloo (a leafy vegetable akin to spinach) and flaked escovietched fish, it makes a fantastic breakfast. ∎

On the Menu

Jamaicans typically forsake corn flakes for more savory fare at breakfast: ackee and saltfish is typical (see the sidebar). The 'average' Jamaican eats a light lunch. One popular snack is a patty, a heavily seasoned, crescent-shaped meat or vegetable pie, in a crusty pastry. Other dishes could be pepperpot stew, fried fish, or 'jerk' pork, or other national dish using island ingredients simmered in coconut milk and/or spices.

Duckunoo is a pudding made of cornmeal, green bananas, and coconut, and enlivened with sugar and spices.

Beef, Pork & Goat

The island staple is rice and peas (red beans), most often served with pork. Goat is also an island staple. It is usually served curried, chopped into small bits with meat on the bone, but it is also the main ingredient of *mannish water* (or 'goat head soup') made from goat offal. You may turn your nose up, but it is considered an aphrodisiac.

Dip and fall back is a salty stew served with bananas and dumplings.

Jamaica's most popular dish (now finding its way onto the world market) is *jerk*, a term that describes the process of cooking meats smothered in tongue-searing marinade. Chicken, pork, or fish are first washed with vinegar or lime juice, then marinated in a hot-sauce of island-grown spices (including volatile Scotch bonnet pepper), and barbecued slowly in an outdoor pit – usually an oil drum cut in half, cleaned out, and hinged so that one half forms a lid – over a fire of pimento wood, which gives the meat its distinctive flavor. The pits are covered with a sheet of galvanized tin, which reflects the heat. Jerk is best served hot off the coals wrapped in paper. You normally order by the pound (US$2 should fill you up).

Jerk supposedly derives from the John Crow Mountain area (see the East Coast chapter), where the runaway slaves known as Maroons first 'jerked' wild pigs, then cooked the meat over a *barbacoa*, from which comes the word 'barbecue.'

Jerk stalls are interspersed along most major roads throughout the country, often advertised with hand-painted signs. You'll find them in the center of towns, too, particularly in Kingston.

Seafood

Naturally for an island nation, there's a strong emphasis on seafood. Snapper and parrot fish are two of the more popular species. Kingfish, grouper, and marlin are also common.

Many fish dishes are heavily spiced or salted. A favorite is *escoveitched* fish, which is pickled in vinegar, then fried and simmered with peppers and onions. Cassava bread, or *bammy*, is a popular accompaniment, as is *festival*.

Pickled herring bears the improbable name of *solomony grundy*. *Rundown* is mackerel cooked in coconut milk and usually eaten at breakfast. *Stamp and go* are saltfish cakes eaten as appetizers.

The term 'lobster' is also used for the local clawless freshwater crayfish, also called *janga*, usually served grilled with butter and garlic, or curried, for as little as US$5 at stalls. Likewise, freshly-caught shrimp *(pepper swimp)* is a favorite in the Black River area, where it is sold by female higglers at the roadside in the village of Middle Quarters.

Avoid turtle eggs in red wine (a specialty of Clarendon Parish). Endangered turtles and their eggs are protected by law. The same is true of booby eggs, taken (illegally) from the rookeries on Goat Island. Eat with a conscience!

Fruits Jamaica is a tropical Eden ripe with native fruits such as the peachlike naseberry, bananas, pineapples, coconuts, the star apple, soursop, ugli, and the ortanique (a citrus crossbred from oranges and tangerines). Tiny roadside shacks also proffer fresh papayas, mangoes, and young or unripe bananas, which are eaten as a staple. *Matrimony* is a salad of star apple and other fruits.

The starchy, rather bland-tasting plantain, closely related to the banana, cannot be eaten in its raw state, but must be cooked. It is treated somewhat like a potato and is usually fried or baked and served as an accompaniment to a main dish. In its unripe form it is used to make delicious chips (English crisps). More mature plantains can develop a delicate sweetness.

I recommend you try the following fruits:

Guava – The guava is a small ovoid or rounded fruit with an intense, musky sweet aroma. It has a yellow-green skin and pinkish, granular flesh studded with regular rows of tiny seeds. It is most commonly used in nectars and

punches, syrups, jams, chutney, and even ice cream.

Mango – This is one of my favorites. Mangoes are a lush fruit that come in an assortment of colors. You should massage the glove-leather skin to soften the pulp, which can be sucked or spooned like custard. Select your mango by its perfume. Ripe mangoes smell unmistakably exquisite.

Papaya – The papaya's cloaks of many colors (from yellow to rose) hides a melon-smooth flesh that likewise runs from citron to vermilion. The central cavity is a trove of edible black seeds. Tenderness and sweet scent are key to buying papayas. They are commonly served with breakfast plates and in fruit salads, and in jams, ice cream, and baked in desserts.

Soursop – This is an ungainly, irregular shaped fruit with cottony pulp that is invitingly fragrant yet acidic. Its taste hints at guava and pineapple. It's most commonly used for puddings, ice creams, canned drinks, and syrups.

Star apples – Star apples are leathery, dark-purple, tennis-ball-sized, gelatinous fruits of banded colors (white, pink, lavender, purple). Its glistening seeds form a star in the center. The fruit is mildly sweet and understated. Immature fruits are gummy and unappetizing: you should feel for some give when buying.

Sugar apple – Sugar apple is a strange name for a fruit that resembles a giant pine cone, with bract-like sections that separate when the fruit is ripe. The gray, juicy flesh is sweet and custard-like and shot with watermelonlike seeds.

Ugli fruit – This fruit is well-named. It is ugly on the vine – like a deformed grapefruit with warty, mottled green or orange skin. But the yellow-golden pulp is delicious: acid-sweet and gushingly juicy.

Guineps

July through November you'll pass children and young men and women holding up bunches of *guineps* (pronounced GI-neps), a small green fruit that grows in clusters, like grapes.

Each 'grape' bears pink flesh that you plop into your mouth whole. It's kind of rubbery, and juicy, and tastes like a cross between a fig and a strawberry. Watch for the big pit in the middle. ■

Vegetables Pumpkin is a staple side dish served boiled and mashed with butter. You may also come across breadfruit in various guises. This starchy vegetable grows wild throughout the island but was first landed in Jamaica only in 1793 following Captain William Bligh's second attempt to procure the fruit from the South Pacific (his first attempt ended in the famous mutiny on the *Bounty*). The vegetable was introduced and raised as a staple food source of slaves. The round 'fruits' weigh up to four pounds.

Young or immature fruit is eaten as a staple, either added to soups or served as an accompaniment to the main dish. The mature (but not yet ripe) fruit is roasted or deep-fried.

Callaloo is akin to spinach and is usually served shredded and steamed or lightly boiled as a side vegetable. It also finds its way into spicy *pepperpot stew*, which dates back to the Arawak period and has been altered over the centuries to become a soup. Local lore says pepperpot can be generations old, as the pot is reheated each day with fresh ingredients added.

Cho-cho, a pulpy squashlike gourd (also known as *christophine*) that hangs on a luxuriant vine in the same way as the cucumber, is served as an accompaniment to meats, in soups, and for making hot pickles.

DRINKS
Nonalcoholic Drinks
Tea Tea is a generic Jamaican term for any usually hot, non-alcoholic drink, commonly referring to the herbal 'teas' popular with locals as aphrodisiacs and medicines. Jamaicans will make teas of anything: Irish moss is often mixed with rum, milk, and spices; and ginger, mint, ganja, and even fish are brewed into teas! Be careful if innocently tempted by mushroom tea: the fungus in question is hallucinogenic and unless you're in search of an LSD-like buzz you should steer clear.

Coffee Jamaican Blue Mountain coffee is considered among the most exotic coffees in the world. It's also the most expensive, fetching up to US$35 a pound in retail shops in the USA and Europe, and double that in Japan! You can buy it in Jamaica for US$2 a pound.

The coffee is relatively mild, light-bodied, and lacks an acrid aftertaste. It has a musty, almost woody flavor, and its own unmistakable aroma. It's delicious.

Most Blue Mountain coffee is exported. Most upscale hotels and restaurants serve it as a matter of course. Unfortunately, the majority of lesser hotels serve either lesser coffees from other parts of the country

or – sacrilege! – powdered instant coffee. Ugh! Be careful if you ask for white coffee, which Jamaicans interpret to mean 50% hot milk and 50% coffee. For more information about Blue Mountain coffee, see the sidebar in the Economy section of the Facts about Jamaica chapter.

Cold Drinks A Jamaican favorite for cooling off is *skyjuice*, shaved ice cones flavored with sugary fruit syrup and lime juice sold at streetside stalls, usually in a small plastic bag with a straw. Sanitation is sometimes questionable. The same is true of *bellywash*, the local name for limeade.

Your best bet for quenching a thirst is to drink coconut water straight from the nut. You'll find them for sale for about US$0.50 from streetside vendors, who will lop off the top and provide a straw. Another refreshing and nutritious drinks to combat the heat is a fruit punch of blended ripe fruits.

Ting is Jamaica's own soft drink, a bottled grapefruit soda. Pepsi and Coca-Cola are also available almost everywhere. Another popular drink with locals is ginger beer, which isn't a beer at all, but a zesty soda.

Alcoholic Drinks
Red Stripe is the beer of Jamaica. In fact, it's synonymous with the island. Crisp, sweet, and lightly hoppy, it's perfectly light and refreshing. It's also the only known antidote to hot spicy *jerk* meats! If you hear locals calling for 'policemen,' don't panic: the beer is named for the natty trim – a conspicuous red seam – on the trouser leg of the uniform of the Jamaican police force.

Heineken is also brewed in Jamaica. Malty Dragon Stout is also popular, and is a favorite of Jamaican women, as is bottled Guinness.

Rum is the libation of choice for poorer Jamaicans, and ranges from dark rums to a mind-bogglingly powerful white (clear) rum. See the Rum sidebar.

Jamaica produces many liqueurs, mostly of rum, but also of coffee beans and fruits. Sangster's rum-based 'Old Jamaica' liqueurs are among the more famous and use natural extracts of Caribbean fruits and spices. The beautiful bottles are enhanced

by the use of traditional lithographic images of historical Jamaica on the labels. (Also see World's End in the Blue Mountains chapter.)

The original coffee liqueur is Tía Maria, which was developed in 1946 by Morris Cargill and a government pathologist, Ken Evans, using Mr Keble Munn's Blue Mountain coffee. The liqueur is named after Cargill's aunt (*tía* is Spanish for aunt). It makes an excellent additive in cakes, soufflés, and pastry creams. The caffeine 'neutralizes' the depressant effect of the alcohol.

ENTERTAINMENT

Jamaica has plenty to keep you amused. Most of the high culture – theater and ballet, for example – is found in Kingston. Elsewhere the key word is *reggae*! If you're a die-hard reggae fan, consider visiting in later July or early August, when Jamaica hosts Reggae Sunsplash and Reggae Sumfest.

Rum Shops Rum shops are the staple of island entertainment. They are funky bars and clubs catering to poorer Jamaicans and where the drink of choice is white rum (often laced with milk). Locals will swear to you that it doesn't give you a hangover, but expect to wake up with a sore head and misty memories. Rum shops are patronized mostly by men, and *de rigueur* decor includes Christmas lights and girlie pin-ups.

Go-Go Clubs Go-go clubs are another staple of Jamaican nightlife. Almost every village has one. Usually it's simply a large bar with a mirrored stage where young women in lingerie and string bikinis dance and perform contortions. Occasionally the dancing is raunchy.

Although the clientele is mostly male, it is not unusual to see couples in the crowd. They're non-threatening places.

Discos & Nightclubs Kingston has more than a dozen discos ranging from earthy dancehall discos frequented mostly by the urban poor to upscale discos playing mostly US and European chart-toppers plus soca. The leading resort towns each have a choice of two or three discos. Many hotels also have their own discos.

Theater Although small-scale theater can be found in all the major towns, Kingston is where the real action is. Jamaica's most beloved theater company is the National Dance Theater Company, which performs at The Little Theater. Almost every performance is sold out.

Cinemas Jamaicans are not big moviegoers. Nonetheless, most large cities have at least one cinema. Entrance generally costs US$1 or US$2.

Gambling There are no casinos in Jamaica. Although hoteliers have lobbied for gambling, in February 1995, the government voted not to allow the introduction of gambling in the country. However, several larger hotels have slot-machine 'casinos' (one-arm bandits), which are legal.

The Story of Rum

Jamaican sugar has been turned into alcohol since Spanish times, when cane molasses *(meleza)* was fermented to make a liquor called *aguardiente*. The British introduced distillation to produce a cane liquor *saccharum*, from which the term 'rum' is derived.

The making of rum involves three stages: fermentation, distillation, and aging. The traditional distillation process used copper pots and produced a heavily flavored rum containing 85% alcohol and 15% water. The distilled liquor was then poured into 40-gallon charred-oak barrels and matured from three to 20 years. Rum derived its distinct flavor and color from the charred barrel as it aged. A small percentage was lost every year to evaporation: the 'angel's share.'

Very little rum is produced in this manner today. The modern, continuous-still method produces a more lightly flavored rum of higher alcohol content. Most modern rum is aged in stainless steel vats for no more than three years, and since all rums are clear after distillation, the color and flavor are 'manufactured' with caramel and other additives.

White overproof is the rum of the poor Jamaican, and it's an integral part of island culture. Overproof rum from homemade stills is virtually pure alcohol (legally overproof rum is 151 proof, but bootleg liquor can be a brain-melting, throat-searing 170 proof).

It is used as a remedy for all sorts of maladies, from toothaches to colds (it was originally called 'Kill Devil'). It's also used to clean newborn babies and to baptize them. Of course, it drowns sorrows and is imbibed liberally at wakes to chase away *duppies* (ghosts). Jamaican gravediggers still sprinkle rum on the ground before digging to consecrate it. White rum is also supposedly good for a man's libido (a popular version is the 'Front End Loader'). ■

Betting on horseracing is permitted at Caymanas Park (the race-track near Portmore) and at betting shops nationwide. Charles Off Betting (☎ 922-3124) and Western Track Ltd (☎ 952-8721) are two of the leading chain branches. See Spectator Sports below.

SPECTATOR SPORTS

Jamaica is relatively devoid of spectator sports. Cricket (see below) is by far the most important sport on the island, and games between leading regional and international teams are played frequently at Sabina Park, Kingston. Polo is played weekly at Chukka Cove, in St Ann Parish.

Crazy about Horses

Jamaicans have always been passionate about horseracing. In 1687 the governor of Jamaica even dissolved the House of Assembly following a riot when the Speaker denied a member permission to attend a horserace. ■

Horseracing takes place at Caymanas Park, in Portmore, 10 miles west of Kingston, each Wednesday and Saturday and public holidays (for information, contact Caymanas Track Ltd, Gregory Park, St Catherine; ☎ 988-2523, fax 998-4635). Track Tours Ltd offers tours from Montego Bay on race days (PO Box 19, Montego Bay, ☎ 952-4657), and JUTA Ltd, in Coconut Grove Plaza, offers tours from Ocho Rios (☎ 974-2292, fax 974-5406).

The Dover Raceway at St Ann hosts the Motor Sports Championship Series of car and motorcycle racing. For more details on sporting events see Special Events earlier in this chapter.

Cricket

Cricket, played virtually year-round, is as much a part of Jamaica's cultural landscape as reefers and reggae. You'll come across small fields and makeshift pitches in even the most remote backwaters, where boys with makeshift bats and wickets practice the bowls and swings that may one day take them from rural obscurity to fortune and fame.

Cricket is a legacy of British rule. The late 19th-century colonialists sponsored cricket as a game of true gentlemen. It was a handy tool for spreading English culture and an admiration for the 'mother country.' In his book *Beyond a Boundary*, CLR James postulated that the level of maturity of cricket was used by the British in the first half of this century as a measure of whether a colony was prepared for self-rule. There's no doubt that it has helped cement a sense of regional identity and unity throughout the English-speaking Caribbean.

Jamaica has no national team. Instead, best players from the cricketing nations of the Caribbean form the West Indies team, which has dominated world cricket for two decades. National feelings run high, however, and cricket fever boils over when the West Indies plays England. Regional competitions feature teams from individual islands.

Jamaicans turn what is in its home country a game without spirit into the most exhilarating cricket in the world. Leading tournaments ignite holy passions. They're also such a social occasion that even if you haven't a clue about the rules of the game, it's impossible not to fall for its magic. The crowds are their own entertainment. Entire families arrive with coolers of beer and hampers stuffed with Jamaican food. Plenty of rum is consumed, and the calls of the crowd make for great theater!

It's easy to get the gist of the game. Here are the basics:

Two teams of 11 players compete. As in baseball, one team fields its entire team while the other team has individuals come up to bat against a bowler (pitcher). The batter attempts to protect a wicket – three wooden stumps (posts), on top of which sit two precariously balanced bails (crosspieces) – with a three-foot-long, five-inch-wide bat, flat on one side and rounded on the other. The bowler attempts to knock the bails from the wicket (home plate), which stands at the end of a 22-yard-long grass pitch in the center of a circular field. The batsman attempts to hit the ball, which may be delivered at a slow pace or even at 100 mph and which usually bounces in front of the batter on delivery. The batter can send the ball in any direction, including behind, and may choose to run to the end of the pitch to score a run. Four runs are automatically earned if the ball passes the boundary of the cricket field; six if it does so without touching the ground (the equivalent of a home run in baseball).

If a fieldsman catches the ball before it hits the ground, the batsman is out (the batsman may also be called out if the ball hits his leg instead of the wicket). A second batsman stands at the end of the pitch. The two batters must run past each other to opposite ends to score a run, and can do so as many times as prudence allows while the ball is being fielded (the equivalent of 'stealing bases;' as in baseball, if the ball is fielded to the wicket before the batsman reaches it, then he is out). After every six balls (pitches), or 'over,' a second bowler bowls from the opposite wicket.

Each team usually plays two innings. An inning is complete when all the team members are out (there are various other ways in which they can be called 'out' by one of two umpires). The team can choose to retire before all its members have batted, in which case the average number of runs per batter can prove strategically useful in calculating a winner (the best batters usually bat first). To hit a 'century' (100 runs) in an inning is considered a great accomplishment. To be 'bowled for a duck' (0 runs) is a disgrace.

Traditionally, test matches (games between international teams) are played over the course of three to five days, not least because the batsmen are so skilled that it can take a long time to get them out.

The rising Jamaican star is Jimmy Adams, who follows in the footsteps of such heroes as George Headley. In the 1930s, Headley dazzled the world with his unique skills (he is considered Jamaica's equivalent of Babe Ruth) and is still the only man to score two centuries in one test match at Lord's, the London cricket ground that is the sport's world headquarters.

THINGS TO BUY

Jamaica has a wide range of arts, crafts, and duty-free items, plus food items and drinks such as Blue Mountain coffee, rum liqueurs, Pickapeppa sauce, and marinades such as Busha Brown's gourmet pickles, relishes, and other gourmet products. I am not aware of any Jamaican foods, drinks, or spices that cannot be exported, though you should check with your home country's customs to see what restrictions they might impose on imports. See Customs earlier in this chapter for more information.

Every resort area has a choice of duty-free stores, crafts shops, and roadside stalls selling a full range of goods. Kingston has a world-class range of shopping centers.

In general, the closer you get to the source, the lower the price.

Cigars

Fine handmade Jamaican cigars give Havana cigars a run for their money. Cinfuentes y Cia Ltd (a subsidiary of General Cigar Co of Connecticut) has been operating in Jamaica for over 40 years. The company specializes in premium Macanudo cigars. You can even buy direct from the factory (☎ 924-7052). You can also buy Cinfuentes or Royal Jamaica cigars at gift shops, duty-free outlets, Norman Manley and Donald Sangster international airports, or the Jamaica Tobacco Retail Store, 31 Upper Waterloo Rd, Kingston 10 (☎ 925-1547).

Duty-Free Goods

Every resort town has a plethora of duty-free shops and most upscale hotels sell name-brand duty-free items. Ocho Rios, Montego Bay, and Kingston have the largest number of duty-free stores. Many items can be bought at up to 30% below US or European retail prices. The same is true of island-made products such as rums, liqueurs, and cigars, which you can buy for 50% or greater saving. Prices vary between stores and resorts, however, so it pays to comparison shop.

By law you must pay for duty-free goods in foreign currency. You can use credit

---

Shopping with a Conscience

Many souvenirs sold in Jamaica are made from protected species of plants and animals that have been acquired illegally. By collecting or purchasing these items, you undermine the wildlife conservation efforts of the Jamaican government and wildlife organizations.

Most sea turtle products, including 'tortoiseshell' jewelry and combs, are made from the highly endangered hawksbill sea turtle. Other species are killed for eggs, food products, taxidermy, leather, and oil for creams. All are prohibited in trade. And all products made of endangered American crocodile are prohibited, as are black and white coral products. Many species of plants – especially orchids – are endemics, also protected by law. Under US and other national laws, violation of a foreign wildlife law is automatically a violation of domestic law.

Everywhere you drive along the north coast, you'll see Queen conch shells for sale. The species is of great ecological importance to Caribbean seagrass ecosystems, but is heavily overcollected in some areas. Historically, the meat has been a staple food item. Today the shells are popular ornaments and the conch population is now declining. Sure, they look pretty. But don't buy!

For further information contact the World Wildlife Fund (1250 24th St NW, Washington, DC 20037). ■

---

cards or traveler's checks. In certain cases you may find that you cannot walk out with your purchase; instead, the goods will be delivered to your hotel or cruise ship.

Arts & Crafts

Tens of thousands of Jamaicans make a living as woodcarvers. Much of the artwork is kitsch, with seascapes and paintings of Rastafarians for as little as US$10, and intuitive hardwood carvings of Bob Marley, glistening with oil, and fishes and animals, often painted in rainbow hues and touched with pointillist dots for anywhere from US$5 to $50.

There's plenty of first-rate art, too. Jamaican art is sought after by collectors worldwide, as it has been for two centuries (decorative Jamaican jewel boxes, furniture, combs, etc, were treasured items in 18th- and 19th-century England). The best works are bought by galleries for sale. Their prices are fixed.

You should look far and wide before making a purchase. You'll know it when you see it. You should carefully examine wood carvings. Avoid green wood, as the carving will split when the wood dries out. Minute holes betray woodworm.

Colorful bead jewelry is a good buy, including bracelets in Rasta colors. Baskets and other straw goods are also great bargains. Styles of baskets are as varied as their uses. The traditional *bankra* is an all-purpose rectangular basket of woven palm thatch. It's an integral part of the rural Jamaican scene. The word bankra, which is derived from the Ghanaian *bonkara*, is now synonymous with basket.

All the resort towns have crafts markets, but you'll find crafts stalls along the roadsides in even remote places. The greater the distance from a craft market or resort town, the lower the prices in general.

Never pay the asking price. *Higgle!* Higgling is expected; if you pay the first price quoted, you'll pay over the odds. Expect to settle on a price at least 20% below the initial asking price. The eventual price is dependent on your patience and bargaining skills. Keep your cool and good humor, which will go a long way towards getting a fair price. Remember, however, that the life of most higglers is hard and you should be willing to pay a fair price. Leave your ego behind when bargaining – it is not a battle! Don't get involved in a serious bargaining if you don't intend to buy – to do so displays crass insensitivity.

Most roadside stalls accept cash only. Few will be able to ship your item home for you.

Remember that it is illegal to buy or sell coral, turtle shell (tortoise shell), bird feathers, and other products derived from endangered species. By buying these products you are assisting in the decimation of the species. *Shop with a conscience!*

Furniture

Jamaican craftsmen are among the world's best at making antique reproduction furniture, and there are several top-notch furniture-making factories that manufacture in mahogany, wicker, and exotic woods, such as blue mahoe, aloe, lignum vitae, and guango. Furniture produced for the export market is top of the line, with an emphasis on Chippendale and Queen Anne styles. Medallion Galleries is one of the leading producers (1 Nanse Pen Rd, Kingston 11, ☎ 923-9017). They even make grandfather clocks!

High-quality, hand-made wicker has also been winning a market for itself in North America, its popularity enhanced by the honey color of the vine (vines from elsewhere tend to be lighter in color). Creative Wicker Ltd (Shop 1, 6 St Lucia Ave, Kingston, ☎ 929-3019) is geared for export and can fulfill orders within a few weeks.

The Jamaica Furniture Guild (13 Dominica Drive, Kingston 5, ☎ 929-1292) represents the leading exporters. You should call them for a recommendation and reference if you plan on shipping furniture home.

Getting There & Away

No problem, mon! Jamaica is easy to get to. Dozens of charter companies and many prominent airlines offer direct service to the island. It's a regular port of call on cruise ship itineraries, and yachters find Jamaica an easy hop from neighboring islands and the eastern seaboard of North America.

AIR

Jamaica enjoys one of the best air feeds in the Caribbean, from both North America and Europe. Its proximity to Florida means regular, relatively inexpensive flights from Miami, Fort Lauderdale, and Orlando, as well as other US East Coast gateways.

Airports & Airlines

Jamaica has two international airports: Norman Manley International Airport at Kingston, and the Donald Sangster International Airport at Montego Bay. Both were undergoing improvements and expansion at press time. In late 1995, consideration was being given to expanding a private airport at Mandeville to handle international flights.

There are also four additional airports for which the government has responsibility. They are Tinson Pen in Kingston, Boscobel near Ocho Rios, Negril Aerodrome, and Ken Jones Aerodrome at Port Antonio. Numerous other small airstrips are scattered around the island.

Norman Manley International Airport

Kingston's international airport is on the Palisadoes, a long sandspit about 11 miles southeast from downtown.

You'll find a JTB information desk facing you immediately you enter the immigration hall upon arrival. There's a money-exchange bureau offering slightly better rates than the banks to the left of Customs. Immigration and Customs formalities are straightforward and usually without long lines. There's a taxi information booth on the left as you exit Customs, beyond which an alley (also on the left) leads to a bank and Island Car Rentals. Straight ahead is the JUTA taxi office and, beyond, a police station and the airport's only eatery – the Otaheitis Café. Fortunately, the airport is hassle free. There are few porters, and plenty of public telephones. For flight arrival and departure information, call ☎ 928-6077 (or the specific airline).

Donald Sangster International Airport

The vast majority of visitors to Jamaica arrive at this airport, about two miles east of Montego Bay. There's a JTB information booth and 'bureau de change' in the arrivals hall. Customs is usually a breeze, although there can be a lengthy wait if many Jamaican nationals are on the flight; customs officials tend to go through their baggage with a fine-toothed comb. Beware also if you travel with heavy carry-on baggage: you may have a long walk to the arrivals hall, depending on where your aircraft berths.

Theft from baggage is a problem at the airport. Ensure your luggage is locked and don't leave valuables in unlocked pockets.

For flight arrival and departure information, call ☎ 952-5530 (or the specific airline). See the Northwest Coast chapter for further details.

Airlines The following major airlines have offices in Jamaica:

Air Canada
    Kingston   ☎ 924-8211
    Montego Bay   ☎ 952-5160
Air Jamaica
    Kingston   ☎ 922-4661
    Montego Bay   ☎ 952-4300
    Negril   ☎ 957-4210
    Ocho Rios   ☎ 974-2566
ALM
    Kingston   ☎ 924-8092
    Montego Bay   ☎ 952-5530
American Airlines
    Kingston   ☎ 924-8305
    Montego Bay   ☎ 952-5950
British Airways
    Kingston   ☎ 929-9020
    Montego Bay   ☎ 952-3771
BWIA
    Kingston   ☎ 924-8376
Cayman Airways
    Kingston   ☎ 926-1762
Continental Airlines
    Montego Bay   ☎ 952-4460
Northwest Airlines
    Montego Bay   ☎ 952-4033
USAir
    Montego Bay   ☎ 940-0172

Buying Tickets

The plane ticket will probably be the single most expensive item in your budget, and buying it can be an intimidating business. There is likely to be a multitude of airlines and travel agents hoping to separate you from your money, and it is always worth putting aside a few hours to research the current state of the market. Start early: some of the cheapest tickets have to be bought months in advance, and some popular flights sell out early. Talk to other recent travelers – they may be able to stop you from making some of the same old mistakes. Look for special offers in newspapers and magazines, consult reference books, and phone several travel agents for bargains. Find out the fare, the route, the duration of the journey, and any restrictions on the ticket. (See restrictions in the Air Travel Glossary.) Then sit back and decide which is best for you.

You may discover that those impossibly cheap flights are 'fully booked, but we do have another one that costs a bit more . . .' Or they may claim to have 'the last two seats available' for the period of your travels, which they 'can only hold for a maximum of two hours.' Don't panic – keep phoning around.

Most airlines charge different fares according to the season (highest fares are normally in the peak season, from mid-December through mid-April). If you are traveling from the UK or the USA, you will probably find the cheapest flights being advertised by obscure 'bucket shops' (called 'consolidators' in the USA), the names of which may not have yet reached the telephone directory. Most such firms are honest and solvent, but there are a few rogues that will take your money and disappear, to reopen elsewhere a month or two later under a new name. If you feel suspicious about a firm, don't give them all the money at once – leave a deposit of 20% or so and pay the balance when you get the ticket. If they insist on cash in advance, go somewhere else. And once you have the ticket, phone the airline to confirm that you are actually booked on the flight. Bucket shops act as clearinghouses for 'unsold' seats, selling tickets for seats that an airline anticipates being unable to fill. Such tickets are discounted at anywhere from 20 to 35% – a handy savings! Before committing to a purchase, call the airline to see if it can match the consolidator's price with a last-fare promotional fare.

You may decide to pay more than the rock-bottom fare by opting for the safety of a better-known travel agent. Firms such as STA Travel, which has offices worldwide, Council Travel in the USA, or Travel CUTS in Canada are not going to disappear overnight, leaving you clutching a receipt for a nonexistent ticket, but they do offer good prices to most destinations. These three companies specialize in fares for students. However, no discount student fares are available to Jamaica from North America.

Once you have your ticket, write down its number, together with the flight number and other details, and keep the information someplace separate. If the ticket is lost or stolen, this will help you get a replacement.

It's sensible to buy travel insurance as early as possible (see Visas & Documents in Facts for the Visitor). If you buy it the week before you fly, you may discover, for example, that you're not covered for delays to your flight caused by industrial action.

Airfares to Jamaica are highest in the winter season. Fares are reduced up to 20% or more in off-peak periods (especially mid-April to mid-December). Traveling on a weekday may also reduce the cost.

Travelers with Special Needs

If you have special needs of any sort – you've broken a leg, you're vegetarian, traveling in a wheelchair, taking the baby, terrified of flying – you should let the airline know as soon as possible so that they can make arrangements accordingly. You should remind them when you reconfirm your booking (at least 72 hours before departure) and again when you check in at the airport. It may also be worth phoning other airlines before you make your booking to find out how they might handle your particular needs.

Airports and airlines can be surprisingly helpful, but they do need advance warning. Most international airports will provide escorts from check-in through boarding, and there should be ramps, lifts, accessible toilets, and reachable phones. Aircraft toilets, on the other hand, are likely to present a problem; travelers should discuss this with the airline at an early stage and, if necessary, with their doctor. See the Disabled Travelers section in Facts for the Visitor for more information.

Guide dogs for the blind will often have to travel in a specially pressurized baggage compartment with other animals, away from their owner, though smaller guide dogs are sometimes admitted to the cabin. All guide dogs will be subject to the same quarantine laws (six months in isolation, etc) as any other animal when entering or returning to countries currently free of rabies such as Britain or Australia. Only animals born and raised in Britain are currently allowed into Jamaica.

Deaf travelers can ask for airport and inflight announcements to be written down for them.

Children under two travel for 10% of the standard fare (or free, on some airlines), as long as they don't occupy a seat. They don't get a baggage allowance either. 'Skycots' should be provided by the airline if requested in advance; these will take a child weighing up to about 10 kg. Children between two and 12 can usually occupy a seat for half to two-thirds of the full fare, and do get a baggage allowance. Strollers and wheelchairs can often be taken as hand luggage.

The USA

The most popular routings are via Miami and New York, but Jamaica is also served by direct flights from a dozen or so other cities.

Most major US carriers, including American Airlines, Continental, United, and USAir, fly to Jamaica, which allows you to use their 'frequent flyer' and other discount promotions. American Airlines has the most frequent service to Montego Bay, continuing to Kingston. It also services many other Caribbean islands, with Puerto Rico as a main connecting hub.

The following toll-free airline information and reservation numbers, are valid anywhere in the USA, Canada, Mexico, and the Caribbean:

Air Jamaica	☎ (800) 523-5585
American	☎ (800) 433-7300
British Airways	☎ (800) 247-9297
Continental	☎ (800) 525-0280
Delta Airlines	☎ (800) 221-1212
TWA	☎ (800) 221-2000
United Airlines	☎ (800) 538-2929
USAir	☎ (800) 428-4322

Air Jamaica flies more people to the island than any other airline, and from more gateways in the USA, too. Formerly govern-

Air Travel Glossary

Apex – Apex, or 'advance purchase excursion,' is a discounted ticket that must be paid for in advance. There are penalties if you wish to change it.

baggage allowance – This will be written on your ticket: usually one 20 kg item to go in the hold, plus one item of carry-on luggage.

bucket shop – An unbonded travel agency specializing in discounted airline tickets.

bumped – Just because you have a confirmed seat doesn't mean you're going to get on the plane – see overbooking.

cancellation penalties – If you have to cancel or change an Apex ticket, there are often heavy penalties involved; insurance can sometimes be taken out against these penalties. Some airlines impose penalties on regular tickets as well, particularly against 'no show' passengers.

check in – Airlines ask you to check in a certain time ahead of the flight departure (usually 1½ hours on international flights). If you fail to check in on time and the flight is overbooked, the airline can cancel your booking and give your seat to somebody else.

confirmation – Having a ticket written out with the flight and date you want doesn't mean you have a seat until the agent has checked with the airline that your status is confirmed. Meanwhile you are 'on request.'

discounted tickets – There are two types of discounted fares – officially discounted (see promotional fares) and unofficially discounted. The lowest prices often impose drawbacks like flying with unpopular airlines, inconvenient schedules, or unpleasant routes and connections. A discounted ticket can save you things other than money – you may be able to pay Apex prices without the associated Apex advance booking and other requirements. Discounted tickets only exist where there is fierce competition.

full fares – Airlines traditionally offer first class (coded F), business class (coded J), and economy class (coded Y) tickets. These days there are so many promotional and discounted fares available from the regular economy class that few passengers pay full economy fare.

lost tickets – If you lose your airline ticket, an airline will usually treat it like a traveler's check and, after inquiries, issue you with another one. Legally, however, an airline is entitled to treat it like cash – if you lose it, it's gone forever. Take good care of your tickets.

---

ment-owned, it was privatized in 1994 and immediately began an ambitious renovation and expansion that incorporates a brilliant new livery of Caribbean colors. Expanded gateways – increased from 73 flights to 136 flights per week by June, 1996 – are part of a new plan for the airline, which also began renovating its fleet (it ordered six new A310 and six A320 jets to replace older 727s and A300s). All flights are entirely smoke-free. Free champagne breakfasts are offered in every class, plus free champagne, beer, and wine with lunch or dinner.

Air Jamaica offers direct service to Jamaica from Atlanta, Baltimore/Washington, Chicago, Fort Lauderdale, Miami, Orlando, New York (Newark *and* Kennedy airports), Philadelphia, Los Angeles and San Francisco. (Nonstop flights from the West Coast take about the same time as flying to Hawaii – about five to six hours.)

Air Jamaica promotes a 'Seventh Heaven Fly Free Program': if you buy six round-

no shows – No shows are passengers who fail to show up for their flight, sometimes due to unexpected delays or disasters, sometimes due to simply forgetting, sometimes because they made more than one booking and didn't bother to cancel the one they didn't want. Full-fare passengers who fail to turn up are sometimes entitled to travel on a later flight. The rest of us are penalized (see cancellation penalties).

onward tickets – An entry requirement for many countries is that you have an onward or return ticket, in other words, a ticket out of the country. If you're not sure what you intend to do next, the easiest solution is to buy the cheapest onward ticket to a neighboring country or a ticket from a reliable airline that can later be refunded if you do not use it.

open jaws – A return ticket where you fly out to one place but return from another. If available, this can save you backtracking to your arrival point.

overbooking – Airlines hate to fly with empty seats and since every flight has some passengers who fail to show up (see No Shows), airlines often book more passengers than they have seats. Usually the excess passengers balance those who fail to show up, but occasionally somebody gets 'bumped.' If this happens, guess who it is most likely to be? The passengers who check in late.

promotional fares – Officially discounted fares, like Apex fares, that are available from travel agents or direct from the airline.

reconfirmation – At least 72 hours prior to departure time, you must contact the airline and 'reconfirm' that you intend to be on the flight. If you don't do this, the airline can delete your name from the passenger list and you could lose your seat. You don't have to reconfirm the first flight on your itinerary or if your stopover is less than 72 hours. It doesn't hurt to reconfirm more than once.

restrictions – Discounted tickets often have various restrictions on them – advance purchase is the most common (see Apex). Others are restrictions on the minimum and maximum period you must be away, such as a minimum of 14 days or a maximum of one year. (See cancellation penalties.)

standby – A discounted ticket where you only fly if there is a seat free at the last moment. Standby fares are usually only available on domestic routes.

transferred tickets – Airline tickets cannot be transferred from one person to another. Travelers sometimes try to sell the return half of their ticket, but officials can ask you to prove that you are the person named on the ticket. ■

---

trip tickets in any two-year period, you get the seventh free (if three tickets were 1st class, then the free ticket is 1st class also). Alternately, you'll receive a 50% discount on a fifth ticket if you purchase four round-trip tickets within two years.

In mid-1995, a new carrier, Caribbean Airlines, initiated service from Miami to Montego Bay and Kingston on Sundays, Mondays, Wednesdays, and Fridays.

Some airlines offer special rates at select hotels in conjunction with the purchase of an airline ticket. Sandals, a leading resort chain, awards its guests who are members of American Airlines' AAdvantage frequent flyer program 1000 miles for stays of three or more nights.

Air Jamaica and Carnival Airlines offer joint fares from Los Angeles via Miami, with daily flights (round-trip economy seats were US$531, off-peak, in 1995).

The *New York Times*, the *LA Times*, and most other major city newspapers all produce weekly travel sections in which you'll find any number of ads quoting air-fares. The monthly *Travel Unlimited* newsletter publishes details of some of the cheapest airfares and courier possibilities for destinations all over the world, departing from the USA. Write to PO Box 1058, Allston, MA 02134.

Charter Flights Charter flights generally offer the lowest fares for confirmed reservations (sometimes one-third or more off of airline prices) and can be booked through most travel agencies. You can sometimes also book one-way tickets with charter airlines for less than half the round-trip fare. Often the charter price is for a package that includes flight and accommodations. They are usually direct flights, without the hub-stop common on standard airlines. Few charters are listed in airline computer reservations systems, as they're operated by wholesale tour operators with whom you or your travel agent will have to deal directly.

Before buying, compare charter prices with an airline's 'sale' fare and a discount ticket from a consolidator.

There are drawbacks to this mode of travel. Firstly, although you can buy the ticket without an advance-purchase requirement, you do have to fix your departure and return dates well ahead of time; a substantial fee may apply for any changes or cancellations (you should consider cancellation insurance in the event of illness, etc). Seating may be more cramped, as planes are usually full, and flights often depart at inconvenient hours. And though US charter operators are bonded with the US government, if the tour operator or airline defaults, you may have problems getting your money back. Also, charter flights are oftentimes less organized than the standard carriers, and processing at airline counters often is more confused and time-consuming, even though the charter operator may be using the service desk and aircraft of a major airline.

Charter operator Tower Air (☎ (800) 348-6937) offers service and a standard

of quality on par with any major North American airline. Sunburst Holidays uses them for round-trip charter flights, offering service from Miami for about US$200, from New York for about US$300, from Boston for about US$360, from San Francisco for about US$500, and from Los Angeles for about US$440. Sunburst's air/hotel packages begin at US$384 for three-nights at Montego Bay or Negril, with round-trip airfare included from Baltimore, Boston, New York, or Philadelphia (you can upgrade to 1st class for US$149 extra; free if you're staying at Sans Souci or Grand Lido resorts).

Sun Splash Tours specializes in spring break and student travel, and has packages starting at around US$399 for seven nights' hotel accommodations, round-trip airfare, airport transfers, and entertainment. Student Travel Services features a seven-night charter package in Montego Bay from US$439 (based on quadruple occupancy), with nonstop flights from Boston, New York, Philadelphia, and Raleigh.

Dozens of charter operators fly to Jamaica from the USA. Check the Sunday travel sections of major city newspapers. Your travel agent should also be able to provide a listing. A good resource is *The Worldwide Guide to Cheap Airfares* by Michael McColl, which provides a comprehensive listing and details of charter tour operators.

Some key charter operators to Jamaica include:

Council Charter
  205 E 42nd St, New York, NY 10017 (☎ (212) 661-1450 or (800) 800-8222)
Island Flight Vacations
  6033 W Century Blvd No 807, Los Angeles, CA 90045 (☎ (310) 477-5858 or (800) 426-4570, fax (310) 410-0830)
Student Travel Services
  120 N Aurora St, Ithaca, NY 14850 (☎ (607) 272-6964 or (800) 648-4849, fax (607) 272-6963)
Sun Splash Tours
  236 W 27th St No 700, New York, NY 10001 (☎ (212) 366-4922 or (800) 426-7710, fax (212) 366-5642)

Sunbird Vacation
    2025 Gateway Place, San Jose, CA 95110
    (☎ (408) 452-0233 or (800) 800-0202,
    fax (408) 452-0475)
Sunburst Holidays
    4779 Broadway, New York, NY 10034
    (☎ (212) 567-2050 or (800) 666-8346,
    fax (212) 942-9501)
    6033 W Century Blvd, Los Angeles, CA
    90045 (☎ (800) 666-8346)
Tower Air
    17 JFK International Airport, Jamaica, NY
    11434 (☎ (718) 553-8500 or (800) 348-6937)

Discount Tickets Many discount-ticket agencies sell reduced-rate tickets to the Caribbean. One of the leading brokers specializing in the area is Pan Express Travel (25 W 39th St, New York, NY 10018, ☎ (212) 719-9292). Student agencies such as College Travel International (☎ (217) 367-0614; email wolvie@prairienet.org) offer airfares at up to 50% savings.

Other leading discount agencies include:

Access International
    101 W 31st St, New York, NY 10001
    (☎ (212) 465-0707 or (800) 825-3633,
    fax (212) 594-6711)
Express Discount Travel
    5945 Mission Gorge Rd No 2, San Diego,
    CA 92120 (☎ (619) 283-6324 or (800) 228-
    0513)
People's Air Tours
    2536 W Peterson, Chicago, IL 60659
    (☎ (312) 761-7500 or (800) 635-7184)

Courier Flights If you're willing to fly at short notice and travel light, courier flights are one of the cheapest ways to go – normally about half the standard fare, but often much less. As a courier, you 'deliver' an item such as a parcel or document on behalf of a company. Usually the handling of the item is taken care of by the courier company: you merely act as its agent by occupying a seat. In exchange, you must give up your baggage allowance, which the courier company uses for the item to be delivered.

Unfortunately, there are very few options to the Caribbean. For information, try

NOW Voyager, the leading booking agency for courier companies, which does book flights to the Caribbean (74 Varick St No 307, New York, NY 10013, ☎ (212) 431-1616). You must pay a one-time US$50 registration fee.

Two good resources are *The Courier Air Travel Handbook*, by Mark Field, and *The Worldwide Guide to Cheap Airfares*, by Michael McColl.

Standby & Last Minute If you can fly at very short notice (usually within seven days of travel), then consider buying a ticket from a 'last minute' ticket broker. These companies buy surplus seats from charter airlines (and sometimes standard carriers) at hugely discounted prices. The airline would rather fill the seat than fly empty – you reap the reward. Discounts can be as great as 40% for a confirmed seat.

One of the leading distress-sale brokers is Last Minute Travel Club, which specializes in air/hotel packages to the Caribbean (1249 Boylston St, Boston, MA 02215, ☎ (617) 267-9800 or (800) 527-8646). Other last-minute ticket agencies require you to become a member of their club; annual fees cost about US$40, for which you receive regular updates. Companies to consider include:

Discount Travel International
    114 Forest Ave, Ives Bldg No 205, Narberth,
    PA 19072 (☎ (800) 334-9294)
Moment's Notice
    425 Madison Ave, New York, NY 10017
    (☎ (212) 486-0500)
Worldwide Discount Travel Club
    1674 Meridian Ave, Miami Beach, FL 33139
    (☎ (305) 534-2082)

Canada

Air Canada (☎ (800) 776-3000) serves Montego Bay four times weekly from Montreal, and Montego Bay and Kingston from Toronto daily in peak season. Air Jamaica (4141 Yonge St, Willowdale ON, M2P 2A6 (☎ (416) 229-6024) flies nonstop from Toronto and Montreal.

Major city newspapers such as the *Toronto Globe & Mail* and the *Vancouver*

Sun carry travel agents' ads. The magazine *Great Expeditions* (PO Box 8000-411, Abbotsford BC, V2S 6H1) is also useful.

Charter Flights Air Transat offers weekly charter flights from Toronto for as little as C$369 in low season. Two other charter airlines – Royal and Canada 3000 – also fly from Toronto.

Regent Holidays (6205 Airport Rd, Building A, No 200, Mississauga ON, L4V 1E1, ☎ (905) 673-3343) offers charter flights and air/hotel packages using Air Transat. Conquest Tours (85 Brisbane Rd, Downsview ON, M3J 2K3, ☎ (416) 665-9255, fax (416) 665-6811) has charter flights plus hotel packages from Ottawa and Toronto, from C$449. Fiesta Sun (111 Avenue Rd, No 500, Toronto ON, M5R 3J8, ☎ (416) 967-1510, fax (416) 967-4951) has charters on Tuesdays and Sundays from C$469 from Toronto.

Australia & New Zealand

STA Travel and Flight Centres International are major dealers in cheap airfares. Check the travel agents' ads in the yellow pages and phone around.

The UK

Jamaica is well served by flights from the UK. Air Jamaica (☎ (0181) 570-9171) introduced direct service from Heathrow in March 1996, with three flights weekly. British Airways also advertises direct service to Montego Bay and Kingston from Heathrow. It also operates a charter service from Gatwick three times weekly (Wednesday, Saturday, and Sunday) in summer, and twice weekly in winter. It's advisable to check seasonal variations by calling British Airways (☎ (0181) 897-4000).

Several airlines feed Miami and Fort Lauderdale from the UK, including American Airlines, Delta Airlines, and Virgin Atlantic. American Airlines has connecting service to Jamaica, while British Airways has onward service from Nassau, Bahamas.

Trailfinders in west London produces a lavishly illustrated brochure that includes airfare details (44–48 Earls Court Rd,

London W8 6ES, ☎ (0171) 938-3366). STA also has branches in the UK. Look in the magazine *Time Out,* the Sunday papers, and *Exchange & Mart* for ads. Also look out for the free magazines widely available in London – start by looking outside the main railway stations.

Most British travel agents are registered with ABTA (Association of British Travel Agents). If you have paid for your flight through an ABTA-registered agent who then goes out of business, ABTA guarantees a refund or an alternative. Unregistered bucket shops are riskier, but sometimes cheaper, too.

The Globetrotters Club publishes a newsletter called *Globe* that covers obscure destinations and can help in finding traveling companions (BCM Roving, London WC1N 3XX).

One of the leading air-only travel specialists is Caribbean Gold (☎ (0181) 741-8491).

Charter Flights Jamaica is a major charter destination from the UK, and many charter operators have contracted with airlines since Airtours first tested the market in 1988. All charter flights are into Montego Bay.

Thomson Holidays has weekly charters year-round with Britannia Airways from Manchester and Gatwick. Airtours (Sunday) and Unijet (Monday) also offer weekly charters from Manchester and Gatwick. Unijet has week-long packages from £399.

All-Jamaica Ltd specializes in travel between the UK and Jamaica. AJL uses Air UK Leisure from Manchester to Montego Bay on Sundays, and London Gatwick to Montego Bay on Mondays, connecting with flights to Cuba.

Leading charter operators include:

Airtours	☎ (0706) 260000
All Jamaica	☎ (0161) 796-9222
	fax (0161) 796-9444
British Airways Holidays	
	☎ (0293) 617000
Caribbean Connection	☎ (0244) 341131
Caribtours	☎ (0171) 581-3517
	fax (0171) 225-2491

Cosmos	☎ (061) 480-5799
Harlequin Worldwide	☎ (0708) 852780
	fax (0708) 854952
Jetlife Holidays	☎ (0322) 614801
Kuoni	☎ (0306) 742222
Simply Caribbean	☎ (0423) 526887
Thomas Cook	☎ (0733) 332255
Thomson Holidays	☎ (061) 839-0202
	fax (0171) 387-8451
Unijet Travel	☎ (0444) 459191
Virgin Holidays	☎ (0293) 617181

Continental Europe

In Denmark, Cruise & Travel specializes in travel to the Caribbean (Bredgade 35C, Copenhagen,1260 K, ☎ (45-33) 119-500, fax (45-33) 119-501).

In France, contact Alternative Travel (8 Ave de Messine, Paris 75008, ☎ 33-1-42.89.42.46, fax 33-1-42.89.80.73) or Austral (29 Rue Dupuits Mauger, Rennes 35000, ☎ 33-993-0300).

LTU Airways flys from Düsseldorf and Munich to Montego Bay on Mondays (LTU International Airways, Parsevalstra. 7a, D-40468 Düsseldorf, ☎ 0211-41-0952; or Eisenhelmerstr. 61, D-80687 München, ☎ 089-57-09-29-30). LTU offers a sky-shuttle service from Düsseldorf to/from Frankfurt airport (US$20 round-trip).

Aeroflot (70 Piccadilly, London W1V 9HH, ☎ (0171) 491-1764) has a weekly service to Montego Bay from Shannon Airport (☎ (06) 47-2299) in Ireland.

Viaggidea SRL operates a weekly charter flight to Montego Bay year-round (via Biondelli 1, Milano 20141, ☎ (2) 895291, fax (2) 846-771). Hotelplan Italia (Corso Italia 1, Milano 20129, ☎ (2) 721361, fax (2) 877558) and Viaggiare (via San Nicola da Telentino 18, Rome 00187, ☎ (6) 4746751, fax (6) 4820022) also specialize in Jamaica.

Asia

Hong Kong is the discount plane ticket capital of the region. Its bucket shops are at least as reliable as those of other cities. Ask the advice of other travelers before buying a ticket.

STA Travel has branches in Hong Kong, Tokyo, Singapore, Bangkok, and Kuala Lumpur.

In Japan you might try one of the following companies:

Alize Corporation
  Aoyama Kyodo Bldg No 803, 3-6-18 Kita Aoyama Minato Ku, Tokyo 107, ☎ (03) 3407-4272, fax (03) 3407-8400
All Nippon Airways World Tours
  Kasumigaseki Bldg, 3-2-5 Kasumigaseki Chiyoda-ku, Tokyo 100, ☎ (03) 3581-7231, fax (03) 3580-0361
Island International
  4-11-14-204 Jingumae, Shibuya-ku, Tokyo 150, ☎ (03) 3401-4096, fax (03) 3401-1629
L & A Tours
  No 608, 3-1-19 Nishi Azabu, Minato-ku, Tokyo 106, ☎ (03) 5474-7723, fax (03) 3746-2478

The Caribbean & South America

Jamaica is linked by British West Indies Airways (BWIA) to Antigua, Barbados, Haiti, and Trinidad. It also serves Puerto Rico, as does ALM Antillean Airlines, which also has flights to Aruba, Bonaire, Colombia, Panama, and St Maarten. Cayman Airlines connects Jamaica with the Cayman Islands. COPA has service to and from Panama. And Cubana has flights from Montego Bay and Kingston to Santiago, Varadero, and Havana in Cuba (also see Organized Tours).

SEA
Cruise Ship

If all you want is a one-day taster of Jamaica, then consider arriving by cruise ship. It's a good way to get a feel for several Caribbean destinations, by which to select a site for a future land-based vacation. Jamaica is one of the most popular calls on Caribbean cruising itineraries and recorded 442,000 cruise ship visitors in 1995.

Montego Bay and Ocho Rios are Jamaica's two major cruise ship ports, and several Florida-based cruise companies include them as stops. Ocho Rios' three deep-water piers were being extended in 1995, with a fourth pier being added; when completed, the piers will be able to handle two megaliners plus two smaller vessels. Montego Bay's modern cruise terminal has five berths. A new 30,000-sq-foot terminal building – about two miles from downtown Montego Bay – features modern immigration and customs facilities, duty-free shops, snack bars, and other visitor facilities. The cruise companies provide buses for passengers, and taxis are available (US$7 to downtown).

Per diem prices vary according to the standard of the ship, but you'll be lucky to pay less than US$1500 for a seven-day cruise. Remember, you get what you pay for, including all meals and entertainment.

The Cruise Line International Association (CLIA; 500 Fifth Ave No 1407, New York, NY 10110, ☎ (212) 921-0066, fax (212) 921-0549) can provide information on cruising and individual cruise lines, originating in the USA or abroad, or you can phone the cruise lines directly, toll free, at the following numbers:

Carnival Cruise Lines	☎ (800) 327-9501
Celebrity Cruises	☎ (800) 437-3111
Commodore Cruise Lines	
	☎ (800) 237-5361
Costa Cruise Lines	☎ (800) 462-6782
Crystal Cruises	☎ (800) 446-6620
Cunard Line	☎ (800) 528-6273
Holland American Line	☎ (800) 426-0327
Norwegian Cruise Line	☎ (800) 327-7030
Princess Cruises	☎ (800) 421-0522
Royal Caribbean Cruise Line	
	☎ (800) 327-6700
Royal Cruise Line	☎ (800) 227-4534
Star Clippers	☎ (800) 442-0551
Sun Line	☎ (800) 872-6400

Freighter

Gone are the good ol' days when passengers could buy passage aboard the banana freighters that plied between Jamaica, North America, and Europe. However, Harrison Line still offers passenger service to the West Indies aboard the MV *Author*, a 27,631-ton vessel that carries eight passengers in two suites, one twin, and two single cabins, each with bath and shower. There's a small swimming pool, plus a lounge with TV/VCR.

The vessel sails on 42-day round-trip voyages from Felixstowe, England, with calls at Ponce (Puerto Rico), Port of Spain (Trinidad), La Guaira and Puerto Cabello (Venezuela), Willemstad and Oranjestad (Dutch West Indies), Santa Marta and Cartagena (Colombia), Puerto Limón (Costa Rica), and Kingston, from where it returns to England. The cost for the full voyage is US$4275 to US$4725. Normally you *must* book the full round-trip, although you may be able to book one-way passage in summer. You'll need to book at least one year in advance through Strand Cruise & Travel Centre (Charing Cross Shopping Concourse, The Strand, London WC2N 4HZ, ☎ (0171) 836-6363, fax (0171) 497-0078).

Yacht

Crewing aboard a yacht destined for the West Indies from North America or Europe is a popular way of getting to Jamaica. You'll need impressive offshore sailing experience to make (or be hired for) an Atlantic crossing. Most sailors heading to Jamaica and the West Indies do so from Florida and other eastern states. Winds and currents favor the passage south through the Bahamas and Windward Passage, which separates Cuba and Haiti. If you plan to travel in summer, keep fully abreast of weather reports, as mid- to late-summer is hurricane season.

Marinas are located in all major resorts and other select points around Jamaica's coast. Upon arrival in Jamaica, however, you *must* clear customs and immigration at either Montego Bay (Montego Bay Yacht Club), Kingston (Royal Jamaican Yacht Club, Port Royal), Ocho Rios, St Ann's Bay, or West Harbour in Port Antonio. In addition, you'll need to clear customs at *each* port of call in Jamaica. It's a hassle, but Jamaica's troubles with drug trafficking are so extensive that you should be willing to cooperate with this policy. Anticipate the possibility of being boarded and searched by the Coast Guard.

In the UK, contact Alan Toone of Compass Yacht Services (Holly Cottage, Heathley End, Chislehurst, Kent BR7 6AB, ☎ (0181) 467-2450). Alan arranges yacht charters and may be able to help assist you in obtaining a crewing position.

Inquire in ports or yacht marinas about any irregular passenger services, via yacht or cargo boat, between Jamaica and other Caribbean islands. Check also the notice boards at marinas; often you'll find a note advertising for crew, or you can leave one of your own. Yachting magazines are also good resources.

Yacht charter companies are listed under Yacht Charters in Getting Around.

Maps & Charts You'll need accurate maps and charts for any voyage through the Caribbean's reef-infested waters. British Admiralty charts, US Defense Mapping Agency charts, and Imray yachting charts are all accurate. You can order them in advance from Bluewater Books & Charts (1481 SE 17th St Causeway, Ft Lauderdale, FL 33316, ☎ (305) 763-6533 or (800) 942-2583).

DEPARTURE TAXES

As of January 1996, the departure tax was J$500, payable at the airport upon checking in for your flight. You can pay in foreign currency or in Jamaican dollars (cash only). The tax is, of course, subject to change.

ORGANIZED TOURS

There are dozens of organized tours to Jamaica. The vast majority are sun-and-sand 'package tours' featuring round-trip airfare, airport transfers, hotel accommodations, breakfasts, and certain other meals, all for a guaranteed price. Sightseeing tours, entertainment, and other extras may also be included.

Package Tours

Dozens of tour companies offer package tours to Jamaica, usually using charter airlines. The biggest companies may operate on a regular basis, often every week. Many companies offer a selection of hotels to choose from, with package prices varying accordingly.

Most per-person rates are quoted based on double-occupancy (two people sharing a room). An additional charge ('single supplement') applies to anyone wishing to room alone.

The USA The following tour operators are among those most active in the Jamaican market:

Adventure Tours USA
    5949 Sherry Lane, Dallas, TX (☎ (214) 360-5000 or (800) 999-9046)
American Airlines FlyAAway Vacations
    Mail Drop 1000, Box 619619, DFW Airport, TX 75261 (☎ (800) 433-7300, fax (817) 967-4328)
Apple Vacations
    7 Campus Blvd, Newtown Square, PA 19073 (☎ (610) 359-6700 or (800) 727-3400, fax (610) 359-6624)
Caribbean Collection
    13902 N Dale Mabry Hwy No 230, Tampa, FL 33618 (☎ (813) 935-8892 or (800) 969-8222, fax (813) 264-5912)
Caribbean Concepts
    575 Underhill Blvd No 140, Syosset, NY 11791 (☎ (516) 496-1678 or (800) 423-4433, fax (516) 496-3467)
Caribbean Travel Planners
    350 Fifth Ave No 2719, New York, NY 10118 (☎ (212) 564-9502 or (800) 323-2020, fax (212) 268-9465)
Changes in L'Attitudes
    4986 113rd Ave, N Clearwater, FL 34620 (☎ (813) 573-3536 or (800) 330-8272, fax (813) 573-2497)
Funjet Vacations
    Box 1460, Milwaukee, WI 53201 (☎ (414) 351-3553 or (800) 558-3050, fax (414) 351-1453)
Island Flight Vacations
    6033 W Century Blvd No 807, Los Angeles, CA 90045 (☎ (310) 477-5858 or (800) 426-4570, fax (310) 410-0830)
Island Resort Tours
    4 Park Ave, New York, NY 10016 (☎ (212) 251-1700 or (800) 527-5982, fax (212) 545-8169)
Jamaica Air Tours
    1150 First Ave No 525, King of Prussia, PA 19406 (☎ (800) 622-3009, fax (404) 261-7282)

Jamaica Travel Specialists
    2827 Mann Ave, Union City, CA 94587
    (☎ (510) 489-9552 or (800) 544-5979,
    fax (510) 797-3820)
Reggae Jam/Calypso
    Box 291685, Tampa, FL 98004 (☎ (813)
    985-7944 or (800) 873-4423, fax (800) 749-
    6616)
Sunbird Vacations
    2025 Gateway Place, San Jose, CA 95110
    (☎ (408) 452-0233 or (800) 800-0202,
    fax (408) 452-0475)
Sunburst Holidays
    4779 Broadway, New York, NY 10034
    (☎ (212) 861-5864 or (800) 666-8346,
    fax (202) 452-0905)
Sun Splash Tours
    236 W 27th St No 700, New York, NY 10001
    (☎ (212) 366-4922 or (800) 426-7710,
    fax (212) 366-5642)
Travel Impressions
    465 Smith St, Farmingdale, NY 11735
    (☎ (516) 845-8000 or (800) 284-0044,
    fax (516) 845-8095)
TravelJam
    6512-A Lisa Lane, Bowie, MD 20720
    (☎ (301) 805-8626, fax (301) 805-9563)
TWA Getaway Vacations
    10 E Stow Rd, Marlton, NJ 08053 (☎ (800)
    438-2929, fax (609) 985-4125)
USAir Vacations
    7200 Lake Ellenor Drive No 241, Orlando,
    FL 32809 (☎ (407) 857-8533, fax (407)
    857-9764)
Vacation Express
    2957 Clairmont Rd No 120, Atlanta, GA
    30329 (☎ (404) 321-7742 or (800) 486-9777,
    fax (404) 248-1237)
Vacation Network
    1370 Washington Ave, No 301, Miami
    Beach, FL 33139 (☎ (305) 673-8822 or (800)
    423-4095, fax (305) 673-5666)

Canada Canadian package tour operators
include:

Air Canada Vacations
    1440 Ste Catherine St W, Montreal, QC H3G
    1R8 (☎ (514) 876-0704, fax (514) 876-3699)
Airtrain International
    ☎ 416) 620-4666, fax (416) 620-4843)
Air Transat Holidays
    300 Leo Pariseau No 400, Montreal, QC
    H2W 2P6 (☎ (514) 987-1616, fax (514)
    987-8029)

Albatours
    ☎ (416) 746-2890, fax (416) 746-0397)
Canadian Holidays
    ☎ 416) 620-8050, fax (416) 620-8700)
Conquest Tours
    85 Brisbane Rd, Downsview, ON M3J 2K3
    (☎ (416) 665-9255, fax (416) 665-6811)
Fiesta Sun
    111 Avenue Rd, No 500, Toronto, ON M5R
    3J8 (☎ (416) 967-1510, fax (416) 967-4951)
Regent Holidays
    6205 Airport Rd, Building A, No 200, Mis-
    sissauga, ON L4V 1E1 (☎ (905) 673-3343)
Sunquest Vacations
    130 Merton St, Toronto, ON M4S 1A4
    (☎ (416) 485-1700, fax (416) 485-9479)

Australia & New Zealand Contours
Travel is Australia's largest tour operator/
wholesaler to the Caribbean islands (466
Victoria St, N Melbourne, Victoria 3051,
☎ (3) 329-5211, fax (3) 329-6314). In New
Zealand, contact Innovative Travel, which
is about the only tour operator with a
nascent Caribbean specialty (PO Box 21,
247 Edgeware, Christchurch, ☎ (3) 365-
3910, fax (3) 365-5755).

The UK The Caribbean Centre (3 The
Green, Richmond, Surrey TW9 1PL,
☎ (0181) 940-3399, fax (0181) 940-7424)
offers packages to Jamaica . Uncle Sam
Travel Agency (295 Sotto Rd, Birmingham
B21 95A, ☎ (21) 5233141, fax (21) 554-
7315) runs its own charter programs into
Jamaica.

Japan Island International (4-11-14-204
Jingumae, Shibuya-ku, Tokyo 150, ☎ (03)
3401-4096, fax (03) 3401-1629) specializes in package tours and special interest
travel to Jamaica.

Specialty Tours
Clothing-Optional Tours Several resorts
welcome nudists, and at least three US
companies cater to travelers seeking an all-
over tan:

Bare Necessities
    1502-A West Ave, Austin, TX 78701
    (☎ (512) 499-0405 or (800) 743-0405)

Travel Au Naturel
    35246 US 19 N, Suite 112, Paul Harbor, FL
    34684 (☎ (800) 728-0185)
Travel Naturally
    PO Box 2089, Mango, FL 33550 (☎ (813)
    648-9990 or (800) 462-6833)

Nature Tours Very few companies offer special interest programs focusing on specific activities such as birding. An exception is Calypso Island Tours, which offers an eight-day 'Eco-Adventure' featuring such activities as hiking, birding, and other rarely visited sites wilderness adventures in the Cockpit Country and south coast (3901 Grand Ave No 304, Oakland, CA 94610, ☎ (510) 653-3570 or (800) 852-6242). Tropical Pleasure Vacations also has a one-week eco-tour in mid-summer (1062 55th St, Oakland, CA 94808, ☎ (510) 428-2765). Its tour visits the Blue Mountains and Portland Parish.

Caligo Ventures (156 Bedford Rd, Armonk NY 10504, ☎ (800) 426-7781) also offers a weeklong nature tour that includes visits to the strange terrain of Cockpit Country, the Great Morass, and the Blue Mountains in search of birds. The

1995 trip cost US$1265. Victor Emanuel Nature Tours (☎ (800) 328-8368) also offers weeklong birding tours for US$1250.

WARNING

The information in this chapter is particularly vulnerable to change: prices for international travel are volatile, routes are introduced and canceled, schedules change, special deals come and go, and rules and visa requirements are amended. Airlines and governments seem to take a perverse pleasure in making price structures and regulations as complicated as possible. You should check directly with the airline or a travel agent to make sure you understand how a fare (and any ticket you may buy) works. In addition, the travel industry is highly competitive and there are many lurks and perks.

The upshot of this is that you should get opinions, quotes, and advice from as many airlines and travel agents as possible before you part with your hard-earned cash. The details given in this chapter should be regarded as pointers and are not a substitutes for your own careful, up-to-date research.

Getting Around

AIR

Intra-island flights offer a quick way to travel between Montego Bay, Kingston, Negril, Ocho Rios, and Port Antonio.

In November 1995, Air Jamaica purchased Jamaica's government-owned domestic airline, Trans-Jamaica (the government retained a 20% stake), and became the country's only domestic airline. The privatized company renamed the airline Air Jamaica Express, and immediately suspended all services while the airline was revamped and new schedules put in place. It was planned to coordinate flight schedules to allow Air Jamaica Express to provide feeder service between Air Jamaica's gateway cities and destinations in Jamaica. Flights to Mandeville were also being considered.

Travelers will now be able to reserve flights from international gateways to their final destinations (eg, New York-Negril), and the booking will show up as one flight in computer reservation systems.

Airports & Airlines

Tinson Pen Most domestic flights use Tinson Pen, Kingston's intra-island commuter airport, handily situated two miles west of the downtown oceanfront at the west end of Marcus Garvey Drive.

Air Jamaica Express (☎ 923-8680, or ☎ 924-8850 at Tinson Pen) operates daily flights either to Tinson Pen or to the international airport from Montego Bay, Negril, Ocho Rios, and Port Antonio. Schedules were being developed at press time; call Air Jamaica to get details on their domestic flights.

Charter Flights A handful of companies offer charter services aboard Cessnas and other small aircraft. Wings Jamaica operates Beechcraft Barons from Tinson Pen (PO Box 380, Kingston 11, ☎/fax 923-6573 or 923-5416). Timair is based at Sangster International Airport in Montego Bay (☎ 952-2516). Both companies offer customized sightseeing tours as well as one-way charter flights to airports island-wide. Airways International (☎ 923-6614) also offers charter services to Miami, Nassau, Turks & Caicos, Haiti, Puerto Rico, and other destinations. It also serves Tinson Pen from Montego Bay (☎ 952-5299) and Negril (☎ 957-4051). Airport Express also operates from Tinson Pen.

Helicopter

Helitours, based both in Ocho Rios (☎ 974-2265) and Montego Freeport (☎ 979-8290), offers sightseeing tours by Bell 206B Jetranger III helicopters. A 15-minute 'Fun Hop' around Ocho Rios costs US$50 per person. The hour-long 'Jamaican Showcase' costs US$190 per person and will take you across the island, over Kingston and Port Royal, and across the Blue Mountains. A day-long 'Island Delight' costs US$2500 for up to four people, and includes breakfast in Port Antonio, a city tour in Kingston, plus a gourmet lunch and beach time at the Grand Lido, Negril.

The company maintains helipads in Montego Bay, Negril, and Port Antonio. The choppers can each seat four passengers and up to 250 pounds of cargo. You can charter a helicopter for transport to any airport, or for personalized tours. From Montego Bay, transfers are about US$400 to Negril, US$550 to Ocho Rios, US$750 to Kingston, and US$1200 to Port Antonio. Charter rates begin at US$500 per hour.

BUS

Traveling by bus could be the best – *or worst!* – adventure of your trip to Jamaica. The island has an extensive bus network linking virtually every village in the country, and this is the way most Jamaicans travel. Traveling by bus is a great way to meet locals and get a feel for the local lifestyle. It's also remarkably inexpensive: you can travel from one end of the island to the other for US$2 or so. Buses are seldom used by foreign travelers, as you need to be somewhat of a masochist to enjoy the experience.

Jamaica's bus 'system' is the epitome of chaos and has been ever since the government-run Jamaica Omnibus Service was disbanded years ago and scores of independent operators rushed in to fill the void. Timetables don't really exist. Buses rarely run to set schedules. They're also terribly overcrowded (and stiflingly hot), often literally overflowing, with people hanging from the open doors. The problem is particularly bad in Kingston. Whether you find traveling by bus fun, frustrating, freaky or infuriating depends on your frame of mind.

Every town has a bus waiting area, usually near the main market. There's no order or plan to most of them however, and you'll usually be on your own to figure out where your desired bus leaves from. Each bus should have its destination marked above the front window. Bus stops are located along their routes at most road intersections, but you can usually flag them down anywhere except in major cities, where they're inclined to stop only at designated stops.

You pay a conductor (or 'sideman') who packs people in until the bus is grossly overcrowded. You should ascertain the fare from an independent traveler, as conductors often quote an inflated price to foreign passengers. Most Jamaicans are scrupulously honest and may pitch in on your behalf. Guard your luggage carefully against theft and to avoid it being seized by an over-eager tout, who will maneuver you aboard his bus in a fait accompli.

Buses depart when they're full. While there's still room to squeeze a few more souls on board, the impending departure is usually announced with a continuous bleating of the horn. Once the bus sets off, the driver usually determines to scare his passengers to death with a hair-raising

display of reckless driving. Time is money! To make matters worse, many buses are badly worn wrecks that ought to have been retired. Things have improved somewhat in recent years with the replacement of many battered old vehicles with sleek new ones. Still, expect to be cramped and to be deafened by blaring reggae.

Minibus

Minibuses (or minivans) are the workhorses of Jamaica's public transport system. Hundreds of private minibus operators are licensed by the Transport Authority, and all major towns and virtually every village in the country is served. Licensed minibuses display red license plates with the initials PPV (public passenger vehicle). They operate like the larger buses, although fares are generally somewhat higher.

Although most passengers are heading to the final destination, the buses may act on a 'collective' basis, stopping along the route to drop off and pick up people, who are usually laden down with sacks of produce, or even a live piglet or poultry.

All the caveats for travel by bus apply.

Hotel Transfers

Many hotels include airport transfers in their room rates. A dozen or so leading tour operators and car rental companies also offer minibus transfers. The following are typical one-way fares from Montego Bay Airport to various destinations:

Downtown	US$7
Negril	US$18
Mandeville	US$21
Ocho Rios	US$23
Port Antonio	US$28
Kingston	US$28

From Kingston Airport to downtown costs US$10

The Jamaican Union of Travelers Association (JUTA) is the largest transfer provider, with services islandwide (PO Box 1155, Montego Bay, ☎ 952-0813, fax 952-5355).

TRAIN

Those railway tracks marked on maps don't mean very much these days, Gone are the days when for a few pennies you could travel aboard the now-defunct Jamaica Railway Corporation's two daily services between Kingston and Montego Bay. The unprofitable railway system was shut down in 1992. In early 1996 there were rumors that private investors might resurrect train service.

CAR & MOTORCYCLE

Jamaica has about 9500 miles of roads, and virtually any part of the island is accessible by car. A paved coastal highway circles the entire island (it runs about 20 miles inland parallel to the shore between Spanish Town and Black River). Three main roads and several minor roads cross the central mountain chains, north to south, linking all the main towns. A web of minor roads, country lanes, and dirt tracks provide access to more remote areas.

About 2400 miles of road are paved. Conditions vary from excellent to awful. The main roads are usually in good condition, although everywhere you're likely to find deep potholes, especially toward the end of rainy season. Keep your speed down! Many of the secondary, or B roads, are in appalling condition. Minor, unpaved roads are usually rutted by rains and lack of repairs; these are best tackled with a 4WD vehicle.

Here are distances and approximate driving times for a few select destinations:

Route	Mileage	Time
Montego Bay-Negril	52 miles	1½ hours
Montego Bay-Ocho Rios	67 miles	2 hours
Ocho Rios-Port Antonio	66 miles	2 hours
Ocho Rios-Kingston	55 miles	1½ hours
Port Antonio-Kingston	61 miles	2 hours

Driving Conditions

Take a deep breath! Many Jamaican drivers rank high among the world's rudest and least cautious drivers. A huge percentage drive far too fast for local conditions. Nor can they stand being behind the car in front. Hence, cars play hopscotch with one another, overtaking with harrowing, daredevil folly. Jamaica has the third highest fatality rate for drivers in the world – behind Ethiopia and India – with a staggering 343 fatalities per 100,000 cars (compared to 26 per 100,000 in the US, and 22 per 100,000 in the UK). You'll see mangled cars from fatal accidents sitting beside the road outside police stations as a reminder of the consequences of reckless driving.

Use extreme caution and drive defensively, especially at night when you should be prepared to meet oncoming cars without lights!

Use your horn liberally, especially approaching blind corners and in heavily congested urban areas, where you may need to weave your way through crowds. Expect to be honked at frequently by Jamaicans, who also yell the foulest cuss words at other drivers for any real or imagined slight. Traffic jams are particularly frequent in Montego Bay, Spanish Town, May Pen, Ocho Rios, and Kingston, especially on market days.

Directions

A good road map is essential. These are usually provided by rental companies; if not, ask for one at the rental counter. Many newer roads are not shown on the JTB's 'Discover Jamaica' map, and directional signs are few and far between. What may appear on a map to be a 30-minute as-the-crow-flies journey, may take several hours due to windy roads. Also see Maps in Facts for the Visitor.

Locals will be more than happy to help with directions, but take their instructions with a grain of salt. Jamaicans tend to underestimate distance and are over-optimistic about road conditions. Believe any Jamaican, however, who tells you a road is bad! Many Jamaicans still measure distance in 'chains,' the old British measure of 22 yards. I've found Jamaicans to be fairly accurate in giving 'chain' measurements. However, all too often 'a few chains' can turn out to be a mile or more!

In recent years, the government's Tourism Action Plan has initiated a program to place road signs on all major routes.

Gasoline

Esso, Shell, and Texaco maintain gasoline stations across the island. In rural areas, stations usually close on Sundays. Almost everywhere, gas stations may close after 7 pm or so. Fortunately, gasoline is very inexpensive by international standards: about US$1.70 per gallon in 1996. Cash only, please! Credit cards are not accepted.

Security

It's always best to park in hotel (or other secure) car parks. Whenever you park on the street, it's a wise idea to remove any belongings, if possible. At the very least, keep them locked in the trunk.

Women should consider not driving alone in remote areas.

Picking Up Passengers

As a visitor, you're a privileged person. Any empty seats in your car will go a long way toward easing the burden of Jamaicans forced to rely on buses and passing cars. However, your rental policy may specifically forbid giving rides to strangers; check the fine print.

You can feel secure giving rides to children and women, who will wave you down with a lackadaisical sweep of the outstretched hand. Use common sense and caution when offering rides to males.

Road Rules

Always drive on the *left*. Remember, keep left and you'll always be right. Here's another local saying worth memorizing: 'de left side is de right side; de right side is suicide!' The speed limit is 30 mph in towns and 50 mph on highways. Observe them. I can't remember ever seeing Jamaican police using radar. In fact, I don't recall *any* overt sign of traffic police. However, a new crackdown on speeding and drunk driving (including breathalyzer testing) was introduced in 1995.

Jamaica has no compulsory seatbelt law (few old cars have seatbelts anyway) nor is it compulsory to wear helmets when riding motorcycles.

Mechanical Problems

There is no national roadside service organization to phone when you have car trouble. The larger rental agencies have a 24-hour service number in case of breakdowns and other emergencies. That's a good enough reason to choose an agency that is a member of JUDA (the Jamaica U-Drive Association), which sets minimum standards for members. If you do break down and must use a local mechanic, you should do so only for minor work, otherwise the car rental company may balk at reimbursing you for work they haven't authorized. If you can't find a phone or repair service, seek police assistance. Use common sense in dealing with offers of unsolicited help. *Never* give your keys to strangers.

Accidents

Hopefully you won't have one, but if you 'mash up' there are a few rules to obey. Firstly, don't move the vehicles, and don't let anyone else, including the other driver. Have someone call the police, and remain at the scene until a police officer arrives. Make sure to get the name and address of anyone else involved in the accident, as well as their license number and details of their vehicle. Take photos of the scene if possible, and get the names and addresses of any witnesses. Above all, don't be drawn into an argument. Jamaican emotions are volatile, so you should do your best to keep tempers calm. Call your rental company as soon as possible.

Car Rental

All the major international car-rental companies operate in Jamaica, along with dozens of smaller local firms. Car rental agencies are listed in the local yellow pages, and the JTB publishes a list of members of the Jamaica U-Drive Association. You'll find plenty of rental companies at the two international airports, in major cities, and even in lesser towns.

Rental rates may give North Americans sticker shock (Europeans will find prices on par with home). In general, companies away from airports tend to be less expensive. High season rates begin at about US$60 per day and can run as high as US$125, depending on the vehicle. Most companies offer slightly cheaper rates in low season. Some companies include unlimited mileage, while others set a limit and charge a fee for excess miles driven. You may be able to negotiate to receive unlimited mileage if this is not automatically included. Most firms require a deposit of at least US$500, but will accept a credit card imprint. Keep copies of all your paperwork.

You can reserve a car upon arrival, but in high season you may find that most vehicles are taken and that the vehicle of your choice may not be available. Consider making your reservation in advance. It's wise to reconfirm before arrival, when your car will be delivered to the airport (or your hotel).

Rental companies can arrange a driver, for an extra fee, if you desire.

Before signing, go over the vehicle with a fine-toothed comb to identify any dents and scratches. Make sure they are all marked up before you drive away. You're likely to be charged for the slightest mark. Don't forget to check the cigarette lighter and interior switches, which are often missing.

What Type of Vehicle? Most companies utilize modern Japanese sedans. A small sedan is perfectly adequate for most conditions; a big car can be a liability on Jamaica's narrow, winding roads. Most companies also rent 4WD vehicles, which I recommend if you intend to do any backcountry exploring, where the roads can be terribly potholed and extra ground clearance may be required.

Your options are between standard (stick) or automatic transmission, and with or without air-con. Stick shift is preferable because constant and sudden gear changes

are required on Jamaica's hilly, windy, roads, where potholes and kamikaze chickens appear out of nowhere; automatic transmissions do not give you the control you'll need. Remember, though, that you'll be changing gears with your *left* hand. This may take a little getting used to for many drivers, but you'll soon get the hang of it.

Insurance Check in advance to see whether your current insurance or credit card covers you for driving while abroad. All rental companies will recommend damage-waiver insurance, which limits your liability in the event of an accident or damage. I recommend this coverage. It should cost be about US$12 per day – a valuable investment. American Express cardholders can waive this requirement; most Jamaican car rental companies recognize AmEx's policy.

Driver's License Although the minimum age to obtain a driver's license in Jamaica is 17, renters must be 21 (some companies will only rent to those 25 or older). For additional details, see the Driver's License & Permits section under Visas & Documents in the Facts for the Visitor chapter.

Rental Companies Jamaica's largest and most reputable car rental company is Island Car Rentals, with its head office at 17 Antigua Ave, Kingston 10 (☎ 926-8861, fax 926-6987; in the USA, ☎ (800) 892-4581; in Canada, ☎ (800) 526-2422). The company also has offices at the Kingston airport (☎ 924-8075), the Montego Bay airport (☎ 952-5771), and in Ocho Rios (☎ 974-2334). I've used several companies, but have found Island Car Rentals' service and vehicles to be exemplary.

Most car rental companies are reliable, although the smaller the company the greater the risks involved.

Fly & Drive Packages If you want to explore Jamaica fully, consider a prepurchased package combining car rental and hotel vouchers. You simply arrive at the airport, pick up your car, and set off to roam the island armed with vouchers good at 48 participating hotels. The program, called 'Fly-Drive Jamaica,' is sponsored by Inns of Jamaica and offered by Vacation Network (1370 Washington No 301, Miami Beach, FL 33139, ☎ (305) 673-8822 or (800) 423-4095, fax (305) 673-5666). The company will reserve your first night's accommodations in advance (you choose the place), plus additional nights for a fee. Alternately, you can book your next stop as you check out of the last, or be spontaneous and show up unannounced.

If you choose to stay at the most upscale places, the package can promise discounts up to 20% off hotels and car rentals booked separately. The standard high-season package costs US$581 per person, including a two-door, subcompact car with standard transmission and unlimited mileage (add an extra US$12 daily for a four-door car, US$15 for an automatic, and US$32 for an air-con automatic).

Motorcycle Rental

There's a special thrill to exploring on two wheels, with the sun on your skin and the wind in your hair. Exploring on two wheels is also a good option for resorts such as Negril (which is spread out and has little traffic) and Ocho Rios (which is congested with cars).

Dozens of companies rent motorcycles and scooters, which are available at any resort town. They're far more lax than car rental companies; I've even rented motorcycles without having to show my driver's license! Motor scooters cost about US$25 per day. Motorcycles cost more, according to size. Expect to pay about US$45 a day for a 750cc machine.

Ride cautiously! Road conditions are extremely hazardous, particularly for novice riders and especially away from major resorts, where you'll encounter potholes, loose gravel, narrow roads, crazy Jamaican drivers, free-roaming cattle and goats, and other hazards. I've ridden my own 1000cc BMW in the Caribbean, so I speak from experience. Check if the rental agency also has helmets. If they do, *wear one*!

BICYCLE

Cycling is a cheap, convenient, healthy, environmentally sound and above all *fun* way of traveling. Very few Jamaicans use bicycles. Nonetheless, most resorts have at least one bicycle rental shop and a bicycle supply shop can be found in most large towns.

If you do take your own bicycle to Jamaica, heed this one note of caution: before you leave home, go over your bike with a fine-toothed comb and augment your repair kit with every imaginable spare. As with cars and motorcycles, you won't necessarily be able to buy that crucial gizmo when your bicycle breaks down in the back of beyond as the sun sets.

Bicycles can travel by air. You *can* take them to pieces and put them in a bike bag or box, but it's much easier simply to wheel your bike to the check-in desk, where it should be treated as a piece of baggage. You may have to remove the pedals and turn the handlebars sideways so that it takes up less space in the aircraft's hold; check all this with the airline well in advance, preferably before you pay for your ticket.

Note the caveats about road conditions and driving habits given in Driving Conditions above.

HITCHHIKING

Most Jamaicans do not own vehicles and the bus service is unreliable. Hence, the majority of Jamaicans who live outside major towns hitch rides. This includes women and children. Jamaican drivers are therefore used to giving rides to strangers as a matter of course.

That said, hitching is never entirely safe in any country in the world, and we don't recommend it. Travelers who decide to hitch should understand that they are taking a small but potentially serious risk. Travel in pairs and let someone know where you are planning to go.

WALKING

Jamaica is small enough that it is entirely feasible to explore on foot. See Hiking in Facts for the Visitor.

BOAT
Charter Yachts
All the major resorts have marinas where you can charter yachts or motorboats, either with a crew or 'bareboat.' Crewed boats come with a skipper and crew, and you don't need any prior sailing experience. With bareboat charters, you rent the boat and are your own skipper. Obviously you'll need to be a certified sailor to do this. Usually you'll have to give a short check-out demonstration of your skills before being allowed to sail away. Boats are normally fully stocked with linens and other supplies. You will be expected to provide your own food, however. You can hire a cook if you want for about US$85 a day. A security deposit will be required.

Bareboat charters are usually rented by the week. Expect to pay upwards of US$1200, depending on the vessel's size. Crewed charters normally cost about double that.

You can arrange a yacht charter on the island from:

Montego Bay Yacht Club
    Montego Freeport, Montego Bay (☎ 979-8038)
Royal Jamaican Yacht Club
    Palisadoes Park, Kingston 1 (☎ 924-8685)
Morgan's Harbour Yacht Marina
    Morgan's Harbour, Port Royal (☎ 924-8464, fax 924-8146).

If you want to prearrange a yacht rental, there are several respected companies that offer both crewed and bareboat charters in the Caribbean. These include:

Barefoot Yacht Charters
    2550 Stag Run Blvd No 519, Clearwater, FL 34625 (☎ (813) 799-1858 or (800) 677-3195, fax (813) 797-3195)
The Moorings
    19345 US Hwy 19 N, Clearwater, FL 34624, ☎ (813) 535-1446 or (800) 535-7289, fax (813) 530-9747)

You can also use the services of a broker, who can secure an appropriate yacht based on your budgetary and other requirements.

They work on commission and therefore won't charge you a fee.

The following are reputable companies:

Ed Hamilton & Co
    PO Box 430, N Whitehead, ME 04353 (☎ (207) 549-7855 or (800) 621-7855, fax (207) 549-7822)
Lynn Jachney Charters
    PO Box 302, Marblehead, MA 01945 (☎ (800) 223-2050, fax (617) 639-0216)
Nicholson Yacht Charters
    432 Columbia St, Cambridge, MA 02141 (☎ (617) 225-0555 or (800) 662-6066, fax (617) 225-0190)

Ferry
A ferry service links Kingston to Port Royal. See the Kingston chapter for details.

TAXIS
Hiring a taxi is a reasonable way of traveling between resorts and for getting around larger towns such as Kingston or Montego Bay.

Licensed Taxis
Licensed taxis – called 'contract carriages' in Jamaica – are not cheap by the standards of other undeveloped countries, but are affordable if you share the cost with up to three other passengers.

There's no shortage of licensed cabs, which you'll find at all the major resorts and towns. They're the ones with red PPV license plates (a blue plate indicates that the owner has applied for a license; those without are unlicensed). The Jamaica Union of Travelers Association (JUTA) also operates a government-approved fleet of taxis. JUTA's fleet is more up to date and includes minivans. They service the cruise lines and hotels, and generally do more tourist business.

The government has established fixed rates according to distance. Licensed cabs should have these posted inside. And ostensibly you can obtain a copy from any JTB office (few have them). If not, then ask to see some documented evidence that the fare you're being charged is correct. Taxis are also supposed to have meters, but few have them.

The following were typical fares in late 1995, based on up to four people per taxi:

Donald Sangster Airport
to Montego Bay (US$7)

In and around Montego Bay (US$5 – $15)

Montego Bay
to Ocho Rios or Negril (US$70)

Negril Airport to Negril (US$7)

Norman Manley Airport
to Kingston (US$15 – $17)

Kingston to Ocho Rios (US$85)

Kingston to Port Antonio (US$89)

Unlicensed Taxis

You won't find a meter in unlicensed taxis, which are operated illegally by freelancers who rent out their own cars or vans. Most of these cabs are beaten-up old heaps.

If you take an unlicensed cab, you should agree on a fare *before* getting in (this is a good rule even for licensed cabs). If you don't, you're most likely going to get ripped off. Many freelance taxi drivers try to charge the same amount as licensed cabs, but you can normally get the price down substantially. Bargain hard! Your hotel desk clerk or concierge should be able to give you a good idea of what a fair fare should be.

Guard your belongings carefully: freelance taxis have a reputation for theft. And don't let yourself be talked into visiting specific shops, where the driver can expect to receive a commission on anything you purchase.

If you're penny-pinching, consider hailing a *colectivo* – an unlicensed taxi that picks up and drops off as many people as it can squeeze in along the route. These are much cheaper than other taxis.

ORGANIZED TOURS
General Interest

There are plenty of organized tours to choose from. More than a dozen reputable Jamaican companies offer guided excursions and tours to leading attractions

islandwide. Popular tours include rafting trips on the Martha Brae and Rio Grande Rivers, visits to Croydon Plantation and other working plantations, and the Appleton Estate Rum Tour, a motorcoach tour over the rugged mountains and into the Siloah Valley to visit the famous rum factory (☎ 997-6077 or 952-5013, fax 923-6981 or 952-0981). The Appleton tour costs US$62 from Montego Bay and US$65 from Ocho Rios, and includes a rum tasting . . . plus a bottle of rum! The JTB can provide information. Virtually every hotel lobby displays brochures.

International Travel Services Ltd, 18 Ripon Rd, Kingston 5 offers an eight-day 'Great Adventure' that takes in the leading sites of the whole island (PO Box 135, ☎ 926-6540, fax 929-6330). It costs US$999, including accommodations at five hotels. A five-day tour (US$699) is also offered.

The following are among the leading tour companies:

Caribic Vacations
Gloucester Ave, Montego Bay (☎ 952-5013, fax 952-0981)

Galaxy Tours
75 Red Hills Rd, Kingston 20 (☎ 931-0428, fax 925-6975)

Glamour Tours
LOJ Commercial Centre, Montego Freeport (☎ 979-8207, fax 979-8168)

Greenlight Tours
Bogue Industrial Estate, Montego Bay (☎ 952-2636, fax 952-0564)

Pleasure Vacation Tours
153½ Constant Spring Rd, Kingston 8 (☎ 924-4140, fax 924-1756)

Pro Tours
8 Lady Musgrave Rd, Kingston 5 (☎ 978-6113, fax 978-6139)

Tourwise
103 Main St (PO Box 17), Ocho Rios (☎ 974-2323, fax 974-5362)

Special Interest Tours

The Touring Society of Jamaica has a series of hikes in the Blue Mountains, with visits to coffee plantations, botanical gardens, and other offbeat sites (☎ 944-8400, ext 210). More demanding hikes in the Rio Grande

Valley are offered by Valley Hikes (PO Box 89, Port Antonio, ☎/fax 993-2543).

Sense Adventures specializes in natural history, birding, kayaking, hiking, and clothing-optional tours for hardy travelers (PO Box 216, Kingston 7, ☎ 927-2097, fax 929-6967). In addition to a range of one-day trips, it has three- and four-day wilderness treks and a nine-day 'Natural History Adventure' into remote areas.

Offbeat tours are also the forté of Treasure Tours, based in Treasure Beach (Calabash Bay PO, St Elizabeth, ☎ 965-0126);

the Teak Tree Co (PO Box 435, Kingston 6, ☎ 977-1936, fax 977-3247); and the Other Company (☎ 990-9410, fax 957-3309), which offers a day-long 'Roots Rock Reggae Express' from Negril to Kingston for US$90, including an I-tal breakfast and dinner. Maroon Attraction Tours offers excursions to Accompong to trace the history of the Maroons (32 Church St, Montego Bay, ☎ 979-0308, fax 952-6203).

Also see the Activities section in the Facts for the Visitor chapter.

Kingston

Kingston, Jamaica's teeming capital city (population 850,000), suffers from a negative image that, though partly deserved, belies its many appeals. At first neither welcoming nor beautiful, the city is diminished by squalor, and its culture can be darned right intimidating. Seething tensions simmer below the surface and often boil over, making for international headlines that have tended to keep visitors at bay in recent years. But I've grown to appreciate this chaotic and vibrant city: the heartbeat of Jamaica and its center of commerce and culture. It hustles. It bustles. Dramatically situated between ocean and mountains, it no longer seems a daunting beginning to a Jamaican vacation.

Its history is intriguing. High culture is as developed as anywhere in the Caribbean outside Cuba. The city boasts attractions that definitely merit a visit, including a first-rate art museum, and the nightlife is the most cosmopolitan and colorful on the island. The city's yearly calendar is replete with festivals and sporting and other events. Good restaurants cater to every taste. A wealth of nearby venues for recreation and exploration, including the Blue Mountains, Port Royal, and the Hellshire Beaches, beckon to travelers. And for every Kingstonian who appears suspicious and surly, half a dozen are sure to be respectful and friendly.

'Kingston' is usually used to refer to the city-parish of Kingston and the surrounding parish of St Andrew, which are jointly administered and also known as the 'Corporate Area.' Together they cover 191 sq miles, although the metropolitan area measures only 45 sq miles (St Andrew extends all the way to the summit ridge of the Blue Mountains).

Regardless of which area you find yourself roaming, reggae music is sure to be blaring. And everywhere goats run free, browsing the garbage-filled gutters totally oblivious to your approach by car until the moment you're about to pass them, when

---

HIGHLIGHTS

- Somber Bob Marley Museum, offering a fascinating glimpse into the life of Jamaica's most revered contemporary hero
- House of Leo, a de rigueur nocturnal hot spot for dancehall music
- The Parade, a pulsing marketplace at the heart of Kingston
- Peaceful Lime Cay, providing a sun-drenched haven from the hustle and bustle
- Historic Point Royal, a disheveled treasure trove of colonial structures
- Pretty Hellshire Beaches, lively on weekends with the Kingston picnic-and-party crowd
- Horseracing at Caymanas Park

---

the kamikaze herd is sure to dash across your path.

The view from the mountains reveals leafy foothill suburbs and, below, the highrise hotels, banks, and office buildings of New Kingston, where the majority of visitors stay. Here, relatively wealthy 'uptowners' lead middle-class lifestyles modeled on those of North America and Western Europe.

Kingston – home to almost one-third of the nation's population – is a city divided, with hovels and highrises side by side. Downtown and in the squalid margins, city life is dominated by the urban underclass: hustlers, streets vendors, and beggars. The drift from countryside to city occurring in much of the Third World has been felt here no less forcefully in the past few decades. Kingston's population doubled from 376,000 in 1960 to more than 800,000 by 1990, making it by far the largest English-speaking city south of Miami. The growth has overwhelmed the city's ability to provide housing and services. The vast shanty towns that push at the city's margins are for the most part hidden from tourist view. Still, in even the more exclusive areas, makeshift homes of cardboard and corrugated tin are anchored against walls along vacant roadsides and on the banks of storm-water gullies.

HISTORY

Kingston's history begins on May 10, 1655, when an English fleet bearing 7000 men sailed into Kingston Harbour and, after desultory resistance from the Spanish defenders at Passage Fort, captured Jamaica for Cromwell. For several decades the future site of the city was used for rearing pigs. When an earthquake leveled Port Royal in 1692, survivors struggled across the bay and pitched camp with the swine. The refugees promptly succumbed to an epidemic of fever that claimed more than 3000 lives. (The city, which arose on the site of a swamp, suffered many epidemics of fevers in ensuing years.)

Within two months of the disaster, the Council met aboard HMS *Richard and Sarah* and decided to build a city 'equal to Port Royall in everything.' A town plan was drawn up on a grid pattern and centered on an open square.

Though devastated repeatedly by earthquakes and hurricanes, the port city prospered throughout the 18th century, becoming one of the most important trading centers in the Western Hemisphere and an important transshipment point for slaves destined for the Spanish colonies. Though Britain later abolished the slave trade, Kingston continued to flourish as an entrepôt for the Spanish empire.

By 1800, the population had reached 11,000. As the city expanded, the wealthier merchants gradually moved to the cooler heights of Liguanea, where they

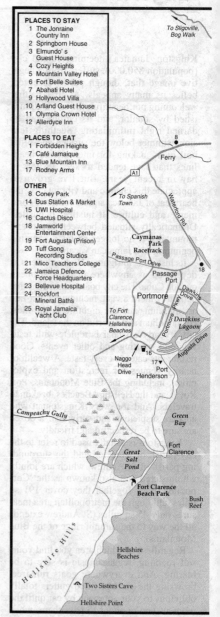

PLACES TO STAY
1. The Jonraine Country Inn
2. Springborn House
3. Elmundo's Guest House
4. Cozy Heights
5. Mountain Valley Hotel
6. Fort Belle Suites
7. Abahati Hotel
8. Hollywood Villa
9. Arrland Guest House
10. Olympia Crown Hotel
11. Allerdyce Inn

PLACES TO EAT
1. Forbidden Heights
2. Café Jamaique
13. Blue Mountain Inn
17. Rodney Arms

OTHER
8. Coney Park
14. Bus Station & Market
15. UWI Hospital
16. Cactus Disco
18. Jamworld Entertainment Center
19. Fort Augusta (Prison)
20. Tuff Gong Recording Studios
21. Mico Teachers College
22. Jamaica Defence Force Headquarters
23. Bellevue Hospital
24. Rockfort Mineral Baths
25. Royal Jamaica Yacht Club

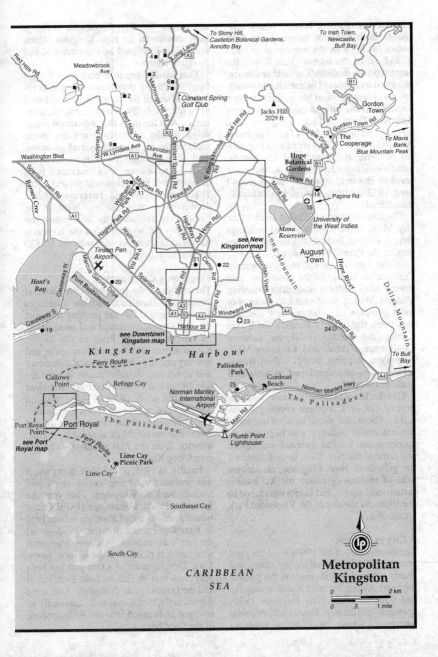

To Stony Hill,
Castleton Botanical Gardens,
Annotto Bay

To Irish Town,
Newcastle,
Buff Bay

Long Lane

A3

Meadowbrook
Ave

B1

Gordon
Town

Red Hills Rd

Constant Spring
Golf Club

Jacks Hill
2029 ft

Gordon Town Rd

The
Cooperage

To Mavis
Bank,
Blue Mountain Peak

Skyline Drive

13

Mannings Hill Rd

Constant Spring Rd

Jacks Hill Rd

E King's House Rd

Hope
Botanical
Gardens

B1

Old Hope Rd

Washington Blvd

A3

Dunrobin
Ave

W Lyndale Ave

A1

14   Papine Rd

15

University
of the West Indies

Spanish Town Rd

Red Hills Rd

Molynes Rd

Waltham Park Rd

Molynes Rd

Hope Rd

Mona Rd

Mona
Reservoir

Long Mountain

Barnes Cree

A1

Hagley Park Rd

Waltham Park Rd

Half Way Tree Rd

Old Hope Rd

see New
Kingston map

August
Town

Hope River

Dallas Mountain

Tinson Pen
Airport

Marcus Garvey Drive

Port Bustamente

20

Spanish Town Rd

Slipe Rd

Camp Rd

22

21

Mountain View Ave

Hunt's
Bay

Causeway N

A1

A3

S Camp Rd

Windward Rd

A4

Windward Rd

Causeway S

19

Harbour St

A4

24

To Bull
Bay

Kingston   Harbour

Ferry Route

Palisades
Park

Gunboat
Beach

Norman Manley Hwy

A4

Gallows
Point

Refuge Cay

Norman
Manley
International
Airport

25

The Palisadoes

Port Royal
Point

Port Royal

The Palisadoes

Main Rd

Plumb Point
Lighthouse

see Port
Royal map

Ferry Route

Lime Cay
Picnic Park

Lime Cay

Southeast Cay

South Cay

CARIBBEAN
SEA

Metropolitan
Kingston

0   1   2 km

0   .5   1 mile

built more expansive homes. Many merchants built lookout towers atop their homes to check on the movement of ships in and out of the harbor (Vale Royal, the current prime minister's official residence, is a good example). The merchants constituted a potent political force. They became peeved that the official capital was sleepy Spanish Town, which Kingston had already eclipsed. In 1755 Governor Admiral Charles Knowles bowed to political pressure and transferred his government's offices to Kingston. His successor revoked the act, however, and it wasn't until 1872 that the capital was officially transferred.

The 1907 earthquake leveled much of the city. Many of the most important buildings were destroyed, and most of the fine houses ringing the Parade burned down.

In the 1960s, the Urban Development Corporation reclaimed the waterfront, and several other historic landmarks including Victoria Market were razed to make way for a complex of gleaming new concrete structures: the Bank of Jamaica, the Scotia Centre, the Oceana Hotel, the Jamaica Conference Centre, and Kingston Mall. A modern shipping facility – Port Busta-mante – was also developed on reclaimed lands to the west.

Overnight, Kingston became a major port of call on Caribbean cruising itineraries. About the same time, Kingston's nascent music industry was beginning to gather steam, lending international stature and fame to the city. This, in turn, fostered the growth of New Kingston, an uptown area of multistory office blocks, banks, restaurants, shops, and hotels developed in the 1960s on the site of the Knutsford Park racecourse.

A City in Decline

The boom years of the 1960s lured the rural poor to Kingston, swelling the slums and shanty towns that had arisen in the preceding years. Unemployment rose dramatically, and with it, crime. The fractious 1970s spawned politically connected criminal enterprises whose trigger-happy networks still plague the city. Commerce began to leave downtown for New Kingston, which was being developed as a commercial and shopping center.

That exodus began a period of decline from which the downtown has yet to recover. Many of the once splendid colonial town houses decayed into 'yards,' or tenements. And the piers that welcomed cruise ships to the waterfront are no more, replaced by an oil refinery and an industrial and commercial area – Newport West – on swampy land reclaimed from the harbor. A redevelopment project in the 1980s was aimed at redeveloping the depressed areas south and west of the Parade, but exploring the area today you can't help but wonder what the Kingston Restoration Company did with the US$30 million investment.

Kingston's Comeback

The city is on the threshold of a potential comeback. Hoteliers and the Jamaican Tourist Board (JTB) are pushing to dispel the city's negative image and to resurrect its tourist industry. Prior to the 1970s, Kingston was a major tourism venue and thriving cruise port, but political turbulence and economic destabilization during the late 1970s and 1980s effectively destroyed the tourist trade. Cruise ships stopped coming. The north-coast resorts disassociated themselves from the capital city and were able to establish a separate market identity. Even the JTB effectively stopped promoting Kingston.

Finally, in 1995, a US$50 million project was initiated to bring cruise ships and tourists back to Kingston. That year the Jamaican Product Exchange (JAPEX), the island's annual travel trade show, was held in Kingston for the first time to show off the city's attractions. A major, long-term restoration is planned in the historic downtown. Development of a free port has been proposed that would include Port Royal and the Fort Augusta Peninsula. And, most significantly, Port Royal will supposedly be restored and turned into the Williamsburg of the Caribbean.

Life on the Edge

On the edge of Kingston huddle extensive shanty towns. Like Dickensian England, endemic rural poverty continues to encourage an enormous pool of starry-eyed youths to seek a better life in Kingston. For most, the illusion ends in one-room dwellings made of packing cases, fish barrels, tin, and cardboard. To deter squatters, the government has refused to supply public amenities, giving rise to illegal and unsanitary pit latrines.

Some slums and shanty towns are occasionally bulldozed by the government. Squatters, however, quickly reclaim land that is cleared, and the lack of basic amenities has not deterred migration from the countryside. Tuberculosis, associated with overcrowded rooms, and typhoid, resulting from inadequate sewage facilities and contaminated drinking water, prevail in the tenements and slums.

Their peripheral location, the social stigma attached to them, and endemic illiteracy have added to the difficulties of their inhabitants in finding work. A great percentage of Kingston's *lumpenproletariat* adapt by 'scuffling' or scraping a living through begging, making handicrafts, and selling the scraps gleaned from garbage dumps such as the 'dungle' on the foreshore in West Kingston. As late as the 1960s, people had actually lived on the dungle. 'Droves of squatters awaited the arrival of the garbage carts, and, as they disgorged their contents, competed for them with the John Crows,' recalls Professor Colin G Clarke of Liverpool University's Center for Latin American Studies. Many others live by pimping, prostitution, and violent crime.

Monsignor Richard Albert lives like Mother Theresa among the poor of Kingston. His '1000 A Month Club' is a foundation that sponsors inner-city projects (supporters join the club for J$1000 a month). ∎

ORIENTATION

The city overlooks the seventh largest natural harbor in the world, with the waterfront on its southern border. It spreads out in a fan shape from the harbor and rises gently toward the foothills and spur ridges of the Blue Mountains, nestled in a cusp. It's a magnificent setting, best seen from the Hellshire Hills looking northeast toward the Blue Mountains across the harbor or looking down from the mountains themselves upon the sprawling city.

A wooded, steep-faced ridge – Long Mountain – rises to the east, with Dallas Mountain, a spur of the Blue Mountains, rising further east, parallel and higher. At the northern end of Long Mountain is Beverly Hills, dotted with upscale homes. To the northeast, the city is hemmed in by Jacks Hill; to the north by Stony Hill; and to the northwest by Red Hills.

Downtown

The historic downtown area just north of the waterfront forms the city center. Ocean Blvd, Port Royal St, and Harbour St parallel the waterfront. King St, the main thoroughfare, leads north from the waterfront to the Parade, surrounding a bustling square at the heart of the historic district.

Most buildings of historic interest lie within a four-block quadrant northeast of the Parade. From here, E Queen St runs east to the Norman Manley airport and Port Royal. W Queen St runs west for four blocks, then tilts and becomes Spanish Town Rd, which cuts northwest (toward Spanish Town) through Tivoli Gardens and the industrial estates of southwest Kingston, an altogether depressing drive lined with slums and shanty towns.

Uptown

Marescaux Rd and Slipe Rd lead north from downtown to 'uptown.' The two roads meet at Cross Roads, a major junction marked with a clock tower that is the unofficial boundary with New Kingston, immediately to the north. Knutsford Blvd, the main north-to-south artery bisects New Kingston. Half Way Tree Rd leads northwest, turning into Constant Spring Rd on the way toward the major commercial

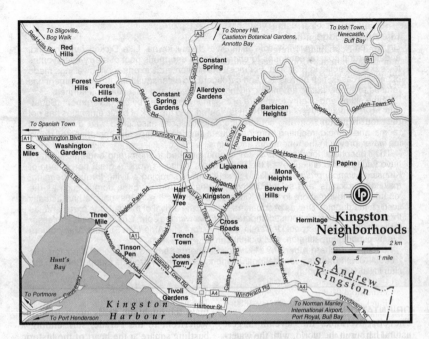

To Sligoville, Bog Walk · Red Hills Rd · Red Hills · To Stoney Hill, Castleton Botanical Gardens, Annotto Bay · To Irish Town, Newcastle, Buff Bay · B1 · A3 · Constant Spring · Forest Hills · Forest Hills Gardens · Red Hills Rd · Constant Spring Gardens · Melyaes Rd · Constant Spring Rd · Allerdyce Gardens · Jacks Hill Rd · Barbican Heights · Skyline Drive · Gordon Town Rd · To Spanish Town · Washington Blvd · A1 · Six Miles · Washington Gardens · Spanish Town Rd · A1 · Dunrobin Ave · A3 · E King's House Rd · Barbican · Old Hope Rd · B1 · Papine · Hope Rd · Liguanea · Mona Heights · Mona Rd · Hagley Park Rd · Trafalgar Rd · Half Way Tree Rd · Half Way Tree · New Kingston · Old Hope Rd · Beverly Hills · Maxfield Ave · Three Mile · A1 · Marcus Garvey Drive · Tinson Pen · Trench Town · Spanish Town Rd · A3 · Cross Roads · Camp Rd · Hermitage · Mountain View Ave · Kingston Neighborhoods · Hunt's Bay · Jones Town · To Portmore · Causeway · Tivoli Gardens · Harbour St · A4 · Windward Rd · A4 · Windward Rd · To Norman Manley International Airport, Port Royal, Bull Bay · To Port Henderson · Kingston Harbour · St Andrew · Kingston · 0   1   2 km · 0   .5   1 mile

center of Constant Spring, and then ascend due north to Stony Hill.

Northeast of New Kingston lies the middle-class residential area of Liguanea, up Hope Rd from Half Way Tree. Hope Rd ascends gradually past Mona Heights to Papine, the gateway to the Blue Mountains.

Maps

You can obtain copies of the Jamaica Tourist Board's 'Discover Jamaica' map from the JTB headquarters (see the Tourist Office section below). It features a good 1:34,000 scale street map of Kingston showing the location of sites of interest and upscale hotels.

The Survey Dept at 23½ Charles St has more detailed city maps designed for planners (see the Maps section under Planning in Facts for the Visitor chapter).

INFORMATION
Tourist Offices

The JTB has its headquarters in the ICWI Building (2 St Lucia Ave, ☎ 929-9200, fax 929-9375). It offers a limited collection of tourist literature, plus a small research library on the ground floor. Another JTB office is located in the arrival hall at Norman Manley International Airport (☎ 924-8024).

The Jamaica Information Service has its headquarters at 58A Half Way Tree Rd (☎ 926-3740). It offers statistical and general information on the island.

Foreign Embassies & Consulates

More than 40 countries have embassies and consulates in Kingston. Some are listed in the Facts for the Visitor chapter. You can also find telephone numbers in the telephone directories.

Money

Banks You'll find more than a dozen banks along Knutsford Rd in New Kingston. Most have foreign-exchange counters as well as ATMs. Very few ATMs are linked to international networks, so it may be difficult to get cash using your cash cards issued by foreign banks. Downtown you'll find a Scotiabank foreign-exchange center in the Jamaica Conference Centre. Banking hours are 9 am to 2 pm Monday to Thursday and 9 am to noon and 2 pm to 5 pm on Friday.

The following banks have branches throughout Kingston:

Bank of Nova Scotia
30 Duke St	☎ 922-1810
105 Red Hills Rd	☎ 925-7560
35 King St	☎ 922-1420
60 E Queen St	☎ 922-8890
2 Knutsford Blvd	☎ 926-1391
6 Oxford Rd	☎ 926-4145
86 Slice Rd	☎ 926-1530
125 Old Hope Rd	☎ 927-4371
10 Constant Spring Rd	☎ 926-3400
4 Ellesmere Rd	☎ 929-4192
88 Half Tree Rd	☎ 926-1520

Century National Bank
14-20 Port Royal St	☎ 922-3313
73 Knutsford Blvd	☎ 968-6796
2 Eureka Rd	☎ 929-3880

CIBC Jamaica
58 Duke St	☎ 922-5295
78 Half Way Tree Rd	☎ 926-7408
1 King St	☎ 922-6120
Manor Park Plaza	☎ 924-2521
6 Newport Blvd	☎ 923-4821

Jamaica Citizen's Bank
4 King St	☎ 922-5850
15A Old Hope Rd	☎ 926-5847
Sovereign Centre	☎ 927-9431
17 Dominica Drive	☎ 929-2602
Premier Plaza	☎ 926-5885
Norman Manley Airport	☎ 924-8666

Mutual Security Bank
18 Trafalgar Rd	☎ 927-3820
14½ Half Way Tree Rd	☎ 926-6531
37 Duke St	☎ 922-6710
134 Old Hope Rd	☎ 977-2075

Traveler's Checks Grace-Kennedy Travel at 19 Knutsford Blvd, Kingston 5 (☎ 929-6290) acts as the local Thomas Cook representative. It cashes Thomas Cook traveler's checks free of charge. Stuart's Travel Service represents American Express; their office is at 9 Cecelio Ave (☎ 929-2345).

Wire Remittances You can have money delivered at short notice via the Western

Union office at 20 Tobago Ave in New Kingston (☎ 926-2454 or toll free 991-2057).

Post & Communications
Mail The GPO is downtown at 13 King St (☎ 922-2120). It's open 9 am to 5 pm Monday to Thursday; 9 am to 4 pm on Friday; and 9 am to 1 pm on Saturday. It gets very crowded. A much better option is the New Kingston Post Office at 115 Hope Rd (☎ 927-7258). Other branches are located on Constant Spring Rd (☎ 925-2815) and Half Way Tree Rd (☎ 926-6803).

Federal Express has an office at 75 Knutsford Blvd (☎ 926-1456). DHL has offices at 50 Knutsford Blvd (☎ 929-2554) and 54 Duke St (☎ 922-7333). UPS offers the cheapest express service; it's open daily 7 am to 7 pm (5 Altamont Terrace, ☎ 968-8288). UPS offers a money-back guarantee of next-day delivery to the USA and Canada. It will cost you about US$11 to send a letter to the USA; you can even send a package up to five pounds for US$17.50.

Telephone & Fax You can make international calls and send faxes from most hotels, but many add a hefty service charge. A cheaper alternative is to make calls from the Jamintel Centre, operated by Telecommunications of Jamaica, at 15 North St, at the corner of Duke St (☎ 922-6031 or 922-9083). It has a message service (☎ 922-9613), and you can also send cablegrams from here. It's open 9 am to 5 pm. You'll also find fax, cable, and telex services in the lobby of the Jamaica Conference Centre at 14-20 Duke St (☎ 922-9160, fax 922-7816).

For Directory Assistance call ☎ 114; for Operator Assistance call ☎ 112; for the International Operator call ☎ 0-980-0000.

Travel Agencies
There are dozens of travel agencies scattered throughout the city. Most are linked by computer with major airline reservation systems and can also assist you with hotel and car-rental reservations. Two reputable

companies are Grace Kennedy Travel at 19 Knutsford Blvd (☎ 929-6290, fax 968-8418), and ITS International Travel Services, which has several offices throughout Kingston, including one on Trinidad Terrace in New Kingston (☎ 926-4841) and another downtown at 9 King St (☎ 922-6114).

Bookshops

Surprisingly, Kingston lacks a really well-stocked bookstore. Most hotel gift shops stock novels by well-known authors, plus a small selection of travel guidebooks and cultural and historical guides to Jamaica. All the Write Things (☎ 968-2307), in the grounds of Devon House, has a comprehensive selection of books on Jamaica and the Caribbean, including local literature, guidebooks, nature, history, and politics. Bookland (☎ 926-4035) at 53 Knutsford Blvd and the Kingston Bookshop (☎ 922-4056) at 70B King St are modestly stocked, as are the Book Shop (☎ 926-1800) at 15 Constant Spring Rd and Times Stores with three locations: at 8 King St (☎ 922-4690), Tropical Plaza, Kingston 10 (☎ 926-7410); and Liguanea Plaza, Kingston 6, (☎ 927-9726). Most bookshops are primarily office supply and stationery stores.

You can buy leading international magazines and newspapers at the above stores, as well as at most pharmacies.

Libraries

The Jamaica Library Service, which operates parish libraries throughout the whole island, is headquartered in the St Andrew Parish Library on tree-lined Tom Redcam Ave (☎ 926-3315). The National Library of Jamaica (☎ 922-5533) at 12 East St incorporates the Caribbean's largest repository of audiovisual aids, books, maps, charts, paintings, illustrations, and documents on West Indian history. The library is open 9 am to 6 pm Monday to Friday and 9 am to 5 pm on Saturday. No bags or briefcases are allowed inside.

The Jamaican National Heritage Trust in Headquarters House at 79 Duke St (☎ 922-1287) maintains archives on the island's architectural history.

The Scientific Research Council (☎ 927-1771) has a public library on Hope Rd. You may also be allowed to use the three libraries of the University of the West Indies; call the loan and reference desk at ☎ 927-2123.

Campuses

'You-wee,' as Jamaicans call the University of the West Indies (UWI; ☎ 927-1660) campus, lies in the lee of Long Mountain, southeast of Mona Heights, in northeast Kingston. Visitors are free to enter the campus, which has several sites of historical interest.

UWI has campuses in Barbados, Jamaica, and Trinidad. The Kingston campus offers degrees in agriculture, arts and general studies, education, engineering, law, medicine, natural sciences, and social sciences, and also includes a teaching hospital with 500 beds on the north side of campus.

From New Kingston, take Hope Rd to Mona Rd. The No 66 bus departs the Parade and passes the UWI campus en route to Hermitage (US$0.20). Buses No 77, 78, and 79 also leave the Parade for August Town, passing the campus en route.

Laundry

You'll be hard-pressed to find self-service laundries. One of the few is Speedy's Laundromat at 108 Red Hills Rd (☎ 924-5846). You may be able to use the self-service laundry in the courtyard of the Chelsea Hotel at 5 Chelsea Ave.

There are plenty of laundry services, however, including Deluxe Cleaners at 30 Constant Spring Rd (☎ 926-8246), Modern Laundry & Cleaners at 44 Waltham Park Rd (☎ 923-7573), and Supercleaners, which has branches in both the Sovereign Centre (☎ 978-5116) and Lane Plaza (☎ 978-0705) in Liguanea. Most laundries offer same-day service as well as drycleaning.

Medical Services

Kingston has more than half of Jamaica's doctors, four public hospitals, and a plethora of medical clinics. Medical Associates

Hospital is a private facility at 18 Tangerine Place, Kingston 10 (☎ 926-8624) that offers emergency ambulance service and medical assistance. Another private company, Deluxe Ambulance Service (☎ 923-7415) offers 24-hour emergency service. Wings Jamaica (☎ 923-5416) based at Tinson Pen airport offers air ambulance.

The following public hospitals all have emergency departments: Bellevue Hospital (☎ 928-1380) is at 16½ Windward Rd, Kingston 2; Kingston Public Hospital (☎ 922-0210) is on North St: and UWI Hospital (☎ 927-6621) is on the University of West Indies campus, Mona.

You can also receive emergency treatment at the Newport Medical Group at 22 Old Hope Rd (☎ 926-5483, or 926-6296 for appointments and emergency only). Other clinics include the Duke St Medical Centre at 57 E Queen St (☎ 967-0135); Eureka Medical Centre at 1 Eureka Rd (☎ 929-1820); and the Professional Medical Centre at 15 Ripon Rd (☎ 929-5843), which is open 9 am to 8 pm Monday to Saturday. If you put your back out carrying all the reggae tapes you've purchased, you can find relief at the Physiotherapy Centre at 12 Tangerine Place (☎ 929-6766).

Biomedical has a clinical diagnostic laboratory at 8A Caledonia Ave, Kingston 5 (☎ 926-4191).

Pharmacies Kingston has no shortage of pharmacies. Try Constant Spring Pharmacy & Medical Centre (☎ 924-2786) at 1418 Constant Spring Rd; Moodies Pharmacy (☎ 926-4174) in the New Kingston Shopping Centre at 30 Dominica Drive; or Kent Pharmacy (☎ 922-3323) in downtown at 55A Duke St.

Medical Services for Women Gynae Associates at 23 Tangerine Place, Kingston 10 (☎ 929-5038) specializes in women's medicine. Doctor Valerie Dean, an obstetrician and gynecologist, also has a clinic at 22 Old Hope Rd (☎ 929-8201). You can have mammograms taken at the Jamaica Cancer Society at 16 Lady Musgrave Rd, Kingston 5 (☎ 978-5898). The Women's

Centre of Jamaica Foundation at 42 Trafalgar Rd (☎ 929-7608) may be able to provide information on specialist medical services for women.

The Crisis Centre (☎ 929-2997) has 24-hour counseling on matters concerning rape and similar crises.

Medical Services for Children If you have kiddies needing medical attention, call the Bustamante Hospital for Children on Arthur Wint Drive, Kingston 5 (☎ 926-5721). There's also a Childcare Medical Center at 6 Portmore Drive in Portmore, west of Kingston (☎ 988-5086).

Emergency
The police maintain a hotline (☎ 927-7778), and a tourism liaison at 79 Duke St (☎ 922-9321). A complete listing of police departments and branches is given in the blue pages of the Jamaican telephone directories. In case of an emergency call the police at ☎ 119. Call the fire department or ambulance service at ☎ 110.

Dangers & Annoyances
Despite its reputation, Kingston is no more threatening to tourists than is Montego Bay, Negril, Ocho Rios, New York, or Chicago, as long as you avoid the 'yards' or ghettoes. Stick to the main streets – if in doubt ask your hotel concierge or manager to point out trouble areas.

New Kingston and upscale residential areas such as Liguanea and Mona are generally safe for walking, as are most main roads. Avoid wandering west of the Parade when exploring downtown. Other trouble areas include Matthews Lane, West St, Foster Lane, Spanish Town Rd, and Maxfield Ave. These areas are rife with tension and crime and the presence of a stranger (especially a white face) invites trouble.

Avoid walking downtown streets at night. Stick to the major, well-lit thoroughfares of New Kingston.

As a foreign traveler, you'll stand out from the crowd. Fortunately, visitors to Kingston are not hassled to anywhere near

The Yards

The ghetto areas of West Kingston are called the 'West.' Acre upon acre of these festering 'yards' or tenements spread out northwest from the Parade. They are no-go zones for out-of-towners. Much of the city's population growth in recent decades has been concentrated here, in areas such as Trench Town and Jones Town, and in sterile housing projects such as Majesty Pen and Tivoli Gardens conceived as 'model communities' by Edward Seaga while he was minister of finance in the 1960s.

As the bureaucrats failed in their attempt at brightening the 'yardies' future, areas became divided politically in a sectarian battle for hearts, minds, and votes curried through patronage. Certain areas were said to 'eat only when their party is in power.' Soon, criminal-politicians and their hoodlums developed strangleholds on the low-income areas.

While I was there in October 1994, a shooting spree left seven people dead; when I was there in March 1995, 12 people died in a blood-letting. Both incidents were blamed on the Shower Posse (named because they 'showered' their victims with bullets) from Tivoli Gardens, a longtime JLP stronghold and the heart of ex-Premier Edward Seaga's constituency.

It's easy to tell which party rules behind the stockades. Up-front, no-nonsense wall murals act as territorial markers that tell the tale of a city at war with itself. Some of the worst ghettoes are in East Kingston, where affiliations have traditionally been with the JLP.

If you want to visit, you *must* seek permission from a guide respected in the area and go with him – not doing so is dangerous business. Sense Adventure (Box 216, Kingston 7, ☎ 927-2097, fax 929-6967) operates a Culture & Reggae trip (day or night) that includes a visit to the 'yards.' ∎

the degree they are in the north-coast resorts. I've walked many miles on Kingston's streets and have never been threatened. Still, many Kingstonians, especially the down-and-outs, are by nature suspicious and at times you may be eyed icily. Don't loiter!

If you feel uncomfortable walking Kingston's streets, it might help to consider whether the threat is mostly what you *perceive* it might be. My comfort level increased markedly as I became more familiar with the city and as I came to realize that my initial lack of comfort was due to my *anticipation* of being threatened.

Note that many Kingstonians respond aggressively to having their photographs taken. Respect their wishes.

Although crime in Jamaica is limited to small pockets beyond the tourist path, the big picture isn't pretty. In May 1995 alone, the police blotter recorded 71 murders and another 39 in the first two weeks of June – a figure of 2.29 murders per day! Sixty percent of Jamaica's murders occur in the capital. In 1993, there were 372 murders in

the Kingston metropolitan area, or 58 murders per 100,000 people (New York had 57 per 100,000). The city ranks as the murder capital of the Caribbean, second among metropolitan areas in the Americas only to Washington, DC (75 per 100,000 population). But more than half of the murders resulted from domestic disputes, and the rest were mostly drug-related murders in the ghettoes.

High walls, window grills, chain-link fences, guard-dog signs, and private-security services point out that crime in Kingston is rife. Much of it is gang-related. For example, business operators in downtown Kingston complain of being harassed by gangs demanding protection money. The situation has grown so bad that in June 1995 businesses in the area closed down for two days to demand government action against the gunmen's reign of terror. In response, the National Security Minister announced a plan to rid the city center of unlicensed street vendors in an attempt to 'better monitor' activities.

Be cautious when driving or crossing the

street. Kingston's streets are narrow and full of potholes that drivers swerve to avoid.

THE WATERFRONT

The harbor is fronted by Ocean Blvd, landscaped with a thin grass strip and shady palms. It's a breezy half-mile walk. The rickety old wharves at the western end are a gathering point for fishing boats. The **Crafts Market** is here, too, in an old iron building constructed in 1872. Although gloomy within (beware of pickpockets), it's a great place to buy wicker and straw goods or carvings.

Virtually nothing remains of the original colonial waterfront that served as a center of social activity centered on a weekend market – known as Christmas Grand Market – held at the foot of King St. In its heyday the market attracted upwards of 10,000 people. It fronted Victoria Pier, where for over three centuries royalty, dignitaries, and other rich and famous folk first set foot in Jamaica.

Negro Aroused

Immediately to the west of the foot of King St stands the statue *Negro Aroused* by Jamaica's foremost sculptor, the late Edna Manley, wife of ex-Premier Norman Manley.

Jamaica Conference Centre

This conference center at 14-20 Duke St (☎ 922-9160, fax 922-7816) was built in 1982 as the venue for meetings of the United Nations' International Seabed Authority. Its impressive architecture and facilities were built to United Nations' standards.

A guided tour is worthwhile, not least to admire the intriguing wicker basket ceilings, others of bamboo resembling waves, and walls that look like upended Murphy beds (closer inspection reveals that they're woven mats).

Two cafeterias offer views over the harbor. The lobby contains a Scotiabank money exchange, Air Jamaica ticket office, and public telephones.

The names of those who worked on the construction of the center are engraved on a mosaic of metal tiles on the facade outside the main entrance. It reads 'One one coco full basket,' which roughly translates as everyone's contribution makes something complete.

Bank of Jamaica

At the east end of Ocean Blvd, on Nethersole Place, is the Bank of Jamaica headquarters, fronted by a tall concrete statue of Noel 'Crab' Nethersole (minister of finance from 1955 to 1969), who earned his nickname for his strange walk. One of his most popular contributions was abolishing the bicycle tax.

Inside you'll find a small **Museum of Coins and Notes** (☎ 922-0750) displaying Jamaican currency through the centuries. Tallies and tokens are also on display, as well as old coins called 'quatties,' recalled in the song lyric: 'Carry me ackee go a Linstead Market, not a quattie wut sell.' It's open 6 am to 6 pm Monday to Friday.

Institute of Jamaica

The Institute of Jamaica (12 East St, ☎ 922-0620) is the nation's small-scale equivalent of the British Museum or Smithsonian. It was established in 1879 for 'the encouragement of literature, science and art.' Also here is a herbarium in the **Natural History Division**, the entrance of which fronts Tower St. The institute hosts permanent and visiting exhibitions, and features a lecture hall, plus reading rooms and libraries where you may browse Jamaican newspapers dating back over two centuries. The institute is open from 8:30 am to 5 pm Monday to Thursday and until 4 pm on Friday. Other divisions are scattered throughout the city, including the African Caribbean Institute at 12 Ocean Blvd and the National Gallery (see below).

National Gallery

Three blocks further west is the National Gallery, opened in 1984 in the Roy West Building at 12 Ocean Blvd (☎ 922-1561).

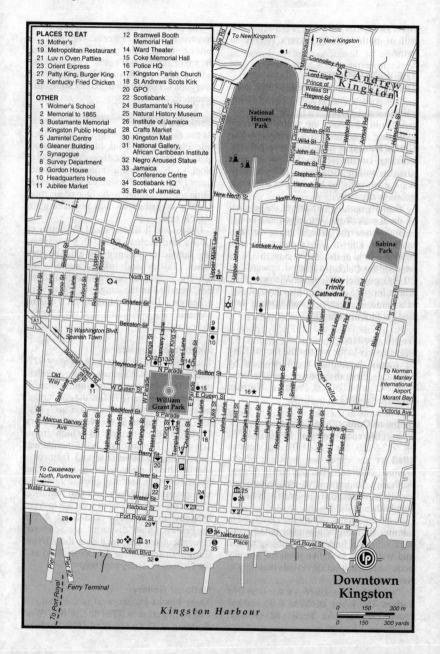

PLACES TO EAT
13 Mother's
19 Metropolitan Restaurant
21 Luv n Oven Patties
23 Orient Express
27 Patty King, Burger King
29 Kentucky Fried Chicken

OTHER
1 Wolmer's School
2 Memorial to 1865
3 Bustamante Memorial
4 Kingston Public Hospital
5 Jamintel Centre
6 Gleaner Building
7 Synagogue
8 Survey Department
9 Gordon House
10 Headquarters House
11 Jubilee Market

12 Bramwell Booth
   Memorial Hall
14 Ward Theater
15 Coke Memorial Hall
16 Police HQ
17 Kingston Parish Church
18 St Andrews Scots Kirk
20 GPO
22 Scotiabank
24 Bustamante's House
25 Natural History Museum
26 Institute of Jamaica
28 Crafts Market
30 Kingston Mall
31 National Gallery,
   African Caribbean Institute
32 Negro Aroused Statue
33 Jamaica
   Conference Centre
34 Scotiabank HQ
35 Bank of Jamaica

To New Kingston

To New Kingston

Connolley Ave

Lord Elgin
Prince of
Wales St
Regent St

Prince Albert St

**St Andrew
Kingston**

Slipe Rd

Marescaux Rd

**National
Heroes
Park**

Heroes Circle

Hitchin St
Wild St
John St
Sarah St
Stephen St
Hannah St

Great George St
Wolmer St
Arnold Rd
Hillington St

Heroes Circle

New North St

North Ave

North Ave

Lockett Ave

**Sabina
Park**

Dumfries St

Upper Mark Lane
Upper Johns Lane

A3

North St

5

6

Charles St

7

8

**Holy
Trinity
Cathedral**

Emerald Rd
S Camp Rd

Beeston St

9

10

To Washington Blvd
Spanish Town

A1

Regent St
Chestnut Lane
Bono St
Pink Lane
Oxford St
Rose Lane
Upper Bellevue
Blevant St

4

Heywood St

Orange St
Tramway Lane
Upper King St
Love Lane
Church St

N Parade

Sutton St

James St
Text Lane
Price Lane
Lissant Rd
Blake Rd

Barnes Gulley

To Norman
Manley
International
Airport,
Morant Bay

Old
Way
Salt Lane
Spanish Town Rd

11

W Queen St

12 13
14

S Parade

**William
Grant
Park**

15

E Queen St

16 ★

Wildman St
Smith Lane

A4

Victoria Ave

Marcus Garvey
Ave

Darling St
Peechi St
West St
Mathews Lane
Princess St
Luke Lane
Orange St
Peters Lane
King St
Temple Lane
Church St

Beckford St

Mark Lane
Duke St
Johns Lane
East St
George's Lane
Hanover St
Rum Lane
Rosemary Lane
Maiden Lane
Gold St
Foster Lane
High Holborn St
Laws St
Ladd St
Fleet St

Camp Rd

17

18

Barry St

20

P

Tower St

21

Water St

22

24

25

26

Harbour St

28

27

Port Royal St

29

Harbour St

Port Royal St

28

30

31

33

32

34 Nethersole
Place

35

Port Royal St

Water Lane

To Causeway
North, Portmore

Pier #1
Pier #2

To Port Royal

Ferry Terminal

Kingston Harbour

**Downtown
Kingston**

(LP)

0   150   300 m
0   150   300 yards

Open 10 am to 5 pm Monday to Friday, it is well worth the visit. The gallery, part of the Institute of Jamaica, displays Jamaican works from the 1920s to the present and boasts particularly good collections by John Dunkley and Edna Manley.

The rooms are arranged by decade. One whole room is dedicated to the contemporary intuitive works of Mallica 'Kapo' Reynolds, a charismatic sect leader whose marvelous mahogany figurines and other works are overtly religious. A collection of particularly interesting works by Osmond Watson melds Christian and Rastafarian imagery. My favorite piece is *Ras Smoke I* by Karl Parboosingh (1972), an evocative oil on canvas of a Rastafarian smoking his chalice. Note the bronze statue of Bob Marley by Christopher Gonzalez in the foyer; it is a draft of a statue that was intended for Celebrity Park.

Entrance is 'by contribution' (US$0.75 minimum). If you would like the services of a guide, ask for Nicky Morris; his profound and enlivening interpretations are a joy to listen to (call ahead; Friday is best). Guides are free, but a tip would be welcome.

An Annual National Exhibition is held every December through spring.

African Caribbean Institute
This institute houses an art museum and a library on Afro-Caribbean culture. It's in the building to the north of the gallery.

KING ST
In colonial days King St was the main thoroughfare leading from Victoria Pier to the Parade. It retains many beautiful old buildings with wide sidewalks shaded by columned verandahs. Note the decorative carvings and long Corinthian columns at the Mutual Security Bank building at the corner of King St and Harbour St, and the ornate wrought-iron railings on the upper floors of the buildings further up the street. The public buildings between Water St and Barry St that house the Treasury and Law Courts, General Post Office, and Accountant General Department (in the old Bank

of Jamaica) were built of concrete after the 1907 earthquake.

THE PARADE
Half a mile up King St you reach the Parade, comprising the streets surrounding William Grant Park at the bustling heart of downtown. The South Parade, packed with street vendors' stalls, is known as 'Ben Dung Plaza' because passersby have to bend down to buy from street hawkers whose goods are displayed on the ground. The place is clamorous and can be daunting!

Barracks once stood on the North Parade, which served as a parade ground for British soldiers. Public hangings took place here in colonial days, when the area was the center of social life. Three blocks west of the Parade lies the **Jubilee Market** (also known as Solar Market), which has been on this site since the 18th century (see the Things to Buy section below).

The Parade is disgustingly littered, and stores blast reggae music loud enough to drive away even the most hardened potential shopper. The wide pavement of North Parade is more placid. Both the North and South Parade are major bus thoroughfares, which adds to the pandemonium.

William Grant Park
This park is an oasis of relative calm amid the downtown mayhem. The site originally hosted a fortress erected in 1694 with guns pointing down King St toward the harbor. The fort was torn down and a garden, Victoria Park, laid out in 1870, with a life-size statue of the queen on a pedestal at its center. She has since been replaced by a bust of Sir Alexander Bustamante. Her Majesty's statue is now a few steps away on the east side of the park. The statue, which faced down King St in its former location, is said to have been turned around 180 degrees during the 1907 earthquake. All important announcements were traditionally proclaimed from its base during British colonial days.

The park was renamed in 1977 to honor black nationalist and labor lead Sir William

Grant (1894 – 1977), who preached his Garveyite message of African redemption here.

You can sit on the red-brick benches to admire the bougainvilleas and note the social life. At the center of the park is a four-tiered whimsical fountain shaped like a wedding cake. It's most often dry, though it's occasionally illumined by spotlights at night. Statues include those of ex-Premier Norman Manley and Edward Jordon (1800 – 1869), a Jamaican patriot who rose to become Speaker of the House of Assembly but who as an abolitionist faced trial for sedition and treason.

Kingston Parish Church

The gleaming white edifice facing the park's southeast corner is the parish church. Within earshot of its bell are born the only true Kingstonians – those 'born under the clock.' Like many structures hereabouts, the original church was destroyed in the 1907 earthquake and was replaced (in concrete) by the existing building. Note the tomb dating to 1699, the year the original church was built. Admiral Benbow, the commander of the Royal Navy in the West Indies at the turn of the 18th century, lies beneath a tombstone near the High Altar. There's also a memorial to Benbow sculpted by John Bacon. The organ, in fine working fettle, dates to 1722.

Coke Memorial Hall

Facing the eastern side of William Grant Park is Coke Memorial Hall, a crenelated building with an austere red-brick facade in the dour tradition of northern England Methodism. The structure, named after Dr Thomas Coke, founder of the Methodist Missions in the West Indies, dates to 1840 but was remodeled in 1907 after sustaining severe damage in an earthquake.

Ward Theater

The impressive sky-blue facade with white trim at the park's northeast corner, on the north side of the North Parade, belongs to the Ward Theater (☎ 922-0453), home to

The Ward Theater is the center of much of Kingston's performing arts events including plays, and dance and folk concerts.

the Little Theater Company. The site formerly housed the Kingston Theater, built in 1774.

The Ward, which dates from 1907, is the fourth theater on the site. It's named for Colonel Charles Ward, Custos of Kingston, who donated the theater to the city in 1912. Ward was a partner in the famous liquor firm of J Wray & Nephew, Ltd, which had its start at the Shakespeare Tavern. At the tavern, next door to the Kingston Theater, John Paul Jones made his debut as a professional actor in 1768 while in-between ships and before going on to become a famous US naval hero.

Bramwell Booth Memorial Hall

West of Ward Theater is the headquarters of the Salvation Army. The little castlelike structure, with its pink, turreted facade, was built in 1933.

DUKE ST

Duke St has several buildings of historic importance. Law firms still have their offices here, as they did in colonial days. At the corner of Water Lane, at 1A Duke St, national hero Sir Alexander Bustamante opened his office from which he wrote his campaign letters to the *Daily Gleaner* and conducted a money-lending business.

Headquarters House

This trim little townhouse of brick and timber is at 79 Duke St. It was originally known as Hibbert House, named after

Thomas Hibbert who reportedly was one of four members of the Assembly who in 1755 engaged in a bet to build the finest house and thereby win the attention of a much sought-after beauty. It seems he lost, but no one is sure if his cronies fared better.

Acquired by the military in 1814, the house became the headquarters of a British general. In 1872, when the capital was moved from Spanish Town to Kingston, the house became the seat of the Jamaican legislature and remained so until 1960, when Gordon House was built across the street. Since 1983 it has housed the Jamaican National Heritage Trust (☎ 922-1287).

Gordon House

Jamaica's parliament meets at Gordon House, immediately north of Headquarters House (☎ 922-0200), at the corner of Duke and Beeston Sts. The rather plain brick-and-concrete building was constructed in 1960 and named after national hero the Right Excellent George William Gordon (1820 – 1865), a 'free colored' son of a Scottish plantation owner. Gordon became wealthy and as a member of the Assembly championed the rights of the poor and oppressed. (For more on Gordon, see the Morant Bay section in the East Coast chapter.)

You can visit Gordon House by prior arrangement to watch how the Jamaica parliament conducts business. The legislature has but a single chamber, where the House of Representatives and the Senate meet at different times. If parliament is in session, you won't be allowed to drive along Duke St between Heywood and North Sts.

Jewish Synagogue

Jamaica's only synagogue sits on the corner of Duke and Charles Sts. The attractive whitewashed building was built in 1912 (the original was toppled by the 1907 earthquake).

ST ANDREWS SCOTS KIRK

This church on Mark Lane is the most intriguing historical gem in Kingston. The octagonal Georgian red-brick structure serves the United Church of Jamaica and

Though the last Arawak died centuries ago, the tribe is immortalized on the Jamaican Seal.

Grand Cayman. It was built from 1813 to 1819 at a cost of £21,000 by a group of prominent Scottish merchants and immediately christened the 'handsomest building in Kingston.' It is surrounded by a gallery supported by Corinthian pillars. Note the blue St Andrews Cross in the stained glass window. You'll be amply rewarded if you visit during a service when its acclaimed choir – the St Andrew Singers – is performing.

HOLY TRINITY CATHEDRAL

This imposing building on North St (nine blocks east of Duke St) is the center of Roman Catholicism on the island. Admiring its dome and four minarets, visitors immediately perceive the Spanish Moorish influence and understand why it has been described as a 'reinforced concrete version of St Sophia,' the famous church in Istanbul. Its pipe organ is said to be unmatched in the Caribbean.

A Jesuit boy's school, **St George's College**, stands next door. The huge building a stone's throw to the east is the **Gleaner Building**, home to Jamaica's leading newspaper.

NATIONAL HEROES PARK

The 74-acre oval-shaped site at the north end of Duke St was formerly the Kingston

Race Course (the first race was run in 1816, the last in 1953). During the 19th century, a traditional rivalry between 'east' and 'west' Kingston often erupted into 'wholesale organized fisticuffs' here. Today it is a forlorn, barren wasteland grazed by goats. The only bright note are the flame trees that burst into bloom each spring.

National Heroes Circle, a small enclosure at the park's southern end, contains a group of statues and memorials, in dreary Soviet-style realism. The tomb of Sir Alex Bustamante is a flat marble slab beneath an arch resembling the handle of a wicker basket. More interesting is the Memorial to 1865 commemorating the Morant Bay Rebellion, with a big rock on a pedestal flanked by bronze busts of Abraham Lincoln and the figure of a black slave with a sword.

Ex-Premier Norman Manley is also buried here. So, too, Marcus Garvey, whose body was flown from England in 1964 and reinterred with state honors.

Note the bust of General Antonio Maceo, the Cuban nationalist hero who was given refuge in Jamaica following the failure of the Cuban War of Independence (the bust is a gift from the Cuban government). The Simón Bolivar Monument, dedicated to the liberator of South America, stands in bronze outside the park, in front of the Ministry of Education. Bolivar survived an assassination attempt while in Jamaica, where he lived in exile for seven months and wrote his famous 'Jamaica Letter.'

MARESCAUX RD

Marescaux Rd is lined with lignum vitae, the national flower. The tree flowers in early summer and begins as a mauve bloom that turns to bright yellow, attracting a species of white butterfly (Kricogonia lyside).

Mico Teachers College

The intriguing wooden colonial structures to the north of National Heroes Park house one of the oldest teacher-training colleges in the world: Mico Teachers College. The college was originally established by the Lady Mico Charity as a primary school in 1834 to educate ex-slaves following emancipation. The main building, which dates from 1909, is one of the most impressive buildings in Kingston.

Mico is the sole survivor of several Mico colleges that were founded throughout the West Indies on the income accrued from a £1000 bequest that in 1670 Lady Mico's nephew chose to forgo rather than marry one of her six nieces. The dowry was thus invested with a portion to be used to ransom Christian slaves from the Barbary pirates. When piracy declined, the money, which had grown to a considerable sum, was used to create the Mico colleges.

Many distinguished Jamaicans were trained here.

Wolmer's School

Immediately south of Mico Teachers College is another venerable educational establishment: Wolmer's School, founded in 1729 at the bequest of a Swiss-German goldsmith. It has also produced many notable figures.

Up Park Camp

'The Camp,' midway down Camp Rd (which runs parallel to Marescaux Rd) is the 200-acre headquarters of the Jamaica Defence Force (and formerly of the British army in Jamaica). The southern entrance is called Duppy Gate for the legend of a colonial officer whose ghost appears at night to inspect the guards. Those interested in Jamaica's military history might pop inside the small **Military Museum** (☎ 926-8121) in front of Up Park Camp.

Gun Court

Immediately south of Up Park Camp is the Gun Court, whose tall barbed wire fences and guard towers have a conspicuous purpose: to keep dangerous criminals in. The Manley government established the high-profile prison in 1972 to house prisoners convicted of gun crimes. Prison conditions are extremely harsh and have been condemned by several human rights organizations.

HALF WAY TREE

What today is an important road junction, major bus terminal, and a bottleneck for traffic was an important colonial-era crossroads village – St Andrew – on the road from Spanish Town to Liguanea and the Blue Mountains. Half Way Tree is named for a venerable silk cotton (kapok) tree that stood here until the 1870s and whose shaded base became the site of both a tavern and market. Today the spot is marked by a clock tower erected in 1813 as a memorial to King Edward VII, whose bust sits on the south side of the tower.

St Andrews Parish Church

This red-brick church (☎ 926-6692), at the corner of Hagley Park Rd and Eastwood Park Rd, is popularly known as 'Half Way Tree Church.' It's thought that a church has been sited here since 1666. The original apparently toppled in the 1692 earthquake, and the foundations of the existing church were laid that year. The exterior is austere and unremarkable, but the stained-glass windows and organ are worth a peek inside. Sunday services are held at 6:30 and 7:30 am; on Tuesday and Friday at 9 am; and on Wednesday at 6:30 am.

HOPE RD

Most of the sites of interest in Uptown are located along this ruler-straight road, which runs from Half Way Tree to Papine, at the foothills of the Blue Mountains.

Devon House

The only site of any great appeal in New Kingston is Devon House, nestled in landscaped grounds on the west side of Hope Rd at its junction with Waterloo Rd. The beautiful ochre and white house is a splendidly preserved example of domestic architecture. It was built in 1881 by George Stiebel, a Jamaican wheelwright who hit pay dirt in the gold mines of Venezuela. The millionaire rose to become the first black custos of St Andrew. Subsequently, the house decayed but was restored after the government bought it in 1967 to house the National Gallery of Jamaica.

Devon House is the site of several noteworthy restaurants.

Most travelers pass by the house itself, but antique lovers will find it worth poking inside. Note the trompe l'oeil of palms in the entrance foyer. Stiebel even incorporated a game room with whist and cribbage tables, a ladies' sewing room, and a gambling room tucked discreetly away in the attic.

The house is a favored spot for wedding photographs, and the tree-shaded lawns attract couples on weekends. Tourists flock to the courtyard behind Devon House, which is ringed by quality souvenir and craft shops, plus the I-Scream ice cream store, and Brick Oven Bakery, which has reactivated the old oven in the original kitchen. Unfortunately, the giant flame tree that once shaded the courtyard was felled in 1995. The former stables and carriage house today are home to two of Jamaica's more famous restaurants: the Grogge Shop and the Devonshire. (See Places to Stay.)

Devon House (26 Hope Rd, ☎ 929-6602) is open 9:30 am to 5 pm Tuesday to Saturday and 11 am to 4 pm on Sunday. It costs US$1.50 to enter.

Jamaica House

Half a mile further up Hope Rd on the left is a one-story structure faced by a columned portico and fronted by expansive lawns. Gladioli fringe the driveway and add a splash of color. Initially built in 1960 as the residence of the prime minister, the building today houses the prime minister's office. You are restricted to peering through the fence.

PLACES TO STAY
1 Mayfair Hotel
2 Terra Nova Hotel
4 Shirley Retreat House
5 Medallion Hall Hotel
7 Sandhurst
8 Christar Villas
12 Central Court Hotel
13 International Inn
25 Four Seasons Hotel
26 Sutton Place Hotel
27 Holborn Manor
   Guest House
28 Indies Hotel

35 The Courtleigh Hotel
41 Island Club Hotel
44 Chelsea Hotel &
   Amusement Centre
49 The Wyndham Hotel
50 Jamaica Pegasus Hotel
51 Altamont Court
52 Sunset Inn
54 Lynn's Guest House
58 Union Square Guest House
64 The Roosevelt
65 Crieffe Court
66 Edge Hill Apartment Hotel

PLACES TO EAT
4 El Dorado Room
6 Queen of Sheba Restaurant
28 Plantation Terrace
29 Pollyanna's, Calcutta
30 Indies Pub & Grill
45 Chelsea Jerk Centre

OTHER
3 German Embassy
6 Bob Marley Museum
9 Jade Palace
10 Post Office

11 Gas Station
14 Countryside Club
15 Gas Station
16 Odeon Cinema
17 Skateland Disco
18 St Andrews Parish Church
19 Post Office
20 Gas Station
21 CIBC Jamaica Banking Centre
22 Police Station
23 Holy Cross RC Church
24 Jamaica Info Service
31 New Kingston
   Drive-in Theater

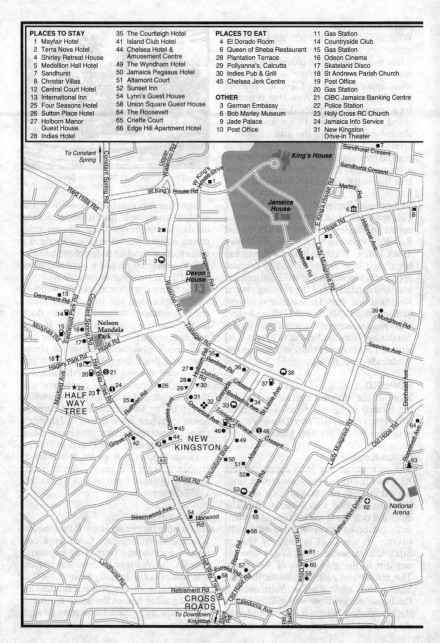

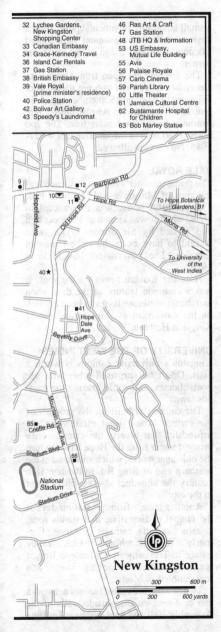

32	Lychee Gardens, New Kingston Shopping Center
33	Canadian Embassy
34	Grace-Kennedy Travel
36	Island Car Rentals
37	Gas Station
38	British Embassy
39	Vale Royal (prime minister's residence)
40	Police Station
42	Bolivar Art Gallery
43	Speedy's Laundromat
46	Ras Art & Craft
47	Gas Station
48	JTB HQ & Information
53	US Embassy, Mutual Life Building
55	Avis
56	Palaise Royale
57	Carib Cinema
59	Parish Library
60	Little Theater
61	Jamaica Cultural Centre
62	Bustamante Hospital for Children
63	Bob Marley Statue

New Kingston

King's House

Hidden amid trees behind Jamaica House is the official residence of the governor general. Reopened to the public in late 1995 after a lengthy restoration, it lies along a driveway that begins at the junction of E King's House Rd and Hope Rd.

King's House (☎ 927-6424) was initially the home of the Lord Bishop of Jamaica. It included a 19-acre property, formerly known as Somerset Pen. The government purchased the grandiose home in 1872 to house the English governor. The original, however, was badly damaged in the 1907 earthquake. Today visitors explore the remake, built in 1909 to a new design in reinforced concrete. The dining room contains two particularly impressive full-length portraits of King George III and Queen Charlotte by Sir Joshua Reynolds. The house sits in a 200-acre setting of park land, which includes a giant banyan tree that legend suggests is haunted by duppies.

You may never get to dine with royalty, but at least the governess hosts afternoon teas as part of the Meet the People program (contact the JTB for information and reservations). Kings House is open 9 am to 5 pm, Monday to Friday.

Bob Marley Museum

Outdoing all other sites as the most visited spot in Kingston is the reggae superstar's former home at 56 Hope Rd (☎ 927-9152). An Ethiopian flag flutters above the gate of the red-brick manse that Marley turned into his Tuff Gong Recording Studios (the studios are now in southwest Kingston; see below).

Dominating the forecourt is a gaily colored statue of the musical legend; in his arms is a guitar, while a soccer ball and portrait of Haile Selassie rest at his feet. The guides are deathly solemn, but the hourlong tour provides fascinating insights into Bob Marley's life, events from which are depicted on a six-panel mural, 'The Journey of Bob Marley Superstar,' painted on the inside of the compound wall.

His gold and platinum records are there on the walls, alongside Rastafarian religious cloaks. One room upstairs is decorated with media clippings about the superstar. Another contains a replica of Marley's original record shop (Wail 'n Soul). And his simple bedroom has been retained as it was, with his star-shaped guitar by his bedside. Marley, you'll note, lived a modest life. During your visit, he'll be talking to you through hidden speakers.

Outside, the guide will point out the bullet holes that ripped through the rear wall of the house during an assassination attempt in 1976. Nearby is the tree beneath which Marley would smoke ganja and practice his guitar. The erstwhile recording studio out back has metamorphosed into an exhibition hall and theater, where the tour closes with a fascinating film of his final days. The Queen of Sheba Restaurant in the forecourt can appease your hunger with I-tal dishes and fruit juices.

The museum is open 9:30 am to 5 pm, Monday, Tuesday, Thursday and Friday; and 12:30 to 6 pm on Wednesday, Saturday, and public holidays (entrance costs US$2, children US$0.30). You're not allowed to wander at will, nor are cameras or tape recorders permitted.

Hope Botanical Gardens

Anyone familiar with Kew or Butchart Gardens may be disappointed in those at the uppermost end of Old Hope Rd. The 200-acre gardens, which contain the Caribbean's largest collection of botanical plants, still haven't recovered from the blow they suffered when Hurricane Gilbert roared through in 1988. Still, it's worth a browse.

The gardens date back to 1881, when the government established an experimental garden on the site of the former Hope Estate, which had been established by Richard Hope, an officer in Cromwell's army that invaded Jamaica in 1655. Part of the Hope Aqueduct, built in 1758 to supply the estate, is still in use. The Ministry of Agriculture, which administers the gardens, maintains a research station and nursery.

Among the attractions of Palm Ave are cycads, or 'sago palms,' from the antediluvian era. There are separate orchid and cactus gardens as well as greenhouses, a small aquarium, ornamental ponds, and a basic children's amusement park called Coconut Park and a zoo at the northeast corner.

The gardens are open from October to December from 6 am to 6 pm daily; from February to April and September until 6:30 pm; and from May to August until 7 pm. Entrance to the gardens is free. The zoo costs US$0.60. For information call ☎ 927-1085. No cars are allowed.

VALE ROYAL

The prime minister's official residence is at the apex of Musgrave and Montrose Rds. The beautiful house was constructed in 1694, when it was known as Prospect Pen and owned by Sir Simon Taylor, who is said to have been the richest man in Jamaica. The government bought it in 1928.

Note the lookout tower on the roof; it was a common feature of the day, when merchants used spyglasses to keep a watch on the movement of ships in and out of Kingston Harbour.

UNIVERSITY OF THE WEST INDIES

Kingston's university campus is worth a visit. Don't be surprised when you see goats, horses, and cattle grazing the campus lawns.

The campus is built on the grounds of the former Mona sugar estate. The old **aqueduct** that bisects the campus once brought water from the Hope River to turn the old sugar works, which still stand at the northern end of Ring Rd. In the late 18th century the aqueduct also supplied water to the city.

Another legacy from plantation days is the chapel of limestone that stands four-square near the campus entrance. Formerly a sugar warehouse at Gales Valley Estate in Trelawny near Montego Bay, it was dismantled stone by stone and reassembled in Mona.

Two of Jamaica's most famous **artworks** can be found on the outside walls of the Assembly Hall and the Caribbean Institute

The UWI campus was built on the grounds of a sugar estate, the operations
of which depended on water flowing through this aqueduct.

of Mass Communications. The elaborate
murals are the work of Belgian artist
Claude Rahir. Also of note is the metal bird
by famous Jamaican sculptor Ronald
Moody on the inner Ring Rd, opposite the
Institute of Social and Economic Research.
It represents *savacou*, a mythical Carib
Indian bird of war.

The **Norman Manley Law School** contains a room dedicated to the ex-premier,
replete with some of his office furniture
and personal memorabilia.

TUFF GONG RECORDING STUDIOS
Bob Marley's son Ziggy Marley runs the
studios at 220 Marcus Garvey Drive
(☎ 927-7103 or 978-0510) in southwest
Kingston. Free tours of the studios are
hosted, and you may bump into your
favorite reggae artist recording his or her
future hit. A gift store sells T-shirts, tapes,
crafts and a miscellany of Marley memen-
tos. You're supposed to be welcome,
though the frigid stares from some of the
tough-looking groupies are daunting.

GOLF
Golfers have two options. Constant Spring
Golf Club (☎ 924-1610) is an 18-hole
championship course at the foot of the
mountains. It boasts a swimming pool;
tennis, squash, and badminton courts; and a
bar. Visitors can use the club facilities for
US$20 daily. To the east of Kingston, Cay-
manas Golf Course (☎ 926-8144) is a
6120-yard, 18-hole course, with club house
and pool (see Around Spanish Town in the
South Coast chapter).

ORGANIZED TOURS
JUTA Ltd (85 Knutsford Blvd, Kingston 5,
☎ 926-1537) has a 'Kingston Highlight
Tour' and also offers customized guided
tours. Galaxy Tours (75 Red Hills Rd,
☎ 931-0428, fax 925-8975) runs a series
of specialty city tours, ranging from cultural outings and shopping trips to 'Reggae
the Night Away.' The Teak Tree Co (PO
Box 435, Kingston 6, ☎ 977-1936, fax 977-
3247) offers an 'Old City Tour' and 'City
Art Tour.' Pro Tours also has a Kingston

art tour and 'Uptown' tour (US$31) each Wednesday, Thursday, and Saturday. Pleasure Vacation Tours (☎ 924-1471, fax 924-1756) offers excursions from Montego Bay, Ocho Rios, and Negril each Tuesday and Thursday.

SPECIAL EVENTS

Kingston has a full calendar of annual festivals and events. Major happenings include, by month:

January

National Exhibition goes all month (see the December listings).

February

Bob Marley Birthday Bash in early February brings reggae fans to the Bob Marley Museum (☎ 927-9152).

United Way Jazz Concert benefits the organization and features regional and international jazz artists. It is held at the Wyndham Hotel mid-month. Contact the Mutual Life Gallery (☎ 929-4302).

UWI Carnival is staged by university students from throughout the Caribbean. It features steel bands, reggae bands, soca jump-up, and Crowning of the Carnival King and Queen. For information call ☎ 927-1660.

March

JAMI Awards feature guest performers from reggae to classical. Contact Pulse Investments Ltd (☎ 968-1089).

April

Carnival Highlights include soca on the waterfront, parades and floats, costumed bands, and the Socin West Fete at Morgan's Harbour (Port Royal). Contact JTB offices worldwide.

Devon House Easter Craft Fair lays out colorful displays of arts and crafts, plus Jamaican foods at Devon House in mid-April. For information call ☎ 929-6602.

May

Jamaica Horticultural Society Show is held each May in the National Arena. Contact JTB offices worldwide.

July

Independence Day Festival & Street Parade features the National Festival Song Competition (held at the National Arena), the Gospel Song Festival (at the Randy Williams Entertainment Centre), and a traditional Jonkanoo street parade with costumed groups, live music and modern dances (☎ 926-5726).

National Dance Theater Company's Season of Dance is a summerlong season of performances that swings into action in July (☎ 926-6129).

Mello-Go-Round is a presentation of various performing arts held at either the National Arena or Ranny Williams Entertainment Centre (☎ 926-5726).

September

Miss Jamaica World Beauty Pageant. The winner represents Jamaica in the Miss World contest. It's hosted at the National Arena; for tickets contact the Spartan Health Club (☎ 927-7575).

October

Oktoberfest celebrates German heritage with oom-pah-pah music, dancing, and, of course, a beer drinking contest. Contact the Jamaica German Society (☎ 927-6408).

December

Devon House's Christmas Craft Fair, hosted by Devon House, promotes a colorful display of arts, crafts, and culinary delights (☎ 929-6602).

LTM Pantomime is a main hightlight with a gala opening on Boxing Day (December 26) at the Ward Theater (☎ 926-6129).

National Exhibition is where Jamaica's finest artists showcase their work each December to February at the National Gallery (☎ 922-1561).

PLACES TO STAY

Kingston has about 1650 hotel rooms, most in small, locally owned properties, B&Bs, and apartments. The classier hotels – all located in New Kingston or the hills above Liguanea – cater mostly to business travelers. You'll find many guest houses in the classified advertising sections of local newspapers. Standards vary widely.

Budget properties are mostly dingy, even depressing. Some accept guests for 'short time' (usually up to three hours) at a lower rate than overnight rates. Given the crowded conditions in which the majority of Kingstonians live (often with several families together), short-time rooms allow brief interludes of privacy. The majority of budget hotels are on the south side of New Kingston; some are on the fringe of trouble-filled districts.

Unlike elsewhere on the island, Kingston hotel rates are usually the same year-round.

Places to Stay – bottom end

Fred Richards runs a 30-room hotel at 2 Goodwin Park Rd, Kingston 4, (☎ 928-1866). Rooms have shared bath and cold water only and fans, alas, are in the hallways. Rates (US$7 to US$15 per room) depend on when you check in. *Hollywood Villa* at 7 W Lyndale Close, Kingston 20 (☎ 969-1518) has five basic rooms, each with fan and TV (US$17, including breakfast) and only cold water. The owners will do your laundry. In the same price range is *Steve's Guest House* at 1 Connolley Ave (☎ 922-1691). The 17 carpeted rooms have private bathrooms (some with hot water), fans, and TV. Rooms with TV and water-bed cost an extra US$3.

Harlem Resort at 2 Walker Ave, Kingston 5 (☎ 926-7872) lies on the northern edge of Trench Town. Some of the 25 rooms (US$14 per room) have private bath and TV. All have fans. Cold water only. 'Short time' rates are available. There's a tiny restaurant.

Another option is the *Chelsea Hotel & Amusement Centre*, next to Chelsea Jerk Centre (5 Chelsea Ave, ☎ 926-5803). The dark, basic rooms feature air-con and hot water but are overpriced at US$20, or US$23 with TV. It is well known locally as a 'love' motel. A sign outside reads: 'No room will be rented to two men!' A public self-service laundry is in the forecourt.

Lynn's Guest House, nearby at 36 Half Way Tree Rd (☎ 929-7047), has seven rooms (US$20) with fans, plus private bath and hot water. Some have TVs (US$25). Also well located on the edge of New Kingston is the *Central Court Hotel* at 47 Old Hope Rd, Kingston 5 (☎ 929-1026), with 32 air-con rooms and one- and two-bedroom suites with fans, TV, and telephone, plus hot water. It has a seafood restaurant. Room rates begin at US$20 (US$2 more for TVs).

A very pleasant hostess, Dorothy Hansen, runs *Arlland Guest House* at 111 Waltham Park Rd on the corner of Molynes Rd, Kingston 11 (☎ 923-4647). She offers 24 rooms in two buildings; the more expensive rooms have air-con and TV (US$11 to US$22), and all rooms have private bathrooms (cold water only). There's a lounge plus small bar and restaurant. A private kitchen can be rented separately. One mile east is the *International Inn* at 14 Derrymore Rd, Kingston 10 (☎ 929-4437), with nine basic cubicle-type rooms (US$15 to US$18) offering air-con and private bath with cold water. It has a small restaurant and bar popular with locals.

Pickings are slim downtown. If you don't mind much more than a box with a bed, then consider the *Bartley Hotel* at 80 Church St (☎ 922-2827), with 33 rooms cooled by fans for US$3. Don't expect much in the way of amenities.

Places to Stay – middle

New Kingston New Kingston has some reasonable options. My favorite option in this price bracket is the *Sandhurst*, in a quiet residential neighborhood at 70 Sandhurst Crescent in Liguanea, Kingston 6 (☎ 927-8244). It verges on the eccentric: note the atmospheric lounge with dark hardwood walls and South American tapestries. Nat King Cole was playing on the PA when I was there. I had images of Miami during the '60s in the 43 spotlessly kept pale-blue rooms with their black-and-white-tile floors, utility furniture, plastic flowers, and copper urns on the wall. Admittedly the rooms are somewhat gloomy and stuffy, but they're well priced at US$25 to US$51 for air-con, TV and telephones. A dining terrace has views toward the Blue Mountains and over an amoeba-shaped pool.

Another reasonable option is *Sutton Place Hotel* at 11 Ruthven Rd, Kingston 10 (☎ 926-1207, fax 926-8443). The contemporary design features unusual classical touches (pediments, octagonal columns, and Mediterranean window grills), but the hotel is rather soulless. The modest-size, air-con rooms (US$58/68 a single/double) do, however, boast cheerful tropical fabrics, and they have TVs and telephones. The hotel has 160 rooms, but the owners plan an expansion. A small pool is on hand, as is an unexciting restaurant and bar. It also has two-bedroom suites with kitchens for US$88.

In the same vicinity is *Holborn Manor Guest House* at 3 Holborn Rd (☎ 926-0296), which has 12 rooms with fans and phones but modest, dowdy furnishings and cold water only. Rooms with TV cost US$35/50 single/double (including breakfast). You'll pay US$5 less without TV, but there's a TV lounge where you can sink into sofas of crimson crushed velvet. Next door is the *Indies Hotel* (☎ 926-0989) 5 Holborn Rd, Kingston 10. It too has utility furniture, plus thick pile carpets and bright floral spreads in its 15 spacious rooms (most with air-con, and all with TVs and telephones) – at least you get hot water here. Low and high season rates are US$35 to US$58 single, US$58 to US$62 double, and US$77 triple. A bar and restaurant is on site.

A popular option with locals is the *Mayfair Hotel* behind Devon House at 4 W Kings House Close, Kingston 10 (☎ 926-1610, fax 926-7741). The columned portico entrance hints at grandeur within, but the 32 air-con rooms – US$40 to $US50 single, US$50 to US$60 double, US$66 to US$110 suites – are fairly basic, though clean and well lit, with utility furniture, TVs and telephones, and a pink motif. Its best feature is the views toward the Blue Mountains. A buffet is hosted poolside on Wednesday and Saturday nights. Nearby is the pleasant but not exceptional *Medallion Hall Hotel* at 53 Hope Rd, Kingston 8 (☎ 927-5721, fax 978-2060), down the road from the Bob Marley Museum. It has 14 rooms with private bathrooms for US$50/60. There's a modest restaurant and English pub-style bar.

The *Sunset Inn* offers an advantageous location in the heart of New Kingston, at 1A Altamont Crescent, Kingston 5 (☎ 929-7283). Alas, the 11 rooms are dowdy with little light, though large bathrooms make amends. Studios (small, with no kitchenette) cost US$35; one-bedroom units with kitchenette are US$40 to US$53. All have TVs, telephones, and fans. Take an upper-story room to catch the breeze.

Albeit boasting contemporary furnishings, *Altamont Court* (also known as Jartena Apartments) at 1 Altamont Crescent, Kingston 5 (☎ 929-4497, fax 929-2118) is an overpriced alternative. It has 36 air-con one-bedroom studios (US$60 to US$75) and suites (US$85), each with telephone and satellite TV, and hot water. Facilities include a small pool and bar.

At the bottom end of Half Way Tree Rd is *Union Square Guest House* at 40 Union Square, Cross Roads, Kingston 5 (☎ 929-9264). It has 15 rooms with color TVs and hot water. Rates range from US$21 with fans to US$30 with air-con.

Puritans may wish to check out the *Shirley Retreat House* at 7 Maeven Ave, Kingston 10 (☎ 927-9208). Operated by the United Church of Jamaica, it has four basically furnished rooms with fans, and the private bathrooms have hot water. There's a TV in the lounge. Rates are US$35/45/55 single/double/triple (half that for Jamaicans).

Further Afield I like the *Abahati Hotel* (7 Grosvenor Terrace, Kingston 8, ☎ 924-2082) for its reclusive setting in a quiet, upscale neighborhood in Constant Spring, at the base of Stony Hill. It offers a cool location at 600 feet elevation. The owners were recently half-heartedly refurbishing the '50s-style Miami hotel. It's painted deep blues and salmons. The 12 rooms – which cost US$30 to US$50 – are carpeted and clean, with lots of light but tired furniture. Some have air-con. Spacious gardens and a pool offer a chance to relax. The hotel's highlight is a pleasing restaurant – Café Jamaique.

Nearby, at 1A Allerdyce Drive, Kingston 8, is the *Allerdyce Inn* (☎ 969-5788, fax 969-5789). This modest though pleasant hotel has 23 air-con rooms (US$40 to US$45 single, US$45 to US$50 double) with burgundy carpet and pink furnishings, lots of storage space, plus TV and telephone in all rooms. The bathrooms, though small, have hot water. An elegant restaurant serves local fare and has a piano bar with live cabaret; happy hour is between 5:30 and 6:30 pm.

Crieffe Court at 10 Crieffe Court (☎ 927-7908) is a well-kept option run by Ron, a super-friendly, courteous, helpful man who opened his 20-room hotel in October 1994. There's nothing inspirational in the basic decor, but the place is spotless and the twin-bedroom rooms (US$40) spacious. Unfortunately, they're also dark (the heavy-screened windows keep out the light). Ron also has studios from US$25. All rooms have fans, TVs, and hot water; upstairs rooms have a balcony. All have double beds. Potted plants abound, and the small gloomy restaurant has a tree growing through the floor.

In the foothills on the northwest edge of town is *Springburn House*, 1 Springburn Ave, Kingston 19 (☎ 969-6850), with 15 rooms, two with shared bath. There's hot water and all rooms should soon have air-con, TV, and telephone. Rates are US$35/45/55 single/double/triple. Another nearby option is *Cozy Heights* at 19A Stilwell Rd, Kingston 8 (☎ 969-5341). It offers six rooms (US$30) with fans and private bathrooms with hot water. There's a dining room, small pool, and a TV in the lounge.

Elmundo's Guest House at 66 Mannings Hill Rd, Kingston 8 (☎ 931-0795) is in the same vicinity. A stone's throw east is the *Mountain Valley Hotel*, a medium-size guest house with 14 rooms for US$25 on Old Stony Hill Rd, Kingston 8 (☎ 924-2313). It's about 400 yards north from the junction with Stony Hill Rd (don't confuse the two). If you continue up the former, which is steep and winding, you'll come to a turnoff for the slate-roofed *Stony Hill Hotel*, five miles north of Half Way Tree. The turnoff is on a dangerous hairpin bend where there's a Texaco gas station; a safer turnoff is a half-mile further uphill. Nearby *Talk's Hotel* has been recommended. Reportedly it's a ramshackle, five-story makeshift place clinging to the hillside at Stony Hill and offering fabulous views.

Fitness devotees should check into the *Olympia Crown Hotel* at 53 Molynes Rd, Kingston 10 (☎ 923-5269), 100 yards east of the Four Roads junction in northwest Kingston. This newly opened motel-style property has 90 rooms (US$30 to US$45). Its main billing, however, is its fully equipped fitness center with steam room and massage. You also get use of tennis courts and even a jogging track. More expensive rooms have air-con and TV.

The *Roosevelt* guest house and restaurant at 17 Roosevelt Ave, Kingston 6 (☎ 927-5214) was closed for renovation when I called by in mid-1995. The old home is in a quiet residential area and promises to be a pleasant addition when finished.

An option for those wishing their own catering facilities is the *Edge Hill Apartment Hotel* at 198 Mountain View Ave, Kingston 6 (☎ 978-1720, fax 978-0779). You'll pay US$53 for studio apartments with kitchenette and sleeping up to three people, but they're modestly furnished with utility furniture. I consider the rooms uninspired and overpriced, but they're clean and feature carpets, two double beds, TV and telephone, and ceiling fan. Edge Hill has a seafood restaurant and rooftop lounge.

Places to Stay – top end

New Kingston Two upscale highrise hotels dominate the New Kingston skyline. The first is the *Wyndham Hotel* at 77 Knutsford Blvd, Kingston 10 (☎ 926-5430, fax 929-7439), in the midst of the financial and diplomatic center. Both it and the *Jamaica Pegasus Hotel* at 81 Knutsford Blvd, Kingston 6 (☎ 926-3690, fax 929-5855), immediately south of the Wyndham, are strongly oriented toward the business traveler. Both boast contemporary architecture and furnishings and a full complement of facilities.

The Wyndham, which was refurbished in 1994, has 300 rooms, including 14 suites. The spacious rooms are elegantly furnished and have a small work desk, direct-dial telephones, and cable TV. Other features include a fitness center, boutique, two tennis courts, 16,000 sq feet of meeting space, and the Jonkanoo Lounge for night owls.

The equally luxurious, 17-story Pegasus (part of the UK-based Forte Hotels chain) has 350 air-con rooms, including 13 suites and three luxury suites. You can choose twin-, double-, queen-, or king-size beds. Cable TV, direct dial telephone, hair dryer, clock radio, and safe are standard. It even has 'female business traveler rooms' and nonsmoking floors. It also offers a panoply of facilities and a selection of restaurants, including the very elegant Pavilion for international dishes. It has a slight edge over the Wyndham with its full-service business center and the Knutsford Club – a more exclusive enclave of rooms, suites, and business facilities. Rates at both begin at about US$150 per room.

The smaller, more intimate *Terra Nova Hotel* at 17 Waterloo Rd, Kingston 10 (☎ 926-2211 or 926-9334) has the most beautiful and sophisticated rooms in town. Though the colonial mansion was built in 1924 (as a wedding gift), the 35 spacious, newly refurbished rooms – US$150 (US$25 additional person) – in three two-story wings have a contemporary feel, with evocative Edwardian decor in deep maroons and dark greens. King-size beds are standard. And thumbs up for the marbled bathrooms. Try to get an upper-story room. The lounge is an Old-World contrast, with 1930s English floral prints and lots of green silks. The El Dorado dining room is the most elegant eatery in town. The hotel is a 10-minute walk from the business district. Cable TVs are standard, with a wider selection than any other hotel in Kingston.

A less glitzy but more atmospheric alternative is the *Four Seasons*, a venerable English-style hotel run by Helga Stoeckert, a delightful German. It's at 18 Ruthven Rd, Kingston 10 (☎ 926-8805, fax 929-5964). The converted Edwardian home exudes an aged European ambiance with its mahogany wall panels and doors, gilt chandeliers, and French curtains. The hotel is comprised of four separate buildings with 39 air-con rooms, all with private bathrooms. Ensure you get a room in the orignal house. Though modest, they're spacious, lofty, airy, and light, with old prints on the walls. Some have half-canopy beds and mahogany furniture. Some have small

bathrooms with showers only; others are larger. Rooms in the garden units are unappealing, with knocked-about utility furniture and a dowdy atmosphere. Telephones and TVs are standard. Rates are US$78/87 year-round (business discounts are offered for longer stays).

Though slightly higher priced, the *Courtleigh* at 31 Trafalgar Rd, Kingston 10 (☎ 929-5320 or 926-8174, fax 926-7801) is lackluster and awaits a renovation. The 40 air-con rooms, though clean, have a 1960s feel and modest furnishings. Some are more pleasant than others. All have TVs, telephones, and wide balconies, but basic bathrooms. Rates are US$79 to US$88 single, US$83 to US$93 double. The Courtleigh also has one-, two- and three-room apartments (US$95 to US$203).

Further Afield An intriguing newcomer is the *Island Club Hotel*, perched at the base of Beverly Hills at 1 Hopedale Ave, Kingston 6 (☎ 978-3915, fax 978-3914; in the USA, ☎ (800) 554-7352) and representing a good bargain at US$76 ($20 additional person, including tax). Its higgledy-piggledy, pink-painted units are offset one atop the other like misarranged building blocks. It's a marvelous design: the units tumbling down the exposed limestone cliff. The red-brick pathways are steep, and there are lots of steps. The air-con rooms are very airy, with lots of windows, lace curtains, and hardwoods. Features include telephones and TVs, and fax machines and computers are available upon request. A tiny fitness center and equally small pool round out the offerings.

The best bargain in Kingston is the *Jonraine Country Inn*, a fabulous millionaire's home leased to hosts Johny Abbott and his wife Lorraine Fong. The exquisite contemporary Spanish-style villa sits 1000 feet above Kingston at Kirkland Heights, on Red Hill, 7 W Kirkland Heights, Forest Hills (☎/fax 944-3513). It stairsteps up the hillside, offering breathtaking views over the city. The main house has seven spacious rooms, and there are a two- and four-room 'cottages' for rent. Johny can arrange almost anything. He loves to host, and you'll be looked after with true hospitality. He and Lorraine are 'real' Jamaicans who can provide you with insights and entrees that would otherwise be hard to come by. It's an incredible bargain at US$70 double, including a full breakfast. They also operate Forbidden Heights, an upscale restaurant. If you want to feel like a millionaire, check in!

The futuristic *Fort Belle Suites* at 211A Constant Spring Rd (☎ 968-2890, fax 926-4729) promises to be the most luxurious of Kingston's hotels. It was scheduled to open in 1996 in the Manor Park suburb as the first major new hotel in Kingston in two decades. It's clearly aiming at business travelers; 'smart' work desks, for example, will feature Internet linkage in all rooms, and there's a full business center and limousine transfer service. The 57 one-bedroom and 20 two-bedroom suites (all with kitchens and balconies) will feature panoramic views. Other highlights include a gym, pool, jogging trail, and tennis court.

Self-catering apartments are a popular option for Jamaicans. Pick of the litter is *Christar Villas* at 99a Hope Rd, Kingston 6 (☎ 978-3933, fax 978-8068). It's handily situated in Liguanea, just below the Sovereign Centre and 400 yards above the Bob Marley Museum. You can choose from modern studio apartments (US$117) and one- (US$93) and two-bedroom suites (US$163 to US$175). Rates include tax and free airport transfer. My suite tended to get hot (suites have air-con in one bedroom, and only ceiling fans in the other rooms), but it was spacious, pleasantly furnished with deep-cushioned chairs, and had a full kitchen and comfy beds. You can always cool off in the pool. A self-service laundry is available. Rooms have satellite TVs but no phones.

If you don't mind a bit of a commute, see *Ivor Guest House* and *Sunset Ridge Guest House*, both in the Guest Houses section under Jacks Hills in the Blue Mountains chapter.

PLACES TO EAT
Budget
Uptown, the *Coffee Terrace Restaurant* (☎ 929-7063) behind Devon House has salads, sandwiches, quiches, and chicken patties, which you can wash down with homemade ginger beer (US$0.60). They serve a late American-style breakfast. Most dishes cost less than US$4. The setting is a breezy verandah overlooking the courtyard. The *Brick Oven*, also behind Devon House, is another popular patty shop.

A more authentic experience is *Minnie's Ethiopian Herbal Health Food* at 170 Old Hope Rd (☎ 927-9207). Minnie is Mignon Phillips, Bob Marley's former personal cook. She creates mouth-watering stews, dumplings, fried fish and festival, and vegetarian I-tal dishes.

The *Chelsea Jerk Centre and Lounge* (☎ 926-6322), at 7 Chelsea Ave, 100 yards east of Half Way Tree Rd, is *the* place for jerk. Mouth-searing jerk pork and chicken dishes cost about US$3. An alternative is *Cleo's* on Kingsway Ave, off Hope Rd. You'll also find plenty of jerk stands scattered along Red Hills Rd. You can smell the spice and smoke as you drive along.

Downtown has a number of places where you can eat for less than US$3. Try *Orient Express* at 135 Harbour St, or the slightly more upscale *Metropolitan Restaurant* on Church St (one block north of Barry St) for Chinese. Office workers favor the *Bench & Bar Restaurant* (☎ 967-4443) on Port Royal St, opposite the Scotiabank Headquarters, for breakfast and lunch; the fare includes sandwiches, patties, seafood, and daily specials. It has a happy hour on Fridays starting at 5 pm. For steamed fish, festival, and other Jamaican fare try *Genise's Restaurant* on Mark Lane. There's a *Burger King* and *Patty King* for cheap patties, both on the corner of Harbour and Duke; and a *Kentucky Fried Chicken* at the corner of Port Royal St and King St. You can buy savory patties for less than $1 at *Luv N Oven* at 22 Upper King St. *Mother's*, on the corner of King St and North Parade, also sells meat patties and burgers.

Jamaican

The *Grog Shoppe* (☎ 929-7027) on the grounds of Devon House serves such dishes as ackee crepes, baked crab backs, roast suckling pig with rice and peas, as well as more *recherché nouvelle* Jamaican dishes for upwards of US$5. You can dine alfresco beneath a huge kapok tree or inside the old stable. Jazz lovers should drop in on Wednesday nights for live jazz.

The *Indies Pub & Grill*, opposite the Indies Hotel on Holborn Rd, and *Polly-anna's*, 100 yards further west, are both popular. The latter also has Chinese specialties. Indies has pizzas (US$7), burgers (US$2), fish & chips, and Jamaican dishes. You can dine outside or in the air-con lounge, which resembles a traditional English pub.

The Courtleigh Hotel offers elegant dining on the *Plantation Terrace*. Despite the cut glass and silverware, the food is mediocre. Caribbean conch salad, pan-fried chicken breast in curry sauce, and vegetarian chop suey are typical. Entrees range from US$5 to US$15. A better option in the same price bracket is the *El Dorado Room* (☎ 221-9334) in the Terra Nova Hotel. The European menu has hints of the Caribbean, as well as steadfast Jamaican favorites such as pepperpot soup and grilled snapper. The hotel also has a less expensive outdoor restaurant; I thought the food was bland, though the Jamaican breakfast is worthwhile (US$7). Also try the *Devonshire Restaurant* (☎ 929-7046) at Devon House, which serves continental dishes with Jamaican accents. It has a dress code and is closed on weekends. Reservations are advised.

Chef Patrick Anderson at *Café Jamaique* in the Abahati Hotel (7 Grosvenor Terrace, Kingston 8, ☎ 924-2082) has won awards for his Jamaican nouvelle cuisine. I recommend the shrimp with curry (US$12).

Several restaurants are good enough to lure Kingstonians a bit out of their way. For lunch or dinner, try the *Rodney Arms* (see Port Henderson, below) or *Ivor Guest House* and *Strawberry Hill*, both in the Blue Mountains (see the Blue Mountains chapter). The *Blue Mountain Inn* (☎ 927-1700), one of Jamaica's most acclaimed restaurants, is on Gordon Town Rd, just below the Cooperage at the base of the Blue Mountains; it was closed for renovation at press time.

Chinese

An inexpensive option is *Lychee Garden* (☎ 929-8619), in the New Kingston Shopping Centre at 30 Dominica Drive. My heartiest recommendation is *Forbidden Heights* (☎ 944-3513), the restaurant of the Jonraine Country Inn, at 7 W Kirkland Heights, way above Kingston on Red Hill Mountain, which easily has the most incredible views for any restaurant in town. The cuisine is superb: chicken in oyster sauce, chicken wings, fish, and shrimp. Entrees begin at about US$10. It's open 11:30 am to 3 pm and 6 to 11 pm (Sundays 4 to 11 pm).

Far more expensive is the *Jade Garden* in the Sovereign Centre at 106 Hope Rd (☎ 978-3476). Despite the prices, it's popular and gets full on weekends. A highlight is the huge aquarium. Don't expect to eat for much less than US$20 a head.

Indian

The Indian legacy is alive and well in Kingston. My favorite restaurant is *Calcutta* (☎ 926-3480), next to Pollyanna's at 11 Holborn Rd. The menu is huge and includes vegetarian dishes for about US$5. Stuffed rotis cost US$3 to US$7. Chicken and beef dishes are US$7 and up. The food is searingly hot – and excellent. The outside terrace to the side is known as the *Mango Tree Café*. It's very romantic at night with trees wrapped in Christmas lights. An added advantage: it's open until 4 am.

Other Cuisines

A visit to *I Scream*, the popular ice-cream shop behind Devon House, will set you back US$2 for a two-scoop cup. The exotic flavors include coconut, chocolate, Devon Stout, grapenut, rum and raisin, fruit and nut, and raisin.

ENTERTAINMENT
Everywhere else on the island the night life is touristy; in Kingston it's not. You won't find limbo or fire-eaters here. Instead, you can savor top-notch discos, ballet, classical music, theater, and down-to-earth reggae concerts performed for locals, not tourists.

The private party scene is intense. Strawberry Hill, where parties are held regularly, is now the center of the upper-crust scene. My friend Michael Fox also hosts popular 'Moonlick' parties at Wildflower Lodge during full-moon weekends (see the Blue Mountains chapter for more details on both).

Cinemas
Three cinemas showing first-run Hollywood movies are located uptown: the *Odeon* at Half Way Tree; the *Carib* at Cross Roads; and *Cineplex 1 & 2* in the Sovereign Centre at 106 Hope Rd. There are also two drive-in cinemas at Harbour View and on Dominica Drive in New Kingston. Entrance is US$2 to US$5.

Discos & Nightclubs
Take your pick from seedy to sophisticated. For local 'color' check out *House of Leo*, on Corgill Rd. It's the dancehall club of choice. Dress code for the ladies is as little as possible, and the more gaudy the better.

An outside street party for the 'masses' happens on Sunday nights near the roundabout at the east end of Norman Manley Hwy on the Palisadoes. Its called *Super D*, named for the sound system with giant speakers that will guide you from afar. I can't vouch for how rough it may get. Another street dance takes place on Tuesday nights at *Front Line* on Red Hills Rd. Inner-city groups play outdoors for free, and vendors set up their stalls. Great fun!

The most unique option is *Skateland Disco*, off Constant Spring Rd at Half Way Tree. An assorted crowd puts its skates on and heads here to roller-dance to booming music. Besides being fun, it provides an insight into the fascinating sociology of Kingston. It has live music on Wednesdays. (No insurance covers accidents.) Nearby is *Countryside Club*, just off Half Way Tree at 19-21 Eastwood Park Rd, Kingston 10 (☎ 926-3010). It's contrived but pleasant, offering wooden dining terrace and lawns, a restaurant and bar, plus dancing to live music.

Upscale discos include *Turntable* at 18 Red Hills Rd (☎ 924-0164); *Peppers* at 31 Upper Waterloo Rd (☎ 925-2219), which plays vintage oldies; *Godfather's Club* at 69 Knutsford Blvd (☎ 929-5459); *Epiphany* at 1 St Lucia Ave in New Kingston (☎ 929-1130); *Illusions* at 2 South Ave, off Constant Spring Rd ☎ (926-7419); and *Mirage* in the Sovereign Centre at 106 Hope Rd (☎ 978-8557), Kingston's most elite disco. The latter has a dancehall night on Tuesday for US$3 entrance (on other nights the cover charge is US$5). *Mingles*, in the Courtleigh Hotel, and the *Jonkanoo Lounge*, in the Wyndham Hotel, both attract an older crowd. One of my favorite discos is *Cactus* (☎ 988-5329), upstairs at the Portmore Plaza in Portmore (see the Port Henderson section below). It features dancehall and reggae, and an oldies party on Sundays (US$2 entrance). Nearby, at Port Henderson, the *Rodney Arms* has a Thursday night jam hosted by well-known DJ 'Junior' Tucker.

Performing Arts
Kingston boasts vibrant performing arts year-round. At the forefront is the highly acclaimed *Little Theater* at 4 Tom Redcam Drive (☎ 926-6129). Founded in the 1960s by the Little Theater Movement, the theater incorporates the Jamaica School of Drama, the island's first. You can watch rehearsals and even take a backstage tour by appointment (☎ 926-6129). The theater puts on plays, folk concerts, and modern dance throughout the year. The main season is July through August, and a 'mini-season' is held each December. The 'Likkle' Theater is famous for its lively slapstick Christmas pantomime, which usually spoofs current events and personalities (see the National Pantomime section under Arts in the Facts About Jamaica chapter). You may not understand much of what's said, but you're guaranteed to have fun.

No less acclaimed is the National Dance Theater Company, which has performed for more than three decades. The company hosts a rich repertory that combines Caribbean, African, and Western dance styles. It has a fiercely loyal following and sells out quickly. The *Ward Theater* (☎ 922-5415 or 922-0453) is home to both the Little Theater's annual pantomime and the National Dance Theater Company. The Jamaica Folk Singers and other companies also perform here on a regular basis. Entrance is US$3 (gallery), US$6 (parquette), or US$7 (dress circle).

The *Barn Theater* at 5 Oxford Rd (☎ 926-6469) also hosts a wide range of top-ranked plays.

Keep your eyes peeled for performances by the University Singers, who are justly acclaimed for their repertoire of Caribbean folk and popular music, choral, madrigals, jazz, African songs, and pantomime.

Go-Go Clubs
At least two go-go clubs on the edge of New Kingston attract a foreign clientele as well as locals. Standard fare is a mirrored stage where a half-dozen or so scantily clad young women gyrate, often acrobatically from the roof rafters. The clubs are hassle free. Both offer free entry on weekdays but cost US$3 on weekends (the fee includes one drink, and there's no minimum-drink requirement). *Palaise Royale* at 14 Ripon Rd (☎ 929-1113) is dispiriting inside, despite its attractive quasi-Arabesque facade. *Gemini*, on Half Way Tree Rd, is slightly more upscale, but the acts are more risqué. Expect to be solicited by the dancers for 'off-duty' pleasure, but your 'no thanks' will be accepted in good grace. The infamous *Centre Pole*, the most popular go-go spot for tourists, closed its doors in 1995.

Jazz
For jazz, head to the *Surrey Tavern* atop the Jamaica Pegasus Hotel on Tuesday and Thursday nights. Live jazz is also hosted in the basement of the *Mutual Life Building* at 2 Oxford Rd every last Wednesday evening of each month (☎ 926-9024).

SPECTATOR SPORTS
Cricket
It's not just cricket! It's West Indian cricket. And the place to see it is Sabina Park (☎ 967-0322). The Red Stripe Cup is played each January, as is the Shell/Sandals Overs competition in February, and the Cable and Wireless Test series in April.

Track & Field
The National Stadium on Arthur Wint Drive hosts major sporting events such as track and field, and cycling. It seats 30,000 spectators. Kingston plays host to the annual Carib Cement International Marathon held each February.

Equestrian Sports
Races have been held in Kingston since 1816, first at Kingston Race Course (the site of today's National Heroes Park). It was moved to Knutsford Park in 1953 (since replaced by the highrises of New Kingston), and in 1959 to Caymanas Park at Portmore on the southwest fringe of Kingston (☎ 988-2523). Racing takes place each Wednesday and Saturday, and on public holidays.

Equestrian fans (and the social elite) head to the Annual International Show Jumping Extravaganza and Horse Trials held each November at Caymanas Polo Grounds at Caymanas Park.

THINGS TO BUY
You wouldn't visit Kingston just to shop, but the city does have some troves. Foremost are the roadside stalls on the Parade and around Half Way Tree. Everything you could want for the home is displayed at the former, along with locally made leather goods at bargain prices.

Craft Stalls & Art Galleries
The waterfront Crafts Market at Pechon and Port Royal Sts hosts dozens of stalls selling wickerwork, carvings, batiks, straw hats, and other crafts. It's hassle-free, but don't expect to be able to bargain much. But no problem! The prices here are lower than anywhere else on the island. Watch

your wallets! Ras Art & Craft, on Dominica Ave at its junction with Knutsford Blvd, is also a good place to scout Rastafarian T-shirts, woolen 'tams,' and leather goods, as are the streets around Half Way Tree.

Several places also sell higher quality art and crafts. Bolivar Art Gallery (1d Grove Rd, ☎ 926-8799, fax 968-1874) has works by Jamaica's leading artists, but it also offers fine books and antiques (including maps). Babylon Jamaica (10A W King's House Rd, ☎ 926-0416) specializes in Rastafarian art. The Art Gallery (10 Garelli Ave, ☎ 926-5097) also has a branch in the Wyndham Hotel and another at Donald Sangster airport. It offers a large range of original paintings by top artists, as well as antique silver collectibles, jewelry, hand-blown Venetian-glass, furniture, and T-shirts exclusive to the gallery.

Also selling the best of Jamaican creative talent is Artisan (106 Hope Rd in the Sovereign Centre, ☎ 978-3514), and Patoo (184 Constant Spring Rd in the Manor Park Shopping Centre, ☎ 924-1552). The latter is a casbah of local treasures (Tortuga puddings laced with rum, Busha Brown sauces, potpourri baskets, reproduction furniture, ceramic tableware and decorative ornaments, and rugs and mats by Faith Centre Weavers). It also has an in-house coffee bar plus a reading nook and art gallery.

Chelsea Galleries in the Island Life Centre on Chelsea Ave displays works by Jamaica's leading artists (☎ 929-0045). Master painter Barrington Watson owns the Contemporary Art Centre (1 Liguanea Ave, ☎ 927-9958), which is a hub of artistic activity . Gallery Pegasus (☎ 926-3690), a small gallery in the basement of the Jamaica Pegasus Hotel on Knutsford Blvd, has revolving exhibitions of works by Jamaica's leading artists. At the Grosvenor Gallery (1 Grosvenor Terrace, ☎ 926-3691), you'll find some of the best art in Jamaica displayed here in five exhibition rooms. Monthly solo exhibitions fill the front rooms, and a permanent exhibition is at the rear, in addition to an antique showroom. The Mutual Life Gallery also maintains exhibits by leading contemporary Jamaican artists; it's located in the Mutual Life Building (2 Oxford Rd, ☎ 929-4302).

For pottery, check out Clonnel Potters Gallery on a quiet corner of Village Plaza on Constant Spring Rd. It sells exquisite thrown and slip-cast pieces in stoneware and porcelain.

Shopping Malls
Constant Spring Rd and Hope Rd are major commercial centers with shopping malls on the North American model. Two of the largest are Sovereign Centre at 106 Hope Rd and New Kingston Shopping Centre on Dominica Drive.

Flea Markets
A flea market is held on Sunday at the New Kingston Drive-In Theater on Dominica Drive. Local markets are best visited for their photography potential. Try Papine Market on weekends at the top end of Old Hope Rd, or the crowded Jubilee Market (also called the Coronation Market), Jamaica's largest market, immediately west of the Parade. Every kind of fruit and vegetable, crafts, cheap clothing, and bric-a-brac are laid out for sale. Be prepared to avoid heaps of rotten fruit, honking cars, and rickety wooden handcarts on tiny wheels being pushed through the throng. You'll be the only out-of-towner and the experience can be daunting! Leave valuables and all but a minimum of money in your hotel safe. And be alert. If you want the *real* Jamaica experience, this is it!

Music Stores
If you're shopping for reggae cassettes or CDs, check out High Times at Shop 42 in the Kingston Mall, next to the National Gallery (☎ 922-5538). There are also several music stores on Orange St.

Liqueur Distributor
Sangster's, purveyors of Old Jamaica rum-based liqueurs, has a factory outlet at 17 Holborn Rd (☎ 926-8888). It's open weekdays, 8:30 am to 5 pm.

GETTING THERE & AWAY
Air
See the Getting There & Away chapter on information on Norman Manley International Airport. You can find information on Tinson Pen Airport, the domestic airport in the Getting Around chapter.

The following international airlines have offices in Kingston. See the Getting There & Away chapter for telephone numbers at Norman Manley International Airport:

ALM Antillean Airlines
   23 Dominica Drive, Kingston 5
   ☎ 926-1762
Aeroflot Soviet Airlines
   2 Grenada Crescent, Kingston 5
   ☎ 929-2251
Air Canada
   Norman Manley Int'l Airport
   ☎ 924-8211
Air Jamaica
   72 Harbour St, Kingston 5
   ☎ 922-4661
American Airlines
   26 Trafalgar Rd, Kingston 10
   ☎ 968-6170
BWIA
   19 Dominica Drive, Kingston 5
   ☎ 929-3771
British Airways
   25 Dominica Drive, Kingston 5
   ☎ 929-9020
Cayman Airways
   23 Dominica Drive, Kingston 5
   ☎ 926-1762
COPA
   23 Dominica Drive, Kingston 5
   ☎ 926-1762
Cubana
   22 Trafalgar Rd, Kingston 10
   ☎ 978-3406

Bus
Buses run between Kingston and every point of the island. Most arrive at and depart from the west side of the Parade or from Half Way Tree. Buses to Ocho Rios and Port Antonio cost about US$1.50; those to Montego Bay cost about US$3. Buses for Spanish Town (US$0.70), Mandeville (US$1), and Black River (US$1.50) depart from Half Way Tree.

The companies that operate the franchises do not publish timetables (see the Getting Around section below). Service is constant and terribly crowded.

Minibus
Minibuses to Montego Bay (120 miles) cost around US$8 to US$12. Minibuses to Ocho Rios cost around US$5 to US$8. You can catch a minibus to almost every town and village in the island from the Parade. There's no logic to the system, so you'll need to ask around (also see the Minibus section in the Getting Around chapter).

GETTING AROUND
Norman Manley International Airport
A couple of robberies in mid-1994 led the US Embassy in Kingston to issue an advisory urging visitors to be cautious while traveling to or from Kingston airport by car, espesially at night, and police patrols have been increased. The advisories are notoriously out of date: check for the latest information (see Dangers & Annoyances in the Facts for the Visitor chapter).

Bus The bus stop is opposite the police station. Bus No 98 operates on a regular basis (usually about every 30 minutes) between Norman Manley airport and the west side of the Parade (US$0.75). The X97 minibus also reportedly operates between the airport and West Parade (US$1.50). It's a 25-minute journey.

Taxi There are plenty of taxis outside the baggage-claim area. JUTA is the only authorized taxi company. A taxi to New Kingston will cost about US$16.

Private Transfer Limo Taxi Tours at 3A Haughton Ave, Kingston 10 (☎ 968-3775, fax 944-3147) offers limousine service from Norman Manley airport, plus regular airport transfers. Pleasure Tours (153½ Constant Spring Rd, Kingston 8, ☎ 924-1471, fax 924-1756), and JUTA Ltd (85 Knutsford Blvd, Kingston 5, ☎ 926-1537) also offer transfers between the airport and Kingston hotels (about US$10 per person one-way). JUTA also has representatives at the airport who can assist you.

Tinson Pen Airfield

Tinson Pen airstrip, off Marcus Garvey Drive, is a basic facility. If you're lucky, a taxi may be waiting outside. Otherwise you'll have to call one, which should cost about US$7 to New Kingston. Tinson Pen is not served by buses. However, buses No P2, P5, and P7 through P14 operate between Portmore and the Parade and pass along Marcus Garvey Drive (the fare to the Parade is about US$0.30).

For information on airline services, call ☎ 923-8680 or 923-9698.

Bus

Only masochists (and the poor) consider traveling by bus in Kingston: the buses are crowded, tropical ovens commanded by cesspool-mouthed 'ductas and 'ductresses.

The chaotic bus system has several major terminuses, the two most important being the Parade and Half Way Tree, where bus stops are scattered along the roadsides. New street signs went up in 1995, making it a lot easier to determine which buses go where. You may still need to ask locally, however.

The city and environs are divided into five zones, including Spanish Town, Portmore, and the Blue Mountains. You may be able to obtain a free bus map from Jamaica Omnibus Service at 80 King St, but don't count on it. Alternately, try the two companies that monopolize services: KMTR at 11 Hillview Ave (☎ 968-2441 or 968-7777) and the National Transport Co-op Society at 26 Lyndhurst Rd (☎ 968-1010). Buses stop only at official stops. Buses start running around 5 am and stop at 10 pm.

Fares are now determined by a six-stage system according to distance: the base rate is J$4 and then 70 cents per mile up to J$11. Children, students, pensioners, and the disabled pay J$2.

Taxi

Taxis are numerous but not when it rains, when demand skyrockets. Use licensed cabs

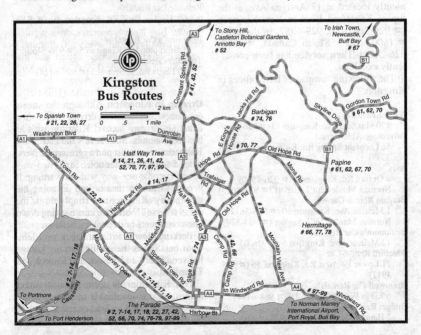

only: they have red PPV license plates. The rate cards quoting government-established rates are often out of date. Ask the fare and determine if the meter is working before you get in (usually it isn't). If not, don't get in until you've settled a rate for the journey (determine whether the quoted fare is in Jamaican or US dollars). You can call a cab from Blue Ribbon (☎ 928-7739), Checker (☎ 992-1777), Metro Cab (☎ 929-6918), and Yellow Cab (☎ 922-6444). Other companies are listed in the yellow pages. JUTA Tours (☎ 926-1537) runs a slightly more expensive taxi/limousine service for tourists. Fares from New Kingston to downtown are about US$3 to US$5.

Car Rental

Many car rental companies have offices downtown and at Norman Manley International Airport. The majority offer free airport shuttles. Jamaica's largest and most reputable car rental company, Island Car Rentals, has its main office conveniently located at 17 Antigua Ave, at the top of Knutsford Blvd in New Kingston (☎ 926-8861, fax 929-6987; in the USA, ☎ (800) 892-4581; in Canada, ☎ (800) 526-2422). Their service has been consistently excellent.

The following companies have offices in Kingston:

A1 Car Rentals
    120 Maxfield Ave, Kingston 13 (☎ 926-4660)
Advantage Auto Rental
    56 Constant Spring Rd, Kingston 10 (☎ 968-3587)
Avis
    3 Oxford Rd, Kingston 5 (☎ 926-1560)
    Norman Manley Int'l Airport (☎ 924-8013)
Bargain Rent-a-Car
    1 Merrick Ave, Kingston 10 (☎ 968-3617
    Norman Manley Int'l Airport (☎ 924-8293)
Beaumont's Car Rental
    12 Melmac Ave, Kingston 5 (☎ 926-0311)
Bluebird Rent-a-Car
    11 Lower Elletson Rd, Kingston 16 (☎ 928-4911)
Bramwell Car Rentals
    6 Kings Way, Kingston 10 (☎ 968-6494)
Budget Rent-a-Car
    7 Hanover St, Kingston (☎ 922-0630)

Cardel Rent-a-Car
    46 Hagley Park Rd, Kingston 10 (☎ 929-0071)
Econocar Rentals
    11 Lady Musgrave Rd, Kingston 5 (☎ 927-0178)
Global Car Rentals
    85 Knutsford Blvd, Kingston 5 (☎ 929-7204)
Hertz
    Norman Manley Int'l Airport (☎ 924-8028)
Island Car Rentals
    17 Antigua Ave, Kingston 5 (☎ 926-8861, fax 929-6987)
    Norman Manley Int'l Airport (☎ 924-8075)
National Car Rental
    19 Carlton Crescent, Kingston 10 (☎ 929-9190)
    Norman Manley Int'l Airport (☎ 924-8344)
Nu-Deal Car Rentals
    30 Shortwood Rd, Kingston 8 (☎ 931-4695)
Pelican Car Rentals
    230 Mountain View Ave, Kingston 6 (☎ 927-6156)
Pleasure Tours
    153½ Constant Spring Rd, Kingston 8 (☎ 924-4140)
    Norman Manley Int'l Airport (☎ 924-8085)
Reliable Car Rentals
    65 Hagley Park Rd, Kingston 10 (☎ 929-7678)
Robinson's Car Rental
    1 Brompton Rd, Kingston 5 (☎ 926-3460)
Travellers Rent-a-Car
    20 Lords Rd, Kingston 5 (☎ 926-6114)

Driving in Kingston Although the streets are narrow and Jamaican driving habits often daunting, driving around Kingston isn't as bad as it sounds. Still, here's the bad news: Kingstonians are fast and aggressive drivers, lane discipline is tenuous, and two-way streets become one-way without warning. It is easy to miss a turn or end up going the wrong way (Kingstonians simply throw the car in reverse). Watch for cars backing down one-way streets or overtaking head-on.

Parking downtown can be a problem. Your best bet is the public parking garage between Barry and Tower, and Church and Temple Sts.

Few Kingstonians seem to know street names, so it is invaluable to have a Kingston map on hand instead of relying solely on the directions of locals.

Kingston Bus Blues

Many things are dysfunctional in Jamaica and chief among them is the Kingston bus system, which devolved into a Kafkaesque nightmare in 1983 when the government shut down the state-owned Jamaica Omnibus Service and turned the system over to hundreds of private bus owners. Timetables became a thing of the past. Overcrowding exceeded 200% at peak hours, when traveling by bus was nightmarish. Bus crews raced one another to reach bus stops first, with bullying touts to usher people on board at each stop. And tickets were rarely issued, leading to wholesale graft. The old system has been called a 'lucrative cash cow,' with no accounting. The day's receipts would simply be handed over in cash to the hundreds of individual bus owners after the crews had taken their cut.

In 1994, Kingston residents barricaded the streets to protest the chaotic and problem-plagued system. The government introduced a new system in March 1995 with a pledge to end decades of overcrowding, lack of timetables, callous treatment by bus crews, and a lack of tight accounting. The Transport Licensing Authority divided Kingston into five franchise areas, with two companies and a cooperative being given the franchises. The companies were supposed to adhere to timetables and issue tickets. However, things seemed only to deteriorate. Angry Kingstonians again barricaded the streets. In September 1995, the chastised government announced that it was reversing a 12-year-old policy and reentering the bus service business. ∎

West of Kingston

PORT HENDERSON

Port Henderson, four miles southwest of Kingston, contains some fine examples of 18th- and 19th-century architecture and is well worth the visit for the views across the harbor. The best time to visit is at sunset, when Kingston's highrises glisten like hammered gold.

In Spanish colonial days, it was here at the mouth of the Rio Cobre that travelers destined for Villa de la Vega (then the capital) would alight. This was the landing site, too, of the English invasion fleet that in 1655 ended Spanish rule over Jamaica. About 1770 the mouth of the river silted up and a village – Port Henderson – was founded further south at the western end of the spit and named for the colonel of the local militia. It rapidly grew into a major port and the embarkation point for Spanish Town. Later, after a mineral spring was discovered, it became a fashionable spa resort.

The Causeway, which links Kingston with Port Henderson, is lined with tumble-down jerk shacks. The harbor is on the left.

On the right is Hunt's Bay, full of discarded rubber tires amid the mangroves. Frigate birds float like kites overhead. You'll see Caymanas Park Racetrack ahead to the right at the north end of **Portmore**, a nondescript middle-income residential suburb. The city (population 90,000) is gradually expanding westward beyond Naggo Head and Braeton under the aegis of the Urban Development Corporation, which in 1965 conceived a plan to develop Portmore as a 'twin city' to Kingston. The project, which calls for the development of 27,000 acres, is just now gathering steam.

As the Causeway nears Port Henderson, it turns into Portmore Parkway. Near the southern end of Portmore Parkway, a turnoff leads to Augusta Drive, which parallels the harbor shoreline and leads to Port Henderson. The breeze-blown shore is popular with Kingstonians, but there's no beach to speak of, and the thin strip of sand is disgustingly littered. Turn left at the roundabout at the west end of Augusta Drive for the remains of Port Henderson.

Passage Fort

East of Caymanas Park, at a site now occupied by the ill-fated Jamworld entertainment complex, are the ruins of Passage

Fort, which once stood at the mouth of the Rio Cobre.

Fort Augusta

This fort, at the easternmost end of Augusta Drive, dates back to 1740, when an existing swamp was partly filled to create Mosquito Point. The fortress – named for the mother of King George III – once guarded the western end of the harbor. What you can see today is not the original fort, which was destroyed when a bolt of lightning struck the magazine holding 3000 barrels of gunpowder. The explosion killed 300 people and shattered windows up to 15 miles away. The huge crater was filled in and the fort rebuilt. It's moderately well preserved. The original limestone turrets are in-place, for example, though recent repairs have been made in red brick, and portions of the outer walls have collapsed into the bay. All you can do is stare at the outside walls as the fort is now a prison.

Forum

Forum is a funky fishing hamlet where weather-beaten pirogues and nets drawn up on the beach make for an intriguing contrast with the skyline of Kingston.

The famous restaurant and pub, **Rodney Arms** is housed in a beautifully restored two-story, Georgian limestone building that was once the Old Water Police Station, where pirates and miscreant marines were detained. It is named after Admiral George Rodney, who commanded the naval station at Port Henderson.

About 200 yards uphill from the Rodney Arms is the well-preserved ruins of a semicircular gun emplacement replete with cannon, and an old fort and battery – the **Apostles Battery** – in various stages of restoration.

Fort Clarence

Continue along the potholed road for a half mile uphill, and you'll reach Fort Clarence. You can't visit the old fortress, which is today the headquarters of the Jamaica Defence Force (JDF). Signs read 'Restricted Area: No Authorized Person

Allowed Beyond This Point.' A barbed wire fence underscores the point. At least the views over the bay are worthwhile from this lonesome spot.

Rodney's Lookout

Between Forum and Fort Clarence is Rodney's Lookout, reached via a trailhead just before the JDF camp. The trail leads uphill to the ruins of Admiral George Rodney's former house. Grasspiece Lookout, used for spying out to sea, is nearby.

Places to Stay

Camping You can pitch a tent at the *World Meditation Centre*, directly below the Apostles Battery. The Rasta owner of the site charges US$5 to camp. Bring your own food and water. The breezy campsites sit on little terraces on the rocky shore over the water, with cactus and agave all around. It's a fantastic setting, with views across the harbor.

Hotels Augusta Drive is lined with hotels. Choose carefully, as some are 'short time' motels (usually hidden behind high walls) that rent rooms on an hourly basis.

The *Arizona Inn* (Lot 8, Block M, Port Henderson, ☎ 998-4666) on Augusta Drive features 11 simply furnished rooms with lofty ceilings, fans, spacious bathrooms, and TVs encased in iron cages! It's a very breezy location. Hold on to your napkin if dining on the outside terrace, where there's a small dance floor and a disco on weekends. The hotel also has an intimate little indoor restaurant with a large wooden bar and lounge with cozy chairs. Rates vary from US$31 to US$49 for a family room, and US$57 for a suite with spa.

In a similar vein is nearby *La Roose* (☎ 998-4654), offering nine clean yet modestly furnished rooms with fans for US$27. An air-con suite costs US$54. All have private bath with hot water; some have TVs and telephones. Its fairly elegant restaurant specializes in seafood. Appropriately named gleaming-white *Jewels*, 430 yards west of La Roose, has 15 air-con rooms

(US$32 to US$43) aired by the breezes that channel down the corridors. Rooms are nicely if simply decorated with bright tropical fabrics, and upstairs rooms have lofty wooden ceilings. Bathrooms have hot water but are small.

Alternately, try the *People's Choice Hotel* (☎ 984-2474) on Sligoville Rd in Portmore. It has air-con rooms with hot water.

Pelican Cove, Occasions, Portmore Inn, and *Happy Time* are all 'short time' hotels located along Augusta Drive (US$6 for three hours; US$9 per night).

Places to Eat

You can hang out with locals at a series of seafood restaurants next to Jewels hotel, including *My Friend's Place*, a popular, narrow little bar with outdoor patio dining. Seafood dishes should cost less than US$2.

Concord Plaza is a small complex midway along Augusta Drive, with a pharmacy, bank, and grocery. You can also buy fresh fish on the beach at Forum.

Don't leave, however, without treating yourself to a meal at the *Rodney Arms*, which deservedly gets packed on weekends. It's a marvelous place to enjoy the views across the harbor or to watch the local fishermen laying out their nets to dry while you sample crab back, seafood platter, shrimp, fish, and other seafood dishes from Mrs Olive Stuart's kitchen. Prices range from US$8 to US$25 for entrees.

Oysters are offered on weekends at the *Rodney Rathid Oyster Bar*, which also serves garlic shrimp, garlic crab, and a special flambé rum drink (US$3). The oyster bar is one of several shady dining terraces on wooden decks on the hillside, which has lots of cactus and aloe and shade trees, and oddities such as a cannon, fountain, and small water cascade. *The Sturdy* is a wooden deck that stands over the sea. At night it's lit by kerosene lamps. Waiters in bow ties add a note of elegance. My snapper was one of the biggest, spiciest, and finest fish dishes I've ever eaten!

Getting There & Away

Port Henderson is reached via the Causeway, which begins at the southern end of Hagley Park Rd (at its junction with Marcus Garvey Drive), leaps across the westernmost point of Kingston Harbour, and traverses a narrow spit. Note, however, that no eastbound traffic *into* Kingston is allowed along the Causeway between 4:30 and 7 pm; no westbound traffic is allowed between 6:30 and 9 am.

Bus Buses to Portmore operate from Half Way Tree and Three Miles (at the junction of Hagley Park Rd and Spanish Town Rd). Alternately, take a minibus (No X20) from the Parade to Port Henderson. Bus Nos 7 to 14 also travel between Portmore and the Parade (US$0.50).

In 1995 the NTCS introduced an air-con executive bus service, with neatly dressed 'ground hostesses' and guaranteed comfort. No standing is allowed. There's even a daily paper and a glass of orange juice. It costs US$1.20 (☎ 968-1010).

HELLSHIRE HILLS

One look at the Hellshire Hills and it is easy to appreciate their great natural tourism potential that lies entirely untapped. The area is a 100-sq-mile, totally uninhabited upland region due south of Spanish Town. The hills are like an inverted circular shield, enveloped on three sides by the Caribbean and covered in knife-sharp limestone and inhospitably thick scrub and tall cactus. The only humans to be found here are occasional wild-pig hunters, charcoal burners, and scientists studying the endangered Jamaica iguana, for whom the Hellshires are a last refuge.

The look of the landscape is determined by the suffocating heat and the composition of the limestone that underlies the hills. The area receives less than 30 inches of rainfall a year. The unusually porous limestone (a variety called honeycomb) soaks up all the rain it receives. What little surface soil exists is suitable only for drought-resistant cactus and

The Jamaican Iguana

The endemic Jamaican iguana *Cyclura collei* is Jamaica's largest land animal, sometimes growing up to two meters long. Once common throughout the southern scrublands and tropical dry forests, during the past two centuries it has suffered from forest degradation and the predation of mongooses, feral pigs, cats, and dogs. The last iguana was seen in the 1940s, after which it was thought to be extinct.

In 1990, however, an iguana was discovered by a hunter in the Hellshire Hills. The 'lost' species had managed to survive for half a century, undetected, within sight of the nation's capital.

A Jamaican Iguana Research & Conservation Group was immediately formed, headed by Dr Peter Vogel, a zoologist at the University of the West Indies in Kingston. Vogel and his team discovered a small remnant population in the central and western section of the hills. Possibly only a few dozen adults have survived. Because the survival rate of young iguanas is very low, many eggs were removed from nests, incubated at Hope Zoo, and the baby iguanas raised for eventual release to the wild.

Unfortunately, hunters are pushing into the remotest regions, threatening to finish off the remaining iguana population. The forest continues to be degraded by charcoal burners, and the iguana is threatened by existing plans for large-scale mining operations and urban expansion on the Hellshire boundaries.

For further information, contact the Jamaican Iguana Research & Conservation Group, Dept of Zoology, University of the West Indies, Kingston 7 (☎ 927-1202, fax 927-1640). ■

thorny scrub, known as 'dry limestone forest.'

The Hellshires are an important habitat for migrant birds, and a last refuge for diverse species of rare plants and animals: the endangered yellow snake, the Mabuya maboua skink, and the coney, Jamaica's only native land mammal (bats excepted). Hunting (and more recently the expansion of towns) has decimated the population of the coney, or Jamaican *hutia*, a large, guinea-pig-like rodent that is now restricted to a few parts of eastern Jamaica. The coney is protected and due to its nocturnal habits, rarely seen.

Although once favored as a haven by runaway slaves, settlement has been retarded by the difficulty of securing water. Thus, the Hellshires have never been populated. The scrub forest is protected under the Forestry Act of 1937, but the law is not enforced. Charcoal burning, slash and burn agriculture, squatting, and other destructive forest uses occur without control. And the area is threatened by encroaching urbanization. The eastern half of the hills has been earmarked for housing and resort development by the UDC. Environmentalists have launched an effort to have the government declare a Hellshire Hills Protected Area that incorporates the wetland fringe.

Hiking

The Hellshires are perfect for hiking. Few trails penetrate any distance from the shore. There are no facilities. If you plan on exploring, hire a guide familiar with the area, take plenty of water, and stay on the trails; the limestone terrain is pitted with scrub covered sinkholes and it is all too easy to break a leg, or worse. Don't underestimate this environment!

Organized Tours

I recommend a one-day 'Iguana Project' trip offered by the Jamaica Iguana Research & Conservation Group (c/o Dr Peter Vogel, Dept of Zoology, University of the West Indies, ☎ 927-1202). The cost of US$60 to US$120 per person (depending on group size) includes transfers from Kingston, lunch, plus an eight-mile guided hike. Proceeds support the conservation project. The trip is also available through Sense Adventure (Box 216, Kingston 7, ☎ 927-2097, fax 929-6967)

HELLSHIRE BEACHES

This series of narrow, white-sand beaches is on the fringe of the eastern Hellshire Hills. A line of batteries once stretched along this shoreline as protection for Kingston Harbour, though virtually nothing remains. They're reached via a well-paved road that leads south from Spanish Town via Braeton Newtown (two miles west of Portmore) to Hellshire Point, eight miles south of Braeton.

The road meets the coast at **Great Salt Pond**, a circular bay overgrown on its perimeter with briny mangrove swamps where snook, mullet, stingrays and reportedly even crocodiles ('alligators') can be seen. Fort Clarence overlooks the northeasternmost point of the bay.

Lying at the southeasternmost point of Great Salt Pond is **Fort Clarence Beach Park** (☎ 968-4409), popular with Kingstonians on weekends. It frequently hosts beauty contests and live reggae concerts. It's open 10 am to 5 pm, Wednesday to Friday, and 7 am to 5 pm weekends, and costs J$50, children are J$20. The park is closed on Monday and Tuesday, except on public holidays. It has showers and toilets plus secure parking. A restaurant and bar are open weekends only. It's reached via a spur road from the first of several roundabouts along the road from Braeton.

A road to the left of the second roundabout leads to the main beach, called **Fisherman's Beach**. Skip it if you want peace and quiet. It's great, however, if you want the 'real' Jamaican experience. The beach is appealing enough and the water warm, but the main interest is the social scene, based around a compact village of ramshackle huts and stalls selling beer, jerk, and fried fish and *festival* (fried biscuit or dumpling). The place gets crowded and noisy on weekends. If you visit before noon you can watch the fishing pirogues come in with their catch.

A reef protects the northern end of the shore, where the swimming is safe.

From Fisherman's Beach, the road winds south along a dramatic, virtually uninhabited shore – one of my favorite pieces of Jamaican real estate – with rocky coves and occasional sandy beaches with turquoise and jade-colored shallows. To the west the cactus-covered land slopes to the Hellshire Hills. Buzzards ride the thermals.

After two miles you'll reach **Two Sisters Cave** and **Arawak Museum**. Both were closed 'for development' until further notice when I last called (mid-1995, there was no 'development' taking place). Blind river bass live in the brackish water that fills the pools at the base of the cave, which is reached by a stairway. Ancient petroglyphs can also be seen in the second cave. A sign nearby warns that bathing is prohibited due to 'bacterial contamination.'

The road dead-ends 400 yards beyond the turn-off for the Arawak Museum. A dirt road continues some miles along the coast. There are no facilities. The only hotel is the *Hellshire Beach Club*, which was still under construction when I called.

Getting There & Away

Buses operate to Hellshire Beaches from Half Way Tree (No 1) and The Parade (No 10) both from Kinston. You'll pay about US$0.40 for the 30-minute journey. You can also catch minibuses from the Parade; there are several to choose from on weekends.

FERRY

Ferry, 16 miles west of downtown Kingston on Spanish Town Rd (A1), was in early colonial days a swamp fed by the Fresh River, which forms the boundary of St Andrew and St Catherine Parishes. In 1677 the swamps were drained and a ferry service initiated. An inn, appropriately named the *Ferry Inn*, became the halfway rest stop for travelers between Spanish Town and Kingston. The building still stands; it was refurbished and reopened as a restaurant in 1989.

Today Ferry is best known for **Coney Park**, which claims to be the largest amusement park in the Caribbean (☎ 933-3398, fax 933-2372). It's a somewhat rundown affair. Still, if you're an amusement park junkie, you can hop on roller-coasters, wet-n-wild waterslides, train rides, a carousel, and bumper cars. It's open 10 am to midnight Saturday and 4 pm to midnight Wednesday to Friday; entry costs US$0.80 (US$0.30 children).

Bus No 21B runs from Half Way Tree to Spanish Town; bus No 22 operates between Spanish Town and the Parade. Both pass Coney Park and cost US$0.30.

East of Kingston

Kingston is hemmed in to the east by Long Mountain, which extends right up to the shore, forming a narrow bottleneck. There's only one road east out of town. Beyond Long Mountain lies a narrow coastal plain. About four miles east of downtown, a road to the right leads along the Palisadoes, a thin scrub-covered sand spit with a few beaches, the Norman Manley International Airport, a nascent wildlife refuge, and, at its tip, Port Royal, which two centuries ago was the setting for Jamaica's most colorful history.

ROCKFORT MINERAL BATHS
These private mineral baths are immediately west of the cement factory three miles east of downtown Kingston. Rockfort (☎ 938-5055) has one public and 11 private pools, all with whirlpools and wheelchair access. Reopened in 1994 after a facelift, it provides pleasant bathing in amiable surroundings. The slightly saline and moderately radioactive water that serves the baths rises from a cold spring that once supplied water to the naval base at Port Royal. One hour is the maximum allowed. The flow is continuous, with water entering the pool from above and exiting below. There's a cafeteria. It's open Monday to Friday 6:30 am to 6 pm, weekends 9 am to 6 pm, and costs US$2 entrance.

Bus No 99B operates from the Parade and travels along Windward Rd as far as Harbour View (US$0.30). The No 99A returns via Half Way Tree. You can also take the No 98, which departs from the Parade and passes Rockport en route to Port Royal.

FORT NUGENT
The English considered the point where Long Mountain comes down to the coast a perfect location for defense. Thus, on the hill sits the ruins of a Martello Tower built in 1806 as part of Fort Nugent, which once guarded the eastern approach to Kingston. Another fort, one mile further west, was also fortified, and you can still see cannons pointing out to sea as you drive by.

THE PALISADOES
The Palisadoes is a narrow, 10-mile-long spit that forms a natural breakwater protecting Kingston Harbour. It extends due west from Windward Rd. At the end, reached via Norman Manley Hwy, lies the historic city of Port Royal, set on a former cay that the Spanish called Cayo de Carena, where they beached their ships.

The spit is underlain by a submerged coral ridge topped by sand, silt, and gravel deposited over thousands of years by westerly currents. It earned its name for the defensive *palisade* that was built across the spit to defend Port Royal from a land-based attack. It consisted of a 'stout wall with a six-gun redoubt.'

The Palisadoes is arid and sparsely vegetated, fringed on its harbor side by extensive mangroves that shelter a small number of crocodiles and nesting colonies of pelicans and frigate birds. Environmentalists are campaigning to have the mangroves protected as a wildlife reserve.

Dangers & Annoyances
In 1994, the US State Department issued a travel advisory for Norman Manley Hwy. Apparently there have been a series of robberies, but I have driven it with no problem numerous times. Police patrols have been increased.

Gunboat Beach
This beach, due east of the airport, is popular with low-income Kingstonians, but the sea is too dirty for swimming. Gunboat Beach is accessed by a spur road that leads from Norman Manley Hwy to the Royal Jamaica Yacht Club. There are jerk stalls

and loud music on weekends. It's a great place to hang out with locals.

Norman Manley International Airport
The airport lies inside the elbow at the spit's widest point. It dates from WWII, when a wide expanse of marshy flats on the harbor side of the Palisadoes' elbow were filled and built up.

Plumb Point Lighthouse
The 70-foot-tall, stone-and-cast-iron lighthouse lies midway along the Palisadoes at its elbow. It was built in 1853 and still functions (it ceased to do so only once during the 1907 earthquake). Where today cactus and scrub grow, there once thrived a coconut palm plantation, established in 1869 by the government. A stone monument near the lighthouse records the planting of the first of 20,000 trees.

Royal Jamaica Yacht Club
The club (☎ 924-8685) is open to bona-fide members of international yacht clubs only.

PORT ROYAL
Port Royal is a dilapidated, ramshackle place of tropical lassitude. Today's funky fishing hamlet was once the wealthiest city in the New World. Later, it was the hub of British naval power in the West Indies, but the remains give little hint of the town's former glory. Its inhabitants tend to be sullen and surly.

Local developers have long touted the city as possibly the prime marine archaeological attraction in the world, and the potential is undoubtedly enormous. Nowhere else does a sunken city lie next to shore in a mere 30 feet of water, and there are colonial remnants on dry land to boot. While much lip service has been devoted to restoring Port Royal, virtually nothing has been done. As it is, it is wasted.

Most tourist sites are open 9 am to 4 pm Monday to Friday and 10 pm to 5 pm on weekends.

In an emergency, you can request assistance from the police station on Queen St (☎ 924-8706).

History
Although the Spanish used to careen their ships on the isolated cay on which Port Royal was later built, they never settled nor fortified it as the English did within one year of arriving in Jamaica in 1655. The English called the island Cagway or the Point. Here they built Fort Cromwell, which was renamed Fort Charles after the Restoration in 1662. Within two years General William Brayne was able to report that 'there is the faire beginning of a town upon the poynt of this harbor.'

Era of the Buccaneers This was the period when England was sponsoring freelance pirates in their raids against Spanish ships and possessions. Almost as soon as the English had captured Jamaica, buccaneers – organized as the Brethren of the Coast – established their base at Port Royal. They were alternately welcomed and discouraged by the authorities according to the dictates of England's foreign policy. (See the Rise of the Buccaneers section under History in the Facts about Jamaica chapter.)

The lawless buccaneers were big spenders who disposed of their loot 'in all manner of debauchery with strumpet and wine.'

Buccaneers made Port Royal their base, and soon it was known as the 'wickedest' place on earth.

The wealth flowing into Port Royal attracted merchants, rum-traders, vintners, prostitutes, and others seeking a share of the profits. Townsfolk even invested in the expeditions in exchange for a share of the booty, and great celebrations took place when the raiders returned. (By tradition, the governor, who then lived at Port Royal, was the first person allowed to step aboard when the ships dropped anchor; he claimed one-tenth of the booty before the whole town descended into wildness.) No number of taverns or whorehouses seemed enough to slake their thirst (forty new licenses were issued for taverns and rum shops in 1661 alone).

The clergy called it 'the wickedest city on earth' and proclaimed that damnation would follow.

Although the governor's court was moved to Spanish Town in 1664, the vice- and violence-ridden town continued its stratospheric growth, aided by an insatiable new trade: that of Guineamen whose ships arrived with reeking holds of 'black ivory' (slaves). By 1682 Port Royal was a town of 8000 people, with 800 houses 'as dear-rented as if they stood in well-traded streets in London,' for as Francis Hanson recorded, 'in Port-Royal there is more plenty of running Cash (proportionally to the number of its inhabitants) than in London.' There were fortresses all around, plus two prisons and, reflecting the town's cosmopolitan nature, two Anglican churches, a Presbyterian church, a Jewish synagogue, a Roman Catholic chapel, and a Quaker meeting house.

During this period, leadership of the Brethren had passed into the hands of Henry Morgan, a barrel-chested Welshman who, with the patronage of Governor Sir Thomas Modyford, organized the buccaneers into a fearsome force and was given letters of marque to lead daring raids on Spanish treasure fleets. Morgan, however, had more grandiose designs and barbarously ransacked the cities of Puerto Príncipe (Camagüey, in Cuba), Porto Bello (in Panama), and Maracaibo (in Venezuela).

Earthquake & Destruction At noon on Tuesday, June 7, 1692, a great earthquake convulsed the island, and the doomsayers were vindicated: Port Royal was destroyed. The wharves and streets nearest the water's edge keeled over like stricken ships. Fort Carlisle, Fort James, Fort Rupert, and Fort Walker sank beneath the waves. Nine-tenths of the town disappeared underwater, where it remains. The massive quake was followed by a huge tidal wave that washed one ship, the *Swan*, into the center of the town, where it rested on the rooftops, providing shelter for those fortunate enough to scramble aboard. More than 2000 people died, many having fallen into great fissures before being 'squeezed to pulp' when a second tremor closed the gaping holes like pincer jaws. Many of the survivors were claimed by the pestilence that followed, caused by the hundreds of unburied corpses.

Resurrection Port Royal's heyday of infamy was over. Even before the earthquake, official English policy had changed, and sea-rovers who would not give up piracy were hounded and hanged at Gallows Point, a promontory at the harbor

Once a ruthless leader of the Port Royal buccaneers, Henry Morgan was later named governor of Jamaica and knighted.

mouth of Port Royal (the last hanging was in 1831). The English government had not written off Port Royal, however. The defensive works were hastily repaired in time to repel a French invasion mounted against Jamaica in 1694. Piracy was briefly revived to help finance the rebuilding. Gradually Port Royal regained its stature as a merchant town and as center of the turtling industry. The town refused to die, despite a great fire in January 1704.

The greatest impetus to Port Royal's resurrection was the near-constant state of war in which England found itself with Spain, France, and Holland throughout the 18th century. The wars marked the beginning of a 2½-century term as headquarters of the British Royal Navy in the West Indies. As the British Navy built up its strength in the Caribbean, the ships came to rely increasingly on Port Royal for repairs and supplies, and as a muster point for battle fleets.

Six forts and a militia of 2500 armed men protected the naval station, which was supported by a prosperous merchant town of 2000 buildings. Alas, the advent of peace in 1815 spelled the end of Port Royal's naval glory, and a fire that year consumed much of the town. Struck by one calamity after another, the old port sank into decline. In 1838, Jamaica ceased to be a separate naval command. With the development of steam warships in the early 20th century, Port Royal's demise was sealed. The naval dockyard closed in 1905, and although the defenses were maintained through both world wars, they have since been left to decay. A rehousing scheme was initiated in 1951, following a devastating hurricane that left just 10 houses standing.

Orientation

Approaching the town, Norman Manley Hwy runs beside a long brick wall enclosing the old British Admiralty Coaling Station, garrison quarters, and naval dockyard. You enter town through a breach in the old town wall to the main square, or Muster Ground, overlooked by the Half-Moon Battery on the left. A parapetted

Restoring Port Royal

In the early 1960s, the Port Royal Company of Merchants planned a development project with Walt Disney Productions to convert Port Royal into a theme park. Nothing evolved then, but suddenly things look promising.

In April 1995 ex-Premier Edward Seaga unveiled an ambitious scheme that would make Port Royal a freeport, with hotels, restaurants, attractions, and entertainment. His plan would also incorporate Fort Augusta, across the bay. Independently, that same month a corporation – Pragma Development Ltd – was formed to restore Port Royal to its former glory. Work was expected to begin in early 1996. In addition to restoring the dilapidated buildings, workshops will be created to make pewter mugs and other period crafts. A special tour boat will be introduced, with underwater portholes for viewing the sunken city. And sound and light shows will bring the past alive, as will reenactments of scenes from the 17th and 18th centuries with townsfolk in period costumes. Plans also involve making Port Royal into a scuba-diving mecca. The plans call for major cruise-ship facilities, and cruise passengers will be ferried to Port Royal from Kingston Harbour. ∎

town wall of cut limestone blocks (popularly known as Morgan's Wall) leads along Tower St to Nelson Square, the old parade ground once known as Chocolata Hole. In 1988 Hurricane Gilbert did much damage to the old barrack buildings here, but Fort Charles still stands, as does the red-brick Garrison Arch, which is all that remains of a former wall. At the tip of the spit is HMJS Cagway, headquarters of the Jamaica Defence Force Coast Guard, which has its patrol boats here. Other historical attractions lie scattered around the perimeter.

Maps

The Institute of Jamaica Publications (2a Suthermere Rd, Kingston 10, ☎ 929-4785) produces an excellent map called 'Port Royal: A Walking Tour.' It includes brief information on the sites to see. The map is included with the book *Port Royal* by Clinton V Black (Institute of Jamaica Publications, 1988), which you can buy in the gift store of Morgan's Harbour (see Places to Stay below).

The Sunken City

Two-thirds of 17th-century Port Royal lies hidden from view, 30 feet deep in the harbor offshore of the naval hospital. A beacon about 100 yards offshore marks the site of one of the sunken forts. The Church Beacon marks Fort James. Legend says that the buoy marks the site where St Paul's Church sank in 1692 (fishermen claim that in rough seas they can hear the tolling of church bells beneath the sea). Another bell dredged from the seabed after the quake – a Spanish-made bronze bell – now hangs in the Institute of Jamaica.

Underwater 'excavations' have been ongoing since 1959, when the National Geographic Society sponsored an expedition. Between 1965 and 1968, marine archaeologist Robert Marx was commissioned by the government to map the sunken city.

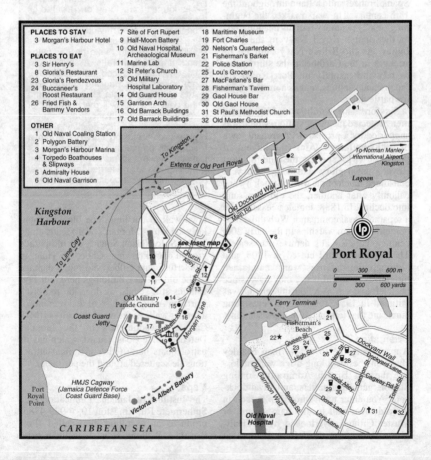

PLACES TO STAY
3 Morgan's Harbour Hotel

PLACES TO EAT
3 Sir Henry's
8 Gloria's Restaurant
23 Gloria's Rendezvous
24 Buccaneer's Roost Restaurant
26 Fried Fish & Bammy Vendors

OTHER
1 Old Naval Coaling Station
2 Polygon Battery
3 Morgan's Harbour Marina
4 Torpedo Boathouses & Slipways
5 Admiralty House
6 Old Naval Garrison
7 Site of Fort Rupert
9 Half-Moon Battery
10 Old Naval Hospital, Archeological Museum
11 Marine Lab
12 St Peter's Church
13 Old Military Hospital Laboratory
14 Old Guard House
15 Garrison Arch
16 Old Barrack Buildings
17 Old Barrack Buildings
18 Maritime Museum
19 Fort Charles
20 Nelson's Quarterdeck
21 Fisherman's Barket
22 Police Station
25 Lou's Grocery
27 MacFarlane's Bar
28 Fisherman's Tavern
29 Gaol House Bar
30 Old Gaol House
31 St Paul's Methodist Church
32 Old Muster Ground

Port Royal

Many expeditions have since explored the 'Sunken City,' which you can explore by glass-bottom boat or on scuba-diving trips from Morgan's Harbour resort.

Old Naval Hospital
The hospital sits at the northwest side of town. It was built in 1742 atop a part of the old city that had sunk in the earthquake, but fire destroyed the original. The existing 380-foot-long structure is remarkable for its prefabricated cast-iron framework especially designed to withstand both earthquake and hurricane; it was shipped as ballast from Bradford, England. The structure dates back to 1819 and remained in use until 1905. Today it is in a desperate state of dilapidation.

The **Port Royal Centre for Archaeological & Conservation Research** has been headquartered here since 1968, but on two recent visits it seemed as inactive as the city it attempts to preserve.

The small **Archaeological & Historical Museum** (☎ 924-8706) in a ground-floor room displays a motley collection of relics – pewter tableware, medicine bottles, a copper still, and even Ming porcelain – dragged up from the Sunken City. One of the more fascinating trinkets is a pocket watch. Its hands rusted away long ago, but they're etched on the face by coral at 11:43 am, the moment of the 1692 earthquake. Check out the model of the planned restoration. Old horse-drawn carts in the forecourt are held together by humidity and bailing wire. Entrance to the museum is by donation.

The Marine Laboratory of the University of the West Indies is immediately south of the hospital. It is not open to the public.

Fort Charles
Jamaica's latitude and longitude are measured from the flagstaff of Fort Charles, a weathered redoubt originally laid in 1655. It alone withstood the 1692 earthquake (the other five forts in Port Royal all sank into the sea). Being 'not shook down but much shattered,' it was rebuilt of red

brick in 1699 and added to several times over the years. It was originally washed by the sea on three sides, but silt gradually built up to form *terra firma* around it. It is now firmly landlocked.

At its peak, 104 guns protected the fort – the most heavily defended in the Caribbean. Many cannons still point out from their embrasures.

Entrance is US$0.15. Brochures cost US$0.15 extra.

Maritime Museum This museum (☎ 925-0355) stands in the courtyard and contains model ships and a miscellany of nautica from the heyday of the British Navy. Nelson lived in the small 'cockpit' while stationed here, and his quarters are replicated. A plaque on the wall of the King's Battery, to the right of the main entrance, commemorates his time here. Local legend suggests that the three cement crosses placed in the outside wall beneath the artillery lookout point mark where Nelson's three wives are buried.

Giddy House A small hut sits alone amid scrub-covered, wind-blown sand 100 yards to the southwest of Fort Charles. The red-brick structure was built in 1888 to house the artillery store. The 1907 earthquake, however, turned the spit briefly to quicksand and one end of the building sank, leaving the store at a lop-sided angle. It is known as the Giddy House because it produces a sense of disorientation to people who enter. There's nothing of interest within; just sand and litter.

Victoria & Albert Battery Next to the Giddy House is a massive gun emplacement and equally mammoth cannon prone by its side. It's the easternmost casement of the Victoria & Albert Battery that lined the shore, linked by tunnels. It also keeled over in the 1907 earthquake.

Old Gaol House
The only fully restored historical structure in town is the sturdy Old Gaol House of cut stone on Gaol Alley. It predates the 1692

Lord Horatio Nelson

Many of England's greatest naval heroes served at Port Royal. Most notable was Admiral Horatio Nelson (1758 – 1805), British Naval Commander during the Revolutionary and Napoleonic Wars.

Nelson arrived in Port Royal in 1777, during the American War of Independence. While awaiting the return of the frigate *Hinchinbrooke*, which he was to command, he was briefly given command of Fort Charles, despite being only 20 years old.

At that time Jamaica was on a war footing and expected a French invasion. Nelson spent much of his time pacing the platform still known as 'Nelson's Quarterdeck.'

The following year, Nelson participated in an expedition to Nicaragua, where he succumbed to fever. He was returned to Port Royal, where he was attended by a famous black faith healer, Cubah Cornwallis, mistress of William Cornwallis (whose name she had taken), the brother of the general who surrendered Yorktown to the Yankees in 1781.

At Nelson's Quarterdeck a marble tablet reminds you that Britain's greatest naval hero was twice stationed at Port Royal. It reads: 'In this place dwelt Horatio Nelson. You who tread his footprints remember his glory.' ■

earthquake, when it served as a women's jail. Today it houses an arts & crafts store and occasionally plays host to poetry readings and live music shows in the Gaol House Bar.

St Peter's Church

Despite its nondescript exterior, St Peter's Church is worth a stop. Built in 1725 of red brick, it today boasts a faux-brick front of cement. Note the floor paved with original black-and-white tiles, and the beautifully decorated wooden organ loft built in 1743. Note, too, the monument by the sculptor Roubiliac that commemorates Lieutenant Stapleton of HMS *Sphinx*, who was killed when a cannon he was firing exploded.

The communion plate kept in the vestry is said to have been donated by Henry Morgan, though experts date it to later times.

Most intriguing of the curiosities is a churchyard tomb of Lewis Galdye, a Frenchman who according to his tombstone 'was swallowed up in the Great Earth-quake in the Year 1692 & By the Providence of God was by another Shock thrown into the Sea & Miraculously saved by swimming until a Boat took him up.' Eventually he grew to become a prosperous *asiento* (slave trader), assemblyman, and the church warden of St Peter's.

Naval Dockyard

The old naval dockyard lies to the east of Morgan's Harbour (see Places to Stay below). Its perimeter walls still stand, as does the Polygon Battery and torpedo slipways, though most of the buildings within are gone. The old coaling station lies immediately to the east. Most of the famous ships of the British Navy from the 18th century to the age of steam berthed here. Today it occasionally hosts live reggae concerts.

Naval Cemetery

Half a mile east of the dockyard, also enclosed by a brick wall, is the intriguing naval cemetery where sailors lie buried beneath shady palms. The cemetery dates back to the earliest days of Port Royal, though the more ancient quarter containing the grave of the famous buccaneer Sir Henry Morgan sank beneath the sea in 1692.

Lime Cay

Lime Cay is one of half a dozen or so uninhabited sand-rimmed coral cays sprinkled like jewels amid the turquoise and aquamarine waters about three miles offshore from Port Royal. It's the perfect spot for nude sunbathing and snorkeling. It's very popular with Kingstonians who flock there on weekends for picnics. A 'picnic park' has even been established.

To get to Lime Cay, you can rent boats

from fishermen in Port Royal for about US$5 round-trip. You can also rent a canoe (US$8) at Morgan's Harbour, which also has yacht charters to Lime Cay (US$13 per person, minimum 10 people). Morgan's Harbour can also arrange packaged lunches and barbecues for you (US$10 to US$14).

Sense Adventure offers a daylong 'Out Islands Odyssey' with skinny-dipping (Box 216, Kingston 7, ☎ 927-2097, fax 929-6967).

Yachting & Sport Fishing

Port Royal has a full-service marina (VHF channel 68; radio call 'Morgan's Harbour') at Morgan's Harbour Yacht Marina & Scuba Center. Fresh water, gasoline, diesel, laundry, showers, chandler facilities, and Customs clearance are offered. The marina has a variety of sport-fishing boats and yachts for rent and offers charter cruises to Lime Cay (US$12 person; minimum four people), plus deep-sea fishing (US$85 per hour).

Scuba Diving

Morgan's Harbour has a full-service scuba diving facility, the Buccaneer Scuba Club (☎ 967-8061, fax 967-8030), offering three- to seven-night dive packages (US$261 to US$669 single, US$186 to US$494 per person double). It also offers a range of PADI courses from basic to open-water certification. A single dive costs US$30. Dive equipment can be rented, as can snorkeling equipment.

The harbor and adjacent waters have abundant coral reefs, such as the **Edge**, where you can swim with nurse sharks, turtles, and dolphins; and explore wrecks such as the *Texas*, a warship covered in black coral. The highlight attraction, however, is the Sunken City, which has been scheduled to open to commercial dive operations. To verify the site's status, call the Jamaica National Heritage Trust (☎ 922-1287).

Exploring the Mangroves

Dive master Gary Carson offers guided trips from Morgan's Harbour by rubber Zodiac to the mangrove swamps in Kingston Harbour. A few crocodiles apparently still inhabit the inner sanctums. The mangroves are also a nesting site for frigate birds and pelicans. When I toured the area, we edged a little too close to the frigate bird rookery and spooked a young bird. It failed to get the wind in its sails and dropped in a panic into the water where it flapped about and kicked madly. Finally it lifted off right in front of us so that I had to duck to avoid being struck by its hooked beak!

You also have a good chance of seeing dolphins, which are once again making regular appearances in the harbor.

You can also rent canoes to explore the mangroves (US$7).

Organized Tours

The Teak Tree Co offers a guided half-day tour from Kingston (PO Box 435, Kingston 6, ☎ 977-1936, fax 977-3247), as does Limousine Taxi Tour Co at 3A Haughton Ave, Kingston 10 (☎ 968-3775, fax 944-3147), and Pro-Tours at 8 Lady Musgrave Rd, Kingston 5, on Wednesdays (☎ 978-6139; US$31).

Places to Stay

Built in 1950 the *Morgan's Harbour Hotel* (☎ 924-8464 or (800) 329-8388, fax 924-8562) is an atmospheric upscale hotel within the grounds of the old naval dockyard. It has 63 spacious, elegant, air-con rooms (US$129/159/172 single/double/triple), all with terra-cotta tile floors and French doors opening onto balconies. Cable TV is standard, as are firm king-size beds with headboards of gleaming dark hardwood. Rooms are decorated with original prints by Jamaican artists. Among the facilities included are fresh and saltwater swimming pools and an octagonal bar with an old anchor chain for its foot rail. It's very romantic at night when lit by ships' lanterns. The hotel offers special dive packages, plus a two-night package (US$125/150 single/double, including breakfast, tax, and service charge).

Places to Eat

Options range from the truly funky to the elegance of *Sir Henry's* in the Morgan's Harbour Hotel.

Vendors sell well-seasoned fried fish and bammy on the main square, where a motley collection of ramshackle stalls lean one against the other. Washed down with beer, your lunch should cost less than US$3. You can purchase supplies at *Lou's Grocery*.

Gloria's Rendezvous at 5 Queen St is famous island-wide for its reasonably priced seafood. Don't confuse it with *Gloria's Restaurant* at the west end of High St. Next door is *Buccaneer's Roost Restaurant*, another down-to-earth eatery serving seafood for under US$2.

Sir Henry's is popular with Kingstonians, especially for Sunday brunch. You can opt to dine on a shaded terrace with views towards the Blue Mountains. The dinner menu includes grilled lobster, jerk pork, and Jamaican specialties, plus salads and sandwiches. Prices begin at about US$6 and go to US$15 for lobster.

Entertainment

Port Royal is a great place to gain a taste of down-to-earth Jamaican life. There are several bars on the square, notably *McFarlane's* (otherwise known as the Angler's Club) and *Fisherman's Tavern*. McFarlane's has tremendous 'color' on weekend nights when a mountain of speakers is built 20-feet-high in the square and the sound of ska music reverberates across the harbor. Then locals wash in and out of the funky watering hole, overindulge in white rum, and pick fights with each other while two older bartenders boogie behind the bar.

'There are a few scalawags, but mostly its harmless stuff,' says Gary Carson, who runs the dive center.

Morgan's Harbour Hotel sometimes has live bands and dancing, as (reportedly) does the Gaol House Bar on Gaol Alley.

Getting There & Away

Bus Bus No 98 operates from the Parade in Kingston to Port Royal via the airport. The journey takes about 30 minutes (US$0.30).

Taxi A taxi ride from New Kingston to Port Royal will cost you about US$25 one-way. Norman Manley International Airport is only a five-minute taxi ride away and should cost about US$7.

Ferry A ferry sails from the No 2 Pier beside the Crafts Market at the west end of Ocean Blvd in Kingston. It's a 30-minute journey and costs about US$0.15 one-way (US$0.35 on Sunday and public holidays). The ferry departs Kingston at 6, 7, and 10 am, noon, and 3, 5, and 7 pm, and departs Port Royal for Kingston 30 minutes later.

CANE RIVER FALLS

These falls are popular with locals, who bathe here, as did Bob Marley who immortalized the place in song: 'Up to Cane River to wash my dread. Upon a rock, I rest my head.' Your presence will generate considerable though usually harmless interest!

From Kingston, just beyond the cement works, you reach a roundabout where a road leads south along the Palisadoes to the Norman Manley International Airport and Port Royal. Continue straight, however, and after two miles (just beyond Seven Mile) a turnoff to the left leads up to Cane River Falls.

CABLE HUT BEACH

A short distance further along the coast road you'll arrive at this uninspiring beach that is, however, popular with Kingstonians. If you want to hang with locals, then this a place to consider. You can eat at any of several jerk stalls and beachside 'recreations centres' highlighted by Paradise Cove.

Hostelries are limited to the *Caribbean Villa Hotel* (Lot 7, St Thomas Rd, Kingston 17, ☎ 928-6541), 400 yards east of the turnoff for the airport and Port Royal. It claims a 'harbor view,' though the view is far from salubrious. It serves local and Chinese dishes in the restaurant. The 10 modest 'bungalow' rooms (US$11 to US$13) were being upgraded in 1995.

BULL BAY

Bull Bay is a small town nine miles east of downtown Kingston. You can take the No 97 bus from Half Way Tree (US$0.30). The town offers little of interest but east of town, beyond a spur of the Blue Mountains called the Queensbury Ridge, a rugged dirt road on the far side of the bridge over the Chalky River will take you into the hills, ending at a **Rastafarian commune** of the Bobo Ashantis. This rather makeshift camp painted in the Rasta colors of red, gold, and green is led by the Right Honorable Prince Emmanuel Charles Edward, revered by his gaily robed followers as a black Christ. Expect to have to pay a donation for your visit and even to be rebuffed: 'Dis not Jamaica, mon. Dis is Jah-mekya (God made her).' You may be able to stay at the Rastafarian commune above Bull Bay.

Beyond Bull Bay, the main road climbs the scrub-covered hill before making a hairpin descent to Grants Pen and Eastern Jamaica. Near the summit, on the left, you'll pass a **monument to Three Finger Jack**, one of Jamaica's most legendary folk heroes. The marker was erected by the National Heritage Trust to recall the deeds of Jack Mansong, who between 1780 and 1781 'fought often singlehandedly, a war of terror against the English soldiers and planters who held the slave territory. Strong, brave, skilled with machete and musket, his bold exploits were equalled only by his chivalry.'

Apparently seven-foot-tall Mansong won his moniker after losing two fingers of one hand in a fight. The slave began his exploits after being sentenced to death for inciting rebellion. He escaped and took to the hills and a life as an outlaw and highway robber. He made the Queensbury Ridge his home and preyed on travelers along the roads near Bull Bay. He was eventually captured in 1781 by three Maroons who stuck his head on a pole and marched all the way to Spanish Town to collect a £300 reward. Mansong's fame was such that a pantomime based on his life ran for nine years in London's West End.

North of Kingston

A crescent of steep-rimmed mountains arc around Kingston to the north. Constant Spring Rd leads from Half Way Tree to the Manor Park roundabout and becomes the A3, or Stony Hill Rd, which ascends north up Stony Hill and crosses the westernmost ridges of the Blue Mountains. From here, the A3 descends through the **Wag Water Valley** to the flatlands of the North Coast. Bamboo lines the valley sides. It's a very windy road with many hairpin turns and potholes. Jamaican drivers do not slow down merely for hairpin bends or because the road narrows, but you should!

About 12 miles north of Half Way Tree, a turnoff to the right at Oakley leads to the **Temple Hall Coffee Estate** (☎ 942-2340), where there's reportedly a fine restaurant.

CASTLETON BOTANICAL GARDENS

Seventeen miles north of Half Way Tree the road bisects Castleton Gardens, which are spread over 30 acres on the banks of the Wag Water River. Castleton Gardens sits astride the boundary of Surrey and Middlesex Counties. Many of the exotic species introduced to Jamaica were first planted here.

The gardens date back to 1860, when 400 specimens from Kew Gardens in London were transplanted on the former sugar plantation owned by Lord Castleton. The gardens, which rise up the hillside on the west side of the road, eventually became the pride of the Caribbean, but they were knocked about by Hurricane Gilbert in 1988 and are still recovering. More than 1000 species of natives and exotics are displayed. The upper level includes two towering Norfolk pines that have grown at over 12 inches a year for more than a century. Nearby are labeled specimens of Strychnos, from which strychnine poison is extracted.

Castleton is open 7 am to 5 pm daily (until 6 pm some months). On the eastern (lower) side of the road is a picnic area with cafeteria and toilets. Entrance is free.

The guides are also unsalaried (they're not allowed to charge), but tips are welcome. Ask for Roy Bennett, who has been the senior guide for almost 40 years. He's very helpful and you'll delight to have him expound on the garden while you explore.

Places to Stay

Reportedly, you can camp on the *riverbank* at Castleton for a token fee of US$2. There's water. A lively little jerk center

called *Desert Rose* is about 100 yards north of the gardens.

You can also camp at *Grass Piece Farm* in the hamlet of Leinster, reached by a road to the left (west) from the bridge 1½ miles north of Castleton. The owners, Annie and Roger Robinson, also rent a cabin.

Getting There & Away

Bus No 52 departs from the Parade and travels Stony Hill via Golden Spring.

Blue Mountains

If you tire of reggae and beach-bumming, and want to cool off in fern-festooned forests, head to the Blue Mountains at the eastern end of Jamaica.

The steep-faced mountains rise northeast of Kingston and soar in green pleats to a knife-edged backbone – the Grand Ridge – that extends west-northwest and east-southeast for about 30 miles. The mountains average 12 miles wide. The chain is flanked to the east by the lower John Crow Mountains; to the west are the less distinct Port Royal Mountains.

The Blue Mountains dominate the eastern parishes of St Andrew, St Thomas, Portland, and St Mary, rising swiftly from the coast to a series of rounded peaks culminating in Blue Mountain Peak (7402 feet), the highest point in Jamaica. Others include Mt Horeb, Stoddard's Peak, Half a Bottle, and Catherine's Peak. The latter, which dominates Kingston and is topped by a tall radio antenna, was named for the first person to climb it, Catherine Long, who reached the top in 1760.

Many of the humble and gracious mountain folk are caught in a culture of poverty. Many villages lack electricity. Most of the children lack shoes. And the majority of grown men (at least those fortunate enough to own a piece of land) get up at the crack of dawn to tend steep-pitched plots where they grow coffee and vegetables. The farms supply Kingston. On weekends the higglers pile into trucks and vans for the journey down the mountain to ply their produce in the markets. Ask a local farmer what he grows and he'll tell you yams, carrots, scallions, and thyme. 'And what about ganja?' you may mischievously ask, for it, too, is an important cash crop hereabouts.

Only one road – the B1 – surmounts the high passes to link Kingston with the north coast, with other minor roads branching off into the mountains. Countless dirt roads link tiny hamlet with tiny hamlet, luring

HIGHLIGHTS

- Lunch, dinner, or better yet, a night of romance at Strawberry Hill
- The trail to Blue Mountain Peak for the greatest high in Jamaica
- Lonesome Cinchona Botanical Gardens
- Old Tavern Estate for the best coffee in the world

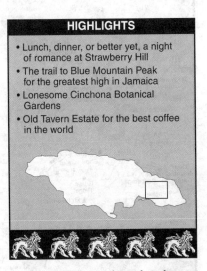

you to escape the tourist path and to see and appreciate life in the mountains. Roads are mostly rutted, rain-washed tracks full of holes and huge rocks. Often they deteriorate into muddy stairways that your car negotiates with wheezing difficulty. Fancy clutch skills are called for, and 4WD is essential.

Fill up on gas in Kingston as there are no gas stations in the Blue Mountains; the nearest is at Papine. You should be able to do all your exploring on one full tank.

Few locals own a vehicle. The wiry old men and women toting baskets of vegetables and bundles of firewood on their heads will be grateful if you stop and give them a ride.

Geology

The mountains take their name from the haze that tints their heights. They're composed of sedimentary, igneous, and metamorphic rocks dating back 140 million years. These are the oldest rocks on the island, born of volcanic convulsions

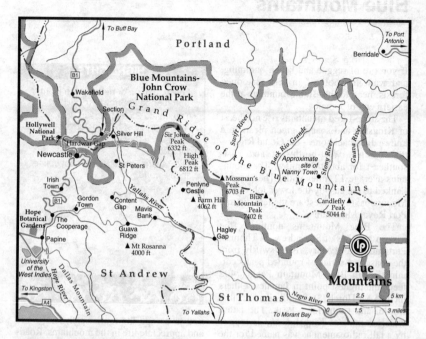

beneath the sea during the Cretaceous period – a result of the jostling of the Caribbean and North American tectonic plates that still occurs. The mountains have been on the rise for at least the past 25 million years, though their major uplift took place within the last five million years.

The range is still imperceptibly rising along major fault lines at a rate of almost one foot per 1000 years. When the faults shift, great landslides tumble into the plunging valleys, leaving raw gashes of red earth and rock. The mountains are of non-porous, igneous origin and since rainfall is high, streams and waterfalls are numerous and the mountains are deeply incised by plunging rivers.

Climate
The Blue Mountains are much wetter than the rest of Jamaica. Moisture-laden trade winds blowing from the northeast spill much of their accumulation on the mountains, which forms a rain shadow over Kingston and the southern parishes. The summer months (June through September) provide the best weather for exploring. December to April is also a good time, though slightly cooler. Temperature drops 3° to 4°F for every 1000-foot rise in elevation (it can freeze in the early morning above 5500 feet). Intervening months experience heavy rains. Torrential rains of 12 or more inches in 24 hours are not unknown, and usually result in serious flooding.

Flora
The Blue Mountains are a botanist's dream, with more than 500 flowering plant species (about 240 of which are endemic to the island), including 65 species of orchid, the majority with flowers so small as to be barely noticeable. An endemic of note is the 'Jamaica rose' (merianias), whose pendulous roselike blossoms glow like tiny lanterns when struck by sunlight. A great many species are exotics introduced by English settlers during the last century as

ornamentals: azaleas, bright-pink begonias, purple melastoma, yellow *Calceolaria* from Central America, sky-blue *Aristea gerrardii* from South Africa, eucalyptus from Australia, bamboo from the Far East, ginger lilies, an import from Asia, and cheesebury and rhododendrons from the Himalayas.

Native tree species include boarwood, whose name derives from the folk belief that wounded hogs tear the bark with their tusks and rub their wounds with the sap. Another is *Chusquea abietifolia*, which remarkably flowers synchronistically, and only once every 33 years. The event was first reported in 1885, when it flowered both in Jamaica and at Kew Gardens in England. It last flowered in 1984 and is due again in 2017.

Vegetation changes with altitude. The upper slopes are swathed in ferns (more than 50 species), bromeliads, and antediluvian tree ferns – *Cyanthea* – that grow to 35 feet tall and live more than 150 years. Toward the summits, cloud forest enshrouds the hiker, opening up now and then to reveal spectacular views.

Fauna

The mountains are home to eight species of frogs and the Jamaican coney, whose essential demise within this century can be blamed on the voraciousness of the non-native mongoose. Birdlife is more prolific. Among the commonly seen species are the 'doctorbird,' Jamaican blackbird, Jamaican tody, rufous-throated solitaire, white eyed thrush, sad- and rufous-tailed flycatchers, the ring-tailed pigeon, and the crested quail dove, or 'mountain witch.' Butterflies are also numerous, including the transparent 'glass wing' butterfly. The large swallowtail is found not in the Blue Mountains, but in the lower John Crows to the east.

Deforestation

Vegetation on the north side of the mountains differs markedly from that on the south. Not only is the north side more lush – the forest begins at about 2000 feet – but, on the south side the forest has been cleared to between 3000 and 4500 feet, mostly for vegetable farming, coffee, and fruit trees. The Blue Mountain ecology is fragile and soil erosion is a major problem.

Deforestation in the Blue Mountains has a long history. During the 18th and 19th centuries much of the hills were cleared to supply the coffee houses of Europe. Since the demise of the coffee industry, eucalyptus and pine have taken hold, while in some places the slopes have been conquered by savanna-type grasses, introduced from Africa early this century. Be careful if you plan on hiking: tangled grass stems hide gullies, causing serious injury to unwary livestock and hikers.

The doctorbird, a species of hummingbird, is the Jamaican national bird.

Every year the pressure increases to cultivate higher slopes. Despite a new attitude towards conservation, both the Coffee Industry Board and Forestry Industry Development Co have been allocated former forest reserve for clearance. The Forestry Dept is beset with political corruption and has been accused of turning a blind eye to ongoing violations. Squatters, charcoal burners, and timber pirates continue to fell trees. Even Mother Nature has been a vandal. The forests suffered miserably during Hurricane Gilbert in 1988, when extensive forest cover was lost.

A good introduction to Blue Mountain ecology is the *Blue Mountain Guide* (ed, Margaret Hodges), published by the Natural History Society of Jamaica.

Blue Mountains-John Crow National Park

On February 28, 1993, a start was made to control logging when the Blue Mountains-John Crow National Park was created to protect 193,260 acres. It is managed under the Protected Areas Resource Conservation Project (PARC), a regulatory body set up in 1991 as a joint venture between the USAID (Agency for International Development) and the Jamaican government.

Currently there are only 15 rangers to patrol the park. Community participation is seen as critical to policing the park. Local advisory committees have been established to involve the communities, so that they derive benefit from protecting the forests. Ecotourism is being promoted, for example, and locals are being trained as trail guides.

Hiking

'To really appreciate the Blue Mountains you must go there, accept the challenge and walk the trail to the summit,' says writer Ivan Goodbody. I agree. The Blue Mountains are a hiker's paradise. Dozens of trails lace the hills, many carved by British soldiers over a century ago. Others were used in the heyday of coffee by mule trains and were kept open by foresters and farmers who used them (until recent

The Windward Maroons

When the English invaded Jamaica in 1655, the Spanish freed their African slaves, who under their elected leader, Juan de Serra, fled to the wild Rio Grande Valley and Sierra de Batistas (renamed the Blue Mountains by the English). Another group became concentrated in the equally wild Cockpit Country of Trelawny Parish. They formed fierce bands known as Maroons, from *cimarron,* a Spanish word meaning 'untamed' or 'wild ones.' The eastern community was called the Windward Maroons; those further west were called Leeward Maroons (see the Northwest Coast chapter for more details).

The Windward Maroons were made up of members of the warlike Ashanti and Fante tribes of Ghana, who were highly skilled in guerrilla warfare in jungle terrain. The thick forest and heavy rainfall aided the Maroons in defending their territory from their remote headquarters at Nanny Town, high atop a spur on the northern slopes of the Blue Mountains. The English soldiers were no match for the Maroons in their own territory.

In 1739, Quao, leader of the Windward Maroons, signed a peace treaty with the British government. The pact ensured the Maroons' freedom. They were also granted 500 acres of land in the Rio Grande Valley. The Windward Maroons split. One group went with Quao to establish Crawford Town near the coast. A second group, under the warrior-priestess Nanny, founded New Nanny Town (now Moore Town). In exchange, the Maroons promised to assist the English in maintaining law and order, and even promised to return runaway slaves, which they did throughout the rest of the century.

The Maroons retain some autonomy even today, governing themselves via a 24-member council headed by an elected 'colonel' who arbitrates minor disputes. They keep alive their lore and legends, and still bring out their *abengs* and talking drums on occasion. Otherwise, modernity has caught up with the Maroons. ∎

decades) to transport their produce to market in Kingston. Many have since become overgrown, but others remain the mainstay of communications for locals, the vast majority of whom do not own cars. No roads penetrate the northeastern slopes, and here it is still possible to savor the isolation that for two centuries made the area a Maroon redoubt.

Trails (called 'tracks' locally) are rarely marked. When asking directions of locals, remember that 'a few chains' can actually mean several miles, while 'jus' a likkle way' may in fact be a few hours of hiking. A guide is highly recommended. Within the Blue Mountains-John Crow National Park hiking trails have been categorized as guided, nonguided, and wilderness. Work is ongoing to complete a 'Grand Ridge of the Blue Mountains Trail' similar to the Appalachian Trail, with huts for sleeping along the way. The trail will run from Morces Gap in the west (access is from Jack's Hill) via Blue Mountain Peak to Corn Puss Gap, in the John Crow Mountains. Some of the most interesting trails lead to active coffee factories such as those at Mavis Bank, Silver Hill, and Wallenford.

You'll rarely be far from a village or homestead where hospitable country folk are certain to assist you.

For locale-specific information, see the Hiking sections below, and the Blue Mountain Peak section.

Maps If you hike alone, I recommend you buy the Survey Dept 1:50,000 or, better yet, the excellent 1:12,500 Ordnance Survey topographic map series, available from Maya Lodge (see Places to Stay, Jack's Hill, below) or the Survey Dept at 23½ Charles St in Kingston (PO Box 493, ☎ 922-6630). Four different sheets – Nos 13, 14, 18, and 19 – cover the area around Blue Mountain Peak, and you may need to buy all four (US$5 each), depending on the route you intend to follow. The maps are also available in England from Ordnance Survey (Romsey Rd, Southampton SO9 4DH).

Michael Fox, owner of Mount Edge (see Irish Town, below), was producing a map showing places where independent travelers can stay and eat.

Guidebooks An absolute prerequisite to hiking alone is *A Hiker's Guide to the Blue Mountains*, by Bill Wilcox, who describes a wide range of hikes. It was published in 1985, but not much has changed. You can buy it at Maya Lodge, which is one of the best places to set out on foot.

Water Although increasing use of pesticides has led to an increase in river pollution, upper-course streams are usually clean enough to drink from (many harbor freshwater crayfish *(jonga)* that can grow up to 12 inches long). Experienced hikers, of course, know to drink from the fresh rainwater in the reservoirs of the cupped leaves of bromeliads. Take a cloth with you to strain out dead bugs and decaying vegetable matter.

Cycling
The Blue Mountains are heaven-made for exploring by bicycle. You'll need a sturdy mountain bike. Take plenty of water, as well as a puncture repair kit. The going will frequently be steep and arduous, but you'll generally be warmly welcomed by locals along the way. If you want a fairly tame organized bicycle tour, call Blue Mountain Tours, which offers a downhill bicycling tour that begins at 5060 feet and descends to the North Coast (PO Box 84, Port Antonio, ☎ 993-2242).

You can also take guided mountain bike tours with Michael Fox at Mount Edge; he offers a one-day trip to Wildflower Lodge (US$120), a two-day trip to Wildflower and Bath (US$160), and a local half-day trip (US$60).

Organized Tours
The Touring Society of Jamaica, based at Strawberry Hill (☎ 944-8400 ext 210, ☎/fax 975-7158), offers a series of Blue Mountains tours, including short walks around Irish Town (US$10 per hour),

and along the Gordon Town and Fairy Glade Trails (US$35 to US$50). It also organizes a half-day birdwatching tour (US$25), and includes the Blue Mountains on an eight-day 'Birding Jamaica' tour each November (US$1350).

Pro Tours Ltd offers a Blue Mountain tour from Kingston (US$31), Montego Bay (US$77), and Ocho Rios (US$67). The office is at 8 Lady Musgrave Rd, Kingston 5 (☎ 978-6139).

The acknowledged expert on the Blue Mountains is Peter Bentley. He and his Sense Adventure staff lead hikes (see Organized Hikes under Blue Mountain Peak below) and canoeing trips using inflatable canoes. They also do a one-day 'Blue Mountain Coffee and Rainforest Tour.'

The Southwest

The Blue Mountains lie northeast of Kingston. Hence, the most visited and easily reached area is the southwestern flank. The B1 snakes up and over the mountains, providing easy access to most places and sites of interest. Simply follow Hope Rd uphill to Papine, a market square and bus station, from where Gordon Town Rd leads into the mountains. A side trip will take you to Jack's Hill.

JACK'S HILL

Jack's Hill is a steep-faced ridge that marks the first step into the mountains north of Kingston. Skyline Drive runs along its crest, providing superb views over the city. Many wealthier citizens have their homes here. The community of Jack's Hill is a scattered hamlet with a couple of rum shops, a post office, and a police station. The Jack's Hill Community Center is the headquarters for **Project Plant** – the Mammee River Agricultural and Environmental Development Project – a community reforestation and environmental education program funded by the United Nations Development Program. Maya Lodge (see Places to Stay below)

acts as a model demonstration site, and its owner, Peter Bentley, is a director of the project, which takes its name from the Mammee River, which flows through the area, and is intended to benefit about 300 local small-scale farmers. The goal is to achieve sustainable management of the watershed and sensitive utilization of the hills north of Kingston for agroforestry and ecotourism.

Hiking

Jack's Hill provides the most easily accessible base for hikes as well as an introduction to the *real* Jamaica. Trails lead uphill to Peter's Rock and the peak of Mt Horeb (4850 feet). Another trail ascends from Peter's Rock to Hollywell National Park. An old trading route, the **Vinegar Hill Trail**, begins here and ascends via Catherine's Peak (5056 feet) before dropping down to Chepstow, near Buff Bay, on the north coast.

Guides can be hired from Maya Lodge (from US$25, plus accommodations and food), which is the headquarters of the Jamaican Alternative Tourism Camping and Hiking Association (JATCHA). You can buy topographical maps here (US$5), and Peter will happily help you plan your vacation and make reservations for US$15. Peter is a fountain of knowledge about Jamaica and alternative travel (his ancestors settled in Jamaica in 1659).

Places to Stay & Eat

Maya Lodge, (PO Box 216, Kingston 7, ☎ 927-2097, fax 929-6967) perhaps the best known 'alternative lodging' in Jamaica, has become an institution among budget travelers. It sits in a trough below the summit of Jack's Hill. Fifteen campsites (US$5) are cut into the steep hillside amid tall grasses and bamboo. You can rent camping equipment for US$2.50 per item. The lodge has an outdoor eating area under thatch with rough-hewn tables and benches. Breakfast costs US$3 and dinner US$7.

A range of indoor accommodations are also offered. Wooden cabins, sleep up to four people but have no electricity. If you don't mind the comings and goings, you can rent a two-person open loft above the office. There's also an open-air 'hammock hut' (US$5 per person) plus double rooms (US$20) with shared bath; one room has a private bathroom. A stay here puts you about as close to the real Jamaica as possible, as Peter's staff are drawn from the local community. He tends to hang around in cutoff Levi's and even these get discarded on occasion. Don't be surprised to find Peter and other guests wandering around nude.

Opposite the entrance to Maya is *Rasta Inn* (owned by 'Baps'), which has basic loft-beds for up to eight people (US$10). There's electricity, a 'sun shower,' and a pit toilet. Baps is partial to blowing on an *abeng* (horn) and playing his bamboo flute.

Make reservations early for a stay at *Ivor Guest House* (Skyline Drive, Jack's Hill, Kingston 6, ☎ 927-1460, fax 977-0033), which squats atop Jack's Hill and offers fabulous vistas over Kingston. The charming house was built in the late 1870s. It was severely damaged by Hurricane Gilbert in 1988 and has since been remodeled and expanded, but has lost none of its traditional style. The three rooms are individually and beautifully furnished. You can relax on rockers on the veranda, which is lit at night by old brass lanterns. The owner, Hellen Aitken, is very charming and helpful. This gem costs at US$80/95 a single/double, including continental breakfast and a free trip to Kingston daily.

Your best bet, albeit an expensive one, is Ivor's. Meals are by reservations only, and you should book well ahead. A four-course dinner costs US$24 per person, and a three-course lunch is US$16. It also serves snack lunches and afternoon teas. The menu changes daily, but typically offers pumpkin soup, jerk shrimp, roast pork, lemon and thyme chicken rolls, snapper with mustard and capers, and such desserts as sherry trifle and cappuccino creme caramel.

If Ivor's is full, try *Sunset Ridge Guest House*, which has 12 rooms at US$60 (20A Skyline Drive, Kingston 7, ☎ 977-1568).

Getting There & Away
Bus You can get to Jack's Hill via minibus (US$0.50) from opposite the Texaco station at Barbican between 5:30 and 10 am, and 3 to 10:30 pm. The No 74 and No 76 buses run to Barbican via Slipe Rd from The Parade, at Duke St and E Queen St.

Car If you're driving from Kingston, take either Skyline Drive from its junction with Gordon Town Rd, half a mile north of Papine (it's about four miles from here to Jack's Hill); or, from Hope Rd, take E Kings House Rd to Barbican and from there, Jack's Hill Rd (half a mile to the right of Barbican). It's three miles uphill. Foxy's Pub sits at the hilltop crossroads in Jack's Hill. From Foxy's Pub, a rugged road – Peter's Rock Rd – leads 100 yards downhill to the lodge, on the left at the bottom.

THE COOPERAGE
Two miles above Papine via Gordon Town Rd is the Cooperage, a hamlet named for its community of Irish coopers who made the wooden barrels in which coffee beans were shipped in the 19th century. On the left is the historic Blue Mountain Inn, an erstwhile coaching inn housed in a former coffee plantation house that overlooks the Mammee River. It was closed for restoration at press time. Hopefully when reopened it will live up to the days when it was ritzy enough to serve Lyndon Johnson and members of the British royal family.

The Mammee River Rd leads left from the T-junction above the inn and follows the river valley uphill. The road was cut in 1896 to link the military camp at Newcastle. It hugs the mountainside and is one switchback after another the entire length. The views are breathtaking, but drivers should leave the gawking to passengers. The road is narrow, overgrown with foliage, and the corners are blind, so honk your horn frequently. Take particular care on weekends when the road gets busy. En route, you'll pass several substantial houses, including Bellencita, the erstwhile home of ex-premier and National Hero Sir Alexander Bustamante. Two and a half miles uphill, a road to the left follows the Mammee River to Maryland and Peter's Rock, overlooking Jack's Hill.

The road straight ahead at the Cooperage leads to Gordon Town, Mavis Bank, and Blue Mountain Peak.

Buses to Redlight, Hardwar Gap, and Gordon Town all pass the Cooperage.

IRISH TOWN

Mammee River Rd climbs to Irish Town, a small hamlet where the coopers lived during the last century. Potatoes are still an important crop, reflecting the Irish influence. Further uphill is **Redlight**. The hamlet was apparently named for the fact that it served as a brothel for soldiers from the Newcastle barracks.

In an emergency, call the Irish Town police station at ☎ 944-8242.

Bamboo Lodge

This private home, just before Irish Town, last century served as a recuperation station for fever-stricken sailors. Lord Nelson came here as a 20-year-old to recover from dysentery and was attended by a noted herbalist, Couba Cornwallis, beautiful mistress of the Earl of Cornwallis, the then-governor.

Craighton Estate

Coffee is still grown at Craighton Estate, a plantation owned by the Ueshima Company of Japan, 6½ miles above the Cooperage. Visits can be arranged by appointment (☎ 944-8224).

Places to Stay & Eat

Strawberry Hill (☎ 944-8400, fax 944-8408) is a superlative retreat suspended 3100 feet up, just north of Irish Town. The property is a brainchild of owner Chris Blackwell, the impresario who launched Bob Marley to fame through his label, Island Records. The 12 Caribbean-style cottages range from studio suites to a four-bedroom, two-story house – 'Highgate' – hand-hewn into the hillside by local villagers who were trained as craftsmen during the property's five-year evolution.

Strawberry Hill is strong on elegance, from hand-molded hardwood sofas, to stereo/CD players, chic bedside lamps, and Sperod's Olive Oil soaps.

Just imagine settling in a hammock on your veranda and listening to reggae riffs carried uphill on the breeze while, far below, Kingston twinkles like myriad fireflies. While I was there, I hopped up into a dark mahogany four-poster bed a mile off the floor. Supermodel Naomi Campbell had slept in this very bed just two weeks prior, I was told. I could still feel the sensuous heat in the crisp linen sheets . . . then I realized it was an electric blanket thoughtfully provided for chilly nights. I settled under a plump down comforter and marveled at the phosphorescent flickering of fireflies flitting about my room.

All this comes at a price. Rates for the one- to three-bedroom units (some with kitchen) range from US$250 to US$775 per night, including continental breakfast. From mid-April to mid-December, rates go down to $175 to $575. For information and reservations, contact Island Outpost: in the USA, 1330 Ocean Drive, Miami Beach, FL 33139, ☎ (800) 688-7678, fax (305) 531-5543; in the UK, 421A Finchley Rd, London NW3 6H, ☎ (0171) 431-4045 or (800) 614-790, fax (0171) 431-7920. Transfers are included (a helicopter is available at additional cost). The staff reflect Blackwell's principle that individual initiative among the mountain villagers is sufficient, and that with professional training and guidance the local labor pool will attain the highest standards.

Many Kingstonians make the longish drive to Strawberry Hill for some of the finest nouvelle Jamaican cuisine on the island. Among the dishes I've savored here are curried pumpkin soup (US$4), soya bean roti stuffed with curried vegetables (US$13), and jerk lamb loin with roasted garlic (US$20).

The modest *Shamrock Tavern Lounge & Villas*, at Irish Town, was closed for renovation at press time.

Getting There & Away

You can take the No 67 bus from Papine (US$0.30). It passes through Irish Town en route to Redlight.

NEWCASTLE

Newcastle hangs invitingly on the mountainside high above Irish Town. The road climbs tortuously to 4000 feet where, 13 miles from Kingston, you suddenly emerge on a wide parade ground square guarded by a small cannon. The settlement is a military encampment that clambers up the slope above the square. Newcastle was founded in 1841 by Field Marshall Sir William Gomm, Commanding Officer of the British Forces in Jamaica. Back then, soldiers stationed on the Liguanea plains were dying en masse of yellow fever. Gomm fought a battle against the British bureaucracy to establish a training site and convalescent center in the more salubrious hills. 'We have carried the hill!' he wrote. With the granting of independence in 1962, the camp was turned over to the Jamaica Defence Force.

The square, named for Gomm, offers a fantastic view of Kingston. With good

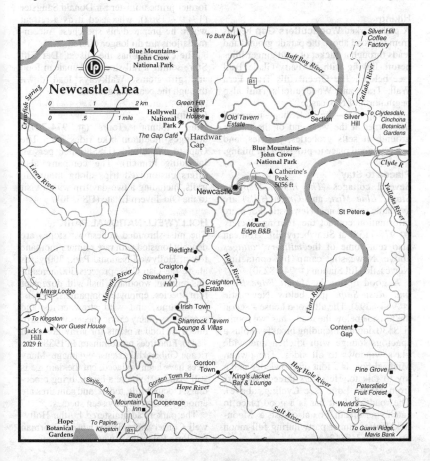

fortune you may even arrive to watch recruits being drilled. Note the insignia on the whitewashed stone wall, commemorating those regiments stationed at Newcastle (it dates back to 1884, when it was started by the North Staffordshire Regiment). The road to the right on the square leads up through the camp and continues to Catherine's Peak.

Reportedly you may nip into the Sergeant's mess for a quick tipple. Since this is a military camp, visitors are only allowed around the canteen, shop, roadways, and parade ground.

Hiking

A path marked **Woodcutters Gap** begins from the road above the parade ground and leads through a thicket of wild ginger lilies before linking with the Fairy Glade Trail (see below). The Green Hills Trail, Fern Walk Trail, and Woodcutter's Trail also begin north of Newcastle.

A camp store – the Tuck Shop – is around the corner at the west end of the parade ground. It sells groceries, pastries, and sodas: a good place to provision for hiking.

Places to Stay

Several cottages *(The Roost, Stepping Stone, Blue Mist,* and *Green Hills)* are available for rent near Newcastle. For more information contact the Touring Society (☎ 975-7158) at Strawberry Hill. You can also rent some of the *military cottages* above Newcastle camp by contacting Newcastle Hill Station (☎ 944-8230).

A good option is *Mount Edge B&B and Rest Stop,* just below Newcastle (☎ 944-8392). The all-wood house – set on the hillside below the road – has two rooms (US$30 double, including breakfast) plus a spacious lounge with kitchen and wide glass windows to all sides. The owner, Michael Fox, is a font of knowledge and a joy to talk to. He offers three bike tours from Mount Edge (see Cycling, above). The roadside fruit bar is a good place to catch your breath. Fox also hosts a 'Moonlick' buffet dinner party during full-moon Fridays for US$12.

HARDWAR GAP

Two miles above Newcastle you reach Hardwar Gap, at the crest of the Grand Ridge. The Gap Café sits on the hillside just below the summit and Hollywell National Park. The Gap is a fabulous place to rest and take in the vistas over a soda or cappuccino (see Places to Eat below). The original house was set up as a way station for buggy traffic in the 19th century. With the advent of motorcars, a 10 shilling charge was levied for overnight stays (guests had to provide their own food and bed linen). It was popularized by the former prime minister Sir Donald Sangster (1911 – 1967), who used it as a retreat where he prepared his speeches. Accommodations are no longer offered.

The café also has the Dis 'n' Dat Gift Store selling a full stock of Jamaican food and gift items. Walkways lead down through the beautiful gardens.

Cycling

Blue Mountain Tours (☎ 974-7075) arranges mountain bike rides from The Gap to Wakefield (US$80 per person, including brunch). The company also offers customized trips along mountain trails, including a two-day trip with a visit to the Old Tavern Estate (US$150).

HOLLYWELL NATIONAL PARK

The mist-shrouded uppermost slopes are densely forested with rare primary montane forest. Hollywell National Park, 200 yards above the Gap Café, protects 300 acres of this remnant woodland, lush with dozens of fern species, epiphytes, impatiens, violets, nasturtiums, and wild strawberries and raspberries (many exotic species were introduced as fodder plants for army horses in 1841). Pine trees predominate. In 1988 Hurricane Gilbert did extensive damage. Many trees have been replaced, but the damage is still visible. If you're a birder, bring binoculars. Doctor birds, todies, and solitaires are among the many easily seen species.

The park is administered by the Hollywell Conservation Trust, whose chairman is Gloria Palomino, owner of Gap Café.

A ranger station is on the right a short distance beyond the entrance. (The toll gate has been unoccupied when I've stopped by.) The park has miradors (view points) and picnic spots.

Hiking

Hollywell is tremendous for hiking. Trails leads off in all directions through the ferny dells, cloud forest, and elfin woodland. With a bit of luck or better-than-average skill at map reading you can even find the Cascade, Jamaica's second highest waterfall, plunging sheer off the north slope off Hartley Hill (4363 feet).

At press time the **Fairy Glade Trail** was due to be closed for rehabilitation; it has been abused by people taking wild plants. This four-hour trail is a rough scramble through the tropical montane and elfin forest to the summit of Mt Horeb (4037 feet).

Another trail – negotiable by 4WD – leads down to Peter's Rock and, eventually, Jack's Hill.

Places to Stay

Camping is allowed (US$3). There are water faucets and toilets.

You can rent rustic cabins with twin beds and basic kitchen a short distance from the entrance (US$5 per cabin for up to four people); bring your own bedding and food. Advance reservations are essential via the Forestry Dept in Kingston, which you must visit in person to prepay and collect your vouchers (173 Constant Spring Rd, ☎ 924-2667). Holiday and weekend stays should be booked several weeks in advance, if possible.

Places to Eat

The atmospheric *Gap Café* (☎ 997-3032 or 923-7055, fax 923-5617). sits on the hillside at 4200 feet, two miles above Newcastle. You can choose elegant dining indoors or alfresco beneath a canopy on a two-tier wooden terrace with wrought-iron furniture. A Jamaican special breakfast costs US$8. High tea is also served. And the eclectic menu includes curried Caribbean

shrimp (US$13), shepherd's pie (US$8), lasagna (US$9), pizzas (US$4), sandwiches, and delicious pastries by Colin ('pastry chef extraordinaire'). Dinner is by advance reservation only. It's open 10 am to 5 pm, Tuesday to Thursday, until 6 pm Friday to Sunday (closed Good Friday). Bring mosquito repellent.

Getting There & Away

Bus No JR75 operates twice daily between Papine and Buff Bay via Newcastle, Hardwar Gap, and Section. It costs about US$0.30 from Papine.

SECTION

Beyond Hollywell the road drops steeply towards the hamlet of Section and then more gently snakes and curls its way down to Buff Bay on the north coast. As soon as you crest the ridge the vegetation is noticeably lusher due to the clouds that normally descend by late morning. You'll pass several cottages with colorful gardens. The most dramatic is Green Hill Guest House (see Places to Stay below), surrounded by azaleas, fuchsias, hydrangeas, rhododendrons, magnolias, and nasturtiums.

Old Tavern Estate

About 400 yards downhill from Green Hill Guest House is a small, anonymous cottage that you would surely pass by if you didn't know that its occupants, Alex and Dorothy Twyman, produce the best of the best of Blue Mountain coffee. The old wooden house is perched on the cliffside at 3900 feet, overlooking coffee groves, with marvelous views towards Buff Bay. The Twymans welcome guests to their Old Tavern Estate (PO Box 131, Kingston 8, 924-2785, fax 929-6777). If you plan on visiting a coffee farm, this one gets my vote.

Although the Twyman's coffee is acclaimed in Jamaica as the best on the island, they can't sell an ounce due to Kafkaesque government regulations. Twyman wants to sell his beans under his own estate label instead of seeing them blended with lesser beans from other Blue Mountain farms. The coffee board has consistently denied Twyman a license to process and roast his own coffee and sell it as 'Blue Mountain' coffee because it is processed on site, not at an official JABLUM processing plant. Laws defining 'Blue Mountain coffee' currently are based on where coffee is *processed*, not where it's grown (see the sidebar Hallowed Grounds, in Facts about Jamaica). Twyman stopped selling his beans to the coffee board in 1982 and has since stored his unroasted beans at a warehouse in the hope that one day he will receive a license. There's good news in this: Twyman has discovered that coffee aged before it is roasted was once highly prized. Apparently aging enhances the bean's flavor; it mellows it. So the Twyman family is sitting on a mountain of the finest and most expensive coffee beans in the world.

The farm currently has 50,000 bushes raised organically and at a low density to protect against disease in the wet climate (other farms have high-density bushes and use lots of fungicides and pesticides). And where other estates pick their berries before or shortly after cool rainy weather sets in, Twyman lets his mature on the bush through winter (as long as eight months), so that they develop a more robust, mellow flavor. The estate produces no more than 30,000 pounds per year. Twyman's estate-roasted coffee is a bargain at US$20 per pound in vacuum-packed bags. Much of the business is direct mail order to clients, including Ronald Reagan and Queen Elizabeth II. You can have orders of five pounds or more shipped by air courier (US$150 to the USA, US$170 to elsewhere). Before buying, you can sample their coffee and their homemade mead, honey, and coffee liqueur. The Twymans are also considering introducing 'roast-your-own' coffee for visitors.

A trail leads down through lush ferns and moist forest to a stream with freshwater crabs and shrimps. The remains of the original tavern can also be seen amid the coffee bushes. In olden days, the journey over the mountains took two days, and travelers would rest at the inn.

Mark Twyman, son of Alex and Dorothy, leads guided walks through the farm.

The Touring Society of Jamaica at Strawberry Hill (☎ 975-7158, ext 210) offers a tour to the Old Tavern (US$75), as does Pro Tours Ltd (8 Lady Musgrave Rd, Kingston 5, ☎ 978-6139) and the Teak Tree Co (PO Box 435, Kingston 6, ☎ 977-1936, fax 977-3247).

Places to Stay
Green Hill Guest House & Cottages (PO Box 467, Montego Bay, ☎ 997-4087, fax 952-6591) is a delightful-looking home with a magnificent setting amid bright-flowering plants, one mile north of Section. Inside is more ascetic. The six bedrooms (US$25 per person) have hardwood floors and are bare but for the beds, one of which is a magnificent antique four-poster. The rooms share one bathroom with a deep tub. There's a small lounge and meals are cooked in a large kitchen. You can enjoy marvelous views from a wide veranda when the clouds fade.

SILVER HILL
A turnoff to the right at Section leads one mile to Silver Hill Gap. The road is lush with ferns that brush against your car. Silver Hill is a ridgetop crossroads where the main dirt road loops south and drops to Content Gap, eventually linking up with the road from Gordon Town to Mavis Bank. A dirt road to the left drops to Silver Hill coffee processing plant (visitors are welcome). After touring the factory, check out the small-time operation of James Dennis, one of scores of small holders who shun the cartel and who have formed the Portland Blue Mountain Coffee Co-Operative Society.

James Dennis has basic rooms at Silver Hill for about US$20. Reportedly, you can also camp here.

The Center

Gordon Town Rd continues straight from the Cooperage and winds east up the Hope River Valley to Gordon Town, Mavis Bank, and Hagley Gap, the gateway to Blue Mountain Peak.

GORDON TOWN
Gordon Town, at 1200 feet, is the only town of any significance in the Blue Mountains. It hardly deserves the moniker. It's a neat village centered on a wide square with a police station (☎ 927-2805), post office, and even a tiny courthouse. It began life as a staging post for Newcastle in the days before the Mammee River Rd was cut from the Cooperage. The old parochial road still exists, though it is really a track; it's now known as the Gordon Town Trail.

Local lore says the town was named for the Scottish regiment, the Gordon Highlanders, who were once billeted here. However, others say its name is derived from that of Dr John Gordon, who purchased the botanical gardens – Spring Gardens – that had been established here about 1770, but have since disappeared. For more information, see *The Botanic Gardens of Jamaica*, by Alan Eyre.

To reach Cinchona, Mavis Bank, and the trail to Blue Mountain Peak, turn right at the square and cross the narrow bridge.

Hiking
The Gordon Town Trail begins in Gordon Town and follows the Hope River Valley via Mt Industry and Redlight. Another trail leads from Gordon Town to Sugar Loaf (7000 feet), Content Gap, Top Mountain, and Cinchona (13 miles). The track is very popular with youth groups and gets quite busy on public holidays and weekends. A third track leads via Flamstead and Bellevue, Mt Rosanna, Governor's Bench, and Orchard to Mavis Bank (10 miles).

Places to Stay & Eat
The *Scorpio Inn* (Gordon Town Square, St Andrew, ☎ 927-1602) has six basic rooms for US$25 with shared baths. Also try the *Tip Toe Inn*, a rum shop just below the square. Reportedly it also has rooms.

The most atmospheric place to eat is *King's Jacket Bar & Lounge*, half a mile above Gordon Town.

Getting There & Away
The No 61 bus operates between The Parade and Gordon Town via Old Hope Rd and Papine (US$0.30). Alternately, you can catch the No 70 at Half Way Tree.

WORLD'S END
At first sight, you'll not be sure what to make of this pretty roadside cottage that clings to the mountainside at 2500 feet, three miles from Gordon Town. Despite its Hansel-and-Gretel appearance and outside walls painted with murals, World's End (Gordon Town, ☎ 926-8888, fax 929-8465) is a factory that produces world-famous rums and liqueurs.

It was created by Dr Ian Sangster, who was born in Scotland and came to Jamaica to teach in 1967. The chemist founded Sangster's Old Jamaica Spirits in 1974. From humble beginnings using a 10-gallon blending pot, an analytical balance, and a Scottish genius for distilling, Sangster parlayed two barrels of aged rum into a thriving business. Sangster concocted his beverages from natural extracts of fruits and spices, cane sugar, and mellow aged rum. You can learn how on tours by appointment. Inside, you can watch how the three ingredients are 'married,' a process apparently helped by the diurnal temperature range (from 50°F at night to 92°F by day).

Sangster's cream liqueurs were touted in the movie *Higglers* as aphrodisiacs. Let me know if they work. You can also purchase Golden de Luxe Rum (winner of the Gold Medal for rum in the 1987 International Wine and Spirits Competition), Coconut Rum, and White Rum (111%

proof) which, claims Sangster, 'adds a little power to the smoothness in cocktails.' Each liqueur has its own reproduction ceramic bottle such as the Port Royal Decanter and a handcrafted flagon, and its own label showing a historic scene by famous Jamaican artists from the Institute of Jamaica and National Gallery.

You can sample the goods on a hillside patio where you can sit beneath shade trees and enjoy the views of the valley.

GUAVA RIDGE

Guava Ridge (two miles above World's End) is the site of a hilltop junction for Pine Grove, Content Gap, and Cinchona (to the left), with Mavis Bank straight ahead. En route you'll pass a turnoff for **Petersfield Fruit Forest**, a special project of the National Water Commission.

A road to the right at Guava Ridge leads through patches of forget-me-nots to several summer homes, including **Nyumbani**, the retreat of the Manley family, and **Flamstead**, a lookout from which Horatio Nelson and other British naval officers once surveyed the Port Royal base, sending their messages with mirrors. Raphael Semmes, the US commander of the *Alabama*, visited Flamstead in 1863 and wrote, 'In those mountains of Jamaica I was in an entirely new world, and was enchanted with everything I saw.' Most visitors to Flamstead today feel the same.

CONTENT GAP

About three miles north of Guava Ridge is the hamlet of Content Gap, a center of coffee production by small-scale farmers. A trail leads downhill from here to Gordon Town.

Another heads uphill from the water tank at Content Gap to **Charlottenburg**, a well-preserved great house with original antique furnishings and still extant slave quarters. The mile-long walk takes about 20 minutes. The house is backed by a forested mountainside. Tours can be arranged by calling ☎ 978-3530 or 927-0752.

Places to Stay & Eat

Lawyer and radio personality Ronnie Thwaites owns *Pine Grove* (Content Gap PA, St Andrew, ☎ 977-8001), a popular Kingstonian family retreat on a bluff with a 360° view. Its 16 small and simply furnished rooms are overpriced at US$70, but they are charming, with two double beds, full kitchens, small verandas, and TVs. Private bathrooms have hot water. The tranquil setting is made more so by the pretty, English-style gardens reached via red-brick pathways and terraces. Bamboo and eucalyptus abound. The all-wood restaurant with wicker furniture is popular with Kingstonians for dinner and Sunday brunch. Meals are by reservation only, even for guests. Pine Grove maintains its own coffee farm.

You may be able to stay at Charlottenburg Great House by prior arrangement (1 Dublin Castle Close, Gordon Town; ☎ 978-3530, 927-0752, or 927-2585).

CLYDESDALE

Clydesdale is a charming old coffee plantation and a popular spot for budget accommodations. The estate was taken over in 1937 by the newly formed Forestry Dept, which established a nursery. The much-battered water wheel and coffee mill machinery are partially intact. It has picnic spots and a small waterfall where you can skinny-dip. The **Morces Gap Trail** begins here.

Places to Stay

Clydesdale has a hostel-type dormitory and modestly furnished cabin. Contact the Forestry Dept for reservations (173 Constant Spring Rd, ☎ 924-2667). Don't expect to arrive unannounced and be welcomed. Pick up your cabin reservations in Kingston before heading into the mountains and bring your own food. You can also camp at Clydesdale, which has water, toilets, and basic kitchen facilities (US$5).

An *Eco-Holiday Village* is advertised north of St Peters (the turnoff is about 500 yards above the turnoff for Cinchona).

Getting There & Away

The turnoff is two miles beyond Content Gap, just above the hamlet of St Peters. Immediately you'll cross the Chestervale Bridge over the Brook's River, where 'Brother' Joseph Wolfe, an old man with a yellow beard and flowing gray dreadlocks, sells superior quality coffee (US$5 a pound) and fresh vegetables from his roadside stand. Immediately beyond Wolfe's is a Y-fork. Take the left, steeply uphill for Cinchona. It's a terribly rocky drive, suited for a 4WD only. After three miles you'll reach Clydesdale.

CINCHONA

Cinchona is one of the most spectacularly situated botanical gardens in the world, with fabulous views north to the peaks and down the valleys of the Clyde, Green, and Yallahs Rivers. It was founded in 1868 when cinchona (an Andean plant) was planted for quinine, which is extracted from the bark, to fight malaria. It proved unprofitable, however, and was abandoned. When the cinchona died out, the grounds were turned into an experimental botanical garden to supply Kingston with flowers.

Cinchona has been kept up rather than maintained. Today it takes up a mere 30 acres, much of the land where cinchona and Assam tea were once cultivated having passed into coffee. It gets virtually no visitors, but is well worth the journey. Cinchona is a veritable world's Who's Who of botanical species: rubber trees, eucalyptus, oleander, rhododendron, juniper, cork oak, pecan, peach, and red-barked Blue Mountain yacca, Canary Island pines, massive rhododendrons, and azaleas that explode riotously in spring. Summer brings blue agapanthus and other lilies out in bloom.

The old governor's house sits atop the gardens, fronted by lawns and looking a bit dilapidated (Hurricanes Allen in 1980 and Gilbert in 1988 gave it a thorough beating). The **Panorama Walk** begins to the east of the gardens. And half a dozen other tracks lead off into the nether reaches of the mountains. No one should attempt to go any further without a guide.

Places to Stay

You can camp here for US$5, but you must reserve in person at the Forestry Dept at 173 Constant Spring Rd, Kingston (☎ 924-2667).

Getting There & Away

Finding Cinchona may prove difficult without a guide. Continue uphill from Clydesdale for two miles until you reach a three-way junction. A house and coffee nursery called Top Mountain sit on a knoll overlooking the junction (there's another farmhouse directly ahead; the Ministry of Agriculture maintains an experimental vegetable farm and temperate fruit orchards here). Take the steep uphill track that leads north past Top Mountain. Keep left at the Y-junction and continue aiming uphill. It's a vertiginous drive, like scaling a mountain, and the track is rutted deep enough to bottom your chassis.

MAVIS BANK

Mavis Bank is a tidy little village with a church at its center. The JABLUM coffee factory here is one of four coffee-processing plants through which all legally defined Blue Mountain coffee must pass. It's owned by Keble Munn, former Minister of Agriculture, and a descendant of National Hero George William Gordon. His coffee is marketed ready-roasted and vacuum-sealed under the Jablum and Mavis Bank labels, though much is sold to the Coffee Industry Board. You can tour the factory by appointment (☎ 924-9503). The factory – brick buildings centered around a huge patio covered with drying coffee beans – is in a hollow below the road on the west side as you approach the village. Also see the sidebar Hallowed Grounds in Facts about Jamaica.

You'll find a small post office at the foot of the village, on the north side where a rough road to the left leads uphill to Westphalia. The police station (☎ 977-8004) is next to the post office.

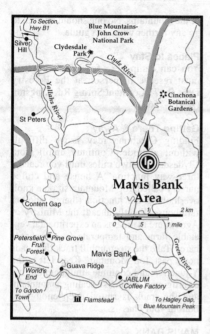

Mavis Bank Area

To Section, Hwy B1
Silver Hill
Clydesdale Park
Blue Mountains-John Crow National Park
Clyde River
Yallahs River
St Peters
Cinchona Botanical Gardens
Content Gap
0   1   2 km
0   .5   1 mile
Petersfield Pine Grove Fruit Forest
Mavis Bank
Guava Ridge
Green River
World's End
To Gordon Town
JABLUM Coffee Factory
Flamstead
To Hagley Gap, Blue Mountain Peak

Hiking

You can rent guides from a small rum shop called Hikers Guide Rest Point. It even offers mules for hikes to Blue Mountain Peak. The trail begins at Churchyard Rd and leads steeply uphill for five miles to Penlyne Castle; see Organized Hikes under Blue Mountain Peak below.

Places to Stay & Eat

There's no hotel in town, but you can rent rooms with locals, as well as with owners Jill and Paul Byles at *Paraiso* (☎ 977-8007 or 924-9505), a farmstead between Guava Ridge and Mavis Bank. *Hikers Guide Rest Point* serves inexpensive I-tal food. It's a great place to chat with locals.

Getting There & Away

The No 62 bus from Papine runs via Gordon Town and Guava Ridge to Mavis Bank (US$0.30). A taxi from Kingston to Mavis Bank costs about US$12. If you're driving, turn left for Mavis Bank at the

unmarked T-junction, one and a half miles east of Guava Ridge (the road ahead leads to Tower Hill).

HAGLEY GAP

This ramshackle village sits abreast a hill east of Mavis Bank, and is the gateway to the Blue Mountain Peak. It's a center for cultivation of pimento, which often lies scattered on the ground to dry. You can take a tour of the Home Spun Art & Craft Workshop, about 200 yards uphill on the road to Penlyne Castle and Blue Mountain Peak.

Beyond Hagley Gap, the 'main' road continues downhill to the Negro River and, beyond, the remote hamlets of Woburn Lawn and Cedar Valley, where Pippa Fray offers rooms for rent; ☎ 925-5651 or 925-4955. By serendipitously following the dirt roads, you'll eventually end up on the coast road near Eleven Mile and Bull Bay.

A post office is located 200 yards beyond the village center, on the left.

Places to Eat

You'll find several funky little restaurants, highlighted by the Rasta-hued *Jah Errol Ital Corner* and *Toppy's Bar* – funky rum shops both serving inexpensive I-tal food. Toppy's also has a small gift store.

Getting There & Away

You can catch bus No LS618 from The Parade. It runs to Hagley Gap via Bull Bay and Cedar Valley (US$0.40).

If driving, continue straight from Mavis Bank and you'll pass through Mahogany Vale and, half a mile beyond, ford the Yallahs River. The road then climbs steeply, deteriorating gradually all the way to Hagley Gap.

PENLYNE CASTLE

Penlyne Castle is the base for hikes to Blue Mountain Peak, seven miles away. Most hikers overnight at two lodges here before tackling the hike in the wee hours, as they have since at least 1925 when a Miss Steadman opened Wilderness Lodge to hikers. The dirt road ascends less than a mile beyond Whitfield as far as Abbey

Green, after which you must abandon your vehicle and hike.

Places to Stay & Eat
Camping Camping (US$5) is allowed at *Whitfield Hall* (see below) if the hostel is full. The campground is on a wide lawn beneath eucalyptus. There are camp tables, benches, and a BBQ pit, as well as water, toilets, and a basic kitchen.

Hostels *Wildflower Lodge* (10 Ellesmere Rd, Kingston 10, ☎ 929-5394/5) is a substantial hardwood structure with an atmospheric dining room with a huge hardwood table and benches . There are hammocks in the dining room and on the veranda, which faces southeast down the mountain. It has 36 bunks in basic rooms with communal bathrooms (US$12), plus three more-appealing private rooms with private bathrooms downstairs (US$25 to US$30), and a two-bedroom cottage (US$60, up to four people) at the bottom of the garden. Meals cost US$6. You also have use of a large but basic kitchen. It offers horseback rides, and guides for the climb, and has a well-stocked gift shop selling film plus arts and crafts. Adult camps are held on weekends year-round, and children's summer camps in July and August.

About 400 yards uphill, nestled amid pine trees, is *Whitfield Hall*, a more basic option with bunks for up to 40 people. It pervades true hostel ambiance (c/o John Algrove, 8 Almon Crescent, Kingston 6, ☎ 927-0986). The large lounge has a huge fireplace (there's a US$3 firewood charge), a smoke-stained ceiling, and aged hardwood floor. An old grandfather clock ticks softly. It also contains a piano and an asthmatic antique pump organ. Brass gaslamps provide illumination. Guests share basic bathrooms with deep tubs (cold water only), plus a small kitchen (bring your own food; you can buy canned peaches here for US$1.75). Bunks cost US$12 per person (US$9 children; US$7 Peace Corps and students). You can hire mules (US$34) and guides (US$3 per person; US$14 to the peak).

Reportedly, *Abbey Green* (☎ 922-8705) also has basic beds and kitchen facilities, plus camping.

Getting There & Away
Penlyne Castle is reached via a dirt road that ascends precipitously from opposite Toppy's Bar in Hagley Gap. Only 4WD vehicles can make the journey, which is dauntingly rugged. You'll reach a T-junction after 2.8 miles, with Penlyne Castle to the left and the hostels to the right. Jeeps can be rented in Hagley Gap to take you up the tortuous, gutted road (reportedly US$20, up to six people).

Whitfield Hall offers transfers by Land Rover from Mavis Bank (US$20 up to six people; US$3 per person for seven or more) or Kingston (US$41; or US$5 per person). Most hotels elsewhere in the Blue Mountain offer 4WD transfers to Penlyne Castle.

BLUE MOUNTAIN PEAK
It's a 3000-foot ascent from Penlyne Castle to the summit of Blue Mountain Peak (7402 feet) – a three- or four-hour hike. It's not a serious challenge, but you need to be reasonably fit, especially to tackle the arduous switchback to a ridge called Lazy Man's Peak (named for the hikers who decide to quit here).

The well-maintained trail is threatened by erosion, and also by trash from those with no respect for the wilderness. Be a responsible hiker! Don't litter or take short-cuts off the trail, which is *illegal* and leads to soil erosion. Wooden signs wisely advise you to 'Stay on the Path.' Rock slides, mud pools, and drop-offs are among the potential hazards if you stray. One of the saddest sights is the graffiti at the halfway hut at Portland Gap.

Most hikers choose to set off from Penlyne Castle in the wee hours to reach the peak in time for sunrise. (It's best not to hike without a guide at night. Numerous spur trails lead off the main trails and it is easy to get lost. The Blue Mountains are not kind to those who lose their way.) Your guide will rouse you at about 2 am, sometimes earlier. Fortified with a breakfast of

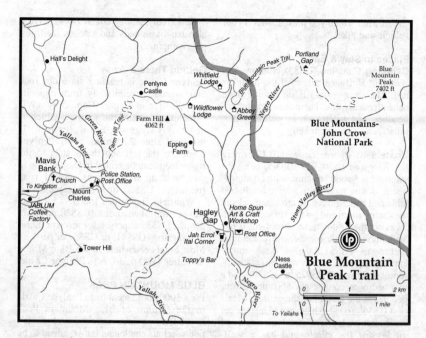

coffee and cereal, you set out single file in the pitch black along the 7½-mile trail (you'll need a flashlight and a spare set of batteries). Midway, at Portland Gap, there's a ranger station on a ridge, surrounded by ginger lilies and hydrangeas.

As you hike, reggae music can be heard far, far below, competing with the chirps of crickets and the *sshhhhh sshhhhh* of katydids singing to attract mates. Myriad blinkies and peeny-wallies will be doing the same, signaling, with their phosphorescent semaphore. With luck, you might pass a 'blinking tree' where the beetles collect and glow en masse, sometimes synchronistically like a lighthouse. Eerie! Even better is if you choose to hike on a moonlit night.

You should arrive at the peak around 5:30 am, while it is still dark. The lights of Kingston glimmer to the southeast, and those of Port Antonio to the north. Dawn is sublime. First, a sliver of pink light arcs across the eastern sky. The star-filled, black

sky soon grades through every shade of purple and blue. Your stage is gradually revealed: a flat-topped hump, marked by a tiny pyramid and metal pole. A short trail leads to the edge of the peak. To the southeast is the distinctive hump of Sugar Loaf. From its peak (which casts a distinct shadow over the land below), Cuba can be seen hovering on the horizon, 90 miles away. After a brief celebratory drink and snacks, you'll set off back down the mountain the way you came. Before you know it, you'll be back at Whitfield or Wildflower in time for brunch.

You don't have to set off at an ungodly hour. By setting out a few hours later, say 5 am, you may still make the top before the mists roll in, and you will have the benefit of enjoying the changing vegetation and unraveling scenery with greater anticipation for what lies ahead (and above). You pass through several distinct ecosystems, including an area of bamboo and primordial giant tree ferns further down. Further

Kingston sunset from the Blue Mountains

LEE ABEL

The Kingston art scene is alive and well.

Well-preserved Devon House in Kingston lures antique lovers and wedding parties.

View toward Newcastle from Strawberry Hill in the Blue Mountains

Wag Water River, en route from
Kingston to Port Maria

At Old Tavern Estate in the Blue Mountains,
the view is stunning and the coffee superb.

up is cloud forest, dripping with filaments of hanging lichens and festooned with epiphytes and moss. Near the top is stunted dwarf or elfin forest, with trees such as hirsute soapwood and rodwood no more than eight feet high – an adaptation to the extremes of cold.

What to Bring

Although hiking boots or tough walking shoes are best, sneakers *(buggas* or *puss boots)* will suffice, though your feet will probably get wet. At the top it can be icy with the wind blowing, and temperatures can approach freezing before sun-up, so wear plenty of layers. Rain gear is also essential, as weather can change rapidly. Clouds usually begin to form in early morning and are sure to be followed by a cold breeze.

Guides

Experienced guides can be hired locally at Hagley Gap, Penlyne Castle, or from Maya Lodge at Jack's Hill; rates are around US$20 per half-day or US$30 for a full day.

Altitude Sickness

A few people experience dizziness and/or drowsiness at elevations as low as 7000 feet, though you'll not be on the mountain long enough for this to be of urgent concern. Don't overnight at the top if you feel sick.

Organized Hikes

Sense Adventure (Box 216, Kingston 7, ☎ 927-2097, fax 929-6967) organizes a one-day 'Blue Mountain Trek' (US$55 minimum) that includes a picnic at 5000 feet on Mount Horeb. It also has a two-day 'Blue Mountain Peak Sunrise' trip.

Places to Stay

Most hikers overnight at *Wildflower Lodge* or *Whitfield Hall* (see Penlyne Castle). A funky 'cabin' (little more than a lean-to) 40 feet below the summit can be rented for US$2.50 from the Forestry Service (173 Constant Spring Rd, Kingston, ☎ 924-2667). A barrel at the summit collects rainwater (it normally has a fair share of dead bugs and detritus – use a clean cloth as a strainer). The Forestry Service also maintains a more substantial cabin halfway up the trail at Portland Gap (2.3 miles above Abbey Green). Latest word was that the shelter is closed. You can pitch a tent outside, where there's a cooking area and water from a pipe. Again, this is by reservation only.

East Coast

The east coast is Jamaica's undiscovered quarter – one geared toward the traveler rather than the tourist. It's the island's least accessible region, and also its wettest. White-sand beaches and colonial-era edifices are relatively few. Hence, the east coast parishes receive far fewer tourists than elsewhere. That's the appeal. It remains off-the-beaten-path. The sparsely populated region (population 160,000) is also ruggedly beautiful, with the Blue Mountains forming a handsome spine separating the parishes of Portland and St Thomas. Exploring is easy, as it's circled by the A4, which hugs the coastline with only brief forays inland. The hinterlands of the John Crow Mountains and Blue Mountains are for serious adventurers only.

St Thomas Parish

The parish of St Thomas lies in the shadow of the Blue Mountains. It's drier than its northern neighbor, Portland; progressively so further west where the narrow coastal plain is covered with scrub. The south-facing coast is also much gentler than that of the northeast, with several appealing gray-sand beaches. Only a limited tourist infrastructure exists, however. Towns are few and far between and life revolves mostly around small fishing villages where the work is still performed by canoe and net. The exception is Morant Bay, which rose to moderate importance in the late 18th century as an export port for sugar grown on the broad alluvial plain of the southeast.

The area is one of Jamaica's poorest, as reflected by the pitiful living conditions of many of the plantations workers on the flatlands east of Port Morant. Conditions have always been harsh here, and the area figured prominently in rebellions during the colonial era.

HIGHLIGHTS

- Morant Point Lighthouse – getting there is half the fun, and you'll have the beach to yourself
- Boston Bay for the best – and hottest – jerk in Jamaica
- Guided hiking in the Rio Grande Valley
- Peaceful, enchanting Blue Lagoon
- Exhilarating Reach Falls for cooling fresh water dips

YALLAHS

East of the parish boundary between St Andrew and St Thomas, the A4 from Kingston makes a hairpin descent to Grants Pen then winds through scrub-covered country, rising and falling until it reaches the coast at the village of Yallahs, 10 miles east of Bull Bay. The word derives from the Spanish word *Ayala*, the name of a local cattle ranch before the English arrived in 1655. Cattle and goats still wander the streets of town.

At press time the finishing touches were being put to a bridge over the wide gully of the Yallahs River, two miles west of Yallahs. It's about time! During heavy rains the ford was often impossible and vehicles had to take a circuitous route up the river valley to Easington and cross an iron bridge to return to the coast. (Note: you can still make the journey to witness Revivalist spirit-cult meetings that are occasionally held on the eastern riverbank near the old bridge.)

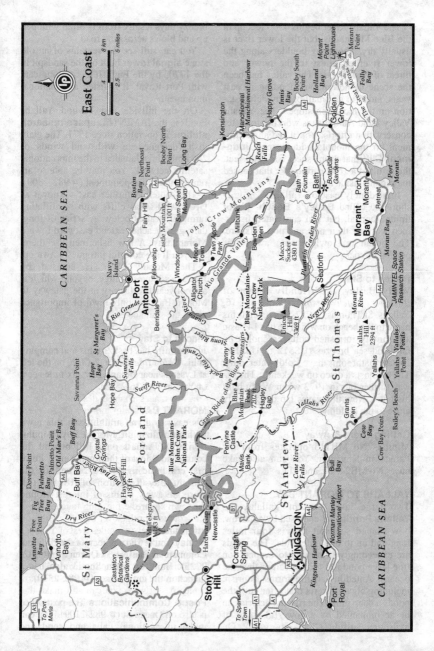

The Yallahs River begins 4500 feet up in the Blue Mountains, but the lower river is usually dry. The many boulders along the lower riverbed attest to the power and threat of flash floods. The valley has been the scene of horrendous flooding in past years, aided in no small part by deforestation on the mountain slopes. The Yallahs Valley Land Authority is working to foster conservation efforts. You'll see an escarpment on the mountainside named **Judgment Cliff** that drops sheer for 1000 feet, the result of a 1692 earthquake that caused the mountainside to collapse.

Immediately east of Yallahs is a gray shoreline called **Bailey's Beach**. It's of limited appeal, but you can watch fishermen working their nets and pots offshore. The ocean is slowly eating away this portion of coast.

Places to Stay

Wally Bailey, the friendly owner of *Bailey's Beach Resort* (PO Box 16, Yallahs, St Thomas, ☎ 982-5056), lends his name to the beach on which he has 14 basic and simply furnished cottages cooled by fans and sea breezes (US$12 to US$14). Private bathrooms have cold water only. The bar hosts a disco on weekends. The sea was further out in 1972 when Wally built his hotel. Now the waves lap dangerously close to the buildings.

Getting There & Away

Minibus No MB115 operates from the Parade in Kingston. You can also take buses No MB24, 27, and 111.

YALLAHS TO MORANT BAY

Two large lakes east of Yallahs, the **Yallahs Ponds**, are enclosed by a narrow, bow-shaped sandspit that is four miles long and up to one mile wide. The ponds are exceedingly briny due to evaporation (the large pond is 14 times saltier than the ocean). Antediluvian life forms flourish, including algal bacteria that often turn the ponds a deep pink. The rise in bacteria can be accompanied by a powerful smell of hydrogen sulfide ('bad egg gas'). On breezy days a salty froth is often whipped up and blows across the road.

You can still see the remains of an old stone **signal tower** built on the sandspit in the 1770s by the English to communicate with Port Royal. It is listed as a national monument.

On the hillside just beyond Yallahs Ponds is the JAMINTEL **space research station**, in operation since 1971. The giant dish (designed to withstand winds of 200 mph) links Jamaica to the international satellite network. You may be able to arrange a tour by appointment (☎ 982-2309).

The shoreline further east – known as **Greenwall** - has cliffs with scintillating turquoise waters below. A series of long, dark-gray beaches extend eastward toward Morant Bay. A few fishermen use them, and you'll see colorful pirogues drawn up.

The Morant River is crossed by Jamaica's longest bridge, beyond which is a Goodyear tire factory at the gateway to Morant Bay, the only town of importance along the south coast.

Places to Stay

Joe Corniffe has basic rooms and camping at his *Gold Mine Camp & Club*, on the left at Lyssons near Botany Bay, six miles east of Yallahs (☎ 926-2548).

MORANT BAY

It's easy to drive straight past this town without realizing it. Morant Bay (population 8000) squats on a hill behind the coast road. Most of the town's early colonial-era buildings were burned in the Morant Bay Rebellion of 1865. Still, there are a few points of interest around the town square.

Information

Money You'll find a branch of the National Commercial Bank at 39 Queen St (☎ 982-2225). Bank of Nova Scotia also has a branch in the town center (☎ 982-2310).

Post & Communications The post office is also on Queen St (☎ 982-2109). You can make international calls and send and

The Morant Bay Rebellion

Following emancipation in 1838, the local black population faced widescale unemployment and extreme hardship. These conditions were exacerbated by heavy taxation and the harshness of local magistrates. In the 1860s, Paul Bogle, a black Baptist deacon in the hamlet of Stony Gut, organized passive resistance against the oppression and injustice of the local authorities and planters in St Thomas. He was supported by George William Gordon, a wealthy mulatto planter who had risen to become an assemblyman.

On October 11, 1865, Bogle and 400 supporters marched to the Morant Bay courthouse to protest the severe punishment meted out to a destitute who had been arrested on a petty charge. An armed militia shot into the crowd and a riot ensued in which 28 people were killed, and the courthouse and much of the town center were burned to the ground. The countryside erupted in rioting. Bogle fled with a £2000 bounty on his head but was soon captured by Maroons and hanged the same day from the center arch of the burned-out courthouse. Meanwhile, Gordon was arrested in Kingston, ferried to Morant Bay, condemned by a kangaroo court, and also hanged.

Governor Edward Eyre ordered reprisals. The militia swept through St Thomas, razing more than 1000 houses and summarily executing more than 430 people. The British government was outraged by Eyre's reaction (a tribunal found that the punishments were 'excessive . . . reckless . . . and at Bath positively barbarous'), and forced the Jamaica House of Assembly to relinquish its power to Parliament. Thus the island became a Crown colony, leading to reforms of the harsh judicial system. ■

receive faxes at the Telecommunications of Jamaica office at 2 Church St (☎ 982-2200).

Medical Services Princess Margaret Hospital can provide emergency treatment (54 Lyssons Rd, ☎ 982-2304). There are numerous medical clinics, including at 4 Queen St (☎ 982-2334) and 14 Queen St (☎ 982-1107); Lloyd's Pharmacy is next door (☎ 982-2400). There's another clinic run by Dr Lampart on Lyssons Rd (☎ 982-2343), and Dr Maurice Stanhope has a clinic at 6 East St (☎ 982-2519). You can have prescriptions filled at Marville Pharmacy (8 Rosemary Ave, ☎ 982-2370).

Emergency The police station is at 7 South St (☎ 982-1265 or 982-2233).

Things to See

The **Paul Bogle statue** stands in a little square in front of the courthouse. The work, by noted sculptor Edna Manley, powerfully depicts the national hero standing grimly, elbows out, hands clasped over the hilt of a machete. Another plaque commemorating Bogle can be found at his chapel at Stony Gut.) The attractive **courthouse** was rebuilt in limestone and red brick after being destroyed in the 1865 rebellion. It's topped by an octagonal wooden belfry.

Kitty-corner to the courthouse is a handsome, ochre-painted **Anglican church** dating to 1881.

Nearby is a plaque commemorating those who died in the 1865 struggle and

Paul Bogle statue in front of
Morant Bay courthouse

whose bodies were left to rot on the refuse dump. In 1965, excavations turned up 79 skeletons in a mass grave between the courthouse and the remains of a small, 18th-century **fort**, which retains three small cannons on their carriages. The bodies were re-interred below the fort, where a memorial in a tiny park records that 'they did not die in vain.'

Places to Stay & Eat
Morant Villas sits amid lawns and tall palms atop a bluff on the coast road just east of town (1 Wharf Rd, ☎ 982-2422). Ten simple yet clean rooms have fans and private bathrooms with hot water (US$30). There are also 10 studios with kitchens (US$35). Its breezy restaurant and bar made of hardwood serves seafood for US$6 to US$12. The hotel offers tours by minibus.

About 400 yards east of Morant Villas is *Chef's Seaview Restaurant* (☎ 982-2449) which enjoys a setting overlooking turquoise waters. Its three rooms are basic with fans. A simple restaurant has an outside patio and a dance floor and stage with go-go dancing on weekends. *Caravan Jerk Pork*, on Hope Rd, is recommended for cheap mouth-searing jerk dishes.

Getting There & Away
Bus No MB27 operates between Morant Bay and the Parade in Kingston, as do minibuses No MB111 and MB24.

SEAFORTH
This modestly prosperous agricultural town is the southern gateway to the Blue Mountains. It's reached via a well-paved road that leads north from the large roundabout immediately west of Morant Bay and follows the wide, level valley of the Morant River inland through banana plantations.

From Seaforth, a paved road leads west and gradually ascends the Rio Negro Valley to Trinity Ville. Further west the road deteriorates as it climbs more steeply to Cedar Valley and Hagley Gap, where the hiking trail to Blue Mountain Peak begins (see Blue Mountains chapter). Another road heads east across the foothills to Bath.

RETREAT
Retreat is a small beachside residential community about three miles east of Morant Bay. It sits between two of the few pleasant beaches along the southern coast. Aptly named **Golden Shore Beach** is hidden from view from the road. Watch for the hand-painted sign.

The beach extends east two miles to **Prospect Beach**, a 'public bathing beach' maintained by the UDC. The area is a popular relaxation spot for locals and Kingstonians, many of whom maintain holiday homes at Retreat.

Places to Stay & Eat
On the main road one mile east of Retreat is *Brown's Guest House* (☎ 982-6205). The bungalow is run as a B&B and has five large rooms painted in gaudy tropical colors. Each has private bath with hot water. Rooms cost US$14. It's a homey place with simple 1960s utility furniture. You walk through a coconut grove to reach the beach. Alternately, try *Saunder's Beach Cottage*, 400 yards further east and reached by a dirt road that leads down to the shore (☎ 982-2215). The modest house has simple rooms for about US$10.

Another appealing option nearby is *Goldfinger's Guest House*, which has modest rooms with private bathroom for US$100 double (Lot 21, Retreat, St Thomas, ☎ 982-2581). There's another guest house – *Visitors Rest* – on the main road, 200 yards before the turnoff for Prospect Beach.

At Golden Shore Beach, *Golden Beach Resort* (☎ 982-9657) has 15 rooms in a condominium-style unit set amid landscaped grounds. They're clean and boast refreshing, contemporary furnishings. Downstairs rooms have patios with grills. Upstairs rooms have air-con. Year-round rates are about US$40 double. A small restaurant for alfresco dining was being built at press time.

For something more elegant, try *Whispering Bamboo Cove* at 105 Crystal Drive, Retreat (☎ 982-2912). It's a gleaming-white, contemporary, villa-style hotel with a columned portico entrance and wrought-iron lamps on the walls. The 10 rooms are airy and spacious and tastefully furnished with tropical fabrics and antique reproductions. Jamaican artwork abounds. Light pours in through wide French doors. Rooms (US$46 to US$66) have cable TV and telephone, plus king-size beds and wide patios or balconies. Solar-powered heating guarantees hot water. The gracious restaurant opens onto lawns. A separate, self-contained, two-bedroom cottage with kitchenette costs US$86.

The UDC has a down-at-the-heels bar and restaurant at Prospect Beach. A funky jerk shack called *Paradise Cove* has heaps more color. The most atmospheric place for miles is a funky bay-front eatery called the *Shipwreck Seafood Bar & Restaurant*, five miles east of Retreat. Traditional Jamaican dishes cost less than US$3, and you can look down over a bay where fishing pirogues are beached and nets hung out to dry.

Getting There & Away
Lee Chong Young operates a minibus (No STBW586) to Retreat from the Parade in Kingston.

PORT MORANT
This small, one-street town lies at the head of a deep bay. It offers nothing of interest except a marina equipped with necessities. It was here that Captain William Bligh introduced the breadfruit to Jamaica following his disastrous trip to the South Pacific in the HMS *Bounty* (it is said that part of the reason his crew mutinied was because he denied them water, which he used to keep the breadfruit plants alive). Bligh survived and went on to try a second time to transport breadfruit to the Caribbean. In 1795 he arrived at Port Morant with his precious cargo covering the deck. The first breadfruit trees were planted nearby at Bath Botanical Garden, where they can still be seen. Bligh received 1500 guineas reward from the Assembly of Jamaica.

Bowden Marina
About 1½ miles east of Port Morant, a road to the right leads to a threadbare marina (☎ 982-8223) rimmed by mangroves in the middle of Bowden Bay. Oysters are farmed here. Berthing costs US$0.50 per foot. There are showers and restrooms, plus gasoline, diesel (J$50 per gallon), and water. I'm not sure why you'd want to anchor here, except by necessity.

There's a National Commercial Bank opposite the gas station, and a police station nearby (☎ 982-2018).

Places to Eat
The best place to eat is *Young's Bar & Restaurant*, opposite the turnoff for Bath. You'll pay about US$2 for curried goat, ackee and codfish, and other staples. Half a mile east of town, *Ace's Beach Club & Restaurant* has an unappealing setting, but its seafood dishes cost less than US$2. It hosts dancehall raves at night and occasionally on weekends.

Getting There & Away
You can take bus No MB127 from the Parade in Kingston. It continues east as far as Golden Grove.

BATH

This down-at-the-heels village, six miles north of Port Morant, lies on the bank of the Garden River, whose valley is dominated by sugarcane and banana plantations. The town owes its existence to the discovery of hot mineral springs in the hills behind the present town in the late 17th century. A spa was developed, and socialites flocked in and built town houses here. The period of splendor was brief. Today, it's a run-down, melancholy place whose poverty attests to the pitiful wages paid to plantation workers.

The one-street town has a post office, police station (☎ 982-2115), and a Shell gas station.

Bath Botanical Garden

At the east end of town is an old limestone church shaded by royal palms that flank the entrance to the second-oldest botanical garden in the Western Hemisphere. The gardens were established by the government in 1779. Many of the exotics introduced to Jamaica were first planted here: bougainvillea, cinnamon, mango, jackfruit, jacaranda, and, most famously, the breadfruit brought at such cost from the South Pacific by Captain William Bligh. Many of the species are labeled. However, the garden has seen better days. It is frequently inundated when the river floods its banks, and Hurricane Gilbert pummeled it badly in 1988.

Bath Fountain

Local legend says that in the 1690s a runaway slave discovered hot mineral springs that cured the injuries he had received while escaping. He was so impressed by the miracle that he returned to tell his master (posterity doesn't record whether the slave was rewarded or punished). In 1699 the government bought the spring and an adjoining 1130 acres, created the Bath of St Thomas the Apostle, then formed a corporation to found the town of Bath and administer mineral baths for the sick and infirm. Thirty slaves built the road and the hospital that offered free treatment to the desperately ill. The waters are high in sulfur, magnesium, lime, and other minerals and have therapeutic value for treating skin ailments and rheumatic problems. Back then, however, it was generally believed that the waters would cure everything from venereal disease to nervous spasms.

By the mid-18th century the springs had been usurped by wealthy planters and English gentry seeking cures for the 'dry bellyache' caused by overindulgence, for as Lady Nugent recorded in her famous diaries: 'they ate like cormorants and drank like porpoises.' It wasn't long before the unusual effects of the water had created a new demand: as the historian Edward Long recorded, drinking the water 'diffuses a thrilling glow over the whole body; and the continued use enlivens the spirits, and sometimes produces the same joyous effects as inebriation. On this account, some notorious topers have quitted their claret for a while and come hither, merely for the sake of a little variety in their practice of debauch, and to enjoy the singular felicity of getting drunk on water.'

Two springs issue from beneath the existing bath house. The water can be scorching (it varies from 115°F to 128°F). You soak in a deep, ceramic-tiled pools (US$2.50 for 20 minutes). The homey spa also offers full-body massages for US$35, plus facial and scalp and other massages (US$25). It's open on Tuesday to Sunday, 10 am to 5 pm. On weekends it's best arrive there early, before the crowds from Kingston arrive. To get there, turn left opposite the church and botanical gardens and follow the winding road two miles uphill.

Hiking

A trail leads from Bath Fountain up over Cuna Cuna Gap to the Rio Grande Valley, Moore Town, and the north coast. You might want to try to hire a guide in Bath. Experienced hikers, however, can obtain Sheet 19 (showing St Thomas Parish) and Sheet 14 (showing Portland Parish) of the Ordnance Survey 1:12,500 map series from the Survey Dept at 23½ Charles St, Kingston. They cost US$5 each.

Places to Stay & Eat

Your only option is the *Bath Spa Hotel* (☎ 982-2132), a recently renovated, pink colonial hotel that dates to 1747 and contains the spa baths on the ground floor. The modestly furnished bedrooms are clinically white (appropriately, the hotel is called 'the hospital' locally). You can choose between rooms with shared (US$22) or private bath (US$30). It has a small restaurant serving Jamaican cuisine. There are no other restaurants, just a few little rum shops serving food. One of the best is the pocket-sized *Smart's Bar*, opposite the post office. Expect the locals to be cool toward you at first.

Getting There & Away

The No MB113 bus to and from the Parade in Kingston stops outside the church. Two other buses – the MB25 and MB90 – also operate to Bath from the Parade. It's about a 90-minute journey (US$0.50 by bus; US$2 by minibus). If traveling from Morant Bay, take bus No LS975, which costs about US$0.10.

Bath is six miles north of Port Morant. The drive is incredibly scenic. From Bath, the road continues east for six miles to the crossroads at Hordley. It is abysmally potholed and makes for slow and frustrating driving.

MORANT POINT

To the east of Port Morant is a large, marshy peninsula – Morant Point – that juts out into the Atlantic Ocean in the shape of the head of a barking dog.

From the A4, a dirt road (two miles east of Port Morant) leads to New Pera, where occasional reggae concerts are held at **Rocky Point Beach**. The road loops west around the headland one mile to the tiny hamlet of Old Pera, where a ruined windmill sits on a hilltop overlooking the rocky coves. There are mangrove swamps east of Rocky Point, so you'll have to turn inland and zigzag through a maze of dirt tracks to the hamlet of Dalvey, from where you can reach Morant Point Lighthouse.

Morant Point Lighthouse

This 100-foot-tall, red-and-white-striped edifice marks Morant Point, the easternmost tip of Jamaica, and the southern end of **Holland Bay**, a lonesome and spectacularly pretty white-sand beach backed by mangroves.

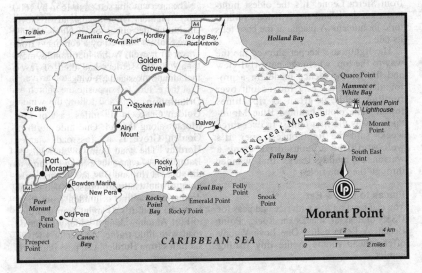

A friendly guide at the
Morant Point Lighthouse

The 18-foot-wide cast-iron tube was erected in 1841 by freed African slaves from Sierra Leone. It's the oldest lighthouse on the island and is listed as a historic monument. A plaque at the base tells its tale.

The lighthouse-keeper showed me the way to the top, where the powerful view and the windy silence made for a profound experience as I looked out over rippling fields as green as ripe limes towards the cloud-haunted Blue Mountains. I was the first tourist in over three weeks said the lighthouse-keeper. It's well worth the arduous drive along a warren of muddy tracks that wander through the cane fields.

Places to Stay & Eat
You can feast on fish with rice and peas for US$3 or less at shacks on Rocky Point Beach. A Rasta called One Love Woody offers cheap rooms in the tiny fishing hamlet.

Getting There & Away
Although you can get there from Dalvey, it is more easily reached by car from the gas station on the A4 in Golden Grove. However, it's a labyrinthine course, and there are lots of lefts and rights to choose from. You'll need a guide to lead you; ask at the gas station. A 4WD is recommended, although I managed the journey in a small sedan.

Minibuses and bus No MB112 (US$0.60) operate as far as Dalvey from Kingston and Morant Bay. Alternately, take bus No LS289 from Port Antonio to Golden Grove (US$0.50).

GOLDEN GROVE
Golden Grove is a desperately poor hamlet of corrugated-tin and wood huts on stilts dominated by the plantations of Tropicana Sugar Estates, east of the road, and the banana plantations of Fyffes to the west. Few dwellings have running water, as the number of people carrying buckets attests. At least it has a gas station.

Many of the locals are descended from Africans from Sierra Leone who settled on the sugar estates in the decades following emancipation.

The area was first settled in 1656 by 1600 white planters from the island of Nevis (including the governor of Nevis, Major Luke Stokes) induced by a command from Oliver Cromwell. Within four months, more than half the settlers had died of fever, including Stokes and his wife.

Orientation
Golden Grove is six miles east of Port Morant along the A4. One mile north of Golden Grove is a crossroads named Hordley. The road going west leads to Bath. The A4 continues east and returns to the shore at Holland Bay, the southernmost point of the windward coast. Much of the dramatic shoreline is hidden from view from the road. It's 31 miles from Hordley to Port Antonio along a wide, well-paved road with little traffic. At Hector's River, six miles from Hordley, you pass into Portland Parish.

Stokes Hall

The Stokes family is commemorated by Stokes Hall (one mile south of Golden Grove), which was built by the Major's three sons who survived the fever and prospered. The thick-stone-walled house is one of few buildings of note in St Thomas Parish, with its fortified towers at each corner. The ruins are protected by the Jamaica National Trust. From on high you have a restricted view over the sugar fields and Duckenfield sugar factory to the southwest. You'll have to hunt to find Stokes Hall, however, as it is hidden behind thick foliage atop a hill; there are no signs, but follow a dirt road toward the ocean for about one mile.

Getting There & Away

You can reach Golden Grove from Kingston by bus No 127, which departs from the Parade, and from Port Antonio by bus No LS289.

Portland Parish

North of the Blue Mountain spine lies Portland Parish, Jamaica's most mountainous parish. This is the island's windward corner, where surf rolls ashore into perfect coves, and waves chew at rocky headlands. The only town of importance is Port Antonio, popular with budget travelers looking for a more offbeat spot. A fistful of world-famous, deluxe resort-hotels centered on the best beaches recall the days when Errol Flynn and other luminaries lent the area renown and panache.

Hurricane Gilbert came ashore here in 1988; tree-littered beaches, torn-up docks, and felled trees are constant reminders that this area took Gilbert's punch on the nose.

Jamaica's coastline is at its most dramatic east of Port Antonio, where a string of white-sand beaches are enclosed by plunging cliffs and set against dramatic mountain backdrops.

History

Portland Parish was one of the last areas of Jamaica to be populated. In the 18th century the government was eager to settle the area as a buffer against raids by marauding Maroons, bands of escaped slaves who lived in redoubts deep in the Blue Mountains. The English offered inducements to settlers, including tax-free land grants, and two barrels of beef and one of flour to each settler so that he could feed himself and his family until he reaped his first crop. Few settlers accepted the colonial government's offer. In 1734 the Maroons were finally subdued and a peace treaty signed. With Port Antonio secure, it became possible to settle the hinterland.

The rich alluvial soil and damp climate of Portland suited bananas, which the Spanish had introduced from the Canary Islands. Sugar plantations arose, but the banana was grown chiefly for domestic consumption. A Yankee skipper named Captain Lorenzo Dow (1840 – 1908) began the banana trade that would boost the economic prospects of eastern Jamaica when he loaded his vessel with the fruit in 1870 and sold them at a fantastic profit in Boston (see History under Port Antonio below). The following year he sailed into Port Antonio and traded his cargo for coconuts and 1450 stems of bananas that earned him a profit of US$2000. Dow and his Boston Fruit Co went on to own 40 banana plantations from Port Antonio to Buff Bay. He also bought up much of Port Antonio and developed Boundbrook Wharf. Bananas were planted throughout the island, but nowhere could compete with Portland Parish.

Portland's brief heyday was doomed in the 1930s by the onset of Panama disease, which ravaged the crops. More resistant strains of banana have since been planted.

Climate

Portland is famed for its high rainfall (to be fair, most of the rain falls at night), and the scent of a recent shower always hangs in the air. Seasonal variations in rainfall are less pronounced in Portland than elsewhere in the country. Here, year-round, moist, northeast trade winds meet the John Crow and Blue Mountains, which force the saturated air to rise and cool. The moisture condenses and falls in torrents. Parts of upland Portland have recorded more than 300 inches of rain a year, some of the heaviest rainfall in the world.

Flora & Fauna
The vegetation is correspondingly lush. The forested mountains with their deep gorges and rushing rivers beckon invitingly, but remain virtually inaccessible to all but hardy hikers. Fortunately, new trails and recreational activities are opening up the Rio Grande Valley and newly formed Blue Mountains-John Crow National Park. The upland regions are a last refuge for the guinea pig-like Jamaican coney, and for the world's largest butterfly, the giant swallowtail.

HAPPY GROVE
Three miles south of Manchioneal you'll pass Happy Grove High School, which stands atop a wild rocky shore. It's a good place to stop and admire the coastal vistas, which grow increasingly dramatic to the north. The village of **Hector's River** is one mile south, on the border of Portland and St Thomas, where the road drops onto the southeastern flatlands. The view from on high is spectacular.

Happy Grove to Port Antonio
While hugging Jamaica's northeastern coastline, the A4 winds around a series of deep bays and privately owned tiny coves. This is where the chic homes are hidden from view amid dramatically lush foliage that brushes up against your car. You can rent many of the private villas; contact the Jamaica Association of Villas & Apartments for a complete list and rates (JAVA, PO Box 298, Ocho Rios, ☎ 974-2508, fax 974-2967; in the USA, 1370 Washington, Suite 301, Miami Beach, FL 33139,

☎ (305) 673-6688, fax (305) 673-5666). You'll find some superb little beaches and there are several unspoiled fishing villages where budget travelers can rent cottages and ease into a laid-back local lifestyle.

REACH FALLS
Although a traditional favorite of JTB posters, these cascades remained virtually unvisited until a year or two ago, when the below-the-falls sex scene in the movie *Cocktail* spawned the waterfall's newfound fame. Now tour buses arrive from Port Antonio and as far away as Ocho Rios (the falls are not worth the long journey from Ocho Rios). Time your visit right and it remains a peaceful spot surrounded by virgin rainforest. A series of cascades tumble over limestone tiers from one hollowed, jade-colored pool to another. A half-mile hike upriver leads to Mandingo Cave, which has a whirlpool. Note the sign that reads: 'Beware of deep pools and strong currents.'

A somewhat-surly squatter named Frank Clarke has parlayed his piece of illicit real estate into a money maker. Frank charges US$1.25 entrance to descend the concrete steps that lead down to the cascades. There are changing rooms above the parking lot, where Rastafarians will attempt to sell you woolen tams, jewelry, and carved calabash gourds.

Places to Stay & Eat
A man called Buckley rents rooms nearby. There are several rum shops and lean-to shacks selling jerk and I-tal food along the road. Frank Clarke has a basic restaurant atop the falls. He serves dishes such as tuna fish stew with potatoes for about US$2.

Getting There & Away
Bus No MB11 operates from the Parade in Kingston (US$1). You can catch any of the other buses that run between Kingston and Port Antonio via Morant Bay; get off in Manchioneal, from where you can walk or hitch uphill to Reach.

The well-paved road up to the falls is half a mile south of Manchioneal. It's a spectacular one-mile drive as you follow the valley of the Driver's River into the foothills of the John Crow Mountains.

MANCHIONEAL

This sleepy fishing village is set in a deep-scalloped bay with calm turquoise waters and a wide (though shallow) beach where colorful pirogues are drawn up. It's a center for lobster fishing and was, in earlier days, important in the banana trade. The name is derived from the poisonous manchineel plant (*Hippomane mancinella*) that once grew profusely along the shoreline (see Fearsome Flora in Facts for the Visitor). It's a cool place to hang if you want a rustic, laid-back experience.

Places to Stay & Eat

Two miles north of Manchioneal is the *Heartical Roots Corner* (☎ 993-6138) where the tiny Christmas River meets the ocean, just south of Kensington. Heartical is run by a friendly one-armed Rasta, Stanford Johnson, and his delightful Austrian-born wife, Gabrielle. They have a thatched, family-sized room for rent for US$25 in a Arawak-style octagonal cabin with hammocks on a wrap-around veranda (additional rooms are being added). You can also camp on the riverbank for US$5 per person. Bring mosquito repellent! You may have to use a pit latrine, which was due to be upgraded. There's also a rustic restaurant where Stanford (a 'superone chef') cooks I-tal vegetarian meals. The tiny golden sand beach is backed by a small lagoon that is safe for swimming. Gabrielle told me the surf here is 'killer,' but I don't think she means literally. July is said to be the best month. Stanford and Gabrielle also rent tents and bicycles.

A local woodcarver called 'Rock Bottom' rents rooms for about US$10 at Long Rd, between Manchioneal and Hector's River.

There are plenty of jerk stalls and rum shops on the coast road in town. Try *Sultan's Place*.

LONG BAY

This is one of the most dramatic settings in all Jamaica. The aptly named bay is a one-mile-wide crescent with rose-colored sand, deep turquoise waters, and breezes pushing the waves forcefully ashore. Canoes are drawn up on the beach, with fishing nets drying beside them. You may be able to hire a fisherman to take you out in his canoe for about US$15 hourly. Note that there's a dangerous undertow if you plan to go swimming. A good place to admire the views and take in the long breakers is from the headland at the east end of the bay. The lifestyle here is laid-back. Long Bay is perfect for budget travelers seeking to ease into a life of leisure in a fishing village that's a total recluse from touristy resorts. Several foreigners have settled here and are now living a counter-culture lifestyle.

Ken Abendana Spencer, a renowned modernist artist, has his studio and home here. His palace-cum-fortress is as fanciful as some of his pricey works. You're welcome to visit if your interest in art is genuine. Take the dirt road inland from the post office near the gas station. Rumor has it, however, that he has recently moved to Morant Bay.

Dangers & Annoyances

Many inhabitants along the entire east coast take a while to warm to outsiders. Drugs are rife locally. You should be very careful when photographing people here. Don't argue the point if you're confronted. Many thefts and burglaries have been reported from houses at Long Bay. I've also heard reports of a rape and several violent thefts to campers hereabouts.

Sam Street Museum

Local resident Dr Sam Street welcomes visitors to his museum (☎ 993-9060), which is incorrectly marked on the JTB's 'Discover Jamaica' road map as being in Moore Town in the Rio Grande Valley. The museum, housed in an old fort, contains a fascinating collection of African tribal art and artifacts accrued over several decades by Dr Street, who also raises medicinal plants. The museum is at Snow Hill.

To get there, take the road that leads inland from the hamlet of Fair Prospect, just north of Long Bay. You can continue along this road to Reach Falls (see above).

Bicycling
You can rent bicycles from the *King George Beer Joint* at the north end of the village for US$15 a day.

Surfing
Long Bay is one of the most consistent surf spots on the island. Rip tides and currents are common. You should stick to the extreme northern end.

Places to Stay
Camping You can camp for about US$3 at *Fisherman's Park*, a rustic Rasta-owned jerk center on the shore in the village center. In a similar vein is *Cutting Edge Park*, across the street. Both are popular hang-outs for locals. Note my comments above, in Dangers & Annoyances: you should never camp 'wild' nor leave your gear unattended.

Guest Houses Many foreigners who now live here rent rooms to travelers. At the north end of Long Bay is *Blue Heaven*, owned by an American called John. It's above a little river estuary with a coral outcrop offshore. The place is basic, but a perfect haven for escape artists who don't mind things spartan. There's a small room (US$4), plus two cabins (US$8) with kitchenette, ceiling fans, and cold water. John plans to upgrade and says rooms will be US$30 or more.

A German named Peter Paul Zahl also rents his *Rose Garden Cottage* for week-long stays. Another German couple maintains a cottage at Commodore, in the hills above Black Rock. And a Dane named Kris Kristensen rents a four-bedroom cottage (PO Box 166, Port Antonio, ☎ 993-3768). Ross Craig and Oscar Lynch also have rooms. Ask around locally for any of the above.

If you're on a really tight budget, try *Precious*, which has basic rooms for US$3. It's next to the post office at the north end of the village.

Hotels *Roylston Villa* (☎ 993-3232), at the southern end of the bay, has six rooms (US$30), each with two single beds plus ceiling fan and private bathrooms. They're simply furnished and clean. Herman Doswell runs *Herman's Holiday Homes*, with modest rooms for US$20 per person. He also has comfortable two-bedroom cottages (US$320 weekly). A small house called *Nirvana* is for rent on the beach, north of the village center.

Places to Eat
Fisherman's Park is a jerk center (see above). *Bamboo Lawn*, 400 yards north of Blue Heaven, is a rustic beachside bar serving seafood dishes for about US$2. It has a disco at night. Another lively spot is the *Sunset Strip Pub*. If you're catering yourself, the *Ocean View Pub* also has a grocery. Nearby is *M&M's Pastry Centre*, selling cakes, patties, fudge, and ice cream.

Things to Buy
Terro's World Productions, 300 yards north of Ocean View Pub at the north end of Long Bay, makes percussion and acoustic instruments for sale.

Getting There & Away
Bus No LS289, which runs between Port Antonio and Golden Grove, will drop you off at Long Bay (US$0.50).

BOSTON BEACH
There are several good reasons to stop at Boston Beach, half a mile east of Fairy Hill. First is the pretty, pocket-sized, golden-sand beach shelving into jewel-like turquoise waters. Second, high surf rolls into the bay and you may join locals who spend much of their time surfing (you can rent boards on the beach). The beach is tucked in a little cove and is easy to drive past without noticing. Look for the jerk stalls immediately north of the beach.

In the 1950s the beach was owned by Robin Moore (author of *The Happy Hooker* and *The Green Berets*), who donated it to the government.

Boston Jerk

Jerk pork, Jamaica's informal national dish, first gained notoriety here as a 'hand-me-down' from the Maroons, who hunted wild boars in the hills of Portland and cooked the meat, well-seasoned, over pimento wood fires. Boston jerk, sold wrapped in paper, is searing. Don't underestimate how *hot* Boston Beach pepper sauce can be. You'll need plenty of Red Stripe beer as an antidote. You can buy the sauce in bottles here for about US$0.60.

Flynn Estates

Much of the land locally was once owned by Errol Flynn. His widow, Patryce Wymore Flynn, still farms red poll cattle on the Flynn estates, where coconuts are also commercially grown. You can tour the plantation on horseback for US$15 by appointment (☎ 993-3294).

Places to Stay & Eat

Cozy Corner First & Last (☎ 993-8450) has three simple, but nicely appointed rooms with fans and TV for US$12 double. Two rooms have hot water. It's half a mile south of Boston, on the roadside overlooking a pasture about 200 yards from the shore. It has a small bar, but doesn't serve food.

Ce-Lee's Restaurant serves seafood dishes, as does *Club Favorita*, a beachside 'party center' that plays ear-splitting music on weekends.

Getting There & Away

Boston Beach is nine miles east of Port Antonio. Allan Witter operates a minibus (No LS702) between the two, but you can hail several others. Expect to pay about US$0.50 by bus, or US$1.50 by minibus. If traveling from Kingston, you can take bus No JR152 from the Parade; it operates via Port Antonio, as does a minibus (No JR140) operated by Hensley Hewitt.

FAIRY HILL

Fairy Hill, seven miles east of Port Antonio, is a small cliff-top hamlet composed of private vacation homes and, juxtaposed, tragically squalid shacks. A dirt road leads steeply downhill to **Winnifred Beach.** The beach is a secluded golden-sand crescent catering mostly to locals and is a great place to escape the tourists and hang with 'real' Jamaicans.

The beach was used as a setting for the Robin Williams' movie *Club Paradise*. A coral reef offshore provides good snorkeling. Parties are held here on some weekends. There are toilets and changing rooms to the right, where there's a small fishing community. Locals will rent boats or bamboo rafts to take you to another tiny beach hidden around the headland, 'if you want a private moment with your loved one,' I was told.

The turnoff to the beach is opposite the Jamaica Crest Resort.

Places to Stay

Camping You can camp on the beach for no charge, although I wouldn't recommend doing so if you're alone. Pablo, at the far end of the beach, rents tents for about US$5.

Guest Houses Two options at Fairy Hill are *Merlen's Place* (☎ 993-8079), which has rooms for rent for about US$20 in a pleasant little concrete cottage; and Zion Hill, where owner Judy Madson plans on offering rooms (see Places to Eat, below). *L&D's Snack Shop* also has a small room for rent 100 yards above Winnifred Beach.

Hotels *Jamaica Crest Resort* opened in 1995 on 17 landscaped acres (PO Box 165, Fairy Hill, Port Antonio; ☎ 993-8400, fax 993-8432). Its six red-tile-roofed villas stairstep up a hillside and have from one to four bedrooms, with kitchenette, cable TV, air-con, telephone, and balcony standard (a housekeeper/cook is optional). Room costs are US$90 to US$180. A full meal plan costs US$25 daily. The complex features an elevated sun deck and pool on stilts, plus a restaurant, bar, disco, conference center, two tennis courts, and a gym. The decor is a strange mix of Chinese and Milanese.

Fairy Hill Garden Villa is one of several private homes for rent at Fairy Hill (☎ 993-8205).

Places to Eat

There's an excellent choice for dining, especially if you're on a budget. Judy Madson, a friendly Californian, serves American breakfasts, plus vegetarian dishes, sandwiches, and omelettes (US$3) at her *Zion Hill Café & Gallery* in the historical Fairweather Building in Fairy Hill (☎ 993-8329). A stone's throw away is *Pearl's Highway Café*, a pleasant little 'bar and fish place' (☎ 993-8445). The *Nazarite Reggae Village Restaurant* is one of the most atmospheric eateries around: it's a marvelous bamboo-and-wood creation overlooking Winnifred Beach from atop the cliffs. On the beach take your pick from a dozen rustic jerk stalls. Near the far end is *Club Paradise Café*, run by Dungus.

There's a supermarket across the street from Merlen's Place.

DRAGON BAY

This beautiful little cove is just west of Winnifred Beach and east of Blue Lagoon. It's the private property of the Dragon Bay Hotel, but the small beach is open to the public for day use (US$1). This is where Tom Cruise set up his beach bar in the movie *Cocktail*. A scuba diving concession is located here.

Places to Stay & Eat

The *Dragon Bay Hotel* enjoys a beautiful setting on the hill overlooking the cove and tiny beach (PO Box 176, Port Antonio, ☎ 993-3281, fax 993-3284; in the USA, ☎ (402) 398-3218, fax (402) 398-5484; in the UK, ☎ (071) 413-8877, fax (071) 413-8883). The resort hotel, originally the creation of the Prince of Marbella, was closed for some years, but reopened a few years ago and recently underwent a complete facelift. The 30 'British colonial-style' villas now have an attractive quasi-Spanish look. Each villa has silent air-con, a kitchenette, plus two downstairs bedrooms that can be rented as separate hotel rooms. Decor features heavy bamboo furniture, beautiful floral fabrics, and pink granite floors. Villa Sevilla is a secluded twin-bedroom, two-story family villa with a private pool and sundeck. You can also rent the Prince's former penthouse. Dragon Bay is popular with Europeans, and local families favor the beach by day. Water sports include paddle boats, windsurfing, beach volleyball, and a full-service dive outfit. There is also a pool, two floodlit tennis courts, a beauty shop, a spa with sauna and small exercise room, and two restaurants. Low season rates range from US$80 for a superior room and US$110 for a one-bedroom suite to US$165 and US$205 for two- and three-bedroom villas.

Dragon Bay offers two dining options: a beach restaurant serving salads and grilled seafood, burgers, and jerk dishes; and a more elegant restaurant serving mediocre continental cuisine.

BLUE LAGOON

Yes this *is* where Brooke Shields swam nude in the movie *Blue Lagoon*. Aptly named, it's embraced by a deep, natural amphitheater with forest-clad sides. It's open to the sea through a narrow funnel, but is also fed by freshwater springs that come in at about 140 feet deep. Its color changes through every shade of jade and emerald during the day. The 180-foot-deep lagoon may well be the crater of an extinct volcano, for the water periodically undergoes a significant rise in temperature. It's refreshing to swim here, passing through cold and warm patches. You may be tempted to swim with your mouth open once you learn from locals that the waters are said to have aphrodisiac properties.

Another piece of local lore says that Hollywood hero Errol Flynn once dived to the bottom using only a snorkel. Millions of tiny fish and even barracuda and squid can also be seen swimming around. Hibiscus *(puia)* drop their pink leaves, which float out on the receding tide. At night, floodlights add to the romantic ambiance.

Bamboo raft trips are available from the Blue Lagoon Restaurant, which lies behind a high wall and has all access rights to the lagoon. It's a great place to wile away time over chess and backgammon boards. It rents snorkeling equipment and paddle-boats (US$10). The original restaurant was demolished by Hurricane Gilbert in 1988; the existing stone-and-hardwood structure opened in May 1995. A US$5 entrance fee for day use is deducted from your bar or restaurant bill with any purchase. A heli-copter pad was planned at press time and heli-tours will be offered from Half Moon, Strawberry Hill, and Round Hill resorts.

Local hustlers will beckon you to park beneath a tree outside the restaurant. They'll try to interest you in jewelry and glass-bottom boat rides. There seems to be some animosity when tourists come to the restaurant and don't purchase their services.

Places to Stay
Crystal Cove, 100 yards west of Blue Lagoon, provides a stunning setting, with a fistful of waterfront villas made famous as a popular locale for fashion shoots. Among them is *Crystal Cove*, a three-bedroom, three-bathroom luxury villa at the water's edge (c/o 11 East Ave, Kingston 10, ☎ 925-8108, fax 925-6248). The one-story villa is staffed with a housekeeper/cook and houseman. It's beautifully furnished and has a book-lined study plus a tree-shaded terrace overlooking the water. Low season rates are US$230 to US$270 daily for two to six people (a five-day minimum is required). Also try *The Pelican* (US$1600 weekly).

At press time the *Blue Lagoon Restaurant* was also planning to rent two villas in the hills, with a 'Jamaican Roots' tour pro-vided upon arrival.

Places to Eat
The *Blue Lagoon Restaurant* (☎ 993-8491) has wide wooden decks overhanging the

famous lagoon. Trees grow through the decks. It serves a creative, yet entirely jerk menu, including jerk crayfish, jerk lamb chops and jerk pork tenderloin. Freshwater lobster is available year round. Food is served on wooden plates made of blue-stained mahoe. You eat with your fingers (a finger bowl and cloth napkin are also provided). I recommend the potentially lethal Blue Lagoon cocktail, served in a half-pint glass. Lunch costs US$15, includ-ing a to-die-for Tía Maria rum cake dessert. A Sunday dinner special is US$20. If you want to impress your lover, you can even request a private dinner on a floating deck in the middle of the lagoon. Fabulous!

It's open from 11 am to 5 pm, Monday to Wednesday, and Thursday to Sunday 11 am to 10 pm.

SAN SAN BEACH
San San Beach, which was used as a setting for the cable movie *Treasure Island*, is a preferred spot for the rich and famous, who have their opulent homes on the peninsula called Alligator Head. A stair-way descends through thick greenery to the private beach used by guests of Goblin Hill, Fern Hill, and the Jamaica Palace hotels. If you're just passing by, however, you can pay a US$2 fee for day use. It has a bar and restaurant and scuba diving facility, and water sports are available.

San San Beach is said to have 'terrific' waves for **surfing** if the wind and swell are right.

Offshore is a tiny islet: **Pellow Island**. Watch out for spiny sea urchins if you can swim out to the island.

Places to Stay & Eat
A breezy hilltop option is *Fern Hill*, '15 chains' up Mile Gully Rd (PO Box 100, Port Antonio, ☎ 993-3222, fax 993-2257; in North America, ☎ (800) 263-4354, fax (416) 620-4843). It offers fabulous views down over San San Beach. The 16 spa-cious, elegant, twin-level units are spread across the luxuriant hillside and boast congenial decor plus balconies beyond

louvered French doors. There are also three villas. Suites have mezzanine bedrooms and their own hot tubs (the ones I saw were dirty). An airy dining terrace atop the hill offers tremendous views. Fern Hill offers a poolside buffet with a dance cabaret when there's a full house. Low-season rates range from US$60 single or double for standard, air-con rooms, to US$110 for a one-bedroom villa. The resort is the only Port Antonio property offering an all-inclusive option.

Goblin Hill Villas is a 700-acre hilltop estate above San San (c/o 11 East Ave, Kingston 10, ☎ 925-8108, fax 925-6248; in North America, ☎ (800) 472-1148). It's popular with families. Its 16 two-bedroom and 12 one-bedroom self-catering villas straddle a ridge and are surrounded by lawns and raw jungle. Those closest to the sea get more breezes and have views down to San San Bay. A nature trail encircles the property. The air-con, townhouse-style villas are huge, and have massive open windows and wide verandas. However, mine had tired furniture, worn bed sheets, and bathrooms and kitchens that were sorely in need of renovation. Each comes with its own private maid and butler (optional). The rooms have neither telephones or TVs, though the resort has a TV lounge and reading room, a large pool enclosed by an arbor, plus two tennis courts. Rates are US$90 to US$185 per one-bedroom villa, or US$165 to US$210.

Other villa options include the five-bedroom *Shoreham Green*, (in the USA, ☎ (403) 264-2604 or (800) 640-7866). The 3800-sq-foot, Georgian-style villa has its own pool and staff (US$3000 weekly). Nearby is the fully staffed *Chateau Exotica*, set in five acres with boating and horses included for US$1795 weekly, off-peak, for up to six people (in the USA, ☎ (407) 433-8176). *Match Resorts* is a five-cottage complex with pool in the hills above San San (c/o Caribic Vacations, 1310 Providence Drive, Ironshore Estate, Montego Bay, ☎ 952-5013, fax 952-0981).

Entertainment

A beach party with limbo and cabaret is held on Monday evenings at the beach.

Getting There & Away

You can take any of the minibuses and buses that run between Port Antonio and Boston Bay (minibus No LS702), Golden Grove (bus No LS289) and points beyond. It should cost you no more than US$0.50 by bus, double that by minibus.

FRENCHMAN'S COVE

This small cove, just east of the hamlet of Drapers, five miles from Port Antonio, boasts one of the prettiest beaches for miles. It became famous in the 1960s when a luxury resort called Frenchman's Cove was built atop the tall headland. The hotel has been closed for some years and seems constantly in the throes of redevelopment. A stream winds lazily to a cozy white-sand beach that shelves steeply into the water. Bring insect repellent, as mosquitos thrive in the moist dale behind the beach. You can sunbathe topless. There's a secure parking lot where you pay J$6 (US$0.15) to use the beach. Immediately west of Frenchman's Cove, Draper's has a few facilities, including Derron's Rent-a-Car (☎ 993-7111) and a small post office (open 8 am to 4 pm, Monday to Friday; 8 am to noon, Saturday). There's a police station half a mile east of Frenchman's Cove (☎ 993-3220).

The cove is reached by a dirt road 200 yards south of the nine-hole San San Golf Course (☎ 993-9345), which was closed for restoration at press time.

Places to Stay

For button-down ambiance check into the *Hotel Mockingbird* (PO Box 254, Port Antonio, ☎ 993-3370, fax 993-7133). It offers a split-level villa plus well-lit bungalows, including nonsmoking options. Most rooms boast ocean views from private balconies. Facilities include a small pool, a TV lounge, plus a variety of health and wellness services, including massage. The owners plan to open an art

The Jamaica Palace, where the stonework is so terribly neoclassical

gallery with works by local artists and art courses with artists-in-residence. They are environmentalists (no paper napkins or plastic straws, for example) and guests are even encouraged to take their non-recyclables home with them. Trails lead through the lush hillside gardens. Low-season room rates (May to mid-December) are US$95 to US$110. To get there, take the private road that leads inland from the church at Drapers.

Draper's San Guest House sits atop the headland above Frenchman's Cove.

Places to Eat

Woody's Place, in Drapers, is a rustic road-side eatery that serves tremendous hot dogs and burgers as well as Jamaican dishes for a couple of bucks. The *Mille Fleurs* restaurant in Hotel Mockingbird offer gourmet Jamaican specialties. It serves a set three-course dinner (US$28), including a vegetarian choice, daily.

TURTLE CRAWLE BAY

Two miles east of town the road circles around this deep bay, which is rimmed by mangroves and is an important nursery for fish. The nursery is now protected as a part of the recently created Port Antonio Marine Park, but you may still see the odd fisherman tending nets.

Squatting atop the western headland is a magnificent gleaming-white castle, an Austrian-style, rococo whimsy with flamboyant stonework (including a pair of enormous crocodiles flanking the front door) built in the 1980s by Baroness Elisabeth Siglindy Stephan von Stephanie Thyssen (now Mrs Nazar Fahmi). This is **Trident Castle**, part of the Trident Villas resort, nicknamed Folly II because it lay unfinished for several years due to financial problems. The architect, Earl Levy, eventually took over the property after a well-publicized tiff with the Baroness. It's now his home. Scenes from *Clara's Heart* were filmed here, and Denzel Washington barely resisted seduction by hotel guest Mimi Rogers in *The Mighty Quinn*.

On the east shore of Turtle Crawle is another fantasy in stone – this one the pseudo-Grecian **Jamaica Palace** – built by the Baroness in 1989. Thus the Baroness trumped the Earl; he has only a castle, but she has a palace. It, too, has appeared on screen: as the setting for Playboy's *Playmates in Paradise*.

Places to Stay

Guest Houses *Faith Cottage* (PO Box 50, Port Antonio, ☎ 993-3703) is a guest house with five rooms (US$70/95 single/double) opposite Trident Villas. Nearby, in the same residential community, are *Match Resort Cottage* (Lot 30, Dolphin Bay, Port Antonio, ☎ 993-9624, fax 993-2700), *Sainte Camette Villas* (☎ 993-2140, fax 993-9393), and *V&K B&B* (Lot 89, Daffodil Ave, Anchovy Gardens, Port Antonio, ☎ 993-2945).

Hotels *East Winds Cove Resort Cottages* (☎ 926-6665) offers six modern little cottages that nestle on a hillside and face west across Turtle Crawle Bay towards Trident Castle.

Trident Hotel & Villas has been an undying favorite of unwinding internationals ever since it opened in the late 1960s (PO Box 119, Port Antonio, ☎ 993-2602, fax 993-2590; in the USA, ☎ (800) 223-6510; in the UK, ☎ (071) 730-7144, fax (071) 938-7493). It has a charming, worn-in feel, and sits atop a cliff overlooking a tiny cove. Peacocks pursue peahens on the croquet lawn and around the topiary firs. Stepping through the lofty mahogany front door is like entering a European mansion. It offers 26 deluxe rooms, villa suites, plus the luxurious Imperial Suite.

Earl Levy runs his property with an aristocratic flair. Trident has a strict dress code for dining. Jackets for men and 'cocktail attire' for women are required (men must also wear ties during winter season). Low-season rates are US$165/220 for rooms;

US$220/340 for suites and villas. High-season rates are about 60% extra. Lottery winners can rent The Castle for US$4750 a day! It is shown by appointment only. Transfers from Kingston are free for week-long stays only. Helicopter transfers are also offered from Kingston and Montego Bay for an extra fee.

Aiming for the same upmarket appeal is the *Jamaica Palace*, a rambling Neoclassical property fronted by white marble columns on the eastern bluff overlooking Turtle Crawle Bay (PO Box 277, Port Antonio, ☎ 993-2020 or 800-472-1149, fax 993-3459). Everything but the black-and-white-checkered floor is gleaming white. The 63 rooms and 20 junior suites are cavernous and come with king-size bed, crystal chandeliers, period antiques, and Georgian bay windows. In the landscaped grounds behind the hotel is a 114-foot-long pool shaped like Jamaica, so you can swim from Port Antonio to Negril if you choose. Rates are US$130 single or double.

PORT ANTONIO

Port Antonio (population 19,000), 68 miles east of Ocho Rios, is the capital of Portland, as it has been since 1723 when the parish was founded. Poet Ella Wheeler Wilcox (1855 – 1919) described the town as the 'most exquisite port on earth,' but it looks decidedly lackluster these days. Back then it was Jamaica's main banana port. Melancholic Port Antonio still has the rakish air and tropical lassitude of a maritime harbor, and there is little of the hustle of Montego Bay or Ocho Rios. Goats snoozing in the shade of verandas sum it all up.

Port Antonio has resisted efforts to develop itself as a tourist resort, despite the limelight provided by socialites who have vacationed here for the past 50 years. In the past decade, it was also the setting of various movies, including *The Mighty Quinn*, *Club Paradise*, *Cocktail*, and a remake of *Lord of the Flies*. More recently it has been favored by Shabba Ranks and other reggae stars for music videos.

Errol Flynn

Errol Flynn, the infamous Hollywood idol, arrived in 1946 when his yacht *Zacca* washed ashore in bad weather. He fell in love with the area and made Port Antonio his playground. In his autobiography, *My Wicked, Wicked Ways*, he described Port Antonio as 'more beautiful than any woman I've ever seen.' Flynn (1909 – 1959) bought the Titchfield Hotel and Navy Island, where he threw wild, extravagant parties – locals like to tell exaggerated tales of Flynn's exploits: 'Remember de day 'im drove de Cadillac into de swimming pool?' Flynn's beguiling ways inevitably attracted the attention of other stars of stage and screen, like Clara Bow, Bette Davis, and Ginger Rogers.

Flynn later established a cattle ranch at Boston Estate, planned a lavish home at Comfort Castle, and had grandiose plans to develop Port Antonio into a tourist resort. Sadly, he died before his plans could be brought to fruition. The wild parties are no more, but his legend lives on. ■

Things are stirring. Efforts are being made to promote the nearby Rio Grande as a major ecotour destination. Modern commercial buildings are arising downtown, providing a newfound sense of vitality. And the purchase of Trans-Jamaica Airlines in October 1995 by a consortium led by innovative tourism figure Gordon 'Butch' Stewart promises the prospects of increased air service and creative marketing schemes in tandem with local hoteliers eager to see their prospects brighten.

History

The Spanish coined the town's name in the late 16th century when they christened the bay Puerto Anton after the governor's son. The Spanish, however, made no serious effort to settle the bay. It wasn't until 1723 that the British laid out a rudimentary town on the peninsula. They named it Titchfield after the estate in Hampshire of the Duke of Portland, who was then Jamaica's governor. The British Navy established a careening station on the island in West Harbour, and in 1729 a fort was built at the tip of Titchfield. However, rampant fevers in the swampy coast lands and constant raids by marauding Maroons deterred all but a handful of settlers.

Once peace with the Maroons was established in 1739, planters began to establish sugar estates and Titchfield expanded. The area proved unsuitable, however (of 138 estates in 1800, none remained a century later), and much of the land passed into the hands of peasants who replaced sugar with sustenance crops, including bananas. Enter Lorenzo Dow Baker, fruit shipping magnate, who arrived in 1871 and established the banana trade that created a boomtown overnight and established Port Antonio as the 'banana capital of the world.' In 1879 an observer noted, candidly: 'but for the fruit trade with America which has sprung up within the last few years, it would now, in all probability, have become as effete and valueless as any part of the whole island.'

Banana Bonanza In its heyday 17 steamer lines were operating here and Port Antonio grew so wealthy that it is said planters would light their cigars with US$5 bills. (Actually, only the fat-cat traders and planters, who soon controlled much of the

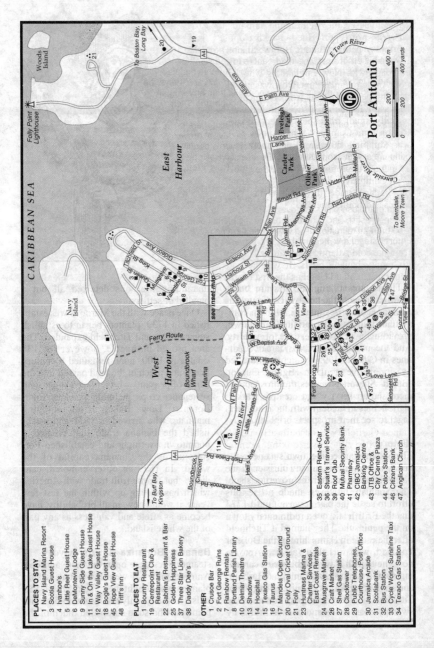

Port Antonio

CARIBBEAN SEA

Woods Island

Navy Island

East Harbour

West Harbour

Folly Point Lighthouse

Ferry Route

Boundbrook Wharf

Marina

Annotto River

Little Annotto Rd

To Boston Bay, Long Bay

To Berridale, Moore Town

To Buff Bay, Kingston

E Town River

Caneside River

Allan Ave

E Palm Ave

Campbell Ave

Evelleigh Park

Harper Lane

Peters Lane

Carder Park

Olivier Park

Victor Lane

Mellad Rd

Red Hassell Rd

Smatt Rd

Manning Ave

French Ave

Summers Town Rd

Gideon Ave

William St

Bridge St

Norman Rd

Love Lane

Grosett Rd

Gale Rd

Portland Rd

Esplanade Ave

To Bonnie View

W Baptist Ave

E Baptist Ave

Musgrave Ave

Natali Ave

Rice Piece Rd

Boundbrook Rd

Boundbrook Crescent

Harbour St

King St

Tilghele St

West St

Valentine

Fort George

see inset map

PLACES TO STAY
1 Navy Island Marina Resort
3 Scotia Guest House
4 Ivanhoe's
5 Little Reef Guest House
6 DeMontevin Lodge
9 Sunny Side Guest House
11 In & On the Lake Guest House
12 Way Valley Guest House
18 Bogle's Guest House
45 Hope View Guest House
48 Trifr's Inn

PLACES TO EAT
1 Bounty Restaurant
19 Centrepoint Club & Restaurant
22 Sabrina's Restaurant & Bar
25 Golden Happiness
37 Three Star Lion Bakery
38 Daddy Dee's

OTHER
1 Crusoe Bar
2 Fort George Ruins
7 Rainbow Rentals
8 Portland Parish Library
10 Delmar Theatre
13 Shadows
14 Hospital
15 Texaco Gas Station
16 Taurus
17 Mandela Open Ground
20 Folly Oval Cricket Ground
21 Folly
23 Huntress Marina & Charter Services, East Coast Rentals
24 Musgrave Market
26 Craft Market
27 Shell Gas Station
28 Clocktower
29 Public Telephones, Courthouse, Post Office
30 Jamaica Arcade
31 Scotiabank
32 Bus Station
33 Cycle World, Sunshine Taxi
34 Texaco Gas Station
35 Eastern Rent-a-Car
36 Stuart's Travel Service
39 Roof Club
40 Mutual Security Bank
41 Pharmacy
42 CIBC Jamaica Banking Centre
43 JTB Office & City Centre Plaza
44 Police Station
46 Citizens Bank
47 Anglican Church

land, amassed the wealth; the Jamaican laborers who performed backbreaking work were paid a pittance, as they still are.) Dow, himself from Cape Cod, staffed his company with New Englanders who lent Port Antonio Yankee airs. Dow was not the first shipper of bananas from Jamaica, but he was by far the most successful. Baker's initially small trade blossomed into the Boston Fruit Company, which, at its peak, was shipping three million bunches of bananas a year from Jamaica. Eventually, by merger, the company became the United Fruit Company and soon came to dominate the banana trade throughout the West Indies and Latin America.

Of a Feather   In the 1890s the ever-enterprising Dow began shipping tourists from the cold Atlantic coast of the USA in his empty banana boats. It was he who built the Titchfield Hotel as the first tourist hotel in Jamaica (it burned down in 1969). The international set followed, including Rudyard Kipling, newspaper magnate William Randolph Hearst, and the world's wealthiest man, financier JP Morgan, who called in regularly aboard his yacht *Corsair III*.

Movie star Errol Flynn and a high-society entourage flocked to Port Antonio throughout the 1940s and '50s. Flynn settled here. In the 1960s, a new, brief heyday occurred when a millionaire named Garfield Weston built a luxurious resort with villas overlooking Frenchman's Cove that rented for £1000 a week. He was followed by Prince Alfonso Hohenlohe's equally exclusive Marbella Club at Dragon Bay. The regal resorts attracted the jet-setting crowd, and the coves east of town were colonized by the very rich.

The upscale resorts and private villas east of town still help keep Port Antonio resolutely old-fashioned. More broad-based tourism has seemed jinxed. Commercialism hasn't yet found this pocket of paradise, and Port Antonio and the surrounding area are pretty much as they were 30 years ago.

Orientation

To get a sense of the town's marvelous setting you have to get up high by following Bonnie View Rd to the hotel of that name. The compact town center is nestled between twin harbors separated by the Titchfield Peninsula. A narrow channel separates the peninsula from Navy Island. All the commercial activity centers on the smaller West Harbour. Another scrub-covered peninsula curls around the eastern shore of the almost circular, mile-wide East Harbour.

East and West Harbours are paralleled by two main drags – W Palm Ave and Allan Ave (called Harbour St at its western end) – which meet at right angles in front of the main plaza and courthouse. Fort George St runs from this junction uphill along Titchfield Peninsula.

Maps   You can obtain copies of the 'Discover Jamaica' road maps, including a small street map of Port Antonio, from the JTB office. Otherwise, head to the clock tower in front of the courthouse: it has a city directory painted on it.

Information

Tourist Offices   The JTB has an office on the 2nd floor of City Centre Plaza at the corner of West St and Harbour St (☎ 993-3051). It's open Monday to Friday, 8:30 am to 4:30 pm, and Saturday 9 am to 1 pm. It's poorly stocked with literature, but manager Cynthia Perry is helpful. If you're seeking generic information on Jamaica, try the Jamaica Information Service across the street in Goebel Plaza (☎ 993-2630).

There are also several travel agencies in town. I recommend Stuart's Travel Service, which has an office at the east end of Harbour St (☎ 993-2609). The Portland Parish Library is in the town center (☎ 993-2793).

Money   You'll find branches of CIBC Jamaica Banking Centre at 3 West St (☎ 993-2785), and Scotiabank at 3 Harbour St (☎ 993-2523), and Citizens Bank next to Hope View Guest House on Harbour St.

All have foreign exchange counters, though Scotiabank is best if you want to make a cash advance against a credit card. There's a foreign exchange booth across the street from Citizens Bank.

Post & Communications You can place overseas calls and send faxes from the Call Direct Center at 29 Harbour St (☎ 993-3174, fax 993-3178), or the Telecommunications of Jamaica office on Allan Ave (☎ 993-2775). The post office (☎ 993-2158) is nearby, next to the courthouse.

Medical Services Doctors' clinics are located at 1 Harbour St (☎ 993-3578), 6 Harbour St (☎ 993-3742), 17 Harbour St (☎ 993-2559), and 50 William St (☎ 993-2338). If you need emergency attention, you'll find the Port Antonio Hospital above town on Naylor's Hill, south of West Harbour (☎ 993-2646). You can buy over-the-counter and prescription medicines at a pharmacy in City Centre Plaza on Harbour St (☎ 996-3624), and another at 11 West St (☎ 993-3629). If you're sorely in need of a massage, call Massage Therapy an appointment (☎ 993-2667). They'll come to your hotel.

Emergency Police stations are located on Harbour St and at the east end of Allan Ave (☎ 993-2527 or 993-2546).

Dangers & Annoyances Port Antonio is relatively free of the hustlers and prostitutes associated with other resort areas. Nonetheless, that's no reason to relax your vigilance. Guard your valuables if browsing Musgrave Market, and use caution if walking the ill-lit streets at night. Stick to the main streets and avoid back alleys.

Walking Tour
It takes two hours at the most to see the few sites of note in the town center. You can walk easily, but watch for fast-moving traffic along sinuous West St.

Port Antonio's heart is the **main square** at the junction of West St and Harbour St. It's centered on a clock tower (out of order) and backed by a handsome red-brick Georgian courthouse topped by a cupola. Near the square, at the end of West St, is the lively and colorful **Musgrave Market**, which has operated since the late 18th century and is supported by thick limestone columns. It was recently restored in period detail. The higglers spill out onto the crowded pavement facing the main entrance opposite a small **cenotaph** on the corner of West St and William St.

At the east end of William St is **Christ Church**, a red-brick Anglican edifice built around 1840 atop a hillock overlooking East Harbour (much of the present structure dates from 1903). Its style is called Neo-Romanesque. The belfry is festooned with epiphytes. The interior architecture is simple; the singular item of note is the brass lectern donated by Captain Lorenzo Dow Baker.

From Harbour St you can follow either Fort George St or Gideon Ave along the Titchfield Peninsula. This hilly peninsula (known locally as 'The Hill') supports several Victorian-style gingerbread houses, most notably DeMontevin Lodge, an ornate rust-red mansion. It is now an atmospheric if simple hotel.

Several large cannons lie semi-buried in the grass nearby. They bear the hallmark of 'Carron Ironworks, Edinburgh, 1813,' and were once part of **Fort George**, built in 1729 to protect against Spanish attack. When the fort was complete, two regiments were transferred from Gibraltar. Alas, their commander died within a few months along with two-thirds of the regiment, who succumbed to fevers. The parade ground and former barracks today house Titchfield School. Beyond the school, several George III cannons can still be seen mounted in their embrasures in 10-foot-thick walls. You can roam freely when class is out. The school and fort lie at the end of Fort George St.

Boundbrook Wharf
This famous wharf lies at the west end of town. It was originally owned by the Boston Fruit Company and freighters still

berth here to supply Europe with bananas (all bananas exported from Jamaica today depart from here). The loading of fruit has been mechanized since 1963 and you'll no longer see the Tallyman tallying bananas or stevedores 'working all night on a drink of rum.' Harry Belafonte's 'Banana Boat Song' was based on truth: the workers *did* sing as they carried bunches of bananas on their heads. The clusters, or 'hands,' of each bunch were tallied, and nine made a 'bunch.' Thus the line in Belafonte's song, 'Six hand, seven hand, eight hand, *bunch*!'

Other Wharves

Adjacent to Boundbrook is the Ken Wright Cruise Ship Pier and Port Antonio Marina (☎ 993-3209), with facilities for yachters. Alas, cruise ships no longer call here, having moved on to Ocho Rios and Montego Bay. Further east is the wharf that serves Navy Island by ferry and, nearby, the small Huntress Marina, named for a yacht that arrived in 1982 for repairs (the owner stayed and now owns the marina).

Navy Island

It's well-worth your time to hop on a ferry and spend a few hours or longer on this small island, which lies almost a stone's throw from the end of the Titchfield Peninsula. The lushly vegetated, 60-acre island is popular with egrets and other waterbirds, as well as day-trippers and nudists.

It was originally known as Lynch's Island after Governor Lynch received it as a gift for services to the Crown. It bore his name until 1728, when the British Navy took over. They used it to careen ships for repair, and eventually built a small battery, plus jetties and warehouses. Nothing remains of their presence. This century, the island has had several private owners, including Errol Flynn. A local legend says that he won it in a poker game, but the truth is less glamorous: he bought it. Rumor has it that his ghost can be seen at night at the dock enjoying sushi and whisky. Flynn's former home is now a hotel (see Navy

Island Marina Resort, in Places to Stay, below) with a fine restaurant. There are three small beaches, one where you can sun your buns. No food or drink is allowed on the island.

A ferry departs from the wharf on W Palm Ave on the hour, 8 am to 5 pm, and after 5 pm on call (there's a phone on the wall to connect you with Navy Island). It costs J$50 round trip. You pay at the office on Navy Island. Of course, you can always swim there if you want, but beware the strong currents.

Folly

According to legend, a millionaire built this classical mansion for his bride. Alas, he built it out of concrete and the cement began to crumble the moment he carried her over the threshold. She fled in terror at the omen and never returned. The legend is nonsense! The two-story, 200-foot-long, 60-room mansion *was* built entirely of concrete in pseudo-Grecian style by a North American millionaire. But Alfred Mitchell and his family lived there happily between 1905 and 1912 (his wife – one of the Tiffany family, the famous New York jewelers – was already a grandmother), and it was in use until 1936, when the roof collapsed. Sea water had been used in the construction causing the iron reinforcing rods to rust.

The shell remains, held aloft by limestone columns that have stood the test of time. The ugly ruin is now overgrown and smothered with graffiti, and despite being a popular spot for magazine photo-shoots it has little to recommend it.

The legend also says Mitchell stocked nearby **Woods Island** with albino monkeys and peacocks. True, he did turn the island into a menagerie, but the animals weren't all white.

Folly is on the peninsula east of East Harbour. Follow the dirt road past Folly Oval cricket ground and veer right at the Y-junction. If you continue straight you'll reach the bright orange **Folly Point Lighthouse**, built in 1888. Visitors are allowed to roam the grounds free of charge.

Beaches

Both the dark-sand beach fronting East Harbour, and tiny Jamaica Reef Beach at the northwest tip of Titchfield were strewn with garbage on my last visit. Several stunning beaches like San San and Crystal Cove lie hidden in private coves several miles east of town. There are also three tiny, but pleasant beaches on Navy Island, plus a pretty little beach called Mother Beck's Beach at Norwich, one mile west of Port Antonio.

Scuba Diving

The shoreline east of Port Antonio boasts eight miles of interconnected coral reefs and walls at an average of 100 to 300 yards offshore. No site is more than 15 minutes away by boat. All dives are drift dives in waters at a near constant 75°F and minimum 60-foot visibility. Dive sites average 30 to 110 feet, with dropoffs of over 300 feet, and little current or surge. Many of the sites are largely unexplored, and the reef, which was recently protected in the Port Antonio Marine Park, remains relatively undisturbed. **Alligator Head** is known for big sponge formations and black corals on a banking reef that drops to extreme depths. You stand a good chance of seeing hammerhead sharks and large pelagic fish at **Fairy Hill Bank**.

Lady G'Diver, a full-service dive shop at Dragon Bay Hotel, offers dives from a Boston whaler and flat-bottom boat (US$65 for two same-day dives). You can rent equipment here (PO Box 81, Port Antonio, 993-3281). San San Beach (see above) also has a scuba facility called Aqua Action.

Sport Fishing

You can charter sport fishing boats from Huntress Marina & Charter Services on West St (☎ 993-3318). Expect to pay from US$250 half-day or US$400 full-day, including bait and tackle. The 41-foot-long *Coral Baby* can also be hired (☎ 993-3511), as can the *Bonita II* (☎ 993-3086).

PEPA's Park Projects

Declining fish stocks, damage to the ecology of Port Antonio's coral reefs, and threats to Portland Parish's natural resources led to the formation of the nonprofit Portland Environment Protection Association (PEPA) in 1988.

PEPA is made up of representatives from over 40 civic and citizens' groups that spearhead environmental projects within their communities. PEPA has worked to foster public awareness of their fragile resources, including setting up 14 Environmental Education Clubs among local schools.

The group's most notable achievement has been the projected establishment of the Port Antonio Marine Park Its boundaries extend over an area of 11 miles, from Ship Rock, west of Port Antonio, to North East Point, south of Boston Bay. Within these boundaries will be two reserves – at Turtle Crawle Bay and San San/Blue Lagoon – where fishing will be prohibited. USAID has contributed funds for ranger training and buoy installation. You can contact PEPA at 6 Allan Ave, Port Antonio (☎ 993-9632). ∎

Organized Tours

JD Tours at the Bonnie View Plantation Hotel has a daily, four-hour tour (US$15) of their 22-acre working fruit and flower plantation (☎ 993-2752). It also offers a Blue Mountains tour (US$35), plus horseback rides into the Shotover Mountains (US$33 per person) and other destinations nearby (US$5 per person per hour). Advance reservation is needed.

Mocking Bird Tours specializes in putting visitors in touch with the local community, especially women in the arts (☎ 993-3370). The company is based in the Hotel Mockingbird (see Places to Stay in Frenchman's Cove). Beach, Mountain & Waterfall Tour Ltd offers a series of tours, including to Somerset Falls (US$25) and Reach Falls (US$15), and a hiking tour of the Blue Mountains (US$40) (7 William St, ☎ 993-9044).

Blue Mountain Tours, in the old railroad station at 2 W Palm Ave, offers a 'Blue Mountain Downhill Bicycle Tour' (PO Box 84, Port Antonio, ☎ 993-2242). The thrilling descent begins high up in the Blue Mountains at 5060 feet and ends at a waterfall. You'll want to take extreme care, as the road is windy and narrow, overgrown, and full of potholes. The US$30 cost includes transfers, brunch, lunch, refreshments, use of a mountain bike, and a guide.

The Navy Island Marina Resort offers four-hour cruises aboard the *Tiki Antonio*, including a visit to Blue Lagoon and snorkeling off Monkey Island (☎ 993-9044; US$25).

Special Events
The week-long Portland Jamboree is held each mid-August, featuring a float parade, street dancing, and live music. Contact the JTB for information. Contestants are lured here each October for the weeklong Port Antonio International Marlin Tournament, one of the Caribbean's most prestigious sport fishing events since 1963 (☎ 923-8724). An annual canoe tournament allows the local fishermen to compete using their dug-out canoes.

Places to Stay
Port Antonio is well-served by hotels. There's something for every budget, and it's one of the few places that has a good choice of inexpensive options.

Consider staying east of town, where a wide choice of accommodations are located near the beaches. Most of the upscale resorts and villas are east of town.

Places to Stay – bottom end
There are a fistful of basic guest houses on the Titchfield Peninsula, each charging about US$10 per room. *Ivanhoe's* has 20 rooms with private bathrooms with cold water, and a homely TV lounge (9 Queen St, ☎ 993-3043). The nearby *Scotia Guest House* has 10 rooms with similar facilities (15 Queen St, ☎ 993-2681). Also on Queen St is *Little Reef Guest House* (no telephone). It has 10 small, basic rooms, some

with private bathroom. Meals are cooked to order. Lastly, *Sunny Side Guest House* is a two-story house almost opposite DeMontevin Lodge, with 10 basic but clean, comfortable rooms with shared bath (13 West St, ☎ 993-2127).

Hope View Guest House offers nine very dingy, dismal, and overpriced rooms (US$12 to US$25), and a TV in the lounge (26 Harbour St, ☎ 993-3040). Two other basic options in the US$10 to US$15 range are *Way Valley Guest House* (11 W Palm Ave, ☎ 993-3267) and *In & On the Lake Guest House* (17A W Palm Ave, ☎ 993-3468). Way Valley was closed for renovation at press time. You might also try *Bogle's Guest House* (28A Summers Town Rd, ☎ 993-2121).

Places to Stay – middle
Guest Houses *DeMontevin Lodge* at 21 Fort George St is a virtual institution (PO Box 95, Port Antonio, ☎ 993-2604). This venerable Victorian boasts a homey ambiance and a blend of modern kitsch and antiques that remind me of my grannie's parlor. A carved stairway leads upstairs to 13 simple bedrooms (three with private bathrooms) that are time-worn, but clean as a whistle. Two rooms have a balcony with views over the bay. Rates are US$25/37.50, US$57 triple with shared bath, and US$50 double with private bath. The Mullingses, a well-known couple who ran it for years, are now dead, but the place is well maintained by Fay Johnson.

Hotels By far the best place to stay is *Bonnie View Plantation Hotel*, which occupies an alluring spot astride a ridge 600 feet above town (PO Box 82, Port Antonio, ☎ 993-2752, fax 993-2862; in the USA ☎ (309) 659-2358, fax (309) 659-2395). Worth the bargain prices alone is the spectacular view. Bonnie View is surrounded by well-tended gardens and a plantation backed by the soaring Blue Mountains. The back garden contains a pool and, amazingly, a small beach. The spotless though modest rooms are done up in pinks and white. A standard room costs US$44/66;

deluxe rooms are US$48/70, and suites US$58/86. A complete meal plan is US$30 extra, and the dining is excellent.

A more modest option is *Triff's Inn* (1 Bridge St, ☎ 992-2752, fax 993-2062). This well-run hotel has 17 spacious and clean air-con rooms with telephone, and private bath with hot water for US$35/50, including continental breakfast. Furnishings are minimalist, but pleasing. A seafood restaurant is open for three meals daily.

Shirley Silvera offers modest rooms with shared bath and cold water for US$30 at *Holiday Home* at 12 French Ave, at the junction with King St (PO Box 11, Port Antonio, ☎ 993-2882). *Shadows* at 40 West St (☎ 993-3823) has five air-con rooms with private bathroom and satellite TVs and telephones for about US$30. If you want self-catering, try *Friends* (☎ 925-6738), which has two chalets in the hills immediately west of town; their bedrooms offer coastal views.

Places to Stay – top end

Navy Island Marina Resort is a cottage resort on Navy Island (PO Box 188, Port Antonio, ☎ 993-2667 or (800) 526-2422, fax 993-2041; or 10 Ruthven Rd, Kingston 10, ☎ 968-5731, fax 960-1533). Accommodations range from standard rooms for US$95/110 to comfy, two-bedroom villas for US$170 to US$280 (two to five people). The 21 rooms are made of hardwoods and have king-size beds. The resort features a private marina, tennis court, volleyball court, freshwater pool, plus the *Bounty Restaurant* and *Crusoe Bar*. It has a Flynn nook in the clubhouse, where Flynn movies are shown weekly. The restaurant is excellent (both the food and setting), though small kitchenettes allow you to cater for yourself.

Port Antonio is renowned for its exclusive rental villas, almost all of which are concentrated at San San Beach (see above). *Evra Jam Villa Rentals* at 38 West St, Shop 10, represents local owners (PO Box 180, Port Antonio, ☎ 993-2325, fax 993-2328).

Places to Eat

My favorite offbeat place is the rickety, thatch-roofed, bamboo bar-cum-restaurant at Huntress Marina that looks like it fell from the Robin Williams movie *Popeye*. It's owned by Sabrina, who calls herself a 'Germaican' and serves steamed fish and other Jamaican seafood for US$2 to US$5. The ambiance is great!

Daddy Dee's, on West St, serves Jamaica staples such as ackee and codfish and curried goat for as little as US$2. Similar prices may tempt you to *Kingslee Bar & Restaurant*, also on West St, serving traditional Jamaican breakfasts for under US$1. *Delicious Delites* leans towards fried chicken, burgers, hot dogs, and ice cream (9 Harbour St, ☎ 993-2169). All these places are popular with locals, as is *Mandala* on West St, which serves Creole chicken, steamed fish, and fish and coconut (US$2.50). Two other good bets for under US$2 are *Atlantis Restaurant* on George St, serving curried goat, rice and beans, and *janga* soup; and *Centrepoint Club & Restaurant*, on a breezy hillside location at the east end of East Harbour. The latter doubles as a dance club at night.

DeMontevin Lodge has a Wednesday night feast of ackee and codfish, suckling pig, and other Jamaican delicacies, plus entertainment later that night at Taurus (US$20). You must phone in your order 24 hours ahead (993-2604).

Craving Chinese? *Golden Happiness*, on the corner of Harbour and West Sts, has reasonable quality dishes. Most meals cost less than US$4, and you can request half-orders. For more cosmopolitan fare, try the bistro-style restaurant at Bonnie View (see Places to Stay), which serves an eclectic variety of dishes, from American to Italian. The view is magnificent; only that from the restaurant of Navy Island Marina Resort competes. The latter has a weekly alfresco buffet with limbo and fire eating.

There are several bakeries selling savories, desserts, and fresh-baked bread. Try *Coronation Bakery* and *Three Star Lion Bakery* at 18 and 27 West St, respectively. *Cream World*, on Harbour St, is the local ice cream parlor.

Entertainment

Nightclubs *The Roof Club*, Port Antonio's famous hang-loose reggae bar, has attracted the likes of Linda Evans and Tom Cruise (11 West St, ☎ 993-2127). You can't hear yourself think, but you're guaranteed a great time. It's hot and steamy . . . I mean the dancing! Young men and women move from partner to partner performing wine on a bummsee, a groin-to-rear-end dance style. You're fair game for any stranger who takes your fancy. The place is small, crowded, and decorated with mirrors, Day-glo squiggles, and UV lighting.

Other happening reggae dance spots are the *Mandela Open Ground* and *Taurus* (☎ 993-2661), both on Summers Town Rd (marked incorrectly on the JTB's 'Discover Jamaica' map as W Palm Ave). *Shadows* is more upscale; you can dance beneath the stars to live music, or in the nightclub, which offers oldies on Sunday (40 W Palm Ave, ☎ 993-3823).

Casino Card sharks should head to *The Players Choice*, upstairs at 3 Market Place (☎ 993-2661).

Cinemas The *Delmar Theater* on Fort George St shows current-run movies (☎ 993-3304). Old Errol Flynn movies are shown at the Navy Island Marina Resort.

Folk Shows Several hotels feature limbo and Caribbean folk shows. See also San San Beach.

Jazz Music Taurus has a jazz night on Sunday. Live jazz is also offered at Blue Lagoon Restaurant (see Places to Eat under Blue Lagoon, above) on Saturday nights.

Things to Buy

Musgrave Market, on West St, is a cacophonous slice of Jamaican life. The colorful and aromatic produce section faces onto West St. Household goods and bric-a-brac are in the center. At the back is a craft market that opens onto the town square. Thursday and Saturday are liveliest.

Jamaica Arcade has craft stalls tucked in a courtyard immediately east of the courthouse. Also check out the sculptures and paintings of Renford Stewart at his studio on 5 William St.

The best quality crafts are sold at Patricia Wymore Flynn's Designer's Gallery, in the Jamaica Palace (see Turtle Crawle Bay, above). Nearby, Zion Hill Gallery (see Fairy Hill, above) displays eclectic artwork in a native style – including jewelry, carvings, and excellent portraits (☎ 995-3005). Judy Madson, the gallery's owner, and local artist Herbie Rose have together designed a program to assist and stimulate pride among local indigent children. They're trying to fund a gallery and art foundation (donations are needed) whereby the income from sales of the children's artwork will fund their education and show them they can make a living through their own efforts.

By the time you read this, a new art gallery should be open at Hotel Mockingbird in Frenchman's Cove. There's also a duty-free shop in City Centre Plaza.

Getting There & Away

Air See the Getting Around chapter for details on Air Jamaica Express. Caribic Vacations may have initiated air charters to Port Antonio from Montego Bay by the time you read this (☎ 952-5013).

Bus A new bus station extends along the waterfront on Gideon Ave. Buses leave regularly for Annotto Bay (No LS287) and Port Maria (where you change for Ocho Rios; minibus No LS916). At least half a dozen buses and even more minibuses operate between Kingston via both Buff Bay and via Manchioneal and Morant Bay (US$1.60 to Kingston). You can get minibuses from West St.

Taxi Government-established taxi fares from Kingston to Port Antonio are US$89 (one to four people). JUTA offers transfers from Montego Bay airport (US$40 one-way), and from Kingston airport for US$30 one way (c/o Destinations, ☎ 993-2609 in

Port Antonio; ☎ 929-6368 in Kingston). Island Car Rentals (☎ 926-8861 in Kingston, or ☎ 924-8075 at Norman Manley International Airport) can arrange a car and driver. JD Tours offers transfers from Kingston (US$80), Ocho Rios (US$100), and Montego Bay (US$180); prices are per vehicle, carrying up to four people (☎ 993-2752, fax 993-2862).

Boat Huntress and Navy Island Marinas both offer customs clearance if you're arriving in Jamaica aboard your own vessel.

Getting Around
The Airport Port Antonio is served by the Ken Jones Aerodrome at St Margaret's Bay, six miles west of town (☎ 993-2673). From here, most upscale hotels offer free transfers. There is no bus service, although you can flag down any bus or minibus passing along the A4.

Car & Motorcycle Eastern Rent-a-Car (☎ 993-3624) has an office on Harbour St, and Don's Car Rental (☎ 993-2241) has an office in the Trident Hotel. Alternately, try Hopeview Car Rental (☎ 993-3040). Individuals with money to burn can even rent a Mercedes Benz from Mercedes Car Rental at 14 Harbour St (reservations, 6 Allan Ave, Port Antonio, ☎ 993-9792, on weekends ☎ 993-8286). A two-day minimum costs US$210, or US$500 per week.

Scooters and motorcycles are available from Rainbow Rentals (☎ 993-2248) next to the DeMontevin Lodge, and from Portland Motorcycle Rentals at 17 Boundbrook Wharf (☎ 993-3653). If you've seen the Lonely Planet video, *The Jamaica Experience*, the scene of negotiating for a motorcycle from Rainbow Rentals won't inspire you with great confidence! Expect to pay between US$30 and US$50 a day, depending on the size of vehicle.

Taxi The Port Antonio Cab Drivers' Co-op (☎ 993-2684), Sunshine Taxi (993-2123), and Tyrell's Taxi (993-3124) all offer taxi service. Most of the vehicles are beat-up old bangers. A typical charge is US$5 to or from San San or the Blue Lagoon. Your taxi driver will gladly wait for you at no charge if you're dining or out for a night of entertainment.

Bicycle Both Stuart's Travel and Cycle World (above Sunshine Taxi at 7 Harbour St) rent bicycles, as does East Coast Rentals (☎ 993-9330) in the Huntress Marina. You can also rent bicycles from Rainbow Rentals.

SOUTH OF PORT ANTONIO
Athenry Gardens & Nonsuch Caves
Athenry Gardens is a former coconut plantation and agricultural research center that today, as a lush botanical garden, boasts many exotic and native species. The highlight, however, is the Nonsuch Cave system of nine separate chambers full of stalagmites and stalactites. Steps lead into the caves, which are gloomily lit by lanterns. The limestone was laid millions of years before Jamaica rose above the sea, as indicated by fossils of fish, coral, and other sea creatures. Now only bats occupy the dank bowels. They hang from the 40-foot-high ceiling in what is called the Gothic-scale Cathedral. Guides call it the Bat Romance Room, which more accurately portrays what goes on. They'll also point out imaginary stalagmite formations: a pope, a bishop, a man in robes upon a camel, and a naked woman emerging from a shell.

The caves and garden are about seven miles southeast of Port Antonio via Red Hassell Rd. After two miles there's a Y-fork. The right fork leads to Berridale and the Rio Grande; take the left for Nonsuch. The road leads uphill all the way and is appallingly rutted. Just when you feel like giving up you see a handsome home sitting incongruously atop the hill. A sign to the right of the house points to the caves and Athenry Gardens.

You can also reach Nonsuch Caves via a road that heads uphill via Nonsuch Village and Sherwood Forest from the Zion Hill Café at Fairy Hill.

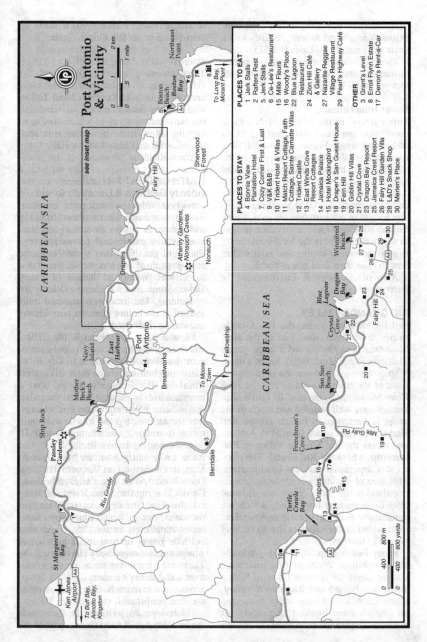

Port Antonio & Vicinity

PLACES TO STAY

4   Bonnie View
    Plantation Hotel
7   Cozy Corner First & Last
9   V&K B&B
10 Trident Hotel & Villas
11 Match Resort Cottage, Faith
    Cottage, Sainte Camatte Villas
12 Trident Castle
13 East Winds Cove
    Resort Cottages
14 Jamaica Palace
15 Hotel Mockingbird
18 Draper's San Guest House
19 Fern Hill
20 Goblin Hill Villas
21 Crystal Cove
23 Dragon Bay Resort
25 Jamaica Crest Resort
26 Fairy Hill Garden Villa
28 L&D's Snack Shop
30 Merlen's Place

PLACES TO EAT

1   Jerk Stalls
2   Rafters Rest
5   Jerk Stalls
6   Ce-Lee's Restaurant
15 Mille Fleurs
16 Woody's Place
22 Blue Lagoon
    Restaurant
24 Zion Hill Café
    & Gallery
27 Nazarite Reggae
    Village Restaurant
29 Pearl's Highway Café

OTHER

3   Grant's Level
8   Erroll Flynn Estate
17 Derron's Rent-a-Car

JD Tours (☎ 993-2752) offers a six-hour trip to Nonsuch and Athenry, ending with a swim at Frenchman's Cove (US$15).

There's a secure car park and toll booth. Entrance costs US$5/2.50. It's open 9 am to 5 pm (☎ 993-3740).

Silver Hills Nursery

This nursery, in the village of Nonsuch, grows fruit trees and mahogany for seeds and seedlings. Frank Swindells, the friendly English agronomist who set up the nursery, will happily give you a guided tour (c/o Look Out PA, Nonsuch, Port Antonio, fax 993-2143). Silver Hill has the ability to produce 20,000 seedlings annually for use in reforestation projects. Frank runs an education and conservation project in which each child in the local community is given a seed or cutting and educated in how to raise their fruit tree at home.

Also see Ecology & Environment, in Facts about Jamaica.

RIO GRANDE VALLEY

Fed by torrential rains, the Rio Grande rushes down from 3000 feet in the Blue Mountains and has carved a huge gorge. This exceedingly lush valley forms a deep, V-shaped wedge between the northeastern flank of the Blue Mountains and the John Crow Mountains to the east. Its fertile alluvial soils are well watered and much of the valley is dominated by banana groves. Red Hassell Rd runs south from Port Antonio and enters the Rio Grande Valley at **Fellowship**, where the Rio Grande Development Corporation has its headquarters. This area of the valley is renowned for its populations of rare, giant swallowtail *(Papilio homerus)* butterflies, which are particularly abundant in early summer. Due to its isolation, the valley is almost entirely devoid of tourists.

From Fellowship, the road gradually winds uphill to **Windsor** (the traditional starting point for arduous hikes to Nanny Town; see below) and **Seaman's Valley**, where the Maroons supposedly massacred an English force in the 18th century. At Seaman's Valley the road forks: to the left is Moore Town; to the right, it leads up through the upper Rio Grande Valley.

Hiking

There are many narrow trails through the valley. All are off the beaten track and many are known only to farmers. Most follow water-supply lines to their intake and link remote hamlets, many of which now exist only in name (ruins can be seen at such places as Brookdale and John's Hall).

You should be prepared for the unexpected. Don't attempt to hike without a guide unless you're an extremely experienced hiker. If you do, don't do so without a machete; although many paths are occasionally cleared, the rainforest quickly reclaims them. Guides are still a good idea, as most trails pass through private property. The Corn Puss Gap trail should never be attempted alone. So, too, the wild path that leads from Windsor to the site of Nanny Town. Some hikes are easy. Others are demanding, with muddy, overgrown trails and small rivers that often require fording and can be chest deep.

Popular hikes include to White Valley, which is known for its large population of giant swallowtail butterflies; to Dry River Falls, reached on a one-hour hike west from the Rio Grande (it's said that a mermaid lives in the cave behind the falls); and to Scatter Waterfalls and Fox's Caves, reached by crossing the Rio Grande on a raft at Berridale, from where you hike 15 minutes, wading across the Sarah River en route. (Alternately you can hike from St Margaret's Bay up to Coopers Hill and Olive Mount, then down to Bourbon and Berridale along the Sarah River.) A steep hike from the base of the waterfall leads to the caves, one of which has many chambers with interesting formations. Another (with the Fox River running through it) has a large population of bats. The owners, the Thaxters, are developing a rest area with toilets and changing rooms, plus a campground and restaurant. The open grounds are ideal for picnics.

Huub Gaymans, a Dutchman, spearheads the Eco-Tourism Action Group, part of the

Sorting bananas for market

C'est la vie at Frenchman's Cove.

A little instruction atop Morant Point Lighthouse

Wandering white-sand beaches at Holland Bay

White River, just east of Ocho Rios, offers an opportunity for leisurely rafting and boating.

DAVE HOUSER

Lovely falls at the privately owned
Enchanted Garden near Ocho Rios

Palm-fringed coast at Ocho Rios

Rio Grande Valley Project that is researching trails, training trail guides, and developing attractions to sponsor tourism and community development.

Valley Hikes (PO Box 89, Port Antonio, ☎/fax 993-2543) offers a series of organized hikes. Those lasting no more than four hours cost US$10. Three-day hikes cost US$150, and a strenuous 10-day hike is US$450. Horseback rides are also available (US$25). Reservations must be made 24 hours in advance. Valley Hikes currently shares an office with the Rio Grande Project in Fellowship, but has plans to move to Port Antonio. They publish a trail guide and rent hiking boots at their office if needed.

Rafting

Errol Flynn supposedly initiated rafting on the Rio Grande during the 1940s, when he organized raft races among locals, who used to ship bananas downriver to Port Antonio on bamboo rafts. Flynn also found the river's leisurely pace perfect for seduction, and had his raft fitted with a cushioned seat (according to local lore, he never took the same woman twice). By the 1960s rafting the Rio Grande had become the rage among the social elite. Moonlight raft trips were considered the ultimate activity among the fashionable . . . until a formally dressed party (including noted novelist and wild-card Truman Capote) tipped over, and grand ladies in chiffon almost drowned.

Today paying passengers make the three-hour, six-mile journey from Grant's Level, near Berridale, to Rafters Rest, at St Margaret's Bay. The 36-foot-long rafts are three feet wide. You sit on a raised seat with padded cushions while an experienced 'captain' poles you through the washboard shallows and small cataracts. The rafts are towed back upstream at the end of the day. It's a marvelous experience. The journey is perfectly scenic. You'll get a taste for rural life along the riverbanks, where women and children bathe and wash clothes, shore-side peddlers strum guitars for a tip, and others sell sodas and coconuts, often from other rafts. En route, you'll pass through

Lovers Leap, a moss-covered stone arch where you can make a wish, and *Betty's*, a lean-to café on a pebbly curve of the river, where you can lunch on Jamaican staples such as ackee and codfish, rice and peas, or *janga* soup.

The trips are offered by Rio Grande Attractions Ltd (PO Box 128, Port Antonio, ☎ 993-2778). They're available 8:30 am to 4:30 pm, and cost US$40 per raft, double for full-moon rides. It's best to make reservations. The put-in is at Berridale, where dozens of rafts are drawn up along the shore. Your car will be driven down to Rafter's Rest to await your return (extra charge). At Berridale, there's a small riverside bar and restaurant where a lively dominoes game is likely to be in progress, plus a gift store with straw hats for sale. You may need one to guard against the sun. And don't forget your sunscreen and an umbrella in case of rain.

A minibus from Port Antonio to Grant's Level will cost about US$2. Expect to pay about US$12 round-trip for a taxi.

Canoeing

Sense Adventures (☎ 927-2097) offers white-water river trips by inflatable canoe on the Drivers River. It's a fairly tame Class II.

MOORE TOWN

This one-street village, 10 miles south of Port Antonio, stretches uphill for several hundred yards along the course of the Wildcane River. It looks like any other Jamaican village, but is important as the former base of the Windward Maroons (see the sidebar in the Blue Mountains chapter). The village was founded in 1739 following a peace treaty whereby the British colonialists granted the Maroons their independence along with 500 acres on which to build a settlement. Moore Town is still run semi-autonomously by a council of 24 elected members headed by an ex-schoolteacher and Jamaica Labour Party (JLP) senator, Colonel 'Teacher' Harris, a powerfully built, self-assured man who has held his post since 1964.

You don't have to request prior permission to visit Moore Town as some sources suggest, but to do so can grease the wheels.

There's a Workers Savings & Loan Bank and a post office (open Monday to Friday, 8 am to 4 pm, and Saturday 8 am to noon) just 50 yards below the school.

Bump Grave
Beyond a derelict church and graveyard at the southern, uppermost end of town is Bump Grave (note the intriguing murals on the school wall, opposite the gravesite). A plaque on the oblong, stone grave reads: 'NANNY of the Maroons/National Hero of Jamaica/Beneath this place known as Bump Grave lies the body of Nanny, indomitable and skilled chieftainess of the Windward Maroons who founded this town.' The grave is topped by a flagpole flying both the Maroon and Jamaican flags.

More Town's inhabitants are a very Christian people, as attested by the seven churches. On one of my recent visits, one of the colonel's lieutenants, Mr Lucky Osborn, became quite vexed when I asked if Nanny was venerated. 'We worship no idols. We worship GOD!' he boomed. He calmed down later and even offered to be my guide to Nanny Town (see below).

Faith Healing
Try to visit on Mondays, when a local faith healer named Mother Roberts performs in the Deliverance Centre. People gather from far and wide for revivalist music, dancing, and lots of hysteria – don't be surprised to see her pull a rusty nail from some one's head! On Wednesdays, Mother Roberts holds more serious, private healings in a shack at the back of her house (a substantial ochre-colored affair that attests to how lucrative her trade is). You take a ticket and wait in line. There's a soda stand to ward off any thirst. When I visited, there were at least 40 people waiting to be 'healed.'

Places to Stay
I'm not aware of any accommodations, but you can try renting a room with a local family.

Getting There & Away
Moore Town is two miles south of Seaman's Castle. The town is unmarked and lies in a hollow to the left of a Y-junction; the main dirt road continues uphill to Cornwall Barracks. In Port Antonio, 'Rev' organizes trips to Moore Town (contact him at Culture Ice, 40 Somestown Rd).

A bus operates to Moore Town from downtown Port Antonio (US$0.30).

TWIN APPLE PARK
This recreational facility was under construction at press time in a hamlet called Cornwall Barracks, two miles south of Moore Town. It will include fish ponds, a restaurant, plus a Maroon craft center and store. The park is reached via an old swing bridge. Other attractions include a waterfall, a small cave, and a mineral spring called Jupiter. Trail guides are being trained to lead hikes locally.

UPPER RIO GRANDE VALLEY
The road leading west from the T-junction at Seaman's Castle leads via **Alligator Church** (named, according to local legend, for an alligator that was seen entering the church, dressed in black) and Comfort Castle to Bowden Pen, 10 miles or so up the river valley.

The ranger station for the John Crow National Park is at Millbank, two miles before Bowden Pen at the end of the dirt road, near the summit ridge of the John Crow Mountains. The dirt road is extremely rough and narrow and you'll need a 4WD. From Bowden Pen, you can continue on foot along what was once a road across the Cuna Cuna Pass, which linked Portland and St Thomas in colonial days.

The area has received more than 400 inches of rain in some years. Needless to say, the vegetation is as thick as it gets in Jamaica.

Places to Stay & Eat
A North American named Royce Brimson runs a small guest house called *Rainbow Valley* at Bowden Pen. It is said to boast great views. Royce cooks I-tal meals. You

can camp here, too. You can also rent a room from an elderly lady called Birdie Bifield (about one mile further). She'll cook if you bring food.

Camp Wimoweh, also at Bowden Pen, is open for camping on weekends for groups of seven or more (The Towers, 25 Dominica Drive, Kingston 5, ☎ 929-3236). It has primitive facilities. US$95 for seven people, all-inclusive, then $40 each additional night.

Getting There & Away
A bus from Port Antonio goes as far as Millbank (US$0.50).

NANNY TOWN
This former stronghold of the Windward Maroons was once a large village of over 140 houses on the brink of a precipitous spur on the northeastern flank of Blue Mountain Peak, about 10 miles west of Moore Town as the crow flies. It is named for an Ashanti woman and warrior priestess who led the Maroons during the early 18th century. Today she's a National Hero. English soldiers searched for Nanny Town for many years until led there by a traitor in 1728. They attacked it several times over the ensuing years, but Nanny proved to be a brilliant military tactician. Legend records that she had supernatural gifts, including the ability to catch bullets and return them 'with fatal effect' with her vagina. (See Moore Town below for more about Nanny.) Eventually, in 1734, a Captain Stoddard led his troops over the Blue Mountains and, armed with swivel guns, took Nanny Town from the rear (Stoddard's Peak is named for him).

The village was soon lost to the jungle. Even the Ordnance Survey maps show its location as 'approximate.'

Local superstitions abound. Nanny Town is said to be haunted by a 'whole heap of duppies' who appear as white birds, and a nearby river flows 'red, red like blood' my guide told me. The town was partially excavated by the Institute of Jamaica in 1973, and pictographs were discovered in caves in the rocks. Another legend says that any European who ventures there will die.

Getting There & Away
It's a tough 10-mile hike over hill and dale from Windsor, three miles south of Moore Town. Valley Hikes (see Hiking, above) has a three-day guided hike that begins in Windsor. The trail leads via the deserted village of John's Hall to a riverside camp site at Makunnu. Nights are spent in huts. In Moore Town, Shadow (alias 'The Professor') or Lucky can guide you.

PASSLEY GARDENS
Passley botanical gardens, two miles west of Port Antonio, is run by Passley Gardens College, which offers degree courses in agriculture. The 600-acre facility is laid out as an idealized village centered around a well-preserved great house. In addition to well-tended gardens, the grounds include an experimental livestock farm and groves of tropical fruit trees. The college has even initiated mariculture along its two-mile shoreline. Visitors are welcome (no admission charge). The college can be toured by appointment only (☎ 993-2631).

ST MARGARET'S BAY
The A4 crosses the Rio Grande two miles west of Passley via a 480-foot-long iron bridge. Beyond is the hamlet of St Margaret's Bay, from where a road loops inland, providing a stunningly scenic drive into the foothills of the Blue Mountains (see below) before returning to the coast at **Hope Bay**, which has an ugly gray-sand beach. Another loop drive can be made from here up the Swift River Valley, where plantations grow cacao.

Ken Jones Aerodrome
Port Antonio is served by the Ken Jones Aerodrome here, six miles west of town, and two miles west of St Margaret's Bay (☎ 993-2673).

The small airport (named for a former minister of communications) has a phone and a small waiting room, but no other services. See Getting Around in Port Antonio for more information.

SOMERSET FALLS

These falls are hidden in a deep gorge overhung with thick foliage. Nine miles west of Port Antonio, the Daniels River cascades down through a lush garden of ferns, heliconias, lilies, crotons, and bright purple plumbergia that grow on a former indigo and spice plantation.

The US$2/1 entrance includes a guided tour and gondola ride to the Hidden Fall that tumbles 33 feet into a jade-colored grotto. You can plunge into the cool waters from a high rock. The property includes a fish farm that raises silver perch, and a small menagerie that includes waterfowl and a friendly emu called Harrison. It's open 9 am to 5 pm daily, and has restrooms and a snack bar next to the car park.

You'll have to negotiate some steep, twisty steps, and when I was last there visitors had to wade through a narrow opening to reach the waterfall.

Places to Stay

Most accommodations near Somerset Falls are in Hope Bay. A Rastafarian couple, Brother John and Sister P, run a rustic retreat called *Content Farm* (☎ 953-2387) at Content, in the mountains above Hope Bay. A stay here offers all-around vistas (mountain and coastal) and provides an insight into the real Jamaican lifestyle. The couple have five bamboo cottages with outhouse toilets, no electricity, and cold water from an outside barrel. You'll bathe in an invigorating mountain stream. Accommodations with all meals (I-tal food and natural juices) cost about US$30. You can camp, too (US$5). The 35-acre farm is planted with avocado, coconuts, and citrus. Content also serves as a tiny primary school, and visitors are encouraged to help with teaching. Content Farm is featured on the Lonely Planet video, *The Jamaica Experience*.

To get there, turn south at the police station in Hope Bay, then turn right after one mile and then second left. A 4WD is recommended. You can write to Sister P at Content, Hope Bay PO, Portland; or c/o Village Cleaners, Shop No 2, 1 Bridge St, Port Antonio.

Rio Sol Mar Guest House features two rooms in a handsome but simple house full of antiques on the banks of the Swift River. One has a four-poster bed. The owner, Paula Espuet, also has two handsome self-catering apartments. You can arrange meals with Ruby, the housekeeper.

Another option called *Rio Vista Villas* (☎ 993-2244) is located near the turnoff for Rafters Rest.

Places to Eat

There are a few funky restaurants and an ice cream stand in Hope Bay, and a fistful of shacks selling jerk chicken and seafood beside the bridge over the Swift River.

For elegant dining, head to *Rafters Rest* restaurant, in a columned Georgian mansion, at the mouth of the Rio Grande, 600 yards downhill from the A4. Rafters Rest is the traditional end point for the bamboo raft trip from Berridale. You dine on a shady veranda lit at night by wrought-iron lanterns. The menu includes salads (US$5 to 10), burgers (US$5), curried chicken (US$9), and steak with garlic butter (US$12). There's also a well-stocked gift store.

Getting There & Away

Buses No LS287 and LS997 pass Somerset Falls en route between Annotto Bay and Port Antonio. Ask the driver to put you down near the entrance (US$0.30). You may also be able to take any of the dozen or so buses that operate between Port Antonio and Kingston.

ORANGE BAY

West of Hope Bay, the A4 winds inland for several miles past Orange Bay and Spring Garden Estate. Near Orange Bay, you'll pass a 600-foot-high ridge that was formed by a prehistoric volcanic fissure eruption.

Spring Gardens Estate

This former sugar plantation, one of the oldest in the region, is today planted in coconuts. It formerly belonged to Viscount Hailsham, whose grandson, renounced the title in 1963. Hailsham's attorney, William

Bancroft Espuet, later bought the property and built Jamaica's first railway in 1868 to convey sugarcane from field to factory. The enterprising Espuet also first introduced the mongoose to the island. Alas, the four male and five female animals he brought from India to control rats have multiplied and their progeny are to blame for the devastation caused over the past century to many native species and livestock.

Crystal Springs
This bucolic recreational site half a mile inland from Spring Gardens boasts a splendid orchid collection and botanical greenhouses in a 56-acre setting of wide lawns, lush bougainvillea, aracauria palms, fruit trees, and forest linked by pathways. It's superb for birding. There's a small folk museum and restaurant, and guided tours are available (☎ 926-6785 or 929-7865; in the USA, ☎ (800) 523-3782). It's open 9 am to 6 pm. Entrance costs US$0.50.

Places to Stay & Eat
Crystal Springs has cabins with electricity and cold water. It's a peaceful haven amid lawns and patches of forest. The rustic cottages cost US$40 double, including Jamaican breakfast. A two-bedroom unit sleeping four is also available for US$120. You can camp for US$5. Tent rentals, previously offered, are no longer available. Meals are served in an open-sided restaurant and cost from US$3 to US$10.

Getting There & Away
Buses running between Port Antonio, Annotto Bay, and Kingston pass by the turnoff for Crystal Springs.

BLUE MOUNTAIN FOOTHILLS
Midway between Orange Bay and Buff Bay, a rough road leads inland through banana plantations to the foothills of the Blue Mountains. The area was earmarked for coffee expansion in the late 1980s, funded by the Japanese Ueshima Coffee Co. The first plantations appear at Skibo.

A bus from Buff Bay goes as far as Chepstow (US$0.20).

Hiking
It's wise to obtain a copy of Sheets 13 and 14 of the Ordnance Survey 1:12500-series topographical maps of Jamaica, showing the Portland Blue Mountains. You'll need both sheets, as well as Sheet 18 (and possibly 19) if you plan on descending to the south of the Blue Mountain crest. You can buy them for US$5 per sheet at the Survey Dept office at 23½ Charles St in Kingston (PO Box 493; ☎ 922-6630), or in England from the Ordnance Survey, Romsey Rd, Southampton SO9 4DH.

BUFF BAY
This small neatly laid town has been entirely bypassed by tourism. It has several colonial-era buildings of modest interest, centered on the Anglican church, one of 15 churches that remain outnumbered by rum shops. Unfortunately, the narrow shingle beach is used by locals as a garbage dump.

There are some modestly attractive beaches west of town, where the road rises away from the coast, with occasional dirt roads leading down to the shore.

Banana plantations extend westward from Buff Bay along the coastal plains spanning the border of St Mary and Portland Parishes. They're owned by Jamaica Banana Producers Ltd, founded by the Jamaican government in 1930 to challenge the domination of the United Fruit Company. The Buff Bay River and Spanish River valleys are also centers of banana cultivation.

Information
The post office is 100 yards east of the church. Buff Bay also has a small hospital (☎ 996-2232), and the police station (☎ 996-2233) is at the east end of town.

Surfing
The coast between Orange Bay and Annotto Bay is good for surfing if there's a swell happening.

Organized Tours
Pro-Tours Ltd offers a daylong excursion to **Fishdone Waterfalls**, a beautiful spot on a

private coffee plantation near Buff Bay. The falls are surrounded by rainforest hugging the slopes of the Blue Mountains, and there are trails for hiking. The cost depends on group size (8 Lady Musgrave Rd, Kingston 5, ☎ 978-6113, fax 978-5473).

Places to Stay & Eat
The *Sea Palace*, one mile east of town at Blueberry Hill, has basic rooms for US$3 (☎ 996-2310). For jerk, stop by *G&B Jerk Centre* on the eastern fringe of town, opposite the *Seawinds Club*, a hotel, restaurant, and disco/bar, which was recently under construction. For breakfast, head to *Pacesetters Café* at 6 Russell Ave (☎ 996-2317). It's run by Earle and Pat Brown, who offer inexpensive meals, including delicious pastries and coffee. At *Rosa's Cantina*, in town, you can savor curried goat, escoveitch fish, and rice and peas for less than US$1.

Getting There & Away
From Kingston or Port Antonio take bus No JR75, which operates twice daily between Port Antonio and Papine via Hardwar Gap (US$0.60). Other buses pass through Buff Bay, including the LS287 from Annotto Bay.

BUFF BAY RIVER VALLEY
The B1 heads south from the Texaco gas station in the town center, and then climbs 20 miles through the valley of the Buff Bay River and into the Blue Mountains. The road ascends via Balcarres, Spring Hill, and Section to Hardwar Gap, at an elevation of 4500 feet, before dropping down to Kingston. The road narrows, climbs, and grows increasingly sinuous, with more and deeper pot holes. Many of the villages that appear on tourist maps are little more than a few shacks, often hidden out of sight in the bush.

These slopes are an important coffee producing area, and you can buy wonderfully aromatic Blue Mountain coffee from roadside stalls for less than US$1 a pound.

Bicycle Tours
About two miles above Spring Hill's police station (12 miles south of Buff Bay) is the office of Blue Mountain Tours (☎ 993-2242), which also has an office between the Esso gas station and Seawind Club in Buff Bay. This is the starting point for guided mountain bike tours which are downhill all the way.

ANNOTTO BAY
This erstwhile banana port once handled the produce of 48 estates. Annotto became a main center for banana production in the late 19th century when a Scottish physician, Sir John Pringle (1848–1923), arrived in Jamaica and reaped a fortune in the area by buying up derelict sugar plantations and planting bananas.

Today Annotto is a downtrodden, one-street town that springs to life for Saturday market. It suffered a severe blow in 1985 with the demise of the Gray's Inn sugar factory and the discontinuation of rail service. Hurricane Gilbert added insult to injury in 1988.

The mile-long main street straddles the River Pencar, which effectively divides the town into east and west Annotto. Depressing shanties line the waterfront. At the town's center is an old blue-and-white courthouse that now houses the office of the collector of taxes. There are also some gingerbread colonial-era structures with columned walkways, and the paltry remains of **Fort George**, which was built on Spanish foundations. The most intriguing edifice is the venerable yellow- and red-brick **Baptist chapel** built in 'village baroque' style in 1894 with cut-glass windows and curious biblical exhortations engraved at cornice height. Little cannons stand in its gateway.

The town's name derives from the Anatto, a dye plant *(Bixa orellana)* that once was grown commercially here. The plant is native to tropical America and Amerindians used the juice from its fruit for war paint.

Information
The town has a small hospital with a primitive emergency department (☎ 996-2222). The post office is on Main St, 50 yards east of the Baptist chapel; the police station (☎ 996-2244), also on Main St, is a stone's throw east of the chapel.

Places to Stay & Eat
Octopus Drive Inn, 200 yards east of the Texaco gas station east of town, is a two-story wooden house facing the sea. It rents very basic rooms for US$6 and has a small restaurant and bar.

You can eat for less than US$2 at *Roots Club*, on Main St, a popular local bar which also has go-go dancing at night.

Back to Eden, across the street, serves I-tal food. Both are good budget eateries, as is the *First & Last Snack Stop* in the old railway station east of town. Roadside higglers congregate immediately east of town. There you can buy grilled lobster, conch, saltfish, and peppered shrimp, washed down with fruit juices or coconut milk.

Getting There & Away
If coming from Ocho Rios take bus No LS916, which costs about US$0.50 one way. Winston Condappa operates a minibus (No 716) between Annotto and Port Maria. Bus LS287 departs Annotto Bay for Port Antonio (US$0.50).

Northeast Coast

This area is replete with attractions. For this reason the main resort, Ocho Rios, is a favorite stop for cruise ships. The region is lusher than Montego Bay and areas further west, and has several botanical gardens and working plantations to visit within a few minutes drive of Ocho Rios. By driving further east, to Oracabessa and Port Maria, you'll escape the crowds and discover such gems as Noel Coward's former home. Few travelers venture inland to discover the scenic beauty of the mountains, or esoteric attractions such as Bob Marley's birthplace and mausoleum.

OCHO RIOS

Ocho Rios (population 8200) is Jamaica's third most important resort (second if you count cruise ship arrivals). First the good points, most notably the setting: Ocho Rios is located in a deep bowl backed by lushly vegetated hills and fronted by a wide, scalloped, white-sand beach – Turtle Beach – and a reef-sheltered harbor. Immediately east of town are other nice beaches, most of them hidden in coves that are ostensibly the private domains of upscale hotels.

Ocho Rios, 67 miles east of Montego Bay, is good for forays along the coast and inland, with many botanical gardens, plantations, and other sites and activities of interest to experience within a short distance. The town also has excellent duty-free shopping. 'Ochi,' as the locals call it, is popular with the cruise ships, which gleams white against its lush backdrop and turquoise waters.

The town, however, has little charm. Most of the palm trees behind Turtle Beach are gone, replaced by hotels. The otherwise-beautiful bay vista is marred by a bauxite-loading facility that now stands idle. In town there are virtually no historic buildings of note. When the cruise ships call in, the compact streets are thronged with passengers, like bees released from a hive.

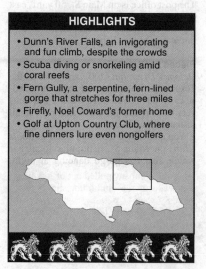

HIGHLIGHTS

- Dunn's River Falls, an invigorating and fun climb, despite the crowds
- Scuba diving or snorkeling amid coral reefs
- Fern Gully, a serpentine, fern-lined gorge that stretches for three miles
- Firefly, Noel Coward's former home
- Golf at Upton Country Club, where fine dinners lure even nongolfers

Cruise ships rarely arrive on weekends; you would do well to plan your itinerary accordingly. Over 400,000 of these passengers flood the streets annually, adding up to 40% of Jamaica's tourist arrivals! Not surprisingly, competition among local hustlers is fierce at these times, and a stroll down the street can wear on the nerves.

The government's revitalization project, aimed at reducing harassment of visitors and beautifying the town, will improve sidewalks and add a boardwalk to Dunn's River Falls. By the time you read this, hardcore hustling may be a thing of the past; the police began clearing illegal vendors and prostitutes off the streets in mid-1995.

History

Ocho Rios (Spanish for 'eight rivers') is an English corruption of *chorreras* ('waterfalls'), the name the Spaniards gave to this section of coast. Ironically, neither the Spanish nor the English settled the bay; pirates, however, thought it a perfect base.

The pirates were sponsored by local plantation owners, partly to keep them focused on foreign not domestic booty, but also in exchange for a share of the profit.

Although plantations were developed inland and along the coast, Ocho Rios never evolved as a fruit-shipping port of any consequence. Things began to change when Reynolds Jamaica Mines built a deep-water pier west of town in the 1940s. The first shipment of bauxite to leave Jamaica did so in 1952 from the Reynolds Pier. An overhead conveyor belt (which still looms over the road) carried the ore 6.3 miles from the Reynolds open-cast mines at Lydford, in the hills south of town. No bauxite has been shipped from the pier since the company pulled out of Jamaica in the wake of the aluminum slump of the 1980s.

Ocho Rios was still just a quiet fishing village in the 1960s when the Jamaican government formed the St Ann Development Council and began a systematic development. The council acquired much of the land surrounding the bay. They dredged the harbor and built a small marina, reclaimed the shore, brought in sand for Turtle Beach, and built a number of shopping complexes and housing schemes. Private developers followed. By the early 1980s, Ochi's character had been established: a meld of American-style fast-food franchises, nondescript shopping malls, and mediocre and upscale English-style hotels.

Orientation

Greater Ocho Rios extends four miles between Dunn's River Falls, two miles to the west of the town center, and the White River, two miles to the east. Almost all the development outside the center is to the east. A good place to get your bearings is Shaw Park Gardens, which offers a bird's-eye view over Ocho Rios.

The main coast road, the A3 (called DaCosta Drive in town), runs through the

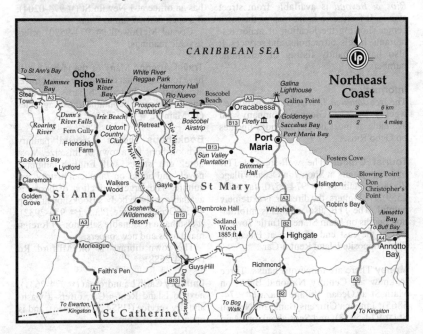

town center. Near the west end of DaCosta Drive is a roundabout. The main road to Kingston leads south from here via Fern Gully. Dominating the center of town are the twin towers of the Jamaica Grande Hotel, at the northern tip of west-facing Turtle Beach. Aptly named Main St runs in an S-curve along Turtle Bay and parallel to DaCosta Drive. Main St and DaCosta Drive meet to the east at a clock tower that marks the busy center of town. James St runs north from here to the west end of Mallards Bay, whose beach is hidden from view; divided up between several mid-range hotels.

The town is small enough to walk everywhere, but you'll need transportation to get further afield. Town center and A3 are subject to horrendous traffic jams. A long-touted bypass is being built to relieve the pressure and may be completed by the time you read this.

Maps A large, fold-out map called *Ocho Rios & Beyond* is available from street stands. It features a basic map of the town center showing the location of major restaurants, hotels, attractions, and services. It also has a handy listing of telephone numbers.

Information

The free *Jamaica Tourist Guide*, published weekly by The Gleaner Company and available at most hotels, includes updates on Ocho Rios.

Tourist Offices The well-stocked JTB office is upstairs at Shop 7 in Ocean Village Plaza on Main St (☎ 974-2570, fax 974-2559). Iva Walters, the director, is extremely helpful. The JTB also maintains information booths on Main St, near Turtle Towers, and at the east end of town at Pineapple Place, opposite Island Rent-a-Car.

Money There are numerous banks. Three to know are Century National Bank, on Main St at Ocean Village Plaza (☎ 974-5865); Jamaica Citizens Bank, on Newlin St (☎ 974-5953); and Scotiabank on Main

St (☎ 974-2311). The Bank of Jamaica has a currency exchange at Shop 2, Pineapple Plaza (☎ 974-5618). You can arrange an urgent remittance of money via Western Union, which has an office immediately west of Ocean Village Plaza (☎ 991-2056). American Express is represented by Stuart's Travel (see Travel Agency below). They can handle any problems that may arise with your traveler's checks. If you want to change money illegally on the black market you'll find plenty of obliging hustlers on DaCosta Drive. The going rate is about 15% above the official exchange rate. Use utmost caution as scams are frequent.

Post & Communications The post office is on Main St, opposite the Ocean Village Plaza; it's open 9 am to 5 pm, Monday to Saturday. You can send faxes and telegrams from here, as well as from the TOJ office (☎ 974-1574). There's a Call Direct Centre at 74 Main St (☎ 974-7595). UPS has an office at 1 Newlin St (☎ 974-0204); it's open daily, 7 am to 7 pm.

Crystal McDowell (☎ 974-9530) offers psychic readings.

Travel Agency Many of the larger hotels have tour desks that can confirm most travel arrangements. In town, Stuart's Travel is one of the more reputable travel agencies (12 Main St, ☎ 974-5369).

Bookshops There's a general paucity of bookshops for a town of this size. Most hotel gift stores sell English-language novels and books on Jamaican history and culture. The largest selection of books is available at Everybody's Bookshop at Shop 44 in Ocean Village Plaza (☎ 974-2932). It also has a reasonable selection of foreign magazines and newspapers.

The town library is on Milford Rd (☎ 974-2588).

Laundry Carib Laundromat (☎ 974-7631), next to Island Rent-a-Car, offers a wash-and-dry service (US$4.50 per load), and is open 10 am to 7 pm.

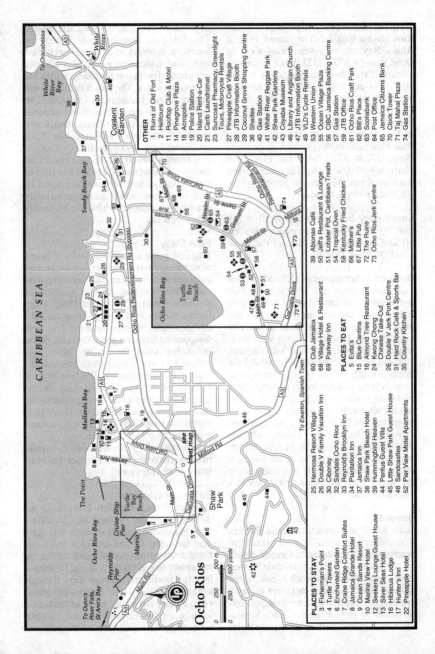

Ocho Rios

PLACES TO STAY

3 Fisherman's Point
4 Turtle Towers
6 Enchanted Garden
7 Crane Ridge Comfort Suites
8 Jamaica Grande Hotel
9 Ocean Sands Resort
10 Marine View Hotel
12 Seekers Lounge Guest House
13 Silver Seas Hotel
16 Hibiscus Lodge
17 Hunter's Inn
22 Pineapple Hotel
25 Hermosa Resort Village
26 Double V Family Vacation Inn
30 Ciboney
32 Sandals Ocho Rios
33 Reynold's Brooklyn Inn
34 Plantation Inn
37 Jamaica Inn
38 Shaw Park Beach Hotel
39 Hummingbird Heaven
44 Pentus Guest Villa
45 Little Shaw Park Guest House
48 Sandcastles
52 Pier View Motel Apartments

PLACES TO EAT

5 Evita's
15 Blue Cantina
16 Almond Tree Restaurant
24 Kwong Chong
    Chinese Take-Out
26 Double V Jerk Pork Centre
31 Hard Rock Café & Sports Bar
35 Country Kitchen
39 Abionas Café
50 Jeff's Restaurant & Lounge
51 Lobster Pot, Caribbean Treats
54 Tropical Oven
58 Kentucky Fried Chicken
66 Mother's
67 Little Pub
72 The Ruins
73 Ocho Rios Jerk Centre
60 Club Jamaica
68 Village Hotel & Restaurant
69 Parkway Inn

OTHER

1 Ruins of Old Fort
2 Helitours
11 Rooftop Club & Motel
14 Pinegrove Plaza
18 Acropolis
19 Police Station
20 Island Rent-a-Car
21 Carib Laundromat
23 Suncoast Pharmacy, Greenlight
   Tours, Motorcycle Rentals
27 Pineapple Craft Village
28 JTB Information Booth
29 Coconut Grove Shopping Centre
36 Shades
40 Gas Station
41 White River Reggae Park
42 Shaw Park Gardens
43 Coyaba Museum
46 Library and Anglican Church
47 JTB Information Booth
49 VLD's Cycle Rentals
53 Western Union
55 Ocean Village Plaza
56 CIBC Jamaica Banking Centre
57 Gas Station
59 JTB Office
61 Ocho Rios Craft Park
62 Bill's Place
63 Scotiabank
64 Post Office
65 Jamaica Citizens Bank
70 Clock Tower
71 Taj Mahal Plaza
74 Gas Station

Medical Services Surprisingly, Ocho Rios has no hospital. The nearest is at St Ann's Bay, about seven miles west of Ocho Rios (☎ 972-2272). You can arrange a doctor's visit, however, by calling ☎ 974-5055, 974-2610, or 974-5913. Ocho Rios has many pharmacies, among them Great House Pharmacy in Brown's Plaza on Main St (☎ 974-2352); Suncoast Pharmacy in Pineapple Plaza (☎ 974-5569); Ocho Rios Pharmacy in the Ocean Village Plaza (Shop 27, ☎ 974-2398); and Pinegrove Pharmacy (☎ 974-5586). The latter is open 9 am to 8 pm, Monday to Saturday, and 10:30 am to 3 pm Sundays.

Emergency In an emergency, call ☎ 119 (police); ☎ 110 (fire). The police station is off DaCosta Drive, just east of the clock tower (☎ 974-2253).

Dangers & Annoyances Ocho Rios is not a dangerous place. The biggest annoyance is the persistent entreaties of young men selling ganja and cocaine. Just say no and move on. Don't argue with them! I've received veiled threats ('Watch your back, whitey!') for losing my cool with pushers.

Avoid the area immediately behind the market south of the clock tower. Use caution at night anywhere, but particularly on James Ave, a poorly lit street where the tawdry air recalls days when there was a go-go bar and brothel here. Although most prostitutes have been cleared off the streets, some still linger in the town center; they can be as pesky as other hustlers. Many are crack users. If you succumb to the sexual lure, be aware that AIDS is a particular risk.

Beaches
Ocho Rios' main beach is **Turtle Beach**. It stretches east from Turtle Towers condominiums to the Jamaica Grande Hotel, on the shore of a half-mile-wide, horseshoe-shaped bay. The beach is public, but the two hotels at either end were recently granted the right to enclose their portions of beach to protect guests from harassment by hustlers. Unfortunately, the noise of jet-skis echoes across the calm waters. The 400-yard-long beach is backed by hotels, with plenty of licensed water-sport and food concessionaires, plus almond trees and a few palms for shade. It also has changing rooms. The beach is maintained by the UDC. Entrance is US$0.30. I've met a few travelers on prepaid vacations who were dismayed by Turtle Beach and wanted to check out of Ocho Rios. It's a sentiment I can understand.

Mallards Beach faces north, east of the Jamaica Grande Hotel. The narrow strip of sand is broken into sections dominated by individual hotels that maintain virtually autonomous control of what are ostensibly public beaches.

Fern Gully
This lush gorge is one of Ocho Rios' prime attractions. A road zigzags uphill through the three-mile-long canyon of an old watercourse that was planted with hundreds of different fern species about 1880. Trees form a canopy overhead, filtering the subaqueous light. Several species of fern have disappeared from the gorge in recent years, ostensibly killed by traffic fumes that collect to form a thick haze beneath the canopy by late morning. It's best to visit early in the day to avoid the smog. Hurricanes have added to the damage due to the funneling effect of the chasm. Don't pick the plants. Fern Gully is a national park and removing plants is forbidden.

Drive slowly and carefully. A bypass road to relieve the traffic pressure has been in the works for years.

Botanical Gardens
Coyaba River Garden Coyaba is an Arawak word for 'heaven' or 'paradise.' This paradise has trails through lush gardens featuring streams, cascades, and pools filled with carp, crayfish, and turtles. A **museum** has displays tracing Jamaica's heritage from early Arawak days through to independence. There's also a gift store, and a gallery boasts the works of Jamaica's leading artists. Coyaba is nearly a mile west of St John's Church, to the left just

before Shaw Park Gardens (PO Box 18, Ocho Rios, ☎ 974-6235). Entrance is US$4.50 and includes a 30-minute guided tour. It's open 8 am to 5 pm (until midnight on Thursday and Friday).

A Moonshine Festival is held on Thursday nights (5:30 to 10 pm). The US$50 fee buys you a Jamaican buffet with African drumming and a jonkanoo show, followed by dancing to ska, rock steady, and reggae.

Carinosa If you wish to brush up on your botanicals, this is the place. The superbly maintained, lushly landscaped gardens (owned by the ex-premier, Edward Seaga) boast an orchid house with 200 species, a fern garden with more than 300 species, and a rainforest that you can explore along paved paths. There are lots of exotic shrubs and 'roses' (as Jamaicans call any plant). Other highlights include a working waterwheel, a small aquarium, a small menagerie, and an aviary with indigenous and exotic birds. There's also a restaurant and gift store. A guided walking tour is offered.

Take the winding road that leads south from the roundabout at the western junction of DaCosta Drive and Main St.

Shaw Park Gardens Last but not least of the botanical gardens is this tropical fantasia of ferns and bromeliads, palms, and exotic shrubs. Shaw Park is a hilltop stunner, with marvelous views down over the 25 acres that once formed the grounds of the now-defunct Shaw Park Hotel, a converted 18th-century great house. Trails and wooden steps lead past waterfalls that tumble in terraces down the hillside. A viewing platform offers a bird's-eye vantage over Ocho Rios, and a bar and restaurant are on hand. The site is thought to have been an Arawak settlement (a skeleton was found here in 1763). Shaw Park is open 9 am to 5 pm (PO Box 17, Ocho Rios, ☎ 974-2552, fax 974-5042).

To get there, turn west opposite the public library on the Fern Gully road (A3), take the right fork at the Shaw Park Dairy, and follow the winding road uphill for one mile.

Ocho Rios Fort
The English built this pocket-sized fort in the late 17th century. The fortress later did duty as a slaughterhouse before being restored in the 1970s by the Reynolds mining company, who fitted it with four cannons (two originally from the fort). It stands next to the Reynolds bauxite installation on the A3 immediately west of town.

Dunn's River Falls
To visit Jamaica and not climb Dunn's River Falls is like touring France without seeing the Eiffel Tower. The cascades, two miles west of town, are the island's most well-known attraction. Forget about trying to avoid the crowd. Join hands in the daisy chain and clamber up the tiers of limestone that stairstep 600 feet down to the beach in a series of cascades and pools. The water is refreshingly cool and the falls are shaded by tall rainforest.

You must buy a ticket before you can climb, then follow the stairs down to the beach. A guide is optional. The powerful current can sweep your feet from the slippery rocks, but your sure-footed guide will hold you by the hand and carry your camera. Signs warn that you climb at your own risk. Yes, occasionally people hurt themselves. Hence, there's a first aid station supervised by St John's Ambulance Brigade. You can always exit to the side at a convenient point if your nerves give out, and there are wooden steps with handrails for the less adventurous. You can also rent rubber sandals for US$5 from booths outside the entrance.

Plan your visit for when the cruises ships aren't in town – weekends are best – otherwise you may have to line up for some time. It's a 30-minute climb; allow 90 minutes in all. Swimwear is essential. The property is managed by the St Ann Development Council, which maintains changing rooms and lockers on the beach. However, it's best to leave any valuables in your hotel safe, as the lockers are reputed to not be secure. At the top there's a huge crafts market – the most impressive in Jamaica, though the hustling is fierce – and there are jerk stalls and snack bars next to the car park. It costs US$5 to climb the falls (☎ 974-5015). It's open 9 am to 6 pm (from 8 am when cruise ships are in town).

Laughing Waters

Less crowded, these cascades are not quite a mile further west. Just like its more famous sibling, a river appears from rocks amid a shallow ravine about two miles from the sea and spills to a fabulous little beach. Alas, the falls, which are also known as Roaring River, are not what they once were since being tapped by a hydroelectricity plant. If you want to impress your friends back home with your travels, rent the old James Bond movie, *Dr No*, parts of which were filmed here (the beach is known as 'James Bond Beach'). Remember the seduction scene with Ursula Andress?

White River

The slow-moving river marks the boundary between St Ann and St Mary Parishes, two miles east of town. It's popular for lazy 45-minute journeys by bamboo raft operated by Calypso Rafting (☎ 974-2527). En route you'll stop for a refreshing dip in a deep pool (US$30 per person). An 'Exotic Night on the White River' is held each Tuesday and Saturday night, when flaming torches are lit along the riverbank; your raft trip ends with dinner and a 'native' cabaret (US$31).

Every Tuesday, Wednesday, and Thursday, Calypso Rafting also has a 'Jungle Bachanaal' (US$40 per person), that includes a buffet on the riverbank beside a lagoon. Drinks cost extra.

To get to Calypso Rafting, turn south at the Texaco station immediately west of the White River bridge. The road curls down to the river past White River Reggae Park. Signs point the way half a mile uphill to Calypso Rafting, to the right up Bonham Spring Rd. Trips are available between 9 am and 5 pm.

Irie Beach

This isn't a beach, but a series of cascades and deep turquoise pools formed by the White River, high in the hills at Bonham Spring Farm two miles south of the river estuary. Irie Beach was named by a Rastafarian who lived here for years. It's a serene and secluded place with a fabulous setting. A tourist resort opened in mid-1995 on a beautifully landscaped riverbank garden with a wooden deck beneath shade trees, and a very tiny sand 'beach' with lounge chairs. There's a rope swing over a 25-foot-deep lagoon, and a trail follows the cascades half a mile upriver. A restaurant of natural stone and wood stands above the river. It serves burgers, jerk chicken, escoveitched fish, and a vegetarian plate (US$5 average). Beach admission is US$5 (J$100 for Jamaican residents). It's open daily 10 am to 5 pm.

Prospect Plantation

Prospect is a working plantation, 200 yards east of Sans Souci Spa & Resort (☎ 974-2058, fax 974-2468). It grows pimento and limes commercially and other produce for show. It was formerly owned by British industrialist and politician Sir Harold Mitchell; it's still run by his family. The old great house that sits atop a hill is not open to the public, but from a distance you can make out the fortified loopholes for protection against pirates and rebel slaves. The estate also includes the Prospect Cadet Training Centre, founded by Sir Harold to educate the youth of indigent families and prepare them for the police force and Jamaica Defence Force.

The youngsters also act as tour guides. You can tour the plantation by tractor-powered jitney that offers some incredible views of the White River gorge and coast. Cuba is visible 90 miles away from Sir Harold's Viewpoint. The tour includes a visit to the nondenominational college chapel, a sturdy stone structure with a timbered roof. You can join such luminaries as Charlie Chaplin, Winston Churchill, and Henry Kissinger by planting a tree for US$50. You'll receive a photo with your name and the date of planting, which is also branded onto the trunk. The tree will be maintained for life. Tours depart at

10:30 am, 2, and 3:30 pm, Monday to Saturday, and 11 am, 1:30, 3 pm on Sunday. It costs US$12. Three horseback tours are also offered for US$20 to US$35.

Harmony Hall

This beautiful great house, on the A3 four miles east of town, dates to 1886 when it was a Methodist manse adjoining a pimento estate. The restored structure is made of cut stone below with a white-painted wooden upper story trimmed with gingerbread fretwork, and a green shingled roof topped by a spire. It has been reborn as an arts and crafts showcase where works by Jamaica's leading artists are sold. Shows are held throughout the year; an exhibition season runs mid-November to Easter.

The grounds are a venue for events during the Ocho Rios Jazz Festival in June. And until recently the lower level housed one of the island's premier restaurants. The bar was still there when I stopped by, and a café was planned to replace the restaurant, which had closed. Artist Graham Davis, one of the owners, plans to open a showroom for bamboo furniture, aromatherapy oils, Reggae to Wear clothing, books and CDs, etc. Upstairs will include a gallery – The Travelers' Tree – for crafts from throughout Central America. For information contact PO Box 192, Ocho Rios (☎ 975-4222, fax 974-2651).

Scuba Diving & Snorkeling

Virtually the entire shoreline east of Ocho Rios to Galina Point is fringed by a reef. One of the best sections is **Devil's Reef**, a pinnacle that drops to more than 200 feet. Nurse sharks are abundant at **Caverns**, a shallow reef about one mile east of the White River estuary; it has many tunnels plus an ex-minesweeper called *Kathryn* that was sunk in 1991 to create a dive site at 50 feet deep.

You can arrange dives at the water sport concessions on Turtle Beach; try Garfield Dive Station (☎ 974-5749). Resort Divers at Shop 6, Island Plaza (☎ 974-5338, fax 974-0577) has dive trips from US$35, plus scuba lessons and PADI certification courses (US$350). It has a full service pro shop and

rents gear, as does Sea & Dive Jamaica at 74 Main St (☎/fax 974-5762). Fantasea Divers has a facility at Sans Souci Resort with a Handicapped Scuba Association instructor on staff (☎ 974-5344). Shaw Park Beach Hotel also has a dedicated scuba facility (☎/fax 974-5762), as does La Mer Dive Resort, at Jamaica Beach (see Boscobel Beach below), and the Arawak Inn, at Mammee Bay. For information on snorkeling cruises see Organized Tours below.

Other Activities

There are plenty of water sport concessionaires on Turtle Beach. Try Water Fever (☎ 974-2587) for **parasailing**. They also have a facility at Shaw Park Beach Hotel.

Several **sport fishing** boats are available for half- and full-day charters from the marina. Try Free Spirit Charters at Shop 6, Island Plaza (☎ 995-3661), or the *Striker* (☎ 975-7036). Resort Divers (☎ 974-5338) offers fishing charters from $300.

The only **golf** course is at Upton Country Club (☎ 974-2528), in the hills four miles southeast of town (turn right at the Texaco gas station beside the White River estuary and follow Bonham Spring Rd uphill past White River Reggae Park). The par 71 course has fairways rippling up and down hills fringed by forest. There's a club house, bar, pro-shop, and one of the most elegant restaurants on the island. It's open 7:30 am to 5:30 pm. Green fees are US$30 (complimentary to Sandals guests). Caddies cost US$10 and cart rental is US$30. Lessons are offered.

You can choose from three **horseback riding** tours at Prospect Plantation (☎ 974-2058), where trails lead through 900 acres. The guided trips vary from one hour to 2½ hours and cost US$20 to US$35. Daniel's Stables at Mammee Bay also offers horse riding.

Try **bungee-jumping** for a different sort of high with Jamaica Bungee, whose office is on James Ave (☎ 974-5660).

Organized Tours

JUTA Tour Company offers a 'Ocho Rios Highlight Tour' and other day excursions

(PO Box 160, Ocho Rios, ☎ 974-2292). Excursions further afield are offered by Tourwise, which has its headquarters at 103 Main St (☎ 974-2323, fax 974-5362), and Greenlight Tours at Shop 16, Carib Arcade, 200 yards west of Pineapple Place (☎ 974-2266). Top Tours, at 73 Main St (☎ 974-1463, fax 974-0005) specializes in tours for Italian tourists.

Pro-Tours Ltd in Kingston (☎ 978-6113, fax 978-5473) offers full-day tours from Ocho Rios that take you over the mountains for breakfast in Mandeville, a swim at YS Falls, and a boat ride into the Great Morass (Thursday and Saturday, US$93).

Caribic Vacations offers excursions throughout Jamaica, but specializes in excursion tours to Cuba (see the sidebar on trips to Cuba in the Northwest Coast chapter). Their local office is at Shop No 23, Coconut Grove Shopping Centre (☎ 974-5871).

Snorkeling & Sunset Cruises Resort Divers has snorkeling trips for US$15, and sunset cruises for US$25. Heave-Ho Charters also has snorkeling and party cruises aboard the 60-foot catamaran, *Cool Jazz* (11A Pineapple Place, ☎ 974-5367, fax 974-5461). You can charter this or three other small catamarans. Also try the *Windsong*, another catamaran which has snorkeling trips (US$35) plus a 'Soca Sunset Dance Party' (US$25) on weekend evenings (☎ 974-2446). *Margarita* is a 41-foot yacht that offers a snorkeling cruise at 10 am and sunset cruise at 2 pm; a cruise to Dunn's River is offered on Tuesday and Thursday. A 51-foot sloop called *Red Stripe* sails daily from the UDC Dock on three-hour snorkeling cruises at 9 am and 12:30 pm (US$38); the cruise includes a visit to Dunn's River Falls. A two-hour 'Soca Sunset Cruise' (US$25) at 4:30 pm (☎ 974-2446). You can play-act the part of a pirate on the *Jolly Roger*, a brigantine that also hosts parties and sunset cruises; contact Tourwise at 103 Main St (PO Box 17, 974-2323, fax 974-5362).

Helicopter Tours Helitours at 120 Main St has aerial tours by four-passenger Bell Jetranger helicopters (☎ 974-2265). A 15-minute 'Ocho Rios Fun Hop' costs US$50. A longer journey takes in the coast east of town, including Firefly and Tacky Falls beyond Port Maria (US$95). You can also charter a chopper. The helipad is just west of the Reynolds bauxite terminal.

Special Events

The biggest shindig of the year is the weeklong Ocho Rios Jazz Festival, held each mid-June. Traditional venues include the Jamaica Grande Hotel, the Little Pub complex, and Harmony Hall and Glenn's Jazz Club, east of town. Many performances are free; afternoon and evening concerts are US$15 and US$20. Island Flight Vacations is the official jazz festival tour operator (☎ (800) 426-4570), and offers package tours. For more information contact the Jazz Hotline (☎ 927-3544, fax 927-3544).

Also worth noting is the White River Reggae Bash, held each February 6 to honor Bob Marley's birthday. The Celebrity Golf Classic, each May, also has live music on hand (Motown artists The Temptations and Smokey Robinson were featured in 1995).

The Jamaica Hotel & Tourism Association hosts an annual fundraiser for charities each May. Contact the JTB (☎ 974-2570) for more information. In late September, Ocho Rios hosts the annual Ocho Rios International Marlin Tournament (☎ 922-7160).

Places to Stay

Ocho Rios flaunts a wide range of accommodations for every taste and budget, from carefree to formal. A fistful of Jamaica's most sophisticated (and expensive) hotels extend east for several miles (also see East of Ocho Rios). Self-catering villas are also a popular option and can be great bargains if you're with a family or group. Many of the villas are quite salubrious; most come with a cook and housemaid.

Places to Stay – bottom end

Camping A popular option among budget travelers is *Hummingbird Heaven* (PO Box

95, Ocho Rios, ☎ 974-5188, fax 974-5202), beside the Tourwise bus park about 400 yards west of the turnoff for Upton-on-Green. The 20 tent sites rent for US$5 double, and have flush toilets and showers. The owner, Audrey Barned, rents tents for US$2.50. She's extremely helpful and will gladly share her listings of cheap accommodations and campsites islandwide. Some of the best I-tal meals on the island are served here, at the Abionas Café (see Places to Eat below).

You can also camp at *Little Shaw Park Guest House* (see Guest Houses below), near the Shaw Park Gardens in the hills above town. Each site costs US$15 double, and tents are available for rent. Owners Trevor and Deborah Mitchell will cook meals on request.

Guest Houses *Marastilda B&B* (☎ 974-2223) is run by Aston Young, a former producer of 'Sesame Street.' He rents three bedrooms (US$20 per night) in his homey bungalow above Rivermouth Beach, 200 meters west of Sans Souci Spa & Resort. Each has its own private entrance and bathroom. You can use the spacious TV lounge and a kitchen, though Aston will prepare meals by prior arrangement. There's a bus stop outside the gate.

Another cozy option is *Pentus Guest Villa*, at 3 Shaw Park Rd (☎ 974-2313) in the hills southwest of town. It has four rooms with shared bath (US$20/30 single/double). Nearby, at 21 Shaw Park Rd, is the *Little Shaw Park Guest House* (☎ 974-2177), a trim place with eight rooms for US$40. Private bathrooms have hot water. Meals are available by request.

If you prefer to be closer to the town center, consider *Carleen's Villa* on the waterfront at 85 Main St (☎ 974-5431). It offers five rooms at US$50. You might also try *Mari-Guil Guest House*, at 94 Riviera Blvd, Tower Isle. Contact Karein Ebner at ☎ 975-4833.

A hot spot for lovers of pool and snooker is *Seekers Lounge Guest House* at 25 James Ave (☎ 974-5763). Its 25 rooms have lots of light, but are basic and a bit run-down.

The hotel has a large billiards room. Rates are US$25 with shared bath, US$30 with private bath with hot water, and US$42 with air-con.

City Center The *Rooftop Club & Motel* (☎ 974-2597), on James Ave, has rooms for US$14 with fans, or US$17 with air-con. The nine rooms are roomy but very basic. Those in the center have no windows. Things get noisy at night as there's a disco overhead.

Pool players could be in heaven at *Hunter's Inn* (86 Main St, 974-5627), which has a huge bar and with four pool tables. The six carpeted rooms have fans and small bathroom with hot water, but are rather gloomy and basically furnished (US$20 to US$27).

Further Afield Another basic option is *Rose Ann Accommodation* (☎ 974-1912), below a hardware store 200 yards west of Sans Souci. It has 12 rooms with ceiling fans and private bathrooms with hot water for US$14 to US$18. Some are very small. The cheapest rooms in Ochi are at the *Rum Barrel Motel & Restaurant* (☎ 974-5909), above the 'El Rancho' grocery store, one mile south of town on the road to Fern Gully. The six basic rooms cost US$9 and have private bathrooms and fans.

A long-time favorite of budget travelers is *Hummingbird Heaven* (see Camping above). The six cabins are hurricane-proof geodesic domes of wood and concrete: simple but clean with private showers with hot water, but only tiny windows (US$20). Audrey was planning to upgrade the rooms, so you can expect the prices to rise.

About a mile further east is *Reynold's Brooklyn Inn* (188 Main St, Ocho Rios, ☎ 974-2480). It's the green-and-ochre building above the roadside 100 yards east of Ciboney. Six basic but clean rooms (US$12 to US$14) share two bathrooms with cold water. Those facing the road are noisy. The restaurant serves Jamaican and Chinese dishes for about US$3.

Places to Stay – middle
City Center One of the best bargains is the *Hibiscus Lodge*, whose breezy cliff-top setting overlooks a coral reef where the snorkeling is superb (PO Box 52, Ocho Rios, ☎ 974-2676). It's handily close to the town center. The rooms, set amid lush grounds, are spacious albeit modestly furnished. There's a small cliff-top pool, an atmospheric bar, plus one of Ocho Rios' finer restaurants – the Almond Tree. Stairs lead down to a boat landing. The hotel offers good value, especially its discounted off-peak rates (US$60 standard, US$80 deluxe).

I also recommend *Ocean Sands* (☎ 974-2605, fax 974-2605), an attractive property on James Ave, with a marvelous oceanfront setting with its own pocket-sized beach and coral at your doorstep. A tiny restaurant sits at the end of a wooden wharf – a marvelous spot for enjoying a cool beer! The 28 pleasant rooms have French doors that open onto private balconies. Again, a bargain at US$45 single, US$65 double (more in winter). There's a small pool.

The strangely named *Double V Family Vacation Inn*, 109 Main St, is a compact property in lush grounds (☎ 974-0174). Its 30 spacious, air-con rooms have large beds but gaudy red carpets and dowdy furnishings. Nonetheless, its bargain-priced at US$20/35. It features a pool, restaurant, and TV lounge.

Two other options include the *Pineapple Hotel* at Pineapple Place (PO Box 263, Ocho Rios, ☎ 974-2727, fax 974-1706), that has 23 contemporary, air-con rooms with private bathrooms and hot water for US$50; and the *Parkway Inn*, with 21 air-con rooms for US$57, including one suite and a family size room (US$75). Rooms at both properties are spacious but bland.

Marine View Hotel at 9 James Ave (☎ 974-5753) has 25 basic rooms for US$35, some with air-con (US$45). All have private bathrooms with hot water. Take a room on the top floor, where you'll have a glimpse (barely) of the sea. There's a small pool and a restaurant. Another option downtown is *Jeff's* (☎ 974-2664), at 10 Main St. Air-con rooms with private bathrooms and hot water cost US$40.

If you want to cook for yourself, check out the *Hermosa Resort Village* near Pineapple Plaza, whose 16 contemporary, one-bedroom, air-con townhouses (US$65) feature kitchens, plus loft bedrooms that sleep up to four (Lot 8, Hermosa Beach, Ocho Rios, ☎ 974-2660). There's a pool and hot tub.

Three self-catering properties are on Turtle Beach. *Sandcastles Apartotel*, next to Ocean Village Plaza, has modest, but pleasantly furnished studios and apartments with fully equipped kitchens or kitchenettes (Villawise, 120 Main St, Ocho Rios, ☎ 974-5877 or (800) 562-7273, fax 974-1517). Yes, the five units do resemble sandcastles. Nearby is *Fisherman's Point*, a condominium resort with 76 simple yet elegant apartments with kitchenettes, satellite TVs, and tiny private balconies (PO Box 747, Ocho Rios, ☎ 974-5317, fax 974-2894; in North America, FDR Holidays, ☎ (516) 233-1786 or (800) 654-1337, fax (516) 233-4815). A personal cook can be arranged. The complex has a pool, bar, and seafood restaurant. Rates begin at US$65/100. *Pier View Motel Apartments* is at 19 Main St, with air-con rooms and fully equipped kitchens from US$40 (PO Box 134, Ocho Rios, ☎ 974-2607, fax 974-1384).

Further Afield For a hilltop setting, try *Pimento Lodge* (☎ 974-1899), a handsome, Spanish-style hotel with studios (US$30) and two- and three-bedroom units, and a dining room and kitchen (US$60 to US$90). The studios have the best views down over the forest towards the distant ocean. A pool provides the same vistas. Rooms are very spacious. There's no restaurant, but the staff will cook meals on request. To get there, take the turnoff to the left opposite Mr Bo Jangles Meat Mart and Mae Mae's Drinking Saloon, one mile south of town on the road to Fern Gully; Pimento Lodge is one mile up Breadnut.

Rio Blanco Village is an apartment-style hotel overlooking the White River estuary

(PO Box 24, Ocho Rios, ☎ 994-1385 or (800) 526-2422, fax 974-5049). The 30 rooms and 38 suites all have kitchenettes (only 20 have air-con), and cost US$55/75. *Bonham Hill Villas* is on Bonham Springs Rd, in the hills below Upton Golf Course. It has two- and three-bedroom units – not villas – with pleasant decor and ocean-view balconies (PO Box 263, Ocho Rios, ☎ 974-5454, fax 974-1706).

Chrisann's Beach Resort (Tower Isle PO, St Mary, ☎ 975-4467 or (800) 526-2422), at Tower Isle near Harmony Hall, has uninspiring condominium apartments on their own private beach. Studios rent for US$490 weekly, low season; and one- to three-bedroom suites for US$525 to US$1470.

Rose Garden Hotel is a modern complex about two miles west of Dunn's River Falls (☎ /fax 972-2825). Its 24 rooms are modestly furnished and clean, with lots of light. Each has private bathroom with hot water, TV, and balcony (US$65, US$70 with air-con). There's a small pool and sundeck. Breakfasts cost US$5.

Places to Stay – top end
You're spoiled for choice, though quality and ambiance vary greatly, especially among all-inclusive resorts. Choose wisely. Most have resident bands and Jamaican cabarets.

City Center A little charmer in town is the modern *Village Hotel & Restaurant* at 54 Main St (☎ 974-9193 or (800) 835-9810, fax 974-5440). Its 34 air-con rooms feature tasteful contemporary decor and vary from standard to deluxe (US$70 to US$108), the latter with hot tubs. Satellite TVs and telephones are standard. Superior rooms and suites have kitchenettes. A tiny courtyard restaurant serves Jamaican dishes. Rates drop with longer stays.

There are several options on Turtle Beach. *Club Jamaica* (PO Box 342, Main St, Ocho Rios, ☎ 974-6632 or (800) 818-2964, fax 974-6644) is a compact all-inclusive resort on a Club Med theme, centered on a small pool and whirlpool

enclosed in a soulless concrete courtyard. It has 95 air-con rooms with satellite TV, telephones, and a vibrant color scheme. Noise echoes down the corridors. Insist on an oceanfront room. The courtyard is used for alfresco dinners (other meals are served in a cafeteria-style dining room). It's small enough that people mingle, and most guests I talked to seemed to be having a good time, but it's devoid of atmosphere and overpriced. A dive operation is on site and there are water sports, a bar-hopping tour, karaoke, crab-racing, and toga parties. Rates are US$175/220 superior to US$210/270 deluxe.

The gleaming white *Jamaica Grande Hotel* is centered on a grandiose open-air lobby overlooking a massive 'fantasy pool' with swim-up bar, swim-through grotto, and a waterfall fashioned after Dunn's River Falls (PO Box 100, Ocho Rios, ☎ 974-2201, fax 974-2162; in North America, ☎ (800) 228-9898, fax (602) 443-6543). There are 720 tastefully decorated rooms and 24 suites in two towers. Facilities include five restaurants, nine bars, the Jamaica'n me Krazy disco, a fitness center, tennis courts, and Club Mongoose to keeps kids under 12 amused. It has the largest conference facilities on the island and therefore gets a lot of convention traffic. Theme parties and live entertainment are offered nightly. All-inclusive plans are available; winter rates range from US$360 to US$380 for either single or double.

Silver Seas Hotel (☎ 974-2755, fax 974-5739) enjoys a breezy oceanfront location on its own private, pocket-sized beach in Mallards Bay. It has a lively atmosphere. The center of action is a huge semi-circular bar facing onto a pool. Natural stone abounds. The spacious, ocean-view rooms cost US$72 single, US$84 double, US$96 triple. It's popular with young German package-tourists.

At the other end of the spectrum is the graceful *Plantation Inn*, nestled above its own private bay (PO Box 2, Ocho Rios, ☎ 974-5601, fax 974-5912; in the USA, Jamaica Reservation Service, 1329 S Dixie Hwy, Suite 1102, Coral Gables, FL 33146,

The Plantation Inn harkens back to the good old days – with slight modifications.

☎ (305) 665-3163 or (800) 526-2422). For many years it was fashionable with international socialites and still retains the air of a country club. However, in recent years the hotel has loosened up (dress code at dinner, for example, is 'casual elegant' though women are still requested 'not to appear in any public area in hair curlers'). Hot consommé is served as 'elevenses' on one of the two beaches in classic British tradition. Decor in the 63 rooms and 15 suites features dark mahogany and white rattan. Low season rates range from US$90 to US$180.

Further Afield *Enchanted Garden*, on Eden Bower Rd in the hills southwest of town, is named for its 20-acre Eden-like setting (☎ 974-1400, fax 974-5823). The grounds are akin to an inner-city park, with 14 waterfalls, huge pools, a fruit orchard, separate fern, spice, cactus, and lily gardens, and a walk-in aviary where you can hand-feed the birds. The 113 air-con rooms, however, have no hint of the tropics. Gardenhouse villas are more elegant, with marble floors and vibrant decor. The 40 suites have mezzanine kitchens, and hot tubs on the patio. Facilities include a full health spa with a gym, tai chi and aerobics, a private beach club, plus a restaurant incongruously set on an East Indian pavilion, containing pool tables, slot machines, and three aquariums. Rates (overpriced) are US$150 to US$320, and US$175 to US$195 per person for suites. Day and evening passes are available for use of the facilities (US$45 per person, US$55 evening, including entertainment).

Nearby is *Crane Ridge Comfort Suites*, offering a breezy hilltop location at 17 DaCosta Drive (☎ 974-8050 or (800) 221-2222, fax 974-8070). The all-suite resort features 79 one-and two-bedroom suites in three-story structures. An airy restaurant on stilts looms over a large amoeba-shaped pool. A shuttle service is offered to the beach, Shaw Park Gardens, and Dunn's River Falls. Per person high-season rates are US$115/130 one-bedroom, US$135/150 two-bedroom.

The Sandals chain has two upscale heterosexual-only couples resorts in Ochi (in North America, ☎ (305) 284-1300 or (800) 726-3257, fax (305) 667-8996; in the UK, ☎ (0171) 581-9895, fax (0171) 823-8758). All rooms have air-con, with king-size beds. Every water sport imaginable is available, as are land activities from bocci ball to basketball. Nightlife means everything from karaoke to toga parties. Rates at both are all-inclusive, from airport transfers to everything that exists within the gates, including all you-can-eat meals and drinks, a tour of Dunn's River Falls, and golf at Upton.

East of town is *Sandals Ocho Rios*, with 237 rooms in five categories (PO Box 771, Ocho Rios, ☎ 974-5691, fax 974-5700). The elegant complex is reminiscent of a Mediterranean village and has its own beach. The vast facilities embraces four restaurants, three pools, a beauty salon, gym, and disco. Low season rates (three nights) range from US$680/1388 standard to US$840/1708 deluxe. Its more upscale sister property is *Sandals Dunn's River*, west of town (PO Box 51, Ocho Rios, ☎ 972-1610, fax 972-1611). A dramatic curving staircase and gleaming marble columns recreate the opulence of an Italian Palazzo. The resort also boasts Jamaica's largest swimming pool with a cascading waterfall topped by a gazebo. The 256 rooms come in seven categories. Low season rates (three nights) range from US$748/1518 standard to US$1133/2300 deluxe.

Another all-inclusive is *Ciboney*, next to Sandals Ocho Rios. This country club – one of only two AAA Four Diamond-award winners in Jamaica (although there are more deserving places) – has rooms in the great house, plus 226 one-, two- or three-bedroom, red-tile-roofed villa suites, each with a private pool and attendant (PO Box 728, Ocho Rios, St Ann, ☎ 974-1027

or (800) 333-3333, fax 974-5838). Six restaurants each have a distinct mood and cuisine. It has its own nightclub, two large pools and a hot tub, plus six tennis courts, two squash courts, and a spa. Water sports include scuba diving. It's a fairly sedate place. Rates are US$290/380 standard, US$305/410 deluxe, and from US$345/460 for villa suites, including round-trip transfers, all meals, free massage, manicure, spa treatment, and use of all facilities.

The other AAA Four Diamond hotel is the *Sans Souci Grand Lido*, which sets the tone for contemporary sophistication (PO Box 103, Ocho Rios, ☎ 974-2353 or 800-203-7456, fax 974-2544; in North America, ☎ (305) 925-0925 or (800) 859-7873; in the UK, ☎ (0992) 447420). Its setting is sublime, with its own golden beach in a secluded, lushly foliated cove backed by lime-green lawns. The resort has a world-class fitness center and emphasizes restorative spa treatments. Every conceivable water sport is featured, and a complete schedule of activities range from scuba lessons to reggae dance classes. All 111 rooms are deluxe. Some are set on the cliff face, with dramatic views through the trees. Bathrooms are glorious, with lots of marble, huge showers, and hot tubs. The service (including 24-hour room service) approaches Asian standards of excellence. A regal Friday-night gala buffet is held on the lawn. Low season rates (three nights) range from US$795 to US$1365 per person, double occupancy, inclusive of everything from meals and alcohol to massage, beauty treatments, and even dry cleaning. Its 'SuperSummer' packages offer significant savings off published rates.

Another popular option is the *Shaw Park Beach Hotel* whose thatch-roofed units are spread along a wide golden-sand beach in a private cove (Cutlass Bay, PO Box 17, ☎ 974-2552, fax 974-5042). Choose from 33 standard, 60 superior, and 13 suites, all with air-con and their own private, oceanfront balcony or terrace. Features include an oval pool and kiddie's wading pool, two tennis courts, games room, and Silks Disco.

Adjoining Shaw Park is the very beautiful, family-run *Jamaica Inn* (PO Box 1, Ocho Rios, ☎ 974-2514, fax 974-2449; in North America, c/o Caribbean World Resorts, 4228 Hermitage Rd, Virginia Beach, VA 23445, ☎ (804) 469-5009 or (800) 243-9420). Some may find its patrician refinement stuffy; others warm instantly to the grace and solitude. No programmed activities are on hand, though scuba diving, and windsurfing are available, and guests have access to the facilities at Shaw Park Beach Hotel. The 45-room hotel occupies six acres, with a 700-foot-long beach tucked into a private cove. Winston Churchill used to relax here in the 1950s. I recommend the West Wing, right on top of the sea. No children under 14 are allowed. Rates are US$220 to US$245 double (US$170 single), including breakfast and dinner. Jackets are required for dinner (plus a tie in winter), and it is not unusual to see guests dining in black-tie formalwear.

Couples, five miles east of Ocho Rios, was the first American-style hotel in Jamaica (originally the Tower Isle hotel) and helped launch tourism on this part of the island in the 1960s (PO Box 330, Ocho Rios, ☎ 975-4271, fax 975-4439; in North America, ☎ (305) 668-0008 or (800) 268-7537, fax (305) 668-0111; in the UK, ☎ (0181) 900-1913, fax (0181) 795-1728). It's nowhere near as wild as the logo of mating lions suggests! Volleyball, squash, horseback riding, tennis, bicycling, catamaran cruises, and complete water sports are on hand. A small island is reserved for nude bathing and weddings. The 172 rooms have king-size beds and large balconies. Low season rates for a week-long stay range from US$2420 to US$3400 per couple. The all-inclusive price covers round-trip airport transfers, all meals, beverages, three sightseeing tours, and anything else that exists inside the gates.

If you want your own place with the luxury of being waited on hand and foot, consider *Somewhere Villa* or *Eight Rivers Villa*, both a stone's throw east of Prospect Plantation. The latter is a 5000-sq-foot property on 1½ acres fronting the beach. It has four air-con bedrooms, each with its own bathroom. Nearby is the three-bedroom *Wag Water Villa*, part of the Prospect Estate. The three villas share a tennis court. They're represented by VHR Worldwide (235 Kensington Ave, Norwood, NY 07648, ☎ (201) 767-9393, fax (201) 767-5510).

Emerald Seas is another elegant two-story, four-bedroom, Georgian villa on two acres of lush grounds, adjacent to Sans Souci Grand Lido, at Prospect. Living areas are built around an indoor rock garden. It has its own pool and tennis court, and is staffed by a butler, cook, housemaid, laundress, and gardener. The weekly rate is US$4500/7000 summer/winter (12 Norbrook Rd, Kingston 8, ☎ 925-9571, fax 925-2931).

And a luxurious 19th-century villa commands the headland where the river meets the sea at *Laughing Waters*. The fully staffed, four-bedroom villa can be rented through Heave-Ho Charters for US$6000 a week (11A Pineapple Place, Ocho Rios, ☎ 974-5367, fax 974-5461).

You'll find several other villas to choose from immediately west of Harmony Hall, including *Happy Lot* (☎ 975-4603) and *Seapalms*, which has fully equipped units in five buildings. There are also several villas at Mammee Bay, west of Dunn's River Falls. Two options that I've heard good things about are *Drabar Villa* (☎ 972-5762), and the *Villa Orchid*, a five-bedroom villa with pleasing decor and a small pool. There are dozens of villas, too, in the Mammee Bay Estate, 200 yards west of Sandal's Dunn's River.

The Jamaica Association of Villas and Apartments (JAVA) is headquartered in Pineapple Place (PO Box 298, Ocho Rios, ☎ 974-2508, fax 974-2967; in the USA, ☎ (800) 221-8830). It lists dozens of villas in the Ocho Rios vicinity. Many local villas are also represented by Selective Vacation Services at 154 Main St (PO Box 335, Ocho Rios, ☎ 974-5187, fax 974-2359).

Places to Eat

Jamaican *Jeff's Restaurant & Lounge* on Main St is an American-style diner with Jamaican and American breakfasts (US$2.50 to US$4), burgers (US$2), sandwiches (US$2 to US$3) served by friendly waitresses. Its dinner menu is Jamaican, but the ambiance is distinctly mid-America. It even has ice cream sundaes.

Ocho Rios has fewer roadside jerk stalls than elsewhere. The *Double V Jerk Pork Centre* (☎ 974-5998) is open 24 hours. For three decades it's been slow-cooking Ochi's best jerk, served with 'festival' dumplings and sizzling hot sauce. Likewise, the *Village Café & Jerk Centre* at Main St Village (☎ 974-9193) serves sinus-searing jerk, plus festival, rice and peas, and seafood.

For a meal with a view, head to the *Almond Tree Restaurant* in the Hibiscus Lodge (☎ 974-2676) where wooden dining pavilions stairstep down the cliff and candlelit dinners are served alfresco. The huge menu ranges from hamburgers and continental fare to steadfast Jamaican dishes. Entrees aren't cheap (budget a minimum of US$15), but the fabulous views are free. It also serves breakfast and lunch.

I-tal *Abionas Café* at Hummingbird Heaven (see Places to Stay above) serves tremendous vegetarian food such as lima beans and broccoli (US$4), stir-fried callaloo (US$3), soya burgers, and mango tarts (US$0.75). It's open 9 am to 9 pm, Tuesday to Sunday.

International The *Little Pub* at 59 Main St (☎ 974-2324) has a cruise-ship-on-land atmosphere. It's totally touristy, yet enjoyable, and serves good American breakfasts. An eclectic lunch and dinner menu is strong on steak and seafood. It has a sports bar with large-screen TV, plus video games and cabaret entertainment. It's open 8 am to midnight.

The restaurant at *Upton Country Club*, at Bonham Springs, provides a terrific, romantic ambiance. You'll dine on Caribbean cuisine with a French accent in a cranberry-red room done up with silks and plantation-style mahogany furniture. Entrees begin at US$16.

Also east of town is *Glenn's Jazz Club* (☎ 975-4360), a swank place at Tower Island a stone's throw west of Couples. It serves breakfast (US$7) as well as lunch and dinner. Its international menu includes fish & chips for a steep US$10.

Chinese A touristy favorite is *The Ruins* on DaCosta Drive (☎ 974-2789). This former sugar mill is now a Chinese restaurant amid gardens with cascades and pools. The food is so-so, though the setting is splendid. It's expensive. *Kwong Chong Chinese Take-Out* (☎ 974-2425), immediately west of Hermosa Resort Village, is a budget alternative.

Italian The best views in town are from *Evita's* (☎ 974-2333), high above Ochi on Eden Bower Rd in a handsome 1860s house. Northern Italian entrees average US$8; half-orders are available.

Seafood Both the *Wagon Wheel* and *Lion's Den Restaurant* opposite the entrance to Dunn's River Falls are reasonable options for seafood prepared the Jamaican way. For reasonably priced lobster, try *Jungle Lobster House* beside the estuary of the White River. Never mind that it's a rustic shack. The food is superb, cooked before your eyes over an open fire.

Fast Food & Snacks For fresh-baked bread, patties, and desserts, head to the *Tropical Oven* bakery, opposite Kentucky Fried Chicken on Main St. Nearby is the *Lobster Pot*, a homey seafood restaurant with entrées from US$5. *Caribbean Treats*, next door, serves ice cream sundaes. *Mother's* is a 24-hour fast food joint where you can enjoy a pre-dawn ice cream; it's beside the clock tower.

Entertainment

Discos The happening scene is at *Acropolis*, on the 2nd floor of Mutual Security Mall at 70 Main St (☎ 974-2633). It's cramped and dark and the mostly Jamaican crowd presses shoulder-to-sweaty-shoulder while rap, world beat, and reggae blare out at deafening levels. The dance floor is usually littered with empty beer bottles. An outside bar and terrace provide relief. No tank-tops are allowed for men; the dress code is strictly enforced. Entrance is US$2 (free on Wednesday).

Jamaica'n me Krazy disco in the Jamaica Grande Hotel is less claustrophobic. It has a squiggly fluorescent, psychedelic decor of pointillist dots, and an all-you-can-drink entrance fee of US$15. A 'Carnival Jump-Up' is held here on Thursday nights. *Silks Disco*, in the Shaw Park Hotel, attracts an older crowd (☎ 974-2554). The small disco is open 10 pm until the last guest leaves, nightly except Tuesdays. Entrance is US$1.25. Fridays is Ladies Night.

A more down-to-earth option for hard-core reggae fans is the *Rooftop Club* at 7 James Ave (☎ 974-1042); admission is US$1. See Places to Stay for more details on where the discos are located.

Bars & Nightclubs The *Vintage Bar* atop Soni Plaza plays oldies, plus soca on Fridays. The older tourist crowd heads to *Bill's Place* at 47 Main St (☎ 974-5371). This placid cocktail lounge is run by a charismatic Californian, Bill Santo. You can listen to old tunes off the jukebox or watch sports on TV; karaoke is held on Wednesday and Saturday.

Shades is a popular go-go club near the Country Kitchen restaurant at Content Hills, just east of Coconut Grove Shopping Centre. It's a favorite with local men, but is also popular with couples and foreign visitors. The US$3 entrance includes one drink. The rooftop bar is often rented for private parties, which can get *very* risqué.

The *Love Club* in town also features go-go dancing.

Live Music The *Little Pub* at 59 Main St offers live, touristy entertainment, including an Afro-Carib musical (☎ 974-2324). Most top-end hotels also have limbo and cabaret shows. If you're a jazz lover, give

Glenn's Jazz Club a call (☎ 975-4360); it has jazz on alternate Sundays.

White River Reggae Park hosts a 'Reggae Bash' once a month.

A 'Reggae Lobster Party' is held each Thursday at *Coconut Grove House*, behind the Coconut Grove Shopping Centre (☎ 974-2619). The US$29 fee includes all you can eat and drink, plus native shows.

Things to Buy
At times you may think Ocho Rios is geared solely to shoppers pouring off the cruise ships. The town has more duty-free shops than anywhere else on the island. There's a fistful of major shopping centers, with stores selling everything from coral and silver jewelry, and straw and leather crafts, to T-shirts for everyone from grannie to the kids. Don't expect any real bargains, however; free-spending cruise passengers inflate the prices. To get the best deals, visit after the cruise passengers have returned to their ships, or head out of town.

The two main shopping plazas are Taj Mahal complex and Ocean Village Plaza, both on Main St. Local designer Ruth Clarage has a store in Ocean Village. Ocho Rios Craft Park, next to Club Jamaica, on Main St, has dozens of craft stalls. Pineapple Place, east of town, and Coconut Village, opposite the Plantation Inn, also specialize in crafts. For the best selection of wood carvings, head to Dunn's River Craft Park, or to Fern Gully, which is lined with stalls selling paintings and carvings at prices marginally lower than elsewhere. The makeshift market opposite the clock tower specializes in leather goods.

For better quality art, check out the Frame Centre Gallery in Island Plaza (☎ 974-2374), and Harmony Hall (☎ 975-4222), four miles east of town. The latter sells superb paintings, sculptures, and ceramics by leading Caribbean artists, including Jamaican Intuitives or Primitives, as well as high-quality kitsch such as painted wooden fish and parrots. It also has a small bookstore (open 10 am to 6 pm). Harmony Hall is also renowned for its Easter and Christmas craft fairs.

Exotic Flowers To Go has a shop in the Jamaica Grande Hotel (☎ 974-2201). A boxed pack of 30 fresh tropical flowers costs US$25.

Watson's Shopping Shuttle is a special luncheon trip that starts at 12:15 pm daily from Main St and runs to Harmony Hall.

Getting There & Away

Air Ocho Rios is served by Boscobel airstrip (☎ 975-3101), about 10 miles east of town. No direct international service lands here. At press time, new services had not been announced for Air Jamaica Express, although they should be in service again by the time you read this.

Timair (☎ 974-0575 or 979-1114) operates charter service from Boscobel, as does Wings Jamaica (☎ 923-5416).

Bus Buses on Harbour St depart Montego Bay for Ocho Rios sporadically throughout the day (US$1.50). Kingston buses depart from the Parade (US$2); you can catch the 40-seat JR21 or STBW11, or several smaller buses. They're crowded and terribly uncomfortable. Minibuses are almost as cheap (US$3 from Montego Bay or Kingston), and usually more comfortable. Avoid older vans (usually a battered Ford from the 1970s) in favor of something modern. It's a two-hour ride from either Montego Bay or Kingston.

Buses depart Ocho Rios from Bijoux Plaza. Minibuses leave from the south side of the clock tower for Annotto Bay and Port Antonio, and from north of the roundabout on DaCosta Drive for Kingston and Montego Bay.

Caribic Vacations (in Montego Bay, ☎ 952-5013; in Ocho Rios, ☎ 974-9106) has bus transfers for US$29 round-trip from Montego Bay airport. Tropical Tours Bus Service (☎ 952-2323) has service from Montego Bay. Econotours has a shuttle to Ochi from Kingston, departing at 8 am.

Taxi Caribic Vacations charges US$110 for a taxi from Montego Bay; JUTA (☎ 974-2292) charges US$80 per car or US$150 by limousine. Bargain Rent-a-Car

(☎ 974-5298) offers transfers to/from Kingston and to/from Montego Bay for US$43 per person one-way (US$18 per person for groups).

Getting Around

The Airport There is no bus service from Boscobel. A taxi to Ocho Rios will cost about US$12.

Bus Ocho Rios has no bus service within town, but you can hop aboard any of the buses that link Ochi with towns further afield and ply the coastal road.

Car & Motorcycle Island Car Rentals at Shop No 2, Carib Arcade on Main St (☎ 974-2666 or 974-2334) has competitive rates and offers a variety of vehicles.

Others with offices in Ocho Rios include:

Bargain Rent-a-Car	☎ 974-5298
Bluebird Rent-a-Car	☎ 974-5617
Caribbean Car Rentals	☎ 974-2123
Gemini Car Rental	☎ 974-1361
Pleasure Tours Car Rental	☎ 974-6583

Companies that rent scooters and/or motorcycles include:

Island Scooters	☎ 974-9510
Motorcycle Rentals	☎ 974-5058
Motor Trails	☎ 974-5058
VLD's Cycle World Rentals	☎ 974-7529

Bicycle VLD's Cycle World Rentals also has a range of bicycles, including mountain bikes, from US$12 to US$16; try also Vacation Wheels, Shop 3 in the Carib Arcade (☎ 974-5021). Cycletronics (75 Main St, Tel 974-1281) is a bicycle repair shop.

Taxi There's a shortage of licensed taxis, whose prices are regulated. You can negotiate better deals with unregistered taxi drivers, whose cars are often beat-up wrecks. You can call a cab from the Maxi-taxi Association at Pineapple Place (☎ 974-2971) or Ocho Rios Cab Operators at 1 Newlin Plaza (☎ 974-5929).

SOUTH OF OCHO RIOS

Five miles south of Ocho Rios, at the top of Fern Gully, the A3 crests a plateau where you can call in at the Swansea Refreshment & Jerk Centre to savor your first stupendous view across the rolling pastures to the hillocks of the Dry Harbour Mountains. For the next seven miles south to Moneague, the road winds through sweeping pastoral country with stone walls reminiscent of the Dales of England.

At Moneague the A3 merges with the A1 from St Ann's Bay. You can continue south, uphill to Mt Diablo, where the road dips dramatically towards Spanish Town and Kingston.

Friendship Farm

Friendship Farm (☎ 972-2465) is a cattle property surrounded by 600 acres of meadows, forest, and orchards. Guided tours of the farm and the old great house are offered, and you can hire horses for rides through the fields. In addition, there's a pool with a view, a playground, and a summer camp for the wee ones. It is signed to the left (east) at Colegate, one mile south of Fern Gully.

Derelict buses have been converted to accommodate overnight guests. Imagine a gaily painted houseboat on wheels! There are communal showers and toilets, and meals are prepared on an open barbecue. You also have access to a restaurant, plus all the facilities of the farm.

Walkers Wood

This village in the cool hills of St Ann is clean and tidy, with attractive cottages and a strong civic pride. At first the country village seems sleepy. Yet Walkers Wood has an active community life, financed partly by USAID small-business development grants, and there are several thriving businesses. **Bromley** great house sits atop a hill southeast of Walkers Wood, which it dominates from on high. Bromley is *not* open to the public, but you can take a tour of the small factory with its huge industrial boiling pans, tucked behind the great house. Here, you'll learn the success story of Cottage Industries' world-renowned Walkers Wood range of sauces and spices.

The playing field in the village center was donated by the Reynolds Mining Company, which had a huge open-cast bauxite mine at Lydford, about two miles west of Walkers Wood (see Golden Grove in the North Coast chapter). When the company ceased operation in 1983, it restored its 80,000 acres to pasture. Reynolds actually maintained the largest herd of cattle in the West Indies, and their offspring still graze the lime-green fields.

Places to Stay & Eat You may well be the only tourist for weeks to call in at *Murphy Hill* (☎ 922-0440), a cozy guest house in the cool hills along Spring Mountain Rd, near Lydford. It has fabulous views, and a swimming pool popular with Jamaicans escaping the heat of the lowlands. You can also rent horses. The rooms are clean and boast genuine antiques (US$30 to US$40). There's a small restaurant, but you can also use the kitchen.

The *Corner Tree Café* is run by a colorful character called Ralph 'Cowboy' Ellis,

---

Spicy Enterprises

For over a decade, worker-owned Cottage Industries has been making products from local ingredients: bales of fresh scallions from St Elizabeth, nutmeg from St Mary, tomatoes, hot peppers, and assorted dried spices from local fields. Initially it experimented with chocolate fudge and pork sausages, but it was jerk seasoning that took hold, launching the cooperative to success and giving birth to a whole range of products – everything from canned ackee and callaloo, solomon grundy, jams, and spices, to dried bananas, coconut run-down sauce, and escoveitch marinade.

Take a factory tour to see workers washing and prepping vegetables, blending and stirring, and packaging and labeling bottles and jars with Walkers Wood's attractive labels. ∎

who serves inexpensive Jamaican dishes. It's a good place to chat over a Red Stripe beer and maybe even challenge a local to a game of dominoes.

Things to Buy There's a craft market in the village center, next to Corner Tree Café. Here too is the workshop of the Walkers Wood Woolspinners Cooperative, and the studio and showroom of Art Beat, a small craft shop owned by Nancy Burke, alias Inanci. She sells jewelry, carnival and duppy masks, painted rocks, and other intriguing creations. Another local artist, Laura Facey-Cooper, paints and sculpts in her family home in the nearby hamlet of Bellevue.

Goshen Wilderness Resort
This lakeside 'wilderness resort,' four miles east of Walkers Wood, happily proclaims: 'You catch it, we cook it.' Its prime attraction is 42 large ponds stocked primarily with *tilapia* (freshwater snapper) just waiting for you to yank them out of the water (☎ 974-7067, fax 974-4379). Hours are 10 am to 5 pm; admission is US$3.

Back in the 1860s, the property was a sugar and coffee plantation that formed part of a 40,000-acre estate owned by Judge Roper. Goshen was the heart of a prosperous district and had a racetrack, polo field, and showground. It is still owned by a member of the Roper family, Alex Lanigan.

The resort is a good place to take the kids. Attractions include many types of birds, both caged and roaming free, a petting zoo, a pool with freshwater turtles, swings, volleyball, paddleboats, and kayaks (US$1). There are also nature trails for hiking and horseback rides around the landscaped grounds and into the surrounding woods.

Lanigan plans to build cabins and introduce a shuttle from Ocho Rios. He currently offers a fishing package (US$20) that includes a drink, tackle, and a guide – the fee is US$9 for catch and release. The chef will prepare your fish with bammy and festival, but burgers, hot dogs, and jerk dishes are also available at the thatched restaurant and bar.

The resort is one mile west of Goshen,

which is now a road junction, not a village. If you don't have a car, you can take either minibus No LS979 or LS1069, which both operate from Ocho Rios. The 30-minute journey should cost about US$1.50.

Moneague
This small crossroads town, 12 miles south of Ochi, was favored during the 19th century as a hill resort, and before that as a staging post on the three-day journey between Spanish Town and the north coast. It sits at the junction of the A3 and the A1. The Moneague Tavern, erected in 1891 to cater to coach traffic, later became a teacher training facility. Today it's the Moneague Training Camp of the Jamaica Defence Force. Two Saracen armored cars are on display at the gate. Call the police station (☎ 972-3211) in case of an emergency.

A road leads northeast from the public works (south of the training camp) to **Moneague Lake**, in a low-lying area subject to flooding. The lake's level fluctuates according to the subterranean water table (local lore says that it disappears altogether when someone drowns). Turtles and perch flourish in the lake and waterfowl flock in.

You can rent pedalboats (US$3) at *Silver Lake Camp Resort*, which has restrooms and rents wooden cabins. They each sleep four people (US$6 per person). You can also camp here for US$5, but you'll need to bring your own equipment.

Faith's Pen
South of Moneague the A1 road climbs steadily to Faith's Pen, 17 miles south of Ocho Rios. The roadside is lined with stalls selling citrus fruits and, 400 yards further south, dozens of jerk stalls at **Faith Pen Vendor Centre**, where you can try oddities such as cow-cod soup, a concoction made of bull's testes, reputed to be an aphrodisiac. Immediately beyond, a road leads east to the bauxite mine of ALCAN (the Canadian Aluminium Corporation Ltd), which began operations in Jamaica in 1960. The ravaged slopes have been replanted in recent years in Caribbean pine

and blue mahoe, and are often mist-shrouded in early morning.

The road continues to rise up the pine-forested slopes of Mt Diablo (2754 feet). At 2250 feet the A1 crests the mountain chain and begins its steep, winding descent to Ewarton and the lush Rosser Valley, breathtakingly beautiful from these heights. The summit also marks the boundary between the parishes of St Ann to the north and of St Catherine to the south. On your left, just below the summit, is a large lake the color of jade; this is a tailings dam for the ALCAN mine. For Ewarton see the South Coast chapter.

EAST OF OCHO RIOS
Rio Nuevo

The Rio Nuevo meets the ocean five miles east of Ocho Rios. The bluff west of the river's mouth was in 1658 the site of the most important battle ever fought on the island. Although the colonial Spanish commander had surrendered to the British invasion army in 1655, many Spanish soldiers refused to lay down their arms. Under the leadership of a guerrilla and fifth-generation Jamaican, Don Cristobal Arnaldo de Ysassi, the recalcitrant Spaniards continued to harass the British. In May 1658, the King of Spain named Ysassi titular governor and sent reinforcements from Cuba. They landed at Rio Nuevo, where they built a stockade on the heights west of the river mouth. The English governor D'Oyley promptly sent a fleet, landed marines, established camp on the opposite bank, and managed to surprise the Spaniards using a classic feint: after sending a small boy under flag of truce to test the depth of the river, D'Oyley's ships made the appearance of launching a full-scale frontal assault while his soldiers sneaked up to the fort from the rear. A plaque records the events:

'On this ground on June 17, 1658, was fought the battle of Rio Nuevo to decide whether Jamaica would be Spanish or English. On one side were the Jamaicans of both black and white races, whose ancestors had come to Jamaica from Africa and Spain 150 years before. The Spanish

forces lost the battle and the island. The Spanish whites fled to Cuba but the black people took to the mountains and fought a long and bloody guerrilla war against the English. This site is dedicated to them all.'

The Spaniards lost 500 soldiers, the English lost 50. Another memorial stands beneath a gazebo on the site of the old stockade. The site is shaded by pimento trees, beneath which are benches for quiet contemplation. The site is open 9 am to 4 pm daily. You can hike down to a gray-sand beach where there's a small fishing community.

Boscobel Beach

Boscobel Beach is the longest and most developed of several beaches east of Ocho Rios. It's dominated by the Boscobel Beach resort. Other tiny coves further east harbor fishing hamlets nestled in turquoise lagoons protected by coral reefs.

Jamaica Beach, west of the Rio Nuevo, is renowned for its dive sites immediately offshore.

Places to Stay *Island of Light Center for Holistic Development* is a B&B at Charles Town, in the hills three miles south of the A3 up Rio Nuevo Rd (turn right at Content). The five-acre estate was once part of Prospect Plantation and the two guest cottages (one with three bedrooms, the other with one) were formerly the plantation accountant's stables. Rooms cost US$40 (PO Box 6, Retreat, St Mary, ☎/fax 975-4268). Vegetarian meals are US$12, using produce straight from the garden. The Center hosts 'consciousness-building workshops' including yoga and meditation, massage therapy, and bodywork, as well as art classes for local children. You can also camp here for US$15.

Guest house *Hunter's Lodge* (☎ 975-4227), 400 yards west of the Rio Nuevo battle site, has six modest rooms with private bathrooms but cold water only for US$15/20. At Boscobel, try the funky-looking *Henry Brothers' Cut Eye View Villa* (☎ 975-7055).

Cottage by the Beach (no telephone),

400 yards east of Boscobel Beach, is set in its own private cove. It has two rooms, each with kitchenette, TV, and private bath with hot water, plus a wide veranda with sofa and hammock (US$40 double). A similar option is *Skip's Place* (☎ 975-7010), half a mile west of Boscobel Beach. It has 16 modest cabins of varying sizes for rent from US$25 to US$75 double. Alternately, try *Villa Boscobel Guest House*, opposite the airstrip.

An attractive self-catering option is *Sea Chalets Villa* (☎ 927-4533), in landscaped grounds 400 yards east of Boscobel airstrip. Four-bedroom, two-story villas with kitchens share a shell-shaped pool and sundeck (US$60 per room).

Lording over Boscobel Beach is the all-inclusive resort *Boscobel Beach*, Jamaica's most complete family resort, operated by the SuperClubs chain (PO Box 63, Ocho Rios, ☎ 975-7330, fax 975-7370; in North America, ☎ (800) 859-7873; in the UK, ☎ (01749) 677200). Educational programs, a petting zoo, computer lab, video games, and a 24-hour SuperNanny keep the kids amused. There are adults-only areas, plus five bars, four tennis courts, gym, volleyball, an Olympic-size family pool, a separate, adults-only pool with swim-up bar, and a disco. Low-season rates begin at US$535/1085 per person (three/seven nights). One child under 14 per adult stays free when sharing with parents.

La Mer Dive & Beach Resort is an upscale hotel on Jamaica Beach, immediately west of the Rio Nuevo (☎ 975-5002, fax 974-2359; in North America, ☎ (800) 262-2727). It's dedicated to scuba diving and has 34 self-contained one-, two- and three-bedroom units set in lush landscaped grounds. A PADI dive center is on site.

If you want your own place in the sun, consider *Seagrape Villas* (☎ 975-4406; in the USA, c/o West Indies Investments, 640 Pearson St, Suite 304, Des Plaines, IL 60016, ☎ (312) 693-6884 or (800) 637-3608), . The villas, perched on the cliff at Jamaica Beach, are very beautiful and very upscale. Each has four bedrooms and four bathrooms, sleeping up to eight people, is

centered on a private pool, and comes with its own cook and maid. They rent for US$2500 per week.

There's also a fully staffed, deluxe three-bedroom house – *Pearl Resort Villa* – for rent at Rio Nuevo.

Places to Eat *Cliff View*, just west of the Rio Nuevo, is a popular upscale restaurant owned by music promoter Har Richards. *Skip's Place* (☎ 975-7010), enjoys a breezy cliff-top setting half a mile west of Boscobel Beach. Both serve seafood and Jamaican dishes upwards of US$5. Next door to Skip's is *Moxoni's* (☎ 975-7219), a modestly elegant place where you can look down on the ocean while enjoying lobster, steak, chicken and seafood dishes (US$20 to US$25, or US$28 for a complete dinner).

Things to Buy If you're tired of seeing the same old woven straw and carved wood souvenirs, check out Irie Ceramics (also called Lloyd's Ceramics), a local potters' workshop selling wind-chimes, casserole dishes, figurines, and vases for a song. It's next to Cliff View at Jamaica Beach. Moxon's Community Projects produces coconut items, especially woodcarvings.

Oracabessa
This small town, which hangs on a hillside 13 miles east of Ocho Rios, takes its name from the Spanish words *oro cabeza*, meaning 'golden head,' probably referring to the way the evening sunlight reflects on the headland. First impressions of Oracabessa are of its main street, lined by an open-air market and ramshackle wooden houses. Look more closely and you'll see that these homes are trimmed with old-fashioned fretwork and complete with verandas. There's hardly a modern building in site.

At the east end of town, immediately beyond the police station, a road leads downhill to the marina that formerly served as a banana-loading port. The marina sits in the lee of a tombolo on whose western flank pirogues and fishing boats bob at anchor. Lobster cages and nets are drawn up on the beach. Keep going west along the waterfront and after half a mile you'll reach a delightful pocket-sized beach.

A deep-water pier has been touted by the Urban Development Council in an attempt to revive the town's fortunes. Jamaica's politics being what they are, this may never happen. However, Oracabessa is set to change in a big way. Much of the waterfront has been bought by the Island Trading Company, which plans to recreate an entire village on a 19th-century theme. The company is owned by Chris Blackwell, who was born in St Mary Parish and who actively promotes local community development.

A Scotiabank is located in the town center (☎ 975-3203). The Oracabessa Medical Centre (☎ 975-3304) is opposite the Esso gas station, 400 yards east of the chalky-blue police station (☎ 975-3233) at the east end of town.

Goldeneye Topped by carved pineapples, the gateposts east of the marina mark the entrance to Goldeneye (☎ 974-5833), former home of novelist Ian Fleming, inventor of the legendary spy, James Bond.

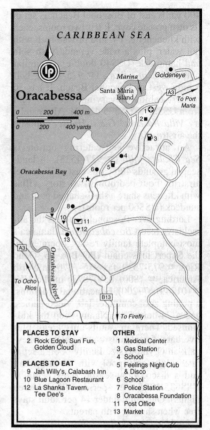

PLACES TO STAY
2 Rock Edge, Sun Fun, Golden Cloud

PLACES TO EAT
9 Jah Willy's, Calabash Inn
10 Blue Lagoon Restaurant
12 La Shanka Tavern, Tee Dee's

OTHER
1 Medical Center
3 Gas Station
4 School
5 Feelings Night Club & Disco
6 School
7 Police Station
8 Oracabessa Foundation
11 Post Office
13 Market

Oh Yes, We Have No Bananas

In the early 1970s an artificial harbor was built on the shore below Oracabessa. It was ill timed. The shipping of bananas – formerly the principal trade of Oracabessa – was in decline, and the harbor was never put to use.

Recently, homegrown promoter and developer Chris Blackwell proposed grander plans for Oracabessa. His Island Trading Company intends to create a planned resort that will 're-energize the traditional architecture of Jamaica' and engage the local community in providing the services and amusements for visitors. The town plan will include a hotel, villas, and apartments stretching the full length of the mile-long harborfront, around a civic center and museums. Architectural plans show a complete town of residential and commercial properties using eco-sensitive materials. ∎

Fleming fell in love with Jamaica after a visit and returned to buy this 15-acre beachfront estate, designing most of the house himself in 1946, with huge jalousies to let in the breezes. All 14 James Bond novels were written here, and five were set in Jamaica. 'Would these books have been born if I had not been living in the gorgeous vacuum of a Jamaican holiday? I doubt it,' he wrote in *Ian Fleming Introduces Jamaica*. Noel Coward, who later lived down the road at Port Maria (see Firefly below), was a frequent visitor, as were Evelyn Waugh, Graham Greene, and others of the beau monde.

Fleming . . . Ian Fleming

Ian Fleming first came to Jamaica in 1942, while serving for British Naval Intelligence. In 1946 he bought a house on the shore at Oracabessa and named it 'Goldeneye,' where he wintered every year until his death in 1964.

It was here that Fleming conceived his secret agent '007,' alias James Bond, whose creation the author attributes to living in Jamaica.

'I was looking for a name for my hero – nothing like Peregrine Carruthers or Standfast Maltravers – and I found it, on the cover of one of my Jamaican bibles, *Birds of the West Indies* by James Bond, an ornithological classic,' he relates in *Ian Fleming Introduces Jamaica.* ■

The house is owned by Chris Blackwell, the famous music promoter. Blackwell has restored the house – a modest, one-story, three-bedroom home overlooking a beach and may start renting it (call ☎ 994-2282 to find out). Fleming's original fan-shaped corner desk, at which he would unstintingly write 2000 words every day, is still fitted into its corner, though most of the furnishings are of contemporary, minimalist design. The house is closed to the public, but may be open by the time you read this.

Places to Stay *Lovely Spot Ocean Villas* (☎ 975-3322), east of town, is a laid-back place run by a friendly owner, Len, who also offers tours of his farm. His four pink-and-white villas (US$24 per person) are modest, though spacious and clean, and sit above a coral shore. Each has a kitchenette, fans, homey furnishings, and hot water. Upstairs rooms have verandas. Little gazebos are scattered around the ramshackle garden.

The *Golden Seas Beach Resort*, half a mile west of Oracabessa, is an attractive historic hotel of cut stone (PO Box 1, Oracabessa, ☎ 975-3540, fax 975-3243). A remake was almost complete when I passed by. Its comfortable rooms are done up in

mauves and overlook an amoeba-shaped pool where you can sit in hammock chairs at the swim-up bar. High season rates range from US$80 to US$105 single, US$100 to US$125 double.

Rock Edge, *Golden Cloud*, and *Sun Fun* are all villas next to each other at the east end of Oracabessa.

Places to Eat For rustic beachside ambiance, head down to the tiny beach on the waterfront, where you can eat at *Jah Willy's Calabash Inn*. Willy serves seafood and jerk for US$2 and less. It's a cool place, and you're virtually guaranteed to be the only out-of-towner . . . a good chance for a game of dominoes or volleyball with the locals. *Dor's Fish Pot* is a popular, lively yet rustic jerk and seafood eatery by the shore east of town. Nearby is *Club Tan Jan Tavern*, serving seafood and I-tal dishes; look for the lively mural on its outside wall. In the town center, *Tee Dee's* sells zesty pasties and soothing ice cream. You can eat basic Jamaican fare for US$2 at the funky *Blue Lagoon Restaurant*, opposite Scotiabank.

Entertainment The only real action around is *Feelings Night Club & Disco* on Wharf Rd (☎ 975-3545); it features oldies on weekends. *La Shanka Tavern*, opposite the market on Main St, is a lively rum shop playing ear-bursting music. Buy the locals a beer or rum and then join them in a lively game of dominoes.

Galina Point & Little Bay

Three miles east of Oracabessa the A3 leaves the coast and winds around Galina Point, the northernmost tip of the island, where the coast takes an abrupt turn south toward Port Maria. A 40-foot-high concrete lighthouse marks the headland. South of Galina you'll pass Noel Coward's old house, **Blue Harbour** (not open for tours; see Places to Stay below) squatting behind a blue-and-white fence on the top of what is called 'the double bend,' where the road and shoreline take a 90° turn and open to a view of Little Bay and

Community Development

Under the umbrella of the Oracabessa Foundation (☎ 975-3393, fax 975-3394), Oracabessa's community spirit is as energetic as anywhere on the island. The key to their community efforts is providing youngsters with options other than prostitution and drugs. The International School of Jamaica (PO Box 36, Oracabessa, St Mary), for example, works to promote self-sufficiency through various enterprises like bee-keeping, composting, solid-waste management, and quilt-making from rag scraps.

A man called Lynx will be happy to tell you about his work visiting schools and markets to educate the community about littering and other environmental issues. His group also helps feed the indigent and elderly. Another community group, Inner Circle, works to ensure that parents send their children to school and assists with providing books, pencils, and other needed supplies. ■

Cabarita Island. The road drops steeply from Blue Harbour to Cocomo Beach, in Little Bay.

The beach is unappealing, despite being popular in the 1950s and '60s with Coward and his illustrious friends. At least the snorkeling is said to be good above the coral reef 50 yards out (check with locals about swimming conditions beforehand).

Places to Stay & Eat A place called *Sea Lawn Coral Beach* reportedly offers camping on the beach.

A colorful character named Busta Prendergast runs *Belretiro Inn* (PO Box 151, Galina District PA, Port Maria). It has a dramatic and secluded setting atop a raised coral shore at Galina. Ten rooms have private baths and cold water, but are overpriced at US$30. It's rather run-down (Hurricane Gilbert walloped it in 1988), but was due to be remodeled as the Galina Country Inn with 30 rooms. There's a small pool and restaurant. The inn is also known as Blue Rock Estate Guest House.

The very beautiful *Caribbean Pearl*, which rests on a breezy hilltop at the southern end of Little Bay (PO Box 127, Port Maria, ☎ 994-2672, fax 994-2043), is run to typical German standards by Hans Jurgens Böcking. I like this elegant and intimate villa-style hotel centered on an amoeba-shaped pool. Eight rooms and two master suites are furnished with hardwoods and white wicker, and mosquito nets over the beds. Wide, louvered windows open to shady verandas where you can relax on wicker hammocks. Ask for Room 2, which has a wicker four-poster bed and Chinese rugs. It's a bargain at US$40/50, including breakfast.

If you want to sleep in the same room as Marlene Dietrich, Katherine Hepburn, Errol Flynn, or Winston Churchill, rent a villa or room at *Blue Harbour* (PO Box 50, Port Maria, ☎ 994-2262; in the USA, PO Box 770, Questa, NM 87556, ☎ (505) 586-1244). Coward bought the property in the early 1950s and built the main house, Villa Grande, for himself, plus Villa Rose, and the smaller, more secluded Villa Chica for his guests. Villa Grande has four upstairs bedrooms with wicker and dowdy utility furniture. Meals are served on a wide wrap-around veranda with fabulous views over the bay. Villa Rose has four rooms with fairly basic furnishings and decor. Villa Chica is smaller, very private, with more pleasing decor in tropical pastels. Blue Harbour comes fully staffed with cook and housekeeper. Pathways lead downhill through tropical foliage to a tiny beach of coral and shingle, where there's also a small seawater pool. You can rent the entire seven-acre estate for US$4000 weekly for up to 12 guests or US$400 per person. Food is extra.

If all else fails, there's the 20-room *Hotel Casa Maria* next to the Caribbean Pearl. The place has lost its panache since Noel Coward and his celebrated guests frequented the bar in the 1950s and '60s (PO Box 10, Port Maria, ☎ 994-2323; in North America, ☎ (509) 547-7065 or (800) 222-6927, fax (509) 547-1265). The rooms are pleasantly, though modestly furnished. Cheaper rooms have garden views; superior rooms have private balconies with ocean views. Rates are US$43 to US$64 single or double, US$54 to US$75 triple. The modestly elegant restaurant advertises 'pizzas and patties.'

A modest resort called *Idlewild on Sea* (☎ 975-3327) was being built at press time beside the road just west of Galina.

The *Kokomo Bar & Grill* on the beach serves seafood dishes for less than J$100.

PORT MARIA

Port Maria (population 8000) is the capital of St Mary Parish. For most travelers, it's merely a place to pass through en route to Port Antonio or Ocho Rios. It has no tourist facilities. As with many other towns along this coast, it prospered in the 19th century as a sugar and banana port. Two centuries prior, the land for miles around were part of Llanrumney Estate, owned by the nefarious Henry Morgan, who rose from fame as a pirate (Port Maria was his base on Jamaica's north coast) to become lieutenant-governor of the island. Nothing much seems to happen here these days, except on weekends when the market is held and the main street turns to mayhem. Stalls sprout like mushrooms on a damp log, and negotiating through town is tricky.

Your first view when approaching from the west is spectacular: you round the headland east of Little Bay, and there's Port Maria nestling in its own turquoise and aquamarine with mountains rising behind. Have your camera ready! The town, however, took a belting from Hurricane Gilbert in 1988 and the appeal may begin to fade as you approach the town center.

Port Maria is divided by a bridge over a small river, with a sleepy residential area to the west and a commercial section immediately to the east. Take care at the tiny roundabout immediately east of the bridge; keep to the left, and exit to the right along Stennet St for Port Antonio.

Information

Money You can change traveler's checks or get advances against credit cards at Scotiabank on Warner St (☎ 994-2265), or at the nearby National Commercial Bank (☎ 994-2219). Western Union has an office opposite the Indian Queen Restaurant, 50 yards south of the roundabout.

Post & Communications The post office is on the north side of the roundabout in the town center.

Medical Services Emergency care is provided at the public general hospital (☎ 994-2228), one mile south of town on Stennet St. For less urgent medical attention call Dr Leonard Jones (☎ 992-2622). Clare's Pharmacy (☎ 994-2386) is in the town center.

Emergencies The police station is 100 yards north of the roundabout, facing the sea on Main St (☎ 994-2223).

Things to See

The pretty St Mary's Parish Church, at the extreme west end of town, was built in 1861 of limestone in quintessential English style. Palms loom over the graves in the churchyard. Opposite the church is the roofless ruin of the **old police station**, destroyed in 1988 by fire. A plaque on the wall is dedicated to the Right Honorable Alexander Bustamante, the labor organizer and former prime minister who once stood trial in the courthouse next door that dates back to 1820. A monument in front of the courthouse commemorates 'Tacky of the Easter Rebellion' (see the Easter Rebellion sidebar below).

A few motley remains of **Fort Haldane** can be seen on a bluff beside the A3, half a mile to the north. If you haven't had your fill of churches, check out the stern brick **Presbyterian church** atop a knoll to the east. It was built in 1830 to Christianize the slaves of Frontier Estate, where the Easter Rebellion was sparked in 1760.

Activities

The town beach, Pagee Beach, sweeps eastward for almost a mile from the river's mouth, and is paralleled by Main St. Fishing pirogues are usually pulled up

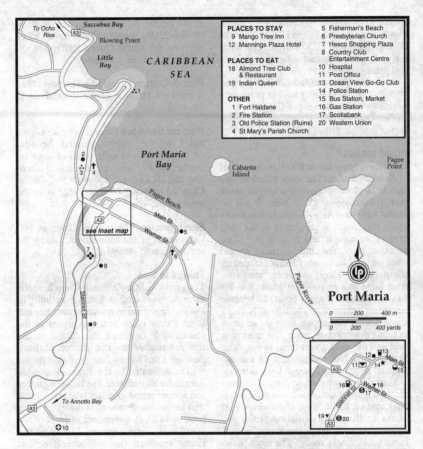

PLACES TO STAY
9 Mango Tree Inn
12 Mannings Plaza Hotel

PLACES TO EAT
18 Almond Tree Club
    & Restaurant
19 Indian Queen

OTHER
1 Fort Haldane
2 Fire Station
3 Old Police Station (Ruins)
4 St Mary's Parish Church

5 Fisherman's Beach
6 Presbyterian Church
7 Hesco Shopping Plaza
8 Country Club
   Entertainment Centre
10 Hospital
11 Post Office
13 Ocean View Go-Go Club
14 Police Station
15 Bus Station, Market
16 Gas Station
17 Scotiabank
20 Western Union

here. You can hire a guide and boat to go **fishing** or to take you to Cabarita Island.

Pagee beach is safe for **swimming**. It is also the most westerly spot for **surfing** along the north coast, with long peelers. The rocks are sharp however, and local surfers advise surfing in front of the point closest to town. The action is said to be best in the morning before the trades kick in.

Organized Tours

Port Maria is the base for a one-week eco-tour that also features hiking in the Blue Mountains and a raft trip on the Rio Grande offered by Tropical Pleasure Vacation (in the USA, 1062 55th St, Oakland, CA 94808, ☎ (510) 428-2765), with accommodations at Blue Harbour for US$1088.

Places to Stay

Pickings are both slim and depressing. *Mannings Plaza Hotel*, 50 yards north of the roundabout, is a very basic, run-down property with rooms with shared bath for US$10. Also very basic is the *Mango Tree Inn* at 49 Stennet St (☎ 994-2687), on the road to Port Antonio. It has 13 rooms with bathtubs made of concrete, and cold water only (US$6). The inn, which doubles as a rum shop, is named for the mango tree out

The Easter Rebellion

St Mary Parish was thinly populated by white people throughout the 18th century, when local sugar estates prospered. Many of the slaves of St Mary were from the warlike Koromantyn tribes of Africa's Gold Coast. On Easter Sunday, 1760, those of Frontier Estate, east of Port Maria, revolted. They were inspired by Tacky, an overseer who had been a tribal chieftain prior to being captured and shipped to Jamaica.

The rebellion was one of the most serious slave revolts to shake Jamaica. That day the slaves killed their masters at Frontier and neighboring Trinity Estate before marching on Port Maria, where they murdered the storekeeper of Fort Haldane and seized arms and ammunition. The revolt lasted one month, during which plantations throughout St Mary were destroyed and the English planters terrorized.

Eventually the militia gained the upper hand in the guerrilla war, and, aided by Maroons, captured Tacky. His head was cut off and displayed in Spanish Town. About 60 whites and 300 slaves perished in the Easter Rebellion, but several hundred more slaves were killed in grim retribution, including two who were chained in Kingston Parade and starved to death in public view. ■

front. About one mile south of Port Maria is the *Welcome Guest House*, just past the bridge at the junction for Sandside. By night it's a go-go club and may rent rooms by the hour.

Places to Eat

Try the *Almond Tree Club & Restaurant* on Warner St. It serves seafood, ackee and codfish, and other Jamaican fare for less than US$3. Alternately, head for the *Country Club*, a rustic restaurant and bar on Stennet St; or the *Indian Queen* immediately south of the roundabout.

Entertainment

The dancers at the *Ocean View Go-Go Club*, on Main St, leave little to the imagination on their mirrored stage. You can let your own hair down at the *Country Club*, which has open-air dancing to live music. Both are good places to mingle with locals.

Getting There & Away

You can catch buses to Port Maria from Ocho Rios. The 40-minute journey costs about US$0.30. Walter Aarons has a Toyota minibus (No LS153) which runs between Ocho Rios and Port Maria for about US$2. Buses also operate from Annotto Bay, from where Winston Condappa also offers rides aboard minibus No LS716 (about US$1.50). If traveling from Kingston, you can hop aboard bus No JR6

or STBW8, which depart from the Parade (US$1.50), as do minibuses No JR154 and JR158. There's a gas station by the round-about immediately east of the bridge.

AROUND PORT MARIA
Firefly

A visit to Firefly is one of the most interesting excursions in all Jamaica. The English-style cottage, set amid wide lawns atop a hill three miles southwest of Port Maria, was between 1956 and 1973 the home of Sir Noel Coward, the English playwright, songwriter, actor, and wit. When he died in 1973, Coward left the estate to his friend Graham Payne, who gifted it to the nation. It soon fell into disrepair. In 1990 the property was leased by the Jamaica National Heritage Trust to Island Outpost, owned by Chris Blackwell, who embarked on a meticulous restoration (it was Blackwell's mother who sold the property to Coward, and both she and her son were considered part of the Coward 'family'). In 1993 the house reopened to the public as a museum, looking just as it did on Sunday, February 28, 1965, the day the Queen Mother visited.

Firefly is approached up a steep drive. You'll be greeted by a guide, who will hand you a fruit punch or rum cocktail and lead you first to Coward's art studio, where he was schooled in oil painting by Winston Churchill. The studio displays

Coward's original paintings, including one (on his easel) of local muscle-boys on the beach. Take time to read the captions of the photographs on the walls telling the tale of his involvement with a coterie of famous friends from around the world.

The former garage has been turned into a screening room where a spellbinding film of Coward's life is shown before you tour the house. The upper lounge features a glassless window shaded by a green awning that stretches the full length of the room and offers one of the most stunning coastal vistas in all Jamaica. Contrary to popular opinion, Coward didn't write his famous song 'A Room With a View' here; it was written in Hawaii in 1928. The room contains a simple workdesk bearing his typewriter, miscellaneous correspondence,

and a bust of Coward. Beyond is the bedroom with his mahogany bed topped by pineapples (symbols of prosperity and peace) and closets still stuffed with his Hawaiian shirts and silk PJs.

Coward lies buried beneath a plain white marble slab on the wide lawns where he entertained so many illustrious stars of stage and screen. A stone hut that once served as a lookout for the pirate Henry Morgan has been restored and is now a gift store, bar, and restaurant (Firefly was then part of Morgan's Llanrumney Estate). Today, musical and theatrical performances are hosted regularly, and a Moonlick party (US$25 all-inclusive) with live jazz band is held on weekends closest to the full moon. During the parties, the estate is lit by candles in brown bags to

Noel Coward's Peeny-Wally

Sir Noel Coward, the multi-talented English actor, playwright, songwriter, and raconteur, first visited Jamaica in 1944 on a two-week holiday. He found so much peace of mind here that he dubbed his dream-island 'Dr Jamaica.' Four years later he rented Ian Fleming's estate, Goldeneye, at Oracabessa, while he hunted for a site to build his own home. He found an incredible view over Little Bay toward Port Maria near Galina, 'a magical spot' 10 miles east of Oracabessa.

In 1948 Coward bought the eight-acre estate and set to work building 'Coward's Folly,' a three-story villa with two guest cottages. He then went back to England and returned to Jamaica only when it was complete. Inspired by the view, he named his home Blue Harbour. He had a swimming pool built at the sea's edge and invited his many notable friends, a virtual Who's Who of the rich and famous.

'His was a most extraordinary, charismatic mind,' recalls Chris Blackwell. 'His wit was so sharp that he controlled a room not only by what he was saying, but by the expectation of what he might say next.'

The swarm of visitors, however, eventually drove Coward to find another retreat. While painting with his friend, Graham Payne, at a place called Lookout (so-named because the pirate Henry Morgan had a stone hut built atop the hill to keep an eye out for Spanish galleons), Coward was struck by the impressive solitude and the vista of bays receding in scalloped relief, backed by distant mountains. The duo lingered until nightfall, when fireflies appeared. Within two weeks Coward had bought the land, and eight years later had a house built big enough for only himself. He named it Firefly.

Coward's most creative years were behind him when he arrived in Jamaica. At Firefly, however, he could write in peace. His only novel, Pomp and Circumstance, his comedy, South Sea Bubble, and his musical, Ace of Clubs, were all written here. Coward lived a remarkably modest lifestyle in Jamaica; he set up the now-defunct Designs for Living shop in Port Maria, the profits from which were put into the training of local schoolchildren in arts and crafts. Coward himself recorded his love of the island and islanders on canvas, in bright, splashy colors.

Coward had spent 30 'delightful years' in Jamaica when he suffered a heart attack at the age of 73. He is buried on the lawns of Firefly beneath a marble slab that simply reads: 'Sir Noel Coward/ Born 16 December 1899/ Died 26 March 1973.' ∎

represent the fireflies (locally called peeny-wallies or winkies) after which the house is named.

Entrance is US$10 (or J$100 for Jamaican residents), including a complimentary drink. The museum is open 8:30 am to 5:30 pm daily (PO Box 38, Port Maria, St Mary, ☎ 997-7201, fax 974-5830). Firefly is well signed and can be reached via three different routes that lead inland from the A3, from Oracabessa, Little Bay, and Port Maria.

Brimmer Hall

This 2000-acre working plantation near Bailey's Vale, six miles southwest of Port Maria, grows bananas, coconuts, sugarcane, and citrus for export. It's centered on a wooden great house with an impressive interior of dark hardwoods, furnished with oriental rugs, antique furniture with Chinese inlay, and even an original suit of armor. An educational tour reveals the workings of the plantation. Brimmer Hall is a popular tour-stop for groups from cruise ships calling in at Ocho Rios. The one-hour tour costs US$15, including a tour of the plantation by canopied jitney pulled by a tractor. A bar/restaurant serves Jamaican dishes next to a large pool surrounded by lush foliage. There's also a small gift shop.

It's open daily 9 am to 5 pm. Tours are offered at 11 am, 1:30, and 3:30 pm (☎ 994-2309).

Sun Valley Plantation

Sun Valley Plantation provides a less commercial alternative to Brimmer Hall. It, too, is a working plantation, at Crescent on the B13, three miles south of Oracabessa and a similar distance west of Port Maria (PO Box 20, Oracabessa, ☎ 995-3075). Owners Lorna or Janese Binns will guide you along trails that border the Crescent River and on through the groves of bananas and other tropical fruits (US$12 including snack). Tours are offered daily at 9 am, 11 am, and 2 pm.

Horseback Riding Horseback rides are available at Sun Valley Plantation with advance reservation (US$20 per hour). Quebec Plantation, three miles east of Port Maria, also offers horseback rides plus a tour of the great house (☎ 994-2532); Follow Warner St east past the Presbyterian church in Port Maria.

PORT MARIA TO ANNOTTO BAY

Fourteen miles east of Port Maria, the A3 (known locally as Junction Rd) turns south through the Wag Water Valley and winds into the Blue Mountains en route to Kingston. The river is named for an English derivation of the Arawak name written as *Guayguata* by the Spanish and mispronounced, in turn, by the English. The coast road continues east as the A4 to Annotto Bay and Port Antonio (see the East Coast chapter).

Midway between Port Maria and Annotto Bay you'll pass **Whitehall**, a tiny village known for its cast-iron pots. It's at the junction with the B2, a rough and lonesome road that leads southeast over the mountains to Bog Walk and Spanish Town.

About six miles east of Whitehall, a turnoff to the north leads past banana plantations via Green Castle, then hugs a lonesome shoreline with gray-sand beaches fringed by almonds and backed by lagoons. After 2½ miles you emerge in **Mt Pleasant Heights**, a tiny, away-from-it-all fishing village atop a wide-open plateau with mountains off in the distance. Mt Pleasant Heights nestles atop Don Christopher's Point, named for the Spanish guerrilla leader, Cristobal Ysassi (see Rio Nuevo above).

Places to Stay

You can camp amid the trees at *Sonrise* (formerly Strawberry Fields), at Robin's Bay, immediately west of Mt Pleasant Heights (Sonrise, Robin's Bay PA, St Mary, ☎/fax 996-2351). Tent sites cost US$15 (US$10 single). There's a bath and shower complex, plus picnic tables and benches. Tents (US$5) and air mattresses (US$2) can be rented. Or stay in one of six standard cabins with two bunks and a double bed in loft bedroom. They cost US$90 double. Discounts are offered for three nights or more. A charming 'honeymoon cottage' has its own private little beach good for skinny-dipping. Sonrise is a very serene, unpretentious place, popular with families from Kingston on weekends, and boasts a private setting above a tiny cove with a pretty, pocket-sized, golden-sand beach. The clear, shallow waters and coral reef are great for snorkeling. At night a big campfire is built in a huge stone fireplace on the shore. Marvelous!

An amphitheater is being added for special events and jazz and spiritual music concerts. Meals are served in a gazebo restaurant. Trails lead along the low cliffs and hikes are offered to a black-sand beach and hidden waterfall. Day entry costs US$3.

Bobby's, next to Sonrise, rents a basic cabin by the beach (US$14). *Coconut Lounge*, one mile west of the turnoff for Sonrise, has a modest guest house (US$9). It also has a bar with go-go dancing. Rooms are very basic and may be rented by the hour to dancers.

About 400 yards west of Sonrise is *River Lodge*, an atmospheric mill-house on a century-old estate, with white-bleached stone walls, blood-red floors, and five spacious bedrooms lit by skylights (US$30 double). The bathrooms (cold water only) are festooned with climbing ivy. Meals are served in a small thatched restaurant in the courtyard. The place is run by a German, Brigitta, and her Rasta boyfriend, Frank (Robin's Bay PO, St. Mary, ☎/fax 995-3003; in Germany, Mrs Fuchslocher, Fladigenfeld 35, 34128 Kassel, ☎/fax 0561-886232). It's said to be haunted by the ghost of the Lady of the manor, who supposedly murdered her husband.

Places to Eat

Try the steamed fish and other Jamaican fare at *Bobby*, a rustic shack next to Sonrise, which has a health-food restaurant serving breakfast (US$5), lunches, and dinner (US$6 to US$12). In Mt Pleasant Heights are *Harbour Light Club* and *Sunrise Lawn*, two rustic eateries and entertainment centers where you can get steamed fish and jerk for a few dollars. You can also bargain for lobster and other seafood from local fishermen.

Getting There & Away

Any of the buses between Ocho Rios and Annotto Bay or Port Antonio will let you off at the junction of the A3 and the road to Robin's Bay. It's a four-mile walk to Robin's Bay. With good timing, you can connect with bus No JR16A which operates between Kingston and Robin's Bay.

North Coast

Travelers have traditionally passed through the coastal areas of Trelawny and St Ann on the way between Montego Bay and Ocho Rios. Tourist development is relatively limited, although Runaway Bay is a well-established if small resort, and individual hotels are now spreading along the coast. Falmouth is of historical interest. The Martha Brae River is known for rafting and Good Hope Estate for horseback riding and fine dining. Travel just a few miles inland and you enter a realm of rolling pastures and thickly forested slopes where small hamlets and market towns are tied to the land. Visitors have yet to discover the fascinating Cockpit Country that lies within minutes of the A1. This is the most scenically appealing region in Jamaica, but it's still virtually inaccessible.

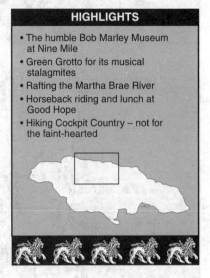

HIGHLIGHTS

- The humble Bob Marley Museum at Nine Mile
- Green Grotto for its musical stalagmites
- Rafting the Martha Brae River
- Horseback riding and lunch at Good Hope
- Hiking Cockpit Country – not for the faint-hearted

Falmouth to St Ann's Bay

Falmouth is an active market town that has been largely ignored by tourist development. Its attractions are largely historical. East of Falmouth the A1 runs parallel to the shore about two miles inland. It again hits the coast at Rio Bueno, a charming historic little town 13 miles east, at the border with St Ann Parish. Few roads lead down to the shore, which remains relatively undeveloped. Beyond Rio Bueno, you'll pass a number of attractive beaches. Discovery Bay (said to be the site of Columbus' first landing in Jamaica in 1494) and Runaway Bay, both known for their white-sand beaches, are booming as centers of resort development.

Low mountains rise to the south of the A1 and ascend gradually to the Dry Harbour Mountains. You can follow another paved road – the 'Great Interior Road' (the

B11) – that parallels the coast about seven miles inland. Built at the turn of the 18th century to facilitate troop movements, it begins at Rock, one mile east of Falmouth, and weaves east via Clark's Town across the sugar plains of eastern Trelawny and the lower slopes of the Dry Harbour Mountains. It's a fabulously scenic drive all the way through Brown's Town to Claremont.

FALMOUTH

Few other towns in Jamaica have retained their original architecture to quite the same degree as Falmouth (population 4000), which has a faded Georgian splendor. The city, 23 miles east of Montego Bay, has been the capital of Trelawny Parish since 1790. It's still an active market town. On Wednesdays, downtown bustles with clothiers and craft retailers, and on weekends farmers come in from miles around to sell their produce, recalling the days when Falmouth was Jamaica's major port for the

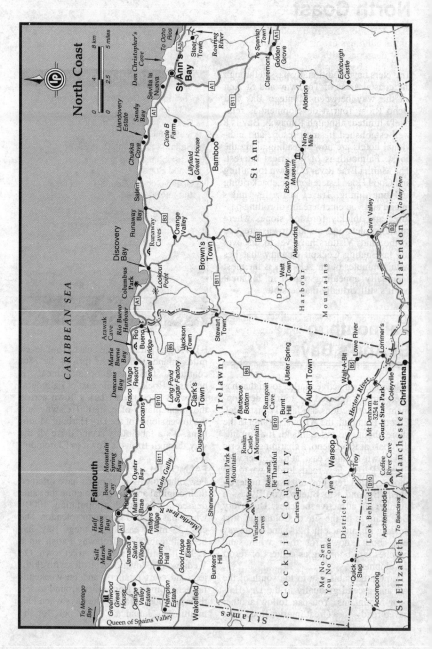

North Coast

export of molasses, rum, and sugar. Many of the buildings dating back to that era are now decrepit. Although slate roofs have long since been replaced with zinc and tin, upper stories of timber atop cut-stone bases remain.

There have been several plans to restore the town as a tourist attraction, but very little effort to that end has been undertaken. One exception occurred during the early 1970s, when several of the buildings along Market St received a tuck-and-fold for the filming of *Papillon*, starring Steve McQueen and Dustin Hoffman.

Falmouth remains off the tourist track, despite its potential appeal. A two-mile-long beach begins east of town and stretches past the Trelawny Beach Hotel. In town, you can watch pirogues still being hand-hewn from the trunks of silk-cotton trees on the scruffy beach along Seaboard St.

History

The land on which Falmouth was founded once belonged to Edward Barrett, who owned vast estates locally. There were almost 100 estates in 1770, when a new parish was formed from the eastern portion of St James. The first capital was Martha Brae, a small port inland from the mouth of the Martha Brae River, one mile south of present-day Falmouth. Gradually, the rivermouth silted up, making Martha Brae unsuitable for cargo traffic. A small village – called Barrett Town – had grown up on the site where, in 1790, Falmouth was laid out as the new parish capital. The new town was named for the English birthplace of Sir William Trelawny, who was then the island's governor and after whom the parish was named. The streets were patriotically named after members of the royal family and English heroes.

The town was planned as a grid. Lots were sold and eagerly bought up by wealthy planters, who erected their townhouses in a simple but charming vernacular style using Georgian elements adapted to Jamaican conditions (one of the best examples is the elegant townhouse that today

accommodates the tax office on the sea front off Tharp St – it was the residence of John Tharp, the largest slaveholder in Jamaica).

Advantageously positioned, Falmouth quickly grew into the busiest port on the north coast. Most of the outbound trade consisted of hogsheads (large barrels) containing wet sugar, and puncheons (casks) of rum, while slaves were off-loaded for sale in Falmouth's slave market. Falmouth was described as a 'pleasant, fashionable seaport' in 1830, when it had a population of almost 3000 – the same as today. Back then, the town was a relatively urbane place, and the city weekly newspaper, the *Falmouth Post*, even had subscribers in England.

It was not unusual for two dozen ships to be in port at a time, alongside scores of smaller vessels that ferried goods to towns along the coast. While the ships waited for the right winds to depart, the sailors caroused, creating such an uproar that they were banned from the town after 6 pm. A special stone cage was even built to house rowdy sailors.

The town's fortunes, however, degenerated when the sugar industry went into decline during the 19th century. Falmouth was dealt a further blow with the advent of steamships, which the harbor was incapable of handling. By 1890 the port was dead, and residents drifted away.

Orientation

The town's node is Water Square, a wide plaza at the east end of town with a roundabout. The A1 from Montego Bay runs into Water Square, from which it zigzags east before continuing to Ocho Rios.

Information

Money You can cash traveler's checks at Scotiabank (☎ 954-3357) at 20 Market St at the corner of Duke St and at National Commercial Bank (☎ 954-3232) on Water Square. You can have money remitted via Western Union (☎ 954-3278), which is represented by Big J's Supermarket on Lower Harbour St.

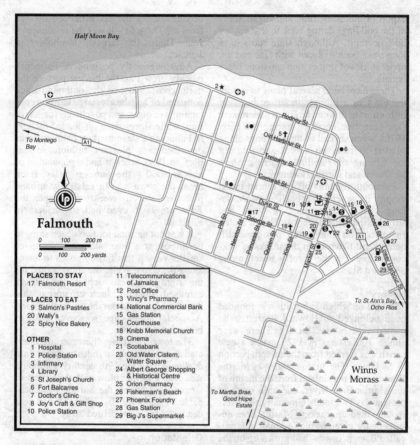

Half Moon Bay

To Montego
Bay

Falmouth

0   100   200 m

0   100   200 yards

Rodney St.

Old Harbour St.

Trelawny St.

Cornwall St.

Duke St.

George St.

Elm St.

Newton St.

Princess St.

Queen St.

King St.

Market St.

Seaboard St.

Lower Harbour St.

To St Ann's Bay,
Ocho Rios

To Martha Brae,
Good Hope
Estate

Winns
Morass

PLACES TO STAY
17 Falmouth Resort

PLACES TO EAT
9   Salmon's Pastries
20 Wally's
22 Spicy Nice Bakery

OTHER
1   Hospital
2   Police Station
3   Infirmary
4   Library
5   St Joseph's Church
6   Fort Balcarres
7   Doctor's Clinic
8   Joy's Craft & Gift Shop
10 Police Station

11 Telecommunications
    of Jamaica
12 Post Office
13 Vincy's Pharmacy
14 National Commercial Bank
15 Gas Station
16 Courthouse
18 Knibb Memorial Church
19 Cinema
21 Scotiabank
23 Old Water Cistern,
    Water Square
24 Albert George Shopping
    & Historical Centre
25 Orion Pharmacy
26 Fisherman's Beach
27 Phoenix Foundry
28 Gas Station
29 Big J's Supermarket

Post & Communications The post office
is at the corner of Cornwall and Market
Sts. You can make international calls and
send faxes from the Telecommunications of
Jamaica office at 23 Market St (☎ 954-
5910). It's open Monday to Friday, 10 am
to 4 pm.

Medical Services Emergency services are
available in the Falmouth Hospital (☎ 954-
3250) on Rodney St. If you need to see a
doctor, Dr Diane Glasgow runs a clinic on
Trelawny St, open Monday to Friday, 8:30
am to 2:30 pm. There are several pharmacies, including Vincy's on Water Square

and the Orion Pharmacy (☎ 954-3392) at
35 Market St.

Emergency The main police station
(☎ 954-3222) is on Rodney St.

Historical Downtown
The spacious **Water Square**, at the east
end of town, is named for an old circular
stone reservoir (dating to 1798) that stored
water raised from the Martha Brae River.
Slaves would arrive in early morning to
draw water, which they carried to their
owners' townhouses. In 1955, a formal
garden and fountain were erected atop the

site, which today forms a traffic round-about. The fountain is topped by a replica of the old waterwheel at Martha Brae (see the Martha Brae section below).

Albert George Market, a grand old market facing Water Square, was built in 1894 and named for two of Queen Victoria's grandsons. Renamed the Albert George Shopping & Historical Center, it still functions as a market and also contains a minor historical museum.

Perhaps the most imposing building in Falmouth is the grandiose Georgian **courthouse** in Palladian style, fronted by a double curling staircase and Doric columns, with cannons to the side. The current building, dating from 1926, is a replica of the original 1815 structure that was destroyed by fire after only two years. The town council presides here. It faces the sea at the corner of Market and Seaboard Sts.

The strange, conical structure at the corner of Thorpe and Lower Harbour Sts was once the **Phoenix Foundry**, built in 1810. Among other things, it supplied iron bedsteads for the British army.

The oldest building in town is **St Peter's Parish Church** on Duke St. This Anglican church was built in 1785 and enlarged in 1842. Take time to browse the graveyard, which has tombs dating back over 200 years. Don't sit on the pew in front of the pulpit; that's reserved for the resident magistrate.

Knibb Memorial Church, at the corner of King and George Sts, commemorates a nonconformist Baptist preacher, William Knibb, who was an active abolitionist. Knibb came to Jamaica from England in 1825 and was branded a troublemaker by privileged whites. His first chapel was burned by the militia following the Christmas Rebellion of 1831, and Knibb was arrested but later released. He was instrumental in lobbying for passage of the Abolition Bill that ended slavery.

On July 31, 1838, the slaves gathered outside the rebuilt chapel for an all-night vigil, awaiting midnight – the most pregnant moment in Jamaican history – and the dawn of full freedom, when slave shackles, a whip, and an iron collar were symbolically buried in a coffin. The scene is depicted in sculpture relief on a marble panel above the baptismal trough inside the chapel. Knibb and other Baptist ministers are buried here.

The Falmouth courthouse is the most imposing structure in town.

Hour of Emancipation

'On the evening of July 31st the chapel at Falmouth . . . was opened for worship . . . . It was crowded. An hour before midnight some verses of a dirge composed for the occasion were sung by the congregation, who then continued in devotional exercises till within a few minutes of twelve o'clock. After a short silence Knibb began to speak: his hearers were wrought to a pitch of extraordinary excitement. He pointed to the face of the clock, and said, "The hour is at hand, the monster is dying." Having heard its first note, he cried out, "The monster is dead: the Negro is free." During these few moments the congregation had been as still as death, and breathless with expectation: but when the last word had been spoken they simultaneously burst of exaltation. "Never," says Knibb, writing to a friend, "never did I hear such a sound. The winds of freedom appeared to have been let loose. The very building shook at the strange yet sacred joy."' – Anonymous ∎

Many of Jamaica's police stations are housed in historic buildings, and Falmouth's is one of the most interesting. It was constructed in 1814 as the **Cornwall District Prison**: a 'house of correction' for defiant slaves, with a separate cell for debtors. The prison on Rodney St contained a treadmill, a huge wooden cylinder with steps on the outside, installed to replace flogging, which the governor, Lord Sligo, had thought too inhumane. Shackled above the mill, slaves had to keep treading the steps as the cylinder turned. If they faltered, the revolving steps battered their bodies and legs. Today the ancient lockups are still in use.

There are several noteworthy buildings along Market St. Among these is the **Knibb Memorial High School** at the corner of Market and Trelawny Sts. Built in 1798, it was originally a Masonic hall and later a Baptist manse. Nearby, at the bottom of Market St, is the **Methodist manse**, a stone-and-wood building with wrought-iron balconies and Adam friezes above the doorways.

There's little to see of **Fort Balcarres**, which is now a school on Charlotte St. The fort was originally sited near the courthouse in the town center. Apparently the firing of ceremonial salutes set roofs ablaze, prompting a move.

Sport Fishing & Boating

The Caribbean Amusement Co (☎ 954-2123) at Rose's-by-the-Sea, at Rock east of Falmouth. It has a dive boat, and you can charter sport-fishing boats to set out in search of marlin and other game fish. You don't need to go far. The rivermouth in Oyster Bay is one of the few places in Jamaica still offering good fishing for tarpon, known as the 'silver bullet' for its feisty defense on a line. No license is required.

The ramshackle wharf nearby doubles as the Falmouth Yacht Club and has gasoline and water for boats. You can also hire a boat here to take you to **World Beach**, a remote strip on the far side of Oyster Bay (you can also walk to the beach from Time 'n Place; see Places to Eat).

Places to Stay

Greenside Villa, two miles west of Falmouth, has studio apartments with kitchenettes fitted with small gas stoves (PO Box 119, Falmouth, ☎ 954-3127). They rent for US$15 and have private bathrooms (cold water only). The rooms are simple but spacious and clean. Nearby *Roi's Travel Halt* rents small cabins for about US$20. *Sober Robin*, on the east of town, also has a few budget rooms.

Anyone seeking off-beat seclusion should head to *Time 'n Place* (Falmouth PO, Box 93, Trelawny, ☎ 954-4371), a funky beach bar. Its delightful and knowledgeable owners, Sylvia and Tony, have a quaint all-hardwood cottage for rent right on the beach. It has louvered windows on three sides, plus hot water, a radio, and bamboo furniture. They charge US$50 for up to three people. You can go strolling along the lonesome beach, and the rustic restaurant and bar is a great place to hang out. Ask Tony to take you to the 'bottomless' Blue Hole, which he discovered.

In town the only place is *Falmouth Resort* at 22 Newton St (☎ 954-3391). It has 12 modest rooms with private bath and hot water for US$35 double. The restaurant is popular with locals. Breakfasts cost about US$1.

Paradise Guest House (☎ 997-5372), on the A1 three miles east of town, has eight rooms for US$40 double. It's half a mile from the shore. There's a small pool in the front courtyard.

Rose's-by-the-Sea – formerly the Fisherman's Inn – is a quaint hotel at Rock Wharf, just east of town (Falmouth PO, ☎ 954-4078, fax 954-3257; in the USA, 534 W Manchester Blvd, Inglewood, CA 90301, ☎ (800) 767-3009, fax (310) 671-8954). The 12 gleaming-white air-con rooms are spacious and pleasingly furnished, with big bathrooms and private patios. There's a pool and two restaurants (one inside, one out). It's not really worth the US$75/100 single/double rate, however, and the location has no great appeal.

If you don't mind its rather ugly '60s-style exterior, try the venerable *Trelawny Beach Hotel* three miles east of town (PO Box 54, Falmouth, ☎ 954-2450, fax 954-2149; in North America, ☎ (303) 832-0335 or (800) 336-1435). The twin-tower high-rise hotel has 350 rooms. It caters to families and is popular with tour groups and a middle-of-the-road crowd. It has its own white-sand beach and a full range of water sports and activities. Rates begin at about US$80 per night, double.

A sports-oriented all-inclusive resort called *Swept Away Trelawny* is expected to open in the winter of 1996/1997, with 250 rooms spread across 40 acres. It's sibling in Negril is fabulous.

If you don't mind being outside town, consider *Good Hope Estate* (see below).

Places to Eat

Time 'n Place (see Places to Stay) resembles a set from *Popeye*, the movie starring Robin Williams. The bamboo beachside hut has tables on the sand. Nearby fantastical wooden sculptures hewn from driftwood decorate a ramshackle wharf. There are swings and hammocks at the bar. Take your pick of burgers with fries (US$3.50), vegetarian pizza (US$4), and an array of Jamaican dishes.

Raphael Brown serves vegetarian dishes and herbal teas at his rustic restaurant and bar west of Falmouth.

Craving Chinese? Check out the *Ponderosa Restaurant* (☎ 954-4153), 200 yards west of the Trelawny Beach Hotel. The Trelawny Beach Hotel itself offers continental and Jamaican fare in the *Jamaican Room* (☎ 954-2450), with a prix fixe menu for US$25. It's closed on Tuesday and Thursday. Shorts are not allowed, but there's a second, more casual open-air restaurant – *Palm Terrace* – that also has entertainment nightly. Entrees range from US$12 to US$25. *Jamaica Hut* and *Country Club Restaurant*, both opposite Trelawny Beach Hotel, are modestly expensive seafood restaurants catering to guests tired of hotel food.

Another option for stylish dining is *Rose's Cha Cha Cha Restaurant* (☎ 954-3427). You can also eat outside on the terrace overlooking Oyster Bay. The menu ranges from salads and seafood to creole specialties such as brown stew; it's also heavy on steaks and lobster. Entrees range upwards of US$10. It's open from 7 am to 10 pm. Several sources recommend the open-air restaurant of *Glistening Waters* (☎ 954-3229), next door. I find it totally soulless.

You can buy fresh-baked breads, pastries, and spicy meat and vegetable patties at *Spicy Nice Bakery* or *Salmon's Pastries* in Falmouth. If, like me, you have to have ice cream daily, head to *Wally's* on Market St, one block south of Duke St.

If you don't mind driving seven miles out of town, consider a splurge at *Good Hope Estate* (see below). It'll be worth it.

Entertainment

The *Country Club Restaurant* has a disco nightly. It's opposite the Trelawny Beach Hotel, which also has a disco. A *cinema*

(☎ 954-4191) at 33 Market St shows current-run movies for US$2.

Things to Buy

Crafts If you haven't seen enough T-shirts elsewhere, you can buy from a handsome selection at Beverly's Funwear, in the venerable Albert George Shopping & Historical Centre, which contains several craft shops. Joy's Craft & Gift Shop at 48 Duke St opposite the church is also worth a browse. A comprehensive selection of arts and crafts is available at Bamboo Village, 200 yards west of the Trelawny Beach Hotel. En route, you can't miss Caribatik (☎ 994-3314), the showroom of the late Muriel Chandler, which has its name prominently displayed on the outside wall beside the A1 just east of town at Rock Wharf. You can tour the workshop and watch the rainbow-hued batiks being made with hot wax and dye by artists-in-training. The wall-hangings are tremendous, though the prices may give you sticker-shock and you may find the clothes outdated. It's open Tuesday to Saturday, 9 am to 4 pm.

Herbal Teas & Aphrodisiacs If your love life is lackluster, call on Raphael Brown, the Jamaican Bush Doctor, who has a roadside healing center west of Jamaica Safari Village (see below). His aphrodisiac juice should do the trick, though the ingredients – seamoss, sarsaparilla, Irish moss, bloodwist vine, ginseng, and 'chenny root' blended and fermented with honey – will probably make you wilt (US$5 per mini bottle, US$18 for half a pint). Raphael also has herbal teas for various illnesses (US$1 per cup). He'll also read your palm for a mere US$21 (30 minutes), and he'll even don white robes and perform a soul-sealing voodoo wedding ceremony.

Getting There & Away

Falmouth is served by buses from both Montego Bay (about 30 minutes journey) and Ocho Rios (90 minutes). Buses for both destinations leave from Water Square and cost about US$0.40 to Montego Bay and US$0.80 to Ocho Rios.

Minibuses leave from Harbour St in Montego Bay; in Ocho Rios they depart from near the roundabout at the west end of Main St. From Kingston, you can take minibus No STBW468 or STBW470 from the Parade; expect to pay about US$6.

The following minibuses operate from Falmouth:

Destination	Route Number
Brown's Town	LS606
Duncans	LS381
Kingston	STBW476, STBW492
Mandeville	LS30
Montego Bay	LS2020, LS972, LS983, LS381
Ocho Rios	LS1019, LS972

JAMAICA SAFARI VILLAGE

If you don't get to see crocodiles in the wild, head to this crocodile breeding farm, nature reserve, and family park (☎ 954-3065) at the eastern end of Salt Marsh Bay, one mile west of Falmouth. Crocs bask in the sun, eyeing you leerily from behind wire fences. Other animals include mongooses and snakes, and there's a bird sanctuary, plus a petting zoo for the kids. The scene in the movie *Live and Let Die* in which James Bond ran across the backs of crocodiles was filmed here; a five-minute clip of the film is shown on arrival. Admission costs US$6.50 (children US$3).

You can take a short boat tour of the mangrove swamp behind the village for a hefty US$15.

ORANGE VALLEY ESTATE

The preserved ruins of this sugar estate are among the finest on the island. The boiling house and slave hospital are in particularly good shape. It's five miles west of Falmouth. To get there, turn inland off the A1 at Dundee toward Adelphi; turn east after two miles.

MARTHA BRAE

Two miles due south of Falmouth, this small village astride the Martha Brae River served as the first capital of Trelawny Parish. Then the rivermouth at Rock silted up and Falmouth was planned and built as the new capital in 1790, the same year that the first bridge over the river was erected. The remains of a Persian waterwheel built in 1798 can be seen on the Falmouth side of the bridge. It was used in the 19th century to divert water to Falmouth.

The river is named for an Arawak priestess who, according to legend, knew the location of a secret gold mine in a cave by the river. She is said to have lured Spanish gold-seekers to the cave, which she sealed by diverting the course of the river, drowning the conquistadores and securing her secret.

The Martha Brae River rises at Windsor Caves in the Cockpit Country and flows 32 miles to Oyster Bay, east of Falmouth. Tropical fish are bred commercially and ornamental water plants are raised in the marshland behind the rivermouth.

From Martha Brae, a well-maintained road winds scenically through the river gorge to Sherwood. Another rougher road leads west to Good Hope Estate and the Queen of Spains Valley (see the Northwest Coast chapter).

Rafting

The rafting trip down a three-mile stretch of the Martha Brae is one of the most exhilarating in Jamaica. The journey takes 90 minutes on long bamboo rafts poled by a skilled guide. The upper reaches tumble at a good pace before slowing further downriver where you can stop for dips in calm pools. En route, you'll pass beneath shady glades. At the end, you'll be driven back to pick up your car.

Trips begin from Rafters Village, situated on a great loop of the fast-flowing river, about one mile south of Martha Brae. There's a picnic ground, bar and restaurant, a swimming pool, bathrooms, changing rooms, and secure parking lot, plus a large gift store where you can buy miniature rafts and T-shirts.

A raft trip costs US$34 per raft (two people), but the guides freelance for half the price if you ask them out of earshot of the management. Do so in the parking lot.

Ask for Ashley, a friendly Rasta. In either case, your raft guide will expect a tip.

Canoeing is possible further upriver; Good Hope is said to be a good put-in site.

GOOD HOPE ESTATE

I love this marvelous great house and working plantation, seven miles due south of Falmouth. The property is set amid a broad valley on the edge of Cockpit Country. It overlooks the lush Queen of Spains Valley, with undulating fields of papaya and lime-green sugarcane framed by a serrated rim of mountains and watered by the Martha Brae.

The estate was settled in 1742 and the house built around 1755 atop a hillock. The property was owned by John Tharp (1744 – 1804), who rose to become the richest man in Jamaica. At one time he owned 10,000 acres and 3000 slaves in Trelawny and St James Parishes (Tharp had seven neighboring estates and reportedly kept a mistress on each). Displeased with all four of his sons, he left his entire estate to his only grandson. Unfortunately, the 21-year-old heir was a fool – but a wealthy fool! Marriage offers were made and a wedding arranged with a titled lady. The fellow found the experience too much and lost his wits on his wedding night. He lived another 67 years, totally unaware of the constant lawsuits that whittled away at John Tharp's fortune. The property went into decline, mismanaged by a series of agents.

The house was recently restored as a stately hotel. One of the four generously proportioned bedrooms in the main house has the original plantation owner's lead-and-tile-lined bathtub and a deep copper basin in which water was heated. The former coach house has five rooms (which can be rented as a self-contained villa complete with cook and housekeeper). If you have the chance, however, opt for the guest house set like a jewel box on its own pedestal on the rear lawn. *Do* get up shortly after dawn to see the valley enshrouded in mist. Service is friendly and relaxed but always professional. Room rates range from US$150 to US$250 per night, including breakfast (Good Hope, PO Box 50, Falmouth, ☎/fax 954-3289; in the USA, ☎ (800) 688-7678).

The tooth-loosening drive from Falmouth is worth it just for the meal alone. It's expensive (budget a minimum of US$20 per person for dinner), but the assured cooking epitomizes the best of nouvelle Jamaican cuisine. Dishes such as jerk roast lamb loin with guava and roasted garlic are worth every cent. Sandwiches and light snacks are also served. Reservations are required.

It's worth a visit simply to admire the architecture: the formal entrance with a double staircase, high-raftered ceilings, Adam frieze, gleaming floor of hardwood the color of pumpkin, and a two-story counting house with a basement lockup for defiant slaves. Breezes ease through the wide jalousies and keep the house cool as a well. The house is fully furnished with period pieces – time-worn cowhide planter's chairs, antique bookcases, and chintz sofas – that preserve the atmosphere of the plantation era.

The estate office and slave hospital are still standing, as is the sugar works by the riverbank, which is today used as a warehouse.

Horseback Riding

Good Hope maintains a stable. You can take rides along trails that lead through the plantation and along the banks of the Martha Brae. Guided tours are offered at 10 am and 3 pm (US$30 one hour, US$40 two-hour; US$25 flat fee for hotel guests). Early morning and later afternoon rides can be arranged upon request.

OYSTER BAY

By day it's a rather ugly place, but at night Oyster Bay (also called Luminous Lagoon) boasts a singular charm – it glows eerily green when disturbed. The glow is due to the presence of microorganisms that produce photochemical reactions like fireflies. The concentrations are so thick that fish swimming by look like green lanterns. The bioluminescence will last up to three days when kept in a jar.

The bay, which is one of the largest lagoons of its type in the world, is located two miles east of Falmouth. It's surrounded by mangroves, many of which were destroyed in the early 1970s as part of an aborted plan to develop the bay for tourism. The move almost killed off the microorganisms, which have only recently recovered.

Boat trips are offered from the wharves behind Glistening Waters and Rose's-by-the-Sea (US$7 per person).

Bear Cay is a spit of land that hooks around the north side of the bay. On the south side it's rimmed with mangroves, but the lonesome beach on the other side is good for snorkeling and sunbathing. You can rent a boat at Glistening Waters and Rose's; picnic meals are available.

DUNCANS

Duncans is a small town centered on an old stone clock tower in the middle of a three-way junction, seven miles east of Falmouth. You'll find several worthwhile places to eat, and the town makes a good halfway stop en route from MoBay to Ocho Rios.

If you find churches (or Jamaican history) interesting, drop by the **Kettering Baptist Church**. Built in 1893, it commemorates William Knibb, a Baptist missionary and a leading abolitionist who founded an emancipation village for freed slaves here in 1840.

Three miles east of Duncans you'll pass a cleft in the roadside cliff face that opens into Arawak Cave, which has intriguing stalagmites and stalactites, plus petroglyphs stenciled onto the glassy walls centuries ago by the Arawaks.

The road that leads south from the clock tower will take you to Clark's Town, gateway to a splendid adventure drive into the Cockpit Country (see the Cockpit Country section below).

Places to Stay

Silver Sands Villa Resort (PO Box 1, ☎ 954-2001, fax 954-2630) has 85 upscale villas and cottages spread out over 224 acres. The enclosed estate backs a private 1000-foot-long white-sand beach. Each unique villa is privately owned and individually decorated. All come with a cook, housekeeper, and gardener. Most have TVs and their own pools. The villas are rated standard, superior, and deluxe and range from one to five bedrooms. Summer rates begin at US$60 nightly for a one-bedroom cottage to US$265 and above for four- and five-bedroom villas. Features include a gym, four-poster beds, a tiny pool with its own rock garden and waterfall, and two double whirlpool bathtubs. A clubhouse restaurant serves local and continental fare. It's half a mile west of Duncans.

Also try the three-bedroom *Beach Haven*, which rents for US$800 a week (PO Box 65, ☎ 954-2423).

Places to Eat
There are several roadside stalls in town, including the rustic *Nicky Beef Patties*, next to the plaza on the west side of the clock tower. It's good for snacks. The *Hillside Bakery*, also on the plaza, is recommended for its 'cocobreads' (rolls spread with butter before baking). If you're in a mood for seafood, try the *Fishpot*, just west of town. The *Aeroplane Jerk Pit*, near Arawak Cave, serves finger-lickin' mouth-searing jerk pork or chicken for about US$2. This open-air restaurant has been conjured from the wreck of a crashed ganja-smuggling plane!

Getting There & Away
All the buses plying the route from Montego Bay to Runaway Bay and Ocho Rios stop here, on the west side of the clock tower. It's about one hour and US$0.80 in either direction. A minibus will cost about US$2.50; No LS531 operates from Duncans to Montego Bay and No LS928 to Ocho Rios.

RIO BUENO
If you saw the 1964 movie *A High Wind in Jamaica*, then this tumbledown fishing village, which appeared as a set, may seem familiar. Rio Bueno is an escape from the faster-paced resorts, a somnolent place where fishermen still tend their nets and lobster pots in front of ramshackle Georgian cut-stone buildings.

The town, 32 miles east of Montego Bay, is set on the west side of a deep, narrow bay that may be the site where Columbus first set foot in Jamaica on May 4, 1494, after anchoring his caravels, *Nina*, *San Juan*, and *Cardera*.

The bay became an active port for coastal traffic during the colonial era but has seen a gradual decline during this century. The A1 loops around the bay, at one point crossing over **Bengal Bridge**, which marks the border of Trelawny and St Ann Parishes. The stone bridge (built in 1789) slopes steeply. The stretch of coast road from here to Discovery Bay (three miles) is known as the Queen's Hwy; it was officially opened by Queen Elizabeth II in November 1953.

Historical Sites
The 18th-century ruins of **Fort Dundas** lie behind the school. Old churches of interest include an **Anglican church** dating to 1833 and a **Baptist church** erected in 1901 to replace another destroyed in the anti-missionary riots of the abolitionist era.

Another interesting feature is a **turtle crawl**, a reminder of days when green, hawksbill, and loggerhead turtles were common along Jamaican shores. The crawl is a bowl atop the coral reef. Turtles were kept alive in the enclosure, where seawater could circulate freely but from which turtles had no escape.

Braco Village Resort
Imagine a time-warp village with a cobbled square and Georgian buildings of cut stone, red brick, and timber in Jamaican vernacular style with shady, columned verandas and gingerbread trim. Introduce artisans, pushcart vendors, and country higglers dressed in period costume. Create a spectacular, jigsaw-piece-shaped Olympic-size pool, lawns crowded with bougainvillea, and a 2000-foot-long beach. Add low-rise accommodations with 180 rooms in a medley of four handsome plantation styles. Then open the gates to paying guests. The

result is Braco Village Resort, a 14-acre all-inclusive resort that opened in May 1995 two miles west of Rio Bueno. A daily pass (US$30) is available for visitors wishing to take advantage of the beach, water sports, and restaurants at this exciting theme-resort (see Places to Stay).

Dornoch Riverhead

Two miles south of Rio Bueno a river springs from the ground at Dornoch Riverhead, where a steep track leads downhill to a thickly wooded cliff face beneath which the Dornoch River wells up silently into a deep pool before rushing off to the sea. It's an enchanting and mysterious place surrounded by trees that hang heavy with epiphytes and lianas. According to legend, a mermaid lived here. On moonlit nights she would sit on a rock combing her hair with the pool as a mirror. One night, a young girl from Stewart Town supposedly disturbed the mermaid, who dove into the pool, leaving her comb. The girl began combing her hair, which began to grow longer and longer and heavier and heavier until its weight pulled the girl into the pool. She drowned. Many locals believe the legend and are wary of the pool. Nonetheless, the famous Baptist missionary, William Knibb, used the pool to baptize converts.

It's thought that the river originates as two separate rivers: the Quashie River and the Cave River, which rise west and south of the Dry Harbour Mountains and disappear underground, where each travels separately for miles before converging and reemerging at Dornoch.

To get to the riverhead, turn south at Bengal Bridge and drive one mile south to Bethel Town. Turn right for Dornoch (one mile).

Places to Stay

Things have improved since the 1870s when a visitor to Rio Bueno's only hotel – the Wellington Inn – reported that 'up in the crazy room where I slept I lay upon an antique bed in the company of lizards, and gazed through holes in the roof upon the twinkling stars.'

The *Hotel Rio Bueno* (☎ 995-3044) has been converted from an old Georgian wharfside warehouse and appeals for its pleasant decor and unique ambiance. The hotel is a museum of Joe James' artwork. All rooms have wide French doors opening onto balconies overlooking the bay. I recommend the huge, atmospheric suite with hardwood floors, open-plan walls and lots of light. Rates are US$48/95 single/double (US$150/175 for a suite). All-inclusive rates are available.

On the eastern flank of the bay is *Bay Vista Village* (☎ 995-3071 or (800) 526-2422, fax 997-7023), which has 38 modern, carpeted one-bedroom and studio suites in landscaped grounds facing the bay and the hotel's own pretty, pocket-size beach. Some rooms have air-con and kitchenettes; some are noisy due to traffic. Facilities include a pool, tennis court, and games room, plus horseback riding and scuba diving. Low-season rates are US$60 studios, US$80 one-bedroom suite, US$70 deluxe room, including continental breakfast.

There are several private homes for rent along the bay.

Braco Village Resort (PO Box 201, Runaway Bay, ☎ 973-4882, fax 973-4839; in North America, ☎ (800) 654-1337, fax (516) 223-4815) is one of the most impressive beachfront resorts in Jamaica. In addition to offering guests such activities as water sports and nude sunbathing, jazz entertainment and golf, this old-time Jamaica theme-resort has 180 rooms in low-rise accommodations in four handsome plantation styles (for more on the 'theme,' see above).

Other facilities include a game room, TV lounge, beauty salon, art gallery where revolving artists give lectures, and top-quality live entertainment. The pool has a large swim-up bar facing onto coral-colored sands. The beach is protected by a natural coral reef, perfect for sheltered water sports; the nude beach even has its own grill and bar. Braco even has 85 acres laced with hiking and jogging trails. There are four tennis courts and a 19-hole golf course.

A three-phase project includes a 208-suite family-only hotel and villa complex with 700 rooms to be completed in 1997. The rooms are somewhat insipid, with daffodil-yellow or strawberry-pink walls and loud floral prints. At least they're huge, with silent air-con and cool tiles underfoot. High season rates are US$186 to US$260 per person, or US$1200 to US$1500 per person weekly all-inclusive.

Places to Eat

The *Lobster Bowl Restaurant* in Hotel Rio Bueno (☎ 995-3044) serves seafood dishes from US$10 in a huge yet elegant hall opening onto a veranda. It's open from 7 am to midnight and on Sunday from 9:30 am, when it serves their Old Time Jamaican breakfast. The property also includes *Joe's Bar* in a gloomy stone-and-timber building that has tons of character. At *International Reggae Beach Club* opposite the post office, you can enjoy seafood (about US$5), jerk dishes, and burgers (US$2). The place comes alive at night.

Rio Brac Rest Stop is an upscale roadside restaurant about 400 yards east of Braco Village. It opens at 7 am and has a gift store and grocery, plus clean bathrooms. *Yow Rest Stop*, a short distance east, is a good place to savor seafood and jerk by the shore. *Travel Halt*, a government-run entity a half mile east of Rio Bueno, has jerk stalls but is mostly dedicated to craft souvenirs for sale in half a dozen little shops.

You get more than your money's worth at *Braco Village Resort*, where a day pass (US$30) buys you all-you-can-eat. The cuisine is fantastic at any of four atmospheric restaurants, including a jerk pit and a 24-hour pasta bar.

Things to Buy

Gallery Joe James (☎ 995-3044), housed in old wharves beside the Hotel Rio Bueno, displays James' famous naive paintings, carvings, and masks. There are some occasional masterpieces, but most pieces are uninspired and overpriced. Small works begin at US$10, and larger, better works

sell for US$500 or more. The place is popular with tour groups.

DISCOVERY BAY

This wide flask-shaped bay with attractive beaches and turquoise shallows is a popular resort spot for both locals and tourists. Originally named Puerto Seco, or Dry Harbour, by the Spanish, it is considered by local inhabitants to be the first place where Christopher Columbus landed on Jamaican soil in 1494 (the actual site of the original landing is controversial; see the Rio Bueno section).

Much land around the bay is owned by the Kaiser Bauxite Company; its Port Rhoades bauxite-loading facility dominates the town. Large freighters are loaded with bauxite at a pier on the west side of the bay (most of it heads off to Russia). They're fed by conveyor belts from a huge storage dome that holds 125,000 metric tons of bauxite – enough for three ore carriers. The facility, which is covered in rust-colored dust, is a blight on the bay and must surely be a brake on tourism development. You can follow the road signed 'Port Rhoades' steeply uphill half a mile to a lookout point offering fantastic views over the bay (there are a pair of high-power, pay-per-view binoculars).

There's a gas station in town, as well as a bank and supermarket at Columbus Plaza.

Puerto Seco Beach

The eastern side of the bay is rimmed with beautiful white-sand beaches. Puerto Seco Beach is the main one. Owned by Kaiser but open to the public, it has tennis courts and rustic eateries and bars. It's open 8 am to 5 pm (entrance costs US$0.65). Enter opposite the gas station.

Quadrant Wharf

A plaque painted in Rasta colors at the west end of town recalls the history of this old wharf and of Discovery Bay.

Columbus Park

Kaiser funded the development of this open-air roadside museum atop the bluff

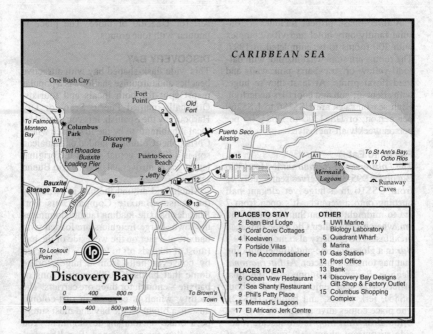

CARIBBEAN SEA

One Bush Cay

To Falmouth,
Montego
Bay

Columbus
Park

Fort
Point

Old
Fort

Discovery
Bay

Port Rhoades
Buaxite
Loading Pier

Puerto Seco
Beach

Puerto Seco
Airstrip

Bauxite
Storage Tank

Jetty

To St Ann's Bay,
Ocho Rios

Mermaid's
Lagoon

Runaway
Caves

To Lookout
Point

Discovery Bay

To Brown's
Town

0   400   800 m
0   400   800 yards

PLACES TO STAY
2 Bean Bird Lodge
3 Coral Cove Cottages
4 Keelaven
7 Portside Villas
11 The Accommodationer

PLACES TO EAT
6 Ocean View Restaurant
7 Sea Shanty Restaurant
9 Phil's Patty Place
16 Mermaid's Lagoon
17 El Africano Jerk Centre

OTHER
1 UWI Marine
   Biology Laboratory
5 Quadrant Wharf
8 Marina
10 Gas Station
12 Post Office
13 Bank
14 Discovery Bay Designs
   Gift Shop & Factory Outlet
15 Columbus Shopping
   Complex

on the west side of the bay. The eclectic historical memorabilia includes anchors, cannons, nautical bells, sugar-boiling coppers referred to locally as 'taces' and used for heating and concentrating cane juice, and an old waterwheel in working condition that creaks and clanks as it turns. There's also a diminutive locomotive formerly used to haul sugar at Innswood Estate, where it remained in service until 1969. A mural depicts Columbus' landing.

The site offers superb views over Discovery Bay. You'll find a craft shop at the western end. Entrance is free.

Marine Biology Laboratory
The University of the West Indies (☎ 973-2241) maintains a marine research laboratory on the west side of the bay (immediately west of Columbus Park), where scientists study coral reefs. It has Jamaica's only decompression chamber. Reportedly, students and academics can rent accommodations.

Runaway Caves
This system of caves and tunnels extends about 10 miles and is accessed via a well-marked entrance two miles east of Discovery Bay. Steps lead down into the chambers, where statuesque dripstone formations are illuminated by floodlights. The highlight is Green Grotto, a glistening lake 120 feet down. The US$3.50 entrance fee includes a guided 45-minute tour, with a boat trip across the lake. It's a fabulous experience, with the stalactites reflecting on the crystalline waters. Your guide may even tap some of them to produce eerie sounds. Seven miles of caverns are said to be negotiable for spelunkers.

In pre-Columbian days the caves were used by the Arawaks, who left their legacy in stencils on the walls. Pirates also used the caves.

The caves are open 9 am to 5 pm. Children under age five get in free; those five to 12 are charged US$2.

Fishing

Mermaid's Lagoon, immediately west of Runaway Caves, has catch 'n cook fishing (☎ 995-3447). The lagoon, which is also known as Discovery Bay Lake, is 170 feet deep. It's stocked with tilapia, a cross between a snapper and freshwater perch. There are hammocks beneath thatch where you can doze while awaiting a tug on the line. Entrance is US$1.50. It's open 10 am to 6 pm.

If you want to try your hand at bigger fry, sport-fishing boats can be rented from the marina at Puerto Seco Beach.

Cruises

Pirate Cruises offers trips aboard *Liverpool*, a replica pirate boat (US$10). Free pickups are offered. It leaves from Portside Villas at Discovery Bay (☎ 973-2007). The company also offers sunset cruises (US$10) as well as sport-fishing charters aboard *Don One* (US$250 for up to six people).

Special Events

A Derby Day sponsored by the Kaiser company is held each August and features live music, marching bands, and dancing. The highlight, however, is the Pushcart Derby, which takes place on the hill rising to Port Rhoades. Dozens of youths representing parish teams compete in a downhill race on their wooden pushcarts that they normally use for transporting goods. Despite their miniature wheels, the carts have been clocked at 60 mph in the homestretch! Now you understand why the road, which is marked out with lanes like a racetrack, is also lined with tire barriers. The event is featured in the movie *Cool Runnings*.

Places to Stay

Portside Villas (PO Box 42, ☎ 973-2007, fax 973-2720) is an attractive little property with a splendid setting overlooking the small yacht marina and a tiny beach. Its 30 rooms and apartments are set in pleasant grounds tight up against the shore; others are on the hillside across the road. There are also efficiency apartments with kitchenettes and two fully staffed villas sleeping up to 10 each, with their own pools. In summer, rates range from US$65 per person for a studio suite and US$75 for a one-bedroom suite to US$2200 weekly for a five-bedroom villa. Facilities include water sports, two pools, whirlpool spa, and a tennis court.

Most of the other options in Discov ery Bay are self-catering. *Spanish Court Apartments* (☎ 972-2235) offers simply furnished units, with kitchens. The *Accommodationer* (☎ 973-2559), 200 yards east of Puerto Seco Beach, has seven rooms with kitchenettes for US$50. *Sundance* is a spacious contemporary villa with a large pool and veranda, lots of light, a pool room, and three en-suite bedrooms. Other choices include *Bean Bird Lodge*, *Coral Cove Cottages*, and *Keelaven*, all three of which are represented by JAVA Jamaica (PO Box 298, Ocho Rios, ☎ 974-2508, fax 974-2967; in the USA, 1370 Washington, Suite 301, Miami Beach, FL 33139, ☎ (800) 845-5376 or (305) 673-6688, fax (305) 673-5666).

Places to Eat

There are many rustic beachside shacks selling cheap Jamaican fare east of Runaway Caves. For a delightful touch of 'real' Jamaica, try Andrea's *Ocean View Bar & Fishpot*, where you can dip your toes in the sea. It's the one painted in blue and white stripes.

In town, *Columbus Park Patty Stand* sells a host of Jamaican fare, including steamed fish. Also serving Jamaican seafood are the moderately priced *Ocean View Restaurant* near the cay; and the *Sea Shanty Restaurant* (☎ 973-2007) in Portside Villas. Both offer bay views. The Sea Shanty also serves steaks and has a four-course dinner that varies nightly.

You can catch your own fish and have it prepared on the spot at a thatched restaurant at *Mermaid's Lagoon* (see Fishing above); take your pick of roasted, steamed, jerked, or curried (the price varies from US$1.50 to US$3 per pound, according to your preference). Fish dishes are served stuffed with vegetables, and you can get bammy for US$1 extra. The restaurant also serves Indian dishes with advance notice.

For jerk pork or chicken, I recommend *El Africano* (☎ 973-2054) opposite Runaway Cave. *Phil's Patty Place* (next to the gas station) has spicy vegetable and meat patties for less than US$1.

Entertainment
Coxon's HQ is the happenin' local night spot.

Things to Buy
Discovery Bay Designs (☎ 973-2565) makes and sells clothing and quality handcrafted wooden housewares. It has a gift shop and factory outlet east of town.

Getting There & Away
If you're traveling by bus, you can catch any of the buses that ply the A1 between Montego Bay and Ocho Rios. They all stop in Discovery Bay (US$1). In Kingston you can hop aboard minibus No STBW504, which goes direct to Discovery Bay for about US$7. Another minibus – No STBW278 – operates to Kingston from Discovery Bay.

Getting Around
A company called G&B (☎ 973-3576) reportedly rents bicycles.

RUNAWAY BAY
Despite its diminutive size, Runaway Bay (five miles east of Discovery Bay) was the first planned resort development in Jamaica and has an impressive array of hotels and tourist facilities. It's a one-street village stretching east for two miles to Salem, which you can drive through in a couple of minutes. Many hotels and facilities are concentrated in Salem (the adjacent villages are synonymous). Several small beaches are supposedly public, although most are the backyards for a few all-inclusive resorts.

The place name derives from the legend that the Spaniards fled the island from here in 1655. It is now thought that the escapees

were African slaves making good their escape to Cuba by canoe. Once there they had a good chance of retaining their freedom; the English authorities demanded their return, but the Spanish apparently replied that once baptized as Catholics the slaves could not be returned to dwell among heretics.

Post & Communications
A small post office is located on the main road in the center of Runaway Bay. You can place international calls or send and receive faxes from the Call Direct Centre (☎ 973-5613) in Salem Plaza. It's open Sunday to Thursday 9 am to 10 pm; Friday 9 am to 5 pm; and Saturday 7 am to 11 pm.

Cardiff Hall
This beautiful great house, one mile east of Runaway Bay, was built in the mid-18th century and is splendidly preserved. The house once overlooked a coconut and cattle estate on property awarded by Oliver Cromwell to Daniel Blagrove, a member of Parliament who voted to condemn King Charles I to death. It remained in the Blagrove family for over two centuries (the Blagroves are still landowners hereabouts). The estate metamorphosed in the 1960s into the Runaway Bay Golf Course, a luxury beachfront hotel (now called Breezes Runaway Bay), and residential and commercial lots.

Dover Raceway
This small racetrack, south of Runaway Bay, is the setting for auto and motorcycle races.

Golf
SuperClubs operates the Runaway Golf Club (☎ 973-2561), which is government-owned but leased to the resort chain; it's now open only to SuperClubs' guests. A low-lying, par 72, 6600-yard course with several elevated tees, it's open daily 8 am to 6 pm. Caddies are mandatory. SuperClubs operates the Breezes Runaway Bay Golf School (formerly Jamaica-Jamaica Golf School) for guests at its resort properties.

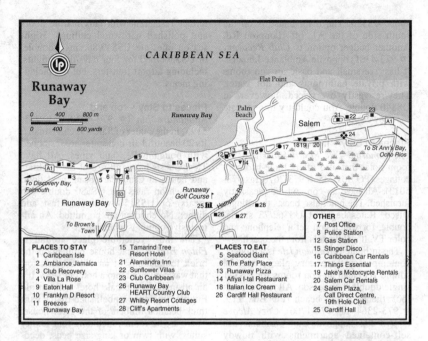

PLACES TO STAY
1 Caribbean Isle
2 Ambiance Jamaica
3 Club Recovery
4 Villa La Rose
9 Eaton Hall
10 Franklyn D Resort
11 Breezes
   Runaway Bay
15 Tamarind Tree
   Resort Hotel
21 Alamandra Inn
22 Sunflower Villas
23 Club Caribbean
26 Runaway Bay
   HEART Country Club
27 Whilby Resort Cottages
28 Cliff's Apartments

PLACES TO EAT
5 Seafood Giant
6 The Patty Place
13 Runaway Pizza
14 Afiya I-tal Restaurant
18 Italian Ice Cream
26 Cardiff Hall Restaurant

OTHER
7 Post Office
8 Police Station
12 Gas Station
15 Stinger Disco
16 Caribbean Car Rentals
17 Things Essential
19 Jake's Motorcycle Rentals
20 Salem Car Rentals
24 Salem Plaza,
   Call Direct Centre,
   19th Hole Club
25 Cardiff Hall

Scuba Diving

Runaway Bay has some of the best diving on the island. Many of the hotels offer scuba facilities. There's a wreck in shallow water in front of the Ambiance Jamaica Resort. A reef complex called **Ricky's Reef** is renowned for its sponges. The best diving is said to be below 80 feet. More experienced divers might try the **Canyon**, beginning at about 35 feet and running between two walls; don't be put off by the nurse sharks that gather here. There are two cars and a plane offshore from Club Caribbean – relics of drug busts – that attract fish and are now becoming overgrown with coral.

Jamaqua is a full-service dive facility at Club Caribbean (☎ 973-4845, fax 973-4875). It offers three dives daily, plus PADI certification and other courses. You can rent equipment here. Sundivers PADI scuba facility is located at Ambiance Jamaica Resort, and Eaton Hall also has scuba diving.

Organized Tours

The major hotels have tour desks and can arrange for you to explore locally or further afield. JCAL Tours Ltd (☎ 973-4106) has a small office outside the Seafood Giant restaurant; the company offers tours islandwide.

Places to Stay – bottom end

You can camp for US$8 on the lawns at *Whilby Resort Cottages* (☎ 944-2701), on a hillside up Hampton Rd south of Salem. The place is owned by the colorful Sister Pat Cassier. There are water and toilets, and kitchen privileges are granted. Sister Cassier also rents simple yet cozy air-con rooms with kitchenettes and private bath and hot water. The place is modestly furnished yet appealing, with views down over the coast. Rates begin at about US$40 and vary according to room.

Cliff's Apartments (☎ 973-2601) offers a collection of houses and very simple rooms, several with shared bath, from about US$20. The main house is on the south side of the A1, off Hampton Rd. Another budget option is *Club Recovery* (☎ 973-4361) opposite Ambiance Jamaica. It has five small and basic air-con rooms with private bathrooms and hot water. They're vastly overpriced, however, at US$40 double. You could try to negotiate for a lower price.

Places to Stay – middle

The *Tamarind Tree Resort Hotel* is a 16-room hotel that also offers three-bedroom cottages (PO Box 235, ☎ 973-2678, fax 973-5013). All have air-con and are pleasantly furnished. The hotel also boasts the Stinger Disco. Rates begin at US$62/73 single/double, for which you get a telephone and color TV. It's 100 yards from the beach.

The intimate *Caribbean Isle* is a modest, contemporary three-story place, with 24 simple yet clean air-con rooms for US$41 single/double, low season. All rooms overlook the pool and beach (PO Box 119, ☎ 973-2364, fax 974-1706). *Cozy Alcove* (☎ 973-2023) opposite Club Caribbean has self-contained apartments with dowdy furniture and kitchenettes. Further up Hampton Rd, with a view over the sea, is *Eagle's Paradise* (☎ 973-2508). Rates begin at about US$20/25 for rooms with shared bath.

If you're looking for a bargain and you prefer a breezy hillside setting, check out *Runaway Bay HEART Academy & Club* (PO Box 98, ☎ 973-2671, fax 973-2693; in North America, ☎ (212) 319-2100), a plantation-style manor with 20 spacious, pleasantly furnished, well-lit rooms with TVs, air-con, and coastal vistas from balconies. Some guests report that the service is excellent, as well it should be: next door is the hotel training school. Others say the service is slow, which is also to be expected since trainees are learning the ropes. In essence, you're a guinea pig. It overlooks the Runaway Bay Golf Course, to which hotel guests have free access. A shuttle runs to Cardiff Hall beach. Amenities include an ice-blue pool, and an elegant

terrace restaurant with faux marble floors and polished hardwood ceilings. High-season rates are US$49/88 single/double, or US$360/600 for four days/three nights, including airport transfers, but not including meals.

Places to Stay – top end

Alamandra Inn (☎ 973-4030, fax 973-5195) in the center of Salem is charismatic. Its 20 beautiful air-con suites are festooned with bougainvillea and vines. All have TVs. Guests have full use of the facilities and beach at Club Caribbean, next door. Low-season rates are US$80 double (no meals) or US$150 with breakfast and dinner. No children are permitted. An all-inclusive option is available.

The most venerable place around is *Eaton Hall*, a great house built upon the brick foundations of an old English fort that was converted into a hotel in 1948. It's an all-inclusive upscale hotel with an old English ambiance embellished by the dark thick-beamed timbers of the great house. There are 52 rooms, including four luxury suites, with twin or king-size beds, decorated in Edwardian-style mahogany furniture and with wooden parquet floors. A pool and sun deck are built atop the coral cliff, and there's a full-service PADI diving facility. Tennis and water sports are available, and nightly entertainment is offered. Rates vary according to month but begin at US$130/180 single/double (PO Box 112, ☎ 973-2738, fax 973-2432 or (800) 526-2422; in North America, Jamaica Reservation Service, 1320 South Dixie Hwy, Suite 1102, Coral Gables, FL 33146, ☎ (305) 667-1174).

Like Eaton, *Ambiance Jamaica* (PO Box 20, ☎ 973-2066, fax 973-2067; in the USA, ☎ (800) 523-6504), a stone's throw further west, has only a small beach, so most of your time may be spent around the pool and sun deck. Its air-con oceanfront rooms and junior suites are set back from the beach. All have balconies and telephones, and king-size beds are available on request. It has a restaurant and large open-air oceanfront bar. A standard room costs US$98/106 single/double, while suites range as high as US$184, including full breakfast (rates are low season). The hotel is popular with Canadian charter groups, as is *Caribbean Isle*, next door at the end of the beach (PO Box 119, ☎ 973-2364, fax 974-1706), which was closed for renovation.

Another favorite of charter groups is *Club Caribbean* in Salem. This Swiss-owned all-inclusive has 130 conical African-style, thatched-roof cottages and 20 one-bedroom suites spread throughout 15 landscaped acres behind a 1000-foot-wide beach with a nude section. The rooms are spacious, with king-size beds and wooden ceilings. There's plenty of activity and nightlife at the disco and three bars. If you hate crowds, you'll not fit in. Activities include a full range of water sports, a PADI dive center, and party cruises on a 40-foot trimaran for an extra fee. Summer rates begin at US$165/210 single/double. Contact PO Box 65, Runaway Bay, ☎ 973-3507 or (800) 647-2740, fax 973-3509; in North America, c/o International Travel & Resorts, ☎ (212) 545-8431 or (800) 223-9815.

A more upscale option is *Breezes Runaway Bay* (formerly Jamaica Jamaica), an elegant 238-room, adults-only resort in the SuperClub chain. It has a massive swimming pool and fronts the best beachfront in Runaway Bay. Think of any activity or facility, and you're sure to find it here, including scuba diving. The price is 'super-inclusive' of everything that exists inside the gates, including unlimited golf at the adjacent Runaway Golf Club. Per person rates begin at US$555 per person double occupancy (three nights) in low season; US$725 in high season. Contact PO Box 58, ☎ 973-2436 or (800) 859-7873, fax 973-2352; in North America, ☎ (305) 925-0925 or (800) 859-7873; in the UK, ☎ (0992) 447420.

In a similar vein, but for families, is *Franklyn D Resort*, a Spanish-hacienda-style, all-inclusive property with 67 suites, including two- and three-bedroom apartments (PO Box 201, ☎ 973-3067, fax 973-3071; in North America, ☎ (800) 654-1337; in the UK, ☎ (0181) 795-1718, fax (0181) 795-1728). Children are provided their own facilities and a variety of activities. And a 'Girl Friday' is assigned to each suite, not just to look after the kids but to tend to your every need, including laundry. The resort has a full range of activities and facilities, including three restaurants and five bars. Note, however, that the beach is minimal. Rates begin at US$1600 per person per week, including all meals, drinks, and activities. Children under 16 stay free.

Villa Carmel (103 Main St, Ocho Rios, ☎ 974-2451), next to Breezes Runaway Bay, is an attractive property with four aircon rooms, each with private bath and modest yet pleasing furnishings. It's surrounded by landscaped grounds and has a pool and sun deck overlooking the beach. A staff of five includes a cook and two housekeepers. Access to Breezes Runaway Bay can be arranged for an additional fee. *Villa la Rose* (☎ 973-3093), at the west end of Runaway Bay, has more modest rooms with beach views at 'low rates.' Another option is *Fairway Villa*, on the Cardiff Hall Estate just west of Salem (c/o JAVA, PO Box 298, Ocho Rios, ☎ 974-2967, fax 974-2967; in the USA, ☎ (202) 488-7107, or JAVA, 1501 W Fullerton, Chicago, IL 60614, ☎ (312) 883-3485 or (800) 221-8830). It's a five-bedroom villa with a spacious lounge and modern if uninspired furniture. It has its own pool and is fully staffed. Weekly rates range from US$2000 to US$2800 summer and winter.

Sunflower Villas (Box 150, ☎ 973-2171, fax 973-2381) has 80 units that range from one- to five-bedroom units; some are Spanish-style three-bathroom villas, with private dipping pools. Cooks and housekeepers are available. There are two pools, plus water sports. Low-season rates for rooms begin at US$65 per person, all-inclusive. Luxury villas range from US$900 to US$2000 weekly. Rates include airport transfers.

Places to Eat

You can't miss *Seafood Giant* (☎ 973-4801) – roadside billboards advertise the restaurant for miles. Typical dishes are jackfish with spinach roasted in foil (US$4) or fried with bammy, plantain, rice and peas (US$2.50); and curried, creole, or braised garlic shrimp (US$12). The filling meals are an excellent value. If you pick your own fish, you'll be charged 'according to size' at steep prices!

Another good bargain is the elegant *Cardiff Hall Restaurant* (☎ 973-2671) at Runaway HEART Academy & Country Club. Reservations are essential. The *Seaview Restaurant* and *Italian Garden Pizzeria* are both good options at Club Caribbean. They're relatively expensive, as is the sea-front restaurant at *Eaton Hall*. Both serve a combination of Jamaican and continental fare and are open to outside guests.

More down-to-earth options in Salem include *Hayden's Seafood Restaurant*, *Island Queen Patties*, and *Pizza! Pizza! Pizza!* (☎ 973-4836). Nearby is *Runaway Pizza*, next to the gas station at the junction for HEART Academy & Country Club. *Afiya* (☎ 973-4266), about 100 yards west of the gas station, specializes in health foods and vegetarian cuisine. Typical dishes include tofu with barbecue sauce, vegetarian pastas (US$4), and veggie burgers (US$2). You can also get soups, natural juices, and desserts such as carrot cake, plus grains, tofu, soy milk, and vitamins. It's open Monday to Saturday 9 am to 7 pm.

There's a shop selling Italian ice cream in Salem. The *Patty Place*, near the junction for Brown's Town, also serves ice cream and has fresh baked bread and pastries. *Northern Jerk* also has a bakery. You'll find supplies at Clarke's Grocery on Main St.

Entertainment

Runaway Bay is not booming with nightlife, although you'll find several rustic rum shops and reggae bars where you can play dominoes with locals. At Salem, check out the *19th Hole Club* (☎ 973-5766), which has pool tables plus dancing to live music. A short distance west is the more down-to-earth *Reggae Palace Club*.

For a more touristy experience, try the live shows at *Club Caribbean* or the *Safari Disco* (☎ 973-2066) at Jamaica Ambiance, which has a happy hour from 10:30 pm, and special attractions on weekends. Mirrored walls and flashing lights provide the ambiance at the *Stinger Disco* in the Tamarind Hotel (it has a two-hour happy hour starting at 6 pm nightly); Monday is rock 'n roll, Wednesday is soca, Friday is dancehall, and Saturday is oldies night.

Things to Buy

You'll find wood carvings, jewelry, and other tourist trinkets for sale on the street. Refrain from buying anything made of protected black coral or tortoiseshell.

Things Essential, at the west end of Salem, has a gift store selling crafts, postcards, books, and swimwear. A broader selection of swimwear and leisure wear is available at Splash, in the Club Caribbean resort. Mingles (☎ 973-2570) in the Breezes Runaway Bay Resort sells top designer items, including crafts and clothing. If you're not staying at the hotel, you'll need to call ahead. A daily shopping shuttle picks up guests from larger hotels for trips to Ocho Rios.

Getting There & Away

All the buses traveling the A1 between Montego Bay and Ocho Rios stop in Runaway Bay, which is about 1½ hours from the former (US$1.20) and 40 minutes from the latter (US$0.50).

Getting Around

Car & Motorcycle Jake's Motorcycle Rentals (☎ 973-5365), 200 yards west of Salem Plaza, rents scooters for about US$30 a day; more for larger bikes up to 750 cc. Salem Car Rentals (☎ 973-2564) and Caribbean Car Rentals (☎ 973-3539) are located 400 yards apart on the main road in Salem.

Bicycles You can rent bicycles from Condor Bike Rentals (☎ 952-5538).

CHUKKA COVE

The name says it all. Polo is the game of choice at Chukka Cove Farm (PO Box 160, Ocho Rios, ☎ 972-2506) at Richmond midway between Runaway Bay and St Ann's Bay. This 50-acre equestrian center has a full-size polo field and hosts regular tournaments. You can also take horseback riding lessons, including polo, dressage, show-jumping, and cross-country.

Chukka offers trail rides through banana and sugar plantations. Other rides include a ride from sea level to almost 2000 feet atop Mt Zion (three hours, US$50) and a Swim Your Horse Trek along the sand (yes, you can even go swimming with your horse; three hours, US$65). A six-hour mountain trek for experienced riders includes a visit to Lillyfield (see the Brown's Town section below), which is also used for accommodations during an overnight trip and a three-day trip.

Chukka Cove has five fully staffed, air-con, two-bedroom, two-story villas sleeping four, from US$99 per person. They're arranged around a pool between the coral shore and polo field. There's no beach, just a rocky cove where scenes from *Papillon*, starring Steve McQueen and Dustin Hoffman, were filmed (it's now called Papillon's Cove).

The Jamaica Polo Association's tournament (☎ 974-2592) is held here in March.

I Say, Polo Anyone?

Polo was introduced to Jamaica by the British army during the late 19th century and today has a fanatical following among the Jamaican elite. St Ann's is a center for polo (see Chukka Cove above). Although refined English accents abound in the spectator stands, where sandwiches and pots of steaming hot tea are de rigueur, money and the appropriate social pedigree are supposedly *not* a prerequisite to participation. All you need is a horse, which, by Jamaica standards, costs an arm and a leg. The St Ann Polo Club (☎ 972-2762) has polo matches every Saturday at 4 pm at Drax Hall. ■

PLANTATION TOURS

If you want to see how a typical Jamaica farm operates, you can take a tour of Circle B Farm, a working plantation that grows avocado, bananas, coconuts, and vegetables (US$10, or US$20 including lunch; ☎ 972-2988). It's near Richmond Hill, one mile south of the A1, reached via a turnoff a half mile west of Sevilla la Nueva at Priory (two miles east of Chukka Cove).

Sleepy Hollow Park, at Blowfire Hills, a half mile south of Circle B, also offers guided farm tours. Owners Con and Patsy Pink also host birders, hikers, and picnickers. It's open 10 am to 6 pm. Entrance costs US$2.

Most of the land hereabouts was formerly part of Llandovery, one of the earliest (and largest) sugar estates on the island, dating from 1674. Llandovery Factory is still intact (you'll see its brick chimney beckoning on the north side of the A1), although it no longer makes rum, as it did for over 300 years. Today it functions as a cattle farm.

SEVILLA LA NUEVA

The modern history of Jamaica began in 1509 at this spot, which was the site of the first Spanish capital on the island and one of the first Spanish settlements in the New World. However, the town lasted only 25 years. Not until 1937 was the Spanish settlement discovered. In 1982, Sevilla la Nueva was declared a Site of the Americas by the Organization of American States, which funds ongoing excavations by the Spanish Archaeological Mission and Jamaica National Heritage Trust. The digging has turned up almost as much information on the Arawaks, as this was also the site of an Arawak village. A plaque here reads: 'The first known Jamaicans, the Arawaks encountered Columbus and the Spaniards at this property.'

Scant traces of the original buildings are scattered throughout Seville Estate, though most of the original Spanish settlement remains buried. A grassy track leads down to the ocean from opposite the entrance to Seville Great House (see St Ann's Bay

The Founding of Sevilla la Nueva

'New Seville' was established in 1509 by orders of Juan de Esquivel, the island's first governor. Esquivel had been with Columbus when returning from Panama on his last voyage in 1503, when Columbus careened his two caravels into this bay and eventually abandoned them side by side (historians agree that this was the same bay where Columbus had first anchored during his discovery voyage in 1494). The ships were so eaten with worms that they immediately filled with water. Unable to repair his vessels, Columbus dispatched his boatswain, Diego Mendez, and a handful of men, who successfully set out in a canoe for Hispaniola. Finally, 369 days after being marooned, Columbus was rescued by Mendez. The *Santiago de Palos* and *Capitana* are thought to be buried under coral and silt to the northwest of the old wharf but have not been found, despite considerable effort.

In November 1509, Don Juan de Esquivel arrived with about 70 colonists. They brought cows, horses, sheep, pigs, and domestic fowl. Christopher Columbus' son Diego was given authority over Jamaica, and it was he who laid out the settlement, which remained the capital until 1534. The settlement spread over 15 acres, with brick-paved streets, a fort, church, sugar mills, and a wharf, where the first African slaves brought to Jamaica were landed.

Sevilla never prospered. It was an ill-chosen site with a marshy shoreline, and malarial fevers were common. Twenty-five years after its founding, the settlers abandoned the city and established a new capital on the site of today's Spanish Town. Sevilla fell into ruin and eventually was entirely reclaimed by vegetation. ∎

below). To the east, fortifications are still visible near the shore behind a restaurant called Seafood Specialists, 400 yards west of the roundabout (squatters have turned it into a fishing hamlet). The eastern extent of New Seville is marked by the Columbus Monument, in the adjacent town of St Ann's Bay. The governor's house stood in the coconut grove that separates the road and the sea. It was decorated with sculptured stone friezes that were removed to Kingston, where they are on display at the National Gallery.

ST ANN'S BAY

This modest-scale town (population 8500) rises up the hillside above the bay that Columbus christened Santa Gloria for its beauty. At first sight there may be little to tempt you to depart from the two-lane bypass (the AGR Byfield Hwy) that skirts the town of St Ann's Bay, capital of its namesake parish.

Despite a relatively illustrious history, the town has long since been eclipsed by Ocho Rios, seven miles east, and today serves as a provincial market town centered

on an old tumbledown market topped by a wooden clock tower.

St Ann's has several sites of interest and is worth a brief browse. It is important as the birthplace of Marcus Garvey, founder of the black nationalist movement. This larger-than-life figure is honored with a larger-than-life monument, as is Christopher Columbus, who first put the bay on the map. And there are several interesting old buildings, especially along Bravo St.

You'll find a small, reasonably attractive beach – Priory Beach – one mile west of town, with water sports and several hotels.

The A1 turns inland at St Ann's and runs south from town to Claremont and, eventually, Kingston. The coast road continues east as the A3. Surprisingly few travelers take time to explore inland south of St Ann's Bay, much of which is given over to cattle estates and pimento farms. The A1 climbs from sea level to 1500 feet in five miles. It continues rising to Mt Diablo (2754 feet) on the border with St Catherine's Parish before dropping down to Spanish Town and Kingston. You can also follow the old coach road that leads south from Claremont. In the mid-18th century it was the only road south across the spine of mountains.

History

St Ann's Bay figures prominently in Jamaican history. During the 18th and 19th centuries, it prospered as a bustling seaport. In 1750 a fort was built west of town using old blocks from Sevilla la Nueva. It was rapidly eroded by seawater, and by 1795 a new fort had been built on the opposite side of the bay at Windsor Point. The fort later served as a house of correction, with separate rooms for debtors, lunatics, and slaves. Following the slave rebellion of Christmas 1831, the local rector, Rev George Wilson Bridges, formed the Colonial Church Union in St Ann's Bay. The organization persecuted non-conformist ministers, and its members rampaged through the northern parishes burning Baptist churches and assaulting abolitionist missionaries.

Information

Money National Commercial Bank (☎ 972-2490) and Scotiabank (☎ 972-2531) both

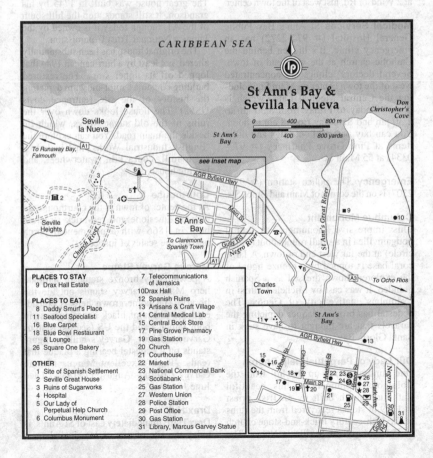

CARIBBEAN SEA

St Ann's Bay & Sevilla la Nueva

To Runaway Bay, Falmouth

Seville la Nueva

Seville Heights

St Ann's Bay

To Claremont, Spanish Town

Don Christopher's Cove

St Ann's Bay

AGR Byfield Hwy

Main St

Gully Rd

Negro River

St Ann's Great River

Charles Town

To Ocho Rios

St Ann's Bay

AGR Byfield Hwy

Market St

Church St

Wharf St

Main St

Park Ave

Negro River

0   400   800 m
0   400   800 yards

PLACES TO STAY
9   Drax Hall Estate

PLACES TO EAT
8   Daddy Smurf's Place
11 Seafood Specialist
16 Blue Carpet
18 Blue Bowl Restaurant & Lounge
26 Square One Bakery

OTHER
1   Site of Spanish Settlement
2   Seville Great House
3   Ruins of Sugarworks
4   Hospital
5   Our Lady of Perpetual Help Church
6   Columbus Monument

7   Telecommunications of Jamaica
10 Drax Hall
12 Spanish Ruins
13 Artisans & Craft Village
14 Central Medical Lab
15 Central Book Store
17 Pine Grove Pharmacy
19 Gas Station
20 Church
21 Courthouse
22 Market
23 National Commercial Bank
24 Scotiabank
25 Gas Station
27 Western Union
28 Police Station
29 Post Office
30 Gas Station
31 Library, Marcus Garvey Statue

have branches in the town center. If you need to have money remitted speedily, you can do so through Western Union on Bravo St.

Post & Communications The post office is just east of the police station. You can make international calls and send faxes from the Telecommunications of Jamaica office (☎ 972-9701) at 11 King St at the east end of town. It's open Monday to Friday 8 am to 4 pm.

Library The parish library (☎ 972-2660) is at 2 Windsor Rd, just west of the town center.

Medical Services St Ann's Bay Public General Hospital (☎ 972-2272) has an emergency clinic. It's hidden behind the Catholic church at the west end of town. Several doctors' clinics are concentrated west of the town center on Main St, including the Central Medical Labs, which is open Monday to Friday from 8:30 am to 2:30 pm and Saturday from 8 am to noon. You can buy prescription drugs and other items at Pine Grove Pharmacy (☎ 972-0334) at 55 Main St.

Emergency The police station (☎ 974-2307) is on the corner of Main and Braco Sts.

Columbus Monument
This impressive monument sits amid bougainvillea in a small roundabout (traffic circle) at the far west end of town. A large coral base is topped by a bronze figure of the explorer shown dressed as a Spanish grandee. It was cast by Michele Geurisi in Columbus' native city of Genoa. The pedestal has bronze plaques depicting the caravels that are thought to have sunk in Santa Gloria Bay.

Our Lady of Perpetual Help Church
One hundred yards up the hill from the Columbus monument is this beautiful Catholic church built by an Irish priest in 1939 of stones recovered from the ruins of the 16th-century brick-and-stone church of Peter Martyr at Sevilla la Nueva. The

contemporary structure is also of Spanish design. It stands in pretty grounds full of palms and bougainvillea and is festooned with climbing plants. Inside, great beams support the organ loft.

Seville Great House
When the English captured Jamaica from the Spanish, the land on which Sevilla la Nueva had been built was granted to Richard Hemming, an officer in Oliver Cromwell's invasion army. Over the next two centuries, Hemming's descendants developed the property as a sugar estate. The great house was built in 1745 by his grandson. It still stands atop the hill south of the A1, though today it is owned by the Jamaica National Trust Commission.

The original house has been substantially altered, not least by a hurricane in 1944 that lopped off its upper story. The restored building contains a mini-museum depicting the history of the site (entrance costs US$2). The house looks down over the ruins of the old sugar works, which lie beside the main road. You can explore the 'English Industrial Works' that include a sugar mill, copra kiln, waterwheel, and boiling house.

Courthouse
At the center of town is the courthouse, an elegant limestone and red-brick structure built in 1866 with a pedimented porch bearing the scales of justice.

Marcus Garvey Statue
A pewter-gray bronze statue of national hero Marcus Garvey stands outside the library. The home-grown hero is considered the father of black consciousness in both Jamaica and the US (see the Marcus Garvey sidebar). Garvey's hulking figure stands on a pedestal bearing a plaque that reads: 'Right Excellent Marcus Mosiah Garvey / Born – August 17, 1887 / Died June 10, 1940'.

Drax Hall
Drax Hall, immediately east of St Ann's, is today the site of one of Jamaica's largest

One God, One Aim, One Destiny

Marcus Garvey was born in St Ann's Bay of working-class parents on August 17, 1887. As a young man he traveled extensively throughout Costa Rica, Panama, and England. He returned well educated and a firm believer in self-improvement. Inspired to raise the consciousness and well-being of blacks, he founded the United Negro Improvement Association (UNIA) in 1914 to unite 'all the Negro peoples of the world into one great body to establish a country and a government exclusively their own.' In 1916 he traveled to the US, where he formed a branch of UNIA in New York and was influenced by another prominent black nationalist, Booker T Washington. Garvey, a gifted orator, established a weekly newspaper, the *Negro World*, and built an enormous following under the slogan 'One God! One Aim! One Destiny!'

Garvey fostered black enterprises. He set up the Black Star Line, a steamship company that eventually aimed to repatriate blacks to Africa. The company, however, failed through poor management.

The American and British colonial governments regarded Garvey as a dangerous agitator. They conspired against him and in 1922 arrested him on mail-fraud charges. He served two years in Atlanta Federal Prison before being deported to Jamaica. Back in his homeland, the black internationalist founded the reformist People's Political Party. Universal franchise did not then exist in Jamaica, and he failed to gather enough support at the polls. In 1935 he departed for England, where he died in poverty in 1940.

His remains were repatriated to Jamaica in 1984 and reinterred with state honors in National Heroes Park. In 1980 the Organization of American States honored him by placing his bust in its Hall of Heroes. He is still revered among blacks throughout the world. ■

deluxe resort developments. The property, however, has an intriguing history. A Barbadian migrant, Charles Drax, established a sugar estate here in the late 17th century. By his will of 1721, Drax left his property for the founding of a charity school. By devious means, the local Beckford family 'captured' the property and only relinquished it in 1804 following two decades of litigation. In 1802 the school was founded near Kingston, and the disputed property was converted to a coconut and cattle plantation. Later still, the old sugar works was converted to a soap factory.

Scuba Diving

The coral reef offshore of St Ann's Bay is said to be one of the most impressive in Jamaica. You can rent equipment from the Island Dive Shop (☎ 972-2519) at Columbus Beach in Priory about one mile west of St Ann's.

Places to Stay

In town, the pickings are slim. *Motel 64* (☎ 972-2308) is very basic. Its 14 small rooms (US$13) have minimal furnishings, but they are clean and have fans and private showers.

At the other end of the spectrum is *Drax Hall Estate*, under construction at press time and aiming to be one of the most prestigious international resorts in the world. Slated to take up 2400 acres of shorefront overlooking Don Christopher's Cove east of St Ann's, the project includes the 27-hole

Doral Drax Hall Golf Course, due for completion in 1998. A master plan includes 180 single family villa lots and 13 condominium and townhouse sites; a 100-slip marina and marina village; plus a 280-room hotel – the Doral Drax Hall – that was due to open by late 1996. For information, contact the on-site information center at ☎ 972-9523, or c/o Drax Hall Estate, PO Box 299, St Ann's Bay, ☎ 972-2438, fax 972-2299; or Drax Hall Holdings, Blue Cross Building No 203, 85 Hope Rd, Kingston 6, ☎ 978-5319, fax 978-5318).

Jamel Jamaica (☎ 972-1031, fax 972-0714) at 12 Richmond Estate in Priory west of Sevilla la Nueva, is a compact property with a strong Mediterranean feel. Bougainvillea spills over whitewashed walls onto a sun deck of colorful tiles. Each of the 24 air-con rooms has a TV, telephone, and private balcony overlooking the beach. Water sports are offered. Summer rates are US$109 double. A two-bedroom family suite costs US$120.

A stone's throw from Jamel is *Priory Beach Cottages* (☎ 972-2323), a complex of five spacious beachfront cottages facing Priory Beach. It's a reclusive place. Each unit (US$700 per week) has two bedrooms, a full kitchen, and wide jalousie windows. There's a small pool.

High Hope Estate (PO Box 11, ☎ 927-2277, fax 972-1607) proves true the adage that you get what you pay for. This interpretation of a 15th-century Italianate villa is set on 40 acres of manicured lawns and woodland high in the hills above St Ann's. It has seven rooms, each individually styled. Five look out over the ocean; two face the mountains. All are decorated with priceless antiques: 18th-century Moroccan harem screens, 19th-century Korean silk screens, a Steinway baby-grand piano, and marble floors. High Hope was built in 1961 as a private residence for a socialite couple who have welcomed such illustrious guests as Charlie Chaplin, Noel Coward, Kurt Vonnegut, and Adlai Stevenson. If it's raining, you can settle in the well-stocked library with a good book. Rates range from US$145 to US$225 per night double,

including breakfast. You can also rent the entire place fully staffed.

Places to Eat

There's no shortage of reasonably priced places to eat. Several of the better restaurants are at the west end of Main St, including *Blue Carpet* (☎ 972-0821), which is open for breakfast, and the *Blue Bowl Restaurant & Lounge*. On the side of the bypass *Seafood Specialist* is a rustic restaurant that serves excellent steamed or fried fish served with yams and rice 'n peas for US$4. Wash it down with natural juices (US$1).

You can buy pastries and snacks at *Square One Bakery* on Braco St (you'll also find at least two other bakeries on Main St). For jerk, check out *Daddy Smurf's Place* on Windsor Rd at the far east end of town.

Things to Buy

The St Ann's Artisans & Craft Village on the north side of the bypass has half-a-dozen or so stalls selling straw items, wooden carvings, jewelry, and the usual array of T-shirts. Among the few stores selling arts and crafts are Gifts Galore & Book Shop and Mind & Body Boutique, side by side at the west end of Main St. You'll find a small selection of international magazines at the Central Book Store (☎ 972-0154), a stone's throw further west.

Getting There & Away

You can take any of the buses traveling along the A1 between Montego Bay and Ocho Rios. Ask to be dropped off by the crafts market on the bypass. At least one minibus (No STBW465) leaves from the Parade in Kingston.

CLAREMONT

Claremont (population 1500) is a regional market town that prospered briefly during the 1960s and 1970s on the income generated by the Reynolds Company's bauxite and cattle-ranching activities. The company has since pulled out of Jamaica. The town, which lies nine miles south of St Ann's, has an attractive town square

Rural market, south of Brown's Town

Rafting the Martha Brae River

Giving Lou Lou a look

Franklyn Taylor leads the way to Windsor Caves.

A guide at the Bob Marley Museum demonstrates the powers of the 'inspiration stone,' where the superstar learned to play guitar.

A view of Cockpit Country from Barbecue Bottom

From the great house at Good Hope Estate, visitors can take in the Queen of Spains Valley, planted in sugarcane.

北

centered on a handsome campanile-like clock tower topped with green shingle.

Claremont is on the main bus route between the north coast and Kingston, and many buses pass through. Ask your driver to drop you in Claremont, which you can also reach by minibus No STBW121 from Kingston (US$5) or minibus No LS1071 from Ocho Rios (US$1).

GOLDEN GROVE

Two miles south of Claremont at Golden Grove along the A1, a road to the left leads through pastures and rusting metal structures that are all that remains of the old Lydford Works, a massive bauxite mine and processing plant that was established in 1952 by Reynolds Jamaica Mines, Ltd. The facility was built near the site where a Kingstonian named Sir Alfred D'Costa (the 'Father of Jamaican bauxite') discovered bauxite ore in 1942 (he had soil samples analyzed because he was concerned for the low yield of his crops). The soils from his estate were declared unusually rich in alumina, with a content of 45 to 50%.

At their peak the conveyors and overhead bucket tramways carried over three million tons of bauxite annually to the pier at Ocho Rios. Reynolds also engaged in agricultural research and light industry. It owned 80,000 acres locally, most of which was grazed by the largest herd of cattle (16,000 head) in the West Indies. The company sold its land to the Jamaican government in 1980 and finally pulled out of the island altogether in 1984, though the cattle remained. The Reynolds company is thought of fondly by locals for its efforts to support community development.

The genesis of Jamaica's bauxite industry is commemorated by an aluminum plaque beside the road at Phoenix Park, five miles south of Claremont. It was cast from the first load of bauxite shipped in 1952.

EDINBURGH CASTLE

One of Jamaica's more gory and fascinating stories surrounds the ruins of Edinburgh Castle, eight miles southwest of Claremont, near the hamlet of Pedro.

The two-story fortified house with two towers at diagonal corners was built by a mass murderer named Lewis Hutchinson, a Scot who in the mid-18th century had left Scotland and settled in Jamaica. The 'castle' stood close by what was at the time the main coach road between St Ann's and Spanish Town. The deranged Scot invited his victims into the house, where he wined and dined them before robbing and murdering them. For years, no one presented evidence against him (no doubt his slaves were too terrified to testify; in any case, their testimony was inadmissible by law).

Eventually the maniac quarreled with a neighboring planter, whom he almost killed. A soldier was then sent to arrest him. He, too, was shot dead and the game was up. Hutchinson fled, managing to elude the militia and escape to sea. The navy was alerted, however, and Hutchinson was caught. He was hanged from the Spanish Town gallows on March 16, 1773.

Although local lore says that the maniac disposed of his victims in a 275-foot-deep sinkhole 400 yards south of the castle, no skeletons have been found. However, 43 watches that belonged to his victims were discovered.

Cockpit Country

Jamaica's most rugged quarter is a dramatic, sculpted 500-sq-mile limestone plateau taking up the whole of southwest Trelawny. The area, which is pockmarked with deep depressions, is a classic example of karst scenery: an area of eroded limestone features studded with thousands of conical hummocks divided by precipitous ravines. The limestone accumulated on the seabed over millions of years before being uplifted about 20 million years ago. It has since been eroded into fantastic formations. Though similar terrain extends east all the way through Trelawny and St Ann Parishes to the border with St Mary, nowhere is it as dramatic as in the area known as the Cockpit Country.

The daunting area is overgrown with luxuriant greenery. Most of the area remains unexplored and virtually uninhabited and unexploited. No roads penetrate the region (although a rough dirt road cuts across the eastern edge between Clark's Town and Albert Town) and only a few tracks make half-hearted forays into its interior. Even by 4WD you can only explore its outer edges. It is otherwise accessible solely by hiking along overgrown trails. The most dramatic way to see it is from above by plane or helicopter, from which you gain a dramatic sense of the Cockpits' scale and beauty. From the sky the area looks like a giant upturned egg carton.

Covered in dense vegetation, the Cockpit Country proved a perfect hideout for the Maroons. The southern section is known as 'District of Look Behind,' an allusion to the Maroon practice of ambushing English soldiers. Much of the vegetation around the perimeter has been cleared in recent years by charcoal burners. And a few valley bottoms are cultivated by small-hold farmers who grow bananas, yams, corn, manioc, and ganja in the deep red earth. It's unwise for foreigners to explore unaccompanied by someone known in the area; you're likely to be considered a DEA (Drug Enforcement Agency) agent and if you stumble upon a major plot, the consequences could be serious (in 1994, a foreign journalist was murdered for his transgression).

Early morning in the Cockpits are magical! Mists float through the eerily silent valley bottoms where you hear only dripping water and birdlife.

Flora & Fauna
The Cockpits are virtually unsullied by humans and the area is replete with wildlife – a temptation for birders and nature lovers. Most of the Cockpits are still clad in primary vegetation that in places includes rare cacti and other endemic species known only in that specific locale. Vegetation differs markedly from top to bottom, and from north- to south-facing slopes. Northern slopes typically are lusher, with rain forests draped with epiphytes, ferns, and mosses. The hilltops are relatively sparsely vegetated due to soil erosion. The Cockpits themselves are generally covered in tall scrub, including brambles and thorns such as scratchbush, the serrated leaves of which can leave you itching for weeks.

Most of Jamaica's 27 endemic bird species are found in the Cockpits, including jabbering crows, black- and yellow-billed parrots, todies, and, more rarely, the endangered golden swallow. If you take a nature trip, keep a sharp eye out for the harmless and now rare Jamaican boa. With luck you may also see giant swallowtail butterflies, the largest butterfly in the Western Hemisphere.

Spelunking
The Cockpits are laced with caves, most of them uncharted. Guides will lead you to the more well-known caverns, where they'll use kerosene-soaked rag torches to light the way. Many caves harbor underground rivers, which can rise dramatically during rains.

Exploring here is for experienced and properly outfitted spelunkers only. There is no rescue organization, and you enter at your own risk. The Jamaica Caving Club has published *Underground Jamaica* by Alan Fincham. This essential compendium provides the most thorough information available on the island's charted caves (Jamaica Caving Club, c/o Dept of Geology, University of the West Indies, Kingston 7, ☎ 927-6661).

Hiking
A few tracks lead into and even across the Cockpit Country. There are no maps, but you can follow overgrown slave trails with a machete and a guide to lead the way. Most trails are faint, rocky tracks. Hiking away from these trails can be dangerous going. The rocks are razor-sharp, and sinkholes are everywhere, often covered by decayed vegetation and ready to crumble underfoot. Never travel alone. There is no one to hear your pleas for help should you break a leg or fall into a sinkhole. Don't

underestimate how strenuous and hot it can be. Don't expect to be able to follow the valley bottoms. Inevitably, you will find yourself winding up the hillocks and down again. Take plenty of water, and drink only sparingly. There is no water to be had locally (except from the bug-filled tanks of bromeliads) due to the porous nature of limestone. Take warm clothing for nights, which can get cold.

The easiest trail across the Cockpits connects Windsor (in the north) with Crown Lands and Troy, about 10 miles as the crow flies. It's a full day's hike with a guide. The trail begins at the fork where you branch right for the Windsor Caves; the trail is the left-hand fork. In Windsor, you can hire either Martell or Franklyn Taylor as guides. (Not many locals know the way across the Cockpits. It may be difficult, but necessary, to ascertain whether your prospective guide really does know the way, as he may merely have convinced himself – and you – that this is the case for the sake of your dollars.)

Organized Tours

Few organized tours operate to this fantastic and primitive region, reflecting the undeveloped state of Jamaica's adventure tourism and ecotourism. The Jamaican Alternative Tourism, Camping, and Hiking Association (Sign Great House, Montego Bay, ☎ 952-9188) can provide you with information.

Robert Sutton of Marshall's Pen in Mandeville (☎ 963-8569) is one of Jamaica's leading ornithologists. He organizes birding and nature hikes from Mandeville, with most activity in the Cockpits focused around Barbecue Bottom (see below). Linda Lee Burkes may still custom-design tours for birders, spelunkers, and hikers through her Touring Society of Jamaica, which used to be based nearby at Sign House, recently moved to the Blue Mountains (c/o Strawberry Hill, Irish Town, St Andrew, ☎ 944-8400, fax 944-8408). SENSE Adventures also operates occasional nature hikes in Cockpit Country (Box 216, Kingston 7, ☎ 927-2097, fax 929-6967).

Also see Clark's Town and Albert Town below, as well as the Northwest Coast chapter.

WINDSOR

This valley surrounded by lushly foliated cliffs on the northern edge of the Cockpits was formerly owned by John Tharp, owner of Good Hope. Tharp built Windsor Great House nearby (half a mile northeast of Windsor Caves). In the 1960s, the Kaiser Bauxite Company bought the estate to resettle farmers displaced by its mining operations. They grow subsistence crops and bananas for sale. You enter the valley from Sherwood at the north end. A narrow two-mile corridor cuts through the limestone outcrops. The paved road dead-ends at Windsor.

Windsor Caves

Though little visited, these off-the-beaten-track caverns are fascinating. A gangway leads along a cliff to the mouth of the cave. About 200 yards beyond the narrow entrance you'll pass into a large gallery full of stalactites (you'll have to step through bat manure, which the locals 'mine' for phosphates). A second passage opens to another huge chamber with a dramatically arched ceiling. In rainy season you can hear the roar of the Martha Brae River flowing deep underground. Further chambers range from a tight fit to, well, cavernous. You can explore safely for more than a mile, beyond which the caves are the terrain of experienced spelunkers.

I strongly recommend you hire a local guide, as several spelunkers have been lost in the caves. Martell and Franklyn 'Doc' Taylor – two elderly and friendly Rastas – are the best guides. They lead the way with smoky kerosene-soaked torches (unfortunately, the soot is having a devastating affect on the limestone, as it accumulates on the walls). You'll find them at the gaily painted hut at the end of the paved road. They charge US$5 to US$10 per person (depending on group size) to visit Rat Bat Cave and a 'likkle more' to the Royal Flat Chamber.

Linger at dusk to watch the bats leave the cave in a great cloud. Apparently, the caves are owned by Lady Rothschild, an entymologist of the famous banking family, who supposedly bought them to study the bat population.

Places to Stay
A Texan called Patrick Kildres has two rooms for rent in a two-story house at Windsor. He charges US$15 for rooms and US$10 to camp beside the river. The simple place has water from a spring, plus solar panels to power the radio and a battery for lighting. You can cook over a simple stove. Martell and Franklyn act as caretakers and will provide food if you wish. They'll even cook lunch and dinner for US$5.

Getting There & Away
Bus There's no bus service to Windsor. However, you can take bus No LS792, which operates between Montego Bay and Brown's Town via Sherwood, from where you can walk or hitch the remaining three miles.

Car If you're driving, the best route is via Martha Brae. From there head south to Sherwood, where Windsor is signed (turn right at Mac's Supermarket, then left 200 yards down the hill). The road is paved all the way through banana groves in the lee of Cockpit valleys; it dead-ends in Windsor.

Finding the correct route from the Queen of Spains Valley or Good Hope is best done with the aid of a 1:50,000 map. One mile east of Bunkers Hill you'll reach a staggered crossroads: the turnoff to the left (north) leads to Good Hope. From Bunker's Hill, you can either continue straight ahead to Sherwood, or alternately take the right fork (south), 100 yards further east of the Good Hope junction; then turn left after half a mile to reach Windsor (the very rough dirt road is partly overgrown with tall grass and often has deep muddy pools; if you miss the turn, you'll end up at an estate called Panteprant).

CLARK'S TOWN
This small market center sits in the middle of sugarcane fields in a bowl on the northern perimeter of Cockpit Country, four miles south of Duncans. The town is centered on St Michael's Anglican Church. Just north of town you'll pass the Long Pond Sugar Factory & Distillery, which manufactures the famous Gold Label Rum (a road leads west opposite the factory and winds through sugarcane plantations to Rock, one mile east of Falmouth).

One of the most adventurous drives in Jamaica begins at Barbecue Bottom, two miles south of Clark's Town.

Getting There & Away
Several minibuses operate to Clark's Town from Water Square in Falmouth (Nos LS706 and No LS607); from Creek St in Montego Bay (Nos LS650, LS705, and LS796); and from north of the roundabout on DaCosta Drive in Ocho Rios (Nos LS562, LS981, and LS1041).

BARBECUE BOTTOM
Thickly forested limestone cliffs close in on this flat ravine planted in sugarcane. From here a very rough road snakes south across the eastern edge of Cockpit Country. The scenery is stupendous as you rise onto the flanks of ravines and look out upon the fantastical shapes. In places, the loftily perched track traces the edge of great abysses so deep that if you drop a stone it may take forever to hear it hit bottom. In places, walls have been built to prevent cars from plummeting over the edge.

Beyond Barbecue Bottom there's not a soul for the next seven miles. It's extremely remote, and you'll feel, correctly, that you're driving along one of the loneliest stretches on the island. A breakdown here is a serious business. The rarely used track is overgrown with bush, and vegetation sweeps up against the car on both sides. In places you may have to negotiate deep muddy pools and in parts, where the gravel gives way to big rocks and potholes, you'll wish your car had hooves. A 4WD vehicle is essential.

Eventually you'll emerge at Burnt Hill and a Y-junction. Take the left turn to Spring Garden and Troy for some of the most dramatic scenery in all Jamaica. The right turn leads to Albert Town (see below), from where you can return to the coast via an easier drive.

If you're arriving via Albert Town and want to drive *north* from Burnt Hill, take the road that begins 50 yards south of the Texaco gas station in Albert Town and leads uphill (southwest) to Spring Garden. After one mile you'll pass a tiny roundabout at the side of the road. A rough road to the right heads to Barbecue Bottom.

RAMGOAT CAVE
This remote cavern lies hidden midway between Barbecue Bottom and Burnt Hill. You'll need a guide to locate it. Take a flashlight. Local kerosene torches give off black smoke that can be uncomfortable in the cavern's confines and does irreparable damage to the cave.

TROY
This nondescript hamlet is a southeastern gateway to the Cockpit Country. From Troy, head to Tyre, an even smaller hamlet on the edge of the Cockpits, about two miles north of Troy. The road north of Tyre is paved for half a mile, then gradually deteriorates and eventually fades as it cuts into the Cockpits.

Surrounded by sugarcane fields, Troy is a center of yam cultivation, which grow on tall runners in the valley bottoms. Mrs Chillie has a small guest house at Tyre.

ULSTER SPRING
South from Rio Bueno the B5 (the main road linking the north coast with Mandeville and the south-coast parish of Manchester) winds uphill via Jackson Town and Vale Royal Mountain, then cuts through a dramatic steep-faced gorge known as the Alps before plunging down through another gorge to Ulster Spring,

20 miles from Rio Bueno. On the edge of Cockpit Country, you'll pass through cockpit bottoms planted in bananas and sugarcane.

About two miles south of Ulster Spring, the Quashie River tumbles down a series of falls into an immense sinkhole, where it disappears, reemerging 10 miles to the north.

ALBERT TOWN
This small market center sits in the hills above and two miles southwest of Ulster Spring. The road climbs through cockpits with dramatic views en route. There's a Texaco gas station (it's closed on Sundays, when the nearest gas station is at Christiana).

South of Albert Town the B5 rises into mountains that form the spine of Jamaica. Beyond the hamlet of Wait-a-Bit you enter a whole different realm, with vistas of lush, rolling agricultural land interspersed with pine forest. It's cooler up here, with clouds drifting langorously through the treetops. You'll crest the mountains (and the boundary with Manchester Parish) just south of Lorrimer's, about nine miles south of Albert Town. The spot is marked by a radio station. Christiana is about two miles further south.

Places to Eat
You can appease your appetite for one or two dollars at *TJ's Snacks & Pastries* at the north end of town, 50 yards north of the post office. *Sunshine Bakery & Grocery* is nearby. Amazingly for this out-of-the-way place, you can buy nutritional foods and vitamins at *Mini-Mart Health Store*, a quarter mile south of town on the road to Christiana. Everything is closed on Sunday.

Getting There & Away
Buses and minibuses operate between Albert Town and Falmouth (No LS630), Kingston (Nos ST873 and ST829), Mandeville (Nos LS868 and LS584), and Spaldings (No LS964).

Dry Harbour Mountains

A paved road – the ever-winding B3 – leads south from Runaway Bay via the old sugar estate of Orange Valley and the important market center of Brown's Town. From there it climbs through the Dry Harbour Mountains to Cave Valley, at the base of the island's backbone and gateway to the south-coast parishes of Clarendon and Manchester. The district south of Brown's Town is known as Wilberborce, after the English abolitionist who steered the Abolition Act through Parliament. Many villages in the wooded folds of the Dry Harbour Mountains were founded as 'emancipation villages' by the Rev John Clark of Brown's Town. Nonconformist churches and their congregations purchased the land to provide homesteads for freed slave communities. One of the most impressive is **Sturge Town**, perched amid woodland four miles east of Brown's Town. The hamlet offers fabulous views down to the coast.

The roads twist and turn through fabulous scenic countryside. The area is off-the-beaten-track, including Nine Mile, the birthplace and resting-place of reggae superstar Bob Marley.

BROWN'S TOWN

Brown's Town is a large and lively market town (population 4000) at the juncture of several valleys, seven miles south of Runaway Bay. Many noble houses on the hillsides hint at its relative prosperity (much of the wealth is reportedly derived from illicit means – the surrounding hills are renowned as centers of ganja production). The town is at its most bustling during market days (Wednesday, Friday, and Saturday), when the tin-roofed, cast-iron Victorian market overflows with higglers, and the streets are thronged. Bring your camera for the whirligig of commotion and color.

Information

Money With all the trade going on, you'd expect to find several banks. National Commercial Bank (☎ 975-2275), Scotiabank (☎ 975-2237), and Jamaica Citizens Bank (☎ 975-2925) all have branches within a stone's throw of each other on Brown's Town Rd. None have currency exchange booths, but you can cash traveler's checks and arrange advances against credit cards.

Post & Communications The post office (☎ 975-2216) is midway down Brown's Town Rd, opposite the police station. You can make international calls and send faxes from the Telephone Call Centre, in a basement opposite Brown's Town Mini Mall; it's open Monday to Saturday 8 am to 1 pm, and Sunday 3 to 10 pm.

Travel Agencies The nation's leading travel agency chain, Stuart's Travel Service (☎ 975-2566), has an office in Nam's Plaza near the Telephone Call Centre.

Bookshops You'll find a small selection of international magazines at Grand Pharmacy, and at Brown's Town Books & Stationery in Brown's Town Mini Mall on Main St.

Medical Services There's no hospital locally, but you can get medical attention at the DeCarteret Medical Centre (☎ 975-2265) at the north end of Main St. Dr Winsome James-Grant also has a clinic (☎ 975-2343) on St Christopher's Crescent.

There are several pharmacies, including Brown's Town Pharmacy (☎ 975-2271) in the Brown's Town Mini Mall on Main St and Grand Pharmacy (☎ 975-2613) at 2 Top Rd. The former is open 9 am to 6 pm Friday to Wednesday and until 4 pm on Thursday.

Emergency The police station (☎ 975-2233), fronted by stone arches, is midway down Brown's Town Rd.

Bicycle Repairs If you're cycling, the Bicycle Shop on the left at the bottom of Brown's Town Rd may be able to make any repairs or supply parts.

Things to See

The town is named for its founder, an Irish estate owner named Hamilton Brown (1776 – 1843), who represented the parish in the House of Assembly. Brown, who owned nine estates locally, also financed the building of **St Mark's Anglican Church** in Victorian Gothic style. Despite such altruistic projects, he allegedly also arranged for the Baptist church to be burned down so that blacks would have nowhere to worship.

Another 19th-century church, the **Evangelical Tabernacle**, is on Top Rd. The founder of the latter, Dr James Johnson (1854 – 1922), was one of the earliest promoters of tourism to Jamaica. In 1903, he published *Jamaica, the New Riviera: A Pictorial Description of the Island and Its Attractions.*

Other buildings of interest include the fine cut-stone **courthouse** with neoclassical columned portico.

Places to Stay

There are at least four budget guest houses to choose from. *Treasure Trove Guest House* (☎ 975-2372) at Minard Heights just north of town features a swimming pool and horseback riding on a farm. A woman named Jean Sharpe (☎ 975-2487) also rents out rooms. Alternately, try *Meditation Height* (☎ 975-2588) on Huntley Ave.

The most atmospheric place is *Lillyfield*, a coffee plantation with an 18th-century great house converted to a guest house. Reportedly it's homey – the old graciousness is long gone – but, nonetheless, it appeals to adventurous, self-sufficient travelers. The house, about five miles east of Brown's Town, has an acclaimed restaurant and tremendous views.

Places to Eat

You can buy patties, pastries, and other snacks, as well as fresh produce at the

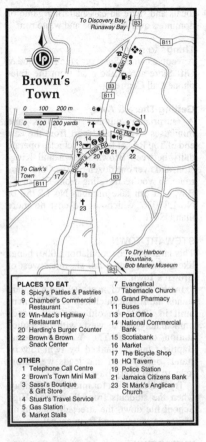

PLACES TO EAT
8 Spicy's Patties & Pastries
9 Chamber's Commercial Restaurant
12 Win-Mac's Highway Restaurant
20 Harding's Burger Counter
22 Brown & Brown Snack Center

OTHER
1 Telephone Call Centre
2 Brown's Town Mini Mall
3 Sassi's Boutique & Gift Store
4 Stuart's Travel Service
5 Gas Station
6 Market Stalls
7 Evangelical Tabernacle Church
10 Grand Pharmacy
11 Buses
13 Post Office
14 National Commercial Bank
15 Scotiabank
16 Market
17 The Bicycle Shop
18 HQ Tavern
19 Police Station
21 Jamaica Citizens Bank
23 St Mark's Anglican Church

open-air market. There are several basic, budget eateries in town, including *Harding's Burger Counter & Restaurant*, 50 yards down the hill from the market; *Brown & Brown Snack Counter* on St Hilda's Drive; *Chambers Commercial Restaurant* and *Spicy's Patties & Pastries* on Top Rd; and the atmospheric, down-to-earth *Win-Mac's Highway Restaurant*, opposite the police station on Brown's Town Rd. I've heard high praise for lunch at *Lillyfield* (by reservation only; c/o Chukka Cove, ☎ 972-2506).

HQ Tavern is a funky place to banter with

locals and share an ear-shattering game of dominoes over Red Stripe and white rum.

Things to Buy
A woman named Sassi runs the Boutique & Gift Store across the road from the Telephone Call Centre.

Getting There & Away
A surprising number of buses and minibuses arrive and depart from the east end of Top Rd. At least six vehicles operate daily between Brown's Town and Kingston, and over one dozen ply the Ocho Rios route. If you're traveling from Discovery Bay, you can take minibus No LS758 or No LS1036, which should cost no more than US$1.

STEWART TOWN
This large village (population 2000) hangs like a citadel atop a hill six miles west of Brown's Town.

In the center of a grassy town square stands the Anglican church of St Thomas, built in 1842. An old saw mill stands immediately to the west, with the police station opposite. The Webb Memorial Baptist Church, flanked by twin towers, stands on the road that leads west from town to Discovery Bay.

Try to time a visit for midday on Sunday, when the students from Westwood High School file down the street dressed in all whites en route to and from chapel.

WATT TOWN
You can count on being the first foreigner in weeks to arrive at Watt Town, 10 miles southwest of Brown's Town in the backwaters of the Dry Harbour Mountains.

The hamlet is known as the birthplace of Revivalism, which began here in the 1880s. It is still a center of the religion, and Revivalists make pilgrimages here to study at the Watt Town Revival Schoolroom. Visitors are welcome, though a gatekeeper will determine whether or not you may enter the consecrated grounds. The village is semiautonomous and ruled over by a body of 'patriarchs.'

ALEXANDRIA
Alexandria, nine miles south of Brown's Town, is a quaint little crossroads village that spreads along the B3 for over a mile. It's of little interest except for those heading to the Bob Marley Museum at **Nine Mile**, which happens to be nine miles east of Alexandria. The road that continues east from Nine Mile passes through a rugged landscape with tiny hamlets in the base of cockpits. The scenery is dramatic, making for a more rewarding drive if you're returning to the north coast. The road leads to Claremont (see below), where you can turn north on the A1 for St Ann's.

The National Commercial Bank in the town center is open only on Tuesday 9:30 to 11:30 am and Friday 9:30 am to 3 pm. There's a small hospital (☎ 975-2372), police station (☎ 975-9011), and gas station.

Alexandria is linked by bus No ST512 to the Parade in Kingston. It's a two-hour journey, costing about US$3. Minibuses also travel to Alexandria from Ocho Rios.

BOB MARLEY MUSEUM
A visit to the birthplace and crypt of Bob Marley at Nine Mile is a must for anyone with the least interest in reggae or the legacy of the 'first Third World superstar, Rasta prophet, visionary and revolutionary artist.' The site is run by the Bob Marley Foundation, which uses some of the proceeds to advance education, health, and social services in the local community of Nine Mile, a small mountain village in the middle of a poor farming district. The area was settled by German farmers at the time of emancipation. The museum gets about 15 to 20 visitors daily.

Upon arrival you're diverted into the gift shop to pay your US$10 entrance fee before your guide leads you up a steep path lined with international flags. Authentic Rastafarian guides lead the 30-minute tours. They speak in reverential tones and often break into renditions of Marley's songs. Between puffs on a spliff of ganja, your guide will tell of Marley's childhood and the simple lifestyle he and his mother shared.

Marley was born on February 6, 1945, in what is now a derelict house below the museum site. He moved into the hut on the hill – called Zion – when he was three months old. The hut, like virtually everything else, has doors and doorjambs painted green, yellow, and red (one wall is also painted with the words 'I BOB LOVE JAH O LOVE'). You'll be told that the colors represent sunshine (yellow), nature (green), and blood (red). Inside the hut there is merely a bed, and walls covered with adoring graffiti and miscellany left by visitors.

Behind the hut is the 'inspiration stone' on which Marley sat and learned to play the guitar. The rock is painted like a tam in Rasta colors. Supposedly Marley even slept here to receive inspiration. My guide took a suck on his spliff and lay down to demonstrate the point.

Marley's body lies buried along with his guitar in an eight-foot-tall oblong marble mausoleum (it was built to accommodate his wife Rita Marley when she dies) inside a tiny church of traditional Ethiopian design that stands next to the hut. You must leave your shoes outside and take your cap off before entering (the guides can get quite animated if you fail to do this). The sun rising to the east casts its rays on Marley's face as it shines through a Star of David window.

A photo of Haile Selassie takes precedence at the base of the tomb, with a smaller photo of Marley to the side. The crypt also contains a large bronze bust of the musician, a stained glass window of a lion of Judah, some of Marley's musical instruments, and a huge leatherbound book full of newspaper clips reporting Marley's funeral (the book is torn and battered and held together with silver tape. Before leaving the crypt you may be asked to stand humbly while a prayer is recited.

No video camera or taping equipment is allowed.

The museum shop sells Marley paraphernalia of every description, from T-shirts to music tapes. You can also buy

Bob was a lion among lions.

simple crafts from locals who hawk carved gourds and other items opposite the museum entrance. The first time I visited, the hustlers were as thick as flies. Some wanted to guard my car, others to wash it, and still others to act as guides, but more recently the hustlers were gone and huge wire fences had been erected. Now the place looks like a military compound.

A memorial concert is held here each February 6, and Ziggy Marley, Rita Marley and other reggae stars traditionally perform. For information about the concert or the museum, contact Cedella Marley Booker Entertainment, Calderwood, PO Box St Ann, ☎ 999-7003; in the USA, Cedella Marley Booker, 2809 Bird Ave, Suite 146, Miami, FL 33133 (☎ (305) 257-3737).

Places to Stay & Eat
You can probably rent a room with a local family for US$15 or so. The museum has a restaurant serving vegetarian I-tal dishes for US$2 and upwards. A local rum shop, the *Dias Pub*, and the *Jahlove Grocery* are both 100 yards downhill from the museum.

Getting There & Away
In the Lonely Planet video *The Jamaica Experience*, host Ian Wright is delivered to Nine Mile by a battered old Ford Transit van. The minibus, run by Carl Hinds, operates between Alexandria and Claremont and should cost no more than US$1 from either.

CAVE VALLEY

This tiny yet strategically located village sits on the border of St Ann and Clarendon Parishes, eight miles south of Alexandria, at the north end of Vera Ma Hollis Savanna, a seven-mile-long valley. Its name is derived from *Los Bermajales*, the Spanish name for 'red lands.' During the early years of the British occupation in the late 17th century, the region was a center of independence for slaves freed by the Spanish and whose descendants became the Maroons. Maroons were still present throughout the 18th century, and the British built a barracks here during the First Maroon War in the 1730s.

A horse trough, erected in the square in 1937 by the Jamaica Society for the Prevention of Cruelty to Animals, hints at Cave Valley's former importance as a horse-trading center. Reportedly, it still hosts a weekend market to which horses and mules are brought from miles around. Tobacco and coffee are also important crops, especially in the valley of the Cave River, which rises in the mountains near Coleyville, 10 miles west of Cave Valley (the Coffee Industry Board has a small factory three miles southwest of Cave Valley at Aenon Town; visitors are welcome to look around).

In the dry season you can see the **Cave River Sinks**, two holes into which the river disappears, reemerging 13 miles north near Stewart Town. During heavy rains, however, the underground river backs up and instead of draining down the natural plug, the waters flood the valley.

The road that leads southeast from Cave Valley through Vera Ma Hollis begins a precipitous ascent to Corner Shop and the summit of the Central Highlands at about 2800 feet. From here you can descend to Trout Hall in the upper Rio Minho Valley (drive carefully; the road drops 1300 feet in less than three miles).

The road through the Cave River Valley eventually reaches Spaldings, Christiana, and Mandeville.

Getting There & Away

You'll find minibuses to Cave Valley in Ocho Rios north of the roundabout on DaCosta Drive. Other minibuses run from Mandeville and Kingston, from where you can also catch bus No ST188 (about US$2). If you're coming from Albert Town, ask for Courtney Hasnon, who operates a minibus (No LS863) to Cave Valley.

Northwest Coast

Northwest Jamaica's node is Montego Bay, the second largest city on the island and by far the most important tourist resort. More than 30% of the country's hotel rooms are here, including those in several of Jamaica's most exclusive hotels, nestled up against their own gilded shores.

Though Montego Bay is as far from the 'real' Jamaica as you can get, you don't need to wander far to escape the madding crowd. Behind the narrow coastal plain is hill country where you can immerse yourself in mountain-village life. Some villages have a remarkable and unique history, such as Seaford Town and Accompong in the Cockpit Country. The region boasts a greater concentration of well-preserved colonial great houses than any other, many of which are working plantations that welcome guests on guided tours. And three championship golf courses, several horse stables, and the island's best shopping add to the region's appeal.

Montego Bay

Montego Bay (population 70,000), capital of St James Parish, exists on tourism and trade. It's also a thriving port city. The wharf activity that used to take place along the city shorefront has disappeared, replaced by the container-shipping trade further west at Montego Freeport.

The town, colloquially called 'MoBay' by locals (native-born Montegonians are called 'bawn-a-bays'), spreads tentacles of light industry west as far as Reading, and east to Ironshore, a total distance of seven miles. Ironshore, formerly a sugar estate, is also a burgeoning resort.

Many guidebooks tout MoBay's natural beauty, and reggae artists have sung the city's praises to the world. It does have its attractions, most notably its golf courses,

historic great houses, and the beautiful private beach resorts east and west of town, but the town itself is not particularly appealing. Downtown, south of the hotel strip, is a crowded, chaotic mishmash of one-way streets full of honking cars and a press of pedestrians (take care when crossing roads; Montegonian drivers give no quarter to tourist pedestrians).

You could walk the entire length of Gloucester Ave – the tourist strip – and not be aware that scintillating white sand lies a stone's throw away. By some historical quirk, two of the city's three 'public' beaches – Doctor's Cave and Cornwall – are in the hands of private owners who hold a monopoly lease. The wire fences and tall concrete walls they've erected are dismal

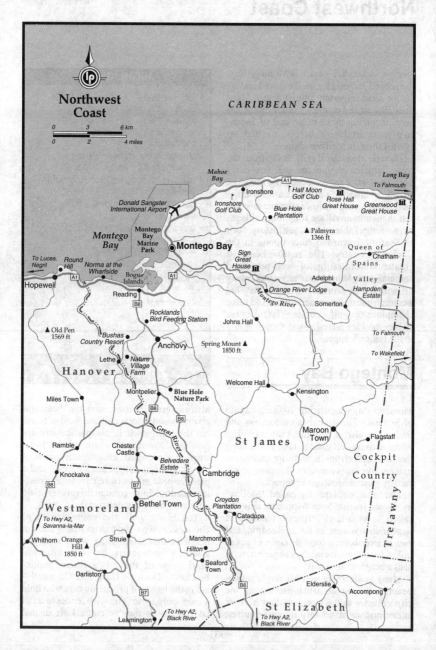

Northwest Coast

CARIBBEAN SEA

To Falmouth

Long Bay

Greenwood Great House

Rose Hall Great House

Half Moon Golf Club

A1

Ironshore

Mahoe Bay

Ironshore Golf Club

Blue Hole Plantation

▲ Palmyra 1366 ft

Queen of Spains

Donald Sangster International Airport

Montego Bay Marine Park

Montego Bay

● **Montego Bay**

Sign Great House

Chatham

To Lucea, Negril

Round Hill

Norma at the Wharfside

Adelphi

Valley

Hampden Estate

Hopewell

A1

Reading

B8

Bogue Islands

A1

Orange River Lodge

Montego River

Somerton

Rocklands Bird Feeding Station

Johns Hall

To Falmouth

▲ Old Pen 1569 ft

Bushas Country Resort

Anchovy

Spring Mount ▲ 1850 ft

To Wakefield

Lethe

Nature Village Farm

Hanover

Montpelier

Blue Hole Nature Park

Welcome Hall

Kensington

Miles Town

B8

B6

Great River

St James

Maroon Town

Flagstaff

Ramble

Chester Castle

Belvedere Estate

Cockpit

Knockalva

B8

B7

Cambridge

Country

Westmoreland

Bethel Town

Croydon Plantation

Catadupa

To Hwy A2, Savanna-la-Mar

Trelawny

Whithorn

Orange Hill ▲ 1850 ft

Struie

Marchmont

Hilton

Darliston

Seaford Town

B7

B6

Elderslie

Accompong

To Hwy A2, Black River

St Elizabeth

To Hwy A2, Black River

Leamington

blights that effectively divorce the beaches from the resort. The same is true of Walter Fletcher Beach, run by the Urban Development Council. Most of the good beaches around Montego Bay are the private domains of resort hotels. A couples-only resort called Sandals Montego Bay, adjacent to the airport, has the best beach in the vicinity, while Jack Tar Village has the best beach in town.

MoBay has also earned a justified reputation as a hustler's city. It's impossible to walk down the road without being approached. To its credit, the Jamaican Tourist Board (JTB) has made recent inroads to reduce the numbers of touts and casual prostitutes who hang out along Gloucester Ave. Hidden amid the hills and valleys behind town are thousands of wood-and-tin hovels usually unseen by tourists. This is where the majority of Montegonians live. Once you've witnessed the conditions, it's easier to understand the competitive tenacity with which hustlers whisper 'Hey, Jake! Smoke? Coke?' or flippantly ask 'You need girl?'

There *are* attractions, however, despite the city's lack of soul. Many admirable Georgian stone buildings and timber houses still stand downtown and are well worth seeking out, as is St James Parish Church. The duty-free shopping is excellent, as is the variety of arts and crafts. Every kind of water sport is represented. And there are several good restaurants to choose from. Those seeking a budget holiday with a lively nightlife and shops and craft markets packed with bargains will be right at home, as will those seeking to spend a week idly sunning at an all-inclusive upscale resort, such as Breezes, Sandals, or Jack Tar Village. However, if you're seeking authentic Jamaica, MoBay has relatively little to offer.

HISTORY
Columbus put Montego Bay on the map – literally. The explorer anchored here in 1494 and called it 'El Golfo de Buen Tiempo' (Gulf of Good Weather). Only in 1655 did a settlement first appear on Spanish maps:

Manterias, after the Spanish word *manteca*, or lard, from the days when the Spanish shipped 'pig's butter' derived from the herds of wild hogs that flourished in the surrounding hills. The English later showed the bay as Lard Bay on their maps. Following the British takeover in 1655, the parish of St James was established and named for the Duke of York, later King James II. The tiny port, however, languished for over a century under constant threat of both pirates and the fearsome Maroons, who maintained their autonomy in the wild Cockpit Country southeast of MoBay.

As sugar was planted in the 18th century, Montego Bay took on new importance, encouraged by a peace settlement with the Maroons. Sugar was planted on every valley floor and St James became the most important sugar producing parish on the island. More than 150 ships a year arrived in Montego Bay, bringing slaves and supplies. Wealthy planters and merchants erected lavish town houses and the parish church. And a cultural life developed: by 1773, the city had the only newspaper outside Kingston, the *Cornwall Chronicle*. Unfortunately, many of the original buildings perished in fires and hurricanes that destroyed many valuable records in the western part of the island, obscuring the early history.

Emancipation & the Launch of Tourism
Montego Bay and its hinterland were the settings for the slave rebellion of Christmas 1831, when estates throughout St James were put to the torch. Militia and regular troops stationed in Montego Bay quickly quelled the revolt, and the courthouse (now destroyed) became a center for savage reprisals.

Following emancipation in 1834, the sugar trade slipped into decline. The city once again languished until revived by the development of the banana trade, pioneered by the local firm of JE Kerr & Co, and by the early tourist trade that developed in the late 1880s when Dr Alexander G McCatty founded a sanatorium at what is today Doctor's Cave Beach. The sanatorium

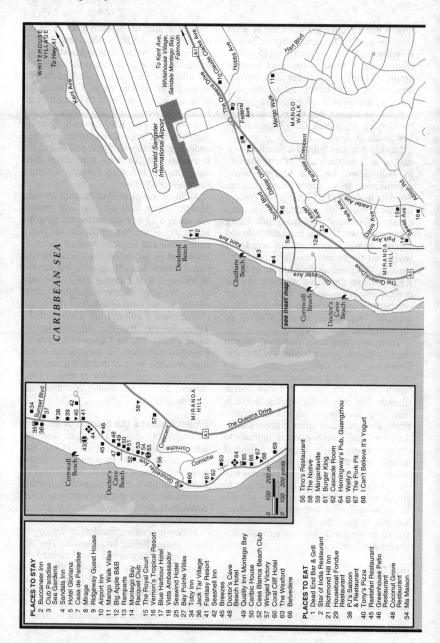

CARIBBEAN SEA

WHITEHOUSE VILLAGE
To Hwy A1
Kent Ave

Donald Sangster International Airport

To Kent Ave, Whitehouse Village, Sandals Montego Bay, Falmouth

The Queens Drive
A1
Claude Ave
Hobbs Ave
Hart Blvd

Mango Walk
MANGO WALK
Federal Ave
Paradise Crescent

Sunset Blvd
Dillinger Drive
Leader Ave
Park Ave
Leader Ave
Albert Rd

Kent Ave
Deadend Beach

Chatham Beach

Gloucester Ave
The Queens Drive
MIRANDA HILL
A1

Denis Ave
Sewell Ave
Park Ave

Cornwall Beach
Doctor's Cave Beach
see inset map

Inset map

Sunset Blvd
Cornwall Beach
Doctor's Cave Beach
Gloucester Ave
MIRANDA HILL
The Queens Drive
A1
Corniche
Crescent

0   100   200 m
0   100   200 yards

PLACES TO STAY

2 Buccaneer Inn
3 Club Paradise
   Sea Gardens
4 Sandals Inn
5 Hotel Gloriana
7 Casa de Paradise
8 Mirage
9 Ridgeway Guest House
10 Airport Inn
11 Mango Walk Villas
12 Big Apple B&B
13 Ramparts
14 Montego Bay Racquet Club
15 The Royal Court
16 Vernon's Tropical Resort
17 Blue Harbour Hotel
18 Vista Ambassador
25 Seawind Hotel
27 Bay Pointe Villas
34 Toby Inn
36 Jack Tar Village
41 Fantasy Resort
42 Seashell Inn
45 Breezes
48 Doctor's Cave Beach Hotel
49 Quality Inn Montego Bay
50 Caribic House
51 Casa Blanca Beach Club
57 Winged Victory
60 Coral Cliff Hotel
63 The Wexford
66 Belvedere

PLACES TO EAT

1 Dead End Bar & Grill
2 The Native
21 Star of India Restaurant
29 Richmond Hill Inn
   Houseboat Fondue
   Restaurant
38 PJ's Saloon
   & Restaurant
40 Tony's Pizza
45 Rastafari Restaurant
46 Greenhouse Patio
   Restaurant
48 Coconut Grove
   Restaurant
54 Ma Maison

56 Tino's Restaurant
58 The Native
59 Margaritaville
62 Burger King
64 Cascade Room
   Hemingway's Pub, Guangzhou
65 Wally's
67 The Pork Pit
68 I Can't Believe It's Yogurt

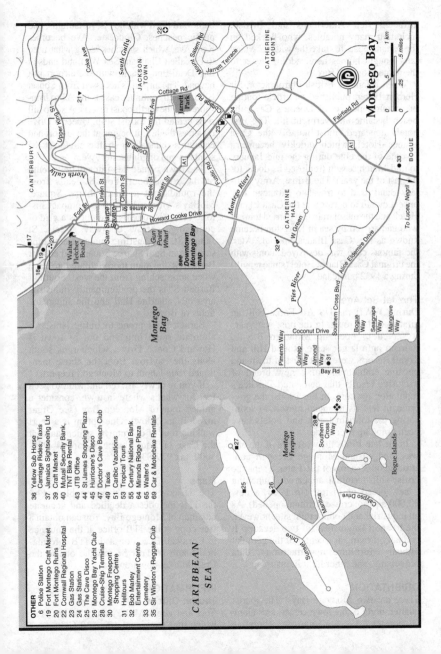

attracted rich Americans and British, including many notables, who flocked on the banana boats to 'take the waters.' Many later bought homes here, adding luster to the name Montego Bay.

When a famous British chiropractor, Sir Herbert Baker, published an article touting the curative powers of Doctor's Cave, the beach became an overnight hit. The first hotels appeared, most notably the Casa Blanca Hotel, which quickly became a favorite of the elite during the mid-January to mid-March season (it closed its doors for the rest of the year). The British Army Military Band used to travel to Montego Bay once a month to perform at the Casa Blanca Hotel, and the diesel train that carried tourists who had arrived by sea in Kingston became known as the 'Casa Blanca Special.' Alas, the famous cave was destroyed along with the original Casa Blanca Hotel (since rebuilt) during a 1932 hurricane.

The Jet-Set Age
During WWII the US Air Force built an airstrip east of town. In the post-war years it served to open up Montego Bay to tourism on a larger scale. Round Hill and Tryall Resorts were built west of town and became emblematic of a new breed of exclusive resorts that cemented Jamaica's reputation for chic. In the 1960s, the government lent its financial muscle to sponsoring the tourism trade, and hotels have been going up ever since.

In the late 1960s the west side of the bay was dredged and Montego Freeport constructed on 35 acres of fill. Later, a separate cruise-ship terminal appeared, launching a new breed of visitor (in 1994, a new 30,000-sq-foot cruise terminal opened). As an industrial and commercial site, however, the freeport languished for two decades. It is finally thriving as a center of the garment industry, furniture manufacturers, data processing, and other light industry.

ORIENTATION
There are two Montego Bays. The tourist quarter, north of the town center, arcs along Gloucester Ave, a narrow shoreline boulevard lined with hotels, restaurants, and public beaches. Gloucester Ave becomes Kent Ave, which stretches along what used to be called Chatham Sea Wall and ends at tiny Dead-End Beach, with the airport just beyond. The airport is accessed from Sunset Blvd, which continues east as the A1 to Ironshore and the north-coast resorts. A steep hill rises behind the tourist strip. Queen's Drive traverses the hill: it begins at the airport and ends at a roundabout (traffic circle) at the southern end of Gloucester Ave.

The town center lies immediately south of the roundabout. Fort St leads from the roundabout to Sam Sharpe Square, MoBay's vibrant heart. The compact historic center is roughly laid out as a grid of confusing, narrow one-way streets. St James St, the bustling main street, runs south from Sam Sharpe Square and ends at Barnett St, the main thoroughfare into town when approaching from the west. South of Barnett St is the predominantly industrial area of Catherine Hall and the sugarcane fields of Bogue.

Barnett St is prone to traffic jams. An alternate route into and out of town is Howard Cooke Drive, which runs south along the bayfront from the above mentioned roundabout to Montego Freeport.

If you're newly arrived and want to get a feel for what's where in town, consider a guided tour of Montego Bay (see Organized Tours below). One option is a short walking tour of downtown, which starts at the Cage on Sam Sharpe Square (☎ 979-3000, fax 979-8368).

Maps
The 'Discover Jamaica' map published by the JTB includes a detailed and accurate city map of Montego Bay. You can obtain a free copy at the JTB office at the entrance to Cornwall Beach or at the JTB information booth on Fort St and the one at the Craft Market downtown.

INFORMATION
Tourist Offices
Your first stop in MoBay should be the JTB, which runs a regional office off Gloucester

Ave, opposite the entrance to Cornwall Beach (PO Box 67, ☎ 952-4425, fax 952-3587). Much of their literature is hidden away in file cabinets, but the staff is helpful.

There's also a JTB information office next to the public library east of the round-about on Fort St, one in the Crafts Market on the corner of Market and Harbour Sts, and another in the immigration hall at Sangster International Airport.

Downtown, Swift Deliveries has a tourist information and booking office inside the Cage on Sam Sharpe Square. There's also a Transport Centre & Visitor Information center (☎ 953-9007) in the Blue Diamond Shopping Center at Ironshore; they operate tours islandwide through Utas Tours & Rent-a-Car.

For general information on Jamaica, call in at the Jamaica Information Service at 16 East St (☎ 952-0544). It's not a tourist bureau: its services and pamphlets are oriented toward Jamaicans and cover issues such as business opportunities and domestic issues.

Foreign Consulates
The US embassy in Kingston maintains a consulate in the St James Shopping Plaza on Gloucester Ave (☎ 952-0160 or 952-5050). Likewise, there's a Canadian consulate at 29 Gloucester Ave (☎ 952-6198), next to the Belvedere Hotel, and a British consulate (☎ 953-2231).

If you overstay or otherwise need assistance with immigration formalities, there's a Jamaican Immigration Office on the 3rd floor of Overton Plaza. It's open Monday to Thursday 8:30 am to 1 pm and 2 to 5 pm.

Money
You'll find a money-exchange bureau immediately beyond the immigration booths in the arrival hall at Sangster International Airport. It's open 24 hours. This is your only chance to change money legally at the airport, though many of the locals lingering outside the customs hall will be happy to change your money into Jamaica dollars; expect to get fleeced if you accept

their black-market rates. You'll do better in town (see below).

Unless you plan on taking the bus into town, you won't need local currency, as taxis accept US dollars. You can obtain Jamaican dollars later.

Banks There are plenty of banks in town, including two on Gloucester Ave: Mutual Security Bank (☎ 952-6320) at the corner of Ewin Drive and a Century National branch (☎ 952-9485) at 166 Gloucester Ave, just north of Burger King. There's also a Scotiabank in the new Half Moon Shopping Centre, east of Ironshore. Downtown branches are centered on Sam Sharpe Square.

I've found the Bank of Nova Scotia (☎ 952-4440) more efficient than Mutual Security Bank. Both have ATM machines, usually with long lines. Downtown banks can get very crowded. To avoid long lines, make your transactions at the Jamaica Citizens Bank in the new LOJ Shopping Centre on Howard Cooke Drive. A branch of National Commercial Bank serves passengers arriving at the cruise-ship terminal.

Most banks are open Monday to Thursday 9 am to 2 or 3 pm and until 4 pm on Friday.

Hotels Most hotels can change international currency for Jamaican dollars, but rates vary widely. A few hotels convert at the official exchange rate; others charge as much as 10% below the official rate.

Street Dealers Although exchanging cash on the black market is illegal, many penny-pinching travelers seek out street dealers, encouraging a significant covert trade. Money-changers linger outside the main banks on Sam Sharpe Square and along Gloucester Ave. The going rate is usually only about 5% (rarely more than 10%) better than the official exchange rate, which is hardly worth risking a potential rip-off. Beware of scams. *Never* hand over your dollars until you've received and counted your Jamaica dollars.

¡Cuba Sí!

You won't be long in Jamaica before noticing posters advertising excursions to Cuba, which lies just 90 miles to the north of Jamaica. The two islands are as different as chalk and cheese. For US citizens, the temptation to visit an island that Washington has dubbed off-limits holds a compelling allure (more than 20,000 US citizens visited Cuba in 1995 – mostly through Canada, Mexico, the Bahamas, Jamaica, and other Caribbean islands).

I've flown into Cuba from Jamaica several times: there have always been *yanquis* on board, alongside Europeans eager to discover how Cuba fits with their image. All you need is your passport and a tourist visa issued on the spot by any of the Jamaican companies that specialize in excursions to this intriguing island of socialism and sensuality. Flight times vary according to the aircraft used: Santiago de Cuba is about 40 minutes from Montego Bay; Havana about 90 minutes.

Despite its hardships and faults, Cuba is a profound experience that far exceeds most visitors' expectations. It is exhilarating in a way that Jamaica is not. It stirs one's passions and deeply touches heart and soul. I recommend Havana, to which visitors reactions widely vary. I *love* this city of tropical charms!

Three decades of negative reporting have led foreign visitors to expect a dour experience. The opposite is true. Sure, the average Cuban's standard of living has plummeted since the collapse of the Soviet Union, Cuba's erstwhile umbilical cord during 33 years of a harrowing and far-reaching US trade embargo that still hangs like an ax over Cuba. And much of Havana is seedy and crumbling and sorely in need of a pot of paint. But you won't see any of the wood-and-tin hovels and grinding poverty of Jamaica. The art, dance, and music scenes far outshine those of Jamaica. Walking Havana's streets is otherworldly surreal, like living inside a romantic thriller. As author Pico Iyer wrote: 'The tourist's exciting adventures have stakes he cannot fathom.'

Havana is a far cry from other Caribbean backwaters that call themselves capitals – including Kingston. The Spanish colonial buildings hard up against the Atlantic are handsome indeed. The edifices are astounding. Old Havana (proclaimed a World Heritage Site by UNESCO in 1982, and currently being restored to haughty grandeur) is an exhilarating 350-acre repository of castles, churches, and columned mansions dating back centuries.

And Cuban communism, you'll soon discover, doesn't mean you can't have fun. Habaneros relish a *joie de vivre* that makes Jamaica's look tame. Cuba blends Caribbean rhythms with Latin sensuality. Music – salsa, rhumba, and hip-swiveling *despolete* – is everywhere. Discos are top-class and throb to the latest sounds: world-beat, hip-hop, and soca. There are bohemian cafes spilling onto colonial plazas. And at bars such as La Bodeguita and El Floridita, you can sit with Ernest Hemingway's ghost and savor the proletarian fusion of dialectics and rum.

You won't want to leave without visiting a cigar factory, permeated with intoxicating tobacco aromas and revolutionary slogans that exhort workers to maintain strict quality: *La calidad es respecto al pueblo*, or 'Quality is respect for people.'

Then there's the countryside – even more beautiful than that of Jamaica. And the Cubans – an incredibly gifted, generous, courteous, and intellectual people – will steal your heart!

Contrary to outdated rumors of 'tourist apartheid,' foreign visitors can travel freely and mingle with Cubans without restraint. Getting around is easy via taxi or rental car, though the numerous public buses are as crowded and dismal as those of Jamaica. Now is a particularly fascinating time to visit. The island is awakening from a political time warp and is inching toward a market economy.

What Uncle Sam Says

The US government's Trading with the Enemy Act, while not actually banning US citizens from traveling to Cuba, prohibits them from spending money there or otherwise engaging in financial transactions with Cuba. To spend even one cent, a US citizen must have a

Treasury Dept license, which is granted only to journalists, academic researchers, and Cuban-Americans with family in Cuba. However, if you purchase an all-inclusive package in Jamaica and don't actually spend any money in Cuba, your visit is entirely legal!

The Cuban government has an open-door policy and welcomes US tourists. Savvy to the complications faced by US tourists, Cuban immigration officials don't stamp passports. If you alert Jamaican immigration officials of your intent on going to Cuba, you risk having them stamp 'Departure to Cuba' in your passport.

Getting There & Away
Getting there is easy! Several Jamaica tour companies offer weekend and longer excursions using Cubana Airline charters from Montego Bay and Kingston. Most include airfare, transfers, city tours, some meals and entertainment, and accommodations for overnight trips. You can pay for your tour with a US credit card. However, US credit cards cannot be used in Cuba.

Caribic Vacations (69 Gloucester Ave, ☎ 979-0322, fax 979-3421) offers weekend, five-day, and weeklong excursions to Havana and Varadero, Cuba's main beach resort. Flights leave Montego Bay each Friday and Sunday (US$179 one-way, US$199 round-trip, including tourist visa). Caribic also has offices on Norman Manley Blvd in Negril (☎ 957-3309, fax 957-3208) and in Ocean Village Plaza in Ocho Rios (☎ 974-9106, fax 974-9107). It offers a choice of hotels, with two-day packages as low as US$289, double occupancy. They even have packages to an all-inclusive resort on Varadero Beach, owned by Jamaica's Super-Clubs chain.

InterCaribe (11½ Ardenne Rd, Kingston 10, ☎ 978-2108, fax 978-2686) offers similar excursions from both Kingston and Montego Bay.

Sunholidays (Fort St, or PO Box 531, Montego Bay 2, ☎ 952-5629, fax 979-0725) also provides one-day and weekend excursions to Cuba. Its 'Cuba for a Day' excursion to Santiago costs US$179 and the 'Weekend in Havana' excursion costs US$269, inclusive of airfare and sightseeing.

Keep an eye out for Lonely Planet's new guide to Cuba. ∎

Wire Transfers If you need to have money wired from abroad, Western Union is at 19 Church St (☎ 979-9125), at the corner with Orange St. American Express is represented by Stuart's Travel at 32 Market St (☎ 952-4350); it's open Monday to Thursday 9 am to 2 pm, and Fridays 9 am to noon and 2 to 5 pm.

Post & Communications

The main post office (☎ 952-7016) is on the west side of Fort St. It's open 9 am to 4:30 pm Monday to Saturday. The lines can be excruciatingly long. If you only want to mail postcards or letters, do it through your hotel's front desk. You can have mail held at the post office (have it sent c/o Poste Restante, General Post Office, Montego Bay No 1, St James, Jamaica).

If you want to mail packages, your best bet is UPS, which has an office at Shop No 3 in the Miranda Ridge Plaza at 36 Gloucester Ave (☎ 979-0292). Alternately, if speed is of the essence and money no object, consider either Federal Express (32 Queens Drive, ☎ 952-0411) or DHL (34 Queen's Drive, ☎ 979-0543). Also see the yellow pages for other air-courier services.

The Jamaica International Telecommunications office, just east of the fort on Fort St, is open 9 am to 7 pm Monday to Friday. It advertises cellular service 8 am to 4 pm Monday to Friday and until noon on Saturdays. You can also make calls and send and receive faxes through the Telephone Centre at Shop No 158 in the City Centre Building; it also offers 'mini postal' and courier services.

Travel Agencies

Montego Bay has plenty of travel agencies. Two of the more reputable agencies include International Travel Services at 26 St James St (☎ 952-2485) and Stuart's Travel at 32 Market St (☎ 952-4350). The concierges at upscale hotels will be happy to make most reservations that a travel agency can arrange.

Bookshops

Most gift stores and pharmacies sell a limited range of leading international magazines, newspapers, and books. Books are usually limited to Jamaican cookbooks, Bob Marley biographies, and tour guides. For a wider variety, including novels, try Sangster's Bookshop at 2 St James St (☎ 952-0319), which is the largest bookstore in town. Also try Ray of Light Bookshop at 11 King St (☎ 979-9154) or Henderson's Book Store at 27 St James St (☎ 952-2551). Most 'bookshops' in Jamaica are primarily stationers and office supply stores.

Libraries

The parish library, opposite the City Centre Shopping Centre on the south side of Fort St (☎ 952-4185), has quiet reading rooms and an impressive collection of books in English on Jamaica.

Film

Four stores sell film and photographic equipment in town: Green's Computer & Photographic Services at 14 Market St (☎ 940-1395), Ventura Photo Service at 22 Market St, Salmon's Colour Lab on Sam Sharpe Square (☎ 952-4527), and Photo Express at 57 St James St (☎ 952-3120). None of the counter clerks I've talked to are the least bit knowledgeable about photography.

Slide film, especially Fuji, is difficult to find. Agfachrome is widely available, as is Ektachrome, but if you use professional film such as Fuji's Velvia, you're out of luck. Ventura, which also has a store three miles east of town in the Half Moon Shopping Centre, has a 15-minute passport and visa photo service.

Laundry

You'll find a self-service laundry at the Fabricare Centre at 4 Corner Lane (☎ 952-6897). It also offers one-hour drycleaning plus laundry service, as does Ucon Laundry & Dry-Cleaners at 3 Love Lane (☎ 952-6105).

Medical Services

Montego Bay has two public hospitals. The main hospital is Cornwall Regional Hospital high above town just off Mount Salem Rd (☎ 952-5100). It has a 24-hour emergency department. Eldemire Hospital is at 3 Orange St (☎ 952-2620). Like all public health facilities in Jamaica, you can expect lengthy delays for all but emergencies.

Doctor's Hospital (☎ 952-1616) is a private hospital in Fairfield southeast of town; it accepts most international insurance coverage.

There are dozens of doctors to choose from. Try Cornwall Medical Centre at 19 Orange St (☎ 979-6107). Doctors on Call (☎ 979-0283), a physicians group, will send a doctor to your hotel. In Ironshore, the Northwestern Medical Service & Microlab (☎ 953-9299) is in the Blue Diamond Shopping Centre. Blue Cross of Jamaica has its headquarters at 3 King St (☎ 952-4448, fax 979-7868); the staff may be able to offer referrals.

Pharmacies are a dime a dozen downtown. Try Hilton's Pharmacy at 27 St James St (☎ 952-2455). It's open Monday to Saturday 8 am to 4:30 pm (until 5 pm on Fridays).

Emergency

In the case of an emergency call:

Rape Crisis Center	☎ 929-2997
Police	☎ 119 or 952-2333
at Ironshore	☎ 953-2229
Air-Sea Rescue	☎ 119
Ambulance	☎ 110
Fire	☎ 110 or 952-2311

Dangers & Annoyances

Although the JTB valiantly tries to counter Jamaica's poor reputation on crime and harassment, the raw reality is that crime is serious enough to warrant caution (I know two locally born Jamaicans who have been robbed at gun point in MoBay, for example), and harassment is a pervasive petty annoyance.

By day there is really no danger to foreign visitors. You can walk virtually anywhere without worries. And Gloucester Ave is safe at night. However, don't walk downtown or on any backstreets at night, especially alone. The streets are ill-lit and you risk being mugged or worse.

Your greatest danger is from traffic. Montego Bay's roads are narrow and often you'll be forced to step onto them. Cars are often driven at break-neck pace. Don't expect the driver to give way, use extra caution when crossing streets, and watch for gutters and potholes in the road and sidewalk.

By far the biggest annoyance is persistent, often pushy importuning by male hustlers trying to sell you something or attach themselves to you as a guide as you walk down the street. Each year the situation improves, but this petty harassment can detract from your enjoyment. Many hustlers will accept 'no thanks' for an answer. A few will attempt to make you feel guilty: 'You a racist?' You'll hear a gamut of crafty lines to get you to open your wallet. Often a hustler will approach you with his hand extended in a greeting. The natural temptation is to shake it, but once you do you're on the hook. 'Remember me?' is one of the favorite lines used on naive tourists, even though you know you've never set eyes on the guy (or woman) before. Both male and female visitors can expect to be approached in none-too-subtle terms by locals offering their services as gigolos and 'good-time girls.'

In 1993, the Ministry of Tourism funded a Montego Bay Resort Patrol, which involves uniformed men and women patrolling the streets. They usually patrol in pairs and wear dark-blue military-style uniforms, with black berets, and truncheons (nightsticks).

Stop by the Jamaica Tourist Board and pick up a little pamphlet on 'Helpful Hints for Your Vacation,' which discusses practical pointers to help you avoid trouble.

CHURCH ST

Many of the most interesting buildings in town are clustered along Church St, the most picturesque street in MoBay. One of these – an octagonal structure – stands at the corner of Water Lane. The two-story plantation-style building today houses a

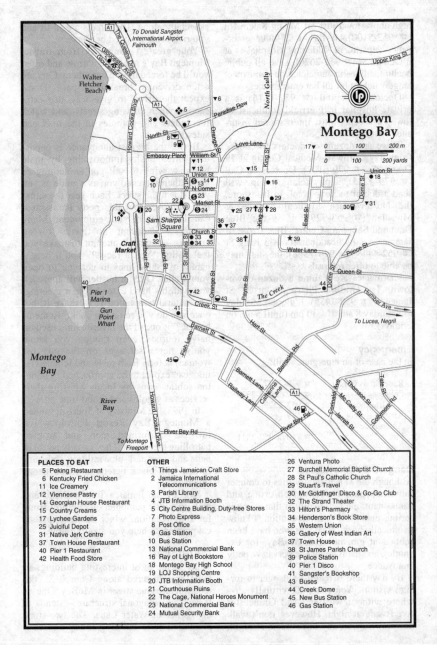

Downtown Montego Bay

0   100   200 m
0   100   200 yards

PLACES TO EAT
5   Peking Restaurant
6   Kentucky Fried Chicken
11 Ice Creamery
12 Viennese Pastry
14 Georgian House Restaurant
15 Country Creams
17 Lychee Gardens
25 Juiciful Depot
31 Native Jerk Centre
37 Town House Restaurant
40 Pier 1 Restaurant
42 Health Food Store

OTHER
1   Things Jamaican Craft Store
2   Jamaica International
    Telecommunications
3   Parish Library
4   JTB Information Booth
5   City Centre Building, Duty-free Stores
7   Photo Express
8   Post Office
9   Gas Station
10 Bus Station
13 National Commercial Bank
16 Ray of Light Bookstore
18 Montego Bay High School
19 LOJ Shopping Centre
20 JTB Information Booth
21 Courthouse Ruins
22 The Cage, National Heroes Monument
23 National Commercial Bank
24 Mutual Security Bank

26 Ventura Photo
27 Burchell Memorial Baptist Church
28 St Paul's Catholic Church
29 Stuart's Travel
30 Mr Goldfinger Disco & Go-Go Club
32 The Strand Theater
33 Hilton's Pharmacy
34 Henderson's Book Store
35 Western Union
36 Gallery of West Indian Art
37 Town House
38 St James Parish Church
39 Police Station
41 Pier 1 Disco
41 Sangster's Bookshop
43 Buses
44 Creek Dome
45 New Bus Station
46 Gas Station

police station. Its wide veranda is supported by square, fluted columns. Fifty yards west, at the corner of King St, is a splendidly maintained, pretty white-fronted building housing the First Life Insurance Co. Its Georgian doorway is lit by brass lamps, and there's an English-style garden behind. Equally impressive is the three-story, pink-stuccoed Georgian building with a soaring hardwood door at 25 Church St, also on the corner with King St, which today houses the headquarters of Jamaica Telecommunications Ltd.

Burchell Memorial Baptist Church
A brief detour one block north along King St leads to this red-brick structure, which dates to 1835. It's not at all pretty, but it plays an important part in local history. Samuel Sharpe, who led the Christmas slave revolt of 1831, was a deacon here. The original church was founded in 1824 by Rev Thomas Burchell. An angry mob of colonialists destroyed the church in reprisal for Burchell's support of the emancipation cause, but the missionary escaped to sea. Sam Sharpe's remains are buried in the vault.

The concrete hulk across the street is St Paul's Catholic Church.

St James Parish Church
Once regarded as the finest church on the island, the parish church of St James on Church St is still impressive. Supposedly, it is *not* named for James II, King of England, as is the parish; the English adopted the name of the original Spanish church on the site, which was dedicated to Santiago (St James), the patron saint of Spain – a handy coincidence.

The current church was built between 1775 and 1782 in the shape of a Greek cross and has suffered greatly with the years. You can still see signs of the extensive damage inflicted by the earthquake of March 1, 1957. The church was so shaken that it had to be rebuilt. By the look of the toppled and desecrated tombs, the graveyard was also badly knocked about.

With luck the tall church doors will be open (if not, call ☎ 952-2775 to arrange a visit) and you can view the beautiful interior, which contains a stunning stained-glass window behind the altar. Note the intriguing marble monuments, including fine works by John Bacon, the foremost English sculptor of his day. One is a memorial to Rosa Palmer, whose virtuous life was up-ended and misshapen in literature to create the legend of the White Witch of Rose Hall. Look carefully at the neck and you'll detect faint purple marks. Locals consider this a sign of the truth of the fable that the 'Witch' was strangled.

The Town House
The most famous historic building in town is at 16 Church St. The Town House's handsome red-brick frontage is buried under a cascade of bougainvillea and laburnum. It dates from 1765, when it was the home of a wealthy merchant. It has since served as a church manse and then as a town house for the mistress of the Earl of Hereford, Governor of Jamaica circa 1850. In this century, it has been used as a hotel, warehouse, Masonic lodge, lawyer's office, and synagogue. An intriguing curiosity is the bullet hole in the mahogany staircase – the result of a feud between a husband and his wife's lover. Today the Town House is home to a splendid restaurant (see Places to Eat below).

Other Buildings
An equally absorbing historic building next to the Town House, on the corner of Orange St, houses the Gallery of West Indian Art. After browsing here, walk two blocks north along Orange St to the Georgian House, at the corner of Union St. This magnificent brick-and-stone house with a bow-shaped frontage is today the Georgian House Restaurant. There are actually two buildings here: the original owner, a wealthy merchant, apparently housed his wife in one and his mistress in the other.

Two blocks west of the Town House, at Church and Strand Sts, is the 1930s-era **Strand Theater**.

SAM SHARPE SQUARE

This bustling, cobbled square – an important center for political rallies and speeches during election times – is centered on a small bronze fountain (painted silver) dedicated to Captain J Kerr, a member of a prominent local family and a pioneer in the banana trade.

The square, formerly called the Parade, is named for national hero the Right Excellent Samuel Sharpe (1801 – 1832), leader of the weeklong Christmas Rebellion that erupted on December 28, 1831,

engulfing much of the region (see the Preaching Resistance sidebar). At the square's northwest corner is an impressive bronze statue of Paul Bogle and Sam Sharpe, Bible in hand, speaking to three admiring listeners. It was sculpted by local artist Kay Sullivan.

The **Cage**, a little cut-stone and red-brick building, was built in 1806 as a lockup for vagrants, disorderly seamen, and runaway slaves. The bell in the tiny belfry was rung at 2 pm every day to provide country slaves with one hour by

Preaching Resistance

The weeklong Christmas Rebellion that began on Kensington Estate on December 27, 1831, and engulfed much of the Montego Bay region was the most serious slave revolt to rock colonial Jamaica. Its impact and the public outcry over the terrible retribution that followed were catalysts for British Parliament passing the Abolition Bill in 1834.

The instigator of the revolt was Samuel Sharpe (1801 – 1832), the slave of a Montego Bay solicitor. He was one of few literate slaves. Sharpe acted as a deacon of Montego Bay's Burchell Baptist Church and became a 'daddy,' or leader, of native Baptists. Religious meetings were the only legal gatherings for slaves, and Sharpe used his forum to encourage passive rebellion. He also formed a secret society dedicated to securing emancipation. After reading about debates over slavery in the British Parliament, he became convinced that emancipation had been granted.

In 1831 Sharpe counseled fellow slaves to refuse to work during the Christmas holidays unless estate owners agreed to address their grievances. Word of the passive rebellion spread throughout St James and neighboring parishes. Inevitably, word leaked out and warships and extra troops were sent to Montego Bay.

The passive rebellion turned into a violent conflict when the Kensington Estate was set on fire. Soon, plantations and great houses throughout northwest Jamaica were ablaze, and Sharpe's noble plan was usurped by wholesale violence. Fourteen colonialists were murdered. The superior military might of the colonial authorities, however, soon suppressed the revolt. Swift and cruel retribution followed.

It is thought that the militia killed more than 1000 slaves during and after the conflict. Day after day for six weeks following the revolt's suppression, magistrates of the Montego Bay Courthouse handed down death sentences to scores of slaves, who were hanged two at a time on the Parade, among them 'Daddy' Sam Sharpe. He was later named a national hero. ■

which to leave town or face imprisonment for breaking a curfew on blacks.

On the southwest corner is the charred ruin of the colonial **courthouse** that burned down a few years ago.

FORT MONTEGO

Virtually nothing remains of the main fort, which once stood atop the hill above Gloucester Ave. The sole remnant, a small battery with three brass cannons on rails, is on Fort St behind Walter Fletcher Beach. Sadly, not much effort has gone into sprucing up even this morsel for the tourist trade.

The erstwhile fort that guarded the bay figured in the history books only for two tragic mishaps. In 1760 during celebrations over the taking of Havana, a cannon exploded, killing the gunner. The only time the fort's cannons were fired on a ship (in 1795) proved equally lamentable. The ship – the schooner *Mercury* – had been mistaken for an enemy vessel. Fortunately no damage was done.

CREEK DOME

The Creek Dome, at the corner of Dome and Creek Sts, was built in 1837 above an underground spring that supplied the drinking water for Montego Bay. Until 1894, when piped water was introduced, slaves would line up at the Dome with *yabbas* on their heads. Despite its name, the structure is actually a sextagon with a crenelated castle turret.

BARNETT ESTATE

The sea of sugarcane south of Montego Bay is part of Barnett Estate, a plantation owned and operated since 1755 by the Kerr-Jarretts, one of Jamaica's preeminent families, whose holdings once included most of the Montego Bay area (Rose Hall and Greenwood Great Houses, east of Montego Bay, were both part of the original Kerr-Jarrett estates). The plantation, still family-owned and operated after 11 generations, was recently opened for plantation tours.

Tours begin at a visitors center, formerly the plantation manager's house, which doubles as a museum charting the development of the area since the day that Colonel Nicholas Jarrett arrived with Cromwell's invasion army in 1655. The family has been at the vanguard of Jamaican history ever since. The **Bellfield Great House**, built in 1735, has been exquisitely restored and is now a showcase of elite 18th-century colonial living. Well-informed guides in period costume lead you from room to room, each one furnished in precise period detail. Mannequins representing members of the Kerr family are intended to add a little 'life' to the settings. You'll want your camera for the view over Montego Bay from the veranda.

You'll then hop aboard a jitney for a ride through the 3000-acre estate to see how bananas, coconuts, mangos, and other exotic crops are grown commercially. Before leaving, take time to sample jerk chicken or pork at the thatched Sugar Mill Bar & Jerk Centre, constructed from the sugar mill built in 1794. Plans for horseback riding, a botanical garden, an aviary, and a gourmet restaurant are in the works.

Entrance with guided tour costs US$12. For information contact Barnett Estates, PO Box 876 (☎ 952-2382, fax 952-6342). The estate is located along Barnett St just north of the Montego River.

BEACHES
Cornwall Beach

This 100-yard-wide swath of white sand is enclosed within a wire-fence compound behind St James Shopping Plaza. It's well served by facilities. The beach (☎ 952-5796) is popular with topless bathers. At its core is the Bird Watcher's Bar, built around a massive almond tree (count your change carefully – I've been shortchanged here twice). On the left are changing rooms, plus a snack bar with lackadaisical service, an ice-cream shop, hair-braiding and manicure shop, and a crafts stall. The snack bar serves sandwiches (from US$2), steam fish fillet (US$5), and fish & chips (US$4.50). There's a volleyball court in the sand, and a dance stage for nighttime concerts. Hustling here is minimal, but you may still be importuned to buy jewelry, trinkets, or drugs. If tempted by the latter, discretion is advised; the beach is small and very public. Entrance costs US$0.50. Lifeguards are on duty from 9 am to 5 pm.

Doctor's Cave Beach

MoBay's main beach (☎ 952-2566) is immediately south of Cornwall Beach. Though crowded on weekends when locals flock here, it's a great place if you want to socialize with Jamaicans without being hassled. The deep, wide, white-sand beach, which is administered as a private bathing club by a group of wealthy Montegonians, is hidden behind a grotesque wall. There's a bar, snack bar, gift shop, and water sports, plus changing rooms, which are rather grubby. It's open 8 am to 6 pm. Entrance costs US$0.60.

Walter Fletcher Beach

This long sliver of white sand is mostly the domain of locals. I suspect this is so because the beach *seems* inaccessible and unwelcoming due to the high wire fences enclosing an unkempt seaside park unimaginatively laid out by the Urban Development Council (the park has been disgustingly littered in years past, though last time I passed by the situation had improved). The beach (☎ 952-5783) is named for Walter Fletcher, who among other achievements brought the first Pan Am charter to Montego Bay. You'll find netball (US$3) and tennis courts (US$1.15). Lockers are available for US$1.60. It's open 9 am to 5 pm, and entrance costs US$1 for adults, US$0.70 for children.

Other Beaches

Two tiny white-sand beaches lie just west of Walter Fletcher Beach and are free of charge. Also free are pocket-size Chatham and Dead-End Beaches, both on Kent Ave. Chatham Beach is opposite Sandals Inn; Dead-End is at the end of the road. They're popular at night with locals who cool off after dark. You may see many local couples clinging tightly semisubmerged. Don't ask what they're doing – living

arrangements are often crowded, and the warm, calm shallows provide perfect cover for lovemaking.

WATER SPORTS

Dream Machines (☎ 952-5675) offers water sports on Cornwall Beach. Take your pick of activities, from a banana-boat ride (US$10) to water skiing (US$20) to scuba diving (from US$35) to sunfish sailing (US$25). MoBay Windsurfing (☎ 952-5505) runs a similar concession at Doctor's Cave Beach. Both concessions also offer parasailing, snorkeling, and sea-kayaking. You can also take a glass-bottomed boat (US$10) out to the reef, where the snorkeling is good amid the turquoise and azure shallows. Mr Joe offers rides from Dead-End Beach (US$10 per hour, including snorkeling).

SPORT FISHING

The waters off Jamaica's north coast are especially good for game fishing. Beyond the north-shore reefs, the ocean floor plummets steeply for thousands of feet. The abyss is part of the Cayman Trench, the deepest ocean canyon in the Caribbean. You can see it from shore, a great river of deep indigo against the lighter blues. Deep-water gamefish use it as a migratory freeway. Kingfish, yellowfin tuna, wahoo, and barracuda run through the channel year-round, as do blue marlin, the grand prize of sport fishing. September to April is best for marlin (June and August are peak months), but 'Marlin Alley,' as the trench is known, offers weighty catches in all months.

Half- and full-day charters can be booked through hotels or at Pier 1 Marina. Expect to pay about US$250 for a half-day charter. Be sure to clarify in advance what the fee includes. A full day's notice and a 50% deposit are usually required.

SAILING & CRUISING

A large selection of yachts and small cruise boats operate party cruises. Most companies charge US$35 for three-hour party cruises, and US$25 to US$35 for sunset and dinner cruises. Check around, as prices vary. Most vessels sail from Pier 1.

One of the better known vessels is the *Jamaica Queen IV* (☎ 953-3992), a double-decked, 61-foot-long, glass-bottom catamaran specially designed as a party boat. You can dance to the pulsating beat of soca and reggae on a day cruise over the coral reefs, or on a sunset cruise, or dinner cruise with open bar. It even has a Saturday night disco cruise.

I like the *Calico* (☎ 952-5860), a 55-foot ketch faintly resembling an old pirate ship. Party cruises sail from Pier 1 at 10 am and 3 pm daily, except Monday. A sunset cruise is also offered at 5 pm Wednesday to Saturday. A similar option is the *Mary Ann*, a 57-foot ketch that also offers day and evening party cruises from Sandals Royal Caribbean (☎ 952-5505). Rhapsody Cruises (42 Fort St, ☎ 979-0104, fax 979-0101) offers three-hour 'fun' (US$50) and two-hour sunset cruises (US$25) aboard the *Montrose*.

Jamaica Rose Ltd offers charters aboard *La Express*, a 54-foot sailing yacht. If you want to travel in style, consider a sunset cruise aboard *Four Stars*, a venerable motor cruiser once owned by band leader Guy Lombardo, author Sloane Wilson *(Man in the Gray Flannel Suit)*, and singers Steve Lawrence and Eydie Gorme. Both are docked at Norma's at the Wharf at Reading, a few miles west of town (see Reading below).

You can charter yachts for private group sailing trips from any of the above companies. To charter a private yacht, contact the Montego Bay Yacht Club (☎ 979-8038, fax 979-8262).

SCUBA DIVING

The site of Jamaica's first marine sanctuary, MoBay offers highly rated dive sites, most of which lie close to shore and vary from shallow patch reefs to awe-inspiring walls. Visibility is usually 60 to 100 feet; water temperature never falls below 68° F.

The large sponges at deeper sites such as **Basket Reef** are spectacular. Another choice site is **Black Coral Alley**, a canyon

---

Montego Bay Marine Park

Destruction of mangroves, sewage and industrial-waste runoff, overfishing, and depletion of coral and shells by collectors have all contributed to a decline in the health of the Montego Bay reef ecosystem in recent decades. In 1992, the Montego Bay Marine Park was established as the first national park in Jamaica with an aim to conserve and manage the coral reefs, mangroves, and seabed grasses (see the Coral Ecology section in Facts about Jamaica).

The park extends from the eastern end of Sangster International Airport westward (nine km) to the Great River and covers an area of 6000 acres (almost 10 sq miles) of bay to a depth of 100 feet.

Regulations are being developed for managing the park and enforcing restrictions. For example, fishing is restricted to designated areas, allowing fish populations to recover. Water sports are also limited to designated areas. Boats are required to use mooring buoys and can no longer anchor at will atop the coral. And collecting shells or coral is now prohibited.

To do your bit, *don't* buy coral jewelry or shells, however great the temptation!

The park is headquartered at the Cornwall Beach Complex (PO Box 67, ☎ 952-9709). ■

---

lined with black coral trees. **Widowmakers Cave** is famous for being swarmed by wrasses, barracuda, and parrot fish. If nurse sharks, hammerheads, and rays appeal, head out to the **Point**. There's even a DC-3 wreck at **Airport Reef**. Beginners explore the shallow reef close to shore off Doctor's Cave Beach. Some of the shallow reefs have been badly denuded over the past few decades and are now protected.

Organized Diving

Half-a-dozen dive companies operate out of MoBay. Most offer dive courses from beginner to dive master and will certify you through the PADI Open Water Dive Course, which costs US$350 to US$375.

Most companies charge US$35 for a single dive and US$55 for two dives. Many of the large resorts have their own operations.

A Dutch couple, Hannie and Theo Smit, operate Poseidon Divers (PO Box 152, Reading, St James, ☎ 952-3624 or (800) 880-5224, fax 952-3079) at Marguerite's Restaurant on Gloucester Ave and at Reading Reef Club. Besides offering dive courses, they also rent scuba equipment for US$15 per item between 8:30 am to 3 pm daily (closed Sunday). Similar dives and courses are offered by Resort Divers Pro-Shop (Shop No 8 in the LOJ Shopping Center, ☎ 952-4285, fax 952-4288). Reef Keeper Divers (☎ 979-0104, fax 979-0101) runs a full range of snorkeling and diving excursions, as well as certification courses; they also rent equipment. Tony Callaghan of Tango Divers (☎ 952-3474) offers a NAUI certification course for US$350, plus a beginners resort course (US$75). Jamaica Scuba Divers is based at the Half Moon Resort (☎ 953-2211, fax 953-2731). Scuba Connection (☎ 952-4780) has an outlet at Club Paradise Sea Gardens and is open from 10 am to 1 pm.

All the above companies offer snorkeling trips, usually for US$15 (one hour).

Dives for Non-Divers
Snuba, available at Cornwall Beach, is an ingenious way for non-divers to commune with the fishes. You dive using a breathing apparatus attached to an oxygen tank that floats above (US$25 for one hour). Another option is the 'Undersea Semi-Submarine Tour' aboard a semi-submersible that operates from Pier 1 (contact Mo-Bay Undersea Tours, ☎ 940-2493 or 997-2893). It departs daily at 9 and 11 am, and 1:30 pm (US$34 adults, US$22 children). The vessel doesn't dive, but you look at the marine life through bubble-dome windows beneath the boat.

GOLF
If MoBay lives up to any boast, it's the excellent golfing. There are three championship golf courses just east of town (but within the city limits) at Ironshore, Half Moon, and Wyndham. A fourth course, the site of the Johnnie Walker World Championship, lies within easy reach at Tryall, a 30-minute journey west (see the Tryall Estate section in the West Coast chapter). Ironshore Golf & Country Club (☎ 953-2800) is a links-type course known for its blind-shot holes. My favorite is the Half Moon Golf & Country Club (☎ 953-2560), conceived by world-renowned coursedesigner Robert Trent Jones. The first nine holes are laid out along the shore; the back nine ripple sensationally uphill through Running Gut, a narrow limestone gorge. The former sugar factory has been turned into a club house. Wyndham Rose Hall Golf & Country Club (☎ 953-2650), home to the Jamaican Open and the International Junior Golf Championship, is known for its tricky windage and superb coastal vistas.

Caddies and clubs can be rented at all three. Don't worry that your caddy may carry your clubs on his head; he's used to it! Reservations are essential.

HORSEBACK RIDING
If you want to experience easy trail rides into the hills or along the beach, call the Double A Ranch at Holiday Inn Village in Ironshore (☎ 953-2319). A more comprehensive facility is Rocky Point Stables, a full-blown equestrian center nearby at Half Moon (PO Box 35, Falmouth, ☎ 953-2286). It offers riding lessons and adventure trail rides into the mountains and along the beach, daily at 9 am and 3 pm (90 minutes, US$40; three-hour rides cost US$50). You must wear long pants and shoes or sneakers. Another option is White Witch Stables (☎ 953-2746) located at Rose Hall Golf & Country Club.

RAFTING
Mountain Valley Rafting runs river trips down the Great River, beginning in Lethe (see Great River below).

ORGANIZED TOURS
Guided City Tours
If you've just arrived and want to get a feel for the town, consider a guided tour of

Montego Bay. Several local companies offer half-day tours. JUTA Tour Company on Claude Clarke Ave (PO Box 1155, ☎ 952-0813, fax 952-5355) and JCAL Tours Ltd, at 8 Queens Drive (PO Box 265, ☎ 952-7574, fax 952-7575), have 'Montego Bay Highlight' tours, as does Tropical Tours Ltd at 81 Barnett St (☎ 952-0400).

Heli-Sightseeing
For a bird's eye view of the MoBay environs, take to the air in a Bell Jet Ranger helicopter. Helitours Ltd at Montego Freeport (☎ 979-8290) offers tours by whirlybird. Options include a 15-minute 'Montego Bay Sun Run' (US$50) and 30-minute tour as far east as Rose Hall and Hampden Estates and west to Tryall (US$95), plus a hourlong trip over Cockpit Country – a fantastic way to see this rugged and stunningly scenic region (US$190). The trips are narrated; you listen through personal headphones (choppers are damn noisy) while looking down over the magnificent vistas through bubble windows. If you're a family or group, you can charter a chopper for a day (from US$2200). The company also has an office at 120 Main St (☎ 974-2265).

Before being taken over by Air Jamaica in late 1995, Trans Jamaica Airlines offered a one-day tour to Port Antonio for US$105 (☎ 952-5401), including round-trip flights, plus options for visiting Reach Falls, rafting on the Rio Grande, or touring the Blue Mountains; lunch is included. It may still do so under its new name: Air Jamaica Express (see Getting Around below).

Further Afield
More than a dozen companies slate options for touring locally and afield. I recommend Caribic Vacations at 69 Gloucester Ave (☎ 979-9387, fax 979-3421; or c/o headquarters at 1310 Providence Drive, Ironshore Estate, White Sands Beach PO, Montego Bay, ☎ 979-0114, fax 952-0981). The company offers a wide range of tour services, including excursions to Ocho Rios, Croydon Plantation, and Negril, plus a two-day all-Jamaica tour every Monday. The company also operates the 'Appleton Estate Rum Tour' in association with Jamaica Estate Tours (every Tuesday and Wednesday, US$65). It also arranges car rentals, transfers, and specialty excursions and tours, plus you can also book sailing trips or rafting trips on the Martha Brae and Great Rivers.

Jamaica Sightseeing, opposite the Toby Inn at 1 Kent Ave (PO Box 467, ☎ 952-4370, fax 979-3821), likewise runs a series of day tours as well as two-day (US$210) and three-day (US$275) tours around Jamaica. Vernon Chin, the owner, is very knowledgeable and helpful. His company specializes in personalized tours and special-interest groups (especially nature-oriented). Utas Tour, located in the Transport Centre in Blue Diamond Shopping Centre (☎ 979-0684), also has a series of full-day excursions to Dunn's River Falls (US$24), Kingston (US$60), and various attractions nationwide (PO Box 429, ☎ 979-0684, fax 979-3465). The company's three-day 'Jamaica Land We Love' tour takes in the whole island (US$391, including accommodations and meals).

Maroon Attraction Tours (32 Church St, ☎ 952-4546, fax 952-6203) offers a 'cultural, educational and historical tour' into Maroon Country. It claims to be 'the only legal tour.' Its all-day excursion from Montego Bay costs US$50, including breakfast in Maroon Town, plantation tour, and a village walk with the Colonel. Ava Simpson, Ken Watson, and Glen Harris run the trips every Tuesday and Thursday morning.

Other local tour and travel arrangers include Jamaica Tours Ltd at 686 Half Moon St in Coral Gardens (☎ 953-3132, fax 953-2107) and Glamour Tours (☎ 979-8207, fax 979-8168) in the LOJ Shopping Centre on Howard Cooke Drive. Jamaica Co-Op Auto & Limousine Tours at 8 Queen's Drive (☎ 952-7574, fax 952-7575) has a south-coast tour featuring YS Falls, the Great Morass, and Lover's Leap. Pro-Tours Ltd in Kingston (☎ 978-6113, fax 978-5473) runs trips from Montego

Bay to the Great Morass and Appleton Rum Estate on the southwest coast (Thursdays, US$88).

SPECIAL EVENTS
Reggae Sumfest
This internationally acclaimed reggae festival was first held in 1993, when Reggae Sunsplash fatefully moved from MoBay to Kingston. The five-day festival, held each August, begins with a beach party on Walter Fletcher Beach, followed by four different theme nights. The 1995 festival included more than 50 world-class reggae artists, including Buju Banton, Bunny Wailer, and Rita Marley.

Its venue has been in flux. It was first held at the Catherine Hall Entertainment Centre, although its permanent venue will probably be the Bob Marley Entertainment Centre on Howard Cooke Drive. In 1995 tickets cost from US$7 to US$25 per night. Tickets go on sale in Jamaica about two weeks before the concert. Full-week bracelets that allow you to attend all events cost US$100 to US$150. For more information, contact Summerfest Productions (☎ 979-1720).

Many tour operators run special Sumfest packages. In the USA, contact Jamaica Travel Specialist (2827 Mann Ave, Union City, CA 94587, ☎ (510) 489-9552 or (800) 544-5979); or Calypso Tours (3901 Grand Ave No 304, Oakland, CA 94610, ☎ (510) 653-3570 or (800) 852-6242). Both companies have special weeklong packages, as does Island Flight Vacations, which in past years has been the official tour operator for Sumfest (2130 Sawtelle Blvd, Suite 309, Los Angeles, CA 90025, ☎ (800) 426-4570). In England, Music Travel Centre (☎ 0171-383-7518) offers organized Sumfest tours.

Miami to Montego Bay Yacht Race
Sailers flock to Jamaica for this race, which takes place in mid-February. Its been an annual event since its conception in 1961, when the Jamaica Yachting Association and the Biscayne Bay Yacht Club of Florida initiated it as a biennial event. The challenging race was soon endorsed as a mandatory event in the World Ocean Racing Championships. Entries are varied by size. The event is also an excuse for four days of partying! Patrick O'Callaghan at the Montego Bay Yacht Club can provide information (☎ 952-0565).

Other Happenings
The MoBay No Problem 10K foot race, first held in January 1996, is intended to be an annual event. The event starts and ends at the Seawind Hotel. Entry is US$15. Contact the JTB for information.

An International Horse Show & Polo Match is held each February at Rocky Point Stables at Half Moon. The event includes dressage and show-jumping, as well as a polo competition (☎ 953-2286).

The Montego Bay Yacht Club hosts an Easter Regatta, or Jamaica Sailing Week, each March or April. The annual Montego Bay International Marlin Tournament is held in September, as it has been since 1967. For information on both events, contact Patrick O'Callaghan at the Montego Bay Yacht Club (☎ 952-0565).

The Heritage & Jazz Festival is held each October during Heroes Weekend at Nature Village Farm on the Great River (see the Nature Village Farm section under Lethe, below). The festival features a Heritage Village, Food Village, and Country Fair, with stalls displaying the culture, cuisine, and arts & crafts of Jamaica. Jazz performers from Jamaica and around the world give concerts and teach workshops in local schools. The festival raises funds for local charitable causes. Admission is J$350. Gates open at 11 am (☎ 979-7963 or 952-6231).

PLACES TO STAY
Montego Bay boasts the largest number of guest rooms of any resort area in Jamaica: over 4500. There's something for most budgets, though true budget accommodations are virtually nonexistent. The great majority of hotels are clustered near the beaches along Gloucester Ave, with a growing number of more exclusive resorts nestled on their own beaches east of town at Ironshore and Mahoe Bay. Many older

hotels are above town on Queen's Ave, where they catch the breezes.

Although many hotels are listed as guest houses, the definition is nebulous; the majority are no different than hotels (and are categorized as such below according to price), and the only self-proclaimed B&B in town does *not* include breakfast!

Several of the most deluxe resorts on the island can be found either side of town. You can also choose from a large selection of private villas. And there is also a wide choice of all-inclusive resorts. You need to research carefully if booking an all-inclusive hotel, however: standards vary markedly, and some resorts do *not* include water sports and certain services in their rates. The best all-inclusives are Breezes, the three Sandals' properties (for couples only), and Jack Tar Village. Many of the town's older hotels are dowdy and seem to be having difficulty competing with the newer all-inclusive hotels.

The following quotations are, with few exceptions, based on summer season rates (mid-April to mid-December); add 20% to 40% for high season. A 10% service charge and 12.5% Government Consumption Tax are automatically added to the bill at most hotels. Reservations are advised for more upscale properties. If you arrive without reservations, the JTB information booth in the immigration hall at Sangster International Airport can provide a list of approved hotels and guest houses. They'll call and make reservations for you.

Places to Stay – bottom end
The cheapest place I know is *Linkage Guest House* at 39 Church St (☎ 952-4546). The rooms are simple but clean. Rates begin at US$15/20 single/double. Discounts are offered for stays of a week or longer. Meals are served, and the owners offer Maroon heritage tours to Accompong and Cockpit Country.

The *YMCA* maintains a hostel on the south side of town at 28 Humber Ave (☎ 952-5368), well away from the tourist beat. Its 15 basic rooms have shared bathrooms (cold water) and cost US$15

to US$25. Fans can be rented. There's a TV lounge and table tennis. Women are welcome.

Alternately, try *Mountainside Guest House* on Queen's Drive, at the corner of Federal Ave (☎ 952-4685). Rooms in the US$15 range are simple but adequate, and they also allow *camping* for US$5 per person.

The cheapest hotel near the airport is *Ocean View Guest House* at 26 Sunset Blvd (☎ 952-2662). It's a bargain at US$23/30 single/double, although rooms are no-frills. Free airport transfers are available on request, but you need to give them advance warning. You could even walk to the airport 400 yards away if your bags are light.

Places to Stay – middle
You'll find several reasonable mid-priced hotels to choose from within minutes of the beaches on Gloucester Ave.

A favorite of Europeans is the compact *Caribic House*, above the Caribic Vacations office at 69 Gloucester Ave (☎ 952-5013, fax 952-0981) directly opposite Doctor's Cave Beach. It has 20 rooms with fans, beginning at US$30 low season. Add US$5 for an air-con room.

Nearby is the *Coral Cliff* (PO Box 253, ☎ 952-4130, fax 952-6532), a venerable hotel built in 1906 by Harry M Doubleday, a member of the famous New York publishing family. The 32-room colonial-style hotel is a charming, modestly furnished warren. Some of the rooms are desperately in need of renovation (mine had rotting floorboards in the bathroom, windows that could easily be pried ajar, and door handles that almost came off in my hand). Still, you might like its funky charm. There's an oval swimming pool at the back, and the atmospheric Veranda Restaurant is enjoyable for its broad, breezy terrace. Rates for standard rooms are US$49/53 single/double (low season).

A nearby alternative is the *Belvedere* near Walter Fletcher Beach at 33 Gloucester Ave (☎ 952-0593 or (800) 814-2237, fax 979-0498), with 27 air-con rooms with telephones and hot and cold water (from

US$35 single/double). The rooms have heaps of light and views over the bay, though bathrooms are small and the furniture is basic. You can cool off in a little dipping pool with poolside bar.

My favorite in this price range is the *Toby Inn* on the corner of Gloucester Ave and Sunset Drive (PO Box 467, ☎ 952-4370, fax 952-6591). The 72 air-con rooms are in several two-story units surrounding a pool and sundeck with bar. Rooms vary, but all are nicely furnished, with faux-marble floors and pine-and-rattan furniture. Most have small verandas. Facilities include a games room, modestly elegant restaurant (food quality is average), and an elevated 'treehouse bar' with a lounge and large-screen TV. The hotel – which charges US$40/45 single/double in low season – is popular with German tour groups and young Europeans. It has live entertainment, including limbo and folkloric shows.

A less elegant sister property, the *Seashell Inn*, is perfectly located off Gloucester Ave, opposite Cornwall Beach (☎ 979-2983, fax 979-9836). Some of its spacious, albeit sparsely furnished, air-con rooms are ready for a renovation (US$35/40 single/double; US$5 extra for superior room). Huge showers are a plus. Request rooms in a newer block. It has a dining terrace beneath a huge fig tree next to a pool.

The *Buccaneer Inn* (☎ 952-6489) is a small, modest property with a homey feel. Rooms – US$66 single or double – have hardwood floors, phones, TVs, and safety boxes, plus large balconies. Its reclusive location at the end of Kent Ave is a five-minute walk from Gloucester Ave, as is *Hotel Gloriana* (☎ 979-0669), in the middle of a roadside shopping complex on Sunset Blvd. It has 10 quaint, large, carpeted, air-con rooms with verandas and telephones (US$42 single/double in summer). TVs can be rented for US$10. Bathrooms are small. It operates a tiny downstairs restaurant, plus a breezy rooftop restaurant from where you can watch airplanes come and go. The hotel was expanding recently and will have 64 rooms when finished.

If you prefer a breezy hilltop setting, Queen's Drive is replete with options, some offering fabulous views. At the north end is *Mirage*, a cozy hotel complex with spacious, carpeted rooms with rattan furniture for US$52/62 single/double. The rooms overlook a tiny pool. Upper-floor rooms have skylights but get warm. Nearby is the *Casa de Paradise* (☎ 952-3163, fax 979-5332); with 25 air-con, carpeted rooms for US$45/55 a single/double. They're unimpressive, but clean. Bathrooms are small.

By far the most atmospheric place is the 10-room *Ramparts* on Ramparts Close (☎ 979-5258), boasting lots of dark timber and natural stone. Its intimate little bar and the TV lounge that serves as a dining room are exquisitely Old-World English. The small pool is a satisfying place to catch some rays. Rates begin at US$45 single or double. *Big Apple B&B*, nearby at 18 Queen's Drive (☎ 952-7240), has 11 carpeted, air-con rooms, all with two double beds and views over the bay. Furnishings are modest and bathrooms are small. Rates are US$40 double with fans (US$50 with air-con) but do *not* include breakfast.

A popular option is *Blue Harbour Hotel* above the fort on Sewell Ave midway up Miranda Hill (PO Box 212, ☎ 952-5445, fax 952-8930). Free shuttles to the beach are available, but it's a stiff climb back up from town. Its air-con rooms are spacious, well lit, and airy. All have TVs; some have king-size beds. Room rates begin at US$29/42 single/double in low season (US$48/56 in high season). A pool and bar are set in a courtyard. Breakfasts are served, but not lunch or dinner. Blue Harbour also has family units for up to 10 people.

The euphemistic *Vernon's Tropical Resort* at 3 Leader Ave (PO Box 18, ☎ 952-2875) offers a secluded spot in the hills with views inland over the Barnett Estate sugarcane fields. The 25 rooms, however, are very modest and homey, albeit clean (US$40/45 single/double). Some have air-con, though check first to see that the one in your room is working. TVs can be rented. The open-air bar is pleasant and

Not far from the hubbub of Montego Bay, life slows down considerably.

A floating shop in Montego Bay –
perfect for snorkelers

Crafts market in downtown Montego Bay

Idyllic Blue Hole Garden centers on a sinkhole that's perfect for cool dips.

It's a Bart & Bob thing at Negril Beach.

A wee patch of shade is better than none.

there's a large pool, but the Kit-Kat Restaurant is rather dull. Vernon's is popular with Jamaican families.

Several small hotels near the airport offer modest accommodations at reasonable prices. They're handy if you're overnighting in transit, but you can also walk to the beaches, about half a mile away. *Seville Guest House*, just down the road from the Ocean View Guest House, offers modest rooms with utility decor for US$35 per room. There's a TV lounge. No meals are served. It also has apartments in a complex called 'Upper Deck,' near the Blue Harbour Hotel; they're rented long-term only (three months or longer at US$550 per month).

My recommendation is *Ridgeway Guest House*, directly opposite the airport. Justifiably popular with Europeans, it's a bargain. The 10 rooms are large and attractive (some have air-con) and feature private bathrooms with hot water. Rates run from US$25/40 single/double, or from US$20 per person per night weeklong, including continental breakfast. You can rent TVs for the rooms. There's a coffee shop and bar on the rooftop, and a pool was planned. Free shuttles to the beach and airport are provided. A worthy alternative is the *Airport Inn* (☎ 952-0260), which has 10 clean and adequate little rooms for US$45 (US$50 with kitchenette).

Places to Stay – top end

The priciest accommodations in town fall into three categories: hotels, all-inclusive resorts, and villa and apartment rentals.

Downtown Four all-inclusive properties stand out on Gloucester Ave, each with its own distinct mood. The first is the low-rise *Casa Blanca Beach Club* (PO Box 469, ☎ 952-0720, fax 952-1424), above the coral shore south of Doctor's Cave Beach. This former hotel of choice for the rich and famous has reemerged as one of MoBay's finest hotels after a long decline. The decor is beautiful. It has its own pocket of sand where free water sports (sailing, surfing, and snorkeling) are provided. The air-con oceanfront rooms with queen-size bed,

private bath, and balcony cost $120/190 single/double, all-inclusive. Facilities include two pools, a games room, TV lounge, and seaside dining terrace.

By far the most appealing resort in the heart of Montego Bay is *Breezes*, a classy, contemporary four-story structure that towers over Doctor's Cave Beach, to which guests have free access (the hotel also has its own private water-sports section). It promises the luxury of a 'cruise ship on land.' By MoBay standards, it lives up to the billing and has upped the ante considerably since it opened in September 1995. Its graciously appointed 124 rooms and suites are centered on an L-shaped pool that at night forms the foreground for a high-tech stage. Avoid the standard rooms, which are very small. The lively entertainment is epitomized by a toga party on Thursday nights. Facilities include two restaurants, beach grill, four bars, rooftop Jacuzzi, game room with pool tables, and an upscale nightclub. Breezes is managed by SuperClubs and is a 'Super-Inclusive' property: *everything* is included in the cost, beginning at US$110/140 midweek/weekend per person per night (☎ 940-1150, fax 940-1160; in the USA ☎ (305) 925-0925 or (800) 859-7873; in the UK ☎ (1749) 677200).

The third attractive all-inclusive is *Jack Tar Village*, a low-rise beachfront hotel with 128 rooms and its own private section of Cornwall Beach. A full renovation was planned for 1996. All rooms have ocean views and wide French doors opening onto a private balcony. A breezy, elegant restaurant faces the beach. The hotel offers a full range of activities and water sports, plus complimentary massage daily. It also hosts a crafts fair each week with vendors setting up stalls along the beach. Rates are US$150/220 single/double.

A stone's throw north on Kent Ave is *Sandals Inn*, an intimate 52-room couples-only resort (☎ 952-4140, fax 952-6913). It's run to the same exacting standards for which the Sandals' properties are famed, and offers similar entertainment, water sports, and top-notch cuisine. The beach, across the road, is tiny – much smaller than the hotel brochure suggests. Three-night packages begin at US$505 per person in low season.

The 88-suite *Quality Inn Montego Bay* (formerly the Gloucestershire Hotel) opened in late 1995 across the street from Doctor's Cave Beach (in North America, ☎ (800) 228-5050). Most rooms feature a balcony. All have air-con and direct-dial phones, room safes, and satellite TV. Rates range from US$80 to US$115.

Two other all-inclusives to consider along Gloucester Ave are the all-pink *Fantasy Resort*, with 119 rooms overlooking Cornwall Beach (PO Box 161, ☎ 952-4150, fax 952-3637); and the *Vista Ambassador*, spread over 10 acres on a hill overlooking Walter Fletcher Beach (PO Box 262, ☎ 952-4703, fax 952-6810). The latter, a family resort (formerly Lifestyles Resort), has had a troubled renovation and was not open at press time. When complete it will boast 116 rooms and villa-suites (the latter with terrace Jacuzzis), a full-service spa, gym, and other facilities catering to a health-conscious clientele. Standard room packages were slated to start at US$220 per person.

The *Club Paradise Sea Gardens* on Kent Ave is also all-inclusive. The beautiful public areas have an Old-World style with lots of antiques and reproductions. It has its own tiny beach. Rates are US$110 per person (☎ 952-4780, fax 952-7543; in the USA, 7501 NW 4th St No 201, Plantation, FL 33317, ☎ (305) 583-4070 or (800) 545-9001, fax (305) 583-3943).

The family-run *Doctor's Cave Beach Hotel* offers a superb location on Gloucester Ave (PO Box 94, ☎ 952-4355, fax 952-5204). Its labyrinthine corridors lead to 78 rooms and 12 suites. Some rooms are dowdy and in need of repair. The lush gardens at the back are tight up against the cliff face, where there's a whirlpool under a gazebo. Other facilities include a small gym, the Coconut Grove Restaurant, and a piano bar opening onto a small swimming pool. A standard room costs US$80/105 single/double in low season (US$10 more for deluxe; US$35 more for breakfast and dinner daily), but I consider this overpriced.

Another venerable but run-of-the-mill hotel in the same price bracket is the *Wexford* on Gloucester Ave between Doctor's Cave and Walter Fletcher Beaches (PO Box 108, ☎ 952-2854, fax 952-3637). The carpeted rooms are modestly furnished and have balconies, telephones, and TVs. One wing has one-bedroom apartments with kitchenettes.

Above Town The *Montego Bay Racquet Club*, above town at the corner of Sewell and Park Aves, has long been a favorite of fashionable society and serious tennis buffs, but it is beginning to look tired. It has 16 air-con villas in the cool hills (US$55/60 single/double) and seven Laykold tennis courts (PO Box 245, ☎ 952-0200, fax 979-7210). Nearby at 5 Queen's Drive is the *Winged Victory* (☎ 952-3891, fax 952-5986), another elderly property with a lush hillside setting, lots of tilework and wrought-iron in the public areas, and a pool with views over the bay. Carpeted rooms are modestly furnished. It was devoid of guests (and life) when I last called in. No smoking is allowed in bedrooms. Rates begin at US$70 single or double. All-inclusive packages are available.

Another hilltop option is the *Royal Court Hotel & Natural Health Resort* at Sewell and Leader Aves (PO Box 195, ☎ 952-4531, fax 952-4532; in the USA, PO Box 20071, Cherokee Station, New York, NY 10021, ☎ (212) 628-0451 or (800) 509-1133, fax (212) 628-0425). This elderly 25-room hotel caters to the health and fitness market. Hence, the old alcohol bar is now a juice and herbal tea bar, the restaurant serves fish and vegetarian dishes exclusively, and the in-house Wellness Centre offers everything from colon therapy and psychotherapy to weight-loss programs and cooking classes. The suites are attractive, albeit homey. Even the standard rooms, which are carpeted, have king-size beds. Summer rates are US$50/60 single/double for standard room. Suites are US$85. Royal Court offers a three-night package (US$270 per person) that includes all meals, bodywork, and massage session. Free airport transfers and shopping trips are offered. Views face inland.

A total contrast is *Mango Walk Villas* (☎ 952-1473, fax 979-3093), where attractive modern units include six studios (US$75), 14 one-bedroom units (US$100), and two two-bedroom units (US$135), each air-conditioned and furnished in rich fabrics, with kitchen, living room, and patio. It's centered on a deep pool and poolside bar. Mango Walk is a reclusive hilltop district 10 minutes by car to the town and beaches.

East of Town East of town you'll find several top-notch resorts, not least *Sandals Montego Bay* (☎ 952-5510, fax 952-0816), a couples-only resort that boasts the distinction of the highest year-round occupancy rate of any hotel in the Caribbean! Here, you and the one you love (as long as you're heterosexual) can put aside the noise of children, seek out the honeymoon sparkle, and snorkel, sail, or soak up the sun to your heart's content along a scintillating white-sand beach that seems endless. The casual resort takes up 19 acres. Be prepared for lots of social activity. Couples are here to have fun! The food is superb and the live entertainment is top-notch. Every kind of water sport is available, including scuba (resort course only, not certification). It has 244 rooms in nine categories. Three-night packages begin at US$625 per person, which is a tremendous value. For reservations, contact:

Canada
    4211 Yonge St No 320, Willowdale, Ontario M2P 2A9, ☎ (416) 223-0028, fax (416) 223-3306
Germany
    Arnulfstrasse 44, 80355 Munich, ☎ (89) 592-106, fax (89) 550-1916
UK
    32 Ives St, London SW3 2ND, ☎ (0171) 581-9895, fax (0171) 823-8758
USA
    Unique Vacations, 6150 SW 76th St, Miami, FL 33143, ☎ (800) SANDALS or (305) 284-1300, fax (305) 667-8996

Sandals Royal Caribbean, one mile east at Mahoe Bay, is an older, more classical, compact, and sedate couples-only property that attracts a slightly older age group (☎ 953-2231, fax 953-2788; see Sandals Montego Bay above for overseas contacts). Its beach is relatively small, but water sports, land sports, entertainment, and cuisine are on a par with its sister property. Highlights include Kokomo Island, with the Indonesian-style Bali-Hai Restaurant. It offers 160 rooms in six categories. Three-night packages begin at US$655 per person, off-season.

Also at Mahoe Bay is *Coyaba*, a compact family-run resort with 50 luxurious rooms furnished 'plantation style' with hand-carved beds, floral drapes, and rich mahogany reproduction antiques (Little River PO, ☎ 953-9150 or (800) 237-3237, fax 953-2244). It sits on a narrow beach in the cusp of a lagoon with a reef just 100 yards offshore. It's a quiet property blending contemporary elegance with a New York clubby feel. The elegant Vineyard Restaurant offers splendid nouvelle Jamaica cuisine but at shocking prices. Room rates range from US$105 to US$198 in low season (US$20 less for single occupancy). A deposit is required. An all-inclusive plan is offered for US$130 extra and includes a deluxe room, all beverages, water sports, and meals.

If it's within your budget, *Half Moon* (☎ 953-2211 or (800) 626-0592, fax 953-2731; in the USA, ☎ (800) 424-5500), is one of the most beautiful and exclusive resorts in Jamaica. This world-renowned resort is named for its private crescent beach that stretches more than a mile, behind which is 400 acres of beautifully landscaped gardens containing 220 rooms and suites (including an Imperial Suite complete with grand piano) in stunning Georgian plantation-era decor. Rates begin at about US$150 per night. Adjacent to the hotel are 20 super-deluxe, five-, six- and seven-bedroom villas with private pools. Each comes with its own cook, maid, gardener, and even its own rental car – for a whopping US$1500 a night.

Facilities include four squash courts, 13 tennis courts, an equestrian center, a championship golf course, and the Half Moon Shopping Village comprising a bank, coffee shop, English pub, specialty restaurants, and 30 upmarket shops.

Coyaba and Half Moon are members of Elegant Resorts of Jamaica, which has an all-inclusive Platinum Plan that allows you to mix and match accommodations at these and any of its other properties: *Round Hill Hotel & Villas*; *Plantation Inn*; and *Trident Villas & Hotel*. For information in the USA call ☎ (800) 237-3237; in the UK, ☎ (0171) 730-7144. (Also see Tryall Estate in the West Coast chapter.)

The nearby Holiday Inn is the second largest property on the island with 516 air-con rooms and suites in unappealing seven-story buildings. It was undergoing a complete renovation and is due to reopen as the all-inclusive *Sunspree Resort* aimed at the family market with special facilities for children. Rates will start at US$125 per person double occupancy (PO Box 480, ☎ 953-2485, fax 953-2840).

Jamaica Rose Resort, located in the hills of Ironshore Estate, offers 10 deluxe air-con bedrooms with TVs and private bath (427 Ferguson Ave, White Sands Beach, Montego Bay; ☎ 953-27141; in the USA (205) 836-2929 or (800) 358-3938, fax 205-836-2931). There's a sun deck and private pool, plus two terrace bars. Guests can use the Ironshore Golf & Country Club. Rates are US$149 per person double (three-night minimum; breakfasts and dinner are US$15 extra).

There's much to recommend the 468-room *Seawind*, despite its ugly rainbow-colored twin towers and uninspired grounds. If you want to be a recluse, then you may like its lonesome location at the end of the Montego Freeport Peninsula. It also has its own beautiful private beach with a nudist's section and a full range of water sports. Five bars and the Cave Disco (a local favorite on Saturday nights) guarantee plenty of life. There are also 104 self-contained apartments known as Bay Pointe Villas to choose from. The hotel closed its doors at the end of 1995 under new ownership and should reopen in 1996 after a thorough restoration (PO Box 1168, Montego Freeport, ☎ 952-4874, fax 952-1839; in the USA, Jamaica Resorts & Hotels, 1320 S Dixie Hwy No 1154, Coral Gables, FL 33145, ☎ (305) 667-8860, fax (305) 665-9035).

Villas & Apartments The hills of Ironshore are replete with snazzy villas and apartments for rent. One of the most exquisite is *Tranquility Villa*, a large three-bedroom house with its own private beach and stunning decor fit for the pages of *Architectural Digest* (US$4500 per week December to April; from US$1950 to US$2800 during low season). For information on this and other villas, contact Exclusive Villa Resorts (PO Box 1372, Montego Freezone, ☎ 951-6232, fax 951-6236).

Russell Villas of Rose Hall (PO Box 80, Montego Bay, ☎ 953-2732, or (800) 238-5289, fax 953-2732) is a conglomeration of deluxe, fully staffed two- to six-bedroom villas, each in its own landscaped grounds (US$400 to $700 nightly in summer). Each comes with transportation services and full membership privileges at Half Moon Golf, Tennis & Beach Club, which they overlook. Villas by Linda Smith (in the USA, ☎ (301) 229-4300) represents the *Oscar Hammerstein Estate* plus 22 other exquisite villas near Montego Bay. The *Atrium at Ironshore* (PO Box 604, Montego Bay, ☎ 953-2605, fax 953-3683) also offers a selection of upscale apartments of various sizes and amenities.

More modest three-bedroom villas are available through Ironshore Resort Villas (PO Box 108, ☎ 953-2501) and Seville Resort Villas & Apartments, at 19 Sunset Ave (PO Box 1385, ☎ 952-2814, fax 952-5509). The latter also has a guest house for US$30/35 single/double.

PLACES TO EAT

You'll not starve in MoBay, which has dozens of restaurants of every stripe, including a selection of sidewalk cafes along Gloucester Ave. Many tourist-oriented restaurants offer free hotel transfers, but far too many eateries geared to the tourist trade serve bland cuisine at high prices. Be prepared to pay top dollar – say, US$20 minimum per person – for meals that satisfy your palate. Many of the best hotels are associated with the upscale resort hotels, and most are open to non-guests. However, there are plenty of inexpensive, down-to-earth downtown restaurants catering mostly to the local trade with bargain-price Jamaican fare.

Street Fare

If you're buying food to prepare yourself, you can buy fresh produce at the colorful street market on Orange St between Union and William Sts and at the bustling Charles Gordon Market on Fustic Rd off Barnett St. Downtown, you'll also find vendors selling pasties and other fast-food fare, including roasted peanuts, from push carts; you'll hear the peanut sellers coming – their roasters whistle away like kettles.

Fast Food

There are plenty of fast-food outlets, including the typical US chains. For burgers try *Hemingway's Pub* at Miranda Ridge Plaza between Walter Fletcher and Doctor's Cave Beaches. Other fare includes buffalo wings, fish & chips, and shepherd's pie.

Tony's Pizza (☎ 952-6365) is a red-and-white-striped mobile-home-turned-kitchen outside the Mutual Security Bank on Gloucester Ave. It stays open until 2 am (3 am on Friday and Saturday).

I Can't Believe It's Yogurt, on Gloucester Ave, serves nonfat frozen yogurts priced from J$40 for a tiny cup – expensive but delicious. Downtown are the *Ice Creamery* on St James St and *Country Creams* on Union St.

Jamaican

One of the more colorful and off-beat downtown eateries where you can fill up for under US$3 is *Lyle's Intensified Inn* at 36 Barnett St (☎ 952-4980). It sells pastries, patties, fried fish, and bammy. Note the mural outside showing police officers harassing a Rasta. 'No loafers, prostitutes

What they do with jerks in Jamaica...

& Pimps Read & Run or Else?' says the sign. Another bargain spot for curried goat, pumpkin soup, and so on is *Smokey Joe's* off St James Ave.

For spicy meat and vegetable patties, I recommend *Butterflake Pastries, Delicious Patties & Pastries*, opposite Lyle's on Barnett St, and the *Viennese Bakery* on the corner of St James and William Sts.

The open-air *PJ's Saloon & Restaurant* at the north end of Gloucester Ave serves jerk pork and chicken from US$2.50. It has live reggae music at night. A more authentic experience is the *Pork Pit* on Gloucester Ave (☎ 952-1046), where you are served through a hole in the wall and can eat at open-air picnic tables beneath a shade tree. Finger-lickin' jerk chicken and pork costs from US$2, with yams, festival, and sweet potatoes extra. Downtown, try the *Native Jerk Centre*, in an old house at the south end of Market St (☎ 979-5063).

I've eaten at *Ma Maison* (☎ 952-5996) several times, not because the food is great (it isn't) but because the service is good and I like dining alfresco in the shade of umbrellas while watching the activity along Gloucester Ave. The huge menu includes Jamaican, Indian, and Chinese dishes from US$5 to US$18. Next door,

Tino's (☎ 952-0886) is similar, with the added attraction of a live band.

Another of my favorite places is the *Dead End Bar & Grill*, at the end of Kent Ave. It has a *cool* ambiance, with a ceiling held aloft by tree trunks. Uniquely, it's open 24 hours. The eclectic menu boasts everything from chicken wings (US$3) and sandwiches to fish & chips (US$3.50). The tiny tuna sandwiches are a rip-off. There's a large-screen TV at the bar. It's as popular with locals as tourists – a good sign. I also like *Walter's Bar & Grill* (alias Wally's; ☎ 952-9391) at 39 Gloucester Ave, a popular and lively place serving Jamaica specials as well as American favorites such as buffalo wings.

The food at *Greenhouse Patio Restaurant* (☎ 952-7838), across from Doctor's Cave Beach Hotel, has bland food, but it's open at 7 am for breakfast. It can be ice-cold inside the faceless air-con restaurant, but there's a small road-front patio. The western menu has Jamaican hints, such as callaloo omelette (US$3).

Pier 1 is a great place to savor Jamaican Sunday brunch (about US$15) on a breezy wooden deck overlooking the pier. Another good place to have breakfast is the *Cascade Room* in the Pelican (☎ 952-3171), a steadfast favorite of upscale locals for over three decades. Its menu of Jamaican dishes includes stew peas with rice, and stuffed conch with rice and peas (US$7). Take a sweater to withstand the air-conditioning. It offers free shuttles.

For nouvelle Jamaican cuisine with an international flavor head to the *Vineyard Restaurant* at Coyaba Beach Resort at Mahoe Bay, east of town (☎ 953-9150). Budget a minimum US$20 per person for dinner. *Norma's at the Wharf*, at Reading west of Montego Bay, is even better – it's one of the best dining experiences in the Caribbean (see the Reading section below).

Asian

There are several Chinese restaurants to choose from downtown. One of the most popular is the *Guangzhou Restaurant* in the Miranda Ridge Plaza at 39 Gloucester

Ave (☎ 952-6200). It's open noon to 10 pm weekdays and 5 to 10 pm on weekends. It serves a huge variety of Chinese dishes (US$5 to US$15) but also has Thai and Mongolian dishes. Discounts are offered between noon and 4 pm. I've not eaten at the elegant *Lychee Gardens* at 18 East St (☎ 952-9428), but it has been recommended for its Sichuan cuisine. It's open noon to 10 pm daily. A more basic and cheaper option is the *Peking Restaurant* at Shop No 132 in the City Centre Building. Dishes at *Le Chalet/Wok Jai* at 32 Gloucester Ave (☎ 952-5240) begin at US$5.

If you're craving Japanese cuisine, check out *Sakura* (☎ 953-9686) in the Half Moon Village. It specializes in *teppanyaki* cooked at hibachi-grill tables. Budget a minimum US$20 per person.

Continental

The *Coconut Grove Restaurant* at Doctor's Cave Beach Hotel (☎ 952-4355) mixes 'European, Italian traditional, and Jamaican nouvelle.' The elegant poolside setting is pleasant, with piano music from the piano bar, but the food is expensive and of moderate quality. Typical dishes are curry of the day with coconut and fried plantain (US$10), and shrimp creole in a spiced tomato and sweet sauce (US$17).

Margaritaville (☎ 952-4777), just south of Casa Blanca Hotel on Gloucester Ave, is a great place to watch the sunset over cocktails, followed by dinner on the elegant cliff-top patio with views west across the bay.

Downtown are two splendid options with a unique historic ambiance. The first is the *Georgian House* at the corner of Orange and Union Sts. This supremely elegant restaurant – faithfully restored in period detail – features silverware and crystal, lace curtains, and gilt chandeliers. You can also dine alfresco at wrought-iron tables in a courtyard shaded by palms. Entrees such as shrimp creole, lobster Newburg, and tenderloin of pork begin at about US$20. In a similar vein, the *Town House*, an 18th-century structure at 16 Church St (☎ 952-2660), offers the choice of dining in the brick-walled cellar or more elegantly upstairs in the Blue Room. Choose from chicken in orange and ginger, or stuffed lobster for US$20. Maybe you'll sit at the same table where such notables as Paul McCartney, Charlton Heston, Barbra Streisand, Marlon Brando, and other illustrious figures have dined.

Several elegant restaurants serving continental cuisine are situated in the hills above Montego Bay. One of the best is the *Native* (formerly the Unicorn) at 7 Queen's Drive (☎ 979-2769) in a great setting replete with a pool and bamboo-columned bar at the cliff face overlooking Gloucester Ave. It features live music at nighttime. The menu ranges from salads (US$3 and up) to 'goat in a boat' (curried goat in a pineapple half, US$9) and stir-fried tofu with vegetables (US$10).

Another longtime favorite is the *Richmond Hill Inn* (☎ 952-3859), where you can dine in a 18th-century great house attended by white-gloved wait staff. It specializes in continental seafood.

I've not eaten there, but everyone raves about the *Sugar Mill Restaurant* at the prestigious Half Moon Golf Club (☎ 953-2314). It serves Caribbean and international cuisine in an exclusively elegant setting. Free shuttles are offered from Sandals and Sea Castle (for pickup reservations, call ☎ 953-2228).

Italian
The moderately expensive *Pastafari Restaurant* on the top floor at Breezes has true Italian flair (☎ 940-1150).

A steadfast favorite for gourmet Italian is *Julia's* (☎ 952-1772) on Bogue Hill, south of town. It offers a tremendous view. Free shuttles are provided.

Vegetarian
I don't know of any vegetarian restaurants in Montego Bay, and only a few restaurants offer vegetarian dishes on their menus. Want to start a business? There's a health-food store (☎ 952-4952) on the corner of St James and Creek Sts. *Juiciful Depot* in a cul-de-sac off Market St serves natural juices.

Other Cuisines
For something out of the ordinary, try the *Houseboat Fondue Restaurant* (☎ 952-7216), anchored in Bogue Bay at Montego Bay Freeport. It bills itself as 'for dippers, dunkers and people who like to eat what they cook and cook what they eat.' A three-course meal (US$20) includes a choice of cheese, filet mignon, chicken and 'chocolate festival' fondue. It's open for dinner only from 6 to 10 pm and offers free shuttle service.

The *Star of India Restaurant* (☎ 952-6489) was due to open next to the Buccaneer Inn. It will serve Indian cuisine with entrees beginning at about US$10.

ENTERTAINMENT
For its premier resort status, Montego Bay's nightlife is surprisingly unsophisticated compared to Kingston's and far less developed than that of Negril. Still, you should find enough to keep you amused for a week. Most upscale hotels have live bands and limbo and carnival-style floor shows for dinner and post-dinner entertainment, and if you're staying at an all-inclusive resort such as Sandals, you may never be tempted to prowl outside the compound at night. That's a pity, because Montego Bay is famous for its raunchy beach parties, which are worth checking out.

Take care at night if you're seeking down-to-earth nightlife such as go-go clubs downtown (Lyle's Intensified Inn, written up in many guidebooks, recently closed its go-go disco). Avoid walking alone downtown at night: if you're unsure of an area, take a taxi.

Bars
Walter's (also known as Wally's) on Gloucester Ave is the most popular and liveliest hangout in town: it's always brimfull, with a good mix of people, including a regular clientele of hoteliers and other local tourism industry figures. It has a TV sports bar. Another popular option is the *Dead End Bar & Grill* at the north end of Kent Ave.

A more sedate option is the *Piano Bar* at Doctor's Cave Beach Hotel, or *Hemingway's Pub* in the Miranda Ridge Plaza on Gloucester Ave, which offers live entertainment (☎ 952-8606).

Beach Parties

Montego Bay has four *boonoonoonoos*, or 'beach parties,' which are only-in-Jamaica affairs with live reggae bands and shatteringly deafening DJ music. Where you should go depends on what night it is.

Gloucester Ave is closed on Monday evenings from 7 pm until midnight for its weekly *street carnival*, with reggae bands and other local cultural entertainment. The bacchanal spills over to the *Cornwall Beach Party* (US$3 entrance). Check with the JTB (☎ 952-4425) for information. On Thursday you can ride de riddims at the *Dead End Jam*, a closed-off street party at the end of Kent Ave where the DJ cranks it up until you can feel the vibrations loosen your fillings. During high season, when the crowds crush shoulder-to-sweaty-shoulder, the air is thick with ganja smoke and the whole street is full of revelers *winin'* en masse. A *Boonoonoonoos Beach Party* is also held every Friday night at Walter Fletcher Beach. The US$29 entrance includes buffet and open bar (☎ 952-5719).

Discos

The most urbane place in town is *Hurricane's* disco atop Breezes on Gloucester Ave. It's small but high-tech and gives you an option beyond reggae music. Modestly sophisticated is *Connections* in the Fantasy Resort, also on Gloucester Ave, and the *Jonkanoo Lounge* at the Wyndham Rose Hall Beach Hotel (☎ 953-2650). The *Cave Disco*, with stalactites and stalagmites, in the Seawind Hotel (☎ 979-8070) at Montego Freeport, attracts a heterogeneous crowd on Saturday nights. I'm told that the new *Diamond Roof Disco* in Blue Diamond Shopping Centre is a mellow option.

On Fridays, everyone heads to *Pier 1* on Howard Cooke Blvd, where you can dance to reggae beneath the stars. It gets packed with a mix of tourists and locals (US$5

entrance; ☎ 952-2452); live bands also play. The dancing goes on well into the wee hours.

The *Flamingo Nightclub* (☎ 953-2257) at Sugar Mill Rd in Ironshore is a disco popular with both tourists and locals, especially on Saturdays. It also has erotic go-go dancing most nights and charges a US$5 cover when it hosts live bands. Go-go dancing is also the forté of *Mr Goldfinger Disco*, downtown at 51 Market St (don't walk here at night; take a taxi).

Cinemas

Montegonians are not movie-goers. The new, upscale *Blue Diamond Cinema* at the Blue Diamond Shopping Center (☎ 953-9020) shows first-run movies. You might also try the *Roxy* on Barnett St and the *Strand* at 8 Strand St (☎ 952-5391), though both are dingy and are not in the best areas for nightime walking.

Other Options

If you love jazz, you can make an evening of it with *Twilight Time* at Rose Hall each Friday evening from 6:30 pm on, offering live jazz, plus dinner and drinks (☎ 953-2323, fax 953-2160). The *Belvedere Hotel* (☎ 952-0593), across from Walter Fletcher Beach at 33 Gloucester Ave, also has live jazz every third Sunday evening.

Special-event evenings further afield are also an option. You might want to check out 'An Evening on the Great River' (see Great River below) and 'Lollypop on the Beach' (see the Sandy Bay section in the West Coast chapter). Ask your hotel concierge or the JTB (☎ 952-4425).

THINGS TO BUY

You can shop till you drop, as there's no shortage of duty-free shops. And the competition among crafts vendors is so great I'm amazed half of them can make a living. At least half-a-dozen major shopping plazas are in town and at Ironshore. The closest to the tourist strip is St James Shopping Plaza, adjacent to Cornwall Beach.

Bargaining is the norm on the street but not in stores.

Arts & Crafts

Montego Bay's streets are virtually spilling over with local arts and crafts.

For the largest selection head to the huge Craft Market extending for three blocks along Harbour St between Barnett and Market Sts. Competition is fierce at the dozens of stalls selling wooden carvings, straw items, jewelry, ganja pipes, T-shirts, and other touristy items. It's open daily 7 am to 7 pm.

There's also a craft market hidden behind the Mutual Security Bank on Gloucester Ave, where a small streetside shopping center also sells everything from duty-free goods to souvenirs. Touts hang outside and will hustle fiercely to get you into the craft market and thus earn their commission on any sale that results. The Fort Montego Craft Market, behind the fort on Gloucester Ave, also has about two dozen stalls, and for cruise-ship passengers who have left things to the last minute, there's Harry's Art & Craft Gallery at Montego Freeport Shopping Centre (☎ 979-8024). Prices at the latter tend to be slightly higher than in town.

The hard-sell hustlers that were once the plague of Gloucester Ave are gradually being forced to set up shop in the sanctioned markets, although a few still make their presence felt. Some of the all-inclusives, such as Jack Tar Village, allow local vendors to set up a crafts market one day a week. A few vendors have hit on a nifty way to bring their wares to tourists ensconced in all-inclusives: they paddle in and sell their jewelry and carvings from within wading distance of the beaches. Most upscale hotels have their own arts-and-craft stores. A general rule is that the more upscale the hotel, the better the quality of items for sale.

If you're seeking *real* quality, save your bucks for the Gallery of West Indian Art (☎ 952-4547) at 1 Orange St in downtown. Here you'll find quality arts and crafts from around the Caribbean, including plantation scenes by local painter Albert Artwell. Images Art Gallery in the Half Moon Club (☎ 953-9043) is an affiliate of the Western

Montego Bay offers shoppers plenty to choose from.

Jamaica Society of Fine Arts. It displays watercolors, antique collectibles, and selected crafts from Jamaica's foremost artists. Ambiente Art Gallery (☎ 952-7919) and Things Jamaican (☎ 952-5605), both immediately east of the fort, also sell high-quality works. Bay Gallery in St James Shopping Centre exhibits works by well-known local artists such as Susan Alexander, Karl Jerry Craig, Gloria Escoffery, and Seya Parboosingh (Shop No 16, ☎ 952-7668).

Duty-Free Goods

Economies of scale operate at the City Centre Building – a modern shopping plaza opposite the library on Fort St, where duty-free shops include Bijoux (☎ 952-2630), Chulani (☎ 952-2158), and Casa de Oro (☎ 952-3502), which also has an outlet (☎ 953-2600) at the Holiday Village Shopping Centre east of town. You'll also find a good selection of duty-free shops in the departure lounge of Sangster International

Airport and at the cruise ship terminal at Montego Freeport.

Reggae Reminders

If the colorful concert posters around town have caught your eye, nip down a narrow driveway on Union St to Party Magic, where Mansion, Dain, Danny, and Whizzy handpaint banners for Shabba Ranks shows, Reggae Sumfest, and other key events (☎ 952-6331). You can buy small-scale signs as souvenirs for U$3.

Most craft and souvenir shops sell popular reggae tapes, but for the widest selection of records and CDs, check out Tee Pee Records & Tape at Shop No 17 in the City Centre Building, or Top Ranking Record Shop (☎ 952-1216) at Shop No 4 in the Westgate Shopping Centre.

GETTING THERE & AWAY
Air

Air Jamaica Express (formerly Trans-Jamaica, ☎ 952-5401, fax 952-1877) operates scheduled flights between Montego Bay and Kingston, Negril, Ocho Rios, and Port Antonio. The airline's schedule was undetermined at the beginning of 1996 pending initiation of new services linking domestic flights to international arrivals and departures.

Wings Jamaica Ltd (☎ 923-6573 in Kingston) and Tim-Air (☎ 952-2516) offer charter service and sightseeing trips.

If you've won the jackpot, or the company is picking up the tab, Helitours offers charter transfers by helicopter (US$500 per hour). Transfers from Montego cost US$525 to Ocho Rios, US$400 to Negril, US$750 to Kingston, US$500 to Mandeville, and US$1200 to Port Antonio.

See the Getting There & Away chapter for a description of international services into Sangster International Airport.

Sangster International Airport

Odds are that as a foreign visitor, you'll arrive at Sangster International Airport, immediately north of town, along Sunset Blvd only about one mile from Gloucester Ave. Over 80% of visitors arrive here.

Construction was due to begin on a new terminal in early 1996. When completed in 1998, there will be 12 gates (currently there are four). At press time, however, most passengers face a very long walk from the tarmac to the arrivals hall – a sweaty ordeal!

Facilities The hall is well laid out, with an information desk at the end of the immigration hall before the immigration checkpoint. The staff can recommend hotels and even make reservations. A money-exchange bureau is immediately beyond immigration before the stairs down to the baggage claim and customs. There's a local transport information desk immediately in front of the exit from customs. Desks representing specific tour companies and hotels are on the left and rental cars on the right. An airport information desk on the right, next to the exit, also provides information on transportation and makes announcements. Porters are available (J$5 per bag).

Bus

Montego Bay is served by buses from towns islandwide. Until recently, most buses arrived and departed from Harbour St, but on my last visit a construction project had dispersed the departure points to the wasteland behind the library between Harbour and St James Sts, and a muddy, potholed lot at the east end of Orange St near the junction with Creek St. It was very confusing. You'll have to ask around to ascertain the departure point of the bus you're seeking.

At press time a bus station was being built off Howard Cooke Blvd, near the site of the old railway station just south of Barnett St. Things should have improved by the time you read this.

Major bus routes include the following:

Catadupa
    Bus LS70, 1 hour, US$0.60
Christiana
    Bus LS72, 1½ hours, US$1.50
Duncans
    Bus LS531, 1 hour, US$1
Kingston
    Bus STBW221/309, 4 hours, US$2.50

Minibuses Minibuses serve dozens of towns islandwide. They depart from Orange and Creek Sts. Major minibus routes include the following:

Duncans
   Minibus LS531, 1 hour, US$3
Falmouth
   Minibus LS2020, 30 minutes, US$2
Frome
   Minibus LS200, 1 hour, US$3
Kingston
   Minibus STBW167/197/315/480/488, 3½ hours, US$8
Little London
   Minibus LS931, 2 hours, US$5
Lucea
   Minibus LS429, 1¼ hours, US$3
Negril
   Minibus LS804, 1½ hours, US$4
Ocho Rios
   Minibus LS972, 2 hours, US$6

Many resorts offer to shuttle to guests from Sangster International Airport as far as Negril or Ocho Rios. Some are complimentary; others cost about US$15 to either destination.

Taxi

Taxis are a feasible and cost-effective way to travel between towns if you're traveling with two or more additional passengers. The fare is about US$60 to Ocho Rios or Negril. Make sure you and the driver reach an agreement on a fare and what it includes *before* setting off.

Several companies offer taxi transfers by minibus. JUTA (the Jamaica Union of Travellers Association), the biggest taxi operator, has a large fleet of minibuses and full-size motor coaches. The office is on Claude Clarke Ave in the Norwood district (PO Box 1155, ☎ 979-0778, fax 952-5355). One-way transfers with Pleasure Tours (☎ 952-5383) cost US$18 to Negril, US$23 to Ocho Rios, US$28 to Port Antonio, and US$21 to Mandeville, based on two or more people.

Boat

Cruise ships berth at a special terminal at Montego Freeport, about two miles south of town. Taxis and minibuses will be waiting to whisk you downtown (about US$8) and to major sites if you haven't already signed up for a tour offered by the cruise-ship company. (See the chapter on Getting There & Away for details of cruise companies serving Montego Bay.)

If arriving under your own steam (or sail), you can berth at Montego Bay Yacht Club (☎ 979-8038, fax 979-8262) at Montego Freeport. It has both 110 and 220 volt electrical hookups, plus gasoline and diesel. There's a pool and a very attractive bar and restaurant.

GETTING AROUND

You can walk between any place along Gloucester Ave and downtown (it's about 1½ miles from Kent Ave to Sam Sharpe Square). It can be hot going during the day, but it's a level walk. You'll need a vehicle for anywhere further afield, including Queen's Drive and Montego Freeport.

To/From the Airport You'll find plenty of taxis outside the arrivals lounge at Sangster International Airport. Freelance taxi touts will descend on you immediately as you exit the arrivals lounge. Don't let yourself be hassled, however. There's an official booth on the sidewalk to the left where you'll be assigned a licensed JUTA taxi. Freelance touts tend to steer you towards unregistered taxis.

Bite the bullet! A US$7 taxi fare applies between the airport and downtown Montego Bay. It may be the most expensive taxi ride you'll take, mile for mile. Even non-licensed drivers may quote you this rate. You should be able to share a *colectivo* taxi for less than US$1; try the gas station just outside the airport.

Buses don't serve the airport, but you can catch a bus or minibus into town from the roundabout on the main road 400 yards from the terminal. The fare is about US$0.20.

A company called Martin's Minibus supposedly offers a transfer service between Donald Sangster Airport and Norman Manley Airport in Kingston (five hours).

If the exorbitant taxi fare rankles, you could even walk to the airport from Gloucester Ave if your bags aren't too heavy.

Bus

There's no effective bus service within MoBay. Most tourist places are within walking distance anyway. At press time, Air Jamaica was planning to initiate a shuttle service to run on a regular schedule between points throughout MoBay.

Taxi

Plenty of taxis cruise up and down Gloucester Ave. You'll be propositioned by taxi drivers almost as soon as you step from your hotel. Licensed taxis have red license plates and meters. Government-determined rates should be posted inside the cab, but not all taxi drivers adhere to this. Establish that the meter is working before setting off.

Unlicensed taxi drivers usually drive battered old Fords, Vauxhalls, or Russian-made Ladas from the 1970s or earlier. Fares are negotiable. The fare should be significantly lower than for licensed taxis, but don't count on it. Hammer out an agreeable fare *before* setting off. If you feel you're being ripped off, get out and hail another cab; that should bring your driver to his senses (I've yet to see a female taxi driver in Jamaica).

Colectivo taxis set off from the south end of Harbour St.

Car Rental

Dozens of car-rental companies serve Montego Bay. Several companies are represented at the airport, including Island Car Rental (☎ 952-5771, in the USA ☎ (800) 892-4581; in Canada ☎ (800) 526-2422), which offers competitive rates and has always provided me with the most reliable and courteous service. Their cars, which begin at US$49 daily (more in high season), are new, which is not always the case with local companies. Other companies have outlets on Queen's Drive adjacent to the airport, and downtown along Gloucester Ave. Most offer discounted rates (usually about 15% to 20% lower) April to

December, as well as free pickup and delivery service.

The following companies have offices at Sangster International Airport:

Avis	☎ 952-4543
Bargain Rent-a-Car	☎ 952-0762
Budget	☎ 952-5185
Gemini Rent-a-Car	☎ 952-8153
Greenlight Car Rental	☎ 952-2769
Hertz	☎ 979-0438
Island Rental Car	☎ 952-5771
	or (800) 892-4581
National Car Rental	☎ 952-2769
Pleasure Tours Car Rental	☎ 952-0960
Sun Tours Car Rental	☎ 952-1943
Thrifty Car Rental	☎ 952-1115

Companies with offices in Montego Bay include:

Anna Rent-a-Car
  Holiday Inn, Rose Hall   ☎ 953-2766
                    or 953-2840
Apex Car Rentals
  32 Queen's Drive   ☎ 952-7587
Avis
  Ironshore Industrial Estate ☎ 952-1481
Budget
  Ironshore Industrial Estate ☎ 952-3838
Caribbean Car Rental
  19 Gloucester Ave   ☎ 952-664
                  fax 974-5760
Chen's Car Rental
  166A Gloucester Ave ☎ 952-3075
CJ's Car Rental
  Ironshore   ☎ 952-1099
Econocar Rentals
  Ramparts Inn Hotel ☎ 952-5538
  5 Ramparts Circle
Galaxy Car Rentals
  32 Queen's Drive ☎ 952-0136
Greenlight Car Rental
  Providence Drive ☎ 952-2636
  Ironshore
Hertz
  1217 Providence Way ☎ 979-0439
  Ironshore Industrial Estate
Horizon Tours & Car Rental
  22 Sunset Blvd ☎ 952-8555
              fax 979-0099
Hot Top Jeeps
  39 Gloucester Ave ☎ 979-9187
        or 953-2820 evening
National
  Providence Drive, Ironshore ☎ 952-2636

Pleasure Tours Car Rental
    32 Queen's Drive   ☎ 952-1441
                              or 952-5383
Praise Tours & Car Rental
    1 Queen's Drive   ☎ 952-6482
Prospective Car Rentals
    28 Union St   ☎ 952-0112
Sun Tours Car Hire
    97 Barnett St   ☎ 952-5185
Sunbird Car Rentals
    19 Gloucester Ave   ☎ 952-3015
Thrifty Car Rental
    57 St James St   ☎ 952-4585
United Car Rentals
    49 Gloucester Ave   ☎ 952-3077
                              fax 952-1081
Yellow Bird Car Rental
    32 Queen's Drive   ☎ 979-2622

Motorcycle Rental

At least a dozen outlets along Gloucester Ave rent motorbikes varying in size from 50cc to 750cc. If you're not an experienced rider, I recommend a small or midsize bike. Scooters normally rent for about US$30 minimum a day; motorbikes begin at about US$40 for smaller sizes (more for larger bikes). Try the following three companies on Gloucester Ave: TNT Bike Rental (☎ 979-0396) outside the Mutual Security Bank; Kryss Bike Rental (☎ 940-0476), next to Walter's; and Montego Bike Rentals (☎ 952-4984) at 21 Gloucester Ave. Hewitt Motorcycle Rentals (☎ 979-0393) has two outlets, one at 2 Queen's Drive and the other at 68 Barnett St.

The most famous house in Jamaica is the setting for one of the island's most famous myths.

Horse-Drawn Carriage

Yellow Sub Carriage (☎ 952-5063) charges US$25 per hour for city tours by horse-drawn cab. The white cabs have seen better days, but that doesn't detract from the romance of clip-clopping your way along Gloucester Ave. Jack Tar Village is the official departure point, but you can hail an empty carraige anywhere along Gloucester Ave.

Montego Bay to Trelawny Parish

East of Montego Bay beyond Ironshore, the A1 hugs the coast all the way east to Falmouth, 23 miles away. It's not a particularly scenic drive, although there are small beaches tucked away behind the shoreline mangroves. The slopes that sweep down to the coast were once covered in sugarcane, but in recent years the sugar estates have given way to private homes, villas, and resorts. However, two fabulous great houses – Rose Hall and Greenwood – still stand foursquare on the hills, and both are worth a visit. Greenwood Great House (17 miles east of MoBay) spans the boundary of St James and Trelawny Parishes.

A more adventurous option chosen by few travelers is to head inland from Montego Bay by following the Montego River east to the pancake-flat Queen of Spains Valley, where a sea of rippling green sugarcane sweeps off into the distance, hemmed in by a serrated bowl of the wild, unexplored Cockpit Country.

ROSE HALL GREAT HOUSE

This stunning mansion, with its commanding hilltop position two miles east of Ironshore, is the most famous house in Jamaica. It's also one of the most magnificent and most visited, enticing over 100,000 callers a year. The imposing house was built in the 1770s by John Palmer, a wealthy plantation owner and custos (the English monarch's representative) of St James Parish. Palmer

The White Witch of Rose Hall

In 1820 John Rose Palmer, the grand-nephew of John Palmer who built Rose Hall, married Anne May Patterson. Although the young woman was half English and half Irish, legend had it that she was raised in Haiti where she learned voodoo. Legend also says that Anne May proved to be a sex-crazed, murderous vixen. The lascivious lady allegedly practiced witchcraft, poisoned John Palmer, stabbed a second husband, and strangled her third. Her fourth husband escaped, leaving her to dispose of several slave lovers before she was strangled in her bed.

This tale – Jamaica's most famous legend – is actually based on a series of much distorted half-truths. The inspiration for the story, originally told in writing in 1868 by John Costello, editor of the *Falmouth Post*, was Rose Palmer, the initial lady of Rose Hall, who *did* have four husbands, the last being John Palmer, to whom she was happily wed for 23 years (she died before her husband at age 72). Anne Palmer, wife to John Rose Palmer, died peacefully in 1846 after a long, loving marriage.

In 1929, novelist HG DeLisser developed the fable into a marvelous suspenseful romance, *The White Witch of Rose Hall*.

Many Jamaicans believe the legend, and various attempts have been made to contact Annie's ghost. The most famous was a séance held on Friday, October 13, 1978, when a psychic named Bambos claimed to have made contact. Apparently, Annie's ghost led him by the hand to a nearby tree where, in full public view, he found a voodoo doll. ■

The three-story building has wings enclosing a courtyard, and a double staircase backed by an arcade leading up to a front door beneath a Palladian portico. Inside, the house is a bastion of 18th-century style. Although the original mahogany staircase and doors were removed long ago (they now grace various homes in Kingston), they have been replaced with magnificent reproductions. Other interior details and furnishings have been restored, or recreated as faithfully as possible, including silk wall fabric that is an exact reproduction of the original designed for Marie Antoinette during the reign of Louis XVI. Don't touch! Unfortunately the fabric is now badly torn and worn by the hands of unthinking visitors. Many of the antiques are the works of leading English master woodworkers of the day, including Hepplewhite, Sheraton, and Chippendale.

Part of the attraction is the legend of Annie Palmer, a multiple murderer said to haunt the house (see the White Witch of Rose Hall sidebar). Upstairs is her bedroom decorated in crimson silk brocades. The cellars now house an old-English-style pub and a well-stocked gift shop where you can buy Rose Hall Plantation Rum, White Witch perfume, and other specialty items made exclusively for Rose Hall.

Tours commence every 15 minutes from 9 am to 6 pm daily. Entrance costs US$10 (US$6 for children under 12). You can also take a 'Rose Hall 5-Star Tour' that combines a tour of the great house followed by a beach party and barbecue; or 'Twilight Time at Rose Hall' each Friday evening from 6:30 pm, with live jazz, dinner, and drinks. For information, contact Rose Hall, PO Box 186, Montego Bay, ☎ 953-2323, fax 953-2160.

Damali Beach

This beach is a tiny, privately owned piece of shore where you can wade to an offshore reef. You can also rent a glass-bottom boat (US$20 per hour per person), parasail, or scuba dive (equipment for rent). Fishermen at Long Bay offer reef rides by boat.

and his wife Rose (after whom the house was named) hosted some of the most elaborate social gatherings on the island. Slaves destroyed the house in the Christmas Rebellion of 1831, and it was left in ruins for over a century. In 1966 John Rollins, a former lieutenant governor of the US state of Delaware, bought the property and lavished over US$2.5 million on it to restore it to haughty grandeur.

Places to Stay & Eat

You can camp on *Damali Beach* (☎ 953-2387; in the US, ☎ (215) 471-0884), but the place still hasn't recovered fully from Hurricane Gilbert.

The *Wyndham Rose Hall Resort*, on the shore just west of Rose Hall Great House, is an elegant 500-room resort on 400 acres fronted by a beautiful 1000-foot-long beach (☎ 953-2650, fax 953-2617; in the USA ☎ (800) 822-4200; in the UK ☎ (0181) 367-5175, fax (0181) 367-9949). The seven-story hotel isn't particularly attractive, though the interior was recently renovated; furnishings are elegant, and the amenities – including a choice of restaurants and the Jonkanoo nightclub – top-notch. The resort boasts its own 18-hole golf course and six tennis courts among the many sports options.

A short distance east is *Sea Castle*, a luxury all-suite resort centered on a magnificent plantation-style great house at the heart of a 14-acre estate. The housing units, ranging from studios to penthouse suites, faintly resemble castles, hence the name. It's a good place for families, offering a Kiddies Club and nanny service. Low-season rates range from US$90/102 single/double for studios to US$342 for a three-bedroom penthouse sleeping six. Sea Castle is operated by Jamaica Resorts & Hotels (1320 S Dixie Hwy No 1154, Coral Gables, FL 33145, ☎ (305) 667-8860, fax (305) 665-9035).

If you prefer a place in the hills, consider *Dunn's Villa Resort Hotel* (Rose Hall, Little River PO, Montego Bay, ☎ 997-5077; in the USA, ☎ (718) 882-3917) in the village of Cornwall, two miles inland from Wyndham. This homey hotel has 10 air-con rooms with wide balconies for US$60 double, including breakfast. The spacious public areas are minimally, albeit graciously, furnished. There's a pool and Jacuzzi on a raised large sundeck. It's run by Howard and Gloria Dunn, who offer a local tour by horse and buggy (they also rent mountain bikes for US$8). The Dunns offer lunches and dinner at the poolside White Witch's Hideaway Pub & Grill

(burgers and jerk chicken are typical, US$2 to US$5).

GREENWOOD GREAT HOUSE

Greenwood sits high on a hill five miles east of Rose Hall. It's a more intimate, smaller-scale property. The two-story stone-and-timber structure was built about 1760 by Sir Richard Barrett, whose family had arrived in Jamaica in the 1660s and amassed a fortune from their sugar plantations. (Barrett was a cousin of the famous English poet, Elizabeth Barrett Browning, whose poetry was supported by the sweat of over 2000 slaves, a fact over which Browning herself expressed great shame.) Greenwood was intended primarily for entertaining guests, hence the large ballroom. Barrett was custos of St James and a member of the Jamaican Assembly. In an unusual move for his times, however, he educated his slaves, as the guides in period costume will tell you (they omit to tell you that Barrett died in compromising circumstances in a 'rooming house' – brothel – in Falmouth).

Unique among local plantation houses, Greenwood survived unscathed during the slave rebellion of Christmas 1831. The house today boasts what it claims is 'the finest antique museum in the Caribbean.' The original library is still intact, as are oil paintings, Dresden china, a rare collection of musical instruments, a court jester's chair, and such somber antiques as a mantrap used for catching runaway slaves. The master bedroom is still used by the current owners. Have your camera ready for the spectacular views down over the coast from the veranda.

Entrance costs US$8. The house is open 9 am to 6 pm daily (PO Box 169, Montego Bay, ☎ 953-1077). Buses traveling between Montego Bay and Falmouth or Ocho Rios will drop you off anywhere along the A1.

MONTEGO RIVER VALLEY

A road that begins at the Westgate Shopping Centre (a quarter-mile south of the junction of Barnett St and Cottage Rd in Montego Bay) leads east along the

Montego River Valley. Almost immediately the road narrows through a wooded gorge beyond which lies the village of Sign, six miles east of MoBay.

A number of hiking trails through the Montego River Valley begin at Sign Great House (Sign PO Box 5, St James, ☎ 952-9188).

Blue Hole Plantation
This beautiful old house at 1200 feet above sea level bills itself as a nature lodge (Little River PO, St James, ☎ 995-2072 or 979-9814 for reservations). The fieldstone-and-timber house was built by the Waite family in the early 18th century; the Waites had sided with Oliver Cromwell and were forced to flee to Jamaica following the Restoration of the English monarchy. They developed their lands as a sugar plantation, although the sugar mill was destroyed in the slave rebellion of 1831. Remnants of the old estate can be seen along trails that lead through the grounds, which abound in signed fruit trees.

Don't stroke the snapper turtles that are kept in a small pool; their bite can severe a finger! There's a small interpretive nature center, and a bar and outdoor restaurant built around a huge rubber tree. The place receives very few visitors. It's supposedly open Monday to Saturday 10 am to 4 pm, though when I called in there was no one around. Call ahead.

It's possible to bike from Blue Hole Plantation to Ironshore. Call Andy's Ride (☎ 952-6070) for a guided downhill tour.

Getting There & Away Turn left in Orange Estate (one mile east of Sign) and follow the road three miles uphill. You can also reach it from Ironshore. The turnoff from the A1 is beside the Coral Gardens Police Station, half a mile east of Coyaba Beach Resort. The road switchbacks uphill for three miles into the hills; your reward is the remarkable vistas along the coast. Turn east at Flower Hill Ave and follow it to a miserable dirt road. The unmarked entrance to the great house (which is out of view) has a tumbledown bamboo hut.

Orange River Lodge
This old great house is at Williamsfield in the hills two miles southeast of Sign. A guided tour of the banana plantation is available, as is horseback riding, and there's a swimming pool and Jacuzzi for refreshing yourself or if you merely want to spend a few hours lazing away from the beach.

The lodge allows camping for US$5 per tent. It also has modest dormitory accommodations (US$10), and more attractive rooms for US$70/130 single/double, including breakfast and dinner (PO Box 822, Montego Bay, ☎ 952-1145, fax 952-6241). The lodge offers a beach shuttle twice daily for guests.

QUEEN OF SPAINS VALLEY
Continuing east through the twisting Montego River Valley, you'll arrive at **Adelphi**, 13 miles east of Montego Bay, at the head of the Queen of Spains Valley. The valley is as flat and green as a billiard table, with sugarcane rippling silver-tipped in the Caribbean light as far as the eye can see. Adelphi is a modest village of no visual appeal. It was here, however, that a Quaker, Isaac Lascelles Winn, bought an estate known as 'Stretch and Set' (the name was derived from the cruel punishment previously meted out there), named it Adelphi, and hired a free-black Baptist minister, Moses Baker, to administer religious instruction and education to his slaves – the first estate owner ever to do so in Jamaica.

Reggae star Jimmy Cliff, who became an international sensation overnight in the film *The Harder They Come*, has a home near Lima, one mile east of Adelphi.

Treasure Queen Transport operates bus No LS79C, which travels through the Queen of Spains Valley via Hampden from Montego Bay (US$0.20).

Hampden Estate
Hampden, three miles east of Adelphi, is a working plantation with a rum distillery, sugar factory, and great house (☎ 995-9870 or 954-3262, fax 995-2184). The house is one of the most impressive and beautiful

buildings in Jamaica, well worth the drive. It's a highly unusual whitewashed structure with dark timbers and mansard roof, and reminds me of old mills in East Anglia, England. The house is enclosed within dry-stone walls with the factory immediately behind, steaming gently.

In colonial days, Hampden was one of several local estates that specialized in producing quality rums with high ether content for the German market (German importers employed expert tasters who went around Jamaica testing for distillers with the right ferment).

The entire property is open for guided tours 9 am to 4 pm Monday to Friday (US$12 adults, US$8 children). The smell of molasses and 'dunder' (the liquid waste from sugar-making) will guide you through the rippling fields of lime-green. The property straddles the border of St James and Trelawny Parishes.

The road beside the estate continues via a bamboo glade to the hamlet of Hampden in Trelawny.

Southeast of Montego Bay

The southeast quarter of St James Parish culminates in Cockpit Country, a region that exemplifies Jamaica's wild side. It stretches eastward through Trelawny Parish (see section on Cockpit Country in the North Coast chapter). This dramatic region has remained virtually unexplored due to its daunting terrain. The Maroons and their descendants settled this reclusive, untamed habitat ,and through their ferocity maintained an uneasy sovereignty from the English colonialists (see A Renaissance of Pride sidebar below). To reach the area from Montego Bay, head out along Fairfield Rd, which leads east from the A1 (about one mile south of Montego Bay) via the hamlets of Johns Hall and Welcome Hall. The potholed road climbs steeply through banana plantations and eventually

divides and runs north and south around the perimeter of the impenetrable Cockpit Country.

KENSINGTON

This hamlet, 13 miles southeast of Montego Bay, is famous as the site where in 1831 slaves set fire to the ridgetop plantation and initiated the 'Christmas Rebellion.' A roadside plaque erected by the Jamaica National Heritage Trust commemorates the event:

On Tuesday night December 27th 1831 the trash house on Kensington estate was set on fire signaling the start of the last slave rebellion in Jamaica when the slaves led by Johnson, Campbell, Gardiner and Dove forced the militia guarding the area to retreat to Montego Bay. Over 150 estates were burnt. In the reprisals, 500 slaves were killed including Sam Sharpe who had organized the slaves to demand freedom. As a result of the outbreak the movement to abolish slavery was greatly accelerated.

MAROON TOWN

Despite its name, this crossroads village (three miles east of Kensington) was never a center for Maroons. There's little of interest here, but two miles east of town is the tiny hamlet of Flagstaff, on the site of a former Maroon capital of Trelawny Town.

In 1739, after decades of fighting a guerrilla war with the Maroons of St James, Governor Edward Trelawny despatched Colonel John Guthrie to make peace with Cudjoe, the Maroon leader. They signed a treaty that granted the Maroons 1500 acres of land around Petty River, which was renamed Trelawny Town. Cudjoe was named hereditary chief of the Maroons, who were granted virtual autonomy, including the sole right to serve justice on their own people. Peace lasted for half a century. Unfortunately, a second Maroon War commenced in 1795 (see the Tide Turn section under History in Facts about Jamaica chapter).

Over 1500 British soldiers were engaged in the guerrilla war that ensued. Eventually, bloodhounds were imported from Cuba and used to track down the Maroons. Under the ruse of negotiating a peace treaty, the British seized the Maroon leaders and loaded them aboard ships for transport to Halifax, Nova Scotia (many died of the cold, and the survivors were eventually shipped to Sierra Leone, becoming the first Africans ever repatriated from the Americas). Trelawny Town was razed and a barracks built for British soldiers. In recent decades, the hamlet of Flagstaff has grown on the spot. Only a few remains of the military site can today be discerned.

The dirt road peters out in the lee of a deep cockpit about a half mile beyond Flagstaff.

ELDERSLIE

This forlorn congregation of meager houses and ramshackle huts is set on the southwest edge of Cockpit Country in what was once a thriving banana producing area, 15 miles south of Maroon Town. Many local youth today earn a living turning lignum vitae and other hardwoods into carvings.

The road that leads west from the village center will take you to Ipswich, YS Falls, and the south coast.

Wondrous Cave, near Elderslie, has an underground lake. Westin Thomas will guide you there. You can find him at the village social center. Mr Thomas allows *camping* beside the river next to Wondrous Cave.

ACCOMPONG

This village (population 1100) scattered along a hillcrest on the south side of the Cockpit Country is the sole remaining village in western Jamaica inhabited by descendants of the Maroons.

The village, which sits atop a very steep hill, is named after the brother of the great Maroon leader, Cudjoe. Accompong, which is a common name among the Akan-speaking Coromantyn tribes of West Africa, had led a band of Maroon's who lived scattered in the surrounding Cockpits during the mid-18th century. The settlement was founded in 1739 following the treaty between the Maroons and the English. In

1795, when a second war with the British broke out, the Accompong Maroons remained neutral. At the end of hostilities, all other Maroon settlements were razed but Accompong was allowed to remain.

Accompong is still headed by a 'Colonel' elected by secret ballot for a period of five years. He appoints a council, which he oversees. Oft-touted reports that the Colonel has absolute authority are exaggerated. So, too, is the concept that the Maroons enjoy virtual autonomy in legal matters, as shown in 1986 when the police raided Accompong and seized a large quantity of marijuana. Despite pleading immunity under the terms of the 1739 treaty, many council members were sentenced to jail. Reputedly, they refuse to pay government taxes, which might explain the dire state of the roads!

Today locals take pride in their heritage and are quick to use it for economic ends. Accompong exists on the largesse of tourists, and you may be hit up for money for the smallest excuse. Local youth may accost you immediately to tout themselves as guides, and you may even be told that there's an entrance fee to the village, which is false. Don't believe any local who tries to play on a long-forgotten custom that visitors can enter the village only by invitation.

Those interested in researching Accompong further should read anthropologist Katherine Dunham's *Journey to Accompong*, in which she recalls her stay in Accompong in 1946.

Post & Communications

A public telephone (☎ 997-9101) serves the whole village. It's cellular and has limited service. You can buy phone cards opposite at Peyton Place.

Things to See & Do

Accompong is centered on a level space called the Parade Ground. A Presbyterian church looks over the square, where a monument honors Cudjoe. The **Accompong Development Centre** is opposite the monument. Here, locals have developed a small craft industry and you can watch local women and children making belts, clothes, and carved gourds. If it's closed, you can request to have it opened; see Tom, whose house is across the road, immediately above the memorial.

Guides can be hired to take you to the **Peace Caves**, where Cudjoe signed the 1739 peace treaty with the British. Maroon Attraction Tours (32 Church St, ☎ 952-4526) organizes a village walk with the colonel.

Accompong Festival

A traditional ceremony is held each January 6 to celebrate the signing of the treaty and their birthright of freedom. *Abeng* horns and drums are played and the lively music, feasting, and dancing in typical Jamaican fashion end with a reggae party. Westerners are welcome.

Places to Stay & Eat

The cellar of *Peyton Place Pub*, a bar and grocery store on the town square, has been converted into a guest house with three small, simple but clean rooms (US$10). They're very cool and even have windows. They share a small shower and toilet. Another small guest house is down the hill. Ask Joshua Anderson, the bartender at Peyton.

The *Star One People of the Culture Club* is another popular, rustic bar that also serves basic meals, as does a colorfully painted shack at Harmony Hall (also called Whitehall), one mile south of Accompong. The *Accompong Cultural Centre* puts on live music.

Getting There & Away

From Montego Bay, buses depart from Creek St for Maggotty (south of Cockpit Country), where you can catch a bus outside Shakespeare's Tavern to Accompong.

The south coast provides the best access to Accompong. The road to the left at the Maggotty roundabout leads to Accompong on the edge of Cockpit Country. Turn right in Retirement (there's no sign, so it's best to ask directions) and follow a horribly rocky road uphill. The road dead-ends in Accompong.

A Renaissance of Pride

The Accompong community faces a difficult task in maintaining its cultural autonomy. The village is recovering from three decades of emigration and the legacy of cultural suppression by European missionaries who tried to convince the community that their African roots, based in spirituality and medicine, were evil. Several prize artifacts (as well as Cudjoe's home) have been destroyed. The Maroon 'Koramanti' language became extinct. Traditional health and sanitation systems have degenerated, traditional agricultural techniques have withered, and as much as two-thirds of the adult population has left. With the nearest school eight miles away and no transportation to it, youth are enticed to find an easier life in the cities.

But the traditional spiritual beliefs and medicines are finally experiencing a revival as young people discover a new pride in their roots. A community center was recently completed, and a Maroon Museum and a skills center are planned. Permaculture (sustainable agriculture) training has been initiated. The village has an ongoing Maroon Health Project that focuses on supporting primary health through the use of traditional medicines and a public health initiative. For more information, contact the Center for Natural & Traditional Medicines, PO Box 21735, Washington, DC 20009 (☎ (202) 234-9632).

You can buy a booklet, *Welcome to the World of Maroon Traditional Medicine*, which is worth the steep price tag of J$200. Ask for Kenroy in the village. ■

South of Montego Bay

The hill country south of MoBay is replete with attractions, including a variety of working plantations, several great houses, evolving eco-resorts, and a village of poor white farmers that is one of Jamaica's strangest anomalies. Most points of interest are reached either via the B8, which winds south from Reading and crosses a broad upland plateau before dropping onto the

Westmoreland Plain, or the B6, which leads southeast from Montpelier (six miles south of Reading).

READING
Reading, immediately west of Montego Bay along the A1, is a small crossroads hamlet at the junction of the B8, which leads south to Anchovy and Savanna-la-Mar. It has several small resorts fronting pocket-size beaches and a gas station and grocery store.

In colonial days Reading was an important shipping port for sugar. During the 1950s, several of the old wharfside buildings metamorphosed into the winter home of Millicent Rogers, an eccentric heir to the Standard Oil Company fortune who arrived in Jamaica with a retinue of Indians from Taos, New Mexico (her warehouse recently opened as Norma's at the Wharf, a top-notch restaurant; see Places to Eat below). The hills above Reading are still popular with the international elite, who maintain fashionable homes here.

Budha's Art Gallery is worth a stop; it's on the left, 200 yards west of the junction to Anchovy.

Scuba Diving
Reading is a good spot for scuba diving: offshore is Reading Reef, at the western extreme of the Montego Bay Marine Park.

The old wharf at the west end of Reading is the setting for Jamaica Rose Ltd (☎ 979-9137), which runs a complete dive shop and offers a range of diving packages (one-tank dive US$30, certified night dive US$45, resort course US$70, PADI Open-Water Course US$250). Poseidon Divers has a dive center on-site.

Sport Fishing
Jamaica Rose Ltd (see above) also offers fishing trips and charters (from $20 per person, 16 people maximum) aboard *Four Stars*, a sleek motor cruiser once owned by band leader Guy Lombardo, Sloane Wilson (author of *Man in the Gray Flannel Suit*), and singers Steve Lawrence and Eydie Gorme. Half-day fishing trips cost US$300

to US$350 for up to four passengers, including beers, sodas, and tackle; a full day runs US$450 to US$650, including lunch.

Places to Stay
You'll find oceanfront cottages for rent at *Beach House Apartments*, opposite Budha's Art Gallery. Nearby is *Chalet Caribe Hotel* (Box 365, ☎ 952-1365), which concentrates on scuba diving and offers 30 studios, apartments and hotel rooms, starting at US$40. Mrs Jarrett runs an unnamed *B&B* on the south side of the road, 2½ miles west of Reading. She has two rooms with single and double beds, plus private bath with hot water. Rates are 'negotiable,' she says.

Two miles west of Reading is *Sahara de la Mer Resort*, a modest two-story hotel built around a coral reef from which the swimming pool – open to the sea – has been cut (PO Box 223, Reading, ☎ 979-0846, fax 979-0847; in the USA, ☎ (213) 292-4803). The hotel also has its own tiny beach, plus a freshwater pool and Jacuzzi. There are 24 spacious rooms with custom furnishings, air-con and ceiling fans, hot water, satellite TV and telephone, and oodles of light. French doors open to a wide terrace; the suite has its own spacious balcony. There's also a beauty shop plus restaurant with wrap-around windows. Summer rates are US$45/65 for a single/double standard; US$55/75 deluxe; US$80/100 suite.

Reading Reef Club is an upscale property tucked cozily on its own small private beach on Bogue Lagoon, immediately opposite the junction to Anchovy (PO Box 225, Reading, ☎ 952-5909, fax 952-7217; in the US, ☎ (800) 223-6510, fax (402) 398-3217). Small and intimate, the elegant hotel has 37 oceanfront rooms and two- and three-bedroom suites (some with king-size beds). All have verandas and louvered windows, air-con, fans, and telephone. There's a breezy terrace bar plus a pool. There is a five-night minimum Christmas and New Year. Rates are US$75/100 a single/double for a superior, US$100/125 deluxe, and US$250/300 suite.

Places to Eat
Exuding ambiance is *Norma's at the Wharf* (Reading PO, ☎ 979-2745), in the old bayside warehouse of the Montpelier Estate. Norma Shirley has justifiably been acclaimed the 'Julia Child of the Caribbean'. The menu includes such dishes as deviled crab-back (US$7) and Château-briand in peppercorn sauce (US$30). It's not cheap, but Norma's food will have you salivating for more. Guests dine on the brick patio and wooden dock with views across the bay or inside the venerable limestone building full of antiques.

The *Safari Restaurant* at the Reading Reef Club is recommended for its seafood, which is delivered fresh each day by local fishermen.

Getting There & Away
You can take any of the buses or minibuses that ply the A1 between Montego Bay and Negril; just ask the driver to let you off. It should cost no more than US$0.10 by bus or US$0.50 by minibus.

GREAT RIVER
Three miles west of Reading the road crosses the mouth of the Great River, which forms the boundary between St James and Hanover Parishes. Snook can reportedly still be caught in small numbers in the lower river course, as can tarpon – one of the Caribbean's most feisty gamefish – at the rivermouth. The watercourse is virtually uninhabited, although women and children gather to bathe and do laundry.

Rafting
Mountain Valley Rafting (Great River Rafting & Plantation Tour Ltd, PO Box 23, Montego Bay, ☎ 952-0527, fax 952-8231) offers tranquil two-hour river trips from Lethe, nine miles upriver (see Lethe, below). You're punted downstream aboard long, narrow bamboo rafts poled by an expert raftsman. The waters are generally calm and, depending on river conditions, good for swimming beside the raft or in calm pools. The journey is about two miles and includes a stop at a riverside garden

and small zoo. You can choose an optional lunch at a riverside park where you can take a donkey ride or laze in a hammock with a rum cocktail or coconut water. An optional plantation tour is also offered. Trips cost US$34 for two passengers (children under 12 are half price). A restaurant provides hot lunches for US$10. The company has an office at 3 Strand St in Montego Bay.

Kayaking
The section from Lethe to the estuary also provides one of Jamaica's best white-water kayak runs. The journey was pioneered in 1983 by Peter Bentley of Sense Adventures in Kingston and John Yost of Sobek Expeditions in California. The locals implored their 11-man team not to canoe downstream. 'Don' go down deh sah. Lawd boss, the ribber she bad. No man, dat a serious ting!' Bentley recalls them saying.

The first five miles lead through spectacular gorges with sheer rock walls festooned with foliage. The waters are usually calm, with a few white-water sections (Class 2 or 3) that give the bamboo rafters an added treat. A sharp bend in the river announces a change of pace. The river tumbles through more than a dozen rapids that increase in difficulty (some are Class 5, listed as 'extremely challenging') and require scouting. The run varies markedly throughout the year. During heavy rains the river can rise as much as 25 feet, reaching the graceful old stone bridge in Lethe. Inflatable rafts are recommended because of the many sharp rocks. Peter Bentley rents tough, inflatable Sea Eagle kayaks (Sense Adventures, PO Box 216, Kingston 7, ☎ 927-2097, fax 929-6967).

Entertainment
Each Tuesday, Thursday, and Sunday, Great River Productions (☎ 952-5047) offers an 'Evening on the Great River.' It costs US$30, including round-trip transfers from Montego Bay. You'll travel by fishing boat up the torch-lit river from its mouth, followed by a barbecue dinner with a calypso

and limbo show, and dancing to live music. Trips depart Montego Bay at 7 pm.

LETHE

This small village is the starting point for raft trips on the Great River. Lethe is in the hills about four miles south of Reading; signs show the way. The graceful stone bridge spanning the Great River was built in 1828, badly damaged in the 1957 earthquake, and has since been restored to its former glory. The cylindrical apertures in the abutments are a clever device meant to provide a spillway during high waters. The overgrown remains of an old sugar mill remain on the riverbank.

Nature Village Farm

This farm-turned-family-resort offers fishing and other attractions. The site is the venue for the annual 'All That Heritage Jazz Festival' in mid-October (☎ 979-7963 or 952-6231). It's reached to the left at a Y-junction two miles north of Lethe. You can't miss the huge sign. After one mile, you'll get to gates where signs announce 'No trespassers!' Disregard them. There's no other sign, but you've arrived at Nature Village.

Rafting

Mountain Valley Rafting runs river trips on Great River beginning in Lethe (see Great River above).

Places to Stay

Busha's Country Resort & Farm (☎ 952-0712) is a modest retreat on the site of a former sugar plantation. It's surrounded by 200 acres of farmland and forest, into which hiking trails lead. The place offers 'holistic' vacations and is popular with religious groups on weekends. Facilities include an outside bar under shade, kiddie swings, and an attractive pool and sundeck with swim-up bar. Condos are planned. Rooms cost US$60/65 single/double; US$65 for studio with kitchenette. Day visits cost US$30 including use of all facilities, plus guided hikes and horseback rides.

To reach Busha's take a dirt road that begins one mile west of the B8 on the road to Lethe.

Getting There & Away

The turnoff for Lethe is two miles south of Reading. Drive carefully up Long Hill, a steep and narrow ascent from Reading; the serpentine road is heavily trafficked with buses and trucks.

ROCKLANDS BIRD FEEDING STATION

Rocklands is a favorite of birders who have flocked here since 1958 when it was founded by Miss Lisa Salmon, a famous artist, writer, and naturalist who has tamed and trained over 20 bird species to come and feed from her hand. Miss Salmon is quite a lively character and her humor is keen. A variety of birds show up reliably in midafternoon at 3:15 pm: ground doves, orange quits, saffron finches, and hummingbirds, including most spectacularly the doctorbird.

Miss Salmon will pour birdseed into your hand or provide you with a sugarwater feeder with which to tempt birds. Seats are arranged theater-style on a stone patio festooned with orchids and other epiphytes and plants, and from where there is a miraculous view over Montego Bay. Guests sit in religious awe as a hummingbird streaks in to hover like a miniature helicopter before finally perching on an outstretched finger – hopefully yours. Soon, half a dozen or more birds may be feeding. Over 140 birds have been recorded. When I last called in, a rare pottoo had established a nest, and a Jamaican owl had recently made an appearance.

Unfortunately the elderly Miss Salmon, with her amazing repertoire of bird lore, is now limited by her health. Her replacement guide, Fritz, is also an expert on birds.

Rocklands (☎ 952-2009) is open 2 to 5 pm or longer depending on the lighting. No calls are accepted after 6 pm, as Miss Salmon is early to bed. You can make a special appointment for an early morning walk with Fritz. Entrance costs US$5.

Miss Salmon offers *accommodations* for up to 10 people (serious birders only) for US$20 per person. Meals are not included, but modest cooking facilities are available.

The turnoff to the east from the B8 is 200 yards south of the signed turnoff for Lethe. The dirt road to Rocklands (400 yards) climbs steeply and was in appalling condition last time I drove it. You can also take a bus from Montego Bay for Savanna-la-Mar or Black River. There's a bus stop on the B8 near the turnoff for Rocklands.

ANCHOVY

Perhaps the only reason to stop at this non-descript village is to view Mt Carey Baptist Church on a knoll on the right about one mile south of town. The church – a replica of the original, destroyed in the 1957 earthquake – was the headquarters for Rev Thomas Burchell (1799 – 1846), a leading missionary in the fight for emancipation. An obelisk commemorates the abolitionist, who founded the Baptist movement in western Jamaica.

In town there is a post office, police station, and several restaurants, including the *Anchovy Progressive Pork Shop* serving jerk pork, grilled fish, and so on.

You might call in at Anchovy Furniture Factory, where you can order handcrafted four-poster beds and other large hardwood pieces for delivery, but at least one couple prepaid for furniture and had not received anything two years later.

MONTPELIER

South of Anchovy you drop down into a broad valley planted in the citrus trees of Montpelier Estates, formerly an important sugar estate now owned by the Jamaica Orange Co. The Ministry of Agriculture also maintains an important cattle research station, assisted by the New Zealand government. It was here, in the 1890s, that Zebu cattle (from Africa) and Mysore cattle (from India) were crossed with native stock to produce a Jamaican breed of draft cattle.

The great house of the old Montpelier sugar plantation burned down a few years back, but St Mary's Anglican Church still stands on a knoll overlooking the remains of the sugar factory.

The B8 splits a stone's throw south of the church. The main road continues south. The road to the southeast (the B6) leads to Seaford.

Blue Hole Nature Park

This family 'eco-park,' three miles south of Anchovy, opened in 1995 on a 800-acre complex in the hills east of the valley (PO Box 26, Cambridge, St James, ☎ 990-5582). A guided plantation tour is offered, and horseback rides are planned through the groves of interspersed pineapple and citrus. There are botanical gardens and picnic groves, plus an impressive 60-foot-wide circular swimming pool with meandering cascades. A bird and wildlife sanctuary are in the planning stage. Meals are served alfresco at a thatched restaurant and bar. The park is open 8 am to 5 pm and costs US$2 (children US$1). Ask for Spence, the superintendent, to show you around.

About 400 yards uphill (beyond the entrance) is the Blue Hole – a jade-colored sinkhole measuring 164 feet deep (but only 12 feet wide). It's been tapped by the Water Commission to supply local communities, so iron fences have spoiled the setting. No swimming!

The park owners had plans to install log cabins and tent sites with toilets and cooking facilities.

To get to the park, look for the signed turnoff 400 yards north of the gas station at Montpelier. You'll see St Mary's Church ahead; keep to the right and follow the pot-holed road steeply uphill for two miles.

CAMBRIDGE

From Montpelier the B6 follows the Great River Valley five miles to this attractive little crossroads town centered on a railroad station in disuse. Cambridge (population 3000) seems small and insignificant, but it's the second largest town in St James Parish and the center of a banana and coffee producing area. It has a bank and gas station. If you want to explore locally, ask for Tony Fitzroy Dove at Lou Lou's (see below). He'll be happy to act as a guide. 'What you give is what I tek,' he says. 'We no rush people here. Leave de visitors to dem mind.'

Places to Stay & Eat
Half-a-mile south of Cambridge at Mount Faith, just beyond the crest of a hill, is *Lou Lou's*, a gaily painted little craft shop and restaurant. Don't fail to stop! Lou Lou is a jovial, charismatic figure. If you're hungry, try her fried chicken and fish, mutton, and pepperpot soup (US$2 to US$5). You can also buy fresh coconuts to slake your thirst (US$0.60).

Lou Lou has a small and basic one-bedroom cottage behind her store. Furnishings are bare, but it's clean and has a small balcony. It rents for US$28 per night (overpriced) or US$50 a month (a bargain), but these rates are probably negotiable.

MARCHMONT
This crossroads (there's no village to speak of) is the gateway to Croydon and Catadupa (east), and Seaford (southwest). Just north of Marchmont lies a Rastafarian retreat, unmistakable for its vividly painted walls. Apparently, only true believers are allowed and casual camera-touting visitors are discouraged.

A grocery store sits at the four-way junction. Fifty yards south of the Marchmont crossroads is *Josy's Ice Cream Parlour & Restaurant*, a pleasant little eatery (closed Sundays).

CATADUPA
In 1978 I recall arriving by train – the Governor's Coach – at this then-lively village, where locals had a thriving trade selling crafts and making clothing to order for passengers en route to the Appleton Rum Estate (you were measured for skirts or shirts en route to Appleton and they were finished and ready for pickup on the way back). Today Catadupa is a collection of aging buildings around the railroad station. A number of locals eke out a living growing coffee and bananas.

The village is named for some nearby cascades and reflects the Greek name for the Nile cataracts in Egypt.

The road from Marchmont (two miles) is in horrible condition. In Catadupa it swings right at the railway station and leads uphill to Mocho and Maroon Town. You'll need a 4WD vehicle to handle the bone-jarring ride. 'Road bad to Hell, mon!' an old timer told me when I unsuccessfully attempted it in an ordinary sedan. What an understatement! You can also get to Catadupa directly by bus Nos STBW466 and 485 from the Parade in Kingston (about US$1.50).

Croydon Plantation
This thriving plantation (also named Croydon on the Mountain) has hillside terraces planted in coffee, citrus, and five varieties of pineapples. Honey is also produced, and a hive under glass allows you to see the busy bees at work. The terrain is too hilly for mechanization, as will be explained to you on a 'see, hear, touch, and taste' tour offered daily from 10:30 am to 3 pm (except Sunday). The tour costs US$45, including lunch and transfers. Advance reservations are advisable. Croydon, reached via a sideroad from Catadupa (one mile), has a fabulous setting and spectacular views.

Caribic Vacations offers a Croydon Plantation Tour from Montego Bay; their office is on Gloucester Ave (☎ 952-5013, fax 952-0981).

From Montego Bay, the plantation is a 45-minute journey by bus No LS70.

HILTON
This beautiful old plantation home has a splendid hilltop location at St Leonards, two miles southwest of Marchmont (PO Box 162, Reading, St James, ☎ 952-3343 or 952-5642). The house is overgrown with thumbergia, which hangs over the veranda, from which you can savor tremendous views. It's very cool inside. Antiques abound.

The house is the venue for the all-day 'Hilton High Day Tour,' which begins with a Jamaican breakfast in the house. You then take a guided walk to Seaford Town (one mile away) and the village of St Leonards, where you'll visit the Basic School. The walk should create an appetite for a roast-suckling-pig luncheon prepared in a brick oven back at Hilton. You're led down to the pigsties, where dozens of little piggies go *oink! oink! oink!*. Say 'hi!' to your future lunch. The meal also features a choice of homemade lemonade (fantastic!), shandy (half lemonade, half beer), or rum punch. For the rest of the afternoon, you're free to relax or roam the 100-acre plantation on horseback before returning.

Tours are offered on Tuesday, Wednesday, Friday, and Sunday (US$35 for call-in visitors, or US$40 including transfers from Montego Bay). Horseback riding costs US$10 for 30 minutes using English saddle. The hot-air balloon rides for which Hilton was once famous are no longer offered.

SEAFORD TOWN

This fascinating village has a singular history. Its scattered tumbledown cottages follow a traditional German design that points to Seaford's unusual origin. The hillside village was settled by northern German immigrants in 1835 as part of the colonial program of establishing European settlements in Jamaica as emancipation approached.

Between 1834 and 1838, more than 1200 Germans arrived in Jamaica, of which an initial group of 251 settled Seaford (along with a dozen or so English families). The land – 500 acres on Montpelier Mountain – was donated by Lord Seaford, who owned 10,000 acres locally (the Germans were promised that they would receive title to their land after five years' labor; they toiled for 15 before the land became theirs). It was hoped that these industrious settlers would create a thriving settlement and act as a model for the newly freed slaves, but others suggest an ulterior motive: if Europeans settled the hills, the ex-slaves would be forced to remain in the lowlands and work on the plantations; the settlements would also act as a buffer between the plantations and the marauding Maroons.

In fact, the settlers had a hard time. The farmland that the Germans had been promised turned out to be a tangled wilderness. And only a few of the settlers were farmers; most were tradespeople or former soldiers. Fortunately, the immigrants received free rations for the first 18 months, but even before the rations ran out, the Germans had settled into a life of poverty. Tropical diseases and social isolation soon reduced the population to less than 100 within two or three years. Only a fraction of the original settlers stayed, although enough did that they established a viable German community the legacy of which is felt to this day.

The initial community was a mix of Protestants and Catholics, but most of the Germans were converted to Catholicism by Father Tauer, an energetic Austrian priest who settled here in the 1870s. Currently, less than 200 Seaford inhabitants can claim German ancestry; the rest have emigrated over the past few decades. Whites are today only 20% of Seaford's population. Still, despite 150 years, there are relatively few mulattos in evidence. Socially, Seaford is integrated; sexually it is not. The fifteen or so families have intermarried for so long that inbreeding has caused problems. Seaford's whites remain practicing Catholics and still practice a few folk customs, though German is rarely spoken.

Seaford Town Historical Mini-Museum

This tiny museum (☎ 995-9399) tells the fascinating tale of Seaford's German origins. There are maps and photographs of the early settlement, plus artifacts spanning 150 years, including such curiosities as cricket bats made from the stems of coconut leaves. Overhead, note the list of original settlers and their trades.

Entrance costs US$1. The town priest, Friar Bobby Gilmore, keeps the key to the museum; he lives in the green-and-white house opposite the museum. However, you should first seek out the caretaker, Spencer Gardner, who lives 100 yards beyond the museum; his house is the last in the row along a dirt road just below the health center. Spencer is planning to expand the museum and to publish a history of the Seaford Germans.

Church of the Sacred Heart

This red, zinc-roofed old stone structure sits atop a rise overlooking Seaford. Its precursor was built by Father Tauer in the late 19th century but was totally demolished in the hurricane of 1912, when the belfry was flung more than 100 yards and even the foundation stones weighing 1000 pounds were picked up and tossed down the hill. Take time to browse the overgrown graveyard.

The road beyond the church continues uphill to a health clinic and the government-run St Boniface Industrial Training Centre, which trains school-leavers in technical trades.

Places to Stay & Eat

I'm not aware of any regular accommodations, but you're sure to find someone who'll rent you a room by asking around. *Johnson's Circle Tree Bar* is 100 yards west of the turnoff for the church in Seaford; it has shaded outdoor dining.

BELVEDERE ESTATE

Belvedere is a family-owned working plantation of 1000 acres, of which 500 are cultivated with tropical fruits (PO Box 361, Montego Bay, ☎ 952-6001, fax 957-4097; in Negril, ☎ 957-4170). Red Poll cattle graze the other 500 acres. There's a waterfall where you may bathe.

The estate offers a fascinating perspective on modern estate life and a touristy but intriguing re-creation of how things were almost three centuries ago, when the estate became one of the first sugarcane plantations in Jamaica. You're welcomed by guides in Jamaican-bandanna prints offering sugarloaf, and pineapple and orange samplers, while a farmhand coaxes a donkey in circles to demonstrate the workings of an old sugar press. If you've arrived under your own steam, a guide will come in your car as you drive through the groves of citrus and coconut palms. She'll also walk you through the botanical gardens and Post-Emancipation Village, featuring huts where a basket-weaver, baker, blacksmith, and coffee and cocoa grinder demonstrate traditional skills.

The entrance with tour costs US$10, or US$15 including a Jamaican lunch in an atmospheric thatched restaurant where a mento band provides entertainment. A tour by tractor-pulled jitney is in the works. And Pat McGann, the owner, is restoring one of the two old great houses (destroyed in the 1831 slave rebellion) as a guest house.

Belvedere is at Chester Castle, three miles southwest of Montpelier (take the B7, which splits from the B8). Organized group excursions to Belvedere are available through tour operators in Montego Bay.

Belvedere is served from Montego Bay by minibus No LS729. You can also take another minibus No LS957, which travels between MoBay and Darliston; ask Trevor Jamieson to drop you at Chester Castle, from where you can walk.

STRUIE

Struie, five miles south of Chester Castle and five miles west of Seaford Town, is known for its roadside tomb of a British solder killed in an ambush during the slave rebellion of Christmas 1831. Legend says that his head was severed and fled the scene. Locals believe the area to be haunted by the soldier's ghost. Listen carefully at night and you may be able to hear the clash of swords!

Last time I drove by, the grave was totally concealed by long grass.

KNOCKALVA

Following the B8 southwest from Montpelier leads to Knockalva, the center of an agricultural training farm that for over a century has been a leading cattle breeding center. The school is centered on a great house built in 1859 and later modified in Asian-Gothic style by a Scottish freemason, Major Malcolm, with pillars and arches echoing Solomon's Temple. The garden he laid out was his version of Gethsemane.

The hills south of Knockalva are festooned with spectacular groves of bamboo. Five miles south of Knockalva you pass through the village of Whithorn. As you round a bend immediately beyond it, the sugarcane plains of Westmoreland are suddenly laid out below, with the twin white stacks of the Frome sugar plantation off in the distance (see the Frome section in the West Coast chapter). The driveway of the Coke View Methodist Church, on the left on the hillside, is a good place to pull over for a photograph. For an even better view, follow the road east from Whithorn to Darliston; it winds in hairpins up Frame Hill.

Places to Eat

Restaurants are in short supply. *Leslie's Place* at Haddo is a colorful if funky rum shop and restaurant where you can sup a Red Stripe and eat curried goat with locals for about US$3. On a bend just south of Haddo is *Capitol*, a bar and gift store owned by Marilyn, a friendly Canadian woman. It's a cool joint. You can't miss its mural of Bob Marley on the outside wall. Marilyn used to offer rooms and meals but during a recent visit she told me she was thinking of selling: she'd recently been robbed at gun point and wanted to pack up and move back to Canada.

West Coast

- Negril Beach, hands-down the best spot for laid-back sunning by day and live reggae by night
- Scuba diving off Negril Beach
- Peaceful Royal Palm Nature Preserve, full of wildlife
- Roaring River, for atmosphere and natural beauty

Many travelers know the West Coast merely as Negril, Jamaica's hippest, most laid-back resort, with the island's most beautiful beach and a nightlife with a buzz. Negril also boasts superb coral reefs and excellent scuba diving, plus a large swamp area – the Great Morass – that as yet remains undeveloped but is a naturalist's paradise.

Other than Negril, the coast is relatively undeveloped, although a couple of Jamaica's finest hotels are here. The region is drier than further east and the vegetation not as lush.

The A1 leads west from Montego Bay and hugs the coast of Hanover Parish virtually the entire way to Negril, at the most western tip of Jamaica. It's a pleasing drive as you wind in and out of tiny coves with occasional dramatic coastal vistas. Visitors rarely explore the roads that lead inland.

From Negril, the A2 turns east, leading through the flatlands of Westmoreland Parish to Savanna-la-Mar. Tourism has bypassed the south coast east of 'Sav.' Densely forested hills edge the twisty road. The few lonesome beaches attract contemplative sorts who like to slumber in hammocks away from the rest of the world. The area is only now awakening from its Rip Van Winkle slumber. Plans are moving ahead for three major resort developments that have many local residents concerned about the disruption of their bucolic ways. The area is politically favored, as it's the constituency of Prime Minister PJ Patterson, so change of some sort is coming.

Great River to Negril

Hanover Parish begins west of the Great River. After crossing the river, the A1 winds uphill to a headland where you should stop to take in the sweeping vista back toward Montego Bay. The road then moves away from the shore and drops down through a dwarf coconut plantation and passes Round Hill (see Places to Stay under Hopewell below), one of two premier resort hotels along this section of coast.

The only town of note is Lucea. Most travelers buzz on by without a second glance at the intriguing historic buildings, but you can happily spend a couple of hours here.

West of Lucea the road wriggles past small fishing villages and around tiny coves with pocket-size beaches hidden along a relatively undeveloped coast once favored as a place of refuge by pirates. Though their sights were on Spanish treasure galleons, they often marauded local plantations. Just beyond Orange Bay, the road swings around a wide expanse of swampland – the Great Morass – before opening onto the stunning seven-mile-long beach of Negril.

If you're driving, be careful on this section of road. Motorists are tempted to

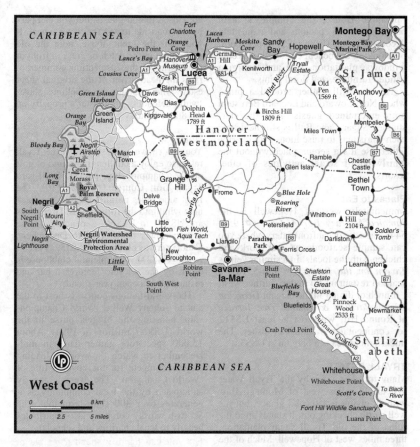

CARIBBEAN SEA

Montego Bay

Fort
Charlotte   Lucea
Orange   Harbour   Moskito   Sandy
Cove   Cove   Bay   Hopewell
Pedro Point   Montego Bay
Lance's Bay   German   Marine Park   A1
Hanover   Hill
A1   Kenilworth   Tryall
Museum   881 ft   Estate   St James
Cousins Cove   Lucea
Lances R   B9   Old   Anchovy
Davis   Blenheim   Pen
Green Island   Cove   Dias   Birchs Hill   1569 ft   B8
Harbour   Kingsvale   Dolphin   1809 ft
Green Island   Head   Miles Town   Montpelier   B6
Orange   1789 ft
Bay   Hanover   B8   B7
Bloody Bay   Negril   Westmoreland   Ramble   Chester
Airstrip   Glen Islay   Castle
The   March   Bethel
Long   Great   Town   Town
Bay   Morass   Grange   Blue Hole
A1   Royal   Hill   Frome   Roaring   Orange
Negril   Palm Reserve   River   Whithorn   Hill   Soldier's
South   A2   Delve   2104 ft   Tomb
Negril   Mount   Sheffield   Bridge   Petersfield   B8   Darliston
Point   Airy
Negril   Negril Watershed   Little   B9   Leamington
Lighthouse   Environmental   London   Fish World,   Llandilo   Paradise   Ferris Cross   B7
Protection Area   Aqua Tech   Park
Little   New   Bluff   Newmarket
Bay   Broughton   Point   Shafston
Robins   Savanna-   A2   Estate
Point   la-Mar   Bluefields   Great
South West   Bay   House
Point   Pinnock
Bluefields   Wood
2533 ft   Newmarket
Crab Pond Point   Surinam Quarters
St Eliz-
abeth
A2
CARIBBEAN SEA   Whitehouse
Whitehouse Point
West Coast   Scott's Cove   To Black
River
0   4   8 km   Font Hill Wildlife Sanctuary
0   2.5   5 miles   Luana Point

speed. Minibuses drivers display particularly reckless abandon, screeching around bends at tremendous speeds.

HOPEWELL

This small wayside village sits at the junction to Cacoon Castle and Miles Town, five miles west of Reading. The skeleton of the *Caribou*, an iron-hulled steamer that ran aground during a storm in the 1890s, still protrudes from the shore one mile west of Hopewell.

For an absorbing browse, stop at the Craft Potters, where wicker, intriguing figurines, and huge pots and vases are for sale.

Places to Stay

The roster of regulars at *Round Hill* says it all: Paul McCartney, Ringo Starr, Jackie Kennedy. The 98-acre resort was created in 1954 as the first cottage-type hotel, and in the early days it opened only in winter (PO Box 64, Montego Bay, ☎ (800) 972-2159 or 952-5150, fax 952-2505; or call Elegant Resorts of Jamaica, ☎ (800) 237-3237). Round Hill has been lauded ever since as one of the best hotels in the world.

The 27 private villas on the hillside are as individual as thumbprints (US$360 double). Most are magnificently furnished and many have their own private pools.

Pineapple House, the complex's main building, has 36 spacious and exquisitely decorated rooms (from US$190 per room) overlooking the beach, each with louvered windows, plantation-style and Georgian antique furniture, and floral prints.

You can still gather around a piano where Noel Coward and Leonard Bernstein both entertained guests. And the star-studded Sugar Cane Ball is still held here each Christmas to raise money for charity. Otherwise it's a serene place without the whirlwind of social activities of other resorts.

Places to Eat
Immediately west of Hopewell is the *Jamaica Micrazy Bar & Grill* (☎ 956-5448), a rustic oceanfront eatery where you can sample seafood and jerk pork and chicken with the locals. In a similar vein is *Tavern on the Beach* (☎ 956-5578), a seafood restaurant 50 meters further west.

Lunch or dinner in the elegant *Georgian Dining Pavilion & Almond Tree Terrace* at Round Hill will cost at least US$12 for continental and Jamaican dishes. The midafternoon tea is a bargain at US$3.

TRYALL ESTATE
Many travelers whiz by the Tryall Water Wheel, 14 miles west of Montego Bay, without giving it a second glance, but it's well worth checking out. It stands amid the ruins of the old Tryall sugar plantation, three miles west of Hopewell. Much of the estate, including the huge wheel that drove the cane-crushing mill, was destroyed in the slave rebellion of Christmas 1831 (see the sidebar Preaching Resistance in the Northwest Coast chapter). Restored to working condition in the late 1950s, the wheel is still turned by water carried by a two-mile-long aqueduct from the Flint River.

The great house atop the hill is today the hub of one of Jamaica's most exclusive resort properties: Tryall Golf, Tennis & Beach Club (see Places to Stay below). The resort is built atop the remains of a small fort and is still guarded by cannons. The great house and 2200-acre resort complex are closed to non-guests, but you can park by the roadside to see the water wheel. If you visit the great house, note the old gravestone in the patch of grass in front of the entrance: the inscription commemorates the head driver of the original sugar estate who was shot by rebellious slaves 'while defending his master's property on the 8th of January 1832.'

Golf
You don't have to be staying at the Tryall resort to enjoy a challenging round of golf on the championship, par 71, 6920-yard Tryall Golf Course (☎ 952-5110). The front nine holes parallel the sea; the back nine wind into the rolling hills. Green fees are US$40 to US$60, depending on the season (lower from April to December). Caddies are available for US$15, as is cart rental (US$27). The splendid clubhouse is down by the sea and features a bar and restaurant. It's open year-round.

The world-famous course is host to the annual Johnny Walker World Championship, boasting the biggest purse in the world (US$2.7 million in 1994). About 15,000 spectators gather daily in mid-December to watch the world's leading players compete for the coveted title of 'World Champion.' The event is eagerly anticipated by the local community as it generates over 300 short-term jobs (the Scottish whisky company also contributes heavily to local charities and schools).

Places to Stay & Eat
Tryall Golf, Tennis & Beach Club (PO Box 1206, Montego Bay, ☎ 956-5660 or (800) 336-4571, fax 956-5673; in the UK, ☎ (0171) 1602-7181, fax (0171) 1938-4793; in Germany, ☎ (089) 642-3015, fax (089) 642-3434) is magnificent. At its heart is the old hilltop great house with a bar and lounge where you can savor a traditional English afternoon tea while enjoying the fabulous coastal views.

The house had its roof ripped off by Hurricane Gilbert in 1988. It has since been restored and new wings include 52 gracious, air-con rooms (from US$230/280 single/double). More than 50 stunning villas (from one to five bedrooms, US$1950 to US$5550 weekly in summer) are scattered throughout the estate. Each is staffed with cook, housekeeper, laundress, and gardener. There's a large pool set into the hillside beside the gourmet Veranda Restaurant.

SANDY BAY

This hamlet immediately west of Tryall began life as a 'free village' founded by Rev Thomas Burchell for emancipated slaves. His Baptist church, dating to 1848, still stands. Many locals are christened Burchell in the Jamaican custom of honoring people they admire. The only tourist appeal is the famous beachfront restaurant and dance spot, Lollypop on the Beach.

West of town watch for **Blue Hole Estate**, a charming old great house backed by hills, fronted by wide pasture, and with a stump of a windmill at the edge of the former polo field. It was once the home of William DeLisser, former custos (the English monarch's representative) of Hanover Parish, who owned a sugar estate and factory here. It's not open to the public.

Places to Stay & Eat

Lollypop on the Beach (☎ 953-5314) has two small, basic but clean air-con rooms with cold water. They're overpriced at US$27 per night and are directly above the stage and dance area, but there's no denying the place has atmosphere! Lollypop is very popular with locals for its mouth-searing jerk pork and chicken, and as a well-known dance hall. It offers packages from Negril, including Carnival Nite on Tuesdays (US$20); Jamaica Beach Party Nite on Wednesdays (US$45 including unlimited beer, glass-bottom boat cruise, and round-trip transfers from hotels in Negril); and a Friday night seafood fiesta.

KENILWORTH

Just beyond the Maggotty River you'll see a turnoff to the left for the Human Employment & Resource Training Trust (HEART Trust), about one mile along a dirt road at

Kenilworth (formerly called Maggotty). The HEART Trust was established in 1982 as a residential academy to provide vocational and personal development training to young Jamaicans. It operates under the Ministry of Education & Culture and today offers courses in data processing, apparel, and, more recently, hospitality skills. It occupies 206 acres of an old sugar plantation acclaimed as the best example of old industrial architecture in Jamaica. The 17th-century ruins are on the left at the base of the hill; the HEART academy rises up the slope. Tourists are welcome. Don't be put off by the daunting wire-mesh gate. The guard will let you in if you ask (no charge).

Most prominent among the estate ruins are the sugar boiling house and distillery and the long rectangular sugar mill, a two-story limestone building with a semicircular flight of stairs leading up to an arched doorway. The walls have oval Palladian windows trimmed in lighter stone that contrasts with the darker masonry. A graveyard, 400 yards up the hill beyond the ruins, includes the tomb of Thomas Blagrove, an early owner whose family also owned Cardiff Hall in St Ann. According to the inscription, 'his humane treatment of his servants, in a region not abounding in such examples, induced their cheerful obedience.'

Plans call for the ruins to be restored – the venerable mill, for example, will be turned into a performing arts theater. HEART is also developing a tour and is planning to build six rooms plus a restaurant and conference center in the old drying house. For further information contact Samuel Boyd, Kenilworth HEART Trust/ NTA Academy, Sandy Bay PO, Hanover (☎ 953-5315).

MOSKITO COVE

This long, slender inlet, one mile west of the turnoff for HEART, is a popular place to anchor yachts. It's rimmed with mangroves and a few rustic jerk stalls and beer shacks. **Bigga's Royal Dwarf Factory** is where a friendly Jamaican named Bigga does naive carvings and masks to order.

Watch for the life-size wooden figure in a yellow shirt and red shorts outside his ramshackle hut.

Beyond Moskito Cove the road crosses a beautiful, wide-open grassy plain that slopes gently towards the ocean. Drive with caution! Cows often wander aimlessly along the road. Look, too, for the stack (rock pillar) offshore that some say resembles Queen Victoria in profile.

LUCEA

'Lucy' (population 6000), as the town is commonly known, is built around a peaceful harbor ringed by hills on three sides. One of them – Animal Hill – is named for the families (the Wolfs, the Lyons, the Mairs, and the Hoggs) who once lived there. Small enough for visitors to walk everywhere, Lucea is a somnolent place except on Saturdays when the market is in full force. Back in early colonial days, however, it was a more active port than Montego Bay.

The town abounds in old limestone and timber structures of a style referred to as 'Caribbean vernacular,' with gingerbread wood trim, clapboard frontages, and wide verandas. The oldest dates back to the mid-1700s. Lucea has appeared as a set in several movies, including *Cool Runnings* and *Wide Sargasso Sea*. The Hanover Historical Society, formed in 1989, is active in the town's preservation. You can walk around with relatively little hassle, although a number of drug-related robberies in recent years have marred the town's crime-free reputation.

Only the 'molasses pier' remains of the once-busy shipping wharves. Molasses is still loaded onto cargo ships from huge tanks next to the pier. More important today is the free-trade zone west of town where several US companies have factories.

Local residents have set up a small-scale 'visitor in the home' program similar to the JTB's Meet the People program.

History

Lucea is one of Jamaica's earliest settlements. The first written record of Lucea dates back to 1515, when King Ferdinand of Spain commended his governor in Jamaica for moving settlers to the site after the capital of Sevilla la Nueva was abandoned. The town grew on the shores of Santa Lucia Harbour, which, according to a local plaque, was 'about three cables wide' and extended inland for one mile. In 1774 historian Edward Long estimated that 300 ships at a time could be sheltered here. Lucea had by then been named a freeport by the English. The infamous pirate Henry Morgan even used Lucea Harbour to shelter his ships and later owned 4000 acres locally.

By the mid-18th century Lucea was the center of an important sugar-growing region and the town prospered as a sugar port and market center. Jews from Europe settled and established themselves as merchants, shopkeepers, clothiers, shoemakers, and goldsmiths (a Jewish burial ground can reportedly still be seen behind a private residence at the corner of Cressy Lane and Main St).

Following emancipation, the free peasants prospered in Hanover Parish and supplied produce to much of the rest of Jamaica, which faced economic destitution. The 19th century saw many fine edifices built by skilled artisans (former slaves) including Lucea market and the town hall and courthouse. Main St still retains a few old merchant residences, with timber columns supporting the upper stories, and a fireproof warehouse with brick arches supporting a double-barrel roof.

Lucea is most famous for lending its name to a locally grown yam, which in the 19th century was exported in large quantities to expatriate Jamaicans working on the plantations and railway construction in Cuba and Central America. 'Lucea yams' are still an important crop, along with pimento and ginger.

Information

Money The Bank of Nova Scotia (☎ 956-2235) and National Commercial Bank (☎ 956-2204) each have branches on Main St where you can cash traveler's checks or arrange cash advances.

Medical Services If you need medical assistance, contact Dr David Stair or Dr Taylor Watson (☎ 956-2930). Lucea hospital has an emergency department (☎ 956-2233 or 956-2911); it's on the headland behind Hanover Parish Church, west of town.

Emergencies There are police stations on Main St (☎ 956-2263) and on Watson Taylor Drive (☎ 956-2222).

Sir Alexander Bustamante Square
This small square with a small fountain fronting the handsome courthouse is the center of town. It was formally opened by Queen Elizabeth II on her state visit in 1966.

The courthouse has limestone balustrades and a clapboard upper story topped by a clock tower supported by Corinthian columns. The clock was sent to Lucea in 1817 by mistake – it was actually intended for the Caribbean island of St Lucia. The residents (who had ordered a more modest clock from the same company) decided to keep the more elaborate godsend and passed the hat around to pay for it. It has supposedly worked without a hitch ever since and is said to still be under the maintenance of the Williams family who were given the responsibility for its running over 100 years ago. If you think the cap on the tower resembles the helmet worn by the Prussian Imperial Guards, you're correct. The tower was donated by a German landowner who stipulated that he be allowed to design it.

Note the vintage fire engine (1932) on display beside the courthouse.

Hanover Parish Church
At the top of the hill west of town is Hanover Parish Church (☎ 956-2253), established in 1725. It's architecturally uninspired but has several interesting monuments. Services are on Sunday at 7:30 and 9:30 am, and Wednesday at 6:30 am.

Hanover Museum
This tiny museum (on the right 200 meters west of the church) is housed in an old police barracks including the burned-out

remains of prisoners' cells, where walls are now overgrown with bougainvillea. Bill Bert Graham, the genteel curator, looks after such exhibits as a prisoners' stocks, wooden bathtub, and a miscellany of pots, lead weights, and measures. There's a tiny gift shop, toilets, and a snack bar. It's open Monday to Saturday 9 am to 5 pm. Entrance is US$2.

Rusea High School
A road beside the church leads to Rusea High School, a venerable red-brick Georgian building constructed in 1843 as an army barracks. It has housed the school since 1900. Before then the school was located in the town center, where it was opened in 1777 as an act of benevolence by a French refugee, Martin Rusea. He had washed ashore in a storm and eventually left his estate to the residents of Hanover for their help in saving him.

Fort Charlotte
The overgrown remains of Fort Charlotte overlook the channel a short distance beyond Rusea High School. It's named after Queen Charlotte, wife of King George III of England. The roughly octagonal fortress had embrasures for 23 cannons, some of which are still in place on rails.

Nearby is a small colony of frigate birds that hover like kites overhead.

Places to Stay
The musty smelling *West Palm Hotel* (☎ 956-2321) is an old wooden building, just behind Hanover Parish Church, with 23 simple rooms of varying sizes from US$26 (US$35 with air-con). Some have narrow single beds; others have queen-size beds. All have basic furnishings and private bathrooms with hot water. The hotel is popular with businesspeople, and locals gather at the bar out back. The restaurant reportedly serves reasonable food.

Driftwood (☎ 956-2370) on Third St is a small guest house with eight modest rooms (US$25 to US$35) in a house dating back to the 1780s. Two other options include *Tamarind Lodge* at the east end of town and

Charlotte Inn Guest House (neither have telephones). There are also simple rooms for rent at *Rudy Perry's Sunset Village*, just west of town. *Crystal View* (☎ 957-9225) is a B&B that recently opened outside town.

Places to Eat

The *Hard Rock Cafe* west of Lucea is *not* part of the internationally famous restaurant chain but a funky little shack serving rice and peas, jerk, and other Jamaican dishes for a few dollars.

Long Acre Restaurant & Nightclub, reached via a long tree-lined driveway two miles west of Lucea, stages reggae shows in an atmospheric oceanfront setting. There's a bar but no food. It's a popular wedding venue.

A 'Moskito Cove Beach Picnic' (☎ 952-5164) is held each Tuesday and Thursday at *Bamboo Bay*, immediately east of Lucea Harbour. The cost of US$50 (half price for children) includes transfers from Montego Bay, lunch, entertainment, a glass-bottom boat ride, and use of watersports equipment.

Things to Buy

Check out the works of Lloyd Hoffstead, a well-known local painter and sculptor who has a gallery on Hanover St (☎ 956-2241), on the left as you enter town. There's also a small workshop for disabled people at the entrance to the fort where you can buy crafts.

Getting There & Away

Buses traveling between Montego Bay and Negril pass through Lucea on a regular basis. You can also find plenty of minibuses, which will cost about US$3. From Lucea, minibuses also operate to Frome (US$1), Savanna-la-Mar (US$2), and Kingston (US$8).

A junction at Kew Bridge (at the eastern end of town) leads south over the mountains. The B9 leads south from the courthouse to Frome and Savanna-la-Mar.

LANCE'S BAY

A farmer named Ron has a **cave** with stalagmites and stalactites on his property at Lance's Bay, four miles east of Davis Cove. He charges US$3 for a two-hour guided tour. The stygian chambers are worth checking out for an off-beat adventure.

Hideaway Cottages offers small, well-kept air-con cabins at Lance's Bay, midway between Lucea and Davis Cove. The pink-and-green cottages are set back from the road in well-tended gardens and have a porch with chairs. *Carolina Sunset Inn* is a rustic eatery on the oceanfront just before Lance's Bay.

For a neat off-beat experience, call on Linda. She runs the very laid-back *Casa Linda Country Inn*, 2½ miles west of Lance's Bay. Her rustic two-room guest house is set amid an orchard in a tiny community of subsistence farmers. You reach it via a very rough and rocky road. The rooms cost US$25 double, including breakfast, and are basic but have electricity, private bathroom (cold water), and ocean-view balcony. Linda hopes to have a telephone soon.

BLENHEIM

This tiny hamlet is too small to appear on most maps, but it's important as the birthplace of national hero Alexander Bustamante, father of Jamaican independence and the island's first prime minister. The rustic three-room wooden shack where Bustamante was born has been reconstructed on the original site as a museum and national monument. The museum collection mostly consists of newspaper clippings and photographs. There are no refreshments, but public toilets are available. When I visited, I was the first person in two weeks to sign the guest book. There's no charge.

'Busta' is revered as a champion of Jamaica's poor and oppressed and a memorial ceremony is held in his honor in Blenheim each August 6 (see the sidebar National Hero Busta).

Getting There & Away

Bus You can catch a bus in Lucea. Most of the buses that travel to Grange Hill and Savanna-la-Mar pass through Kingsvale, from where you can walk to Blenheim.

National Hero Busta

Alexander Bustamante, one of Jamaica's most revered national heroes, was born on February 24, 1884, on the Blenheim Estate, where his father was an impoverished overseer. The boy – christened William Alexander Clarke – left Jamaica with limited education in 1903 and worked in several countries before returning to his homeland in 1932 (with the surname Bustamante).

He was already in his 50s when he entered public life by speaking out against the appalling social and political conditions of colonial Jamaica. This charismatic figure organized the local labor force and formed the Bustamante Industrial Trade Union, for which he was imprisoned by the British colonial government following islandwide riots in 1938.

In 1944, he formed the Jamaica Labour Party (JLP) to contest the island's first general election held under universal adult suffrage. The JLP won a resounding victory. 'Busta' thus became Jamaica's first prime minister, a post he held until 1954, the year he was knighted by Queen Elizabeth II. Busta enjoyed unusually cordial relations with the Queen: at a state reception for Commonwealth prime ministers at Buckingham Palace, he once greeted the monarch with the words 'Hello honey!' and a warmly received embrace.

When Jamaica became part of the West Indies Federation, Bustamante was the Jamaican representative of the Democratic Labour Party that assumed power in the federal elections. In 1962, however, he steered the nation to independence following a special referendum in which Jamaicans voted to secede from the federation. Bustamante then led the JLP to victory in the Jamaican general election later that year, thereby becoming the first prime minister in an independent Jamaica. He retired from active politics in 1967 but remained influential. He was named a national hero prior to his death in 1977. ■

Herbert Myers operates a minibus (No LS864) between Negril and Montego Bay via Kingsvale.

Car Blenheim is easiest to approach from Lucea via Dias, where a road leads west to Blenheim. Here you turn right, or west, at June's Pastries. Signs along this road point the way.

From Davis Cove, take the road that leads inland immediately west of the bridge over Davis Cove River (two miles east of the village of Green Island). The road passes through cane fields before climbing through heraldic stands of bamboo. You'll come to a T-junction after two miles; take the left road and continue to a steep dirt road to the right that begins immediately before the second of two tiny bridges. The road looks like it hasn't been used in years but continue uphill half a mile to the Bustamante House.

GREEN ISLAND HARBOUR

Three miles west of Davis Cove (and 12 miles east of Negril) you drop down to the shores of a deep cove – Green Island Harbour – where bright colored pirogues line the thin, gray-sand shore. There are oyster beds here and a forlorn Presbyterian church.

Rhodes Mineral Springs & Beach

Two miles west of Green Island Harbour, a turnoff to the right leads down to this recreational site, where you'll find several thatched bars and restaurants plus a Scuba World Dive Shop (☎ 997-5580) fronting on a small but attractive beach where hot mineral springs bubble up. There's a beach party on Sunday nights.

Places to Stay

JJ's Guest House, just before Green Island Harbour, is a modest yet comfortable place atop a breezy hill with distant views of the ocean (contact Allan and Margaret James, Green Island PO, Hanover, ☎ 956-9159: in the USA, ☎ (718) 968-7469). There are eight rooms, each with two single beds, ceiling fans, and private bathroom with hot water. You can sip your cocktail and dine on Jamaican dishes atop a rooftop patio. There's a swimming pool. It's 400 yards up a dirt road from the highway. Summer rates are US$22/30 single/double (US$30/40 in winter).

Rhodes Mineral Springs & Beach (☎ 956-9230) has four handsome two-bedroom cottages right on the beach. *Rhodes Hall Plantation* (Green Island PO, Westmoreland, ☎ 957-4232) reportedly has inexpensive accommodations on the 550-acre estate.

At Orange Bay, Jasmine McGregor rents *Falcon Crest* (☎ 957-6072), a house for up to six people. There's a kitchen and lounge plus three bedrooms with private bath, hot water, and ceiling fans. Rooms rent for US$25/35 without/with cooking facilities. The price for the house is negotiable. Jasmine also has smaller, self-catering rooms nearby from US$15.

Places to Eat

You can eat cheaply at the jerk stalls along the roadside at Green Island Harbour, where you'll also find *Mandela Green* (☎ 956-2607), a popular bar and dance spot.

Negril

Negril, 52 miles west of Montego Bay, is Jamaica's fastest-growing resort and the vortex around which Jamaica's fun-in-the-sun vacation life whirls. Tourism is Negril's only industry. The village (population 2000) is so small, however, that hotel workers are drawn from miles around; many commute daily from as far afield as Lucea and Savanna-la-Mar, 20 miles away. Despite phenomenal growth in recent years Negril is still more laid back than anywhere else in Jamaica (it's one of the few places in Jamaica where you can gain an all-over tan). There's far less hustling here, although it occurs often enough to be an annoyance. You'll probably interact with locals more here than other resort areas.

It's remarkable to think that only two decades ago you could walk a mile on the beach before chancing upon Man Friday

footprints. What a pleasure it was to arrive in Negril in the mid-1970s, before the world had discovered this then-remote sensual Eden. For one buck a night you could sleep in a Rastafarian's hut beside the jungled shoreline, aided in slumber by thick clouds of ganja and the cheep-cheep of geckos calling from the eaves. Back then Negril was an off-the-beaten-track haven: nirvana to the budget-minded, beach-loving crowd who rented basic rooms for a pittance. It was a 'far-out' setting where you could drool over sunsets of hallucinogenic intensity that had nothing whatsoever to do with the 'magic' mushrooms that still show up in omelettes and tea on restaurant menus.

However, Negril's innocence is long gone. The red-eyed hippies have decamped, replaced by neatly groomed youths who whiz about on rented motor scooters, often with a local lass or dreadlocked lad clinging tightly behind. Topless European women lie semisubmerged on lounge chairs in the gentle surf. And it's impossible to avoid the entreaties of drug-dealing locals: 'Psst! Wan' some ganja, mon?' 'A likkle smoke for you, mon?' 'Hey, Tom Jones! Grass for you?'

Fortunately, hints of the 'real Jamaica' linger on. Woodcarvers still hawk their crafts on the beach. Makeshift stalls selling I-tal health foods and jerk pork line the roads. And the years seem only to have mellowed the greetings proffered freely by locals: 'I'rie . . . Respect . . . No problem, mon!' Tourists and 'yardies' commingle peaceably. You'll soon find yourself falling in love with Negril's insouciance and its scintillating seven-mile-long beach shelving gently into calm waters reflecting a palate of light blues and greens. Coral reefs lie like a forest of gems just offshore. And you'll want your camera to record the consistently peach-melba sunsets that get more applause than the live reggae concerts for which Negril is equally famous.

HISTORY

The Spanish called the bay and adjacent headland Punta Negrilla, referring to the black conger eels that used to proliferate in

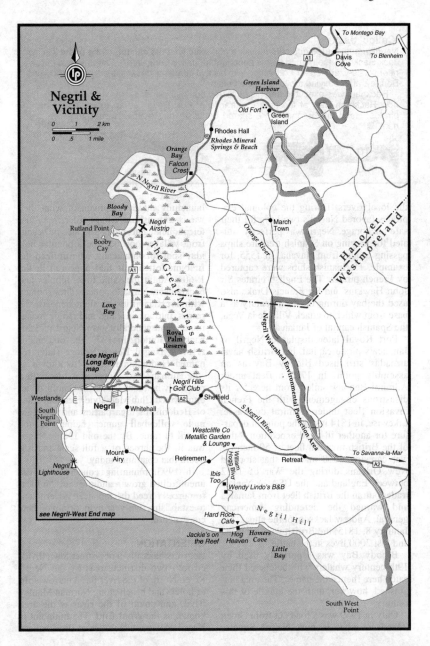

Negril & Vicinity

0   1   2 km

0   .5   1 mile

To Montego Bay

To Blenheim

Davis Cove

A1

Green Island Harbour

Old Fort

Green Island

Rhodes Hall

Rhodes Mineral Springs & Beach

Orange Bay

Falcon Crest

N Negril River

Hanover

Westmoreland

Orange River

March Town

Bloody Bay

Rutland Point

Negril Airstrip

Booby Cay

A1

The Great Morass

Long Bay

Negril Watershed Environmental Protection Area

Royal Palm Reserve

S Negril River

see Negril-Long Bay map

Negril Hills Golf Club

A2

Sheffield

Westlands

Negril

Whitehall

South Negril Point

Westcliffe Co Metallic Garden & Lounge

To Savanna-la-Mar

A2

Mount Airy

Retirement

Ibis Too

Retreat

William Hogg Blvd

Wendy Lindo's B&B

Negril Lighthouse

see Negril-West End map

Hard Rock Cafe

Negril Hill

Jackie's on the Reef

Hog Heaven

Homers Cove

Little Bay

South West Point

'Calico' Jack

Negril's most touted and colorful piece of history was the capture of the pirate 'Calico' Jack Rackham (so named for his penchant for calico underwear). The amorous buccaneer was seized here in 1720 along with his two pirate mistresses, Mary Read and Anne Bonney, after dallying too long on the beach.

Rackham was executed and his mutilated body suspended in an iron suit on what is now Rackham Cay, at the harbor entrance at Port Royal, as an example to other pirates. Read and Bonney were spared because they claimed to be pregnant. ■

the local rivers. During the colonial era, pirates favored Negril's two bays for their safe anchorage. Negril was perfectly situated for preying on Spanish treasure ships passing to and from Havana. In 1555, for example, 15 Spanish ships were captured by French pirates. The English pirates Sir John Hawkins and Sir Francis Drake also used the bay during the 16th century as a base from which to attack Villa de la Vega, the Spanish capital of Jamaica.

Port Royal later displaced Negril as Jamaica's pirate capital, but British naval armadas still used Bloody Bay as an assembly point. In 1702 a fleet under Admiral Benbow sailed from here for its disastrous engagement with the French invasion fleet under Admiral du Casse. Likewise, in 1814 it was the point of departure for another ill-fated expedition – that of the British invasion fleet of 50 men-of-war carrying 6600 marines that stormed New Orleans during the War of 1812 between England and the USA. A Yankee trader outran the British fleet from Jamaica and warned the defending American general, Andrew Jackson, of the attack. On January 8, 1815, the British were repulsed and lost 2000 lives in the battle.

Bloody Bay was reportedly used by 19th-century whalers who butchered their catch here (hence the name). The area languished, however, until the middle of this century.

Only in 1959 was a road cut from Green Island to what is now Negril Square,

launching the development of what then was a tiny fishing village. Electricity and telephones came later. The sleepy beachfront village soon became a popular holiday spot for Jamaicans, who utilized the first modest hotels that appeared in the 1960s. About the same time, hippies and backpackers began to appear. They roomed with local families or slept beneath the palms, partook in ganja and magic mushrooms, and generally gave Negril its laidback reputation. In 1977, the first major resort – Negril Beach Village (later renamed Hedonism II and also known as the Human Zoo) – opened its doors to a relatively affluent crowd in search of an uninhibited Club Med-style vacation. Tales of Hedonism's toga parties and midnight nude volleyball games helped launch Negril to fame. By the mid-1980s, Negril was in the throes of a full-scale tourism boom that continues today.

In 1993, mounting concern over the uncontrolled growth and pressure on local resources forced the Jamaican government to establish a two-year moratorium on new construction.

ORIENTATION

Negril is basically a one-street town divided into two distinct areas by the Negril River. North of the river lies a narrow strip of hotels and beach along Norman Manley Blvd, and south of the river is the area known as the **West End**. The midpoint is Negril Village, which lies at the southern end of Long Bay. Its center is a small roundabout immediately south of the South Negril River. Negril village consists of little more than two shopping plazas, a gas station, and a handful of banks and other commercial ventures. Houses and wood-and-tin shacks lie dispersed among the forested hills behind.

Sheffield Rd leads east from Negril Square and heads to Savanna-la-Mar, 19 miles away.

North of the River

To the north is Long Bay and its blindingly white, seven-mile-long beach fringed by sea-grapes and palms. The beach is paralleled by Norman Manley Blvd, a two-lane highway that leads to Lucea and Montego Bay. In Negril the road is lined with hotels almost its entire length, a fistful of upscale, all-inclusive resorts clustering at the northern end. A 400-yard-long section between Cosmo's Restaurant and Mahogany Inn is undeveloped and has been set aside as a public beach park (this area is popular for nude bathing).

Immediately east of Norman Manley Blvd and stretching its entire length is the Great Morass swamp. Midway down Long Bay, the boundary between Hanover Parish and Westmoreland Parish crosses the Great Morass and Norman Manley Blvd, ending at the sea.

Long Bay is anchored to the north by the low rocky headland of Rutland Point. Beyond is a smaller yet more deeply scalloped cove, Bloody Bay, once called Negril Harbour. The bay is more exposed to winds and the beach not as pretty as its neighbor. As in Arawak days, narrow canoes made from large cotton trees are still pulled up on the beach in the early morning, when local fishermen bring in their catches of parrot fish, red snapper, and angel fish.

South of the Village

A rocky limestone plateau rises immediately south of the South Negril River and extends south for several miles. You'll find a few pocket-size beaches at the northern end. The area is known as the Rock or West End. Scenes from *Papillon* and *Doctor No* were filmed here. West End Rd snakes south along the dramatically sculpted cliff top (be careful walking – it's narrow, with many blind corners and fast-moving vehicles). About one mile south, the road becomes Lighthouse Rd, which leads past Negril Lighthouse and changes name again to Ocean Drive.

INFORMATION
Tourist Offices

The Negril Chamber of Commerce (☎ 957-4067, fax 957-4591) publishes a *Guide to Negril*, a comprehensive compendium that includes a useful map. You can pick up a copy at the NCC office next to the post office (open Monday to Friday 9 am to 4 pm).

The JTB office (☎ 957-4597 or 957-2243) is on the 2nd floor of Adrijan Plaza, on the southwest side of Negril Square. The staff is helpful and can provide information on excursions and hotel availability. The selection of maps and literature is meager. The office is open Monday to Friday 8:30 am to 4:30 pm, and Saturday 9 am to 2 pm.

The JTB also maintains visitor information booths at the Negril Crafts Market on West End Rd (200 yards north of Rick's Cafe), and just south of the turnoff for Summerset Village. A third booth is at Long Bay Beach Park.

Negril, Negril: Where to Stay, Dine and Party is published twice yearly; it's available free of charge at most hotels. Keep your eyes open, too, for *Negril Beat*, another free biannual guide to what's happening in town.

Money

There are several banks, all open Monday to Thursday 9 am to 2 pm and longer on Friday. The exception is Workers Bank (in Plaza de Negril), which is open from 9:30 am to 3:30 pm weekdays and 9:30 am to 1 pm Saturdays. Scotiabank (☎ 957-4236), 100 yards west of Negril Square, is the most central; the new Century National Bank midway along Norman Manley Blvd is handy for travelers staying at Long Bay.

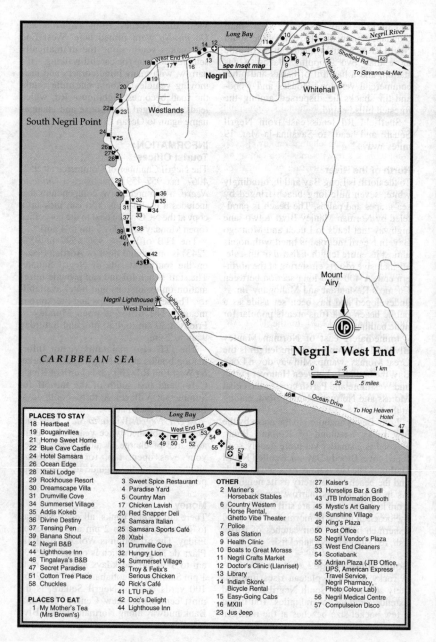

Negril - West End

PLACES TO STAY
18 Heartbeat
19 Bougainvillea
21 Home Sweet Home
22 Blue Cave Castle
24 Hotel Samsara
26 Ocean Edge
28 Xtabi Lodge
29 Rockhouse Resort
30 Dreamscape Villa
31 Drumville Cove
34 Summerset Village
36 Divine Destiny
37 Tensing Pen
39 Banana Shout
42 Negril B&B
44 Lighthouse Inn
46 Tingalaya's B&B
47 Secret Paradise
51 Cotton Tree Place
58 Chuckles

PLACES TO EAT
1 My Mother's Tea
   (Mrs Brown's)
3 Sweet Spice Restaurant
4 Paradise Yard
5 Country Man
17 Chicken Lavish
20 Red Snapper Deli
24 Samsara Italian
25 Samsara Sports Café
28 Xtabi
31 Drumville Cove
32 Hungry Lion
34 Summerset Village
38 Troy & Felix's
   Serious Chicken
40 Rick's Café
41 LTU Pub
42 Doc's Delight
44 Lighthouse Inn

OTHER
2 Mariner's
   Horseback Stables
6 Country Western
   Horse Rental,
   Ghetto Vibe Theater
7 Police
8 Gas Station
9 Health Clinic
10 Boats to Great Morass
11 Negril Crafts Market
12 Doctor's Clinic (Llanriset)
13 Library
14 Indian Skonk
   Bicycle Rental
15 Easy-Going Cabs
16 MXIII
23 Jus Jeep

27 Kaiser's
33 Horselips Bar & Grill
43 JTB Information Booth
45 Mystic's Art Gallery
48 Sunshine Village
49 King's Plaza
50 Post Office
52 Negril Vendor's Plaza
53 West End Cleaners
54 Scotiabank
55 Adrijan Plaza (JTB Office,
   UPS, American Express
   Travel Service,
   Negril Pharmacy,
   Photo Colour Lab)
56 Negril Medical Centre
57 Compulseion Disco

All the banks have money-exchange counters and offer cash advances against Visa or MasterCard. On Norman Manley Blvd, you can also change money at *Timetrend* (☎ 995-2538 or 997-5655), a money-exchange bureau 20 yards south of De Buss. It's open 9 am to 5 pm weekdays and until 3:30 Saturdays. The National Commercial Bank (☎ 957-4117), in the Sunshine Village Complex, has a 24-hour ATM.

Most hotels can change money. If you want to save a few pennies, you can try to negotiate a worthwhile rate with hustlers, who congregate near Adrijan Plaza. Be cautious. Rip-offs are frequent. The rates aren't that attractive anyway, only 5% to 10% better than the official exchange rate.

Post & Communications

The post office is in Kings Plaza on West End Rd. It's open Monday to Friday from 8 am to 5 pm. Anticipate long lines. United Parcel Service (UPS; ☎ 957-9498) has an office next door to the JTB in Adrijan Plaza; it's open 7 am to 7 pm. UPS delivers letters internationally (US$11 to the USA, for example), as well as packages. It also offers photocopying and fax services, as does the Negril Chamber of Commerce (see above).

You can make international calls from the main JTB office (the operator will monitor the time and you'll be charged accordingly) or from Negril Calling Service at Shop 19 in Negril Plaza. Office Solutions, in the forecourt of the Bougainvillea Hotel (☎ 957-4109, fax 957-3388) has similar services, including secretarial services; it's open 9 am to 9 pm. The Negril area code is 957.

Bookshops

You can buy European and North American novels, magazines, and newspapers at most gift stores in upscale hotels. In town, Top Spot (☎ 957-4542) in Sunshine Village is well stocked with international publications.

Photography

Photo Colour Lab (☎ 957-4594), next to the JTB office in Adrijan Plaza, offers developing (US$1 processing per B&W roll), video production, and custom B&W work. It also provides passport and visa photos (US$5) and sells film. It's open Monday to Friday from 8 am to 5 pm, Saturday 8 am to 4 pm.

Laundry

You can have your dirties washed and ironed at West End Cleaners (☎ 957-0160), 20 yards behind Scotiabank. Pants cost US$1; a shirt costs US$0.70.

Medical Services

The nearest hospitals are at Savanna-la-Mar and Lucea. However, there are several small clinics in Negril.

The Negril Medical Centre (☎ 957-4926) runs a family practice Monday to Friday from 9 am to 8 pm; it's 100 yards east of the Shell gas station on Sheffield Rd. If your hotel is on Norman Manley Blvd, try the 7 Mile Medical Clinic (☎ 957-4888); it can perform diagnostics, blood-testing, and so on. There's also a clinic and 24-hour emergency service (☎ 957-4259) at Llanriset at the north end of West End Rd; clinic hours are Monday to Friday from 9 am to 5 pm and Saturday 9 am to 1 pm. Another clinic (☎ 957-3047) is next to Compulseion Disco in Negril Plaza (Monday to Friday 8 am to 8 pm and alternate Saturdays 9 am to 3 pm). There's also a dental clinic here, open Monday to Saturday, noon to 6 pm. Most clinics accept credit cards.

The Negril Pharmacy (☎ 957-4076) at Shop 14 in Adrijan Plaza fills prescriptions. It's open daily 9 am to 7 pm, Sundays 10 am to 4 pm.

Emergency

The police station (☎ 957-4268) is 100 yards east of the gas station on Sheffield Rd. There are two Tourism Liaison Officers, and a police boat now operates in Long Bay. For the fire brigade, call ☎ 110 or 957-4242.

Dangers & Annoyances

Sun & Heat The sun will probably be your biggest headache or at least the source of it.

The temptation is great to spend all day lazing on the beach. Beware! Use sunscreens liberally. If you burn, any of a dozen or so local women patrol the beach selling healing aloe. The price is negotiable; for US$5 or so you can have a soothing aloe massage on the spot.

Insects The Great Morass provides a breeding ground for mosquitoes, which are not usually much of a problem by the sea where the breezes blow. Wander a few dozen yards inland, however, and you'll be happy to have insect repellent.

Hustlers & Drugs The peskiest annoyance is the droves of young Jamaicans who traffic in drugs, attracted by Negril's *laissez* reputation. It's non-threatening, but if drug use isn't your thing, then the sales pitch can wear on the nerves. Cocaine and crack have appeared in recent years, and ganja is still a steadfast part of the Negril scene (marijuana is the most important crop in Negril's

---

Here's the Dope

Ganja is illegal in Jamaica. Though it's smoked in plain view in Negril, undercover police agents are present, and rarely a day goes by without one or more visitors being arrested.

Be aware that if you use ganja or mushrooms, you risk double jeopardy: I've heard reports of tourists suffering harmful or disturbing side effects, especially from ganja cakes. This is also true of hallucinogenic wild mushrooms, which are legal and grow wild in cow pastures (psilocybin is the active agent). Apparently, drinking alcohol while on mushrooms can induce a 'bad trip.' ■

---

hinterland). Tourists and locals alike smoke spliffs openly at concerts and even on the beach. I advise being more circumspect by daytime.

If you're not interested, give a firm 'no thanks!' The Negril Chamber of Commerce and citizens' groups have taken

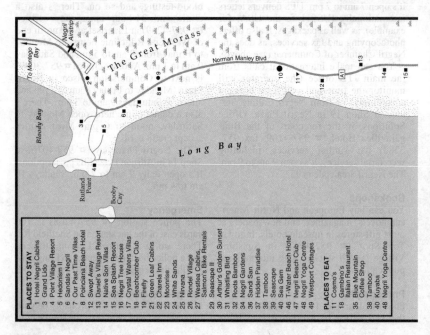

PLACES TO STAY
1   Hotel Negril Cabins
3   Grand Lido
4   Point Village Resort
5   Hedonism II
6   Sandals Negril
7   Our Past Time Villas
8   Poinciana Beach Hotel
12 Swept Away
13 Daniel's Village Resort
14 Native Son Villas
15 Sea Splash Resort
16 Negril Tree House
17 Crystal Waters Villas
18 Beachcomber Club
19 Firefly
21 Green Leaf Cabins
22 Charela Inn
23 Moonrise
24 White Sands
25 Nirvana
26 Rondel Village
27 Westlea Cabins,
    Salmon's Bike Rentals
29 Arthur's Golden Sunset
30 Seascape II
31 Whistling Bird
32 Roots Bamboo
34 Negril Gardens
36 Sandi San
37 Hidden Paradise
38 Tamboo
39 Seascape
40 Sea Gem
46 T-Water Beach Hotel
47 Negril Beach Club
48 Negril Yoga Centre
49 Westport Cottages

PLACES TO EAT
11 Cosmo's
18 Gambino's
    Italian Restaurant
35 Blue Mountain
    Coffee Shop
38 Tamboo
40 Kuyaba
48 Negril Yoga Centre

measures in recent years to cut down on harassment by drug pushers, unlicensed vendors, and 'undesirable elements.' Even the hair braiders have been licensed and are now relegated to specified booths along the beach.

Prostitution Prostitution is common. Male tourists entering discos or walking at night are almost sure to be approached. Local males also pimp themselves to foreign females, many of whom indulge in the 'rent-a-Rasta' trade.

Most hotels frown on unregistered guests, which usually means you'll have to pay an 'extra guest' charge. Alternately, a discreet tip to the security staff is often what's called for.

Crime Negril is no worse than other resort destinations in reported crime. Nonetheless, there is plenty of opportunistic theft. Take particular care of items left on the beach. Burglary is common in budget and

moderate-priced properties. Several muggings have occurred. At night, take a taxi rather than walking long distances on the dimly lit roads (at press time, the Chamber of Commerce was planning to install solar lights along the beach). I've also heard of at least two hotel robberies in which tourists were robbed at gunpoint; never open your hotel door to strangers without ascertaining their identity.

NEGRIL LIGHTHOUSE

You won't find much of historical interest in Negril, but the gleaming-white, 66-foot-tall lighthouse (three miles south of Negril Village on West End Rd) is a worthy place to check out. At 18° 15' north, 78° 23' west, it illuminates the westernmost point of Jamaica. The lighthouse, erected in 1894 with a prism made in Paris, was powered by kerosene until 1956, when it was replaced by acetylene. It has been solar powered since 1985. The automatic light flashes every two seconds. The lighthouse

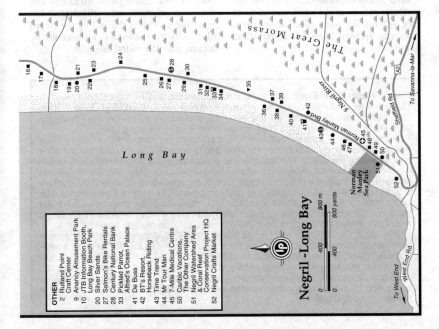

OTHER
2 Rutland Point Craft Center
9 Anancy Amusement Park
10 JTB Information Booth, Long Bay Beach Park
20 Silver Sands
27 Salmon's Bike Rentals
28 Century National Bank
33 Pickled Parrot, Alfred's Ocean Palace
41 De Buss
42 B'Ts Resort, Horseback Riding
43 Time Trend
44 Mr Tour Man
45 7-Mile Medical Centre
50 Caribic Vacations, The Other Company
51 Negril Watershed Area & Coral Reef Conservation Project HQ
52 Negril Crafts Market

Negril -Long Bay

Long Bay

The Great Morass

S Negril River

To Savanna-la-Mar

Norman Manley Blvd

Sheffield Rd

Norman Manley Sea Park

To West End

West End Rd

is built atop a tank of pressurized water, which acts as a shock absorber in the event of infrequent earthquakes.

You can visit the lighthouse free of charge. Henry Woodcock, the superintendent, will gladly lead the way up the 103 stairs for a bird's-eye view of the coast. Note the original brass lantern on display. Don't touch the brass fittings, however, or Henry will chew your head off!

A small brass cannon sits in the grounds. Note, too, the two huge, bulbous silk-cotton trees at the gate.

BOOBY CAY

This small coral island lies half a mile off-shore from Rutland Point. You may recognize the island as a South Seas setting in the Walt Disney movie *Twenty Thousand Leagues under the Sea*. The island is named for the colony of blue-footed booby birds that nest here. Unfortunately the bird population is endangered following years of egg collecting by local fishermen.

Boat shuttles operate daily from the all-inclusive resorts at the north end of Long Bay. Alternately, water-sports concession-aires can arrange boats for about US$5 one-way.

NEGRIL HILLS

A drive into the Negril Hills that rise south-east of Negril reveals a bucolic Jamaica miles removed from the hedonistic beach scene. The hourlong drive makes a clockwise loop via Sheffield Rd. From Sheffield Rd turn south opposite Sweet Spice along Whitehall Rd, which climbs into the limestone hills through remarkably pretty cattle country and tiny hamlets. (Watch for cattle wandering in the road.) Two-and-a-half miles south, turn right onto William Hogg Blvd, which eventually connects with Ocean Drive and loops around to the West End.

THE GREAT MORASS

Behind the shore of Long Bay, a virtually impenetrable two-mile-wide swamp of mangroves – the Great Morass – stretches north 10 miles from the South Negril River to Orange Bay. The swamp, said to be the remnant of a primeval forest, is the island's second largest freshwater wetland system and forms a refuge for endangered waterfowl. A few endangered manatees and American crocodiles may still cling to life here. The swamp is drained by the Negril River, which is stained a sickly tea color by tannins from the underlying peat.

Negril Watershed Environmental Protection Area

This protected wilderness zone, the first of its kind in Jamaica, has finally come to fruition after years of lobbying on the part of local conservationists. At press time, the final details were still being drawn up, though the conservation area is already a reality.

The conservation area extends from Green Island on the north coast to Salmon Point (south of Negril) and inland to the Fish River and Orange Hills. It also includes a marine park extending out to sea. The intention is to protect the entire Negril watershed, including the Great Morass swampland and all land areas that drain into the Caribbean between Green Island and Salmon Point. One of the area's best remaining fish-nursery grounds and the area's most extensive remaining mangrove forest will be included, and future hotel construction will be controlled. Once approved by the government's Natural Resource Conservation Authority, the conservation area will be managed by the Negril Area Environmental Protection Trust (NEPT) made up of community activists.

The Negril Coral Reef Preservation Society (NCRPS), formed in 1990, has been spearheading conservation efforts (see the Fragile Coral Reefs sidebar for contact information). The NCRPS recently received a J$22 million (US$620,000) grant from the European Union for hiring and training rangers, community education, mariculture projects, coral reef restoration, water-quality monitoring, placement of zoning and reef mooring buoys, and the creation of a central sewage system considered vital to the success of the marine park project. ■

In 1958, the Norman Manley administration set up the ineffectual Negril Land Authority to drain the 6000-acre morass and develop the area as part of its Peat Mining for Energy Project. Excavations in the 1950s washed sediments out to sea, killing large portions of the reef system. The coral has since grown back, but the reefs remained at the forefront of an ecological battle between conservationists determined to preserve the swamps and the government-owned Petroleum Corporation of Jamaica, which wanted to mine the peat. Local opposition to the project, however, gained international support and the project was shelved in 1987.

Drainage channels cut into the swamp in past decades have lowered the water levels, and as a result, water quality has been gradually deteriorating. Sewage, pesticides, and other commercial byproducts have seeped into the region's shallow water table, making their way to sea where they have poisoned the coral reefs and depleted fish stocks.

The Great Morass is critical to the Negril environment. It acts like a giant sponge and filters the waters flowing down to the ocean from the hills and mountains east of Negril. It's also a source of much-needed freshwater. Negril's meteoric unplanned development during the past two decades has resulted in severe water shortages (the area receives 2.5 million gallons of water daily, but needs six million to operate efficiently). Construction of a water desalination plant is being considered. Still, the creation of the Negril Watershed Environmental Protection Area (see sidebar) and a much-needed sewage treatment plant (under construction in late 1995) are considered essential to protecting the area's fragile watershed.

Touring the Great Morass
Locals have been slow to utilize the Great Morass for tourism, but the creation of the Negril conservation area has provided a focus on natural attractions away from the beach. Channels are now being opened up for wildlife excursions by small boat.

There are virtually no organized tours; you'll need to negotiate with villagers who have their boats moored along the South Negril River immediately west of the bridge. It costs approximately US$35 for two hours.

An airboat called the *Swamp Dragon* reportedly operates from 9 am to 5 pm.

ROYAL PALM PRESERVE
This 351-acre reserve, on the southern border of the Great Morass, was created in 1989 to protect the largest population of Jamaican royal palms in the world. It's named for the swamp royal palm (*Roystonea princeps*) native to Jamaica. Ospreys and sea hawks use the palms for vantage points, and the reserve is a home for the Jamaica parakeet and Jamaica woodpecker.

Two observation towers provide views over the tangled mangroves and sea-grape swamps, into which wooden walkways lead. Unfortunately, since it opened, the reserve has lain idle.

Illegal logging still takes place in the reserve due to insufficient monitoring. The Negril Area Environmental Protection Trust (NEPT) wants to develop it as a center for ecotourism, and it's campaigning to make the reserve a national park and seeking international support. Mail or fax your signed letter of support to NEPT, c/o the Negril Coral Reef Protection Society (NCRPS; see the Fragile Coral Reefs sidebar).

The reserve is not signed from the main road. The turnoff is about 400 yards beyond Cool Runnings Entertainment Centre, one mile east of the golf course. After 200 yards, turn left at the Y-fork. The gates are sometimes locked.

NUDE BATHING
Topless bathing is common all along the Negril shoreline. A small section of public beach near Cosmo's Restaurant is a favorite of nudists, and Booby Cay is also a popular spot. Hedonism II, Grand Lido, and Point Village Resorts all have nude beaches.

The Fragile Coral Reefs

Negril's offshore reefs provide a habitat for over 1000 species of coral, fish, sponges, and other fauna in the near-shore waters. They have been severely damaged in recent decades by the resort boom and human tinkering with the Great Morass.

Reef restoration is an important part of the Negril Conservation Area project, and pilot projects have recently been established at Banana Shout and Tensing Pen on Lighthouse Rd. Both are sites for artificial coral cultivation through mineral accretion stimulated by a low-voltage electrical current passing through an underwater iron mesh. Unfortunately, nothing can be done to bring back the marine turtles that once favored the beach for nesting.

The Negril Coral Reef Preservation Society (NCRPS) has established a code of conduct for snorkelers and scuba divers:
• *Don't touch the puffer fish!* This removes the protective mucous film that prevents infection.
• *Don't turn over rocks.* They form homes for many species.
• *Don't remove or kill long-spined black urchins.* They serve a good cause by controlling algae and are themselves recovering from a devastating virus.
• *Don't catch or purchase lobster between April 1 and June 30.* This is the lobster's peak reproductive time.

Other NCRPS projects include demarcation of a swimmers' lane 300 feet from shore along the beach, and designating areas for jet skiing, water-skiing, parasailing, and large boat anchoring. Local children are also being trained as Junior Environmental Rangers and educated to care for the environment they will inherit.

The NCRPS publishes a quarterly newsletter, *Negril Reef Rap*, which you can receive by becoming a member (US$15 per year; NCRPS, PO Box 27, Negril, Westmoreland, ☎ (809) 957-4473, fax (809) 957-0053). The NCRPS headquarters are in the community center, in the car park at the Negril Crafts Market on Norman Manley Blvd. ■

GOLF

Mid-1994 saw the opening of the Negril Hills Golf Club, a 220-acre facility landscaped into the base of the Negril Hills at Sheffield, three miles east of Negril Square. The 18-hole, par 72 course borders the Great Morass. Lagoons, swamps, and forest are an integral part of the design, as are lots of water hazards. There's a clubhouse, a pro shop, a restaurant, and a tennis court. A hilltop villa resort and great house are planned. Green fees are US$15 (JGA members, US$7.50). Carts are mandatory and cost US$15. Caddies cost US$7, club rentals US$10. For information call ☎ 957-4638.

HORSEBACK RIDING

Babo's Riding Stable, near Sandals, offers lessons and two-hour rides (US$25) into the Negril Hills and the ruins of Whitehall Great House, which burned down in 1985. Babo bills himself as the 'Rasta Cowboy.' Country Western Horse Rental (☎ 957-4439), next to the police station on Sheffield Rd, and Mariner's Horseback Stables (☎ 957-4474), on Whitehall Rd, also offer guided rides into the hills (US$25 for two hours). Rhodes Hall Plantation (☎ 957-4258) has two-hour rides (US$30) at 7 and 10 am, and 1 and 3 pm, including hotel transfers. The sedate rides lead through banana and coconut groves on the 500-acre estate, ending with a beach ride.

BOAT CRUISES

Taking a cruise provides an excellent perspective on Negril, especially at sunset. There are several yachts and catamarans offering two- and three-hour excursions daily. Most trips include snorkeling and plenty of booze, but don't mix the two!

Aqua-Nova Water Sports at the Negril Beach Club has a three-hour party cruise (US$35) and other boat tours daily, including a lunchtime party cruise to Booby Cay (US$35). The *Checkmate*, a splendid 68-foot yacht, also hosts a two-hour sunset cruise daily at 4 pm for US$20, including hotel pickup (☎ 957-4218). *Reggae II* also sets sail at 4 pm daily from Bloody Bay on a sunset cruise.

Glass-bottom boat rides are a great way to see the fish life and coral if you hate getting wet. There are several to choose from on the main beach, including Best Boat Reef Tours (☎ 957-3357) next to the Pickled Parrot. In the West End, glass-bottom boat rides are offered from the little beach opposite Tigress.

WATER SPORTS

The waters off Negril are usually mirror-calm – ideal for all kinds of water sports. The beach shelves so gently into the calm waters that you can wade out to the coral reef. Snorkeling is particularly good south of Long Bay, where plentiful coves and deep lagoons with crystalline waters offer excellent coral reefs. Dozens of concession stands along the beach rent masks and fins, as well as jet skis and water-skiing equipment. Expect to pay US$5 an hour for snorkeling equipment, and US$10 to US$15 for sailboards and Sunfish.

Scuba Diving

Negril's extensive offshore reef and its coral cliffs with caves and grottoes south of the Negril River make it a leading scuba-diving center. Visibility often exceeds 100 feet, and seas are dependably calm, with an unusually high level of marine life. Most dives are in 35 to 75 feet of water. There are several sites of interest:

Coral Gardens is a shallow near-shore dive (also good for snorkeling).

The Throne is a 50-foot-wide cave with massive sponges, plentiful soft corals, nurse sharks, octopi, barracuda, and stingrays.

Aweemaway, a shallow reef area south of the Throne, has tame stingrays that may allow you to stroke them.

Sands Club Reef lies in 35 feet of water in the middle of Long Bay. From here, a drift dive to *Shark's Reef* leads through tunnels and overhangs with huge sponges and Gorgonian corals. Placid nurse sharks, moray eels, and spotted eagle rays are commonly seen.

Airplane Wreck is the remains of a Cessna airplane intentionally sunk and lying at 70 feet in Bloody Bay. Corals and sponges have taken up residence in and around the plane, attracting an abundance of fish, including deadly scorpion fish. Nurse sharks hang out at a nearby overhang.

Sundivers Jamaica has a five-star PADI facility at both the Poinciana Beach Hotel (☎ 957-4069) and Rock Cliff Hotel (☎ 957-4834). PADI certification and introductory 'resort courses' are offered by the Negril Scuba Centre (PO Box 49, ☎ 957-4425, fax 957-4425) at the Negril Beach Club; Scuba World (☎ 997-5580) at Hotel Negril Cabins (and at Orange Bay); Mariner's Inn & Diving Resort (☎ 957-4474, fax 957-4472); Seahorse Watersports (☎ 957-4478) at Home Sweet Home; Dolphin Divers (☎ 957-4944); and Blue Whale Divers (☎ 957-4438). Expect to pay US$30 to US$50 for introductory, one-tank, and night dives, and US$300 to US$400 for PADI Open-Water certification. Mariner's Inn has a free Discover Scuba class in their swimming pool.

Some operators also rent underwater video cameras (US$40). The Negril Scuba Centre rents 35 mm underwater cameras (US$25). All the outfits rent wet suits and equipment. Most upscale all-inclusive resorts have scuba facilities at no extra charge.

Sea Kayaking

Sea kayaking is a fantastic way to explore the Negril shoreline. Call on Negril Kayak Tours (☎ 957-4474) at the Mariner's Inn on West End Rd. The company offers guided sea-kayaking tours to hidden beaches on the south coast.

Banana Boat Rides

On Long Bay, Irie Watersports (☎ 957-4670) has banana-boat rides – an inflatable raft shaped like a banana and towed by a speedboat. It's great fun, a sort of bucking bronco ride with a cushioned seat instead of a saddle.

Parasailing

If a bird's-eye view of Negril sounds good, try parasailing (being harnessed into a parachute and towed aloft by a speedboat). Ray's Parasailing (☎ 957-4349), Aqua-Nova Water Sports (☎ 957-4323) at the Negril Beach Club, and Pringle Watersports (☎ 957-4893) all offer parasailing as well as a complete range of other water sports.

ORGANIZED TOURS

There's not much to see or do locally. The most popular excursions are to Roaring River and the Blue Hole (see the Petersfield section below), to the Black River Great Morass (not to be confused with Negril's Great Morass), and to the Appleton Rum Estate (see the Southwest Coast chapter). Caribic Vacations (☎ 957-4760) on Norman Manley Blvd offers scheduled tours by minibus into the Negril Hills on Thursday and Saturday for US$30, to Black River on Tuesday for US$75, and to other far-flung spots. JUTA Tours (☎ 957-3117), next door to Caribic Vacations, also offers excursions. Mr Tour Man (☎ 990-9608), near De Buss bar, also runs tours to YS Falls and Black River for US$22; it's open 8 am to 10 pm.

The Other Company Ltd (☎ 957-3309) specializes in ecological and cultural tours. Options include workshops in tropical agriculture, dance, and holistic lifestyles, plus a Roots Rock Reggae Express tour (US$90) to Kingston, including a visit to the Bob Marley Museum and an I-tal breakfast and dinner. Alvin's Country Tours (☎ 957-6129) also offers tours of the 'real Jamaica.'

Fancy a thrilling, albeit expensive, adventure by whirlybird? Then call Helitours (☎ 979-8290), which offers flight-seeing tours by Bell Jetranger helicopters from Negril Airstrip. Its 10-minute Negril Hilite trip costs US$50. It also has longer Westend Adventure and South Coast Magic trips.

SPECIAL EVENTS

Negril has relatively few special events. If you want to see the resort at its liveliest, then visit in mid-March during the Negril West End Reggae Festival. First held in 1993, the highlight of the Negril calendar is now an annual event hosted by the Hog Heaven Hotel (☎ 957-4991). Ziggy Marley, Judy Mowatt, Gregory Isaacs, Freddie McGregor, and Yellowman are typical of the featured talent.

The Negril Carnival (☎ 957-4220) is held in May and features a float parade, concerts, soca party, competitions, and dancing. It's not quite the bacchanal of Kingston, but it's fun nonetheless. The Negril Spring Triathlon is held each January at the Swept Away Sports Complex. For further information contact the JTB.

PLACES TO STAY

Negril boasts a dizzying kaleidoscope of hostelries – a wider assortment of accommodations than any other Jamaican resort town. There's a good selection of budget properties and several places catering to campers.

Many of the hotels and restaurants are operated by foreigners who arrived in the early days and fell under a spell from which they could never escape. The tradition of cottages lingers, though they're no longer cheap. Most of the funky shacks have evolved into guest houses, and the guest houses into hotels, which continue to multiply like mushrooms. Fortunately a strict building code has kept the resorts from growing taller than the tousled palm trees that rise majestically over the beach. South of the village, hotels continue to spread beyond the lighthouse where the gaps are gradually being filled in.

Many properties offer a combination of rooms, cabins, and/or self-catering units. Hotels given below are listed roughly from north to south beginning at Bloody Bay within each price range.

In general, beach properties are more expensive than hotels of equivalent standard in the West End. The most exclusive properties congregate at the northern end of Long Bay. Rates quoted are for summer (low season) unless otherwise noted. Winter (peak season) rates can be 20% to 60% higher.

Because electricity supply is sometimes interrupted, hotels provide candles in your room. Locate them when you check in, but note that they're not there for romantic nights.

In the USA, Vacation Network acts as a reservation agent for over 50 properties featured in the company's Negril brochure (1501 W Fullerton, Chicago, IL 60614, ☎ (312) 883-1020 or (800) 423-4095, fax (312) 883-5140).

Places to Stay – bottom end

Camping On the beach, *Roots Bamboo* is one of the most popular options and gets fairly busy (Ted Plummer, Negril PO, Westmoreland Parish, ☎ 957-4479). It has a communal shower block. Sites cost US$9/16 single/double, US$21/28 triple/quad. Tent rental costs US$2. Roots has a small beachside bar and restaurant. Also check out *Seascape II* (☎ 957-9225), a short distance north. You can camp here for US$10 double, with kitchen facilities, water, outside toilets, and security.

You'll also find a couple of places atop the cliffs: *One-stop Camping*, with sites for US$10, and *Lighthouse Park* (PO Box 3, ☎ 957-4490), just south of the lighthouse, with tent sites (US$15 for one or two people, US$2.50 additional) and communal toilets and cold showers in nicely kept grounds. No children allowed. The owners of One-Stop have a little rancho bar and will cook for you.

Guest Houses The term 'guest house' is used liberally in Jamaica and does not necessarily mean that the owner will be on site, nor that meals are served, as is usually implied. The vast majority of 'guest houses' are merely small hotels.

One exception, if you don't mind being out of town, is *Wendy Lindo's B&B*. It's a great bargain at US$40 double, including breakfast (US$500 for two weeks). Offbeat types probably won't appreciate it, but

if you're turned on by quaint, this could be for you. Wendy, an expat from the Isle of Scilly, offers three rooms (two share a bath) in her charming house – a little piece of England built atop a coral outcrop with views slanting down over the forest to the ocean. Her cottage is full of antiques and cozy couches, frilly curtains, and porcelain china. Guests have full use of the house. The clean, airy rooms have private patios, ceiling fan, screened windows, and hot water. Wendy offers free taxi service. The house is on Beaver Ave, about eight miles south of Negril, off William Hogg Blvd.

Hotels – at the beach *Green Leaf Cabins* (☎ 957-4677), opposite Silver Sands, offers 10 basic, modest-size two-story cabins with patio and outside shower (some with private bath; some with outside shared bath). Two villas are available. Rates are US$20 shared, US$30 to US$35 with hot water, US$60 to US$70 villas. *BJ's Resort* (☎ 957-4744), south of Seascape Hotel, also has eight small, basic but well-kept cabins in the same price range.

Seascape II (☎ 957-9225) has nine tiny rooms – basic but clean – in a house built in quasi-alpine fashion (US$20). Another popular option is *Roots Bamboo* (☎ 957-4479), with 32 basic and soulless cabins right on the beach. Some have showers; others share a communal shower block with campers. Rates are US$22 single, US$30 to US$40 double (slightly more with a porch and shower). There's a small beachside bar and restaurant.

Don't make a decision until you've checked out the eight very rustic and charming rooms and cottages that make up the *Negril Yoga Centre* (PO Box 48, ☎ 957-1397; in the USA, ☎ (813) 263-7322). The rooms surround an open-air, wood-floored thatched yoga center set in a garden. Options range from a two-story Thai-style wooden cabin to an adobe farmer's cottage (US$25 to US$50 double, US$10 additional). The center makes its own yogurt, cheese, and sprouts and will custom-cook on request. Yoga classes are offered Monday and Wednesday at 5:30 pm.

Arthur's Golden Sunset (PO Box 21, ☎ 957-4241, fax 957-4761) is a longtime favorite of the budget crowd. Originally built in 1977, it has since expanded from a group of rustic cottages and now offers 'economy' rooms from US$27 to US$32 (some with shared bath). Standard rooms cost US$36 to US$40, with shared kitchenette but private bathroom; 'superior' rooms with kitchenettes, private bathrooms, and hot water cost US$47 to US$50. In all there are 27 rooms and 15 two-bedroom cottages.

If you're seeking a very off-beat experience, check out *Westport Cottages* (☎ 957-4736), which is popular with the laid-back backpacking crowd (particularly Europeans). A communal feel pervades the place, which Joseph Mathews, the wise and witty owner, says is approved for 'roach people.' Joseph has very rustic huts with outside toilet and shower with cold water. The nine rooms (US$15/20 a single/ double) have mosquito nets and fans. A communal kitchen is available and free bicycles and snorkeling equipment are provided. A funky bar is out front.

A popular no-frills favorite of budget travelers is nearby *Westlea Cabins* (☎ 957-4422). Its 18 skimpily furnished wooden cabins are clean but overpriced at US$40 (low season). Smaller units share outside toilets in scruffy grounds where chickens run around.

Hotels – West End *Lighthouse Park* (PO Box 3, ☎ 957-4490), immediately south of the lighthouse, offers six rustic but clean bamboo cabins (US$25 single/double, US$5 additional) and A-frame cottages (US$35/45 single/double) with kitchenettes. Breakfast is provided. Steps lead down from the sunning platform to the sea.

You'll find several other inexpensive cottages for rent along West End Rd.

Places to Stay – middle
Hotels – at the beach For atmosphere I recommend *Negril Cabins* on Bloody Bay (PO Box 118, ☎ 957-4350 or 957-4381; in North America, ☎ (800) 382-3444). It's also one of the best bargains around. It has 24 standard and 26 air-con superior rooms. The all-hardwood, Thai-style cabins are raised on stilts and set well apart amid lush grounds with abundant waterfalls. Facilities include a fitness center and tennis court plus game room, Jacuzzi, pool with swim-up bar, and Coconut Palm restaurant. A path leads to the beach. It's popular with German tour groups. Summer rates are US$64 to US$71 single, US$92 to US$109 double, including breakfast, tax, and service charge (children under 16 free).

Daniel's Village Resort is a gleaming-white 45-room structure that seems to have been airlifted from Spain's Costa Brava (☎ 957-4394). You can choose studios with kitchenette, or standard or deluxe rooms (US$55 to US$85), each with large kitchens and living areas. Furniture is dowdy. It also has apartments (US$100), plus a large pool and the Swamp Thing Bar, which hosts women's mud wrestling.

A nearby option is *Beachcomber Club* (PO Box 98, ☎ 957-4171, fax 957-4097), a 45-room hotel that charges from US$80 upwards in summer; winter rates are almost double. It runs an open-air beachside restaurant and Gambino's Italian restaurant, plus a nightly entertainment schedule. Next door, *Firefly* (PO Box 54, ☎ 957-4358; in the USA, 1320 S Dixie Hwy, Suite 1102, Coral Gables, FL 33146) rents four handsome all-hardwood cottages, each different but all with kitchenette (US$65 to US$75). Its other offerings range from a one-bedroom studio to penthouse suites with bedroom, dining room and veranda (US$85). A minimum one-week stay is required in winter.

Moonrise (PO Box 57, ☎ 957-4344, fax 957-4675) offers six studios and 17 comfortable rooms with private bathrooms and hot water. Louvered windows let in lots of light. Utility furniture adds an institutional feel, however. Rates without kitchenettes are US$55/77 single/double (US$88 with air-con) or US$110 double with kitchenette. Its neighbor is *White Sands* (PO Box 60, ☎ 957-4291, fax 957-4674), an attractive property where options range from one-bedroom apartments to a four-bedroom, four-bath villa. Studios and apartments are simple yet elegant; apartments and villa are exquisite. Summer rates based on double occupancy are studio US$54, deluxe room US$75, apartment US$92, and villa US$240 for eight people. The units sit in a well-maintained garden with a pool. White Sands is popular with tour groups.

Rondel Village (PO Box 96, ☎ 957-4413, fax 957-4915) has nicely appointed beachfront rooms (US$70) clustered around a small pool and Jacuzzi. You can also choose octagonal shaped one-and two-bedroom villas that sleep up to six (US$115 to US$165 double) and feature air-con, marble floors, French doors, satellite TV, fully equipped kitchenettes, and Jacuzzi. A seafront cafe and juice bar sells ice cream, cappuccino, and the like.

Nearby, *Hidden Paradise* (☎ 957-4404) offers four pink-and-white twin-room cottages with air-con, fan, refrigerator, private verandas, and hot water (US$75). Two cottages have kitchenettes. It also features eight rooms in a house amid well-tended lawns. Next door, also in lush gardens, sits the French-owned *Seascape Hotel* (☎/fax 957-4303), offering one- and two-bedroom studios and apartments. Seascape has a restaurant and bar with Jacuzzi in the backyard. Summer rates are US$40 to US$70 for rooms or US$90 for a self-contained apartment.

Others to consider include the *Tamboo Inn* (☎ 957-4282), south of Sandi San, with 20 one- and two-bedroom condos from US$46 (one-bedroom with no kitchenette) to US$150 for two-bedroom cabins with kitchenettes. Next door, in a similar vein, is *Sea Gem* (☎ 957-4318), which offers quaint though rustic cabins and villas. It features the thatched Kuyaba on the Beach restaurant.

Sandi San (PO Box 47, ☎ 957-4487, fax 957-4234) is an intimate and pretty property; its seven studios, 15 rooms, and one suite all feature air-con with fans, hot water, and attractive decor, including hand-carved beds of native mahoe. It has its own beachside bar and open-air restaurant, plus beach

volleyball. Rooms cost US$65 to US$100 double (US$20 additional) or US$130 for a cottage. Of a similar standard and intimacy is *Gold Nugget*, sequestered amid a garden of bamboo and hibiscus across the street (PO Box 91, ☎ 957-4388, fax 957-4269). You can choose from rooms with verandas or fully equipped apartments, or two honeymoon suites (rooms US$52/62 a single/double; apartments US$62/72; suites US$100). It has a pool with bar.

T-Water Beach Hotel (PO Box 11, ☎ 957-4270, fax 957-4334) is one of the oldest hotels in Negril. Its 70 air-con rooms and beachfront suites are handsomely furnished, with patios or balconies, some with kitchenette. It has a beachfront restaurant and beach bar, plus two Jacuzzis, a pool, TV lounge, and water sports. Another good option is T-Water's neighbor, the *Negril Beach Club Hotel* (PO Box 7, ☎ 957-4222, fax 957-4364). Its 'smorgasbord' of rooms include 65 air-con, modest yet nicely furnished rooms, plus studios and deluxe suites in two-story blocks. A full range of water sports is offered. Other facilities include two tennis courts, a pool, coffee shop, boutique, and health club. Summer room rates are US$56 to US$89 single, US$67 to US$100 double; suites US$110 to US$167 single, US$122 to US$167 double, including tax.

Hotels – West End If you prefer to be in the heart of downtown, check out *Cotton Tree Place* (☎ 957-4450), 100 yards west of Scotiabank. This modern complex has 30 units, including air-con studios with kitchenettes for US$80. The rooms with fans are better (US$60) although carpeted. All rooms have a TV, sofa, and balcony. Bathrooms are small. A roomy 'Stone House' with lofty wooden ceiling and a loft bedroom sleeps up to five people (from US$60 double).

If you don't mind the odd location (on the hillside behind Negril Village), consider *Chuckles*, boasting flashy modern condo-style units in lush landscaped grounds centered on a large pool and sun deck (☎ 957-4250, fax 957-9150). It has

75 luxury air-con rooms (US$70 to US$105, depending on size and view). More expensive rooms have king-size beds. You can also choose from a pair of two-bedroom villas (US$225). The resort offers a Jacuzzi, tennis courts, bike rental, and a shuttle to the beach. Rates include tax, service charge, and breakfast.

Heartbeat offers one of the most romantic options atop the cliffs in its thatched, all-hardwood octagonal cabins (PO Box 95, ☎ 957-4329, fax 957-0069). You can also choose self-sufficient studio apartments or a three-bedroom cottage, beginning at about US$30. To the south is *Home Sweet Home* (☎ 957-4478; in the USA, ☎ (800) 925-7418), with 14 rooms with private balconies, fans, and private showers (US$40 single or double). It features a cliff bar and restaurant, pool, Jacuzzi, and a boat pickup for fishing or snorkeling trips. There are sunning platforms on the cliff face. Nearby is *Bougainvillea* (☎ 957-4882), which charges US$40 per night for studios with kitchenette; long-term rentals cost US$400 a double per month.

A tremendous option for atmosphere is *Blue Cave Castle* (☎ 957-4845), which looks like a castle from *Ivanhoe*, as Ian White described it in *The Jamaica Experience* (a Lonely Planet video). This crenelated concoction squats on the cliff face. It's the creation of a Czech who has spent almost a decade on his pet project. The eight bedrooms (each with refrigerator) cost US$35/45 single/double and are made of natural stone. Stairs lead down to Blue Cave, a sparkling grotto with swallows nesting on the overhang. It has a small restaurant. Further south, *Ocean Edge* (Box 71, West End, ☎ 957-4362, fax 957-4849) offers 30 rooms – some with air-con – and is also poised on the cliffs. The hotel has a pool and Jacuzzi, plus glass-bottom boat and other water sports. Summer rates are US$55 to US$65, suite US$70 double.

Although it's one of Negril's most popular options, I find the *Hotel Samsara* uninspired, particularly its ugly concrete sun deck spanning the cliff top (PO Box 23, ☎ 957-4395, fax 957-4073). Options include any of 50 air-con oceanfront rooms, cottages, or more charming thatched tree houses on stilts (US$45 to US$85, US$10 additional). Samsara boasts tennis and volleyball courts and PADI scuba-diving center, a pool, a unique water slide into the ocean, plus the Jah Beer Garden/Sports Café with satellite TV. It hosts a Sunset Happy Hour and live reggae concerts every Monday.

A much better bargain is *Xtabi* (PO Box 19, Lighthouse Rd, ☎ 957-4336). The name – an Arawak word – means 'meeting place of the gods.' You can choose quaint garden cottages or octagon-shaped bungalows perched atop the cliff or in the gardens. The cliff-top cabins are tremendously atmospheric; the garden cottages are more simple. The bar is lively and the restaurant is one of the best around. Steps lead down to sunning platforms by the water's edge. Sea-front bungalows cost US$40 to US$99 (summer), and garden bungalows for US$33 to US$40 double are excellent bargains.

Another good bargain with tremendous off-beat ambiance is *Rock House* (PO Box 24, ☎ 957-4373; in North America, PO Box 78, Park Ridge, IL 60068, ☎ (708) 823-5226), boasting a covey of thatched rondavels dramatically clinging to the cliff side above a small cove. Each has a hot plate and refrigerator, plus electric and kerosene lamps. The rustic cabins (US$35 to US$45 per person double) have outside showers and private verandas. Catwalks lead over the rocks to a dining room, and stairs lead to the ocean.

Further south, *Coral Seas Cliff Hotel* has elegant, red-tiled villas with nicely furnished rooms. I like the hotel's relaxed feel and consider it a bargain at US$60 to US$90 single, US$65 to US$105 double. It has an impressive pool and airy restaurant and bar (worth the stop to admire the mural) in well-tended grounds (PO Box 91, ☎ 957-9226, fax 957-4269).

Both *Rock Cliff Resort* (PO Box 67, ☎ 957-4331, fax 957-4108) and nearby *Mariner's Inn* (PO Box 16, ☎ 957-4348, fax 947-4472) specialize in scuba packages and have dive centers on site. The former offers 33 elegantly furnished, air-con ocean-view rooms and suites. The latter's 52 rooms are appealing and represent a bargain at US$35 to US$45 (double occupancy in summer), including tax, tips, and an introductory scuba course. It also has apartments for US$58.

Drumville Cove is one of the more dramatically landscaped properties (PO Box 72, ☎ 957-4369, fax 929-7291). Its 19 rooms are cramped but clean and romantic; deluxe rooms are larger. Some rooms have air-con. Another option is three cozy cabins with four beds (two in a loft) and a kitchenette. You can sunbathe nude atop the rugged limestone crags where there's a cliff-top bar. Drumville also boasts a saltwater bathing pool and kiddy pool, and a small restaurant. Summer rates are US$60 to US$65 single, US$70 to US$75 double, US$110 suite.

Opposite Drumville, a road leads inland about 300 yards to two moderate hotels. The first is *Summerset Village* (PO Box 4, ☎ 957-4409; in North America, ☎ (312) 883-1020), on seven acres of landscaped grounds centered on a large pool. Ten air-con 'superior' rooms (US$50 to US$60) are in a condo-style unit; eight others are in a 'chateau.' One- and two-story octagonal cottages (US$65 to US$110) have wide verandas, and there's a five-bedroom Thatch House with a suite and kitchen, and a four-bedroom octagonal house (US$225) that can also be rented by the room. Summerset offers a shuttle to the beach. Nearby is *Addis Kokeb/New Star Guest House & Cottages* (PO Box 78, ☎/fax 957-4485), a more rustic option steeped in tremendous atmosphere. Six cabins are set in a garden full of fruit trees, and guests share a communal kitchen and lounge. Cottages include private bath, kitchen, and screened porch with hammocks. Guests have access to the pool at Summerset.

Among the more acclaimed hotels is *Tensing Pen* (PO Box 13, ☎ 957-4417). The owner, Richard Murray, created the stunning garden – a tropical Fantasia of bromeliads, ferns, orchids, and other flowering plants – for which the hotel is renowned. It has 12 thatched cottages on two acres, plus a communal rock-walled kitchen, an aquarium, and steps that lead down to the crystal-clear ocean.

Negril B&B (☎ 957-4850), one block west of Rick's Café, is also surrounded by a beautiful garden. You may choose either a standard (US$65) or deluxe (US$75) room with king-size beds plus air-con, two fans, and louvered windows.

South of the lighthouse, hotels thin out. Keep going a couple of miles and you'll reach *Secret Paradise* (PO Box 56, West End, ☎ 957-4882), a secluded property that offers one- and two-story octagonal units with full kitchens (US$75 double), plus a two-bedroom ranch house (US$85 to US$181) and a five-bedroom house that can be rented by the room (US$48). A personal cook is available, though there's a small restaurant. A freshwater pool overlooks a small cove for nude sunbathing.

Ibis Too is a cottage for rent atop the hill at the junction of Beaver Ave and William Hogg Blvd. It has a pool plus three rooms in the villa.

Places to Stay – top end
Hotels – at the beach If reggae and limbo don't appeal, consider the ritzy *Grand Lido*, the flagship of the SuperClubs chain (PO Box 88, ☎ 957-4010, fax 957-4317; in the USA, ☎ (800) 858-8009; in Canada, ☎ (800) 553-4320). Grand Lido hugs Bloody Bay and has a second beach for an all-over tan. The 200 suites and split-level junior suites (some with in-room whirlpool) are spread through 22 acres of gardens featuring three 24-hour bars, each with Jacuzzi. Grand Lido outdoes all contenders in its 'ultra-inclusions.' Even wedding ceremonies, 24-hour room service, and dry cleaning, laundry, and pedicures are included in the price. A full range of water sports includes cruises on glass-bottom boats. Sunset and dinner cruises are offered aboard *M/Y Zien*, a 147-foot motor yacht that was once a wedding gift from Aristotle Onassis to

Prince Rainer and Grace Kelly. Adult singles are welcome. Per person rates are US$845 to US$1105 (summer) based on three-night minimum. Add US$100 per night for single occupancy.

Rutland Point is also the stage for the *Point Village* (Rutland Point, ☎ 957-9170, 957-4351). Studios, and one-, two- and three-bedroom suites in Mediterranean-style, two-story limestone villas are scattered throughout the 14 acres. Its wave-pounded shoreline holds pocket-size beaches, including a diminutive nude beach. Furnishings are modest though kitchens are roomy and well appointed. Water sports, picnic trips to Booby Cay, and guided bicycle rides are all included. Facilities include a pool, tennis courts, barber and beauty shop, boutique, beachside massage 'parlor,' and nanny service. A studio costs US$118 double; a two-bedroom suite is US$239. An optional all-inclusive package is US$50 per person per day.

Another SuperClubs property, the aptly named *Hedonism II*, lies nearby (PO Box 25, ☎ 957-4200, fax 957-4289; in North America, ☎ (800) 859-7873; in the UK, ☎ (0992) 447420). This no-holds-barred adults-only resort is world-famous for its risqué theme parties. Its 280 air-con, carpeted rooms have no in-room telephones or TVs, but they do boast king-size beds (twin beds for singles) and mirrored ceilings. Two beaches (one nude), five bars, a game room, tennis and squash courts, volleyball, basketball, and a complete range of water sports are among the attractions. It even has a Circus Workshop! Guests include more single males than females and a surprising proportion of seniors, too. Per person rates are US$535 to US$725 for a three-night minimum (US$75 per night single supplement), depending on season.

Hedonism's neighbor is *Sandals Negril*, part of the all-inclusive, couples-only resort chain (PO Box 12, ☎ 957-4216, fax 957-4338; in North America, ☎ (800) 726-3257 or (305) 284-1300, fax (305) 667-8996; in the UK, ☎ (0171)-581-9895, fax (0171) 823-8758). The 21-acre deluxe property reminds me of a Disneyland village, with

wide lawns trimmed to perfection and music piping softly from speakers hidden amid the palms. At its node is a huge pool with swim-up bar. In all, there are 219 rooms in six categories. Sandals also features tennis, squash, and racquetball courts. Summer room rates begin at US$1580 for a three-night minimum.

Another Sandals' property, *Beaches*, was scheduled to open in late 1996 one mile further south. It's slated to be the first Sandals property open to families and singles as well as couples, with 225 rooms (39 junior suites), a 12,000-sq-foot pool, and five restaurants.

Also near the north end of Long Bay is *Our Past Time Villas* (☎ 957-4931, fax 957-4224), with 16 pleasantly furnished rooms – some have air-con – with satellite TV and patios. It has a bar and restaurant. Rates are US$80 to US$90 for rooms or US$150 for a two-bedroom apartment with kitchenette.

Poinciana is a family resort popular with Jamaican couples (one child per adult stays free with parents). Children and teens can make the most of a game room, organized activities such as arts and crafts, beach volleyball and a basketball shootout, and Anancy Park, Poinciana's own amusement complex. The resort's six acres include three-story accommodation blocks and villas in Georgian-plantation style. The exterior is rough around the edges, but newly renovated rooms in tropical mauves make amends. Summer rates are US$165 per person, all-inclusive (three-day minimum), villas US$188 to US$276. Five-night honeymoon specials begin at US$2145 (PO Box 44, ☎ 957-4100).

You could be swept away by *Swept Away*, an all-inclusive couples-only resort that boasts the island's most replete sports and fitness facility (☎ 957-4040, fax 957-4060; in North America, ☎ (800) 545-7937). The 134 suites are housed in 26 two-story villas. The gym, aerobics studio, 10 tennis courts (all lighted), two squash and two racquetball courts all come with professional instruction. When you're done with your workout, you can recuperate in the spa and beauty parlor. Per couple summer rates are US$1320 to US$1650 for three nights, US$395 to US$500 additional per night. Free golf at Negril Hills Golf Club is included.

Another of my favorites is the *Negril Tree House*, an unpretentious resort with 16 octagonal bungalows and oceanfront villas nudging up to the beach (PO Box 29, ☎ 957-4287, 957-4288 or toll free, (800) 634-7451, fax 957-4386). They're modestly furnished. More elegant one- and two-bedroom suites feature kitchenette, king-size beds, and a Murphy bed in the lounge that opens onto a wide veranda. The beachside bar is a popular place for locals and tourists to mix and features hammocks beneath thatched umbrellas. Water sports are offered, and the resort also has a tour desk, gift store, masseuse, and manicurist. Guests have day privileges at Swept Away's sports complex (US$10 daily). Rates are US$80 to US$110 (rooms), US$140 to US$180 (suites). A 'repeaters' month' in September/October offers a 50% discount to guests who have visited twice before.

Native Son Villas (☎ 957-4376; in the USA, 315 Northview Terrace, Springfield, NJ 07081, ☎ (201) 467-1407, fax (201) 379-1918) offers four modern two-story villas (two share one duplex) sleeping four to nine people. It's a bargain for families or groups at US$115 to US$240 per night (summer), including a housekeeper/cook and a bottle of rum.

The elegant *Sea Splash Resort* is bargain-priced at US$120 to US$130 double, including tax and transfers to/from Montego Bay (PO Box 123, ☎ 957-4041 or (800) 254-2786, fax 957-4049). Exquisite decor highlights 15 air-con suites, each with large balcony, fully equipped kitchenette, satellite TV, and telephone.

Crystal Waters Villas offers very attractive one-, two- and three-bedroom air-con villas, each with lounge, kitchen, and patio (PO Box 18, ☎ 957-4284, fax 957-4889). Amenities include a swimming pool, kiddies pool, and Jacuzzi. A housekeeper and cook are included in the rates

of US$90 (one-bedroom), US$130 to US$180 (two-bedroom), US$250 (three-bedroom). The office is across the road.

Another good bet is *Charela Inn* (PO Box 33, ☎ 957-4277, fax 957-4414), where the 39 air-con rooms (14 deluxe) feature beautiful contemporary decor with lots of hardwoods. It resembles a Spanish hacienda and surrounds a courtyard with garden and a large circular pool. The US$80 to US$100 single, US$96 to US$113 double rates include a cruise plus use of water sports, free Sunfish and sailboard instruction, and a sunset cruise. Children under 10 stay free.

If you're seeking meditation, check out *Nirvana* (☎ 957-4314; in the USA, contact Lonnie & Stanely Gottleib, RD 1 Morley Rd, Box 411, Ashville, NY 14710, ☎ (716) 789-5955), with seven two- and three-bedroom cottages set in beautifully landscaped Zen-like tropical gardens. The all-hardwood cabins cost US$100 to US$150 based on double occupancy in winter. Each has a dining room and kitchen, and screened wrap-around windows. *Whistling Bird* (☎ 957-4403; in the USA, PO Box 7301, Boulder, CO 80306, ☎ (303) 442-0722) is similar, with 24 rooms in 12 deluxe little cottages (US$81 in summer). It's low-key and a great place to relax beneath shady bamboo. There's a restaurant and beach bar.

Of a similar standard is the *Negril Inn* (PO Box 59, ☎ 957-4209, fax 957-4365), a 1960s Miami-style property that's divorced from the beach by an ugly wall. Its 46 rooms are nicely decorated, however, and facilities include an outdoor gym, massage, a pool and two Jacuzzis, floodlit tennis courts and a basketball court, a TV lounge and billiards room, and a disco. It's overpriced at US$130 single, US$170 double. A better option is *Negril Gardens* (PO Box 58, ☎ 957-4408, fax 957-4374; in the USA, ☎ (800) 752-6824), with 65 nicely appointed air-con rooms and two suites in two-story villas with balconies. Garden-view rooms across the road overlook a pool. Summer rates begin at US$105/120 single/double, US$10 additional.

Hotels – West End *Dreamscape Villa* has five voluminous and very beautifully furnished deluxe rooms, plus a studio and one suite, all with satellite TV and refrigerator (PO Box 51, ☎ 957-4495; in North America, ☎ (312) 883-1020). It has a pool, outdoor Jacuzzi under a gazebo, and a private lawn with its own pleasant cove and sun deck. Rates are US$80 to US$120, including continental breakfast in your room.

Divine Destiny is a self-contained resort located 500 yards inland from Drumville Cove (PO Box 117, ☎/fax 957-9184). A beach shuttle is provided. The 40 standard and superior rooms (some with air-con) all have kitchenette. The resort boasts a huge swimming pool with swim-up bar.

South of the lighthouse is *Tingalayas B&B* (☎ 957-0126; in Canada, 440 Ontario St, Toronto, Ontario M5A 2W1, ☎ (416) 924-4269). This marvelous creation of an eccentric Canadian artist and video producer, Lynda Perry, resembles a tiny African village. You can choose from four thatched adobe cottages painted earth-brown and blue. Lynda also rents her beautiful all-hardwood cottage. The property slopes down through a grove of sea grapes to fabulous coral formations with pocket-size sandy areas. Lynda was planning a beachside cafe and bar serving bush teas and I-tal food. A natural fruit and vegetable and herb garden supplies the kitchen. Meals are served beneath a high-pitched thatch restaurant. Rates are US$75 to US$100 per room, including breakfast.

Another unique and tranquil option is *Jackie's on the Reef*, seven miles south of the roundabout (General Delivery, Negril PO Box, ☎ 957-4997; or Jackie Lewis, 364 Washington Ave, Brooklyn, NY 11238, ☎ (718) 783-6763). It operates as a New Age haven focusing on spiritual renewal. A natural stone cottage is divided into four rooms, each with two handmade wooden beds and an outdoor shower and bathroom enclosed within your own private backyard. Massages are given on a veranda, and meditation, tai chi, and spa treatments are offered. Summer rates are US$80 per person, including breakfast and dinner. Day packages (lunch and massage) are offered to non-guests.

At the end of Ocean Drive is *Hog Heaven* (☎ 957-4991). It offers 13 clean, well-appointed self-catering units (US$80 or US$160 for suites) set in attractive grounds but less salubrious than the prices may suggest. Wide patios have hammocks and chairs. Free snorkeling equipment is available, and you can sunbathe nude. Across the street is the famous Hard Rock Café.

PLACES TO EAT

There are almost as many places to eat as to lay your head. Though jerk and patty stalls are being squeezed off the beach, a plethora of rustic eateries along Norman Manley Blvd and West End Rd offer budget snacks and meals. Most are reliable (I've never had a stomach problem). Still, many food stands have no access to running water and *may* pose health problems. Several restaurants, especially on the cliff top, close after sunset. Others may close during the day in the off-season. Don't neglect the hotel restaurants, which tend toward continental cuisine.

Local delicacies (besides mushroom omelettes) include crab pickled in red peppers.

Fast Food

For fast food try *Shakey's Pizza* and *King Burger* in Sunshine Village Plaza. *Archway Café* (☎ 957-4399) on West End Rd serves pizza, fish & chips, and burgers, and has free delivery.

I-tal

For Rastafarian health food, you have several options. *Desi Dread's*, on the beach near Negril Crafts Market, and *Hungry Lion*, on West End Rd, specialize in I-tal dishes and juices. The latter has a mural of Marcus Garvey and various musical idols to amuse you while you enjoy dishes such as lasagna with callaloo. *Mr Natural* (☎ 957-9181), opposite Kaiser's Cafe, is a seafood juice bar serving vegetarian pastas.

At the junction of Whitehall and William Hogg Rds is *Westcliffe Co Metallic Garden & Lounge*, a funky bar and I-tal vegetarian restaurant in a little well-tended garden with lots of plants and huge plastic plants and pterodactyls.

Jamaican

Chicken Lavish (☎ 957-4410) on West End Rd and *Troy & Felix Serious Chicken* opposite Drumville Cove are both bargain eateries with great atmosphere. The latter (look for carved chickens on the garden posts) serves curry chicken (US$6), pepper shrimp (US$10), and fish brown stew (US$9). I recommend the 'call & blow' (white chicken meat wrapped in bacon, stuffed with cheese and onions, fried as a ball, US$7). The *Castaway Restaurant*, next to the Rock House, features tasty 'angel & horseback' (ripe banana wrapped in bacon and fried, US$2.50), as well as lobster (US$12), conch steak (US$6.50), Kingfish steak (US$6), and bargain-priced breakfasts. Nearby *Pastries & Food* (☎ 957-4460) sells a wide variety of pastries, patties, and loaves.

The *Negril Yoga Center* offers Jamaican health-food dinners such as Rasta pasta, chicken Jamaican style, and curry vegetables in coconut milk (US$5 to US$7). If you fancy the drive, head to the *Hard Reggae Cafe* (☎ 957-4991), at the southern end of West End Rd. It has a large breakfast menu (from US$2), plus lunches from US$5, and daily specials.

Sheffield Rd contains several authentic Jamaican restaurants favored by locals. *Country Man* (☎ 940-5219), which serves jerk and BBQ, is a popular 24-hour eatery. Nearby is *Paradise Yard*, 'House of the Rasta Pasta.' Try the whole-wheat pastas. It's also a good place for Jamaican breakfasts, and coffee and ice cream enjoyed in a shaded open restaurant. My favorite is *Sweet Spice Restaurant* (☎ 957-4621), with a menu that includes conch steak (US$7), pepper steak (US$4), curried goat (US$5), and fish (US$5).

Mrs Brown's Fine Food (almost as famous a Negril landmark as Rick's Café)

Legal Lobster?

By law, no lobster can be landed, captured, purchased, or sold between April 1 and June 30. At this time you'll see 'Lobster Closed Season' flyers posted all over Negril. Many restaurants, however, continue to serve lobster (which they claim to have stockpiled before closed season). In 1996, the NCRPS declared a moratorium on serving lobster in the Negril Environmental Protection Area. Obviously, some restaurants are serving illegally caught lobster. Use your conscience: stick to fish or shrimp! ■

---

has been closed but should reopen. However, her daughter runs *My Mother's Tea* and serves 'mushroom daiquiris,' mushroom omelettes (US$12 to US$20), and mushroom tea (US$6). Be warned – *they're hallucinogenic*. It's on Sheffield Rd a half mile east of the roundabout.

Seafood

The most popular place on the beach is *Cosmo's* (☎ 957-4330), with three thatched bars and dining areas specializing in conch soup, curried conch, and curried shrimp. Prices range from about US$5 to US$12. The owner, Cosmo Brown, is known as 'the mayor of Negril.' Though 'born on the beach' in 1945, he trained as a restaurateur in Chicago. Cosmo charges US$0.30 to use his beach facilities and changing rooms. It's open 9 am to 10 pm.

The many options atop the cliffs include *Drumville Cove*, where you can savor such delights as snapper Drumville (baked filet with creamy sauce, US$7), escovitched fish with sautéed onion (US$7.50), and lobster (US$12). *Summerset Village* offers an all-you-can-eat lobster buffet on Thursdays. The *Lighthouse Inn* (☎ 957-4052) serves an excellent red snapper stuffed with callalloo, and steamed or brown-stewed kingfish, tuna, or barracuda.

Italian

Expect to pay US$15 for dinner at the Italian restaurant at *Hotel Samsara*

(☎ 957-4395). *Summerset Village* has an Italian 'extravaganza' on Saturday nights. The Italian-owned *Red Snapper Deli* (☎ 957-0010), an atmospheric bamboo-and-thatch bar and restaurant on West End Rd, serves from a huge menu of seafood and pastas. It offers free shuttles to and from your hotel.

Other Cuisines

Negril is synonymous with *Rick's Café*, to which scores of visitors skitter lemminglike to watch the sunset. This erstwhile rustic bar has gone upscale since it struck pay dirt in the 1970s, and today it's one of the most sophisticated eateries in town. The elegant restaurant is lit by Tiffany lamps and graced by 1920s-era Hollywood posters. Prices have gone upmarket, too. Burgers cost US$6! The varied menu also includes pompano Jack filet, conch steak, charbroiled fish platter, linguini Bolognese, plus exotic desserts ranging from carrot cake and Black Forest cake to candy apple walnut cheese-cake (all are US$3). Entrees begin at about US$10 and run to US$21 for curry shrimp. Rick's is open 2 to 10 pm, and has a two-for-one happy hour from 8 pm onwards.

As an alternative, I recommend the *Xtabi* restaurant, which offers a marvelous setting on the cliff face and has a varied and reasonably priced menu. The chef at *Doc's Delight* restaurant in the Negril B&B (☎ 957-4850) cooks gourmet international dinners (baked chicken in honey-peanut sauce, lobster Thermidor, Châteaubriand, and so on). It's a good option, too, for breakfasts of Belgian waffles and home-made muffins.

A more homely option is the *LTU Pub*, 100 yards south of Rick's Café. The decor at this small cliff-side open-air bar consists of a fabulous mural of an underwater scene with an octopus guarding a treasure chest. The eclectic menu includes a wide range of speciality burgers (from US$6) and spaghetti dishes, fish & chips, and chicken Bombay, all for about US$8.

My favorite place on the beach is *Tamboo Inn* (☎ 957-4282), a magnificent bamboo and thatch, two-story restaurant lit

by brass lanterns at night. Its varied menu includes a breakfast of 'pigs in a blanket' (US$7), pancakes and sausage (US$6), or a fruit platter with ice cream (US$5). The huge lunch/dinner menu ranges from grilled cheese sandwiches to deep-fried lobster niblets and nine types of pizza (US$5 to US$22). You might also try the *Kuyaba*, at the nearby Sea Gem Hotel. *Runaway's Beach Bar & Grill*, next to Crystal Waters Villas, is also popular.

If you're up early, you can breakfast from 7 am at *Hotel Samsara Sports Cafe*. The service is slow, so it's a good thing there's a TV to watch. Lunch options include esco-vietched fish, burgers, sandwiches, and Jamaican specials for less than US$3.

Peking House, on West End Rd, is the only Chinese restaurant in Negril.

Desperate for a cup of fresh coffee? The *Blue Mountain Coffee Shop* is a roadside stall opposite Negril Gardens; it serves dynamite cappuccinos, espressos, and ice coffees.

ENTERTAINMENT

Negril is Jamaica's most party-conscious resort town. Reggae Sunsplash in Kingston and Reggae Sumfest in Montego Bay may be the biggest bashes of all, but at any other time of the year Negril is the place to 'ride de riddims.' In fact, it's the only place in Jamaica with live concerts every night in peak season, and there's sure to be some big talent in town. There is also a handful of discos, plus a couple of earthy go-go clubs, but no cinema and nothing in the way of high culture.

Reggae Concerts

The following venues offer weekly live concerts featuring leading reggae stars such as Third World, Yellowman, Ziggy Marley, and Bunny Wailer: *Hotel Samsara* (☎ 957-4395) on Monday, *De Buss* on Friday with US$8 entrance, *Kaiser's* (☎ 957-4070) on Wednesday and Friday, and *MXIII* (☎ 957-4818) on Thursday and Saturday. To keep noise disturbance to a minimum, the promoters do their best to start shows promptly at 9:30 pm and end by

1:30 am. Entrance is about US$2 to US$6. *Summerset Village* also hosts live bands on Wednesday, and several other hotels, including the *Negril Tree House*, follow suit. The *Negril Inn* has a live reggae show and disco on Saturday night (US$3).

You'll find information about upcoming events posted on streetside poles.

Bars

Negril has dozens of bars, most of them catering to foreign travelers. If you're chasing local color, *Ragabones* in Red Ground, on the hill above Negril, is a favorite of locals. It pulsates with reggae riffs. *Mampf Jazz Club* is another earthy option, a half mile south of Sheffield Rd along Whitehall Rd.

My favorites on the beach include *Kuyaba*, for atmosphere (it's a beautiful thatched restaurant, almost Indonesian in style) and the *Boat Bar*, a tiny place formed around an old fishing boat turned into a bar, with a floor of bottle tops. The *Pickled Parrot* is also fun; it has a two-for-one happy hour from 3 to 5 pm. *Alfred's Ocean Palace* (☎ 957-4735) has live music on Sunday and Tuesday.

North Americans who miss their Monday night football should head to *Risky Business* (☎ 957-3008), a 24-hour sports bar near Sandi San.

You can savor the almost carnal sunsets from any bar along the shoreline, but *Rick's Café*, atop the cliffs on West End Rd, is the prime gathering place. The restaurant-bar also offers fire-eaters, jugglers and musicians to hold the crowd after Mother Nature's show is over. The happy hour at Rick's begins *after* sundown, when the crowd begins to drift away. Several bars have happy hours about 5 or 6 pm, timed to steer you away from Rick's. *Horselips Bar & Grill* at 251 Summerset Rd, for example, has a two-for-one happy hour daily at 5 pm.

Discos

The best disco in town is *Compulseion* (☎ 957-4416), above Negril Plaza. The US$5 entrance fee buys two drinks. It's open nightly until 5 am and has a three-hour-long

happy hour 10 pm to 1 am. It gets hot inside and the dancing can get decidedly raunchy. Local women are unabashed, and the opening gambit of many is to sidle up to men and begin *wining*.

The *Private Affair* disco at Hotel Samsara and *Limits* at Negril Inn are also both modestly upscale. Admission to Private Affair (US$15) includes 'all you can drink.' *Hotel Samsara Reggae Club* is open Wednesday to Sunday from 10 pm. Non-guests can also obtain passes for entry to the private discos in upscale resorts such as Sandals Negril, Hedonism II, and Grand Lido.

Local men head to *Close Encounters*, upstairs in King's Plaza. It's described in official JTB literature as a 'sophisticated dance club.' But if you want to dance, you'll have to join the go-go dancers performing ribald acts on stage. It stays open until 4 am and has no entrance fee (beers cost US$2). *Swamp Thing Bar*, at Daniel's Village Resort, hosts female mud wrestling.

Cinema

There's no cinema, but *Ghetto Vibe Theater* (opposite Paradise Yard on Sheffield Rd) is a funky shack showing movies.

Beach Parties

Blue Whale Divers (☎ 957-4438) hosts a beach party every Tuesday, with kayak races, three-legged races, egg and spoon races, and wet T-shirt contests.

Children's Entertainment

Anancy Park (☎ 957-4100, ext 381), opposite Poinciana Hotel, is a children's entertainment complex. It features a learning center, folk museum, heritage museum, donkey cart rides, fishing and boating lakes, nature trail, carousel, go-cart track, miniature golf course, and video arcade. Guests at the hotel can buy a US$50 per week 'Anancy Package' (open 1 to 9 pm weekdays and 10 am to 9 pm weekends).

THINGS TO BUY

A few dozen itinerant locals hawk carvings, woven caps, hammocks, jewelry, macramé bikinis, and T-shirts on the beach and especially along West End Rd, where there are some splendid carvings and wicker items. You can't walk by without a sales pitch, often quite heavy. Don't be hustled into a purchase you don't want! Partly for this reason, the Negril Chamber of Commerce has been moving vendors off the beach and streets and concentrating them in craft centers.

Craft Centers

There are three such centers: Rutland Point Craft Centre, opposite Hedonism II; the Negril Crafts Market just north of the river; and the newly constructed 56-room Negril Vendors Plaza in Negril Village. All have a wide range of stalls selling every kind of wood carving, crocheted woolen tams, straw baskets, hash pipes, and so on. Competition is fierce. So, too, the sales pitch. Haggling is part of the fun. Look at it that way and you'll get further without losing your cool.

Negril Plaza, Adrijan Plaza, and Sunshine Village also have good souvenir shops.

Art Galleries

Lloyd Hoffstead presides over Gallery Hoffstead II (☎ 957-3015) in Shop 23 on the upper floor of Negril Plaza, next to Compulseion disco. His work is of varying quality, but there are some fabulous sculptures and paintings (open Monday to Friday 9 am to 5 pm). Another option for more naive yet masterful art is *Mystic's Art Gallery*, run by a Rastafarian named Mystic, south of the lighthouse.

Other Items

Most upscale hotels have well-stocked general gift stores and/or boutiques. Tajmahal's has two duty-free stores at the Grand Lido Hotel and Beachcomber Club selling duty-free jewelry, watches, and the like.

The guys at Town and Country Music Store in Hi-Lo Plaza can outfit you with enough reggae tapes to keep you grooving.

The famous Negril Candle Factory was recently purchased and has been shipped lock, stock, and barrel to Treasure Beach (see the Treasure Beach section in the Southwest Coast chapter).

GETTING THERE & AWAY

Air

Just before press time, Trans-Jamaican Airlines' services were suspended following the company's purchase by Air Jamaica. The new schedule should include a route between Negril and Montego Bay, timed to connect with international flights.

Airways International has charter flights. You can also charter a helicopter through Helitour (☎ 979-8290). It costs US$400 one-way from Montego Bay for up to four passengers, US$750 from Kingston.

Bus

In Negril, buses for Montego Bay, Savanna-la-Mar (US$1), and Kingston (about four hours) depart from Sheffield Rd, just east of the roundabout in Negril Village. You can also wave down the Montego Bay bus on Norman Manley Blvd. Caribic Vacations (☎ 952-5013, fax 952-0981) arranges transfers between the Montego Bay airport and Negril for US$29 round-trip.

Bus service between Negril and Montego Bay is frequent. The two-hour journey costs about US$1.50. A better option is to hop aboard a private minibus – approximately US$3 one-way – that operates informally. These buses can be waved down anywhere along the coast road. Be prepared for a hair-raising ride – the drivers are singularly reckless. Minibuses also leave for Negril from Donald Sangster International Airport in Montego Bay (the price is negotiable, but expect to pay about US$10).

Taxi

A licensed taxi to Montego Bay will cost about US$50 to US$60. The price isn't bad considering the exorbitant fares for in-town rides. You should be able to negotiate a rate for half this price with an unlicensed driver. Negril is 52 miles east of Montego Bay or approximately a 90-minute drive.

GETTING AROUND

Walking short distances is OK, and it's especially pleasant to stroll the beach. However, Negril stretches along more than

10 miles of shoreline, and it can be a withering walk to many destinations. At some stage you'll most likely need transport. Upscale resorts at the north end of Long Bay have shuttles into town, and several hotels on the West End run shuttles to the beach. I've walked the length of Norman Manley Blvd and West End Rd several times, but it's a hot and sweaty business.

The Airport
The Negril airstrip is just north of Long Bay, about seven miles from Negril village. There's no scheduled bus service at press time. However, I've heard that Air Jamaica Express may inaugurate a hotel shuttle service in 1996 timed to coincide with its departures and arrivals.

A taxi will cost a whopping US$8 to US$10 for a journey between the airport and the village. Even a half mile journey to Rutland Point will cost US$7. You can rent a car at the airstrip from Don's Car Rental (☎ 957-1366).

Minibuses
Minibuses cruise Norman Manley Blvd and, to a lesser degree, West End Rd. You can flag them down anywhere; rides usually cost less than US$2. The majority of vehicles are heading to Montego Bay, and your request to go a few miles may be viewed with disdain.

Car & Motorcycle
A large percentage of visitors rent a Jeep, motorcycle, or motor scooter once they arrive in Negril. Cars and Jeeps are more expensive than elsewhere in Jamaica. Consider renting one in Montego Bay. In Negril, expect to pay US$60 per day for a small car and US$85 per day for a convertible Suzuki from Jus Jeep (☎ 957-4835), Coconut Car Rental (☎ 957-4291), or Vernon's Car Rentals (☎ 957-4354) at Shop 22 in Negril Plaza. At least a dozen other car rental booths line Norman Manley Blvd and West End Rd. Most require a hefty deposit of up to US$1000.

There are plenty of places renting motorcycles up and down Norman Manley Blvd

and West End Rd. Scooters average US$35 to US$40 a day; motorbikes US$40 to US$55. A few companies to consider are Carol's Bike Rental (☎ 957-4207) at Silver Sands on Norman Manley Blvd; Tyke's Bike Rental (☎ 957-4963) near Rick's Café on West End Rd; and Rambo Bike Rental (☎ 957-4711) on Norman Manley Blvd across from Negril Beach Club. Dependable Bike Rentals (☎ 957-4764) offers free pickup and delivery. Happy Bike (☎ 957-3181) on Norman Manley Blvd has 90cc scooters for US$33 per day and 175cc ones for US$39. It also offers guided motorcycle tours to Black River.

Helmets are not mandatory and hardly anyone wears one. Be warned, though, that the roads are potholed and often have patches of sand and gravel. The accident and injury rate is high. Wear a helmet! Remember, too, that you may not feel the effects of the sun while riding with a breeze to cool you down. Use sunscreen.

Taxi
Taxis are in short supply. As elsewhere in Jamaica, licensed taxis display a red license plate. Fares are supposedly regulated by the government, but you may need to bargain the fare *before* getting in the taxi. You can order taxis from Will's Taxi Service (☎ 957-5249), Easy Going Cabs (☎ 957-3227), or Dependable Taxi Service (☎ 957-4764). There are taxi stands at the Negril Crafts Market and in front of Adrijan Plaza. A much cheaper bet is a local colectivo taxi – usually an aged and battered vehicle – that will probably cost one-third the fare of licensed taxis. It will pick up as many passengers as it can hold en route.

Bicycle
You can rent mountain bikes for about US$8 a day from any of a dozen or more roadside rental offices. All the motorcycle rental agencies listed above also have bicycles, as does Salmon's Bike Rental, in the grounds of Westlea Cabins. Indian Skonk Bike Rental (☎ 957-3227) rents for US$5 per day. If you rent a bike overnight,

make sure that it is securely locked in a well-lit area. Consider taking a large chain and padlock with you. Check to ensure that insurance will cover any loss.

Westmoreland

The little-visited parish of Westmoreland extends east of Negril. Tourism has been slow to develop here, although it is finally stirring along the coast east of Savanna-la-Mar, the regional capital. Sometime before 1998, the south coast is slated to get its first major resort – an US$85 million Sandals all-inclusive property – near Whitehouse, where another 200-room property is rising. Many local residents are active in sponsoring self-reliant community development and see the arrival of the large-scale resorts as a threat. Others look forward to the employment opportunities, regardless of the cost to community life.

Roads fan out from Savanna-la-Mar along the coast and through the Westmoreland Plains, which dominate the western portion of the parish. This flat, mountain-rimmed area, planted almost entirely in sugarcane, was the scene of much violence during the labor agitation of the 1930s that helped reshape Jamaican politics. The plain is drained by the Cabarita River, which forms swamplands at its lower reaches. The fishing is good, and a few crocodiles may still live in more secluded swampy areas, alongside an endemic fish – the God-a-me – that can live out of water in moist, shady spots. The river is navigable by small boat for 12 miles. I expect this area will develop facilities for ecotourists over the coming years.

The eastern portion of Westmoreland is hilly and modestly populated. You'll discover several slender beaches with active fishing communities that provide a slice of Jamaican life relatively uninfluenced by tourism development.

LITTLE LONDON
This small village, 11 miles east of Negril, once had a significant number of East Indians whose ancestors were brought as indentured laborers following slave emancipation in 1834. The Indians suffered high rates of mortality. Their living conditions were so bad that in 1914 the Indian government forbade any further emigration to Jamaica. Today, their ancestors are little in evidence.

Many villagers still work in the sugar fields. Rice has also been grown in the marshlands east of town since the late 19th century.

A rough road leads south from Little London to Hope Wharf, a poor fishing hamlet where you can watch the fishermen mend their nets.

I'm not aware of anywhere to stay in Little London, but you should be able to rent rooms here and at Hope Wharf for US$10 or so by asking around.

Winnie's Kingfish Kitchen, a half mile west of Little London, is about the only eatery of note. It serves seafood and pasties, plus natural juices.

Any of the buses traveling between Negril and Savanna-la-Mar will drop you in Little London, from where you can catch bus No ST577 to Montego Bay. Anthony Vicianna also operates a minibus (No LS931) to Montego Bay for about US$4.

FISH WORLD & AQUA TECH
If you've wondered what it's like to fish for tarpon, then this fish farm and evolving nature park (☎ 955-4929) is the place to cast your lure. The sport fishing is said to be excellent. The place is on the site of an old government rice and inland fisheries project. The feisty tarpon and snook live in large ponds, although you can also fish the river, as well as the ocean by boat. Call ahead if you want your fish fried fresh after you catch it (you can also 'fish' for crayfish called *janga*). Fish World is extremely popular with locals who fish using home-made bamboo rods.

The 600-acre property is beside the Cabarita River about four miles east of Little London (three miles west of Savanna-la-Mar). It's a swampy place, part of the morass that once took up much of the Westmoreland Plains before being drained for King Sugar in the 18th century. The plains still flood occasionally, when the Cabarita River overflows its banks. The birding is fabulous. And crocodiles might be seen on guided nature tours.

Horse riding is available, and go-carts, a water slide and swimming pool, and landscaped gardens are planned. It's open 10 am to 6 pm.

Fish World offers *camping* (US$10), with outside toilets and showers, access to the kitchen, and even a restaurant for non-cooks.

SAVANNA-LA-MAR

With a population of 16,000, Savanna-la-Mar ('the plain by the sea'), the capital city of Westmoreland, is the largest town in western Jamaica. However, 'Sav,' as it is locally known, offers few attractions. Countless shops do lend a sense of prosperity to the otherwise sleepy town.

The town was founded around 1730 and grew modestly as a sugar shipping port during the colonial era. Sav has an unremarkable history, except where Mother Nature is concerned. Hurricanes swept the town in 1748, 1780, 1912, 1948, and 1988. Great George St has acted like a great gutter for wind-driven swells, and in 1912 the schooner *Latonia* was left high-and-dry a mile from shore. A whirlwind of a different kind erupted in the early 1970s during the PNP administration of Michael Manley, when a Cuban medical team arrived to perform duties at the Sav hospital as a gift of the Cuban government. Conservatives immediately created a controversy. The Cubans were asked to leave when Edward Seaga took power and ended diplomatic relations with Cuba.

Orientation

Sav is virtually a one-street town. Its axis is mile-long Great George St, which runs perpendicular to the A2. Great George St leads south to the old sea-front fort. The market is immediately east of the fort on the foreshore of Wisco Pier, which was until recently a

---

Little Bay Mangrove Project

The shoreline between Salmon Point and Hope Wharf is rapidly disappearing due to sand mining and the bulldozing of mangroves for development. Locals say a lot of beach has vanished. The mangroves once trapped sediment that flows from the New Savannah River, and today the mud is flowing out to sea, where it is adversely affecting the reefs and fisheries.

Locals have formed the Little Bay Citizens Association, and alongside NEPT/ NCRPS, the group has begun to replant mangroves and other shoreline trees to stabilize the beach, reduce erosion, and trap sediment. ■

---

sugar loading wharf for many decades. Most other roads extend off Great George St.

Information

There's no tourist-board office. The parish library (☎ 955-2795) may be of assistance; it's open Monday to Friday 9 am to 6 pm, Saturday 9 am to 1 pm.

Money Most of the national banks are represented. The Scotiabank has a branch at 19 Great George St (☎ 955-2601). Nearby in Citizen's Plaza you'll find the Jamaica Citizen's Bank (☎ 955-3300). Mutual Security Bank is at 46 Great George St (☎ 955-2338).

Post & Communications The post office (☎ 955-2680) is on the west side of Great George St, 200 yards north of the courthouse. If you want to send a letter or package with greater assurance of prompt delivery, consider UPS (☎ 955-9637), which has an office at 82A Great George St. It's open daily 7 am to 7 pm. A letter to North America costs US$11, with a money-back guarantee of delivery within 24 hours.

You can make telephone calls and send faxes from the Telecommunications of Jamaica office (☎ 955-2520) at 43 Great George St, opposite the Mutual Security Bank. Another office (☎ 955-9700) is located in the Savanna-la-Mar Commercial Plaza.

Medical Services Sav-la-Mar Hospital, northeast of town, has a 24-hour emergency service (☎ 955-2533). For less urgent matters you'll find several doctors' clinics near Uptown Mall, including the Western Medical Centre, which is open daily 8 am to 11 pm. The Greysville Pharmacy (☎ 955-9427) on Great George St opens 9 am to 9 pm daily.

Emergency The police station (☎ 955-2758) is adjacent to the courthouse on Great George St. Call ☎ 110 for an ambulance or fire brigade. Call ☎ 119 for the police.

Great George St

The English colonialists never completed the **Savanna-la-Mar Fort** at the foot of Great George St. Parts of it collapsed into the swamps within a few years of being built. Although much of its stone walls are still mostly intact, the fort is not worth the drive. Its innards are drowned by the sea to form a small cove where locals swim.

Many of the old stores that line the entire length of Great George St retain their wide, shady piazzas. The most interesting building is the **courthouse**, built in 1925 at the junction of Great George and Market Sts,

Savanna-la-Mar

To Frome,
Lucea

To Roaring
River

To Negril

To Montego Bay,
Kingston

Dunbars
Corner

CARIBBEAN SEA

PLACES TO STAY
1 Orchard Great House
4 Hendon House
9 Lochiel Guest House

PLACES TO EAT
2 Flaming Wok
13 Ann T's
14 Yvonne's Restaurant & Pub
15 Calypso Bay Restaurant
24 J's Jerk Centre
33 Fish & Produce Market

OTHER
3 Manning's School
5 Uptown Mall
6 Western Medical Centre
7 Hospital
8 Gas Station
10 Market
11 Savanna Plaza
12 Gas Station
16 Gas Station
17 Sav-la-Mar Commercial Plaza
18 Backra Services
19 Library
20 Post Office
21 Police Station
22 St George's Parish Church
23 Courthouse
24 Foote's Bike Rental
25 UPS Office
26 Wesley Methodist Church
27 Fire Station
28 National Commercial Bank
29 Telecommunications of Jamaica
30 Mutual Security Bank
31 Jamaica Citizen's Bank
32 Scotiabank
34 Ruins of Fort

A pier-perfect view

Cliff-hanging in Negril's West End

The Gut River percolates out of limestone cliffs and meanders
to the sea through mangroves and reeds.

Positive vibration

A typical rural store

One love stirs the crowd at Reggae Sumfest.

where there's a fountain made of cast-iron and inscribed on each side with the words 'Keep the pavements dry.'

St George's Parish Church, opposite the courthouse, was built in 1905. It's uninspired, although you might be impressed by the stately pipe organ that was dedicated in 1914.

At the north end of town by the roundabout known as Hendon's Circle is **Manning's School**. It was built in 1738 after a Westmoreland planter, Thomas Manning, left his land and buildings 'for keeping a free school in the parish of Westmoreland to instruct the youth.'

Places to Stay
The pickings here are slim. *Hendon House* (☎ 955-3943) is a 250-year-old, blue-and-white two-story timber house, about 50 yards north of Hendon Circle. The entrance is to the side, not at the locked front door, as appears. The place has a funky charm. A spiral wooden staircase leads upstairs to 12 rooms. They're lofty and spacious, with fans and jalousie windows, and cost US$15 and US$18 with shared bath, or US$21 with private bath and decrepit plumbing.

Another old stone-and-timber two-story great house that looks delightful from the outside is the *Lochiel Guest House*, on the A2, east of town. Inside, it's gloomy and rundown, however. Still, some of its 14 rooms (US$30) are appealing for their size and jalousie windows (try the one at the front on the ground floor). All have utility furniture and hot water in private bathrooms. No meals are served, but across the road is the ominously named Club Cancer rum shop and restaurant.

In a similar vein is *Orchard Great House* (☎ 955-2737) beside the road at Strethboghe (also known as Hertford), about three miles northeast of Sav. This aged stone-and-wooden home has 22 meagerly furnished rooms (US$16 with fans or US$25 with air-con). It also has four octagonal self-contained cottages for monthlong rental. There's a restaurant and bar, plus a swimming pool and expansive pool deck.

Places to Eat
I recommend *J's Jerk Centre*, a tiny outdoor place with little thatch umbrellas to eat under. The jerk chicken costs US$2.50 per quarter (add US$1.50 for festival). The owner also serves steam fish for US$2.50. For desserts, check out *Hammond's Pastry*, where Russell and Dorna Hammond make the best traditional coco-bread around.

The *Calypso Bay Restaurant* is another colorful jerk joint popular with locals. *Ann T's Country Kitchen* sells natural juices, fish, and lobster on the shady veranda of an old house. Across the street is *Yvonne's Restaurant & Pub* (☎ 955-9563), a well-kept place serving vegetarian meals for less than US$5.

For Chinese, try the *Flaming Wok* (☎ 955-2235), which does take-out as well as sit-down meals.

Getting There & Away
Half a dozen buses and a similar number of minibuses operate daily to both Montego Bay and Negril. Buses also depart on a regular basis from the Parade in Kingston; the three-hour journey will cost about US$1.80 (or about US$8 by minibus).

If you're coming from Black River, you can hop aboard minibus No LS324, which also operates in the opposite direction as far as Mandeville.

Getting Around
Taxi Several companies offer taxi services. Try Pat's Taxi Service (☎ 955-3335), opposite the Methodist church. Backra Services (☎ 955-3660) has a 24-hour taxi and rent-a-car service. Island Taxi (☎ 955-9722) also offers 24-hour service; it's at 126 Great George St.

Bicycle Foote's Bike Rental (☎ 955-4029) behind J's Jerk Centre rents bikes for US$6 per day. You can also have your bike repaired here.

FROME
Frome lies at the heart of Jamaica's foremost sugar estate. It sits in the center of the

rich alluvial plain that has made West-moreland the island's most productive sugar-growing parish. The plains are dominated by a sugar processing factory built in 1938 by the West Indies Sugar Company and owned by the Jamaican government. The factory, which is just south of the town of Grange Hill, still processes the entire sugar crop of Hanover and Westmoreland Parishes and employs over 2500 people directly and some 7500 indirectly.

When the factory opened, it became the setting for a major labor dispute that spread nationwide. During the Depression of the 1930s, many small factories were bought out by the West Indies Sugar Co (then a subsidiary of the English company Tate & Lyle). Unemployed workers from all over Jamaica converged seeking work. The majority were disappointed. Although workers were promised a dollar a day, those hired received only 15 cents a day (women received only 10 cents). Workers went on strike for higher pay, passions were running high, and violence erupted. When the crowds rioted and set fire to cane fields, the police responded by firing into the crowd, killing four people. The whole island exploded in violent clashes. The situation was defused when Alexander Bustamante (born locally in Blenheim) mediated the dispute. His efforts gave rise to the island's first mass labor unions and the first organized political party under his leadership (see Government & Politics in Facts about Jamaica).

A monument at a crossroads north of the factory gates reads 'To labour leader Alexander Bustamante and the Workers for their courageous fight in 1938. On behalf of the Working People of Jamaica.'

Free tours of the sugar-processing factory can be arranged by reservation (☎ 955-2604 or 955-2641). No high heels or sandals are allowed.

Buses and minibuses marked 'Grange Hill' operate on a regular basis from Savanna-la-Mar, Lucea, Negril, and Kingston (if coming from Kingston, be sure not to take a bus headed for Grange Hill in St Thomas Parish). Almost 40 minivans are registered with the Transport Licensing Authority to operate to and from Grange Hill!

ROARING RIVER & BLUE HOLE

What a surprising treat! Nature lovers and anyone seeking an off-beat experience should spend at least a half day at Roaring River, a natural beauty spot where mineral waters gush up from the ground in a meadow full of water hyacinths. It's a marvelous setting presaged by a towering silk-cotton tree overgrown with epiphytes. An old stone aqueduct takes off some of the water, which runs turquoise-jade. Steps lead steeply up to a cave in a cliff face that is the mouth of a subterranean passage. Inside you'll find a pool said to have mineral properties and good for swimming. Entrance is US$5, including a guide.

The guides (who lead you by kerosene torch) are registered in a cooperative. A tip is expected. Ask for Joseph, a Rasta who is secretary of the Roaring River Citizens' Association. Unregistered touts will try to stop you as you approach Roaring River. They may tell you that you can't go into the village without their permission. It's a ruse to get you to hire one of them as a guide.

There are lots of little stalls selling craft items, fruits, and refreshments.

The narrow lane to Roaring River from Petersfield continues beyond Roaring River for about one mile uphill through the village to **Blue Hole Ital Gardens**, a beautiful sinkhole, surrounded by a landscaped garden on the private property of Esau, a Rasta, and his French-Canadian-born wife I-Rise. Entry costs US$2, but it's worth it for a cool dip with the fishes in the turquoise waters. The source of the Roaring River is about 400 yards further up the road, where the water foams up from beneath a matting of foliage.

Places to Stay & Eat

Blue Hole Ital Gardens has two rustic but utterly charming cottages for rent (US$30 per night) at the edge of the tumbling brook (the 'waterhouse' cabin sits *over* the stream). Each has a spacious veranda. Bamboo-enclosed toilets and showers are alfresco. It's the quintessential alternative-lifestyle retreat. Fabulous!

There are two great places to eat. Both are rustic, rough-hewn affairs. *Jungle Cotton Tree View* sits atop a hill overlooking the silk-cotton tree and burbling spring. It serves Jamaican fare for a few dollars. Better still is *Lovers Cafe*, overlooking Blue Hole Gardens, one mile north. It's tremendous! Papaya and other fruit juices cost US$2. It also serves veggie and cheese patties (US$1), I-tal stew (US$3), and vegetarian omelettes, washed down by herb teas. Try Esau's 'Herbal Roots Tonic' love potion (US$1.50 per bottle). He claims it's a potent aphrodisiac.

Getting There & Away

Petersfield is a modest little town in the center of the sugarcane fields, five miles northeast of Savanna-la-Mar. Roaring River is at Shrewsbury Estate, about one mile north of the main crossroads in Petersfield. You can catch a bus in Savanna-la-Mar as far as Petersfield. From there it's a hot walk down the potholed road through the cane fields.

Organized tours to Roaring River are offered by companies based in Montego Bay and Negril. Check at the JTB offices for suggestions.

FERRIS CROSS

Ferris Cross is a major crossroads hamlet on the A2, five miles east of Savanna-la-Mar. Here, the A2 turns southeast and follows the coast to Black River and the south coast. Another road – the B8 – leads northeast to Galloway (three miles), where it begins a steep climb to Whithorn and Montego Bay.

Paradise Park, a 1000-acre working cattle ranch (PO Box 44, Savanna-la-Mar, ☎ 999-5771, fax 955-2997), offers 90-minute horseback rides through its 400 acres of pasture and forest for US$20. 'Busha' Clarke will take you on rides down to the beach and through palm jungle used as a setting for the movie *Papillon*. It's open 9:30 am to 4 pm, Monday to Saturday. The

small 18th-century wooden great house is open to visitors by appointment only. Paradise Park is along the banks of the Sweet River, one mile west of Ferris Cross.

BLUEFIELDS

This small, somnolent fishing village has a long sliver of beach barely 10-feet deep. It's popular with locals and Kingstonians escaping the mayhem of the capital city for weekends at local guest houses. Six miles southeast of Ferris Cross, the town has a rich history despite its off-beat appearance. The Spanish built one of the three settlements in Jamaica on this site (the others were Sevilla la Nueva and Villa de la Vega); they named it Oristan after a town in Sardinia, which they then ruled.

Bluefields Bay provided a safe anchorage and reliable source of freshwater for Spanish explorers and, later, British naval squadrons for over four centuries. The earliest landfall was made by Juan de la Costa, a mapmaker who sailed with Columbus in 1494. Many pirates based themselves here, including Henry Morgan, who in 1670 set out from Bluefields Bay to sack Panama City. In fact, Bluefields is supposedly named after Bleevelt, a French pirate. With diligent searching you can still see the ruins of a private fort built in 1767 by the owner of Belmont Estate (at the southern end of the bay) to protect against pirate attacks. The town was eventually abandoned following attacks by French and British pirates, and the ruins have entirely disappeared.

Today scant relics of the area's dramatic past remain, though side roads from the placidly rural one-road village lead into the green hills to ramshackle old plantation homes. The English naturalist Philip Henry Gosse (1810 – 1888) lived at Bluefields House in 1844 and 1845, where he gathered materials for his two books, *A Naturalist's Sojourn in Jamaica* and *The Birds of Jamaica*. The house has a breadfruit tree in the garden said to be one of those originally brought from the South Seas by Captain William Bligh in 1793.

Six-mile-long Bluefields Bay consists of a series of small coves. Mangrove

The Bluefields Project
Like many areas in Jamaica, the Bluefields region (population 7000) has seen agricultural, housing, and other development that has resulted in degradation of forests, soils, and other resources. Locals fear the coming of tourism, which poses new threats: farmers are being forced from their lands by rising real estate prices, and fishermen are subsisting on dwindling fish stocks resulting from mangrove destruction and overfishing.

Unlike most other areas, Bluefields' residents are taking charge with an initiative that promotes sustainable development within the communities of Cave, Memsville, Brighton, Belmont, and McAlpine.

The Bluefields Project started in 1988, when the Bluefields Trust was formed by Terry Williams. In 1989 the Bluefields People's Community Association (BPCA) was formed to promote small businesses and establish links between environmental and economic sustainability. A Resource & Training Centre was opened, and local farmers were given courses in permaculture (sustainable agriculture). Local women have been trained in dressmaking and childcare, and a horticultural nursery and environmental education center were set up. For information, contact the Bluefields Project, Box 22, Bluefields PO, Westmoreland (☎ 955-9828).

Donations can be made though the following international organizations:

Co-Operation for Development
  118 Broad St, Chesham, Bucks HP5 3ED, UK
CUSO
  Finance Dept, 135 Rideau St, Ottawa, Ontario, Canada
The Nature Conservancy International Program
  1815 N Lynne St, Arlington, VA 22209, USA ■

forests separate narrow beaches where colorful fishing boats are drawn up on poles and nets hung out to dry like laundry in the shrubbery. Booby birds, frigate birds, and pelicans roost in these bushes. You can even see fishing boats and pirogues being carved from cotton trees in the traditional manner. Villages are few and far between, and fishing is the way of life for most families. Those interested in deep-sea fishing should see the Whitehouse section below.

In town a small mausoleum filled with memorabilia honors slain Belmont-born reggae superstar Peter Tosh. Locals sell reggae tapes, and may ask for a donation to view the tomb. A small reggae festival is held here each mid-October.

Information
The police station is opposite the turnoff for Shafston Estate Great House at the east end of town. If your emergency is stress-related, Terry Williams, founder of the Bluefields Trust, offers massage.

Places to Stay – bottom end
Shafston Estate Great House is a budget traveler's dream. This run-down historic house has a stunning hilltop setting that is well worth the arduous climb. You're rewarded with fabulous views from the veranda down over the coast and forested hills as far east as Negril. You can't see the house until the final approach, when it suddenly appears amid pimento fields framed by a huge silk-cotton tree (one of the biggest in Jamaica).

Camping here costs US$3. Water and toilets are available. You can cook for yourself in the kitchen when its not in use by the chefs, who prepare meals for about US$3. Wooden bunk beds in a dormitory cost US$17/30 single/double, including three meals daily. There are also 10 basic rooms. Those with shared baths cost US$30/50 (US$60 triple). Rooms with private bath are US$10 extra. The place is popular with European youth, who have discovered how relaxing it is to simply swing in hammocks on the veranda or laze in a cool dipping pool. There's also a pool table and darts and a small bar. The eclectic decor adds to the ambiance.

To get there, turn north off the A2 opposite Bluefields police station. After 200 yards, turn left at a Y-fork, then turn right 400 yards further uphill. From here it's a steep two-mile climb up a horrendously pitted dirt road. If you can't make it, call the house for a free pickup from the public telephone outside the police station. For information or reservations, contact Frank & Rosie Lohmann, Bluefields PO, Westmoreland (☎ 997-5076).

The *Casa Mariner* (☎ 957-4348 for reservations) at Cave, two miles west of Bluefields, is a modern but modest property. Ten rooms have private bath with hot and cold water (US$23), and three rooms have air-con. Facilities include a large bar with pool tables and a breezy upstairs mirador restaurant. Another restaurant on a jetty over the water is good for watching herons feeding amid the mangroves.

Wilton House (☎ 955-2852) is a small guest house with four bedrooms and a small cottage.

Places to Stay – top end
If you hanker for the tranquil life and have money to burn, contact Braxton and Debbie Moncure (726 N Washington St, Alexandria, VA 22314, USA; ☎ (202) 232-4010, fax (703) 549-6517). They run five deluxe, fully staffed waterfront villas in Bluefields: *San Michele*, *Milestone Cottage*, *Cottonwood*, the *Hermitage*, and *Mullion Cove*. Rooms are decorated with carved and inlaid sideboards, mahogany rockers, antique armoires and dresses, and hand-embroidered Irish linen on canopied mahogany beds. Asian rugs are thrown on floors of stone, polished guango wood, and terra-cotta tile. Each villa has a private pool (except Cottonwood), plus bicycles, snorkeling and fishing gear, sailboat, and croquet sets; they share a competition-sized tennis court. Each has its own resident chef. Birdie, the manager, will take you touring in the minibus for an additional fee. Weekly low-season (May to December) rates range

from US$2400 to US$3750 double (depending on villa) and up to US$9000 for 12 people at Mullion Cove. High-season rates are approximately 30% more.

The rather ambitiously named *International Yacht Club & Lounge*, also east of Cave, has villas for rent.

Places to Eat
Bluefields is a good place to buy jerk fish, pork, or chicken and enjoy a picnic with your toes in the water and a Red Stripe in hand. A dozen or so jerk stalls line the beach. The most substantial is *Bluefields Jerk Centre* at the West End. *Jerry's Meals on Wheels* sells jerk, seafood and natural juices from an old bus turned into a funky restaurant and bar.

At the far east end of the bay is *Pedro's Paradise*, run by Paul 'Pablo' Fenlator. His thatched bar is a cool spot to hang out and shoot the breeze. Paul makes a dynamite fruit cocktail for US$1.20. His menu includes fried fish, chicken, and rice 'n' peas (US$2), and breakfast of ackee, saltfish, and dumpling (US$2.50), which you can eat on a little pier with a thatched hut over the mangroves. Nearby is the rustic *KD's Keg & Fish Joint*, specializing in seafood.

At Cave, try *Ocean Park Seafood Restaurant*, which doubles as a nightclub.

Entertainment
There are several local reggae bars where you can sup white rum and beer and enjoy a game of dominoes with locals. *Casa Mariners*, *Belmont Sands*, and *KD's Keg* are all fun, especially on weekends.

Getting There & Away
Buses that operate from Negril and Savanna-la-Mar to Whitehouse, Black River, and towns further west all pass through Bluefields. Ask the driver to let you off.

SURINAM QUARTERS
This area, inland from the coast southeast of Bluefields, is named for the colonists who were settled here after the English evacuated Surinam in 1667; they handed the South American territory to the Dutch

in exchange for New Amsterdam (New York). The colonists were mostly involved in raising indigo and, later, sugar (planters here gave the first impetus to sugar production on the island). Many Scottish, who came over from Darien in Panama where a settlement they had founded failed, also settled the area. If you closely examine a map, you'll see many Scottish place names in the area (Auchindown, Kilmannoch, and Culloden, for example). Campbell – a common Scottish name – is a familiar name hereabouts.

You'll see kids standing by the roadside holding lobsters up for sale to passersby. Colorful hammocks are also strung up for sale along the road.

Places to Stay & Eat

White Castle (c/o Clarence Hughes, White Castle, Whitehouse PO, Westmoreland, ☎ 963-5406) is a gleaming white modern building with blue awnings on the forested hillside about four miles east of Bluefields. It has fabulous views from the 10 modestly furnished air-con rooms (US$30). You can use the kitchen, although there are also three rooms with their own kitchens (US$50). A pool is in the works. The turnoff to the hotel is unmarked; it's 50 yards west of the 'Fishpot' roadside stand.

Auchindown Restaurant, one mile further east, is in a farmhouse on a cattle and pimento estate with the ruins of an old great house behind. It's easy to miss: the sign is overshadowed by another reading 'Lumber Yard.'

WHITEHOUSE

Whitehouse is the largest of the fishing villages along this section of coast and a great place to sample provincial coastal life. It stretches for about one mile along the A2, parallel to a series of beaches. Dirt roads lead down to the shores, where large motorized boats and hand-carved pirogues are drawn up, massive lobster pots lay in great piles, and trucks unload huge blocks of ice. The Whitehouse Fishing Cooperative supplies much of the island with wahoo, tuna, barracuda, bonito, snapper,

kingfish, marlin, and lobster taken on the Pedro Banks, about 80 miles to sea.

Follow the dirt road past Alexander's Seaview Shopping Plaza to reach the main beach, where dozens of locals gather when the night's catch is brought in. The fish market is a colorful, bustling sight as higglers bargain with fishermen. A craft and vegetable market is held on Wednesday and Saturday.

Just west of town is South Sea Park, an upscale residential community with villas and homes along the coral shorefront.

The area is expanding and is slated as the site for an all-inclusive resort to be built by the Sandals chain. This will be the area's first large-scale resort, and many locals are concerned about the impact on the local environment. Sandals promises to spend considerable sums to minimize the resort's environmental impact. For example, a section of the beach will be preserved as a nesting site for turtles. Will they have signs directing turtles to that portion?

Local developer Ronnie Thwaites and hotelier Peter Probst are also developing a 200-room housing resort east of Whitehouse, which will include an 18-hole golf course.

Information

There's a Jamaica Citizens' Bank on the main road at the west end of town. You can buy over-the-counter medicines at the Whitehouse Pharmacy (☎ 963-5409), next to the bank. You'll also find South Sea Pharmacy (☎ 963-5489) in the village center near Alexander's Seaview Shopping Plaza.

About 200 yards west of the gas station is a handsome little cottage with gingerbread trim that houses Linda's Massage Centre, which doubles as a boutique and gift shop. Linda offers facials, manicures, and health tonics.

Activities

You can hire a fishing boat to go snorkeling for around US$15 per hour to a local reef. Better yet, hop aboard with local fishermen for a trip to the fishing banks, but be prepared for some arduous work at sea, pulling up lobster and fish pots on lines. This will definitely test your sea legs. The price will entirely depend on your negotiating skills. Herman, a local boatman in Bluefields, provides rods and reels and can take up to four people for about US$20 per hour. It's best to leave at dawn.

Peter Probst at Natania's (see Places to Stay) can arrange snorkeling or fishing with locals for guests.

Places to Stay

You can camp on the lawn at *Roots Uprising Guest House* at South Sea Park for US$10. Laundry services are available, and there's an I-tal restaurant and bar. See below for more details. *Pear Tree Pub*, in the center of Whitehouse, has basic rooms for about US$5.

You'll not regret a stay at *Natania's*, a true home-away-from-home run by live-in owners Peter Probst – a friendly New Yorker – and his Jamaican wife, Veronica (Little Culloden, Whitehouse PO, Westmoreland, ☎/fax 963-5342; in the USA, ☎ (800) 330-2332). It's the most stylish and atmospheric place for miles, as well as a great bargain. The eight rooms (six with king-size beds) all have ceiling fans and wide jalousie windows. A wide outdoor dining veranda looks over well-tended lawns and lush gardens that fall to the rocky shore, where multitiered teraces are built above the coral and fitted with artificial beaches for sunning (clothing optional). Water sports are offered, and there's a large pool and sun deck and separate beachside bar. Room rates are US$50 a double in summer and US$10 for a third person. Natania's is at Little Culloden, one mile west of Whitehouse.

Despite its funky name, *Roots Uprising Guest House* at 139 South Sea Park (☎ 963-5550 or 995-9164) is a contemporary home owned by a Swiss woman named Jenny Húeskn. She has five spacious rooms that share a large bathroom (US$30 to US$50 per room, depending on size). Jenny prefers to rent to families and groups: her house can accommodate up to 10 people (US$1500 weekly with a housekeeper). There are mosquito nets over the beds.

Two other options at South Sea Park are *White House Beach Villa* (which happens to be pink), and *Tan Tan Beach Villa* (☎ 963-5176), fronting a tiny cove with a beach that you're sure to have to yourself. The latter has five modestly furnished rooms with fans and cold water only. It's overpriced at US$50 a double including breakfast.

At the far east end of South Sea Park is the *South Sea View Guesthouse* (☎ 963-5172, fax 963-5000). This modern villa has eight air-con rooms, each with private bath, king-size bed, cable TV, and hand-painted tropical murals. There's a swimming pool and steps lead to a rocky cove good for bathing. Upstairs rooms cost US$50/55 single/double (it also has a package for US$750 per couple per week including two meals daily).

Places to Eat

The *Red Snapper Restaurant* at South Sea View Guesthouse offers breezy alfresco dining overlooking the ocean. Its Jamaican fare includes curried or grilled lobster (US$16), and chicken 'n' chips or steam fish (US$7). *Natania's* also welcomes nonguests for meals in a more homey environment on the patio. It serves breakfasts for under US$5. Lunch includes tuna melt, burgers, and other American fare in the same price range.

A thatched bar and small I-tal and Italian restaurant were being built on the front lawn of *Roots Uprising Guest House* when I last called by.

Dawn Hot Spot & Beer Joint and *Justice Bar & Restaurant* are two rustic eateries in the center of Whitehouse. You can buy breads, patties, and the like at the *Seaview Pastries, Bakery & Snack Counter*, and there's a grocery store plus produce market (Wednesday and Saturday) near Alexander's Seaview Shopping Plaza.

SCOTT'S COVE

Twenty miles east of Savanna-la-Mar, the A2 sweeps around this deep little inlet where dozens of food and beer stalls line the shore. It's a good place to buy fried snapper and bammy (a pancake of fried cassava) with onions and peppers for a dollar or two. The cove is full of brightly painted fishing boats. It was here in 1655 that Spanish ships landed supplies for the guerrilla leader Ysassi, who held out against the English invaders for two more years.

Immediately east is an area of bull-thatch palms that extends into the Font Hill Wildlife Sanctuary. The most important tree economically, it is used for weaving baskets and other straw-work regarded as among the best on the island.

Scott's Cove forms the parish boundary between Westmoreland and St Elizabeth. Beyond lies the south coast, where the landscape takes a dramatic turn.

FONT HILL WILDLIFE SANCTUARY

This 3150-acre wildlife reserve – one of the least disturbed natural ecosystems in Jamaica – is owned by the Petroleum Corporation of Jamaica. It stretches along two miles of shore. The property, once a cattle estate, was acquired by the government in 1973 as part of a proposed development project that never got off the ground.

Much of the sanctuary is made up of scrubby acacia and logwood thickets. Closer to the shore is a maze of interconnected lagoons and swamps, with water colors varying from deep blue to jade green and brown. The birding is fabulous. Herons and egrets are common, as are jacanas, whistling ducks, blue-winged teals, and eight endemic bird species that include the pea dove, white-bellied dove, and the ground dove – the smallest dove in the world.

More than 200 American crocodiles still exist at Font Hill – one of the densest populations in Jamaica. Their numbers, however, continue to decline. A tagging and census of crocodiles was initiated in 1989, led by the well-known Jamaican crocodile expert Charles Swaby. As a boy, Swaby used to hunt crocodiles in the Black River, Parrotee Swamps, and Font Hill (he has captured no less than 2000 crocodiles in his career but has never been bitten). Swaby has since become involved in conservation. Until recently he had a crocodile farm at his home in Mandeville, where he raised the animals for research purposes. He has moved his operation to Font Hill.

The swamps are accessible by canoe at high tide. Be careful – the water level drops at low tide.

The beach is a magnificent little strip of golden sand shaded by sea grapes and fringed by reef. Offshore you'll find great snorkeling and bathing. Dolphins even come into the cove. A great spot for picnics, the beach is very popular with locals who once used it for trysting. Anthony Anderson, the gracious and friendly overseer, says he's put a stop to that 'nonsense!' Anderson plans to convert old derelict houses into a restaurant, gift store, and bar. He also hopes to build a boardwalk, interpretive center, and marina.

Peter Marra is the resident ornithologist. He recommends making reservations for birding trips via Richard Sutton at Marshall's Pen in Mandeville (☎ 963-8569).

Font Hill is two miles east of Whitehouse. Watch for the sign that reads 'Fonthill Private Property – Wildlife Sanctuary.' A dirt track leads to Font Hill Beach.

Southwest Coast & Central Highlands

The southwest coast and central highlands are together Jamaica's new tourism frontier. The region comprises St Elizabeth and Manchester Parishes. The former is a flatland rimmed by mountains; the latter, immediately east, is a wedge-shaped upland plateau the ruler-straight western slope of which forms the boundary between the two parishes. They are marketed together as the 'South Coast' by the Jamaica Tourist Board and in many regards feel like a single unit.

The central highlands were popular last century as a cool vacation retreat. The towns of Christiana and Mandeville became social centers for wealthy Jamaicans and Europeans. The trade has since died though the charms remain. Jamaica's more recent resort-driven tourism has totally bypassed both the uplands and sparsely populated southern coast, where there are few picture-postcard beaches. The shore is much rockier, the water murkier, and the sand darker than on the north coast.

Still, the area is replete with attractions. The most well known of these are the Great Morass, Bamboo Avenue, and YS Falls, a beauty spot to rival the world-famous Dunn's River Falls near Ocho Rios. The lifestyle is virtually unsullied by tourism (the area appeals to travelers whose idea of a good time is watching fishermen return to the beaches, where women wait with tubs filled with ice). Two of Jamaica's prime wildlife-rich ecosystems are also here, and the area is establishing itself as a node for the nation's nascent ecotourism. The spotlight is increasingly shining on Treasure Beach, with its deserted long beaches brightened by colorful fishing boats hauled up to the dunes. It also has a unique lazy calm based on a traditional life that keeps locals rooted and hopeful. Its people are

HIGHLIGHTS

- Black River Great Morass, teeming with wildlife and accessible by boat
- YS Falls for a refreshing dip among splendid scenery
- Lonesome, laid-back Treasure Beach
- Funky Alligator Pond, where fishing is still the way of life and tourists are rare
- Sprawling Long Bay, a secluded haven for crocodiles and manatees

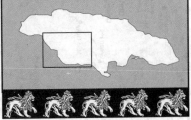

mellower than anywhere else in Jamaica: everyone wishes you a safe journey, fewer people ask you for money, and the ones who do are more inclined to offer thanks.

The southwest coast is poised for change. It's also shaping up as a battleground between developers and environmentalists. Several chain resorts have staked out patches of beach, and electricity and telephone systems are being installed in preparation. Many locals think the region's future lies in a more sensitive kind of tourism, different from the hustle-and-concrete-resort tourism of the north coast. They don't want another Negril or Montego Bay. They'd prefer to benefit from the prosperity that tourism provides without irrevocably changing their environment and lifestyle. Several community-based movements are evolving to help define the region's future.

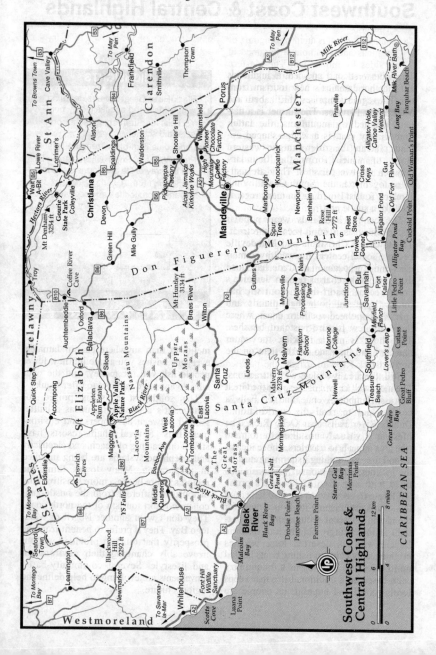

Southwest Coast &
Central Highlands

Geography

The southwest coast is an intriguing mix of dry savannas and swampland hemmed in on all sides by mountains. The western plains, centered on the town of Black River, are known for the Great Morass, a swampy marsh and forest that is a rare habitat for crocodiles and waterfowl. Further east, the plains are lush with cattle pastures, market gardens, and to a lesser degree, sugarcane fields. The area was one of the first cleared by the Spaniards for cattle, and it is still possible to see buildings of 'Spanish Wall' (masonry of white lime, sand, and stone between a wooden frame), a construction method passed down from the 16th century. Santa Cruz, in particular, was known for its vast droves of cattle and horses; the tradition lingers.

The plains are divided north to south by the Santa Cruz Mountains, a steep-faced chain that slopes to the sea and – *whoosh!* – drops 1700 feet at Lover's Leap. The chain forms a rain shadow over the land to the west. This area receives little rain, and westward as far as Black River the plains are covered in savanna and cactus. As yet, no attempt has been made to utilize the waters of the Black River to irrigate the parched plains. Remarkably, however, the area is an important center of market gardening. St Elizabeth is Jamaica's breadbasket: melons, peppers, scallions, tobacco, corn, and similar produce grown here supply the rest of Jamaica. Slash-and-burn agriculture, however, is a threat around Treasure Beach: two or three crops are often all that can be grown in the soil, which is then abandoned and left exposed to rains.

The central highlands stand in total contrast. Parts of England or Germany come to mind around Mandeville and Christiana, with rolling hills, tight valleys grazed by cattle in fields fringed by hedgerows and stone walls, and intensively farmed mountain slopes that rise northward to almost 3000 feet. Both towns are agricultural centers. Mandeville, the prosperous regional capital for the entire south-coast area, has a strong English feel that has attracted a large number of English retirees in recent

decades, alongside North Americans who have arrived with the bauxite industry.

St Elizabeth has its own cultural anomalies. Miskito Indians from Central America were brought to Jamaica to help track Maroons during the 18th century and eventually given land grants in St Elizabeth. They and 19th-century Scottish castaways and German settlers are partly responsible for the high percentage of mixed-race peoples concentrated in regional pockets. This century the area has suffered from high rates of emigration; many of the laborers who migrated to Panama, Costa Rica, Guatemala, and Cuba to work on railway construction and banana plantations came from this area.

Climate

The area has two distinct climates associated with the temperate uplands and the relatively dry, yet hot, plains. When you tire of the humidity of the north and east coast, this is the place to come. The southwest coast has a balmy climate, while the highlands are refreshingly springlike. It can be cool – even cold – at night around Mandeville, and in the Santa Cruz and Nassau Mountains amid the pine and stunted oak forests. Take a sweater or warm jacket.

Organized Tours

Pro-Tours Ltd at 8 Lady Musgrave Rd, Kingston 5 (☎ 978-6113, fax 978-5473), offers full-day tours from Ocho Rios that take you over the mountains for breakfast in Mandeville, a swim at YS Falls, and a boat ride into the Great Morass (Thursday and Saturday, US$93). Another trip from Montego Bay combines the Great Morass with a visit to the Appleton Rum Factory (Thursdays, US$88). Jamaica Co-Op Auto & Limousine Tours at 8 Queen's Drive, Montego Bay (☎ 952-7574, fax 952-7575) also has a south-coast tour featuring YS Falls, the Great Morass, and Lover's Leap. Similar tours from Kingston are offered by Galaxy Leisure & Tours at 75 Red Hills Rd (☎ 931-0428, fax 925-6975).

A US-based company, Calypso Island Tours, offers a nine-day Outback Jamaica eco-adventure focusing on the south coast (3901 Grand Ave, No 304, Oakland, CA 94610, ☎ (510) 653-3570 or (800) 852-6242, fax (510) 653-8314). It includes visits to Moravian churches in Christiana, nature walks in Gourie State Park, visits to YS Falls, San Pedro Bluff, and Alligator Hole, plus a boat trip on the Black River for US$1200.

Black River

Black River (population 4000) is the principal town of St Elizabeth Parish. It sits on the west bank of the mouth of the aptly named Black River in the nape of Black River Bay, where waters are a scintillating jade-blue.

Peaceful and picturesque now, with plenty of snoozy charm, the town is a far cry from the heady days of the 18th and 19th centuries when it prospered from the logging trade. Black River was a center for the export of logwood (introduced to Jamaica from Central America in 1715), from which a Prussian-blue dye was extracted for export; even English lords had their ermine robes stained by logwood dye. Logwood still grows extensively hereabouts, though the ships stay away since the port closed in 1968 (a few fishing trawlers still land their catches here).

Early prosperity brought electric power to Black River in 1893, when it was installed in a house called Waterloo, the first such installation in the country. In 1903 the first motorcar was imported to Jamaica by Waterloo's owner. Back then, the town even had a horse-racing track and an active gambling life, and a mineral spa at the west end of town was popular with the well-to-do.

INFORMATION
Tourist Office
The JTB (☎ 965-2074) runs an office on the upper floor of the Hendriki Building beside the bridge at 1 High St. It has plenty of tourist literature.

Money
You can cash traveler's checks or arrange cash advances at Scotiabank (☎ 965-2252), which has a branch at 6 High St, or at Mutual Security (☎ 965-2207) across the road. Global Travel (☎ 965-2651 or 965-2203) at 46 High St acts as a Western Union agent. They'll help you get cash transferred swiftly from abroad.

Post & Communications
The post office (☎ 965-2250) is next to the police station on North St. You can make international calls at the Telecommunications of Jamaica office nearby (☎ 965-9915).

Medical Services
Emergency services are available at the Black River Hospital (☎ 965-2212), a half mile west of town, housed in an old army barracks. Dr John Brown has a clinic (☎ 965-2544) at 48 High St. You can also receive medical assistance at Seaview Medical Center, 100 yards further east; it's open 24 hours.

Emergency
The police station (☎ 965-2232) is on North St, 200 yards from the shore. For emergencies, call ☎ 119 (police) or ☎ 110 (fire and ambulance).

THINGS TO SEE & DO
High St is lined with ramshackle, colonnaded, Georgian-style timber houses with gingerbread trim. At the east end of this main street is the **Hendriki Building**, dating from 1813. Beyond that an old iron bridge is a good spot for watching great swathes of hyacinths floating out to sea. You might even see the occasional crocodile waiting for tidbits thrown by tourists from the riverside berths. The huge, rusty cranelike scale on the west bank was once used for weighing logwoods.

Historic structures worth checking out include the porticoed **courthouse**, facing the ocean on Main St, and the **town hall** with lofty pillars and fronted by an enormous banyan tree. Nearby is the yellow-brick **Parish Church** of St John the

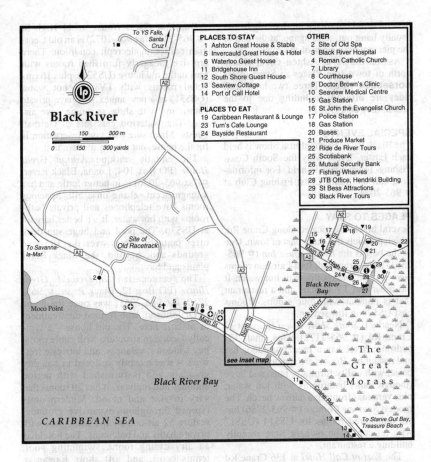

Black River

PLACES TO STAY
1 Ashton Great House & Stable
5 Invercauld Great House & Hotel
6 Waterloo Guest House
11 Bridgehouse Inn
12 South Shore Guest House
13 Seaview Cottage
14 Port of Call Hotel

PLACES TO EAT
19 Caribbean Restaurant & Lounge
23 Turn's Cafe Lounge
24 Bayside Restaurant

OTHER
2 Site of Old Spa
3 Black River Hospital
4 Roman Catholic Church
7 Library
8 Courthouse
9 Doctor Brown's Clinic
10 Seaview Medical Centre
15 Gas Station
16 St John the Evangelist Church
17 Police Station
18 Gas Station
20 Buses
21 Produce Market
22 Ride de River Tours
25 Scotiabank
26 Mutual Security Bank
27 Fishing Wharves
28 JTB Office, Hendriki Building
29 St Bess Attractions
30 Black River Tours

To YS Falls, Santa Cruz

To Savanna-la-Mar

Moco Point

Site of Old Racetrack

Main St

North St

High St

Black River Bay

Black River

see inset map

CARIBBEAN SEA

Black River Bay

The Great Morass

Crane Rd

To Starve Gut Bay, Treasure Beach

Evangelist, built in 1837 at the main road junction. Note the tombstones outside the west entrance. They commemorate local merchant Duncan Hook (1741 – 1779) and his four children by a 'free mulatto,' who lies beside him. Like many white men of his time, Duncan had a special Act of Assembly passed to grant his mistress and children the same legal status as white people. Without it they could not have been buried in the churchyard.

One of the most impressive buildings is the **Invercauld Great House & Hotel**. Another is the **Waterloo Guest House**.

Both are splendid examples of the classic Jamaican vernacular style, with shady wooden verandas and gingerbread trim (see Places to Stay).

Unfortunately, many buildings disappeared in a huge explosion that leveled the town center in 1900, and a good number of those that remain are on their last legs.

The main reason most people visit Black River is to take a boat ride into the Great Morass in search of **crocodiles** and birds (see Boat Tours under Great Morass below). You don't have to take a cruise into the morass to see crocodiles, however.

Several timid but menacing-looking beasts usually hang out, jaws agape, at the end of the piers on both sides of the river.

Ashton Stable at Ashton Great House north of town (see Places to Stay) offers **horseback rides**. Three two-hour trail rides are offered, including one to the beach; they cost US$14.

SPECIAL EVENTS

The Black River Horticultural Show is held each Easter. Every May the South Coast Fishing Tournament is held. For information, call the South Coast Fishing Club at ☎ 965-2074.

PLACES TO STAY

Several hotels are located along Crane Rd, which parallels the shore east of town. One of the best is the *Bridgehouse Inn* (☎ 965-2361) at 14 Crane Rd. Its 14 air-con rooms have private bathrooms with hot water. It has a bar and TV lounge, and a restaurant that is popular with tour groups. Rooms cost US$29 in low season.

Nearby is *South Shore Guest House* at 33 Crane Rd (☎ 965-2172). This small 12-bedroom hotel has a breezy outdoor bar and restaurant. Rooms are spacious, though basic, with utility furniture, fans, and large (though dark) bathrooms with hot water, plus verandas fronting a narrow beach. The modest *Seaview Cottage* (☎ 965-2756) has six uninspired rooms for US$14 (US$17 with air-con). The owners were recently building a restaurant.

The *Port of Call Hotel* at 136 Crane Rd (☎ 965-2360, fax 965-2410) has 19 rooms, plus a restaurant and bar, and pool and Jacuzzi. It looks appealing from the outside, but the interior is disappointing, with meager utility furnishings and a restaurant resembling a military mess hall. Most rooms have TVs and telephones. Those upstairs have air-con. Rates are US$40/50 single/double downstairs, or US$50/65 upstairs. The hotel charges US$60 one-way for airport transfers (US$30 for each additional passenger). It rents bicycles.

Waterloo Guest House at 44 High St (☎ 965-2278, fax 965-2072) is an old Georgian edifice in decrepit condition. There are five meagerly furnished rooms with fans in the old house (US$21), plus 16 carpeted rooms with TV and hot water (US$31) in a new annex. All have private bathrooms with showers; some have air-con. The Waterloo gets lots of German guests. Make sure that your reservation is for the house, not a more modern unit.

The equally antique *Ashton Great House* (PO Box 104, Luana, Black River, ☎/fax 965-2036) is in better fettle and has a magnificent setting on a hill. Spacious rooms have telephones and private bathrooms with hot water. It's a better bargain at US$30. The pool and huge sun deck offer fantastic views over the 185-acre grounds and, beyond, the Black River plains and bay.

The centenarian *Invercauld Great House* (PO Box 12, Black River, ☎ 965-2750, fax 965-2751) was once the home of Dr Johnson, who refined the treatment of malaria here. The old house – a typically Georgian structure with gable roofs, bay windows, valances, and intricate fretwork – was recently restored to haughty grandeur and is furnished with period antiques and replicas. It has 20 rooms that vary in size and mood. Modern units (spread throughout expansive grounds) feature 52 air-con rooms and suites with private baths and balconies. The hotel has an airy dining room, swimming pool, tennis court, and gift shop. Executive suites have king-size beds and private verandas. Room rates begin at US$56, US$82 for junior suites, and US$488 for superior suites. A wide range of tours and activities are offered.

You can also rent a private bungalow, *Kariella Villa* (☎ 965-2725), at 44 Crane Rd. It sits in a lush, landscaped garden and has three bedrooms with marvelous views. Another rental option is *Kenchrismar Beach Cottage* (☎ 997-6000), which costs US$50 double, US$10 per additional person.

You can arrange *villa and cottage rentals* through Ferne Spencer at South Coast Rentals (☎ 965-2651, fax 965-2697) at 17 High St, above Bayside Restaurant.

PLACES TO EAT

The best place around is the *Bridge House* on Crane Rd. It serves excellent seafood and Jamaican dishes such as curried goat, washed down with health drinks made of beetroot juice and Irish moss (entrees begin at US$8).

In town, the *Caribbean Restaurant & Lounge* is a clean, shady outdoor eatery serving Jamaican specialties for less than US$5. If you have little to spend, try *Turn's Café Lounge* at the corner of High and North Sts; it's open 24 hours. A more elegant option popular with locals is *Bayside Restaurant*, which calls itself a 'pastry & pub.' You'll find the *Bayside Jerk & BBQ Centre* at the rear, overhanging the sea. For inexpensive spicy patties and pastries, I like the *Pastry Palace*, just north of the Hendriki Bldg at the east end of High St.

If you crave a cooling ice-cream soda (US$2.50) or milk shake (US$1.50), head to the ramshackle bar at the front of the *Waterloo Guest House*. If you're stocking your refrigerator, try your bargaining skills for fish, meat, or produce at the colorful market on Friday and Saturday, when the town comes alive.

A barbecue party with live music is held at the *Jerk Pit*, at Ashton Great House, each Friday, Saturday, and Sunday evening (US$15). Here you'll dine alfresco surrounded by pasture, with the great house illuminated on the hillock above.

GETTING THERE & AWAY

You can catch buses to Black River from most major towns, as it's on the main route between Kingston and Negril. Several buses originating in Montego Bay also pass through. Buses arrive and depart Black River from behind the market, just west of the river.

South Coast Rentals at 17 High St (☎ 965-2651) rents cars.

North of Black River

THE GREAT MORASS

This 125-sq-mile wetland – Jamaica's largest extant marshland – extends inland from the mouth of the Black River. It is separated by the narrow Lacovia Gorge into the Lower Morass and Upper Morass. Several rivers feed the Morass, including the Broad River, which rises in the Santa Cruz Mountains to the east. The main source, however, is the Black River, Jamaica's longest river, which rises near Coleyville and flows west as the boundary between Manchester and Trelawny Parishes before disappearing underground near Troy. It makes a brief reappearance near Oxford in Manchester Parish before disappearing again and finally reemerging near Balaclava. From here it flows 44 miles to the sea. Many tributaries add to its considerable size as it meanders through the flatlands of the Great Morass. It is navigable for about 12 miles upriver.

The Spanish called it the Río Caobana (Mahogany River), because of its inky black color. Although the waters are lightly stained by tannins from decomposed vegetation in the Great Morass, most of the blackness you see is not the water; its the dark peat of the riverbed.

The Morass is a complex ecosystem and a vital preserve for more than 100 bird species. With luck you'll see cinnamon-colored jacana, egrets, whistling-ducks, water hen, seven species of herons, and red-footed coots strutting atop the lily pads. The Morass also forms Jamaica's only remaining significant refuge for crocodiles. About 300 live in the swamps. They're not hard to see: don't be surprised to find nine feet of crocodile dog paddling alongside your boat and begging with a cold-eyed stare for a treat. Feisty game fish are plentiful, including snook and tarpon. The Morass even has its own endemic fish: a small species called a God-a-me that can live out of water among the moist leaf litter

What a Croc!

Saltwater crocodiles, once common around virtually the entire coast of Jamaica, are now relegated to a few areas along the south coast, most notably the Great Morass. They were once so numerous that one of the earliest laws in Jamaica proclaimed that an 'alligator' should be on the Coat of Arms.

They're formidable looking beasts. An average adult male grows to 12 feet, although such sizes are rarely seen; they're usually killed before they have a chance to attain full maturity.

The American crocodile – called an 'alligator' in Jamaica – is very different from the larger and very aggressive Nile crocodile. The former is shy, afraid of people, and eats relatively small amounts (mostly fish) utilizing conical teeth well-adapted for capturing slippery prey. It goes long periods without eating, and can survive on 10 pounds of food a week.

Early morning is a good time to see crocodiles, when they are sunning on the banks to restore the heat lost at night. The animal, an antediluvian legacy of the dinosaur period, maintains a body temperature of 77°F by alternating between shade, water, and sun. It hunts at night.

When it's submerged, you may see its beady eyes keeping a watch above the water; they can keep their sensory organs above water while submerged. When it sinks, special valves seal the orifices.

The animal inhabits mangroves and can be seen at Alligator Hole (Canoe Valley), Font Hill Reserve, and in the Great Morass of the Black River and, to a lesser degree, Negril. Like the virtually extinct manatee, crocodiles were once abundant in the Black River. Ruthless hunting has greatly reduced their numbers. The crocodile has a very high death rate in Jamaica, primarily due to deterioration in swamplands, overfishing (ironically, since crocodiles cull the slowest and weakest fish members, they improve fish productivity), and alteration of estuary configurations, which has altered water flows adversely. They have been protected since 1971.

and mud. On rare occasions, endangered manatees may even be seen near the river estuary.

The vegetation changes upriver as the watercourse narrows. In places the mangroves are so thick and tall that aerial roots form tunnels. Beyond the confluence of the YS, Middle Quarters, and Black Rivers, red mangroves give way to salt-grass marsh and jungle-thick swamp forest rooted in peat, and the vista broadens into marshy meadows of tall sedges, reeds, and saw grass. Between the mangroves and marsh are a variety of riverine plants such as wild cane, bulrush, wild ginger, quaco, potato slip, floating water hyacinth, and the insect-eating bladderwort. The decaying vegetation gives off methane gas, which bubbles up.

Taming & Saving the Great Morass

In recent years, several corporations have established commercial shrimp and fish ponds, the latest business ventures in a 200-year history of converting the swamps to commerce. Local fishermen also gain access in their dugout canoes, tending conical, funnel-shaped shrimp pots made of bamboo in the traditional manner of their West African forebears.

In 1783 loyalist refugees from the North American colonies were settled in the Morass and unsuccessfully attempted to produce rice and indigo (to this day, locals take pleasure in telling how one of the Carolina settlers named Frogg found the land too wet). For two centuries, the region was heavily logged. In the 1970s the government-owned Black River Upper Morass Development Company was formed to develop the Morass. The company partly drained the Morass and laid roads in preparation for rice cultivation. The project eventually fell through.

The Black River & Great Morass Environmental Defense Fund is spearheading an attempt to have the area declared a national park. Conservationists have been pitted against developers. The marsh is heavily polluted by pesticides and other agricultural runoff from the draining. Plans have been proposed for a manatee and yellow-snake breeding program.

For more information, contact the Forestry & Soil Conservation Dept (☎ 924-2612), Ministry of Agriculture, 173 Constant Spring Rd, Kingston.

Boat Tours

South Coast Safaris (PO Box 129, Mandeville, ☎ 965-2513, fax 965-2986) at 1 Crane Rd in Black River offers 90-minute journeys seven miles into the wetlands as far as Salt Spring Bridge. Owner Charles Swaby guides many of the trips himself aboard his *Safari Queen*. His tours leave daily at 9 and 11 am, and 2 and 4 pm Trips cost US$15 per person, including drinks; US$26, including buffet lunch and a visit to YS Falls; or US$60 including transfers from Negril, US$65 from Montego Bay, and US$80 from Ocho Rios. The trips leave from the large old warehouse on the east bank of the river near the bridge. The midday tours are best for spotting crocodiles, the early and later tours for birding.

St Bess Attractions (☎ 965-2374 or 965-2229) offers a similar tour – the St Elizabeth Safari – at 9 am, 11 am, 2 pm, and 3:30 pm. The office is in Black River behind the Hendriki Building on the west bank of the river opposite South Coast Safaris. Other operators offering similar tours include Jacana Aqua Tours (☎ 965-2211); Black River Tours (☎ 965-2774), run by a charismatic American named Charles Wills; and Ride de River (☎ 965-2466), which has a 'resident' crocodile called Freddie.

Caribic Vacations (☎ 952-5013) offers a boat safari each Wednesday from Ocho Rios (US$82) and Negril (US$75), and on Thursdays from Montego Bay (US$74).

You can also hire a guide to take you upriver in his canoe or boat for about US$5 to US$10 round-trip. Ask near the bridge in town. Donovan Bennett at St Bess Attractions will also rent you a boat and oarsman. Take a shade hat and plenty of mosquito repellent. Ganja is grown in significant quantities in the Morass, and stumbling accidentally on a major plot is a damn good reason not to go exploring solo. You could end up chopped up into crocodile meat!

MIDDLE QUARTERS

This small village on the A2, eight miles north of Black River, is renowned for its women higglers who stand at the roadside selling delicious 'pepper shrimps' cooked at roadside grills. Be warned, though, that they're well named. Have a bottle of beer ready to put out the fire! Also make sure that they're fresh that day. Local fishermen still set out from Middle Quarters to catch mullet and freshwater shrimp (actually, they're crayfish, not shrimp) in traps made in centuries-old African tradition from split bamboo. US$0.15 will buy a good-sized shrimp; US$1 will buy a bagful. Ask for a free sample.

To get there, you can hop aboard any of the buses plying the A2. Minibuses ST728 and ST814 also serve Middle Quarters from Kingston (US$8).

NEWMARKET

A road to the west at Middle Quarters leads uphill eight miles to Newmarket (once known as Lewisville). Newmarket formerly lay to the west of the Westmoreland Parish boundary, but residents always considered themselves part of St Elizabeth Parish. In 1960, after lengthy petitions, the House of Representatives passed a special law granting the town its desired status and slightly altered the parish boundary. In 1979 the small country village was flooded and remained so for an entire year when the underlying rock became saturated and the water table rose above ground level. Forty-one people drowned. The town was relocated and custom-built further up the valley.

The road continues north to Struie and Montego Bay.

YS FALLS

These unspoiled cascades are the most enchanting of Jamaica's falls. Eight beautiful cascades fall 120 feet, separated by cool pools perfect for swimming. They're hemmed by limestone cliffs and surrounded by towering trees lush with epiphytes and orchids. The falls are on private property – the YS Estate, 3½ miles north of the A2 (the turnoff is one mile east of Middle Quarters). The entrance is just north of the junction of the B6 toward Maggotty (this road is horrendously potholed). Look for the YS House and the remains of an old sugar mill near a bridge over the river. Today the estate raises racehorses and a herd of 700 hardy native Jamaica Red cattle, a cross between Red Poll, Zebu, and Devon cattle.

A tractor-drawn jitney takes visitors from the car park to a parking area beneath a giant guango tree near the cascades. Alternately, you can walk (it's a mile-long trek through grassland to the falls; in parts you might have to wade in the river). You may be able to drive to the falls with permission. There are eight iron gates to be opened and closed (your vehicle will need high ground clearance).

You'll find picnic grounds and a tree house. After sipping a rum punch you might be inclined to play Tarzan and swing on a rope into the pools. Be careful! The eddies are strong, especially after rains, when the falls are torrential. A stone staircase and pathway follows the cascades upriver.

YS Falls is one of the few spots in Jamaica without any hustlers, and the owner, Tony Browne, intends to keep it that way. Browne is descended from the Marquis of Sligo, the colorful governor of Jamaica when slavery was abolished in 1834. Back then, old maps of Jamaica spelled the property Wyess, which according to Inez Knibb Sibley's *Dictionary of Places Names in Jamaica*, is thought to be derived from a Gaelic word for 'winding.' Browne, however, believes the name YS comes from the initials of a Captain Scott, who received the grant for services during Oliver Cromwell's invasion in 1655. Scott took a Mr Yates as his partner and together they began producing sugar and rum. Their produce was branded Y&S for Yates and Scott.

The property usually closes for the last two weeks of October, though that may soon change, as YS Falls is now firmly on the tourist map. Entrance costs US$9 for drop-in visitors, including a guide. There's a gift store, a grocery store selling quality Jamaican items, and *Micky's Grill*, a thatched restaurant and bar serving fish and chicken dishes, plus burgers (J$50 to J$70).

Organized Tours

St Bess Attractions (☎ 997-6055) operates tours to YS every half hour from 9 am to 3:30 pm from Black River, as does South Coast Safaris (also in Black River).

Getting There & Away

Buses travel via YS Falls from outside the Shakespeare Tavern in Maggotty. You can walk to YS Falls from the junction on the A2. Buses will drop you there. If you're coming from Mandeville, take minibus No LS2005; it costs about US$2.

IPSWICH CAVES
These cool limestone caverns are full of stalactites and stalagmites, but they are badly stained by soot from kerosene torches and cigarettes.

Ipswich is a nondescript village on the railway line that runs between Montego Bay and Kingston. In 1987 I took a ride on the Governor's Coach Tour, a tourist-oriented railway journey that for many years trundled from Montego Bay to the Appleton Rum Estate and stopped at Ipswich for a peek inside its beautiful limestone caverns. The train no longer operates, but you can still hire a guide to lead you into the stygian chambers for a small fee.

BAMBOO AVENUE
This photogenic archway of towering bamboo has been made famous on tourist-board posters and brochure covers. The 2½-mile-long tunnel shades the A2 between Middle Quarters and Lacovia and is quite calming. Bamboo Avenue was planted by the owners of Holland Estate, which formerly belonged to John Gladstone, father of the British prime minister (you can see the Holland sugar factory to the south). The bamboo has been battered by hurricanes, but it still forms an enchanting tunnel. The grove is maintained by staff from the Hope Botanical Garden in Kingston.

LACOVIA
Lacovia is a one-street village, two miles east of Bamboo Avenue. It straggles along the A2 for almost two miles and is divided into West Lacovia, Lacovia Tombstone, and East Lacovia. The town was the site of a former Spanish ford across the Black River, and a skirmish between the Spanish and English was fought here in 1655. (The name is derivedfrom the Spanish word *la caobana*, meaning 'mahogany,' which was an important local export product.)

You may find it remarkable that this nondescript hamlet was the capital of St Elizabeth in the mid-18th century. Actually, the role alternated with Black River. They had a great rivalry, and official meetings moved between towns. During the late 19th century, an important fiber-making industry was based here using bamboo as the raw material. The industry was run by Jews, who formed the majority of the population since Spanish times. Today, cashew nut farming is important, and locals stand at the roadside selling nuts.

The only site of interest is at Lacovia Tombstone, named for its two side-by-side tombstones in the center of the junction at the east end of town in front of the Texaco gas station. An unlikely legend says that the two young men who lie buried here killed each other in a tavern duel in 1738. One of them, Thomas Jordan Spencer, was a member of the family of the Duke of Marlborough, according to the coat of arms – that of the Spencers of Althorp, of Princess Diana fame – on the marble-topped tombstone.

Places to Stay & Eat
Carlyn Resorts (☎ 966-6636) at the east end of Lacovia is a wood-and-stone two-story structure with five rooms. They're small and basic but clean, and have private bathrooms (no hot water) and fans for US$25. There's a restaurant downstairs that serves seafood; it's a good place to dine while watching the Black River flow by.

Alternately you can buy burgers and other snacks at *Best One Pastries & Bakery*, a fast-food joint 20 yards west of Carlyn Resorts.

Getting There & Away
All the buses running along the A2 pass through Lacovia, which is served directly from Kingston by bus No ST808 (about US$1.50).

SANTA CRUZ
Santa Cruz (population 4000) is an important market town and a dormitory community for the Alpart alumina plant nearby at Nain to the southeast. During the past few decades it has grown modestly wealthy on revenues from the local bauxite industry. Before that it was a market center for

horses and mules bred locally for the British army. A livestock market is still held on Saturdays on the road that leads south into the Santa Cruz Mountains.

Santa Cruz is bounded to the north by the swamp of the Upper Morass. The area was extremely unhealthy in centuries past, and many early settlers succumbed to fever. In the 18th century, several plantation owners granted land north of Santa Cruz to Moravian missionaries from central Europe, and several churches that still stand may be of interest to travelers. The area is accessible by road from **Wilton**, three miles east of Santa Cruz; the road continues north into the Nassau Mountains.

Information

Scotiabank (☎ 966-2230), National Commercial Bank (☎ 966-2204), and Jamaica Citizens Bank all have branches in the town center.

Dr Oliver Myers (☎ 966-2106), at 23 Coke Drive, and several other doctors have clinics near the police station. You'll find Premier Pharmacy (☎ 966-9032) nearby at 26 Coke Drive and Philip's Pharmacy (☎ 966-2113) at 72 Main St. The police station (☎ 966-2289) is 200 yards south of the town center on the road to Malvern.

Places to Stay

The only place I know in town is *Danbor Guest House* (☎ 966-9382), a beautiful home in secluded gardens at the west end of town. It's a bargain at US$16. It has five rooms cooled by fans. Some share a bathroom with cold water only. The homey lounge is a surrealistic zoo of gaily painted ceramic animals. Heaps of plastic flowers do little to enhance the ambiance, but the mood is welcoming. Meals can be prepared to order.

Another option is *Chariots Hotel* (☎ 997-6230) at Leeds, four miles south of town at the base of the Santa Cruz Mountains on the road to Malvern. The place is modern and spacious albeit modest. It has 10 rooms for US$24 or slightly more for air-con and king-size bed.

Places to Eat

If you're craving a break from jerk chicken and rice 'n peas, try the *Rotiraja* for Indian cuisine. *Paradise Patties* is a clean, pleasant enough place to enjoy patties or burgers. *One-a-Way Drive Inn* serves roast and steamed fish; it's three miles east of town.

Entertainment

At the east end of town is *Blinking Safari Club*, a bar and disco. Another rustic nightclub popular with locals is *Occasions* at Braes River, two miles north of the A2 (the turnoff is at Wilton, three miles east of Santa Cruz).

Getting There & Away

Santa Cruz is a main stop for buses going between Kingston and Black River. If you can't bear the thought of traveling shoulder to sweaty shoulder on a rickety old bus, you'll find plenty of more roomy Toyota Hiace minibuses serving Santa Cruz from Black River (US$1.50).

If you want to head into the Nassau Mountains, you can catch bus No LS38X to Balaclava (about US$0.30).

Buses leave from the south side of the junction of the A2 and Centre Drive at the east end of Santa Cruz. Minibuses leave from opposite Scotiabank at the west end of town.

Getting Around

Several companies rent cars. Most of their business is with executives from the local alumina factory, but they'll be happy to take your tourist dollars. Two to consider are Praise Tours & Auto Rental (☎ 966-9019) on Main St at the east end of town and Southern Comfort Car Rental at Shop No 45 in Santa Cruz Plaza (☎/fax 966-9725).

GUTTERS

Gutters, 10 miles east of Santa Cruz, sits astride the border of St Elizabeth and Manchester Parishes. There's no village here, but the site is a major crossroads on the A2 at the foot of Spur Tree Hill – a long, steep climb up the Don Figuerero Mountains to Mandeville. Another road runs south to the Alpart alumina factory at Nain, and to Alligator Pond and Treasure Beach (see below).

Gutters is the unlikely location for one of Jamaica's hottest nightspots – *Jim's HQ Lounge*. It's elegant by rural Jamaican standards. Many Jamaicans proclaim it the top nightclub outside Kingston (see the Entertainment section under Mandeville below).

All the buses plying the A2 between Mandeville and Black River pass through Gutters. You can also get there from Kingston by minibus No ST719 from the Parade for about US$5.

Nassau Mountains

The plains of St Elizabeth are bordered along the north by this low, narrow range of deeply forested mountains. North of these mountains is the wide Siloah Valley, lushly carpeted with sugarcane. Above this valley lies the rugged Cockpit Country that extends north into Trelawny. Few roads penetrate the hills, where the sparse population is mostly involved in subsistence farming.

MAGGOTTY

The regional center of the Nassau area is this small town laid out on a bend of the Black River at the western end of the Siloah Valley. This regional market center is now a source for hydroelectricity generated by a series of 29 waterfalls. The rusty, ghostly skeleton of an alumina plant (closed in 1973 after only four years operation) stands amid the canefields northeast of town. The plant, which was owned by Revere Ltd, was once responsible for polluting the Black River.

Outside town Glenwyn Hall (☎ 997-6036) is a craft center, with a restaurant, bar, and stone-and-bamboo shops strung along the path.

Apple Valley Park

This 418-acre family nature park on the south side of Maggotty surrounds an 18th-century great house. The park is centered on two small lakes full of fish, geese, and ducks, and offers fishing (the owners charge for each catch; US$1.50 per pound) and a variety of touristy activities that seem to appeal mostly to Jamaicans. There are paddle-boat rides, and canoe rides are available on the Black River. There's traditional mento-band entertainment and other shows, plus occasional films. The bar and restaurant atop the canopied causeway are good places to relax over a Jamaican meal. Much of the park is a forest reserve good for birding. The owners also operate a tractor-pulled jitney from the old railway station in Maggotty: it travels through a spectacularly gloomy gorge of the Black River to a series of roaring cascades and calm pools.

It's open daily except Monday and Wednesday from 10 am to 5 pm (☎ 997-6000).

A 'World Family Festival' of family fun in held here in late July and features top Jamaican performers and crafts (contact Desmond Green or Dawn Vaz at ☎ 929-4630).

Canoeing

Sense Adventures arranges trips by inflatable canoes and raft trips on the upper Black River around Maggotty (Maya Lodge, PO Box 216, Kingston 7, ☎ 927-2097). The river is modestly challenging with Class III rapids. The company also offers guided hikes through the valley.

Places to Stay

There are good camping sites (US$10) at *Apple Valley Park*. You can rent tents for US$3. Apple Valley also has rustic cabins for US$15/18 single/double. Patrick and Lucille Lee, the charming Jamaican-Chinese couple who run Apple Valley, also have rooms in their 18th-century great house, now called *Apple Valley Guesthouse* (☎ 997-6000). It has 10 pleasant bedrooms (US$40 double, US$5 per extra person, including use of Apple Valley Park), plus a lounge. Lucille will cook for you, but guests also have kitchen privileges. It's reached from behind the police station.

Nearby is *Poincianna Guesthouse* (PO Box 1, ☎ 966-2270, fax 997-6036), a delightful old house on the hill behind the post office, 100 yards south of Apple Valley Park. It has six modestly furnished rooms with private bathrooms for US$9 to US$12, with hot water when the heater works. There's also a homey TV lounge. Six more rooms are in an annex. Meals are prepared. Ask for Miss Williams at the Shakespeare Tavern.

Places to Eat

The open-air restaurant at Apple Valley Park sits on a causeway between two lakes. It has a menu of traditional Jamaican dishes. You can be sure of enjoying fresh carp, silver perch, or red snapper by catching it yourself (US$2 per pound to cook). The Lees also run the pleasant, air-con *Valley Restaurant* (☎ 997-6000) opposite Apple Valley Park. It has a large Jamaican menu, including vegetarian dishes. Set breakfasts are US$3, and dinners US$6.

More basic options include the *Seven Stars Restaurant* and *Happy Time Club & Restaurant* in Shakespeare Plaza at the northernmost end of the village.

There's a *supermarket* in the village center, opposite the Seven Star Restaurant. You can buy bread, patties, and pastries at the *Sweet Bakery*, next to the Valley Restaurant.

Getting There & Away

Maggotty is seven miles north of Lacovia. The road is well paved. There's a roundabout half a mile northeast of town. The road to the northwest leads to Accompong; the one to the east leads through the Siloah Valley to Balaclava and Mandeville. A badly potholed road leads west from the Seven Star Restaurant in Maggotty to YS Falls. If your fillings are loose, it's better to take the much longer route via Lacovia and the A2.

Buses run along the A2 and stop opposite Shakespeare Plaza.

APPLETON RUM ESTATE

The Appleton sugar estate and rum factory (one mile northeast of Maggotty) enjoy a magnificent setting in the midst of the Siloah Valley of the Black River. The valley is ringed by the Nassau Mountains to the south and the escarpment of the Cockpits to the north (with keen eyes you may be able to see the village of Accompong visible at the highest point to the northwest). The yeasty smell of molasses hangs over the cane fields, luring you toward the largest and oldest distillery in Jamaica. The factory has been blending the famous Appleton brand of rums since 1749. It is owned by J Wray & Nephew, Jamaica's largest producer of rums.

Organized Tours

A guided factory tour is a must! Most visitors arrive on a tour, but individuals are certainly welcome. You'll view a video in the hospitality lounge before setting out on a walking tour of the distillery, where your guide will provide arcane details on fermentation that make you realize how little has changed since founder John Wray perfected his rum technique in the mid-18th century. You'll finish up by tasting rum samples. Factory tours cost US$12, including rum tasting and a bottle of rum.

The famous Governor's Coach Tour (a journey by railway from Montego Bay) no longer operates, but it has been replaced by a similar motorcoach excursion, the Appleton Estate Rum Tour. It departs from Montego Bay daily, and from Ocho Rios (US$65) and Runaway Bay (US$62) on Tuesdays and Wednesdays. The excursion includes a distillery tour, plus a boat ride into the Great Morass. For information, contact Caribic Vacations (☎ 974-9106) or Jamaica Estate Tours Ltd (c/o Appleton Estate, Siloah, St Elizabeth, ☎ 963-2210, fax 963-2243).

SILOAH

The village of Siloah is scattered along an old railway track immediately east of the Appleton factory. Virtually the entire population of the town is employed by the factory. You can drive north from here to get to Quick Step (see below). Take the paved road to the left immediately east of Siloah.

The village is divided into an older section and a more modern (westernmost) one. There's a Scotiabank at the west end of town on the main road.

Dragon's Inn is a basic restaurant and bakery; the *Bamboo Cove* is rustic but more atmospheric. You can buy ice cream, fudge, and desserts across the road at the *Ultimate Snack Counter*.

A minibus (No ST799) runs between Kingston and Siloah.

QUICK STEP

This remote mountain hamlet, eight miles north of Siloah, offers magnificent views over a portion of the Cockpit Country known as the District of Look Behind. It's eerie and extremely forbidding: a chaos of honeycombed limestone cliffs hewn into bizarre shapes and cockpits (deep forested bowls up to 500 feet across). Look Behind is so named because English soldiers involved in the guerrilla war against Maroons had to look over their shoulders to avoid being ambushed.

Trails lead into the heart of the Cockpits, but you are well advised to hire a guide. One trail traverses the area and takes you to Windsor Cave, a full-day's hike. Don't attempt it alone. You may be able to rent rooms locally.

BALACLAVA

Balaclava sits atop a ridge at the east end of the Siloah Valley. If you're climbing uphill from the west, it's worth resting at the ridge crest to take in the view of the valley laid out below, smothered in sugarcane as flat and as green as a billiard table surrounded by a dark curve of hills. Around Balaclava sugarcane gives way to citrus groves.

The town has a bucolic Jamaican charm, although an attractive Anglican church and the disused railway station are about the only buildings of interest. It's

divided into two distinct parts by a bridge over the Black River. For information, stop and inquire for Mrs Myrtle MacFarlane, a self-appointed tourism information officer.

Places to Eat

An inexpensive, basic place to eat is *Freddie's Place Club Restaurant* at the east end of town. Two more basic budget options are *Le Grand Club & Restaurant*, opposite the old railway station, and *JC's*, next to the police station, just east of the bridge. For groceries and fresh bread and pastries try *Bala-Ramadama* near the gas station.

Getting There & Away

Buses stop at the gas station in the center of town. Bus No LS30 departs at about 11 am for Mandeville (US$0.60), and for Montego Bay at 3:30 pm (US$1). Balaclava is also served by bus No LS38X, which runs to Santa Cruz. Patrick Morris operates minibus No ST673 to Kingston (US$5).

AUCHTEMBEDDIE

Two miles northeast of Balaclava, the main road (B6) turns east to Mandeville; another road leads north and climbs into and through the Cockpits via Auchtembeddie and drops to Troy in Trelawny Parish (see the North Coast chapter). Though the B6 is scenic, the latter is one of the most spectacular drives in the country. You climb up through a series of dramatic gorges, with the road clinging to the sheer face of the Cockpits.

This limestone country is a choice spot for spelunkers, who head for **Coffee River Cave** at Auchtembeddie. The Jamaca Caving Club (c/o Dept of Geology, University of the West Indies, Kingston 7, ☎ 927-6661) has mapped about 9000 feet of passages, many of which are totally underwater. They are totally undeveloped for tourism, but local guides will be willing to escort you for a negotiated fee.

Treasure Beach Area

The off-the-beaten-track coastal strip southeast of Black River is unique in several ways. The area is sheltered from rains for most of the year by the Santa Cruz Mountains, so there is none of the lush greenery of the north coast. Instead, you'll find acacia trees and cactus towering up to 30 feet. In places, the landscape is reminiscent of an East African setting. Nonetheless, much of the flat plains inland are planted with crops. Because of the extremely dry climate, farmers have had to apply ingenuity to make the most of the land. They've developed a 'dry farming' technique of laying guinea grass on the soil for mulch.

Most importantly, the region is unsullied by tourism. It's possible here to slip into the kind of lazy, no-frills tropical lifestyle almost impossible elsewhere on the island's coast. The area's residents have a countrywide reputation for honesty and conviviality. Treasure Beach's residents have a graciousness unique to the island.

The Santa Cruz Mountains divide southern St Elizabeth in two. They rise from the sea a few miles east of Treasure Beach and run northwest in a great wedge. The mountains were a popular holiday spot during the late 19th century and earlier this century. Today the steep green slopes are intensively farmed and the area is relatively prosperous. In parts the scenery is reminiscent of England, with roads lined with limestone walls. Many beautiful homes enjoy hillside settings, with spectacular views westward over the southern plains.

The most dramatic route into the mountains is up the west-facing slope from the village of Mountainside. The road switchbacks steeply for several miles, offering marvelous views. The more leisurely route is via Southfield, eight miles east of Treasure Beach.

STARVE GUT BAY

This area southeast of Black River is dominated by marshlands and two large freshwater lakes – Great Salt Pond and Wallywash Pond – that attract large numbers of waterfowl (especially grebes, ducks, and waders). Birders may find it of interest, though Great Salt Pond is sadly littered with trash.

You can follow marshlands south about five miles along the coast to a rustic fishing village called Parrottee Beach. The dirt road deadends half a mile south of Parrottee. Beyond lie a series of lonesome beaches totally undiscovered by travelers. They're difficult to get to but worth the effort if you're seeking total seclusion. You can camp amid the sand dunes, although I don't recommend this if you're alone. A few spots are used by fishermen to land their catches.

You can hike from Parrottee (you may need permission, as there's a barbed-wire gate barring the way south). If you're driving, follow the paved road that winds inland through the marshes from Parrottee. You'll reach a crossroads. Head straight across up the hill if you're heading for Treasure Beach (this is a dramatic drive as the road winds and dips along cliff tops studded with yucca and agave). Otherwise, take the road to the right through parched savanna; just before you reach the closed gates to a private cattle ranch, take a left and follow the muddy track to a T-junction. The low hills in front of you are coastal dunes smothered in vegetation. If you turn left and follow the track past lonesome dark-sand beaches, you'll eventually merge with the Treasure Beach road.

Touch Class Beach Club is, despite its name, a rustic but atmospheric bar at Parrottee. It's a cool place to hang out at night, playing dominoes with locals and listening to reggae music.

TREASURE BEACH

Treasure Beach is a gem for travelers in search of the off-beat. You won't find a more authentically charming and relaxing place in Jamaica.

Treasure Beach is the generic name given to four coves – Billy's Bay, Frenchman's Bay, Calabash Bay, and Great Pedro Bay – that stretch for several miles south of Starve Gut Bay. Their rocky headlands separate romantically lonesome, dark coral-colored sand beaches. The long palm-backed curve of Treasure Beach is the node. Although there have been several rental villas and hotels here for a few years, the area remains largely untouristed. The sense of remoteness, easy pace, and unsullied graciousness of the local people (mostly farmers and fishermen) attract small handfuls of foreigners seeking an away-from-it-all, cares-to-the-wind lifestyle. Many have settled – much to local pride. To think that someone would leave behind the USA or Europe to live in their remote little place!

Each morning 'donkey women' ride down from the hills to sell their freshly picked fruit and vegetables, while fishermen prepare their boats to sail out to the Pedro Keys, a teeming fishing ground from which they return at sunset to land their catch. Each of the bays has its own fishermen's cooperative.

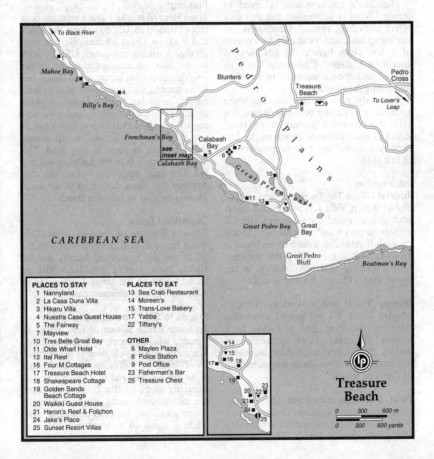

PLACES TO STAY
1 Nannyland
2 La Casa Duna Villa
3 Hikaru Villa
4 Nuestra Casa Guest House
5 The Fairway
7 Mayview
10 Tres Belle Great Bay
11 Olde Wharf Hotel
12 Ital Rest
16 Four M Cottages
17 Treasure Beach Hotel
18 Shakespeare Cottage
19 Golden Sands Beach Cottage
20 Waikiki Guest House
21 Heron's Reef & Folichon
24 Jake's Place
25 Sunset Resort Villas

PLACES TO EAT
13 Sea Crab Restaurant
14 Moreen's
15 Trans-Love Bakery
17 Yabba
22 Tiffany's

OTHER
6 Maylen Plaza
8 Police Station
9 Post Office
23 Fisherman's Bar
25 Treasure Chest

Treasure Beach

0   300   600 m
0   300   600 yards

Amenities are limited. At night the lanes are unlit. Water sports haven't yet caught on here, although the waves are good for body-surfing (beware of a sometimes vicious undertow). Calabash Bay is said to be kindest to swimmers, and it's backed by the Great Pedro Ponds, which are good for birding. This portion of coast also draws hikers who follow trails used by fishermen. And with luck you may even see marine turtles coming ashore to lay eggs (the endangered creatures are protected by law, but many local fishermen still catch them for their meat and shells).

The area's reclusiveness is about to change. Word is getting out that this area offers something special. Developers are buying up land, and it can only be a matter of a few years before the first resorts appear. A Citizens' Committee has been formed and meets monthly to regulate impending development.

Curiously, virtually everyone has white ancestors to a greater or lesser degree. It's said that Scottish sailors were shipwrecked near Treasure Beach in the last century, accounting for the preponderance of fair skin.

Information

Tourist Office The Treasure Chest outside Sunset Resort Villa acts as a tourist information center and travel agency (they'll arrange airport transfers, plus bicycle and car rental). Also check the bulletin board at Trans-Love Bakery, which is the morningtime gathering spot for residents in the know; Jake's Place is favored at night.

Money You'll find a Workers Bank in Maylen Plaza. It's not geared to serving travelers, however, and you may have trouble obtaining large quantities of dollars. The nearest major bank is located in Southfield, a town about five miles east of Treasure Beach.

Post & Communications The International Telecommunications Center (☎ 965-0062) offers telephone and fax service. It's 100 yards east of Jake's. The Treasure

Beach post office is housed in a tiny hut on a hillside about two miles from shore, just west of Pedro Cross.

Massage Joshua Stein offers massages during winter, when he winters at Treasure Beach and does the rounds on his tricycle with folding massage table in tow (US$15 per hour; ☎ 965-0486, or inquire at Trans-Love Bakery).

Emergency There's a police station on the hillside three miles east of Calabash Bay.

Fishing

Jason Henzell at Jake's Place arranges boat rides (US$30 to US$50) along the coast and into the Great Morass. He can also arrange a fishing trip (about US$20) with locals. You can attempt to negotiate for a fishing boat from locals on the beach, but I recommend using someone with experience to negotiate on your behalf. A night at sea is tiring business, and you will probably be expected to pull fish traps. If you negotiate by yourself, avoid asking the fishermen as soon as they land. The best way to do it is to put the word out in a bar. The local grapevine will do the rest. Arrange the trip a day or so in advance. There's no rush in Treasure Beach!

Organized Tours

Rebecca Wiersma of Treasure Tours (Calabash Bay PA, St Elizabeth, ☎ 965-0126) offers one-day excursions locally and far afield, from golfing in Mandeville to boating trips on the Great Morass and at Alligator Hole to see manatees.

Places to Stay – bottom end

Treasure Beach is one of few places in Jamaica where campers will feel at home. The most intriguing option is *Nannyland*, an off-beat, counterculture kind of place at the far western end of Treasure Beach. Camping costs a hefty US$20, but there are outside bathrooms, water, a kitchen, hammocks slung between trees, and trails leading down to a lonesome red-sand beach with coral tidepools. It also has two intriguing, albeit rustic, options: a tree house and a cabin perched at the edge of the cliff. Both cost US$20.The cactus garden is full of beat-up antique trucks, while a museum boasts an eclectic array of miscellany: bottles, a Singer sewing machine, and honorifics to Bob Marley and other black heroes.

Four M Cottages has camping about 400 yards from the beach for US$10. You can also camp under a thatch-roof shelter at *Ital Rest*, where there are cooking facilities plus outdoor showers and toilets (US$10 per site); tents and foam mattresses are rented for US$3 (see below for details).

Shakespeare Cottage (☎ 966-2091), 200 yards east of the Treasure Beach Hotel, has the cheapest rooms around, starting at US$5.

At Calabash Bay you'll find *Golden Sands Beach Cottage* (☎ 965-0167), a budget guest house with four basic but well-kept rooms with kitchenettes and private bathrooms (cold water only) for US$20 to US$25. In the center of Treasure Bay is *Waikiki Guest House* (☎ 965-0448), a simple place with four rooms, each with fans and cold water in a private bathroom (US$15 per room). It faces a tiny beach. Another option is *Mayview* (☎ 965-0014), where 16 simply furnished rooms with shared baths cost US$14 per person for a twin room or US$20 single. The hand-carved headboards are a nice touch. The owner can arrange meals.

Reportedly, *Le Corner Beach Club*, half a mile east of Treasure Beach Hotel, has a few very basic rooms. It's said to be noisy at night.

Places to Stay – middle

Effie Campbell has a modern house with six rooms of varying size at her *Four M Cottages* (PO Box 4, Mountainside, St Elizabeth, ☎ 965-0131, fax 965-2544), opposite the Treasure Beach Hotel. Windows are screened, and there are mosquito nets over some beds. Reportedly, the rooms get hot (they have fans, but no air-con). Each has a private bathroom; water is tepid. Guests have kitchen privileges. The outdoor bar is a popular spot for sunset drinks

with locals. Effie charges US$25/35 single/double (no credit cards accepted). Four M is popular with German tourists.

A more atmospheric but out-of-the-way place is *Ital Rest* (Great Bay District, Calabash Bay PA, St Elizabeth, ☎ 965-0248), run by two Rastas, Jeanne Myers and Frank Genus. It's surrounded by pastures and scrub forest amid grounds full of fruit trees about 400 yards from Great Bay, with the ponds behind. The couple rent four exquisite, rustic, two-story, all-wood thatched cabins with no electricity for US$40 low season. They have outside toilets and showers, and verandas facing both to the sea and mountains. Kitchen facilities are shared. The couple also have a beautiful 'treetop' room with its own separate entrance in their contemporary house (US$25 double, low season). There's a small thatched bar and Jeanne serves home-cooked Jamaican fare. The local beach, about a five-minute walk, is known hereabouts as Cottage Beach.

Nuestra Casa Guesthouse (☎ 965-0152; in the UK, contact Roger Chamberlain, 24 Wavel Place, Sydenham Hill, London SE 26 6SF, ☎ 0181-761-6292)at the west end of Billy's Bay could be the best bargain around. It's run by Lillian Brooks, a delightful English lady who exudes typical Yorkshire hospitality. A wide veranda has rockers, and a rooftop sun deck is shaded by umbrellas. Her three-bedroom house, in a reclusive hillside setting, is tastefully decorated. Two rooms share a bathroom; a third has its own. All have lofty wooden ceilings and are thoroughly charming. It's a tremendous bargain at US$30 double per room. Rates go down the longer you stay (US$27 per night for a two-week stay; US$21 for three weeks). Breakfasts (English or Jamaican) are US$5. Lilly prefers couples and cricket fans.

The least salubrious place is *Olde Wharf Hotel* (PO Box 189, Mandeville, ☎ 962-4471 or 962-3126, fax 962-2858), at the far eastern end of Calabash Bay. Rooms are spacious but modestly furnished and gloomy. Take an air-con room; those with fans get hot (US$30 for a standard room;

US$45 for a superior with air-con and TV; US$100 for executive and two-bedroom suites). It has a tennis court, basketball hoop, volleyball courts, and a pool.

The Sutton family (of Mandeville fame) rents two homes: *Heron's Reef* and *Folichon* (☎ 963-8569). The former is a one-bedroom cottage, with a living and dining area plus kitchen (US$40). The latter, next door, is a four bedroom, two bathroom home that sleeps up to eight people, with a kitchen and housekeeper (US$80).

Tres Belle Great Bay (☎ 965-2651, fax 965-2697) is a new six-bedroom hotel next to the fishing village of Great Bay.

Places to Stay – top end

Jake's Place gets my vote for most endearing off-beat 'hotel' between Negril and Kingston (Calabash Bay, Treasure Beach, PA, St Elizabeth, ☎/fax 965-0552; in North America, ☎ (800) 688-7678 or (305) 531-8800, in the UK ☎ (0800) 614-790). Eclectic is an understatement for this rustic, rainbow-colored retreat. The place is run by Sally (a Jamaican of English ancestry) and her son Jason. There are five charming cliff-top cottages, but seven more are planned along with a three-bedroom villa (winter prices: US$50 for cottages, US$475 for the villa). The decor follows Greek and Moslem motifs, with onion-dome curves, blood-red floors, and walls and rough-hewn doors inset with colored bottles and glass beads. The beds are rickety old contraptions. At night bullfrogs sit on your porch grabbing bugs attracted by the porch light. A small sun deck above the coral shore looks down on a tiny beach. The pool is shaded by a spreading tree, with a cascade falling into a fishpond and then the sea. Jason operates fishing trips and plans to introduce scuba diving. Jake's has its own restaurant that is the trendiest place around at night. In case you're wondering, Jake is a parrot! He now resides at Trans-Love Bakery, where he fell in love with their female parrot.

Another pleasant, more traditional option is the *Treasure Beach Hotel* (PO Box 5, Black River, ☎ 965-2305, fax 965-2544), nestled on a hillside overlooking the beach and formerly known as a nudist resort. The 36 air-con rooms include 16 spacious oceanfront suites with king-size beds and tile floors. A large lounge has a TV for rainy days. There's a swimming pool and volleyball court, and sailing and snorkeling are offered. The dining terrace overlooks the gardens. Standard rooms start at US$70/80 single/double (summer); deluxe rooms are US$130. The hotel has an all-inclusive plan (US$138 per person) and an Eco-Adventure Plan (US$165) featuring daily nature tours.

Treasure Beach has several rental villas and cottages to choose from. *Hikaru Villa* (c/o Mr & Mrs Noel, 141 Ridgefield St, Hartford, CT 06112, ☎ (203) 247-0759) is a fully staffed four-bedroom beachfront villa with private tennis court and a sun terrace overlooking the beach. It rents from US$800 weekly for up to four people, more for additional people. Summer rates are lower. Another fully staffed option is *Villa Caprice* (PO Box 7, Black River, ☎ 965-2265, fax 965-2032), set in lush gardens with a pool. It has four air-con bedrooms.

Sunset Resort Villas (☎ 965-0143; in North America, c/o South Enterprises, 2875 S Main St No 203, Salt Lake City, UT 84115) takes up five acres on Calabash Bay and has a fully staffed six-bedroom villa (US$4200 per week) and a two-bedroom villa (US$1500 per week) with 11 bathrooms between them. The villa can be rented whole or by the room; an upstairs master suite is touted for honeymooners (US$110 double, room only, or US$750 to US$850 per week per person, including airport transfers and all meals). The two spacious and elegant whitewashed villas share a pool. There's even a basketball court.

Other places to consider include *La Casa Duna Villa*, a modern three-bedroom villa with cook and housekeeper at Billy's Bay (in North America, ☎ (215) 297-5642, fax (215) 297-0255, PO Box 21, Solesbury, PA 18963); *Rainbow Tree* (in North America, ☎ (703) 759-5333), a splendid, contemporary five-bedroom villa on six acres; *Fairway* (☎ 965-0125), a handsome modern cottage 100 yards east of the turnoff for the Olde Wharf Hotel; and *Unforgettable Inn*, about three miles east of Treasure Beach at Fort Charles, where rooms cost US$850 a week for two people including all meals; the per person price drops with additional people, up to eight.

Other villas are available through South Coast Rentals at 17 High St in Black River (☎ 965-2651) and through Treasure Tours (Calabash Bay, St Elizabeth, ☎ 965-0126), with prices from US$150 a week.

Places to Eat
The place to savor a leisurely breakfast in typical Treasure Beach fashion is *Trans-Love Bakery* (☎ 965-0486), run by Julie, a transplanted American, and Ralph. It opens at 8 am and serves omelettes (US$2.50), muesli (US$2.50), and fruit salads. The portions are huge! You can also buy fresh-baked sugar buns, cakes, sesame rolls, quiche, and French bread. It does a special Sunday breakfast when an elderly local named Martin plays slide guitar.

At night everyone heads to *Jake's*, an open-sided wooden restaurant featuring gingerbread trim, low lighting, and hip music. The menu varies, but typical Jamaican gourmet dishes include lobster sichuan (US$14), stuffed crab backs (US$7), and vegetable pasta (US$4). Try the killer rum punch or rum coconut with pineapple juice.

For a change of mood, head to *Tiffany's Restaurant* (☎ 965-0300), an elegant and romantic eatery named after the movie *Breakfast at Tiffany's*. It's open noon to 10 pm. The eclectic menu includes burgers (US$3), T-bone steaks (US$8), curried goat (US$6), and salads. The equally pleasant *Yabba Restaurant* at Treasure Beach Hotel serves Jamaican dishes in the US$5 range on an open veranda overlooking the sea.

More rustic options include *Sea Crab* at Great Bay, serving tasty seafood dishes for less than US$5; the charming *Moreen's Restaurant & Bar*, next to Trans-Love; and *Blossom's Supermarket Restaurant*, midway between Jake's and the Treasure

Beach Hotel, where you'll also find a *Pizza Parlour* (☎ 965-0170).

You can stock up your refrigerator at the *Great Bay Co-op* and at the supermarket at Maylen Plaza, on the main road behind Calabash Bay. Fresh fish is always available on the beach.

Entertainment
Most of the locals go to bed early, except on weekends. *Fisherman's Bar* (up a dirt road behind Tiffany's) is the only disco around. It has a bamboo bar at the front. Go-go dancers occasionally perform, and there's a pool hall at the back. *Jake's* also has a dance floor under floodlit trees. Locals hang out listening to reggae and swigging stiff shots of overproof rum at *La Corner Beach Club*.

Things to Buy
You'll find several craft stores, including the Treasure Chest, outside Sunset Resort Villa. Monique's Variety Store sells souvenirs and T-shirts, as does Tropical Treasures in the Maylen Plaza.

When I last dropped by, Jason Henzell (of Jake's; see Places to Stay) was setting up the Caribbean Candle Factory. He plans to continue making the famous wax pineapples, Rastas, peeled bananas, and life-size phallus candles made famous by Henriette Hofman and Stephano Corleone at the factory they established in Negril (but which Jason recently bought and moved to Treasure Beach).

Getting There & Away
From Montego Bay, take a minibus to Savanna-la-Mar from the Fowler Bridge on Creek St (US$2). From here, a minibus to Black River costs US$2; then catch 'Yellowbird,' 'Audley,' or 'Cherry B' bus to Treasure Beach (US$1). Minibuses also operate from Santa Cruz (US$1.50).

Getting Around
There's no bus service. Hitching is a popular option, but there's not much traffic along the single shoreline road. Renting your own wheels is the best option.

There's no car rental agency in town, but Tanka Rentals (☎ 957-4400) offers jeeps, delivered all the way to your hotel from Negril. It also has motorcycles. You can rent bicycles and motorcycles from Native Bike Rental (☎ 965-0140) in Maylen Plaza: bicycles cost US$5 daily with a US$50 deposit; motorcycles begin at US$30 for a 80cc Honda, with a US$200 deposit. They also have larger motorcycles (up to US$70 per day for a 750cc machine). You can also rent motorcycles, scooters, bicycles, and windsurfing boards from Rebecca at Treasure Tours (☎ 965-0126). Jake's Place offers transfers by taxi (US$70) and rents jeeps (US$50 daily), small motorcycles (US$40), and scooters (US$25).

LOVER'S LEAP

You need a head for heights to stand by the cliff edge at Lover's Leap, one mile southeast of Southfield. Here the Santa Cruz Mountains plunge over 1700 feet into the ocean. The views along the coast stretch for miles. The best views are from the upper-story veranda of the unfinished restaurant. The blunt mountain face causes warm onshore winds to rise, and John Crow buzzards soar on the thermals at eye level. Far below, waves crash ashore on the jagged rocks.

Lover's Leap is named for two young slaves who supposedly committed suicide here. According to legend, the girl was lusted after by her owner, who arranged for her lover to be sold to another estate. When the couple heard of the plot, they fled and were eventually cornered at the cliffs, where they chose to plunge to their deaths.

The Jamaica Attraction Development Company has plans to develop Lover's Leap as a tourist site. For now, however, there are no facilities. The half-complete restaurant – a real eyesore – has languished for years, but it may soon be finished.

A red-and-white-hooped **lighthouse** stands next to the parking area. The Jamaica Defence Force maintains a mobile radar in the grounds; it's used to track drug traffic. Smoking ganja here would *not* be a good idea!

Horseback Riding

Mayfield Ranch (☎ 965-6234, fax 965-6166) at Southfield has been breeding horses for over a century. It offers trail rides (US$20 per hour) along bridle trails that lead through savanna grasslands, dry forest, and farmland. It also has a riding ring. The place is a little piece of country-and-western style.

Places to Stay & Eat

The only option nearby is *Lover's Leap Guest House & Eating & Drinking Lounge* (☎ 965-6004), about 400 yards north of the lighthouse. The modest hotel has 10 carpeted rooms for US$16. They're well lit and clean, with fans and private bathrooms, but when I dropped in, they smelled heavily of mothballs.

MALVERN

Years ago, Malvern was favored as a summer resort for its temperate climate, which rarely exceeds 80°F. The village straddles the Santa Cruz Mountains at a refreshing 2400 feet. The tourist trade died long ago, and today Malvern serves as an agricultural and educational center. If you're traveling from Kingston, you can take minibus No ST776 from the Parade.

Malvern is dominated by the cream-colored Hampton College (a girls school founded in 1858), which has a beautiful setting looking across the deep vale toward the Don Figuerero Mountains. It's the building with the blue-and-red roof, about one mile south of Malvern Square, the village center. Munro College (a boys school founded in 1856) is four miles further south. Both were established by charitable trusts: the endowments were intended for the education of indigent children, but the two private schools served the well-to-do, although this is no longer the case. Blenheim Teacher Training College is also in Malvern.

A small number of other interesting historic houses remain, including pretty and photogenic Deep Dene, 200 yards west of the junction in the village center.

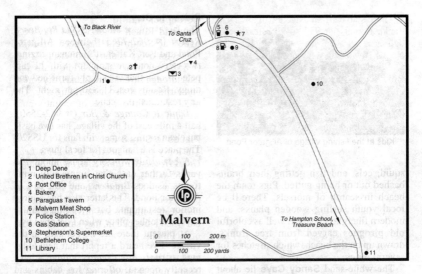

1 Deep Dene
2 United Brethren in Christ Church
3 Post Office
4 Bakery
5 Paraguas Tavern
6 Malvern Meat Shop
7 Police Station
8 Gas Station
9 Stephenson's Supermarket
10 Bethlehem College
11 Library

Malvern

0   100   200 m
0   100   200 yards

To Black River

To Santa Cruz

To Hampton School, Treasure Beach

The slopes around Malvern are flecked with pine forest. A precious stand of bull, or sasal, thatch also grows in the hills above town. The material is still used locally to make straw hats and baskets, as it has been since Arawak days.

Information

The tiny Workers Savings Bank is next to the post office. It serves the needs of the local community, so don't anticipate being able to change large sums of money (open Monday, Wednesday, and Friday 9 am to 2 pm, and Thursday and Saturday 9 to 11 am). The post office is 50 yards west of the junction in the town center. The police station (☎ 966-2355) is immediately east of Malvern Square.

Places to Stay & Eat

I'm not aware of a hotel in town, although you can ask around for a room. Guests have been accepted at *Deep Dene*, which was recently restored as a retreat for Moravian ministers; I'm told it is now a hostel for girls from Hampton College.

You can buy produce and groceries at *Stephenson's Supermarket*, behind the gas station on Malvern Square. *Paraguas*

Tavern and the *Malvern Meat Shop*, which sells patties and pastries, are both at the main junction in town. You'll find a bakery just east of the post office.

ALLIGATOR POND

Alligator Pond – the most authentically unspoiled coastal spot in Jamaica – is about as far from Montego Bay and packaged tourism as you can get. Although Kingstonians crowd in on weekends, this large fishing village remains totally undiscovered by foreign travelers and offers a genuine, off-beat Jamaican experience. Part of the reason is its lonesome location: Alligator Pond is hidden at the foot of a valley between two steep spurs of the Santa Cruz and Don Figuerero Mountains. Both run right up to the coast, effectively cutting Alligator Pond off from the rest of the country.

The village is set behind a deep-blue bay backed by dunes. The main street is smothered in wind-blown sand. Each morning local women gather on the dark-sand beach to haggle over the catch delivered by fishermen. Be sure to bring your camera! It's not for the squeamish, however, as you're likely to see octopus,

Kids at the fishing village of Alligator Pond

squid, eels, and fish getting their brains bashed out or being gutted. Pigs roam the beach in search of morsels. There'll be local youth surfing wooden planks, and modern fiberglass boats as well as colorful old pirogues carved from tree trunks, drawn up on the beach, which stretches for several miles.

The white-sand **Sandy Cays** lie about 20 miles offshore. They poke out of the ocean a few feet, and fishermen sometimes retreat there to process their catch. They're an excellent location for scuba diving, snorkeling, and nude bathing.

On the coast two miles west of Alligator Pond is **Port Kaiser**, dominated by an alumina plant and shipping facility owned by Kaiser Bauxite Company.

Fishing
You can hire a fisherman to take you out fishing for a negotiable fee. If you join local fishermen on their forays, be prepared to witness a disturbing disregard for the law, such as fishing the coral reefs with line and trapping and taking lobster (protected seasonally) year-round.

Scuba Diving
You can scuba dive at Sandy Cay to see coral mounds such as Drop-Drop and Saletsat, where nurse sharks and giant rays gather to feed on the waste fish processed by fishermen at sea. Sea Riv Beach Resort arranges dive trips (see Places to Stay), including ones to the swampy, crocodile-infested shallows of Long Bay Morass.

Places to Stay
The largest place around is *Sea Riv Beach Resort* (☎ 962-7265) between Alligator Pond and Port Kaiser. It's an unappetizing, two-story concrete structure with 22 carpeted rooms that are simply furnished and dingy. Rooms cost US$30 per night. The airy restaurant is ascetic.

Triple R Cottage & Bar (☎ 962-2550), half a mile east of the village, has five basic but clean rooms, some with fans for US$20. The place is a hangout for local guys.

A beautiful two-story house about 200 yards further east also supposedly rents rooms, as does *Breakers*, one mile east of Alligator Pond. The latter also has a large indoor restaurant, but I couldn't rouse anyone at either place when I dropped by.

At present there are no cottages in the village. I've heard a report that new lodgings – *Wards Bay Country Village* – have recently opened, offering log cabins and picnic spots (ask for Tony Freckleton).

Places to Eat
The beach is lined with funky stalls catering to fishermen. Take your pick of a dozen or so places selling fish and lobster dishes. By far the best is *Little Ochie Pub*: it has tremendous atmosphere, with thatched tables and chairs on the beach, and even a thatch-roof old boat raised on stilts, which functions as a dining and drinking terrace. Locals gather here to play dominoes. Specialties include curried conch (US$6) and roast fish (US$4.50).

Another atmospheric spot is the *Red Lobster Seafood Pub*, one mile north of Alligator Pond, at the junction for Port Kaiser. You can't miss it – it's painted bright orange and green.

You can buy lobster for US$6 per pound from local fishermen, but refrain from doing so between April 1 and June 30, when catching, selling, and purchasing lobster are illegal; the fishermen don't heed the law, but you should set an example. Endangered marine turtles are also caught by locals, despite being protected by law. *Don't* buy turtle meat or turtle jewelry!

Cacti reach for the sky at the western end of Long Bay on the south coast.

Sorting the day's catch at Alligator Pond...

...an easier task for some.

The laid-back life at Treasure Beach

Treasure Beach, where tourists are rare

North of Black River, Bamboo Avenue stretches 2½ miles.

Tourists provide plenty of amusement.

Getting There & Away

Bull Savannah, which squats on the eastern brow of the Santa Cruz Mountains, is en route to Alligator Pond, which nestles at the mouth of the valley far below. The road winds down to Alligator Pond with plenty of tight turns. Drive carefully.

Dave South operates a minibus (No ST789) between Alligator Pond and Kingston. Alligator Pond can also be reached via a paved road from Mandeville via Gutters (at the base of Spur Tree Hill on the A2) or via Newport and Plowden Hill. You can travel with Delroy Daley, who runs minibus No LS1017 from Mandeville via Gutters (about US$2). Another minibus, a beat-up old Ford Transit (No LS487), runs from Mandeville and continues to Gut River on weekends.

Claude Simpson operates a minibus (No ST459) between Bull Savannah and Kingston.

LONG BAY

Long Bay, east of Alligator Pond, is one of the most pristine spots in Jamaica. Virtually the entire 15-mile shoreline, which is hemmed in by mountains, is composed of mangroves and reeds that make up the Long Bay Morass – a nirvana for birders. Blue crabs, African perch, and freshwater tropical fish are abundant. There are crocodiles, too. And the swamp is the last refuge in Jamaica for endangered manatees, which can easily be seen at Canoe Valley at the far east end of Long Bay.

With boardwalks and an interpretive center, this could be an ecotourists' mecca. For years the government has talked of creating the Canoe Valley Wildlife Refuge. The area begs for national park status, which would head off the developers.

A coast road begins in Alligator Pond and extends eastward behind the Morass, linking St Elizabeth Parish with Clarendon Parish. Until recently this route was a tortuous track that defied passage to all but the sturdiest 4WD.

I consider this highway one of the pre-eminent drives in Jamaica. For the first few miles, the road dips and winds past tall cacti and scrubby savanna, and the coastal vistas are fantastic. Watch out for goats grazing the scrub (signs read: 'We love our kiddies'). After about three miles the cacti and scrub give way to swampland towered over by thatch palms. The sheer face of the Don Figuerero Mountains edges right up to the road on one side, with the swamp right up against it on the other. Drive carefully – take a corner wide and you'll end up with the crocodiles!

The area is totally uninhabited. There's absolutely nothing for 15 miles, with the exception of a meager facility at **Gut River**, six miles east of Alligator Pond. Gut River is one of half a dozen spring-fed streams that percolate out of the limestone mountains and meander to the sea through a morass of mangroves and reeds. Here the mineral spring emerges from a deep cleft and feeds a miraculously azure pond where the occasional flash reveals mullet and big crabs 20 feet down. Large dragonflies hover over the jewel-like water. The pool grows shallower toward its mouth, where the water is trapped behind a sand spit that hides a lonesome red-sand beach extending for two miles or more. The setting is spectacular with the steep mountains behind.

The site is run by two fellows from Mandeville: Patrick Reid and Mitch Burey. On weekends Jamaicans crowd in from Kingston and Mandeville for ear-splitting reggae. Lots of jerk chicken and curried goat served at a small, funky restaurant gets washed down by Red Stripe beer. When the crowd leaves, garbage is strewn everywhere, and nobody bothers to clean it up.

Scuba Diving

A local company called Sea-Riv, based at the Sea-Riv Resort in Alligator Pond (see above), operates scuba-diving trips to Gut River and God's Well, a sinkhole in the Morass that drops to a cave at about 158 feet. (God's Well is for experienced divers only – the first diver to tackle it died.)

For an additional shot of adrenaline, Sea-Riv will take you on the 'Suicide Run,' a two-mile swim to the ocean through the seemingly impenetrable swamps. Yes, the chance of bumping into a crocodile is very real, but I've been told, 'Dem alligators no problem, mon . . . Dem coward. 'Im see you come close, mon, 'im run fast, fast can go!'

Getting There & Away
Unless you're driving, you'll probably have to take a taxi from Alligator Pond. It should cost no more than US$8 round-trip. Otherwise, you can take minibus No LS487, which travels to Gut River from Mandeville on weekends.

Mandeville

The all-important city of Mandeville sits in the very center of Manchester Parish, a quadrangular wedge running north to south, east of St Elizabeth Parish. Manchester Parish, established as a separate parish in 1814, was named for the Duke of Manchester, who was governor of Jamaica from 1808 to 1827; he was a gambling man and hard drinker, and he sired a large number of offspring all over the island.

Mandeville – the most prosperous and pleasant town on the island – spreads across a rolling plateau on the east of the Don Figuerero Mountains. This range has west-facing, ruler-straight escarpment the base of which forms the political and physical boundary between St Elizabeth and Manchester Parishes. The deeply forested northern slopes of the Don Figureros drop into a narrow and incredibly scenic valley that runs northwest to Balaclava. The valley reminds me of a setting from England's Yorkshire Dales and provides for a fabulous excursion from Mandeville. To the north, the farmed mountains rise again to crest at Mt Denham (3254 feet) on the border with the north-coast Trelawny Parish.

In the 18th century, the area became an important center for coffee cultivation. Sugar estates were entirely absent. Although slaves worked the coffee estates, the harsh plantation system never took hold. Following emancipation, the newly freed slaves settled as independent farmers and continued to grow coffee. In latter years, citrus farms became important, and healthy cattle now grow fat on the lush pastures. Bauxite is also mined on a large scale near Mandeville, bringing further prosperity to the region.

The relative wealth of the area is evident in the scores of immaculate white houses, farmsteads, and ostentatious villas spread across the hillsides around Mandeville, Christiana, and Spaldings. At higher elevations crisp breezes blow through quasi-alpine forests. Combined with the bucolic pastoral valleys below, the area presents an entirely appealing but relatively untouristed Jamaica.

HISTORY
Mandeville began life as a haven for colonial planters escaping the heat of the plains. The town was established only in 1816, following a petition from the region's isolated coffee planters. It was named after Lord Mandeville, eldest son of the governor. The parish authorities laid out the town according to a strict order: first the courthouse, then a parsonage, jail and workhouse, and lastly a church (all four buildings still stand).

The city continued to grow throughout the century as a holiday retreat for wealthy Kingstonians and planters. Over ensuing decades Mandeville also attracted a considerable population of English retirees from other colonial quarters. Many early ex-pats established the area as a center for dairy farming and citrus and pimento production. Jamaica's unique, seedless citrus fruit, the ortanique, was first produced here in the 1920s and is now grown in large quantities by Alcan, the North American bauxite company, which owns considerable acreage locally.

Alcan opened operations here in 1940, when it bought up the surrounding lands, forcing many residents to move into town. Relatively high wage levels lured educated Jamaicans, turning what was then a sleepy retreat into a city of cultured energy. Alcan has built large residential areas for its employees, many of them North Americans whose presence is having a distinct 'Americanizing' effect. Today Mandeville's economic fortunes are tied to those of the bauxite industry.

ORIENTATION
Mandeville is spread across rolling hills. The center, however, is compact enough to walk almost everywhere. At its heart is a historic village green, now called Cecil Charlton Park after a former mayor. From here, roads radiate out like spokes on a wheel. The main artery is Manchester Rd, which leads south from the green. The library, hospital, parish council offices, and leading commercial plazas are nearby. Another commercial artery – Caledonia Rd – runs parallel. The two roads are linked by North Racecourse and South Racecourse, the legacy of a horseracing track that stood here in the 19th century.

A major bypass – the Winston Jones Hwy (A2) – skirts the northern edge of town, dropping eastwards downhill to Williamsfield and the junction of the main roads to Christiana and Kingston.

The JTB's Discover Jamaica road map publishes a separate and accurate map of Mandeville.

INFORMATION
Tourist Offices
The JTB (☎ 962-1072) has an office at 11 Ward Ave. It's open 8:30 am to 4:30 pm, Monday to Friday. The Central & South Tourism Committee is based at the Astra Country Inn, whose owner, Diana McIntyre-Pike, runs a Visitor Information Service (☎ 962-3265). The latter has a meager supply of brochures and seems to be only occasionally staffed.

The Jamaica Information Service (☎ 962-0827) has an office in Shop F3 at Caledonia Plaza, although most of its information is of practical use for local citizens. The Mandeville Hotel publishes a handy pamphlet-type guidebook to the town.

Money
There are plenty of places to change foreign currency or arrange cash advances. Scotiabank has branches at Manchester Shopping Centre (☎ 962-3139), 17 Park Crescent (☎ 962-2842), and Caledonia Mall (☎ 962-9373). Century National Bank also has a branch in Caledonia Mall, Mandeville Plaza, and Manchester Shopping Centre. If you need to receive or send money by remittance, contact Western Union (☎ 962-1037) at 11 Manchester Rd.

Post & Communications
The post office is on South Racecourse. If you need to send packages use UPS (☎ 962-5135), which has an office at Shop 33 in the Manchester Shopping Plaza. You can also send letters to North America for US$11 (more to Europe). UPS offers guaranteed next-day delivery service; it's open daily 7 am to 7 pm.

Travel Agencies
If you need to make travel reservations, you'll find lots of agencies around town. Try Sterling Travel (☎ 962-2203) in Caledonia Plaza, International Travel Services (☎ 962-2123) at 36 Manchester Rd, or Global Travel Service (☎ 962-1183) in the Manchester Shopping Centre.

Bookshops
There are several stationery stores that sell books and magazines, including the Book Shop (☎ 962-9204) in Villa Plaza on Main St and Books & Things (☎ 962-0049) at 1 Buena Vista Circle. Haughton's Pharmacy on the northwest side of the village green also has a reasonable selection of international magazines.

Library
To brush up on local history, drop by the Manchester Parish Library (☎ 962-2972) at 34 Hargreaves Ave.

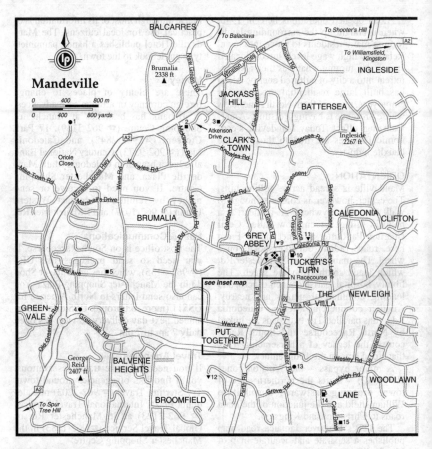

Medical Services

With its elderly expatriate community, Mandeville is well served by nine medical centers and about 40 doctors. The town's two hospitals – Mandeville Hospital (☎ 962-2067) and the Hargreaves Memorial Hospital (☎ 962-2040) – are both on Hargreaves Ave and have emergency centers. For less urgent treatment, I recommend the Caledonia Medicare Centre (☎ 962-3939).

Pharmacies include the Caledonia Mall Pharmacy (☎ 962-0038) at Shop G5, 3 Caledonia Rd; and Haughton's Pharmacy (☎ 962-2246) at 18 W Park Crescent, which is open 8 am to 8:30 pm Monday to Saturday, and 9 am to 7 pm on Sunday.

Emergency

Call the police at ☎ 119. For an ambulance or firetruck call ☎ 110. The police station (☎ 962-2250 or 962-2744) is housed in the old jail and workhouse on the north side of the village green.

CECIL CHARLTON PARK

This tiny, rather disheveled, English-style green, also known as Mandeville Square, lends a charming village feel to the town center. On the north side of the square is

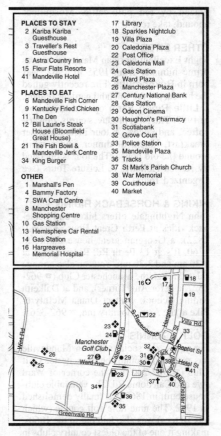

PLACES TO STAY
2 Kariba Kariba
   Guesthouse
3 Traveller's Rest
   Guesthouse
5 Astra Country Inn
15 Fleur Flats Resorts
41 Mandeville Hotel

PLACES TO EAT
6 Mandeville Fish Corner
9 Kentucky Fried Chicken
11 The Den
12 Bill Laurie's Steak
   House (Bloomfield
   Great House)
21 The Fish Bowl &
   Mandeville Jerk Centre
34 King Burger

OTHER
1 Marshall's Pen
4 Bammy Factory
7 SWA Craft Centre
8 Manchester
   Shopping Centre
10 Gas Station
13 Hemisphere Car Rental
14 Gas Station
16 Hargreaves
   Memorial Hospital

17 Library
18 Sparkles Nightclub
19 Villa Plaza
20 Caledonia Plaza
22 Post Office
23 Caledonia Mall
24 Gas Station
25 Ward Plaza
26 Manchester Plaza
27 Century National Bank
28 Gas Station
29 Odeon Cinema
30 Haughton's Pharmacy
31 Scotiabank
32 Grove Court
33 Police Station
35 Mandeville Plaza
36 Tracks
37 St Mark's Parish Church
38 War Memorial
39 Courthouse
40 Market

the **Mandeville Courthouse**, a handsome building of cut limestone with a horseshoe staircase and a raised portico supported by Doric columns. The green is ringed by Park Crescent.

The **Rectory**, the oldest home in town, stands to the left of the courthouse. Both it and the courthouse were completed in 1820. The original rector gained a considerable income from selling baptismal certificates. In addition, he caused an outcry by also renting out the building as a tavern. It later became a hotel and is now a private home.

On the south side is an old iron market that bustles on Wednesday, Friday, and

Saturday. Civic leaders believe that it is too congested and may soon relocate it.

St Mark's Church, which stands on the south side of Cecil Charlton Park, was also established in 1820. It's not Westminster Abbey, but the timber clerestory is impressive. During the slave rebellion of Christmas 1831, non-conformist missionaries suspected of inciting the rebellion were jailed in the organ loft. Take time to browse the churchyard, which includes graves of English soldiers who died during a yellow fever epidemic.

HUNTINGTON SUMMIT

Among the many stunning homes on the hills outside Mandeville is this mansion at 25 Racecourse in May Day, two miles southeast of the town center. The octagonal home is of palatial proportion, with wraparound plate-glass windows and artificial cascades tumbling into a swimming pool where waters feed into a pond in the lounge. The centerpiece of a farm and stables called Manchester Green, the home is fascinating for its eclectic and ostentatious furnishings reflecting the catholic tastes of its owner, Cecil Charlton, a self-made millionaire, farmer, politician, philanthropist, and self-promoter who served as Mandeville's mayor for 20 years during the 1970s and 1980s. He made much of his money as owner of the Charles-Off betting shops, but he also served as chairman of the corruption-ridden National Water Commission (see Government & Politics in the Facts about Jamaica chapter).

The home is open to the public daily except Wednesday and Saturday. Call to make an appointment (☎ 962-2274). There's no charge, but a donation to a charity is urged.

MARSHALL'S PEN

This 18th-century great house is Mandeville's most impressive historical edifice and nature retreat. It stands in the midst of a former coffee plantation turned cattle-breeding property on the northwest side of town. The house is fronted by beautifully landscaped gardens beneath huge fig trees hung with epiphytes and vines. Marshall's Pen is splendid for birding: more than 100 species have been recorded here, including 25 of the 27 bird species endemic to Jamaica.

The property was formerly owned by the Earl of Balcarres (governor of Jamaica from 1795 to 1801) when it was an estate of 4000 acres. Today the 300-acre property is owned by Robert Sutton, Jamaica's leading ornithologist, and Anne Sutton, an environmental scientist. (Mr Sutton, who is in his 90s, can trace his ancestry to the first child born to English parents in Jamaica in 1655.) The couple are gracious hosts who are happy to share their encyclopedic knowledge. Mr Sutton has been described as someone who 'could coach Alistair Cooke on urbane civility.'

It's a treat to don rubber boots and binoculars and set out with the Suttons, with their several dogs swarming happily at your heels. Mr Sutton is co-author with Audrey Downer of *Birds of Jamaica: A Photographic Field Guide*. He also escorts a weeklong birding trip that includes Marshall's Pen, the Cockpit Country, and Blue Mountains. For information contact the Touring Society of Jamaica, Salt Gut, Boscobel PO, St Mary (☎/fax 975-7158).

You can also tour the old stone-and-timber house, which has wood-paneled rooms brimming with antiques, leather-bound books, artwork, and other museum-quality pieces. Entrance costs US$10 and is by appointment only (☎ 963-8569). Early morning and evening are best. Overnight stays can sometimes be arranged in advance, if convenient for the family. Contrary to prevailing information, horseback rides are *not* available.

There are no signs to the house, which is north of the Winston Jones Hwy, about three miles from the town center. Take Oriole Close off the highway opposite the sign (on the *south* side of the road) for 'Marshall's Pen Estate.' Turn right onto a main road after 100 yards; the entrance – a substantial cut-stone gateway – is about 400 yards farther on the right. Follow a dirt road half a mile up to the house, past fields

grazed by red poll cattle. Mosquitoes abound; take repellent.

OTHER SITES
Right Excellent Norman Manley, who was prime minister from 1955 to 1962, was born in **Roxborough**. Fire recently gutted the house, but the splendid gardens remain.

Little Ripon Farm opened to visitors in 1995. The farm produces citrus, flowers, coffee, and cocoa. A tour includes either breakfast, lunch, or dinner, and a whirl around the old house. The tour is operated by Kariba Holidays & Leisure Tours (see Organized Tours).

HIKING & HORSEBACK RIDING
John Nightingale offers hikes and horseback rides at Perth Great House (☎ 962-2822), a Georgian great house dating to 1760. It's at 13 Perth Rd. Rides depart at 9:30 am and 3:30 pm. You can also arrange rides through the Manchester Club (☎ 962-2527, ask for Ann Turner), and at Dalkeith Riding School; contact Diana McIntyre-Pike at the Astra Country Inn, ☎ 962-3265.

GOLF & TENNIS
For years, *the* social scene in Mandeville has revolved around the Manchester Golf Club (☎ 962-2403) at the corner of Ward Ave and Caledonia Rd. The venerable clubhouse built in 1868 was finally demolished in 1992. The nine-hole golf course (which has 18 tees) was also laid out in the 1860s, making it one of the oldest country clubs in the Americas. It's a tight layout and quite challenging despite being relatively short, I'm told. Guests of local hotels can use the facilities, including the tennis courts.

The club becomes a gathering spot for the island's well-to-do during Golf Week and Tennis Week, held each July and August.

ORGANIZED TOURS
Kariba Holidays & Leisure Tours (☎ 962-8006, fax 962-5502), based at Kariba Kariba Guesthouse, offers sightseeing excursions to most places of interest in the south-coast region, as well as a Wicker, Leather &

Woodcraft Tour that visits the studios of local artisans. A two-day Jamaica Off the Beaten Track tour features visits to Black River, YS Falls, Bamboo Avenue, Mandeville, and the Appleton Rum Estate (US$180, including accommodations and meals).

Countryside Ltd at the Astra Country Inn (PO Box 60, Mandeville, ☎ 962-3725, fax 962-1461) has specialist guides for US$10 per hour. They're not official tour guides but ordinary people who show guests their way of life.

SPECIAL EVENTS

The Manchester Horticultural Society Show is held in late May (contact Carmen Stephenson at ☎ 962-2909). Golf enthusiasts time their visit to coincide with Jamaica's oldest golf tournament, the Manchester Golf Week, held in late July at the Manchester Club; contact the Jamaica Golf Association (☎ 975-4287). It's followed in August by Tennis Week at the same location. The Jamaica Horse Show is also held at the Manchester Club in July.

PLACES TO STAY

Mandeville is one of the few places in Jamaica with genuine guest houses, where you're a guest in a family home.

Traveller's Rest Guesthouse (☎ 962-8294) is a beautiful contemporary home owned and operated by Ted and Hyacinth Mitchell (he an Englishman, she a Jamaican). It's very much a home away from home. The tastefully decorated four bedrooms are huge, with sizable bathrooms. It's a bargain at US$40/50 single/double, including breakfast (less if you pass on breakfast). It's on the north side of town at 2 Harriott Meadows, off New Green Rd.

Nearby at 39 New Green Rd is *Kariba Kariba Guesthouse* (PO Box 482, ☎ 962-8006, fax 962-5502), which has a more homey atmosphere. It's run by Derek and Hazel O'Connor, a friendly English couple. Their modestly decorated home has a TV lounge, plus three bedrooms with private bathroom for US$45, and two with shared

bath for US$35, including breakfast. Dinners and lunch cost US$5 each. The couple also prepares barbecues on the lawn.

Joan Fearon, a delightful Englishwoman, runs the *Hillside Guesthouse* (☎ 962-7838) south of town on Manchester Rd. Her contemporary hillside home has fabulous views. Most of the eight rooms have a private bathroom and cost US$23. Breakfast is extra. Alternately, consider *Caledonia Guesthouse* (☎ 962-0406) at 6 Great House Drive; and *Roday's Guesthouse* (☎ 962-2552) at 3 Wesley Ave. Both have modest rooms with private bathroom for about US$30.

If you prefer more standard accommodations, stay at the *Mandeville Hotel* (PO Box 78, ☎ 962-2460, fax 962-0700), tucked at the bottom of 4 Hotel St on the east side of the green. The landmark hotel, the island's oldest, dates to the 1890s, when it was called the Waverly, but before that it served as a barracks for English troops. A renovation has brought it up to par. Self-contained units with kitchenettes are also available nearby. The restaurant is popular with locals and overlooks a pool. Rooms begin at about US$45.

There's a homey charm to the *Astra Country Inn* (PO Box 60, ☎ 962-3265, fax 962-1461) at 62 Ward Ave on the western outskirts of town. It has 20 rooms, including suites with kitchenettes for US$60 to US$90 per room, and the decor is rather jaded. Facilities include a pool, an English-style pub, and a pleasant dining room serving Jamaican cuisine made from produce grown in the hotel's organic garden (a food plan costs from US$20 daily). The staff are friendly, though in need of training. Coffee is supposedly delivered to your room as a wake-up call. The hotel is run by Diana McIntyre-Pike, who spearheads the local 'community tourism' (see sidebar).

Fleur Flats Resorts offers spacious, fully furnished, two-bedroom apartments that sleep four people in comfort (US$31). Rooms have TVs and phones. The very family-oriented resort is a short walk from the town center at 10 Coke Drive (PO Box

Community Tourism

You won't be long in the south coast before you hear the term 'community tourism.' The movement is an attempt to foster opportunities at the community level for locals wishing to participate more fully in Jamaica's tourism industry. Key to the movement is the desire to promote tourism throughout the central highlands and south coast while avoiding the mistakes of other resort areas.

The dynamo behind the movement is Diana McIntyre-Pike, co-owner and manager of the Astra Country Inn, and director of Countrystyle Ltd (PO Box 60, Mandeville, ☎ 962-3725, fax 962-1461), a company that specializes in providing alternatives to 'sea and sand' vacations. She and other civic leaders have formed the Central & South Tourism Committee, funded in part by the national Tourism Action Plan. The group sponsors special interest tours, community guides, skills training, and assistance with tourism development at the village level.

Promoters of small-scale community tourism fear that as south-coast tourism blossoms, government bureaucracy will spoil things. 'Whatever development takes place, it must complement our lifestyle, not change our way of life,' says McIntyre-Pike. A common complaint, however, is that the government is not listening to the locals. This is especially true for the area around Whitehouse, Bluefields, and, potentially, Treasure Beach, where big developers are finding favor with politicians in Kingston.

Organizers such as McIntyre-Pike are hoping to avoid overdevelopment by forging a connection between tourists and the citizenry. Many local citizens have opened their properties as guest houses. Others are taking visitors on family outings or guided excursions. Plans involve attracting small cruise ships to Port Kaiser or Black River, from which passengers would be taken to villages and eco-attractions. And as the big resort chains move in, the program aims to foster cooperative exchanges for resort guests wishing to overnight with local families. In addition to promoting an interchange of cultures, small businesses are also being fostered, such as a village program to manufacture 'South Coast Fashions.' ■

485, ☎ 962-1053; in Canada ☎ (416) 445-0209; in USA ☎ (305) 252-0873; in the UK ☎ (0171) 964-0047). The couple who owns it are extremely gracious and friendly.

You may be able to stay at *Marshall's Pen* (PO Box 58, ☎ 962-2260, fax 962-2770), which has three bedrooms in the main house, plus five self-catering apartments in a converted coffee warehouse. Costs range from US$25 per person per night. Meals can sometimes be arranged. Note, however, that this is not a hotel or guest house; rooms are made available at the owners' discretion, and then only to serious birders or nature lovers.

Other options you might pursue include the *Golf View Hotel* (PO Box 189, ☎ 962-4471, fax 962-2858) at 7 Caledonia Rd; the *International Chinese Hotel* (☎ 962-0527) at 17 Manchester Rd; and *Haven Apartments* (☎ 962-0849) at 3A Clarks Town Rd.

PLACES TO EAT

Among the town's several dozen restaurants, you'll find a variety of international cuisines. And there's no shortage of shopping plazas and groceries around town. None are as much fun, however, as buying fresh produce from the higglers at the market off the square.

Fast Food

If you need a fast-food fix, *Kentucky Fried Chicken* has an outlet on Caledonia Rd, opposite the Manchester Shopping Centre. Or try *Hungry Jack's* at Villa Plaza on Main St, *King Burger* on Caledonia Rd, and *Tweetie's Fried Chicken* also on Main St in the Brumalia Towne Centre.

Jamaican

Try the *Buss Stop*, a colorfully painted bus on Perthwood St, for down-to-earth Jamaican favorites such as ackee soursop soup.

Potpourri (☎ 962-2403), opposite the Odeon Cinema at 1 Caledonia Rd, also serves tasty traditional Jamaica dishes as well as North American fare.

The *Mandeville Hotel* and *Astra Country Inn* both have notable restaurants. At the former I recommend the chicken and red snapper in a piquant sauce. The Astra grows much of its produce in a private garden. Its natural health breakfast costs US$4, and Jamaican dishes begin at US$6.50, though you can have snacks for US$2.

For its mountain location, Mandeville surprisingly has several fish restaurants. *Mandeville Fish Corner* (☎ 962-9213) behind Mandeville Shopping Centre is an outdoor eatery serving fish prepared any way you want it from US$2. The *Fish Bowl*, nearby, is in similar vogue, as is *Miss Bennett's Fish Hut* on Caledonia Plaza.

You can buy a supply of bammies (cassava cakes) from Clem Bloomfield's home at 40 Greenvale Rd (☎ 962-2821) on Tuesday and Wednesday. For other baked goods head to *Lynn's* on Ward Ave, or *Flakey Crust* at 11 Manchester Rd. Both sell fresh-baked breads, pastries, and patties.

International

Bill Laurie's Steak House (☎ 962-3116), one of Jamaica's most well known restaurants, is a piece of Americana in the tropics. The place is extremely popular with locals. The food, which ranges from pumpkin soup to tenderloin steak (US$2 to US$15), happens to be good, but folks come for the setting (the former Bloomfield great house), the panoramic vistas, and the fabulous decor. An atmospheric bar has barrels as bar stools and plenty of beer mugs and old bottles. Hundreds of license plates from around the world add to the charm, and there are several vintage cars and old buggies, including a 1951 Armstrong Sidderley Hurricane convertible. You won't hear reggae here; prepare yourself for old big-band music.

Asian

My favorite eatery is *Den* (☎ 962-3603) at 35 Caledonian Rd, which specializes in a variety of Asian dishes. Thursday and Friday it offers curry dishes, chicken tandoori, and shrimp simmered in coconut cream. It has a happy hour from 5:30 pm. It's closed on Sunday.

Other reasonably priced options include the *Bamboo Village Restaurant* (☎ 962-4515) at 35 Ward Ave and the *International* (☎ 962-0527) at 117 Manchester Rd. Both serve Chinese cuisine; entrees cost between US$5 and US$15.

ENTERTAINMENT

The hottest thing around is *Jim's HQ*, an upscale disco 10 miles west of town at the base of Spur Tree Hill. Half of Mandeville seems to pour downhill to it on weekends, and it gets packed. Entrance costs US$3 and includes one drink. An outdoor terrace relieves the pressure and provides for cooling breaks. DJs play oldies on Sundays, and there are occasional fashion shows and beauty contests on an outdoor stage.

Other more down-to-earth discos include *Sparkles, Penthouse*, and *Tracks*, a popular reggae club.

The *Odeon Cinema* (☎ 962-2177) on Caledonia Rd and the new *Cecil Charlton Centre* both show first-run Hollywood movies. A movie house seemingly more unfit for conservative Mandeville is *Planet Disco* (☎ 962-0360) at 10 Mandeville Plaza. The show varies nightly, with comedies and X-rated movies midweek. It becomes a disco after the show.

The *Capri Restaurant* (☎ 962-1806) next door to the Odeon has live bands on weekends and canned music other nights.

If your taste runs to earthy go-go clubs, join the local men and couples at the *Governor's Club* and *Club Cariba*, both about four miles east of town at Russell Place Gardens along Caledonia Rd.

THINGS TO BUY

Mandeville has 12 major shopping plazas, ensuring that you can find whatever general merchandise you want. The largest is Manchester Shopping Centre on Caledonia Rd.

The town is well off the tourist map, so the supply of crafts is meager. A notable exception is the SWA Craft Centre (☎ 962-2138) on North Racecourse behind the Manchester Shopping Centre. It trains young adults with only basic education to make a living from crochet, embroidery, weaving, and so on. Its most appealing item is the famous 'banana patch' Rastafarian dolls, complete with a Jamaican passport.

Tropical plants make a great buy (you may want to check Customs restrictions relating to agricultural products, however). You can buy anthuriums at the Paul Cross Nursery beside the Catholic Church on Manchester Rd near Newleigh Rd. Alternately, try Carmen Stephenson's garden on New Green Rd, or her flower shop (☎ 962-2909) at Shop 14, Manchester Shopping Plaza.

GETTING THERE & AWAY
Plans are in the works to build an airport capable of accepting international flights, possibly using Alpart's airfield southwest of town. Until then, Mandeville is served by bus service from virtually every major town in Jamaica. Take your pick of more than one dozen buses and minibuses that run daily from Kingston. Minibuses depart Kingston from Half Way Tree (about US$5) and buses from the Parade (about US$1.50). You can catch a bus from Montego Bay on Creek St.

Buses and minibuses depart Mandeville for Albert Town (buses No LS400 and LS691), Black River (minibus No LS947), Cave Valley (minibus No LS865), Christiana (bus No LS46), Falmouth (bus No LS30), Kingston, Montego Bay, Spanish Town, and elsewhere from near the market on the main square. For information call Superior Omnibus Service (☎ 962-2421) at Caledonia Plaza. Bargain Rent-a-Car offers transfers from Kingston for US$35 per person one-way.

GETTING AROUND
There is no local bus system. You'll find taxis near the market on Cecil Charlton Park. Otherwise call Manchester Taxi Service (☎ 962-2021) for a pickup at your hotel.

To rent a car contact the following:

Candi Car Rental (☎ 962-3153), Caledonia Rd; Hemisphere Car Rental (☎ 962-1921) 51 Manchester Rd; Maxdan Car Rental (☎ 962-5341) Shop 8, Manchester Shopping Centre; Prams International (☎ 962-1051) 4 Newleigh Rd; and National Car Rental (☎ 962-0074) 3A Caledonia Rd.

Around Mandeville

SPUR TREE HILL
Four miles southwest of Mandeville is Spur Tree, atop the steep west-facing crest of the Don Figuerero Mountains. From Spur Tree the A2 falls precipitously in a dizzying switchback to Gutters and the plains of St Elizabeth. In the colonial era, carriages were hitched to strong draught mules or oxen for the ascent and descent, while occupants transferred to ponies.

At the top of the hill you can look out over the Essex Valley (forming the eastern part of St Elizabeth Parish) and the Santa Cruz Mountains. If you pull into the car park of Alpart Farm, you can look down into the Alpart bauxite mine, said to be the largest open-pit mine outside Chile. The valley floor is dominated by the company's alumina plant, five miles to the southeast at Nain. Check it out at night, when it glitters with lights. Alpart maintains an orchid sanctuary atop Spur Tree Hill.

NEWPORT
Following Manchester Rd south from Mandeville you'll arrive in six miles at this very quaint and photogenic village, centered on a large triangle where there are two brightly painted pubs (the *Capricorn Pub* and *Grand Duke Bar)* and a police station.

En route, you'll pass **Knockpatrick**, where the road is crossed by a great cable conveyor belt used to deliver bauxite from Alpart's mines to the processing plant at Nain, 15 miles to the west. A Rastafarian named Sam operates a roadside thatched bar called *Nature Village*. He's a colorful character!

REST STORE

This tiny hamlet nestles atop the southern crest of the Don Figuerero Mountains. From Newport (five miles north) the road carries you through a strange and powerful landscape of towering rocks. Bring your camera for the spectacular view down over Alligator Pond, the Essex Valley, and the Santa Cruz Mountains.

From Rest Store, the road begins its winding descent to **Rowes Corner**, one mile north of Alligator Pond. Rowes Corner was the site of the first elementary school for black children in Jamaica, established by Moravian missionaries in 1823 (a memorial commemorates the event). If you turn east at Rest Store, you can loop back to Newport via **Cross Keys**, which has a magnificently preserved Georgian courthouse and police station atop a hill, fronted by topiary bushes.

WILLIAMSFIELD

This village lies 1000 feet below Mandeville at the base of the Winston Jones Hwy (A2), which links with the B4 and B6 at a roundabout east of Williamsfield. The area was once part of a 10,000-acre estate given to Captain Alexander Woodburn Heron, a soldier in Oliver Cromwell's invasion army. **Williamsfield Great House** was built by his grandson, Captain George Heron, who built three other great houses and maintained a mistress and family in each. You can tour the restored great house by appointment. Alexander Heron is buried in a grave next to the lookout point on Shooter's Hill (see below).

You can take a free tour of **High Mountain Coffee Factory** (☎ 962-4211), where coffee and herbal teas are produced. It's adjacent to the old railway station just west of the roundabout.

Chocoholics will think they're in nirvana on a visit to the **Pioneer Chocolate Factory** (☎ 962-4216), which is also open for free tours. It's 400 yards east of High Mountain. You can watch the seeds from the cocoa bean being processed into chocolate bars, which you can sample.

There's a factory outlet on the roadside, next to Robbie's Bar.

SHOOTER'S HILL

Shooter's Hill, two miles northwest of Williamsfield, marks the base of a steep four-mile-long climb ascending almost 1400 feet to Christiana and the central highlands. A lookout point midway offers splendid views as far as Blue Mountain Peak, 60 miles to the east. Near the top of the hill is **Walderston**, where a road to the rights leads off to Spaldings.

Kirkvine Works

Just north of Williamsfield you'll pass the massive tailings lake full of rust-red liquid toxic waste from the Kirkvine Works, further down the road at Shooter's Hill. The alumina plant is owned and operated by Alcan Jamaica, the largest of the four multinational mining corporations operating in Jamaica. It's a joint venture between the Jamaican government and the Aluminium Company of Canada Ltd. The company is the largest single contributor to the Jamaican economy and government coffers. The processing factory, which was completed in 1957, is also the country's largest alumina plant.

Huge bauxite (aluminum oxide) deposits underlie much of the surrounding land. The rust-red earth is scooped from open-pit mines and ferried by dump truck and aerial ropeway to the factory to be crushed, washed, kiln-dried, powdered, and refined into alumina (well over 500,000 tons of alumina are produced annually). The burnt lime required to process alumina is supplied from a local source of limestone. Alcan maintains its own rolling stock to transport the processed ore to Port Esquivel at Old Harbour Bay on the south coast. It's shipped from here to North America and Scandinavia for smelting into aluminum.

The company mines only a small portion of its land holdings at one time. Once mined, the land is restored with pasture and forest and returned to grazing. About 8000 acres is given to livestock and citrus, while another 23,000 acres are farmed by almost 5000 tenant farmers.

You can arrange free weekday **factory tours** through the Astra Country Inn or Mandeville Hotel, or through the Kirkvine Works office (☎ 962-3141). A full day's notice is usually required.

Pickapeppa Factory

Yet another free tour is available by appointment at this factory (☎ 962-2928), which produces Jamaica's sinus-searing world-famous sauce (similar to England's Worcestershire sauce). The factory is at the foot of Shooter's Hill.

Magic Toy Factory

This factory (☎ 964-9723 or 997-6652) in Walderston makes handmade wooden toys and puzzles. The setting, in a great house surrounded by palette-bright gardens and offering fabulous views, is worth the tricky uphill drive. This is a great place to stock up on Christmas gifts for the kids. Jigsaw puzzles and other quality toys go for US$1 and up.

SPALDINGS

Spaldings is a small and often mist-shrouded town at about 3000 feet elevation on the crest of the central highlands at the top of Shooter's Hill. The agricultural center plays second fiddle to neighboring Christiana. The hills are planted in market gardens. Ginger and yams are important local crops.

Spaldings is also the site of Knox College, a coed religious school founded in 1940 by a progressive educator, Rev Lewis Davidson, who believed that a school should serve to benefit its local community. Hence, the curriculum includes practical studies. The school also has its own print works, farm, and meat-processing plant!

Information

Money There's a National Commercial Bank (☎ 964-2268) next to the gas station west of the town square.

Post & Communications There are public telephones at the post office, which is 100 yards east of the town center. A better bet for making direct overseas calls is Dawn's Telecommunications Service on the main street, just west of the town square. It's open 9 am to 8 pm, except Sundays from 3 to 8 pm.

Medical Services For emergencies, contact the Percy Junior Hospital (☎ 964-2222) at the west end of town. If you need less urgent treatment, Dr Glen Norman Day has a clinic (☎ 964-2361) next to the gas station. It's open on Monday, Tuesday, Thursday, and Saturday from 9 am to 3 pm. There's a medical laboratory next door. Dr J Hayman also has a clinic above the Mid-Island Pharmacy (☎ 964-2209) in the town center. It's open Monday to Friday 8 am to 3 pm (Saturday 10:30 am to 1 pm).

Emergency The police station (☎ 964-2260) is at the east end of town.

Places to Stay

Spaldings is not set up for visitors, although Mr Clinton Blackwood has a small guest house at 8 Main St (☎ 964-2719).

The best bet, however, is *Glencoe B&B*, a delightful piece of old England at Nash Farm, one mile south of Spaldings (Spaldings PO, Clarendon, ☎ 964-2286). The two-story stone farmhouse is run by Lucy Nash, whose family founded the farm in 1891. The interior is simply marvelous! The four quaint little upstairs bedrooms boast mahogany floors, antiques, and private bathrooms with hot water. An enclosed wide upstairs veranda forms a wrap-around lounge with a TV and a small library. Rates are US$40/60/80 single/double/triple, including a farmhouse breakfast.

Places to Eat

Take your pick of several clean, modest restaurants serving Jamaican fare, including *Variations Restaurant*, *Goatee Restaurant*, and the *Little Link Pastry Shop* for pasties and burgers. They're all in the town center.

Getting There & Away

Spaldings is most easily reached by bus from Mandeville, where vehicles depart from beside the market on Cecil Charlton Park. If you're traveling from Kingston, you can ride with Clayton Burrell in his minibus (No ST855), which departs from the Parade; the journey will cost about US$5.

Buses from Ocho Rios and Runaway Bay to Mandeville pass through Spaldings.

CHRISTIANA

Arriving from the lush lowlands, visitors are often surprised by the cool, cloud-swept heights around Christiana. You'd be forgiven for imagining yourself in the Pyrenees or the highlands of Costa Rica. The air is crisp, clouds drift through the vales, and pine trees add to the alpine setting.

Lying northwest of Spaldings at an elevation of 3000 feet and one mile south of Jamaica's mountain backbone, the town is the heart of a richly farmed agricultural region where gently undulating hills and shallow vales are speckled with trim white houses with red roofs. Christiana receives very few foreign visitors, but it's worth the drive for an altogether different Caribbean experience.

The area is an important center for Irish potatoes (first introduced to Jamaica in the mid-18th century by a minister of the nearby Bethany church). Cacao, yams, and coffee production are also important, and during picking season you can watch women with baskets moving among the rows, plucking the cherry-red coffee berries. Christiana is a fairly sleepy place, but on Thursday when the higglers come into town to sell their produce, the roads are so thick you can hardly drive through town. If you're in town on Thursday, stay through the evening for Higgler's Night.

The area was settled by German farmers during the 18th and 19th centuries. Many had fought as mercenaries for the English army during the American War of Independence, and they were rewarded with land grants in Jamaica. Their legacy is evident in the fair skin and blue and green eyes of the locals. Moravian missionaries

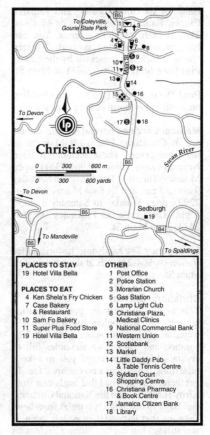

Christiana

0   300   600 m
0   300   600 yards

To Devon

To Devon

To Mandeville

To Coleyville, Gourie State Park

Swan River

Sedburgh
■ 19

To Spaldings

PLACES TO STAY
19 Hotel Villa Bella

PLACES TO EAT
4 Ken Shela's Fry Chicken
7 Case Bakery & Restaurant
10 Sam Fo Bakery
11 Super Plus Food Store
19 Hotel Villa Bella

OTHER
1 Post Office
2 Police Station
3 Morarian Church
5 Gas Station
6 Lamp Light Club
8 Christiana Plaza, Medical Clinics
9 National Commercial Bank
11 Western Union
12 Scotiabank
13 Market
14 Little Daddy Pub & Table Tennis Centre
15 Syldian Court Shopping Centre
16 Christiana Pharmacy & Book Centre
17 Jamaica Citizen Bank
18 Library

were also active during that era, and a Moravian church looks down over the town from the northern end of sinuous Main St. During the 19th century, Christiana became a hill-town resort popular with European dignitaries and Kingstonians escaping the heat of the plains. They'd stay for months. The marvelous Hotel Villa Bella recalls that era.

Information

Money Three bank branches are located along Main St, including Scotiabank (☎ 964-2223) and National Commercial

Bank in the town center, and Jamaica Citizen Bank on the south side of town. They'll cash traveler's checks. You can have money remitted through Western Union, which is represented by the Super-Plus Food Store (☎ 964-2465) on Main St.

Post The post office is in a modern building on Main St just north of the police station.

Medical Services Several doctors' clinics are in Christiana Plaza, off Main St in the town center. These include Dr Glen Norman Day's clinic (☎ 964-2361), open Monday, Tuesday, Thursday, and Saturday 9 am to 3 pm; and Dr Paul Morris' (☎ 964-2299), open Monday to Saturday 8 am to 5 pm. The Christiana Pharmacy (☎ 964-2424) is on Main St.

Emergency The handsome, historic police station (☎ 964-2250) is at the north end of Main St.

Christiana Bottom
This beautiful riverside spot, in a valley bottom 800 feet below the town, has a waterfall plus picnic spots surrounded by bamboo and lilies. Two sinkholes full of crystal-clear water tempt you to take a refreshing dip. There's no entrance fee. To get there, take the road that leads east from Kirby Hardware and the National Commercial Bank in town; it's two miles from here. Take the first left and then go left again. If you still get lost contact Monica Zijdemans at Hotel Villa Bella (☎ 964-2243).

Martin Hill Orchid Sanctuary
Jamaica has scores of orchid species, and more than 100 of them can be admired and photographed at this orchideum south of town. The 25 Jamaican endemics represented include the *Epidendrum scalpeligerum*, not seen for 17 years until recently. The place is as still as a cathedral.

Organized Tours
Monica Zijdemans, owner of Villa Bella Tours, leads excursions to places of interest near Christiana, including trips to the Oxford Caves (US$30) and Martin Hill Orchid Sanctuary (US$10), plus trips to Lorimar Coffee Estate, the Gourie Caves, and the Moravian churches at Bethany and Mizpah. The company is located in the Hotel Villa Bella.

JJ's Tours offers guided **mountain bike tours** from Hibernia Property, an great house near Devon, three miles west of Christiana. JJ, a delightful Canadian, and her husband offer three routes of one, two, and three days (US$60/70/80), with accommodations (extra) at Hotel Villa Bella. A support van is provided. Contact the Villa Bella for information.

Special Events
On Christmas Eve the streets are closed and farming families pour in from miles around for a Jonkanoo called 'Grand Market Night.' The tradition has died out elsewhere in Jamaica, but here the town puts on a grand Jonkanoo with men on stilts and general festivity in the streets. Even the shops stay open until dawn! For more information on Jonkanoos, see the sidebar in the Facts for the Visitor chapter.

Places to Stay & Eat
Hotel Villa Bella (PO Box 473, ☎ 964-2243, fax 962-2765) is a gracious old country inn perched on a hill at the south end of town. The charming owner, Monica Zijdemans, has overseen the restoration of the former grande dame, which retains its original mahogany floors and 1930s art-deco furniture. Gracious and efficient service recalls the days when Christiana was a center for 'old-style tourism.' The place is gradually being brought back to life. Facilities include a reading room and TV lounge, and an elegant dining room and antique furniture. The 18 rooms, with deep bathtubs, rent for US$60 including breakfast.

The hotel offers one of the best and most reasonably priced dining experiences on the island. The menu merges Jamaican cuisine with Japanese and Chinese. Typical dishes include chicken teriyaki (US$7), chicken sichuan (US$8), and poached fish chinese style in ginger and soy sauce

(US$8), all using herbs and vegetables from the hotel's own garden. If you can, eat on the veranda or the garden terrace, where you can sip homemade ginger beer and look out over the flower-filled, six-acre hillside garden. High tea is at 4:30 pm, and a Jamaican barbecue is held each Thursday and Friday night.

At the other end of the scale is *Ken Shela's Fry Chicken*, a rustic eatery near the police station on Main St. There's a bakery 50 yards to the east, and Sam Fo Bakery *is opposite Scotiabank*.

Entertainment

Christiana is relatively dull on weekdays. It's a farming community: farmers go to bed early and get up around 4 or 5 am. There are a few reggae bars, however, most notably the *Lamp Light Club* and the *Little Daddy Pub* in the town center.

The town suddenly comes alive on Thursday nights, when the higglers are in town.

There's a *table-tennis club* next to Little Daddy Pub.

Getting There & Away

This important market town is well served by buses operating on a frequent if somewhat erratic basis from Kingston and Mandeville. You can also take a bus from May Pen (No LS619) and Montego Bay (No LS72).

Getting Around

You can walk most places. There's no bus service to speak of. If you arrived in Christiana by public transport and you decide you need wheels, try Lloyd's Auto Rental (☎ 964-9626) in Syldian Court at the southern end of Main St.

COLEYVILLE

This small mountain-crest farming village at 2952 feet is two miles north of Christiana, astride the border of Manchester and Trelawny Parishes. It's cool and windy up here, and Coleyville is often shrouded in swirling mists. Bring a sweater! On a clear day you have sweeping views of both

coasts. Many of the slopes are covered with pockets of pine. Irish potatoes grow well in the temperate climate, as do strawberries, for which the village is noted.

North of Coleyville, the B5 begins its descent into Trelawny. Another road winds westward, descending through the Hectors River Valley for 10 miles to Troy on the eastern edge of the Cockpit Country. The river marks the boundary with Trelawny Parish.

Gourie State Park

About one mile northwest of Coleyville is this forest reserve of candlewood, pines, mahogany, and mahoe. Orchids grow profusely. The park is laced with good hiking trails. Gourie, however, is most noteworthy for having Jamaica's longest cave system. The cave entrance is about half a mile downhill from the cabins.

Two spelunking routes have been explored and laid out through the **caves**. One is easy; the other is difficult and made more so by the presence of an icy river that runs underground all the way to Oxford, 15 miles to the west. Rubber-soled shoes are required and a guide is essential. Entrance is free, and there are no facilities.

If you're not a serious caver, a good way to visit is with Villa Bella Tours (US$30 for three hours). Calypso Island Tours includes a visit to Gourie in its nine-day 'Outback Jamaica' eco-adventure (see Organized Tours at the beginning of this chapter).

The Forestry Department of the Ministry of Agriculture rents two well-equipped wooden cottages. The office is on Main St (☎ 964-2065), but you can reportedly get the keys from the caretaker.

Getting There & Away

You can walk to Coleyville from Christiana (take a sweater or jacket in the event of fog). Buses operate between Coleyville and the Parade in Kingston (Nos ST712 and ST465); expect to pay about US$2. Errol Thomas also runs a minibus to Mandeville (No LS2044). Buses to Albert Town from Mandeville or Christiana will also drop you in Coleyville.

MILE GULLY

This modestly prosperous agricultural town sits in the midst of a dry valley that runs northwest from Mandeville in the lee of the forested north face of the Don Figuerero Mountains. The B6 leads west from Shooter's Hill, winding, dipping, and rising past lime-green pastures dotted with guango and silk-cotton trees and criss-crossed with stone walls and hedgerows. The area is very reminiscent of the Yorkshire Dales.

The limestone valley is pitted with caves, including Oxford Caves near Mile Gully. They're said to be pretty. If you intend to explore, hire a local guide. You can also visit on a tour offered by the Hotel Villa Bella in Christiana, about 10 miles northeast.

Mile Gully is perhaps best known for the 160-year-old Bethany Moravian church – a simple gray stone building dramatically perched on a hilltop – and, beside it, a beautiful late 19th-century police station topped by a courtroom.

Getting There & Away

You can take bus No LS30, which operates twice daily between Mandeville and Balaclava via Mile Gully. It should cost less than US$1 to any point you wish to get off.

If you're driving, be forewarned that the B6 continues west five miles to Green Hill and a T-junction marked 'St Paul's 5 miles' (left) and 'Balaclava 6½ miles' (right). One mile north (right) of the junction is a very dangerous spot: you'll climb a short hill that tempts you to accelerate. Unfortunately there's a railway crossing atop the crest, and a hairpin bend *immediately* after. You can't see either. *Drive slowly!*

South Coast

This is the least known and least visited part of the island, despite its historic importance as the 'bread basket of Jamaica.' Clarendon Parish and, to a lesser degree, the neighboring parish of St Catherine were in colonial days the wealthiest parishes on the island. The southern part of Clarendon was a separate parish known as Vere – a center for the manufacture of indigo dye, made from the root of the indigo plant. The banks of the Rio Minho had many indigo works during Spanish days, when the Spanish panned for gold in the river they called Rio de la Mina (River of the Mine). They never found any significant quantities of the precious metal, but they did develop a prosperous cattle industry.

The upland region opened up only in the 1920s and 1930s when a railroad was extended into the Minho Valley, giving farmers access to market. Banana plantations were swiftly established. Later, sugar estates expanded into the Minho Valley and into the hills of Upper Clarendon. Sugar remains the mainstay of the area.

The Rio Minho rises in the mountains near Spaldings and flows down to Carlisle Bay. Before reaching the ocean the river drains into the sandy soils of the Clarendon Plains, and the riverbed is usually dry at May Pen. During heavy rains the river becomes a raging torrent. The situation has been aggravated in recent decades by severe deforestation and poor farming practices in the Minho Valley. The area has been totally bypassed by tourism and displays considerable poverty.

Immediately east of Mandeville the A2 begins a 2000-foot, nine-mile descent down Melrose Hill to Porus, an important market town one mile west of the border of Clarendon Parish. The mountainside catches the rains and is densely foliated. Papaya, green oranges, yams, and bananas hang at stalls all along the roadside. The road continues south more gradually

HIGHLIGHTS

- Pristine Canoe Valley Wetland (Alligator Hole), a last refuge for endangered manatees
- Historic Spanish Town, rundown but replete with historical edifices
- White Marl Arawak Museum for a low-key primer to indigenous culture

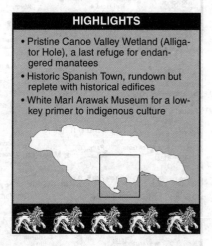

through the Milk River Valley, crosses the normally dry bed of the Milk River at Clarendon Park, and emerges at Toll Gate onto the vast flatlands of the Clarendon Plains (a toll-gate formerly stood at the site of the present village). The B12 runs south from Toll Gate to Milk River and the south coast. The A2 continues eastward almost ruler-straight to May Pen, which lies 36 miles west of Kingston.

The plains south of May Pen are smothered in sugarcane fields and cattle pastures. Mangroves line the south-coast shores, which hold little appeal for tourists in search of beaches. Nature lovers and hikers can find solitude, however, on the vast hook of Portland: a totally undeveloped hilly area covered with dense shrub and used as a bird hunting ground. The Milk River, which forms the boundary between Clarendon and Manchester Parishes, was once used to irrigate the sugar estates of the Clarendon Plains in the days when crocodiles splashed about in the muddy banks. It is said that there are still 'alligators,' but if so, they're very rare.

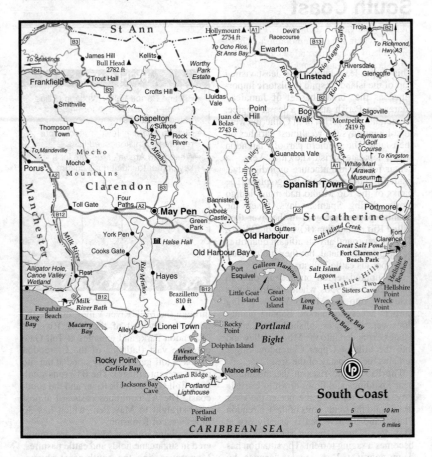

MAY PEN

The large capital city (population 41,000) of Clarendon Parish has a strategic economic location midway between Spanish Town and Mandeville, on the banks of the Rio Minho. It is a major market town and light industrial center at the heart of a prosperous agricultural district. The town center teems at any time of day and week, but especially on Friday and Saturday when the market is held. Be prepared for terrible congestion, honking horns, and pushy drivers who attempt to squeeze in and out and add to the general mayhem.

The town takes its name from the 18th-century estate owned by Rev William May. The nucleus of the early village was centered on two inns on either side of the river and, later, a railway station built in the 1880s.

There's little of interest to see or do. However, an annual agricultural show is held on the Denbigh show ground two miles west of town during Independence weekend each August. For information, contact the Jamaica Agricultural Society (☎ 922-0610). The only historic building of interest is the ramshackle remains of an old fort that can be seen south of the main square, where the pandemonium reaches a pinnacle. The commercial center stretches from here westward along the A2 for more than a mile.

Information

There's no tourist office, but the Jamaica Information Service has an office on Storks St (☎ 986-2193).

Money Take your pick of Mutual Security Bank (☎ 986-2592), National Commercial Bank (☎ 986-2343), and Scotiabank

(☎ 986-2212), all with branches near each other on Main St close to the main square. There's a money-exchange bureau in the plaza opposite the police station on Main St.

Post & Communications The post office (☎ 986-2302) is 100 yards northeast of the main square. You can make international calls and send faxes from the Telecommunications of Jamaica office (☎ 986-2342) on Fernleigh Ave at the west end of town.

Travel Agencies Try Stuart's Travel Service in May Pen Plaza (☎ 986-4542),

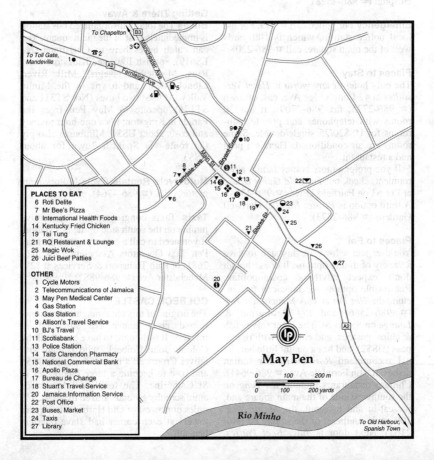

PLACES TO EAT
6 Roti Delite
7 Mr Bee's Pizza
8 International Health Foods
14 Kentucky Fried Chicken
19 Tai Tung
21 RQ Restaurant & Lounge
25 Magic Wok
26 Juici Beef Patties

OTHER
1 Cycle Motors
2 Telecommunications of Jamaica
3 May Pen Medical Center
4 Gas Station
5 Gas Station
9 Allison's Travel Service
10 BJ's Travel
11 Scotiabank
12 Police Station
14 Taits Clarendon Pharmacy
15 National Commercial Bank
16 Apollo Plaza
17 Bureau de Change
18 Stuart's Travel Service
20 Jamaica Information Service
22 Post Office
23 Buses, Market
24 Taxis
27 Library

May Pen

0   100   200 m
0   100   200 yards

Rio Minho

To Old Harbour,
Spanish Town

International Travel Services at 43 Main St
(☎ 986-4946), or BJ's Travel at 2 Bryant
Crescent (☎ 986-6247).

Medical Services May Pen residents must
be a sickly bunch, as there are dozens of
pharmacies, including Tait's Clarendon
Pharmacy at 34 Main St (☎ 986-2324),
open 8 am to 8 pm, and Sunshine Pharmacy
at 7 Fernleigh Ave (☎ 986-9085). May Pen
Medical Center can assist with routine
diagnosis and prescriptions; it's at 10 Manchester Ave (☎ 986-2717). If you need
emergency attention, call the May Pen
Hospital (☎ 986-2528).

Emergency For police call ☎ 119. For the
local police station, which is 100 yards
west of the main square, call ☎ 986-2208.

Places to Stay
The only hotel of any worth is *Hotel Ver-
sailles* at 42 Longbridge Ave, east of town
(☎ 986-2775, fax 986-2709). It has 30
rooms with telephones and private bathrooms for US$20/25 single/double. Some
rooms are air-conditioned. There's a pool
and a restaurant.

If you prefer a more homey family environment, check out *Fairfield Guest House*
at Lot 63 on Fairfield Drive (☎ 986-4344).
A third option is *Pirates Hotel* at Hartwell
Gardens (☎ 986-2873).

Places to Eat
You'd expect a town of this size to have
a variety of dining options. It does, though
don't expect anything cosmopolitan.
Reasonable options for Jamaican fare include the *Hot Pot* at 18A Manchester Ave
(☎ 986-2586) and *RQ Restaurant &
Lounge* on Storks St. The latter serves fish
& chips, pastries, and chicken with rice 'n
peas (US$2), and has a quaint little bar.

I recommend *Roti Delite* for Indian
dishes; it's on Ferndale Ave (☎ 986-9641).
Chinese restaurants include *Tai Tung* on
the southwest side of the main square and,
for eat-in and take-out, the *Magic Wok*,
100 yards southeast of the square (☎ 986-
2161). Next door is *Juici Beef Patties*,

serving a Jamaican version of the Big Mac.
Kentucky Fried Chicken has a franchise
100 yards west of the main square. If
you're craving pizza, try *Mr Bee's Pizza* on
Ferndale Ave (☎ 986-2127). You can buy
all manner of nutritional products at *International Health Foods*, next to Mr Bee's
(☎ 986-4640).

Entertainment
The new *Temptations Nightclub* at Omni
Plaza is a good place to practice your
reggae moves. It has dancehall on Thursday nights; entrance is US$3.

Getting There & Away
Buses The totally disorganized bus station
is immediately east of the main square. You
can catch buses here to Christiana (No
LS619), Spanish Town and Kingston, Ocho
Rios, Mandeville, Negril, Milk River,
Lionel Town, and towns in the Minho
Valley. At least two buses (Nos ST311 and
ST176) operate to May Pen from the
Parade in Kingston; it's a one-hour journey
and costs about US$1. Minibuses also ply
the route via Spanish Town for about
US$3.

Motorcycle Rentals Cycle Motors rents
motorcycles (☎ 986-4764).

Taxis Taxis congregate in a disruptive
jumble on the south side of the bus station.
If you need to call a cab, try either the May
Pen Taxi Operators Association (☎ 986-
2681) or Path Transport & Services at 12½
Manchester Ave (☎ 986-9882).

COLBECK CASTLE
The origins of this once-magnificent, now-
ruined great house are shrouded in
mystery. It is thought to have been built by
Colonel John Colbeck, who landed with
Oliver Cromwell's invasion army in 1655
and rose to become a large landowner in
St Catherine. The fortified relic stands
amid scrubby grounds grazed by goats, 1½
miles northwest of Old Harbour. Its square
towers at each corner had slave quarters
beneath.

OLD HARBOUR

This nondescript town is famous for its iron clock tower in the town square. The Victorian tower is marvelously preserved, as is the clock, which amazingly was installed shortly after the English invasion in 1655 and, even more amazingly, still keeps good time. The belfry and other renovations date from the 19th century. Other points of interest are the Church of St Dorothy, one of the oldest on the island. Anyone with an interest in agriculture might call in at the Bodles Agricultural Station, which is famous for its leading research in breeding hardy cattle strains. It offers tours by appointment (☎ 983-2308).

Information

Scotiabank has a branch on the north side of the square (☎ 983-2205); there's a National Commercial Bank on the south side (☎ 983-2279). You can have money remitted from your home country via Western Union in Salmon's Pharmacy at 9 East St (☎ 983-2483).

The post office is on the south side of the town square (☎ 983-2383).

The nearest hospital is in Spanish Town. There's a doctor's office on Darlington Drive. It's open Monday to Friday, 9 am to 5 pm, and until 2 pm on Saturday.

The police station (☎ 983-2255) is next to the post office.

Places to Eat

A wide choice of eateries serve inexpensive Jamaican fare. Try *Midnite City Restaurant*, the *Paddock*, or *Tee Gee's*. You can satisfy your sweet tooth at *Homey Crust Bakery* or the *Topic Ice Cream Parlor*. *Juici Beef Patties* serves burgers, sandwiches, and spicy patties.

Entertainment

The *Border Line Lagoon Niteclub*, on the main road east of Old Harbour, is a reggae club that also has go-go dancing.

Getting There & Away

Buses traveling to Kingston or Spanish Town from Mandeville pass through Old

Harbour. If you're coming from Kingston, look for Kenneth Dennis' minibus (No ST641); he charges about US$2.

OLD HARBOUR BAY

This large fishing village two miles south of Old Harbour is the site of the south coast's largest fish market. The access road from the A2 is opposite Bodles Agricultural Station. Fishermen land their catch midmorning, and it makes a photogenic sight with the nets laid out and the colorful pirogues drawn up on the somewhat ugly shore. The village itself is a squalid place of tin and wood shacks and is prone to flooding in rainy season.

Christopher Columbus was here in 1494 and named the bay Puerto de la Vaca (Cow Bay) for its large population of manatees (sea cows). The animals have since been decimated. It became an important port for the Spanish, who established a shipbuilding facility at Port Esquival, one mile west of Old Harbour Bay. The name recalls Juan Esquival, Jamaica's first Spanish governor (1509 – 1519). Today it's the site of a bauxite shipping terminal owned by Alcan Jamaica Ltd.

Places to Eat

You can sample fried fish and boiled lobster prepared on the beach at any of several dozen rum shops and steamed fish joints of varying grades of rusticity. *Cacique* is one of the better places; another is *Ocean Breeze Restaurant* at the rear of the fish market. The most salubrious place is *Auntie's Hot Spot*, half a mile inland from the shore. *Seamech Restaurant*, 200 yards before the shore, is also recommended. You can buy ice cream nearby at *Taste Right*.

Getting There & Away

You can catch a bus from Old Harbour. There's also one bus daily (No ST158A) from the Parade in Kingston.

GOAT ISLANDS

Offshore of Old Harbour Bay are two large islands, Little Goat and Great Goat, sheltering Galleon Harbour to the east. The last endemic Jamaican iguana was seen here in the 1940s, and the animal was considered extinct until 1990 when a small population was discovered in the Hellshire Hills (see the Kingston chapter). There are a few beaches along the mangrove-lined shores.

During WWII, the US Navy built a base on the larger island. The barracks are used nowadays by a few fishermen; otherwise the islands are uninhabited. You can hire a boat to take you out or negotiate a fee to join the lobstermen for a day or night at sea.

HALSE HOUSE

This attractive great house three miles south of May Pen is situated on a hillock surrounded by pastures. During the Spanish colonial period the property was known as Hato de Buena Vista (Ranch of the Beautiful View). After the English invasion in 1655, the land was granted to Major Thomas Halse, who built the house on an old Spanish foundation. The house continued in the family for many decades. For a time it was occupied by Sir Hans Sloane, the famous doctor and botanist whose collection of Jamaican flora and fauna formed the nucleus of what later became the British Museum of Natural History in London.

Today Halse House is owned by Alcoa Minerals, which processes the bauxite-rich earth of Clarendon at its Jamalco aluminum processing plant near Hayes. The company calls it Halse Hall and uses it for conferences and social functions, including community events. Tours can be arranged by appointment (☎ 986-2561).

LIONEL TOWN

Lionel Town is a busy market town, 13 miles south of May Pen. It's totally off the beaten path in the midst of sugarcane fields of the West Indies Sugar Company (a subsidiary of Tate & Lyle Ltd). You'll know you've arrived because of strong odors from the **Moneymusk Sugar Factory**, one mile west of town.

Beyond Moneymusk is the ramshackle hamlet of **Alley**, with a notable Anglican church – St Peter's – shaded by giant silk-cotton *kapok* trees, and an old windmill

now housing the town library and looking like a great mushroom with its wide-flanged roof.

At least one minibus (No LS1066) links Lionel Town with May Pen, and bus No ST864 runs daily from Kingston (US$0.50).

PORTLAND RIDGE

The southernmost extension of Jamaica is a rugged upland scrub-covered ridge rimmed by mangrove swamps and offshore coral reefs, and there have been proposals to make the peninsula into the Portland Ridge National Park. It's totally away from the tourist path and difficult to access. Adventurous sorts will find it good for lonesome hiking and camping (use caution; I do *not* recommend camping alone), and the area has many caves considered excellent for spelunking. Arawaks have adorned the walls of many with their petroglyphs. One of the best is Jackson's Bay Cave, with about 12,000 feet of passageways, underground lakes, and stygian chambers festooned with spectacular formations (you can get there via Jackson's Bay).

A very rough single-track road continues past the turnoff for Jackson's Bay and leads to Portland Lighthouse. En route you pass through marshland and mangroves, teeming with birds such as oystercatchers. A 4WD vehicle is recommended. After eight miles you reach the boundary of the PWD Hunting & Sporting Club. A sign reads 'No Trespassing!'

CARLISLE BAY

Carlisle Bay, seven miles south of Lionel Town, has been touted in some guidebooks for its stretches of coral-colored sand, such as at Jackson Beach. The few mangrove-backed beaches lack the beauty of their north-coast counterparts, however. They are the province of fishermen. The main village is Rocky Point, a melancholy, down-at-the-heels place with lots of burned-out shacks. It's a good place, however, to view the large commercial fishing fleet coming and going. You can even hire a boat or ask to be taken on for a night of fishing with the locals.

The bay is reached by a winding and decrepit road through scrubland grazed by goats.

Places to Eat

There are lots of earthy bars to choose from. The friendliest are *Black Thunder HQ* and *Beachwave Beachfront Tavern*. *Splendor Height Restaurant & Lounge* as you enter town is one of the better places to eat.

Rocky Point is known for a local delicacy: turtle eggs in red wine. Endangered marine turtles (and their eggs) are protected by law. Don't support the illegal harvest!

MILK RIVER BATH

Fourteen miles southwest of May Pen is this well-known spa, fed from a saline mineral hot spring that bubbles up at the foot of Round Hill, two miles from the ocean. The waters are a near-constant 92°F (33°C). An immersion is said to cure all kinds of ailments, from gout and lumbago, to rheumatism and nervous conditions.

A spa first opened to the public in 1794. The current spa is owned by the government and supervised by the Ministry of Tourism (☎ 924-8990). There's a clinical feel and smell to the place. The six time-worn public mineral baths and three private baths are cracked and chipped, though clean.

These waters are the most radioactive waters in the world (50 times more so than Vichy in France and three times those of Karlsbad in Austria). Hence, bathers are limited to only 15 minutes, though you are allowed three baths a day. Imbibing the waters is also recommended by the spa staff as a stirring tonic. They don't mean for you to swig from the pool; they'll give you a tumbler.

Very few tourists visit, but the spa is popular with Jamaicans, who tend to hang out in their dressing gowns. It gets crowded on weekends. It's open 7 am to 9 pm daily. Admission is US$1.25 per bath (children half-price). Massages are offered for US$15 per hour (less for guests). For information call ☎ 924-9544.

Much of the surrounding scrubland is threatened by charcoal-burners, whose work is arduous and pays little more than bare subsistence. You'll see basic kilns and possibly the dust-covered workers themselves begging rides along the road.

About 200 yards north of the spa is the **Milk River Spa Mineral Pool**, an open-air swimming pool open to the public weekends and public on holidays from 10 am to 6 pm.

The rambling *Milk River Mineral Bath Hotel* is a homey, white-porched hotel with shady verandas, well-worn pine floors, and 20 modestly furnished rooms (Milk River PO, Clarendon, ☎ 924-9544, fax 986-4962). Rooms cost US$35/45 with shared bath, US$5 extra for private bathroom. A US$50 deposit is required at check-in. Guests are not charged for using the mineral spa. Meals are served in a cozy dining room, where the menu includes Jamaican favorites such as mutton stew and stewed fish. Breakfasts include a health-food Country House Special (US$5).

Milk River Bath is accessed off the A2 along a well-paved road via Cook's Gate and Rest. It can also be reached via the B12 from Toll Gate (on the A2 nine miles west of May Pen). A bus operates from May Pen.

FARQUHAR BEACH

Beyond Milk River Bath, a dirt road lined with tall cacti leads 1½ miles to a funky, colorful fishing village at the river mouth. The gray-sand beach backed by mangroves is not very appealing. The village life is fascinating, however, and you can wile away hours watching the fishermen tending their nets and pirogues.

There are a handful of rustic rum shops run by Rastas. You can hire a boat and guide to take you fishing or to the mouth of the Alligator Hole River in search of crocodiles and the elusive endangered manatees.

ALLIGATOR HOLE

A government-owned wildlife reserve of extreme importance, Alligator Hole (also known as Canoe Valley Wetland) is well known for its manatees. They live amid dense, three-foot-tall reeds in the jade-blue pools fed by waters that emerge at the base of limestone cliffs forming the northern edge of the Canoe Valley. Herons, grebes, jacanas, gallinules, and other waterfowl are abundant. Both marine and freshwater fish also survive in the waters, which are lent a mild salinity by the seepage of sea water through the limestone bedrock. The Canoe Valley Wetland was set up as a feeding station for four manatees that inhabit the diamond-clear water in which crocodiles also hover.

There's a very good interpretive center established by the Natural Resources Conservation Department. After reading the well-done displays, you can take an

hourlong trip to the sea by canoe with a guide. The price is based on 'satisfaction' says Paul, one of the site wardens. There's no entrance fee.

Alligator Hole is reached via the B12. The turnoff is one mile north of Milk River, three miles east of steep Round Hill. A newly paved road also parallels Long Bay, linking the site with Alligator Pond and St Elizabeth, 15 miles west.

CHAPELTON
This picturesque if scruffy little town is very rural-English in feel. It's laid out around St Paul's Parish Church and an old

Mermaid or Manatee?
Long Bay Morass is a rare and precious haven for the West Indian manatee. Many thousands of these elephantine marine mammals inhabited the coastal waters of Jamaica and other Caribbean islands in the days before Columbus. When European ships began arriving in Caribbean waters, sailors told tales of mermaid sightings, but there have been musings that manatees may have inspired the rumors. Over the past five centuries they have been hunted voraciously for their meat, blub-

ber, and hides. Today they are protected under the Wildlife Protection Act, but that is no shield against Jamaican fishermen, who still kill them. Less than 100 are thought to remain.

The animal belongs to the order *Sirenia*, the only aquatic mammals that subsist on vegetation. Three species of manatees – including the West Indian manatee – and the marine dugong of the Indo-Pacific make up the order. All face extinction.

The manatee is an extremely gentle and loving creature that spends much time nuzzling. Little is known of its reproductive behavior, although the manatee is known to engage in homosexual acts. They are extremely slow to reproduce; mature females produce a single calf once every two or three years, and the cow-calf bond is extremely close. The animals have deep-set eyes, blunt snouts and whiskered lips, bodies like plump wine sacks, and paddlelike tails. They have no external ears.

The slow-moving beasts normally cruise at two or three miles per hour, feeding on sea grasses in shallow coastal waters and estuaries. Each individual can daily consume up to 10% of its body weight (they can weigh up to 2000 pounds). Manatees can grow up to 15 feet long. They also like to drink the freshwater that bubbles up from subaqueous springs, such as at Canoe Valley. You're not likely to see one elsewhere in the wild.

For more information, contact the Natural Resources Conservation Department (☎ 929-5070), 53 ½ Molynes Rd, PO Box 305, Kingston 10. ■

clock tower that has a war memorial at its base. One of the earliest slave revolts on the island occurred in 1690 at Suttons Plantation, two miles southeast of Chapelton. These runaways joined up with slaves who had been freed by the Spanish and went on to form the nucleus of the Maroons. Chapelton is 12 miles north of May Pen.

There's a gas station in town, plus a National Commercial Bank, post office (☎ 987-2222), and police station (☎ 987-2244).

Dr Arlene Henry-Dowle has a clinic (☎ 987-2215) west of the church; it's open weekdays (except Wednesday) between 7:30 am and 7 pm. The regional hospital has emergency services. It's signed, on the right, 200 yards south of the village square. Chapelton Pharmacy is just before the hospital gate (☎ 987-2126).

Restaurants are also few. *Dixon's Restaurant & Bar* and *Sunshine Bar* are both very basic.

From the Parade in Kingston you can catch bus No ST46, which travels via May Pen. Several buses also pass through Chapelton en route to Frankfield from Kingston.

TROUT HALL

The village of Trout Hall, in the upper Rio Minho Valley six miles north of Chapelton on B3, is the regional center of a major citrus plantation owned by the Citrus Company of Jamaica Ltd. You can visit the plantation by prior arrangement (40 Manchester Ave, May Pen, ☎ 986-2201, or ☎ 923-4282 in Kingston). North of Trout Hall the B3 climbs 1300 feet in less than three miles to James Hill at the crest of the nation's backbone. From here it descends into St Ann Parish.

FRANKFIELD

West of Trout Hall the B4 follows the Rio Minho through citrus groves and fields planted with yams to the regional agricultural center of Frankfield, centered on a tiny traffic circle at a three-way junction. The disheveled town has a 'lost in the hinterland' feel. You'll be the first foreign visitor in a while, and eyes will follow you as you move through town.

West of town the badly potholed B4 begins a precipitous climb to Spaldings. The road is prone to mudslides in rainy season.

There's a gas station, bank, and pharmacy in town. Otherwise there's no reason to stop here.

If you do choose to stay overnight, a new guest house – *Bonnick's Hideout* – was due to open in 1996.

Bus ST483 is one of a half-dozen buses and minibuses that travel daily between Kingston and the Minho Valley. You can catch these in May Pen, where you can also hop aboard buses No LS311 or LS468 (the journey costs about US$0.40).

SPANISH TOWN

The fascination of Spanish Town lies in its troubled, colorful past. The island's third-largest urban center (population 87,000) and the capital of St Catherine Parish, it boasts a wealth of historic buildings, most in a sad state of repair. Vandalism, demolition, fires, hurricanes, and time have taken their toll on a city that was the capital of Jamaica between 1534 and 1872.

Walking its streets on overcast days, you may sense a malaise. Michael Crichton, author of *Jurassic Park*, was partly correct when he wrote in his autobiographical book, *Travels*, that 'Spanish Town was startling in its sprawl and squalor. A shanty-town west of Kingston, it was poor, colorful, and charged with menace. There were no tourists here: indeed, there were no whites at all.'

This negative view is not entirely fair. Streets once trodden by Spanish señoritas and sandal-footed friars hold strong appeal. The fine craftsmanship that went into building the town can still be seen if you stop and take time to note the ornate fretwork and carvings that decorate both mansions and humble homes. None of the historic buildings date back to the Spanish era, however, but many Georgian public edifices and townhouses still stand, with 'piazzas' or front galleries, and what were once well-fruited courtyards beyond the high red-brick garden walls.

History

After the settlement at Sevilla la Nueva failed in 1534, the Spanish established a new capital at Villa de la Vega – 'the town on the plain' – atop foundations that had been laid down earlier by Christopher Columbus' son, Diego. The town grew modestly as the administrative capital, helped along by a silk-spinning industry (today's Mulberry Gardens district recalls the era when the Spanish planted mulberry trees). However, the town never grew prosperous. Villa de la Vega, later called St Jago de la Vega, languished; at its peak the town had a population of only about 500 people. The Inquisition operated here for a while and even went so far as to imprison the governor and abbot.

The town was poorly defended and was ransacked several times by English pirates. Eventually, in 1655, an English invasion fleet landed and captured St Jago de la Vega. The Spaniards stalled the English advance by requesting time to consider their surrender terms. Instead, they used the time to pack up before wisely fleeing north with all their possessions. The English commander – presumably miffed! – ordered his troops to destroy much of the town that the English would rename Spanish Town and make *their* capital.

For the next 217 years, the town prospered as Jamaica's administrative capital. The menacing Victorian prison and gallows were here. So, too, a slave market, Jewish synagogues, and theaters. Taverns served the planters, their families, and entourages, who flocked to Spanish Town from all over the island during the 'dead season' (October to December) on the sugar estates, when the legislature was also in session.

Eventually Spanish Town was outpaced by Kingston, the mercantile capital. The latter's merchants resented Spanish Town's status as administrative capital and in 1755 managed to strong-arm the governor into forcing a bill through the legislature transferring the title to Kingston. The archives

were transferred east to Kingston. The people of Spanish Town, however, petitioned King George II of England, who proclaimed the bill illegal. The Archives were duly trundled back to Spanish Town (one wagonload was lost when a ferry overturned and the wagon sank into the swamps east of Spanish Town).

Decline had already set in, however. When novelist Anthony Trollope called on the governor in the 1850s, he described Spanish Town as 'stricken with eternal death.' Kingston was officially named the capital in 1872, and Spanish Town sank into a century of sloth. In 1988 Hurricane Gilbert did considerable damage to the historic town center. In 1989 an elaborate development plan was unveiled. However, lack of vision and common purpose, and an inadequate infrastructure have held it back. Still, most major banks have opened offices here and the past decade has seen the establishment of light industrial factories.

Fortunately, a small group of Spanish Town residents have formed the Restoration Committee to encourage a sense of pride in the town's historical landmarks. The group is pushing for zoning of commercial activity and promoting 'Heritage Tourism,' with guided historic tours. The hope is that as tourists return, old-time guest houses will reopen. In 1987, the Jamaica National Heritage Trust petitioned the United Nations' World Heritage Committee to list Spanish Town as a World Heritage Site. It has received 'provisional acceptance.' If recognized, the Jamaican government will receive much-needed funding to restore the city.

Orientation

The town sits on the west bank of the Rio Cobre. At its center is the park on the site of the original Spanish plaza between King and White Church Sts and Adelaide and Constitution Sts. The Spanish laid out the town on a quadrangular grid around the plaza. The Georgian square (formerly called the Parade) is centered on a prim Victorian garden surrounded by iron railings, with a fountain shaded by stately

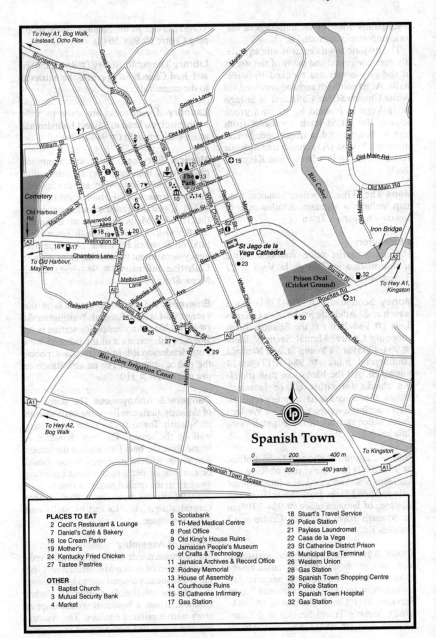

Spanish Town

0   200   400 m
0   200   400 yards

To Hwy A1, Bog Walk, Linstead, Ocho Rios
Brunswick St
Cross Pen Rd
Brunswick St
Monk St
Smith's Lane
Old Market St
William St
Prince's Lane
Cumberland Rd
French St
Young St
Martin St
King St
Nugent St
Manchester St
Adelaide St
Constitution St
The Park
Cemetery
Manchester St
Silverwood Alley
Ram Rd
Wellington St
White Church St
Red Church St
Monk St
Old Harbour Rd
Chambers Lane
Ellis St
St Jago de la Vega Cathedral
To Old Harbour, May Pen
Melbourne Lane
Bullocks Lane
Barrett St
Barrett St
Railway Lane
Bourkes Rd
Condrads Ave
Morrison Rd
Young St
Long St
Salt Island Rd
Salt Pond Rd
Port Henderson Rd
Prison Oval (Cricket Ground)
To Hwy A1, Kingston
Rio Cobre Irrigation Canal
Match Pen Rd
Old Harbour Rd
Spanish Town Bypass
Rio Cobre
Iron Bridge
Sligoville Main Rd
Old Main Rd
Old Main Rd
To Hwy A2, Bog Walk
To Kingston

PLACES TO EAT
2 Cecil's Restaurant & Lounge
7 Daniel's Café & Bakery
16 Ice Cream Parlor
19 Mother's
24 Kentucky Fried Chicken
27 Tastee Pastries

OTHER
1 Baptist Church
3 Mutual Security Bank
4 Market
5 Scotiabank
6 Tri-Med Medical Centre
8 Post Office
9 Old King's House Ruins
10 Jamaican People's Museum of Crafts & Technology
11 Jamaica Archives & Record Office
12 Rodney Memorial
13 House of Assembly
14 Courthouse Ruins
15 St Catherine Infirmary
17 Gas Station
18 Stuart's Travel Service
20 Police Station
21 Payless Laundromat
22 Casa de la Vega
23 St Catherine District Prison
25 Municipal Bus Terminal
26 Western Union
28 Gas Station
29 Spanish Town Shopping Centre
30 Police Station
31 Spanish Town Hospital
32 Gas Station

royal palms. Most of the buildings of historic importance surround it.

The historic town center is one sq mile. It's very congested and many of the streets in the city center are blocked by street stalls. At its southern end and accessed via White Church St, the Cathedral of St Jago de la Vega is fronted by its own green square. Barrett St leads southeast from here to Bourkes Rd, a major commercial street to a bypass (A1) connecting Spanish Town with May Pen (west) and Kingston (east).

Maps The JTB's 'Discover Jamaica' road map includes a separate, detailed map of downtown Spanish Town.

Information
There is no tourist office. Your best source of information is Casa de la Vega at 27 Barrett St (☎ 984-9684).

Money Scotiabank (☎ 984-2384) has a branch at 27 Adelaide St, Jamaica Citizens Bank (☎ 984-2939) at the Spanish Town Shopping Centre, Mutual Security Bank (☎ 984-4235) at 54 Young St, and National Commercial Bank (☎ 984-3017) at 14 Nugent St. All the banks can cash traveler's checks for either US or Jamaican dollars. If you need to have money remitted from your home country, there's a Western Union office in front of the bus station on Bourkes Rd.

Post & Communications The post office (☎ 984-2082) is at the corner of King and Adelaide Sts. You can make international calls and send faxes from the Telecommunications of Jamaica office (☎ 984-7010) in the Spanish Town Shopping Centre at 17 Bourkes Rd.

Travel Agencies If you want assistance with airline, hotel, or car-rental reservations, there are several agencies to choose from, including International Travel Services at 1 Cumberland Ave (☎ 984-2762), Stuart's Travel Service at 5 Cumberland Ave (☎ 984-3285), and Apollo

Travel Service in the Spanish Town Shopping Centre (☎ 984-5040).

Library The public library (☎ 984-2356) is at 1 Red Church St, opposite the entrance to the cathedral.

Laundry If your socks are about to walk by themselves, head to Payless Laundromat at 13 Wellington St (☎ 984-7779).

Medical Services There are plenty of pharmacies, including Carr's Pharmacy at 58 Young St (☎ 984-6469), and the Spanish Town Pharmacy at 19 Bourkes Rd (☎ 984-1314). If you need medical attention, go to the Tri-Med Medical Centre at 35 Young St (☎ 984-2179). The Spanish Town Hospital on Bourkes Rd has a 24-hour emergency department (☎ 984-3031), as does St Catherine Infirmary (☎ 984-3600) at 13 Monk St.

Emergency The police station is at the corner of Oxford Rd and Wellington St (☎ 984-2305). Another police station is on Bourkes Rd, just west of the junction with Port Henderson Rd. In emergencies, phone the police at ☎ 119. For an ambulance or fire truck, call ☎ 110.

Dangers & Annoyances The stereotype of the surly Jamaican has some basis in truth in Spanish Town, It can *seem* threatening walking the streets. The bark, however, is worse than the bite. I've walked the streets downtown without mishap, but you should be cautious of petty theft. Avoid exploring away from the main downtown streets.

Avoid driving near the market, where several streets are blocked by stalls and piles of garbage.

House of Assembly
On the eastern side of the plaza is the red-brick House of Assembly, erected in 1762 but subsequently altered and today housing the offices of the St Catherine Parish Council. It has a beautiful wooden upper story with a pillared balcony. The Assembly and Supreme Court sat here in colonial

days, when it was the setting for violent squabbles among parliamentarians. During one debate in 1710, the Speaker adjourned a rowdy meeting. However, members who wished to carry the vote locked the doors and held swords to the Speaker's throat while the Assembly carried their motion. The Speaker's father (Peter Beckford, the elder) heard the commotion and summoned the guards, who rushed to the younger Beckford's aid. Unfortunately, in the general excitement, Beckford senior fell down the stairs and was killed.

Rodney Memorial & Jamaica Archives

This fine structure stands on the north side of the plaza. The elaborate monument was built in honor of Admiral George Rodney, who crowned his four-year service as Commander in Chief of the West Indian Naval Station in 1782, when he saved Jamaica from a combined French and Spanish invasion fleet at the Battle of the Saints. In gratitude, the House of Assembly voted £1000 to erect a monument. They commissioned John Bacon, the leading English sculptor of the time. Bacon's marble statue depicting Rodney dressed as a Roman emperor ended up costing £30,918. It weighs over 200 tons. One of Rodney's hands is missing; it dropped off when the statue was moved to Kingston during the feud over the capital. Irate Spanish Town residents stormed Kingston to bring Rodney 'home.' He stands within

Inside a protective cupola lurks a 200-ton statue of Admiral George Rodney.

a cupola temple, with sculpted panel reliefs to each side showing the battle scenes. The monument is fronted by two finely decorated but tarnished brass cannons from the French flagship.

The building that wraps around the memorial is the Jamaica Archives & Record Office. It preserves documentation recording centuries of parochial administration, plus such intriguing gems as secret files kept on National Hero Marcus Mosiah Garvey. The Clinton Black Reading Room is open to the public Monday to Thursday 9 am to 4:30 pm, and Friday 1 am to 3:30 pm.

Old King's House

On the west side of the plaza is the impressive porticoed Georgian red-brick facade of Old King's House, a once-grandiose building erected in 1762 as the official residence of Jamaica's governors. The proclamation emancipating slaves was made from the front steps on August 1, 1838. The building was destroyed by fire in 1925, leaving only the facade and the stables.

Jamaican People's Museum of Crafts & Technology

Also on the west side of the plaza, this small museum (☎ 984-2452) is operated by the Institute of Jamaica and is housed in the stables of Old King's House. A reconstructed smith's shop and an eclectic array of artifacts from carpenter's tools to Indian corn grinders provide an entree to early Jamaican culture. A splendid model shows how Old King's House once looked. The museum receives few visitors. There's a small bar and restaurant. Entrance costs US$0.15 (US$0.05 children). It's open weekdays from 10 am to 4 pm.

Courthouse Ruins

Opposite the Rodney Memorial across the plaza is the ruined shell of the courthouse, destroyed in 1986 by fire. The Georgian building dates from 1819, when it was used as a chapel and armory, with the town hall upstairs. The Spanish Church of the White Cross had stood here prior to the English invasion.

St Jago de la Vega Cathedral

This Anglican cathedral is the parish church of St Catherine and the oldest cathedral in the former British colonies. It's also one of the prettiest churches in Jamaica, boasting wooden fluted pillars, an impressive beamed ceiling, a magnificent stained-glass window behind the altar, and a large organ dating to 1849 (donations are being sought to restore it). The church stands on the site of one of the first Spanish cathedrals built in the New World: the Franciscan Chapel of the Red Cross, built in 1525. English soldiers destroyed the Catholic church and used the original materials to build their own cathedral. The current structure dates from 1714 and has been damaged and restored several times. Note the handsome octagonal steeple with faux-Corinthian columns.

Its baptism and marriage registers date from 1668, and many of the key events of the early colonial period are recorded here. Many leading personalities are buried within its precincts. The oldest tomb dates to 1662 and is inset in the black-and-white transept aisle laid by the Spanish.

St Catherine District Prison

There's hardly anything endearing about the historic St Catherine District Prison, with its adjacent cricket oval, behind the cathedral off Barrett St. Hangings have been carried out here since 1714, when the prison was known as the Middlesex and Surrey County Gaol. Many prisoners are on death row in narrow cells that date back almost three centuries. Conditions in the prison were condemned in 1994 by the United Nations Human Rights Committee, and a British Member of Parliament described a recent visit as 'like something out of a nightmare.'

Iron Bridge

There's a stately grandeur to this narrow bridge spanning the Rio Cobre on the southeast outskirts of town. The span was made of cast iron prefabricated at Colebrookdale, England, and erected in 1801 on a cut-stone foundation dating to 1675.

Historic iron bridge, Spanish Town

The only surviving bridge of its kind in the Americas, it is still used by pedestrians.

Baptist Church

This dour church at the corner of William and French Sts was built in 1827 by abolitionist James Phillippo on the old artillery ground. It was faithfully restored after being badly damaged by a hurricane in 1951.

Organized Tours

Professionally guided historic walking tours are offered by Spanish Town Heritage Tours, housed in a charming old building kitty-corner from the cathedral (Casa de la Vega, 27 Barrett St, ☎ 984-9684, or c/o Destinations, 9 Cecelio Ave, Kingston, ☎ 929-6368). The Teak Tree Co also offers a guided walking tour called 'A Journey into the Past' (PO Box 435, Kingston 6, ☎ 977-1936, fax 977-3247).

A full-day tour by Limousine Taxi Touring Co (3A Haughton Ave, Kingston 10, ☎ 968-3775, fax 944-3147) highlights 'Kingston to Ocho Rios.'

Places to Stay

The only hotel I'm aware of is the rather basic *People's Choice Hotel* on Sligoville Rd (☎ 984-2474). It has air-con rooms and a restaurant and bar.

Places to Eat

Spanish Town has little in the way of fine dining, although there are plenty of modest restaurants. The Spanish Town Shopping Centre includes a food court. *Cecil's* is one of the better-looking places; it's on Martin

St, near the corner of Old Market St. For fast food, try *Mother's* on Ram Lane, *Tastee Pastries* just east of the bus station on Bourkes Rd, or *Kentucky Fried Chicken*, across the street. *Daniels' Cafe & Bakery*, at the corner of Adelaide and Martin Sts, serves fresh-baked pastries and breads. If the heat is sweltering, stroll down Wellington St, where you'll find an ice-cream parlor next to the gas station.

Entertainment
Movie buffs have the *Astor Cinema* on Brunswick Ave for amusement. The aircon *Sips Lounge*, at the intersection of Oxford Rd and Wellington St, is modestly upscale (certainly by Spanish Town standards). For a more uptempo evening, try the *Max Club*, just off the A1 in Green Dale east of the Rio Cobre.

Getting There & Away
Bus There's no shortage of buses serving Spanish Town. Bus No 21B (marked 'Spanish Town') departs from Half Way Tree in Kingston. The No 22 bus runs between the Parade and Spanish Town via Spanish Town Rd. The journey takes 30 minutes and costs about US$1.30. Buses Nos 31 through 35 also serve Spanish Town from the Parade.

You can also catch buses for Spanish Town from Black River, Mandeville, Montego Bay, and Ocho Rios. In Spanish Town, buses leave from the Municipal Bus Terminal on Bourkes Rd. It's one of the few organized bus stations in the country.

Car You can reach Spanish Town from Kingston via Norman Manley Blvd, a ruler-straight highway that bypasses Spanish Town to the south and continues to May Pen. The exit is signed: after crossing the Rio Minho, turn right at the Shell gas station onto Barrett St to enter the historic town center.

Arriving on the A2 from Mandeville and May Pen, you'll see the exit sign at the José Martí roundabout, from where Old Harbour Rd will take you downtown. The A1 turns north from this roundabout and leads to Bog Walk and Ocho Rios on the north coast.

Getting Around
There is no bus system within town. Walking downtown is practical, if seemingly intimidating. Guard your valuables!

Driving in Spanish Town is a frustrating nightmare, a maze of narrow, congested lanes and one-way streets. However, you can rent cars from Mac's Trucking & Car Rental at 32A Old Harbour St (☎ 984-8225) and Trev Car Rental at 12 Greendale Blvd (☎ 984-6708). I can't vouch for the reputation of either.

AROUND SPANISH TOWN
White Marl Arawak Museum
Contemporary Jamaican culture owes much to the Arawak influence, as displayed at this rather modest museum sited atop a large pre-Columbian settlement. Archaeological research has been ongoing here since the 1940s. The well-done displays describe Amerindian life and decimation at the hands of the Spanish. Hunting and agricultural implements, jewelry, and carvings are featured. It's administered by the Institute of Jamaica. A reconstructed Arawak village is up the hill behind the museum.

It's open weekdays from 10 am to 4 pm; entrance is US$1. The museum is 200 yards north of the Nelson Mandela Freeway about two miles east of Spanish Town. When traveling eastbound, you'll have to cross the freeway; be extremely cautious of oncoming traffic!

Caymanas Golf Course
This 18-hole course (6844 yards) was home to the Jamaican Open until 1987. It's set amid low hills three miles east of Spanish Town. There's a clubhouse with only limited clubs available for rent. Caddies can be hired. There's a swimming pool. For information call ☎ 926-8144.

COLEBURNS GULLY
This off-the-beaten-track valley extends northwest from Spanish Town into the Central Highlands. The road via Guanaboa

Vale leads north five miles to **Mountain River Cave**. Guides Percival Pierson or Linton Wright will lead you down one steep mile and across the river, where the cave entrance is barred by a grill gate to which they have the key. Inside, you'll find about 200 Arawak petroglyphs painted in black on the walls and ceiling. Many date back up to 1300 years. There are birds and beasts such as frogs and turtles, as well as human figures and abstract designs. Many have been documented by the Archaeological Society of Jamaica and the Smithsonian Institute.

At the top of the valley is the village of **Lluidas Vale**, set in a beautiful green trough (also called Lluidas Vale) filled with cane fields of the old Worthy Park Estate. A roadside monument commemorates Juan Lubolo, a former slave turned 17th-century guerrilla leader. His band of escaped slaves lived autonomously during the Spanish occupation near Lluidas Vale. Lubolo switched sides after the English invasion of Jamaica in 1655 in exchange for full citizenship. His people thus formed the first free black settlement in the New World. After he died, English settlers seized their land. The Juan de Bolas Mountains, which reach 2743 feet, are named after him.

Lluidas Vale is served by buses from Falmouth and Ocho Rios, and from Half Way Tree (No STBW399) and the Parade (Nos ST34 and STBW362) in Kingston. You can also catch buses in Spanish Town.

BOG WALK GORGE

About seven miles north of Spanish Town the A1 cuts through a great limestone canyon – Bog Walk Gorge – carved by the slow-moving jade-colored Rio Cobre. The road parallels the river for several miles. You drop down into the gorge and cross the river via the Flat Bridge, an old stone bridge built to replace an original structure that washed away in the 18th century.

The gorge is several hundred feet deep and littered with massive boulders. Every rainy season there are landslides that block the road, causing considerable disruption. Occasionally, rockfalls add to the damming

effect of the narrow gorge. Flat Bridge is frequently under water after heavy rains; the high-water mark of August 16, 1933, is shown on the rock face, when the river rose 25 feet above the bridge!

Bog Walk

One of Jamaica's oldest towns, Bog Walk was an important rest stop during early colonial days. Today it's a center for food processing and has a Nestlé milk condensery, sugar factory, and citrus-packing plant. The town lies at the confluence of the Thomas, Pedro, and D'Oro Rivers, which combine to form the Rio Cobre, five miles north of Bog Walk Gorge. The one-street town stretches along the old highway for more than a mile but is bypassed by a modern highway that runs parallel to the old road.

If you need the police, call ☎ 119 (emergency) or ☎ 985-2233. There's a post office (☎ 985-2217), plus a pharmacy in Bog Walk Plaza (☎ 985-2658).

Places to Stay & Eat

I'm not aware of any guest houses in town, but half a mile south of Flat Bridge in the gorge is *Riverside Drive-Inn* (☎ 983-5714), a thatched-roof bar whose hostess, the saucy Queen-I rents very basic rooms by the night (US$17) or by the hour. (The rooms are barely worth the US$6 charged for 'short time.') At night, go-go dancers perform on a stage down by the river.

In town, *Big Tree Restaurant*, opposite the police station, is the only decent-looking place to eat. Roadside vendors sell bags of oranges along the A1 bypass.

Getting There & Away

Bog Walk is served by buses from Spanish Town (you can also hop aboard buses for Linstead and Ewarton). The town is also served by buses traveling between Ocho Rios and Kingston. In Kingston there are at least two minibuses (Nos ST803 and ST822) that operate from the Parade. If traveling to Kingston from Bog Walk, you can catch ST791, a Toyota minibus operated by Nevis Blackwood.

SLIGOVILLE

This small village sits on the upper slopes of Montpelier Mountain (2419 feet) five miles east of Bog Walk, at a junction with roads for Kingston (via Red Hills) and Spanish Town.

During the colonial era the area was a popular summer retreat for the well-to-do white society, and the governor traditionally had a home here. When emancipation was proclaimed in 1834, things changed overnight. Sligoville was established that year as the first of dozens of 'free villages' created islandwide. The village was named for the second Marquis of Sligo, governor of Jamaica from 1834 to 1836.

Newlyn Martin operates a minibus (No STBW389) between Kingston and Ocho Rios via Sligoville. It should cost no more than US$1.50 from Kingston and about US$5 from Ocho Rios. You can also catch a bus in Spanish Town.

LINSTEAD

An important market town in the mid-19th century, Linstead has retained its role as a regional market center and is celebrated in the popular song 'Linstead Market':

Carry mi ackee go a Linstead market
Not a quattie worth sell.

On Saturday higglers descend on the town from far and wide, and the streets are packed with women selling their yams, corn, tomatoes, and other produce.

The compact and bustling little town is centered on an old clock tower. Also in the center is an Anglican church that held Jamaica's public records during the threat of French invasion in 1805. The church has been destroyed by hurricanes several times, and the current structure dates from 1911.

A highway (the A1) bypasses Linstead, which sits astride the old road.

Information

You'll find a Scotiabank at 42 King St (☎ 985-2277) and a National Commercial Bank nearby (☎ 985-2257). The post office is on Main St (☎ 985-2218). The highly respected Stuart's Travel Service has an office at 60 King St (☎ 985-2781).

For medical emergencies, call Linstead Hospital at ☎ 985-2241. There are several pharmacies in town, including Gayle's at 93A King St (☎ 985-9858) and Dixon's at 43 King St (☎ 985-2202).

The telephone number for the police station is ☎ 985-2285.

Places to Stay & Eat

If all you need is a dirt cheap place to rest your head, try the *Restwell Guest House & Pub* (☎ 985-7425), down a cul-de-sac half a mile north of town on the old road that parallels the bypass. Six rooms each have private bathroom, with cold water only, and cost US$3 (more with a radio). They're basic but clean.

Getting There & Away

At least six buses operate between Linstead and both Half Way Tree and the Parade in Kingston, where you'll also find minibuses. Any of the vehicles traveling between Ocho Rios and Spanish Town will also take you.

DEVIL'S RACECOURSE

East of Linstead, the B13 leads through a broad valley planted with sugarcane and bananas before beginning a tortuous climb north to the mountain-crest village of Guy's Hill, straddling the border of St Catherine and St Anne Parishes. The road is precipitous, with dangerous hairpin bends that account for its name. Drive with caution!

The salubrious climate hereabouts is also supposedly responsible for the renowned longevity of the local population.

EWARTON

Ewarton, on the A1 seven miles north of Linstead, is a modestly wealthy town that owes its relative prosperity to the Ewarton Works, a bauxite processing plant south of town owned by Alcan Ltd. Many of the locals are employed here.

North of Ewarton the road begins its steep ascent over Mt Diablo and the border with St Anne Parish.

Places to Stay & Eat

Although Ewarton's commercial importance suggests it would have guest houses
catering to business travelers, I'm not
aware of any accommodations. I'd like to
hear from readers who discover any.

The best place to eat is the *International
Whitehouse Seafood Restaurant* (☎ 985-
0319) at 40 Main St on the southern fringe
of town. Main dishes cost about US$4. *Life-
line* (☎ 985-0142) next door is a small health
food store that sells a modest range of nutritional items, tonics, and vegetarian foods.

Entertainment

For a taste of earthy local entertainment,
check out *Living Colours*, three miles south
of Ewarton. This lively bar has reggae
music and go-go dancing. The fascinating
mural on the outside wall tells the tale.

Getting There & Away

A bus journey from either Ocho Rios or
Kingston will cost about US$1.20 (triple
that amount by minibus). Bus No STB-
W406 departs Ewarton for Kingston. Also
see Linstead.

Index

MAPS

TEXT

LONELY PLANET PHRASEBOOKS

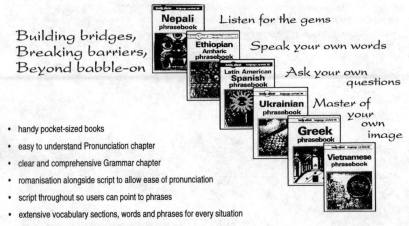

Building bridges,
Breaking barriers,
Beyond babble-on

Listen for the gems

Speak your own words

Ask your own
questions

Master of
your
own
image

- handy pocket-sized books
- easy to understand Pronunciation chapter
- clear and comprehensive Grammar chapter
- romanisation alongside script to allow ease of pronunciation
- script throughout so users can point to phrases
- extensive vocabulary sections, words and phrases for every situation
- full of cultural information and tips for the traveller

'...vital for a real DIY spirit and attitude in language learning' – Backpacker

'the phrasebooks have good cultural backgrounders and offer solid advice for challenging situations in remote locations' – San Francisco Examiner

'...they are unbeatable for their coverage of the world's more obscure languages' – The Geographical Magazine

---

Arabic (Egyptian)
Arabic (Moroccan)
Australia
  Australian English, Aboriginal and Torres Strait languages
Baltic States
  Estonian, Latvian, Lithuanian
Bengali
Brazilian
Burmese
Cantonese
Central Asia
Central Europe
  Czech, French, German, Hungarian, Italian and Slovak
Eastern Europe
  Bulgarian, Czech, Hungarian, Polish, Romanian and Slovak
Ethiopian (Amharic)
Fijian
French
German
Greek

Hindi/Urdu
Indonesian
Italian
Japanese
Korean
Lao
Latin American Spanish
Malay
Mandarin
Mediterranean Europe
  Albanian, Croatian, Greek, Italian, Macedonian, Maltese, Serbian and Slovene
Mongolian
Moroccan Arabic
Nepali
Papua New Guinea
Pilipino (Tagalog)
Quechua
Russian
Scandinavian Europe
  Danish, Finnish, Icelandic, Norwegian and Swedish

South-East Asia
  Burmese, Indonesian, Khmer, Lao, Malay, Tagalog (Pilipino), Thai and Vietnamese
Spanish (Castilian)
  Basque, Catalan and Galician
Sri Lanka
Swahili
Thai
Thai Hill Tribes
Tibetan
Turkish
Ukrainian
USA
  US English, Vernacular, Native American languages and Hawaiian
Vietnamese
Western Europe
  Basque, Catalan, Dutch, French, German, Irish, Italian, Portuguese, Scottish Gaelic, Spanish (Castilian) and Welsh

LONELY PLANET JOURNEYS

JOURNEYS is a unique collection of travel writing – published by the company that understands travel better than anyone else. It is a series for anyone who has ever experienced – or dreamed of – the magical moment when they encountered a strange culture or saw a place for the first time. They are tales to read while you're planning a trip, while you're on the road or while you're in an armchair, in front of a fire.

JOURNEYS books catch the spirit of a place, illuminate a culture, recount a crazy adventure, or introduce a fascinating way of life. They always entertain, and always enrich the experience of travel.

'Idiosyncratic, entertainingly diverse and unexpected . . . from an international writership'
– The Australian

'Books which offer a closer look at the people and culture of a destination, and enrich travel experiences'
– American Bookseller

FULL CIRCLE
A South American Journey
Luis Sepúlveda
Translated by Chris Andrews

Full Circle invites us to accompany Chilean writer Luis Sepúlveda on 'a journey without a fixed itinerary'. Whatever his subject – brutalities suffered under Pinochet's dictatorship, sleepy tropical towns visited in exile, or the landscapes of legendary Patagonia – Sepúlveda is an unflinchingly honest yet lyrical storyteller. Extravagant characters and extraordinary situations are memorably evoked: gauchos organising a tournament of lies, a scheming heiress on the lookout for a husband, a pilot with a corpse on board his plane . . . Part autobiography, part travel memoir, *Full Circle* brings us the distinctive voice of one of South America's most compelling writers.

Luis Sepúlveda was born in Chile in 1949. Imprisoned by the Pinochet dictatorship for his socialist beliefs, he was for many years a political exile. He has written novels, short stories, plays and essays. His work has attracted many awards and has been translated into numerous languages.

'Detachment, humour and vibrant prose' – El País

'an absolute cracker' – The Bookseller

This project has been assisted by the Commonwealth Government through the Australia Council, its arts funding and advisory body.

LONELY PLANET TRAVEL ATLASES

Lonely Planet has long been famous for the number and quality of its guidebook maps. Now we've gone one step further and in conjunction with Steinhart Katzir Publishers produced a handy companion series: Lonely Planet travel atlases – maps of a country produced in book form.

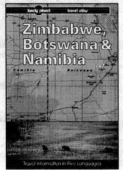

Unlike other maps, which look good but lead travellers astray, our travel atlases have been researched on the road by Lonely Planet's experienced team of writers. All details are carefully checked to ensure the atlas corresponds with the equivalent Lonely Planet guidebook.

The handy atlas format means no holes, wrinkles, torn sections or constant folding and unfolding. These atlases can survive long periods on the road, unlike cumbersome fold-out maps. The comprehensive index ensures easy reference.

- full-colour throughout
- maps researched and checked by Lonely Planet authors
- place names correspond with Lonely Planet guidebooks
  – no confusing spelling differences
- legend and travelling information in English, French, German, Japanese and Spanish
- size: 230 x 160 mm

Available now:
Chile & Easter Island • Egypt • India & Bangladesh • Israel & the Palestinian Territories •Jordan, Syria & Lebanon • Kenya • Laos • Portugal • South Africa, Lesotho & Swaziland • Thailand • Turkey • Vietnam • Zimbabwe, Botswana & Namibia

LONELY PLANET TV SERIES & VIDEOS

Lonely Planet travel guides have been brought to life on television screens around the world. Like our guides, the programmes are based on the joy of independent travel, and look honestly at some of the most exciting, picturesque and frustrating places in the world. Each show is presented by one of three travellers from Australia, England or the USA and combines an innovative mixture of video, Super-8 film, atmospheric soundscapes and original music.

Videos of each episode – containing additional footage not shown on television – are available from good book and video shops, but the availability of individual videos varies with regional screening schedules.

Video destinations include: Alaska • American Rockies • Australia – The South-East • Baja California & the Copper Canyon • Brazil • Central Asia • Chile & Easter Island • Corsica, Sicily & Sardinia – The Mediterranean Islands • East Africa (Tanzania & Zanzibar) • Ecuador & the Galapagos Islands • Greenland & Iceland • Indonesia • Israel & the Sinai Desert • Jamaica • Japan • La Ruta Maya • Morocco • New York • North India • Pacific Islands (Fiji, Solomon Islands & Vanuatu) • South India • South West China • Turkey • Vietnam • West Africa • Zimbabwe, Botswana & Namibia

The Lonely Planet TV series is produced by:
Pilot Productions
The Old Studio
18 Middle Row
London W10 5AT UK

For video availability and ordering information contact your nearest Lonely Planet office.

Music from the TV series is available on CD & cassette.

PLANET TALK

Lonely Planet's FREE quarterly newsletter

We love hearing from you and think you'd like to hear from us.

When...is the right time to see reindeer in Finland?
Where...can you hear the best palm-wine music in Ghana?
How...do you get from Asunción to Areguá by steam train?
What...is the best way to see India?

For the answer to these and many other questions read PLANET TALK.

Every issue is packed with up-to-date travel news and advice including:

* a letter from Lonely Planet co-founders Tony and Maureen Wheeler
* go behind the scenes on the road with a Lonely Planet author
* feature article on an important and topical travel issue
* a selection of recent letters from travellers
* details on forthcoming Lonely Planet promotions
* complete list of Lonely Planet products

To join our mailing list contact any Lonely Planet office.

Also available: Lonely Planet T-shirts. 100% heavyweight cotton.

LONELY PLANET ONLINE

Get the latest travel information before you leave or while you're on the road

Whether you've just begun planning your next trip, or you're chasing down specific info on currency regulations or visa requirements, check out Lonely Planet Online for up-to-the-minute travel information.

As well as travel profiles of your favourite destinations (including maps and photos), you'll find current reports from our researchers and other travellers, updates on health and visas, travel advisories, and discussion of the ecological and political issues you need to be aware of as you travel.

There's also an online travellers' forum where you can share your experience of life on the road, meet travel companions and ask other travellers for their recommendations and advice. We also have plenty of links to other online sites useful to independent travellers.

And of course we have a complete and up-to-date list of all Lonely Planet travel products including guides, phrasebooks, atlases, Journeys and videos and a simple online ordering facility if you can't find the book you want elsewhere.

www.lonelyplanet.com
or
AOL keyword: lp

LONELY PLANET PRODUCTS

Lonely Planet is known worldwide for publishing practical, reliable and no-nonsense travel information in our guides and on our web site. The Lonely Planet list covers just about every accessible part of the world. Currently there are eight series: *travel guides, shoestring guides, walking guides, city guides, phrasebooks, audio packs, travel atlases* and *Journeys* – a unique collection of travel writing.

EUROPE

Amsterdam • Austria • Baltic States phrasebook • Britain • Central Europe on a shoestring • Central Europe phrasebook • Czech & Slovak Republics • Denmark • Dublin • Eastern Europe on a shoestring • Eastern Europe phrasebook • Estonia, Latvia & Lithuania • Finland • France • French phrasebook • German phrasebook • Greece • Greek phrasebook • Hungary • Iceland, Greenland & the Faroe Islands • Ireland • Italian phrasebook • Italy • Mediterranean Europe on a shoestring • Mediterranean Europe phrasebook • Paris • Poland • Portugal • Portugal travel atlas • Prague • Russia, Ukraine & Belarus • Russian phrasebook • Scandinavian & Baltic Europe on a shoestring • Scandinavian Europe phrasebook • Slovenia • Spain • Spanish phrasebook • St Petersburg • Switzerland • Trekking in Spain • Ukrainian phrasebook • Vienna • Walking in Britain • Walking in Switzerland • Western Europe on a shoestring • Western Europe phrasebook

Travel Literature: The Olive Grove: Travels in Greece

NORTH AMERICA

Alaska • Backpacking in Alaska • Baja California • California & Nevada • Canada • Florida • Hawaii • Honolulu • Los Angeles • Mexico • Miami • New England • New Orleans • New York City • New York, New Jersey & Pennsylvania • Pacific Northwest USA • Rocky Mountain States • San Francisco • Southwest USA • USA phrasebook • Washington, DC & the Capital Region

CENTRAL AMERICA & THE CARIBBEAN

Bermuda • Central America on a shoestring • Costa Rica • Cuba • Eastern Caribbean • Guatemala, Belize & Yucatán: La Ruta Maya • Jamaica

SOUTH AMERICA

Argentina, Uruguay & Paraguay • Bolivia • Brazil • Brazilian phrasebook • Buenos Aires • Chile & Easter Island • Chile & Easter Island travel atlas • Colombia • Deep South • Ecuador & the Galápagos Islands • Latin American Spanish phrasebook • Peru • Quechua phrasebook • Rio de Janeiro • South America on a shoestring • Trekking in the Patagonian Andes • Venezuela

Travel Literature: Full Circle: A South American Journey

ANTARCTICA

Antarctica

ISLANDS OF THE INDIAN OCEAN

Madagascar & Comoros • Maldives • Mauritius, Réunion & Seychelles

AFRICA

Africa - the South • Africa on a shoestring • Arabic (Moroccan) phrasebook • Cape Town • Central Africa • East Africa • Egypt • Egypt travel atlas • Ethiopian (Amharic) phrasebook • Kenya • Kenya travel atlas • Malawi, Mozambique & Zambia • Morocco • North Africa • South Africa, Lesotho & Swaziland • South Africa, Lesotho & Swaziland travel atlas • Swahili phrasebook • Trekking in East Africa • West Africa • Zimbabwe, Botswana & Namibia • Zimbabwe, Botswana & Namibia travel atlas

Travel Literature: The Rainbird: A Central African Journey • Songs to an African Sunset: A Zimbabwean Story